The Letters of
Virginia Woolf

Volume I: 1888-1912
(Virginia Stephen)

For my new grandson, William James Bodhi Morrissey.

*Darling Bo, may you come to know and love the
wonderful land of the opal, with all its diversity
and uniqueness, as much as I do. And may
we share journeys of discovery together.*

The Letters of Virginia Woolf

Volume I: 1888-1912
(Virginia Stephen)

Editor: Nigel Nicolson
Assistant Editor: Joanne Trautmann

Harcourt Brace Jovanovich
New York and London

Originally published in England as *The Flight of the Mind*

Library of Congress Cataloging in Publication Data

Woolf, Virginia Stephen, 1882–1941.
The letters of Virginia Woolf.

First published under title: The flight of the mind.
Includes bibliographical references and index.
CONTENTS: v. 1. 1888–1912.–
1. Woolf, Virginia Stephen, 1882–1941–Correspondence.
PR6045.072Z525   1976   823'.9'12 [B]   75-25538
ISBN 0-15-150924-7

Contents

Illustrations

Plate 1 is reproduced by courtesy of Sussex University.
Nos. 3a, 3b and 7b are the property of Dame Janet
Vaughan. 10c was photographed in 1974 by Meyer, Lewes.
The remaining photographs were loaned by
Professor and Mrs Quentin Bell.

Editorial Note

VIRGINIA STEPHEN, as she is from the first page of this volume until she becomes Virginia Woolf on the last, wrote many thousands of letters during her lifetime, and some 3,800 of them survive in public and private collections. People kept them because they were fond of her, and because she wrote as she talked, brilliantly. But would so large a correspondence stand total publication more than thirty years after her death? Readers might be crushed by the weight of the material, and her most light-hearted letters might lose their sparkle when solemnized by print and annotation.

On the other hand, Virginia Woolf will be read and written about for centuries to come. Her letters preserve her personality, the very tone of her voice, even more faithfully than her books. They explain many incidents in her life, and the genesis of her ideas and style. Everything she wrote, even on a postcard, had her special mark upon it. Some of her letters now in private hands may disappear with the death of their owners. A single volume of Selected Letters would be more manageable, but future generations would rightly think that an opportunity had been lost if nothing more than that were published now.

So the decision was taken, with the encouragement of The Hogarth Press in London and of Harcourt Brace Jovanovich in New York, to publish all the letters unabridged. Not quite all, for a few of them, making or cancelling social engagements (a score in the period covered by the present volume), have been omitted because they add nothing to our knowledge of Virginia Woolf. Replies to her letters, of which she kept a considerable number, have not been printed because they would have added intolerably to the size of an already massive correspondence.

The plan is to publish the letters in six volumes, annually from 1975:

Vol.	I	1888-1912
	II	1912-1922
	III	1923-1928
	IV	1929-1931
	V	1932-1935
	VI	1936-1941

Few of them have been published previously. Some have been quoted in the biographies of Virginia Woolf by Quentin Bell and Aileen Pippett, others in memoirs of the period. In 1956 Leonard Woolf and James Strachey published her correspondence with Lytton Strachey, omitting some names and short passages, most of which we have been able to restore in this edition without fear of giving offence.

The letters have been transcribed either from the originals, or from Xerox or microfilm copies of them. All except one (as it happens, the second) were handwritten. Virginia learnt to type early in life but seldom used the typewriter until after her marriage. In childhood and early youth her handwriting was small and irregular, and the deciphering of it has been one of our major difficulties, but in only half a dozen instances have we been obliged to confess defeat by substituting *illegible* for a single word. Her spelling and grammar were occasionally eccentric. She wrote the past tense of 'eat' as 'eat', never 'ate'; the possessive of landlady becomes 'landladies'. We have left her spelling unchanged, adding *sic* only when it seems highly improbable, and made only one major alteration throughout, by substituting 'and' for the ampersands which occur naturally in her manuscript but would speckle a printed page disturbingly.

Her punctuation was erratic. In her early letters dashes normally did duty for full-stops, and she used commas, colons and semi-colons at random, but we have retained them all, because they are additional evidence of the careless affection with which she wrote. Occasionally a missing quotation-mark has been silently replaced, when the sense would be lost without it. We have also made one assumption, in the paragraphing: Virginia was apt to leave longer spaces to indicate a change of subject, but continued writing on the same line. Where these spaces occur, we have normally inserted a new paragraph.

Apart from orthography, our main problem has been to place the letters in their correct chronological order. Often Virginia would not date them at all: sometimes she wrote 'Thursday' at the top; seldom would she add the month, almost never the year. Envelopes were rarely preserved to help us with their postmarks. From internal evidence, such as the address or an illness, or the mention of some public event, like a play which she had seen, the publication of a review or a book, a coronation or a revolution, we have always been able to date a letter to the right year, usually to the month, often to the exact day. When her father and brother were dying, we have arranged her frequent bulletins by the assumed development of the crisis, but much of this is careful guesswork.

She usually wrote letters from her permanent addresses on headed notepaper. In these cases we have reproduced the address in the style which she had had printed. When she wrote on blank sheets, we have added the address in brackets, or expanded a single handwritten name like 'Manorbier' by a fuller identification of the place.

At the foot of each letter we have printed the present location of the original, and by doing so we express our thanks to the owners for the loan of the letters or Xerox copies of them. The great majority of the letters are already in public collections, of which two deserve special mention: The Henry W. and Alfred A. Berg Collection of English and American Literature in The New York Public Library (Astor, Lenox and Tilden Foundations), which owns the many letters which Virginia wrote to her sister Vanessa and to Violet Dickinson, and those (to be published in subsequent volumes) to V. Sackville-West and Ethel Smyth: and the University of Sussex Library, which owns the greatest collection of Woolf manuscripts in England. It is possible that even before this volume is published some of the letters now in private hands may have been given or sold to public libraries or other private collectors. We offer in advance our apologies to the new owners, and hope to include as an Appendix to the final volume an up-to-date summary of the location of all the originals.

The notes attempt to identify minor characters and explain obscure allusions without too much interruption to the text. As this edition has been printed simultaneously for British and American readers, we have left unexplained what would be obvious to either. For example, we have not stated at the foot of the first letter that the Adirondacks are mountains in New York State, since this information would be as insulting to an American as to identify the Cotswolds for an Englishman. In other cases we have left a few trivial references unexplained, either because we could not explain them ourselves, or because a note would be pedantic. Short editorial narratives have been added at intervals in italics, mainly in order to reduce the number of footnotes, and to remind readers of incidents in Virginia's life to which her letters make no allusion.

The copyright in all the letters belongs to Virginia Woolf's nephew and niece, Quentin Bell and Angelica Garnett. It is on their invitation that we have undertaken the editing of these volumes. Professor Bell and his wife Olivier have given us indispensable help. His biography of Virginia Woolf has formed the basis of our chronology and our interpretation of her character. It must be seldom that a biographer's material is published *in toto* for scholars to judge the accuracy of his research, and when the six volumes of letters have appeared, together with the companion volumes of Virginia Woolf's Diaries (which Olivier Bell is editing), very few factual inconsistencies will be found between them and the Life. Their help, however, has gone far beyond the published biography. Olivier Bell's careful indices of Virginia's friends and activities have supplied us with clues available from no other source, and her patience with us has been unflagging and generous. She has also provided us with the majority of the illustrations.

There are others to whom we are much indebted. B. J. Kirkpatrick's *A Bibliography of Virginia Woolf* has been invaluable for identifying her early journalism, and Dr Suzanne Henig has kindly shown us the fruit of her researches in the same field. Dr Lola L. Szladits, curator of the Berg Collection in New York, arranged for us the Xeroxing of its entire archive of Virginia Woolf letters. Peter Lewis and A. N. Peasgood have done the same for the letters at Sussex University. George A. Spater has helped us with many references to letters which we would otherwise have missed. Paul Levy has helped with microfilms in the ownership of the Strachey Trust. Henry Duckworth has lent us letters written by Virginia to his father (her half-brother) George Duckworth, and Elizabeth Hambro letters to her parents Gwen and Jacques Raverat. Robin Harcourt Williams, the librarian at Hatfield, helped with Virginia's letters to Lady Robert Cecil, and Dame Janet Vaughan with photographs from her family album. Our other benefactors are acknowledged at the foot of individual letters.

The Editors wish to thank the Department of Humanities, the Pennsylvania State University College of Medicine, Hershey, Pennsylvania, for their generosity in allowing Dr Joanne Trautmann to spend part of her academic year working on this volume, and for funding her journeys from the United States to England.

Norah Smallwood and Ian Parsons of The Hogarth Press have been the most understanding and helpful of publishers.

All too often the Acknowledgements at the beginning of a book omit any reference to one of its essential practitioners, the printer. This has been a particularly difficult book to set and impose, with its frequent changes of type-size, constant breaks in the text, and Virginia Woolf's errors in spelling and punctuation. T. & A. Constable Ltd of Edinburgh have taken endless pains with it, and the Editors and publishers are much indebted to them for their skill and care.

Several people have worked hard on the deciphering and typing of the letters, and preparing the text for publication. We wish particularly to thank the following. In England, Valerie Henderson, Pamela Kilbane and Lyn Dunbar; and in the United States, Gretchen Hess Gage and Gwendolyn W. Pierce.

NIGEL NICOLSON
JOANNE TRAUTMANN

Introduction

IT is remarkable that so many of Virginia Woolf's letters have survived. But it is even more remarkable how many were written. To quote a single example, on 7 August 1908 she wrote to her sister Vanessa a letter which ends: "I must now write to Nelly, Violet, Dorothea, Nun, Aunt Mary and ... Olive". Only the letter to Vanessa has been preserved.

The accident of survival has been a rough-and-ready process of selection, but sometimes a disappointing one. The high proportion of letters to Violet Dickinson in this volume is partly due to Virginia's love for her, but mainly to Violet's care in keeping almost all of them. There are no letters to Vanessa before her marriage to Clive Bell, none at all to her brother Adrian, none to friends like Rupert Brooke, Walter Headlam or Mary Sheepshanks, and only two in this period to Maynard Keynes and one to Desmond MacCarthy, though we can be certain that more were written. Important incidents in her life, like her childhood holidays at St Ives, later journeys to Greece, Turkey and Italy, and early meetings of the friends who later became known collectively as the Bloomsbury group, go almost unrecorded in her surviving correspondence. A particularly unhappy loss is the total destruction of her letters to Bruce Richmond, Editor of *The Times Literary Supplement* during the period when Virginia was beginning her writing career.

Enough remains, however, to show that she was a compulsive letter-writer. When she sought solitude, as she did but seldom, she warded off loneliness by maintaining conversations in writing. She wrote letters because she enjoyed it, and to stimulate replies. She was very affectionate by nature, and she demanded affection in return, hungry for a picture of the beloved person in circumstances which were unknown to her but imaginable. Friendship must be fed in absence, and the only food (before the telephone replaced it) was the written word. There must be news and gossip, a remembered tone of voice, a reminder of manner and gesture. By a sustained process of alternatively teasing and loving, she evolved an attitude to life which she presumed was shared, and the sharing of it bound her friends to her, her to them. One should allow oneself occasional spurts of strong feeling or descriptive narrative, but they must be broken off before they became too solemn, too contrived. One must not bore. A letter is a light kiss, a paper dart tossed in a friend's direction, to be thrown away or playfully returned.

Her second motive was to practise writing. She described people as if they had no substance until their differences from other people had been analysed, and events as if none had really taken place until it had been recorded, and recorded in a manner unmistakably her own, imagining the smile, the

xiii

frown, of the recipient, rarely repeating a phrase, so grateful for the wealth of the language that she scatters it wilfully, as lavish with words as a pianist is with notes, knowing that it is inexhaustible.

Despite the misleading tranquillity of this printed version of her letters, one can still sense the excitement and pleasure with which she wrote them, and with which they were received. They were read slowly and at intervals of at least a day. The reader of a collected edition does not have these advantages. The letters arrive on his table congested. He does not share Virginia's friends or private language, the memory of recent meetings and the anticipation of the next; nor, as he reads, do the phrases of reply come to his mind as they did to the first recipients. A letter from Virginia was bound to be provocative and at the same time reflective. "I like *thoughts* in a letter", she wrote to Emma Vaughan when she was still a child, "not *facts* only." But thoughts none the less take second place to facts, or rather grow out of them, for how can you distinguish between the carbuncle on a man's nose and the personality which it suggests? How describe the New Forest without seeing it with a new eye? "A true letter", she once wrote to Clive Bell, "should be a film of wax pressed close to the graving in the mind." It must record oscillations, the high notes and the low. There must be laughter in it and affection, and a hint of the tragedy and imperfections of mankind.

Mockery too: self-mockery, and the mocking of others, for to Virginia every new acquaintance was slightly ludicrous. It was difficult to retrieve her good opinion once it was lost. She liked and disliked exaggeratedly. Even affection was best expressed by ridicule. She was not cruel, but she could be malicious. The character-sketches which she drew of one friend when writing to another must have led her correspondents to wonder what she was writing about them. Lady Cromer becomes "like some Matron on the Parthenon", Virginia's aunt Caroline Emelia "a gloomy evergreen", when she was very fond of both of them. One can sympathise with Walter Lamb when he complained that Virginia "made things into webs, and might turn fiercely upon him for his faults". But her teasing was often direct, a literary artifice. She fired volleys of rhetorical questions and instructions. "Are you a fine character?" "Write me a sonnet about eyelashes". She challenges her friends to take impossible risks, like marrying. She can flatter by insult. "Are you exquisite or shabby?" "Adrian thinks he met you today. The lady smiled. Was it you, or a prostitute?" Nobody minded this sort of thing from Virginia. It was an aspect of her wit to place her friends in ridiculous situations. She called it "my curt and mordant style", but it was also an expression of her delight in the manifold variety of human nature. Her portraits of people were made up of innumerable lines which built into recognisable caricatures.

The portrait of herself which emerges is less clear. She wanted to know everything about her friends, and invented it when they would not tell her, but about herself she was guarded. From these letters one would not recognise Virginia if one met her at a party or in the street. One would not know her pace of walking and talking, whether she crossed Bond Street or a coastal field in an amble or a stride, nor whether she gave an immediate impression of aloofness or curiosity. Could she, did she, weep? What were her fantasies? Her letters are often garrulous, but in company she could be very quiet. Once, when shyness crippled me as a child, she consoled me by saying that friendship was like a still mountain-lake, into which a silver stream of talk should be allowed occasionally to trickle.

In her young womanhood she was hesitant, envious of other people's accomplishments in her own field, "desiring this man's art, and that man's scope", but of the world outside her own world of imaginative literature and music, the discussion of ideas and the enjoyment of the countryside, she could be contemptuous, not least of editors whose business it is to date letters and explain obscure allusions in them. She rarely mentions the convulsions of contemporary England. She classes politicians with journalists as "the lowest of God's creatures", despising their masculine self-approbation, and accusing them of "shrivelling all the best feelings". Only in the Women's Suffrage Movement did she identify herself with a political cause, and then not very intensively. She needed the harness of a disciplined political brain, like Leonard's. When she taught at Morley College, in South London, she felt more irritation than pity for the narrowness of uneducated minds. She shared many of the prejudices of her upper-middle class. "One has to be so cheerful with the lower classes", she could write, "or they think one diseased." Her letters are not free from xenophobia, nor from an occasional anti-Semitic smirk.

In other ways she reacted strongly against the assumptions of her times. Given the chance to enter the fashionable world, she hated it. She crept miserably into the corner of a ballroom to read *In Memoriam*, while Vanessa was partnered in every dance. She had no desire for the social success which her beauty and intelligence could so easily have won. She despised a fine country-house (having no eye for architecture) because of the grand style of living that went with it. The sharpest arrows of her wit were reserved for people who gave themselves airs and dressed expensively, and for those who disguised their uncharitableness in the trappings of religion. She resented strongly the degradation of women in a masculine society, censuring her own father for not having given her a proper education, while her brothers were sent automatically to school and university. She thought it outrageous that a clever woman like Madge Vaughan should be forced into the stultifying role of a headmaster's wife, which prevented her from writing. She was determined that the man she married would be as worthy of her as she of him. They were to be equal partners.

Virginia was at intervals insane, and this volume will be scanned for indications of it. There are not many. When she was not mad her mind was crystal sharp. Her bouts of insanity seem actually to have clarified it, like a storm the sky. Each time she recovers from one of her early attacks, she seems slightly more mature. Her handwriting improves: she drops childish expressions. The prospect of another did not particularly alarm her. It was a disease which she had learnt to live with, and it even had its advantages, for it expanded her imagination into fields of pure fantasy. "The insane view of life has much to be said for it", she told Emma Vaughan. The letter which she wrote to Violet Dickinson in 1904 (No. 182) indicates what torments she endured, but soon afterwards she was able to subject her lunacy to self-mocking retrospect. Only one letter in this volume (440) is written apparently under its influence, but it merely skirts the borderline between her genius and her folly, rendering her jokes hysterical and her imagination wild. But who can tell whether a phrase like "We laughed till the spiders waltzed in the corners, and were strangled in their own webs" is the sane Virginia or the mad, a wandering of the mind or a literary exercise in the bizarre? They have much in common. Her letters from the Twickenham mental home in 1910 reveal the transition: "I have been out in the garden for 2 hours; and feel quite normal. I feel my brains, like a pear, to see if its ripe; it will be exquisite by September" (531). She was courageous and patient during her attacks, and as little affected by them afterwards as a normal person is by pneumonia. If one calls sanity clarity, and insanity turmoil, then she could pass from one state to the other as easily as sit down to a hearty breakfast after a nightmare. She was not embarrassed by what had happened to her, finding no difficulty in re-establishing her friendships and occupations. She was simply 'restored'.

She remained a virgin until her marriage, and found the idea of sex with a man frightening if not abhorrent. She warned Leonard at the time of their engagement, "There are moments—when you kissed me the other day was one—when I feel no more than a rock". Quentin Bell suggests that George and Gerald Duckworth's "nasty erotic skirmishes" in childhood may have terrified her into "a posture of frozen and defensive panic", and he quotes considerable evidence for his view, notably the letter (576) which describes Janet Case's reaction to Virginia's revelations about George's conduct. Professor Bell had not however read Virginia's letters to George (e.g. 12, 13, 21, 29, 30) written during or soon after these alleged incidents. If he had read them, it is unlikely that he would have worded his condemnation of George quite so sharply. It is difficult to believe that so innocent a child would have retained this degree of affection for a man guilty of an 'incestuous relationship' with her (the term appears in the Bell index), nor that Vanessa, the other victim of his endearments, would have gone happily to Paris with him in April 1900, and to Rome two years later. Something must have happened to explain Virginia's later disgust, but she may have exaggerated it in recollection. Let us imagine what may have occurred. At that time the two young men were sharing the house at Hyde Park Gate with two exceptionally pretty girls, related to them only through their dead mother. If George and Gerald did caress their half-sisters occasionally, perhaps lean over their desks or their beds to stroke their hair and shoulders, it would not seem to us unnatural nor too shocking. But to the girls, especially to Virginia, who was exceptionally modest, it would appear appalling in retrospect, particularly when she had drifted apart from George, and grown contemptuous of his smart clothes, smart friends, smart marriage, and social self-importance. "The excellent George" had become "a mere lump of flesh, veined with sentiment" (481). Her silent revulsion from his covert sexuality had hitherto co-existed with family affection and appreciation of his genuine kindness, generosity and amiability. Later she exploded in indignation.

Virginia and Vanessa had many admirers. Leonard Woolf in *Sowing* describes them as "young women of astonishing beauty. . . . It was almost impossible for a man not to fall in love with them", and Virginia received at least four offers of marriage before she accepted Leonard's. But for several years after she grew up, her deepest affections were reserved for her family and two or three women friends.

First in order, then as always, came Vanessa. "There is no doubt that I love you better than anyone in the world", she wrote to her. "You are the most complete human-being of us all." Sometimes she loved her almost to the point of thought-incest. They were like a pair of fox-cubs with their verbal licks, little growls, a tumbling of limbs, the nipping of ears. Vanessa was the more powerful person of the two. "She has volcanoes underneath her sedate manner", and it was this combination of audacity and tenderness in her nature which made her so strong an influence in Virginia's life, stronger even than Leslie Stephen, in whom Virginia found parts missing, imagination, for example, and a sense of fun. Her brother Thoby was to her what Branwell had been to Charlotte Brontë before he became dissolute. He was her friend and leader and (within certain limits) her confidant. Her childhood letters to him are like those which most girls write to their elder brothers, only longer, and they are of interest mainly because they reveal Virginia's ebullience as a child, her normality, and her burgeoning gift for comedy. For Adrian her feelings were less strong, and perhaps she underestimated him, for he was a good, clever and affectionate man, whose quality was best revealed by the quality of his friends. Perhaps Virginia was thrown too much into his company after Thoby died and Vanessa married. Adrian was quite a lump to have around, but Virginia still thought of him as a "poor little boy" when he was 6 feet 5 inches tall and aged 23.

Two of her friendships with older women aroused in her a strength of feeling indistinguishable from love. One was Madge Vaughan, a daughter of John Addington Symonds, who married Virginia's cousin, William Wyamar Vaughan, the headmaster successively of Giggleswick, Wellington College and Rugby. There is more baby-talk in Virginia's letters to Madge's sister-in-law Emma Vaughan (Toad), and from them one might deduce that it was Emma whom Virginia loved. But it was to Madge, 13 years older than herself, that Virginia first opened her heart about her literary ambitions, and Madge who became Sally in *Mrs Dalloway*. She had a crush on her, though one would never guess it from the letters alone. Virginia described her as "a charming woman, full of theories and emotions, and innumerable questions, like a child of 2". Another source, David Newsome's *History of Wellington College*, speaks of her as "brilliant and impulsive, unconventional and sensitive". She was herself a writer, but schools and children monopolised her time, and Virginia thought her rare talent wasted.

The second was Violet Dickinson. More than half the letters in this volume were written to her, and but for them she might be quite forgotten. The facts of her life are simple. She was born in 1865, the daughter of Edmund Dickinson, a Somersetshire squire, and her mother was the daughter of the 3rd Lord Auckland. Violet lived most of her adult life at Welwyn with her brother Oswald (Ozzie) who became Secretary to the Commissioners in Lunacy and godfather to the present Editor. Neither she nor Ozzie ever married, and when she died in 1948, she left the whole of her modest fortune (£25,000) to him. She published one book, the letters of her great-aunt Emily Eden, in 1919. She was 6 feet 2 inches tall, gawky, even graceless, but everybody who knew her, in the literary and fashionable world which she frequented, adored her.

Virginia had known Violet since childhood. She had been a friend of Stella Duckworth and a frequent visitor to Hyde Park Gate, but it was not until 1902, when Virginia was 20 and Violet 37, that they began to correspond as intimates. In her early letters Virginia barely conceals the passion which she had conceived for this awkward but lovable woman. She creates a menagerie of aliases for herself—Sparroy (sparrow + monkey?), Kangaroo, Wallaby; calls Violet My Aunt, My Child, My Woman; invents a husband for her, who seems to have been Ozzie or a neighbour, Walter Crum, of whom she pretended intense jealousy, and even more of Mrs Crum. Their intimacy may have gone further than childish endearments. Virginia writes and demands letters which she describes as 'hot': examples are Nos. 91 and 296. But their romantic friendship was based on something more profound. "You are the only sympathetic woman in the world. That's why everybody comes to you with their troubles." It was with Violet that Virginia took refuge for three months when she went mad in the summer of 1904. It was again to Violet that she turned for comfort when her father, and then her brother, lay dying, and she showed her reciprocal concern most dramatically by concealing from her for a month the news of Thoby's death (going so far as to invent his menus, his fluctuating temperature, his conversation and his plans for convalescence) until Violet should recover from her own illness sufficiently to stand the shock. They had many friends in common, notably Beatrice Thynne and Lady Robert Cecil, with whom Violet went on a world cruise; and many interests, like book-binding, music, and the whole world of literature. Virginia sent her early manuscripts to Welwyn, and Violet introduced her to Mrs Lyttelton, Women's Editor of *The Guardian*, the first to publish Virginia's work. Gradually, from about 1907, Virginia's passion faded. Violet could not compete with Bloomsbury. But Virginia continued to write to her, now more as a receptacle than a confidant—"It becomes necessary to empty the brew on someone" (380)—and as her infatuation drained, her letters became stronger and less embarrassing. Their correspondence was maintained throughout Virginia's life, and towards the end of it Violet sent her the entire collection, some 450 letters recording a love that had grown cold.

Her letters to Lady Robert Cecil are among the best in this volume. A daughter of the Earl of Durham and married to one of Lord Salisbury's most distinguished sons, she belonged to a world which Virginia would have scorned had Nelly not been a woman of unusual gifts. Her nephew Lord David Cecil thus remembers her: "Exquisitely pretty, with small fine features and large dark eyes, she combined a sharp, strong, witty intelligence with a delicate artistic and literary sensibility". She was a writer, although she published nothing except reviews, and Virginia respected her judgement well enough to submit her own manuscripts for comment, and to propose that they should contribute a joint literary column to the *Cornhill*. They soon established a close friendship, stranger for the fact that Nelly was very deaf, and their conversation must have been less fun than their correspondence. In these letters we see at its best Virginia's teasing solicitude, her provocative affection, her instinctive feeling for the borderline between banter and impertinence—her gift, in fact, for friendship, which consisted in risking little moves towards another person, moves which can be retrieved if they evoke no response, the light scratch of a kitten that draws no blood. Nelly Cecil was an important woman, grand, rich, involved in great affairs, but behind Virginia's letters is the suggestion that Nelly is nicer than all this implies, would at any moment exchange Hatfield for a cottage, a tiara for a Tauchnitz, and that she shares with Virginia an articulate simplicity, a faint derision of pomp and circumstance, but because she could manage both when required to by her position, she had an extra dimension which Virginia somehow envied.

When a man (apart from her relations) was first added to Virginia's correspondents, she was already 24 years old, and then she wrote to him only because he too had become a relation, Clive Bell. She found it curiously difficult. She resented Clive's intrusion between herself and Vanessa, but there was something more. She did not know what tone of voice to adopt with men. To many readers of this volume it may come as a surprise to find how slowly she discovered her lifelong friends among Thoby's, how indifferent she remained for several years to the Bloomsbury style of living and talking. Letter 512 illustrates this well. Her first long letter to Clive (345) was a disaster, stilted and arch, the only one, as far as we know, for which she wrote a draft. Clive must have wondered what sort of woman he had for a sister-in-law as much as Virginia was wondering about him. Realising that she had adopted a pose untrue to herself, she abandoned it. A few months later they got on to terms which were not merely natural, but flirtatious. Her jealousy and fear of him turned into complicity. They became allies to save Vanessa from domesticity, from babies who leaked unpleasantly from every orifice; and failing, turned to each other. Clive was her most responsive correspondent. She enjoyed his enjoyment of duelling with a woman, and it is only with him that she ventures to discuss her work unflinchingly. Her letters to him and other men developed a tauter style: she honed her wit upon their rougher texture, and gave her letters more sinew. She took more trouble with the choice and cadence of words, wrote seriously about serious things, and was more sensitive to a man's reaction than she was to a woman's. After pages of Toad and Sparroy, they come as a relief.

With Lytton Strachey she was not flirtatious, although for the space of a few hours she found herself engaged to him. Each, as Leonard Woolf remarked in his bowdlerised edition of their correspondence, was a little wary of the other. "They were always on their best behaviour, and never felt so much at ease as they did in their dealings with people whom they admired and respected less." This needs some qualification, for Virginia's behaviour was not at its best in any sense except the literary. In writing to Lytton she became inordinately malicious. She wished him to think her clever more than delectable. The slide of her ski turns into the cut of a skate. There is a certain defensiveness in her manner towards him, a touch of conceit tempered by her fear of appearing ridiculous, of finding her irony turned against her. She was alarmed by him, and faintly jealous.

The letters of Virginia Woolf are of supreme interest because she became a writer of genius. The origins of her style and the newness of her vision are all to be found here. "The way to get life into letters", she wrote to Vanessa, "is to be interested in other people." The same is true of her novels. It was not so much other books which influenced her, as talk, the observation of the way people behave, her friendship with men and women who enquire, challenge, dissect, and her own fluctuating feelings about them, theirs about her. This is the subject-matter of her letters as it is of her fiction. Her literary achievement was to analyse in a new way the mysterious differences which form 'character': the blemishes on a mind are as real to her as the blotches on a face. The letters are a record of her daily observation: the novels a distillation of it. In both she sought 'clarity', avoiding triteness of thought and expression, disdaining convention and humbug. What mattered to her (as she once defined it for Vita Sackville-West), was "the central transparency", by which she meant the precise analysis of common circumstances. She was not interested in the weird, but in the mystery of the normal.

In one of her letters to Clive Bell (429), commenting on Lytton Strachey's poems, she complains, "I do not feel that I am breasting fresh streams", and in illustration she quotes four pairs of words which he had written: 'enormous mouth'; 'unimaginable repose'; 'mysterious ease'; 'incomparably dim'. She thought it a violation of language to re-use it in this way. Words must be sought in crevasses, strung like beads, their shapes and colours tried against each other, in order to "achieve in the end some kind of whole made of shivering fragments; to me this seems the natural process; the flight of the mind" (quoted by Quentin Bell, Vol. I, p. 138). One can watch her experimenting with this process in her letters.

She wrote only one novel, her first, during the period covered by this volume. It was *The Voyage Out*, to which she refers throughout as *Melymbrosia*. The similarity between the style of the novel and the style of her letters is evident, but it is a measure of the unquenchable springs of her inspiration that so little is repeated from one into the other. It would be difficult to find a single phrase which they have in common. When one searches the novel for incidents in her own experience, one finds but few: the parallel between Thoby's and Rachel's deaths is the most striking, but the circumstances are much changed; and Rachel's fantasies may be reflections of Virginia's own during her fits of madness. Her plot develops during a long voyage by cargo-boat, and then moves to a South American coastal resort, with a jungle behind. Virginia had made only one sea-voyage, and it was by liner to Portugal: she had never seen the tropics. The story did not require this odd setting: it could have been told against the background of the Mediterranean, which she knew well, or even of Cornwall, which she knew intimately. But places that she had never seen were as real to her as people whom she had never met.

Her friendships are echoed in certain characters: Vanessa in Helen (but Helen was at least 15 years older); Lytton in St John; Kitty Maxse in Mrs Dalloway; Jack Hills in Mr Dalloway; possibly Thoby in Terence; Virginia herself in Rachel. The resemblances are slight; she was too proud an author to refashion the materials nearest to her hand. But she does use the book to air her opinions: her resentment of the role allotted by men to women; her contempt of Christian humbug; her sense of the hugeness of nature compared to the smallness of man. It is a novel of protest and compassion. One hears the snapping of Victorian shackles. But it is also an enquiry into the nature of love. The sexual element plays only a small part in it, as of a thing observed with curiosity more than a thing experienced. But she wonders outloud whether wedlock was a desirable, an endurable, state, for this was the question uppermost in her mind at the time, and the death of Rachel is her way of leaving it unanswered.

In her own life it was answered a few days after she finished the manuscript. At the age of 30, and on the last page of this volume, she married Leonard Woolf.

NIGEL NICOLSON
Sissinghurst Castle, Kent

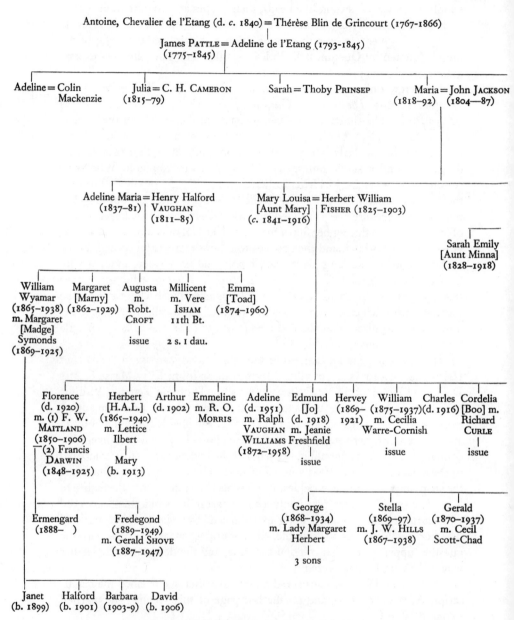

Antoine, Chevalier de l'Etang (d. *c.* 1840) = Thérèse Blin de Grincourt (1767-1866)

James PATTLE = Adeline de l'Etang (1793-1845)
(1775–1845)

Adeline = Colin Mackenzie

Julia = C. H. CAMERON (1815–79)

Sarah = Thoby PRINSEP

Maria = John JACKSON (1818–92) (1804—87)

Adeline Maria = Henry Halford (1837–81) VAUGHAN (1811–85)

Mary Louisa = Herbert William [Aunt Mary] FISHER (1825–1903) (*c.* 1841–1916)

Sarah Emily [Aunt Minna] (1828–1918)

William Wyamar (1865–1938) m. Margaret [Madge] Symonds (1869–1925)

Margaret [Marny] (1862–1929)

Augusta m. Robt. CROFT

issue

Millicent m. Vere ISHAM 11th Bt.

2 s. 1 dau.

Emma [Toad] (1874–1960)

Florence (d. 1920) m. (1) F. W. MAITLAND (1850–1906) (2) Francis DARWIN (1848–1925)

Herbert [H.A.L.] (1865–1940) m. Lettice Ilbert

Mary (b. 1913)

Arthur (d. 1902)

Emmeline m. R. O. MORRIS

Adeline (d. 1951) m. Ralph VAUGHAN WILLIAMS (1872–1958)

Edmund [Jo] (d. 1918) m. Jeanie Freshfield

issue

Hervey (1869– 1921)

William (1875–1937) m. Cecilia Warre-Cornish

issue

Charles (d. 1916)

Cordelia [Boo] m. Richard CURLE

issue

Ermengard (1888–   )

Fredegond (1889–1949) m. Gerald SHOVE (1887–1947)

George (1868–1934) m. Lady Margaret Herbert

3 sons

Stella (1869–97) m. J. W. HILLS (1867–1938)

Gerald (1870–1937) m. Cecil Scott-Chad

Janet (b. 1899)

Halford (b. 1901)

Barbara (1903-9)

David (b. 1906)

Based upon the Family Tree in Quentin Bell, Vol. I.

TREE

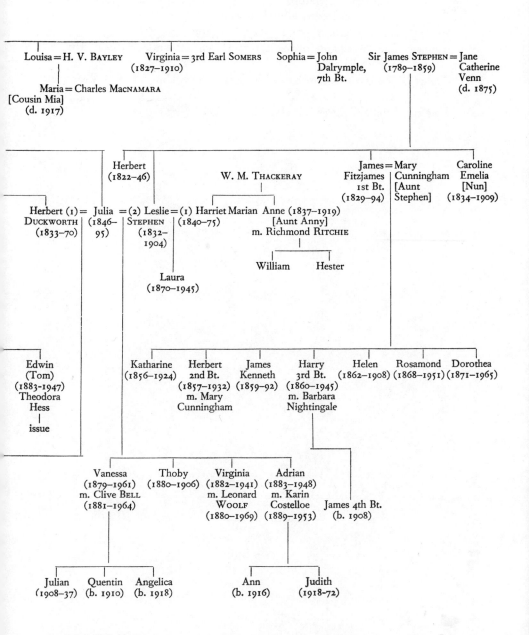

Louisa = H. V. BAYLEY   Virginia = 3rd Earl SOMERS   Sophia = John   Sir James STEPHEN = Jane
                             (1827–1910)   Dalrymple,   (1789–1859)   Catherine
                                             7th Bt.   Venn

Maria = Charles MacNAMARA   (d. 1875)
[Cousin Mia]
(d. 1917)

Herbert   W. M. THACKERAY   James = Mary   Caroline
(1822–46)   Fitzjames   Cunningham   Emelia
                                                  1st Bt.   [Aunt   [Nun]
                                                 (1829–94)   Stephen]   (1834–1909)

Herbert (1) =   Julia   = (2) Leslie = (1) Harriet Marian Anne (1837–1919)
DUCKWORTH   (1846–   STEPHEN   (1840–75)   [Aunt Anny]
(1833–70)   95)   (1832–   m. Richmond RITCHIE
                     1904)

                                              William   Hester

                    Laura
                (1870–1945)

Edwin   Katharine   Herbert   James   Harry   Helen   Rosamond   Dorothea
(Tom)   (1856–1924)   2nd Bt.   Kenneth   3rd Bt.   (1862–1908)   (1868–1951) (1871–1965)
(1883-1947)   (1857–1932)   (1859–92)   (1860–1945)
Theodora   m. Mary   m. Barbara
Hess   Cunningham   Nightingale

issue

          Vanessa   Thoby   Virginia   Adrian
          (1879–1961)   (1880–1906)   (1882–1941)   (1883–1948)
          m. Clive BELL   m. Leonard   m. Karin
          (1881–1964)   WOOLF   Costelloe   James 4th Bt.
                                       (1880–1969)   (1889–1953)   (b. 1908)

Julian   Quentin   Angelica   Ann   Judith
(1908-37)   (b. 1910)   (b. 1918)   (b. 1916)   (1918-72)

Abbreviations at foot of letters

Berg: The Henry W. and Alfred A. Berg Collection of English and American Literature in the New York Public Library (Astor, Lenox and Tilden Foundations).

Sussex: University of Sussex Library, Brighton.

Hatfield: The Marquess of Salisbury (Cecil Papers), Hatfield House, Hertfordshire.

Texas: The Humanities Research Center, The University of Texas, at Austin, Texas, U.S.A.

King's: King's College Library, Cambridge.

Letters 1-7

Adeline Virginia Stephen was born on 25 January 1882. Her first surviving letter was written when she was 6 years old. In 1888 her sister Vanessa was 9, her brother Thoby nearly 8, and her younger brother Adrian 4. They lived with their parents Leslie Stephen (aged 55) and Julia (42) in Hyde Park Gate, a respectable cul-de-sac in Kensington. The other members of the family were Julia's three children by her first marriage to Herbert Duckworth, George (20), Stella (19) and Gerald (18), and for a time Laura (18), Leslie's weak-minded child by his first marriage to Harriet Thackeray, who had died in 1875. There were also seven servants in the household. Thoby and Adrian went in turn to preparatory schools, followed by Clifton College (Thoby) and Westminster School (Adrian), and thence to Cambridge, but the girls were educated at home, mainly by their parents and partly by borrowing books from their father's library. Each summer until 1894 the whole family went on holiday to St Ives in Cornwall. The tragic incidents in Virginia's otherwise happy childhood were the deaths of her mother from rheumatic fever in May 1895, and of her half-sister Stella from peritonitis in July 1897, only three months after her marriage to Jack Hills. The first of these disasters caused Virginia to have a mental breakdown when she was aged 13.

1: To James Russell Lowell
FROM LESLIE STEPHEN AND VIRGINIA STEPHEN

20.8.88   [22 *Hyde Park Gate, S.W.*]

My dear Lowell,
    This is a spontaneous production of Miss Stephen, on seeing a picture of the Adirondacks and hearing that you had been there. She expresses the sentiments of the family in the last clause of the document. You will see that I am lazy in the mornings and amusing myself by reading lessons with the children instead of dictionarying.[1] I am thereby growing fat and shall be glad indeed if I can bestow some of my idleness upon you. We are all well—the children in exuberant spirits and we have better weather here than elsewhere in these islands. So come and have your share.

Ever yours afftely,
L. Stephen

1. Leslie Stephen began editing the *Dictionary of National Biography* in the year of Virginia's birth, 1882.

MY DEAR GODPAPA[1] HAVE YOU BEEN TO THE ADIRONDACKS AND
HAVE YOU SEEN LOTS OF WILD BEASTS AND A LOT OF BIRDS IN
THEIR NESTS YOU ARE A NAUGHTY MAN NOT TO COME HERE GOOD
BYE

YOUR AFFECT[e]

VIRGINIA

Houghton Library, Harvard University

2: TO THOBY STEPHEN   [*22 Hyde Park Gate, S.W.*]

Typewritten
Friday March 6th [1896]

My dear Thoby,

How does the [family] Museum get on? Father says that they have
discovered an ape which is nearer to a man than anything else which has been
yet found.[2] Of course they mean the genus "Sambo", which doubtless you
remember capturing twenty years ago with me. Mr Gibbses Butlers wife,
keeps a venerable dachshund. This animal resolutely refuses to wear a
muzzle, she says it screams at the sight of one, and so they are going to buy
a cage to take it out in!

It is so windy to day, that Miss Jan [Virginia herself] is quite afraid of
venturing out. The other day her skirt was blown over her head, and she
trotted along in a pair of red flannel drawers to the great amusement of the
Curate who happened to be coming out of Church. She swears that she
blushed the colour of the said drawers, but that must be taken for granted.
I have nothing to tell you, Your Highness; and my candle insists upon
tumbling over every five minutes; and Nessa is snarling at the noise; and my
Virgil must be looked out; and I expect that you must go into school; so
Good Bye, your Mightiness; write to me when feel so inclined; your loving
Goatus Esq. . . .

Are you interested in the Italians, and what is it all about, and which side
am I?[3]

Dictated by father
I want to see how quick this wretched girl can typewrite. I think that she

1. Although the Stephen children were not baptized, they had 'sponsors', of whom
   Lowell, the poet and critic, and American Minister in London 1880–1885, was
   Virginia's. In 1888 he was 69.
2. *Pithecanthropus erectus*, of which the fossilised remains were discovered by
   Dr Eugene Dubois in Java in 1891, and first published by him in 1894.
3. On 1 March 1896 an Italian invading force was crushed by the Abyssinians at
   Adowa. The battle led to a treaty which acknowledged the independence of
   Ethiopia.

does it rather better than I had expected. My cold is better and I hope that I shall see you on Thursday.

Leslie Stephen

King's

3: To Thoby Stephen   22 *Hyde Park Gate, S.W.*

[26 January 1897]

My dear Thoby,[1]
    The size of the film is $3\frac{1}{2} \times 2\frac{5}{8}$. We have just finished the remains of my cake,[2] which was an extremely good plumless Madeira one! Gerald [Duckworth] tipped me £1, Stella [Duckworth] gave me the arm chair in which I am now sitting, Adrian [Stephen] a holder for my pen, father a Lockhart's Life of Scott (which has not yet come), cousin Mia[3] a diary, and Mrs [F. W.] Gibbs a most gorgeous gilt edged, wide margined beautifully printed and engraved book by Mr Creighton[4]—a life of Queen Elizabeth— which I shall have to try and get through—
    Adrian was very much pleased when I told him of Georgie's [Duckworth] 10 shillings, which came this morning—We are eating Aunt Marys [Fisher] jams—How do you like your lot?
    This is not supposed to be a *proper* letter, such as you are going to write me, but there is nothing much to say. It is quite freezing today, with the coldest wind *I* ever felt—I have taken to wearing red woollen cuffs, and sit over the fire all day long—
    Goodbye,

Your loving,
Goat

King's

4: To Thoby Stephen   22 *Hyde Park Gate, S.W.*

[1 February 1897]

My dear Thoby,
    Your films came last night, and I found them awaiting me on my supper plate—Two beautiful packets of superfine celluloid Films! A thousand thanks (as the French say) my dear Herbert for this munificent gift—I shall devote not a few to your remarkable face—at no distant date I trust—Till

1. Thoby was now at Clifton College.
2. Virginia was 15 on 25 January.
3. Maria Macnamara, daughter of Louisa Pattle and Henry Vincent Bayley.
4. Mandell Creighton, *Queen Elizabeth*, 1896.

that inducement arrives to lure them forth to the light of day, they are securely locked up in the darkest draw [*sic*] of the "oak davenport".

Gradually all my presents have arrived—Fathers Lockhart came the evening I wrote to you—ten most exquisite little volumes, half bound in purple leather, with gilt scrolls and twirls and thistles everywhere, and a most artistic blue and brown mottling on their other parts. So my blinded eyesight is poring more fervidly than ever over miserable books—only not even you, my dear brother, could give such an epithet to these lovely creatures. Then Jack [Hills] gave me a pair of "Monier Williams" skates, the best on the market, sir, costing 17s 6d (I had the buying of 'em!) and screwed on to your feet by 8 little screws. They are going to be honoured by a special pair of boots, reserved entirely for them during the winter months— a stout but elegant pair, laced, with strong new soles—Such a pair was pre*pared* (quite unintentional) for me just as the frost departed this land, and now the skates along with the films and other precious things are shut up in the oak Davenport—Then a day or two ago I had a letter from Georgie offering me an enclosure, which however was not enclosed—But this morning came a second letter, and a cheque for £1. So our finances are looking up, and will be able to bear the strain of Stella's wedding presents,[1] tolerably well. How does thy purse conduct itself My Herbert? I hope that the six pots of jam have saved it something as yet—indeed it will require a little time for you to dispose of that jam—our pots were very juiceless and inferior.

There mi-lord! I have just written a long letter to George,—terrible discovery! The leather of one of my Scotts is scratched and shows a bloody red line—I suspect Pauline.[2]

Goodbye, milord, mind you write an answer to this letter, the first half only of which is a letter of thanks.

Your loving,
Goatus Esq

A libel I protest—my skating is particularly graceful and I never once have come to grief this winter—Maria [Vanessa] shall not ornament *my* letters again in a hurry—

[See drawing opposite]

King's

1. Stella Duckworth married John Waller Hills on 10 April 1897.
2. The Swiss maid at Hyde Park Gate.

N. Stephen fecit.

5: TO THOBY STEPHEN   [22 *Hyde Park Gate, S.W.*]

[24 February 1897]

My dear Thoby,

It is almost halfway through the term now, and no letter has reached me from my beloved brother. "Gather ye rosebuds while ye may", as your favourite poet says—which is not a very apt quotation I grieve to find on examining my meaning—but the long and short business like non-poetical sum total—is that you must mend your pen without delay, and despatch to dear Viginea (as her friends call her) as many epistles as you can—

The beauty of my language is sick, that I am driven to confess the reason o't—Mr Payn[1] sent father a book which is a great help to him (Mr Payn) in his writings—called the Thesaurus of English Words—Perhaps you can

1. James Payn, novelist and Editor of the *Cornhill Magazine* 1883-96.

5

explain Thesaurus—but the object of the Work is to provide poor scant languaged authors, with three or four different words for the same idea, so that their sentences may not jar—This father took as an insult, and accordingly handed it over to me—and I have been trying to make use of it—

This afternoon Stella and I walked through the Park in hopes of catching a glimpse of Her Majesty the Queen—who is in London for a drawing room. We did not meet her however, and had given up all hopes of bowing to her or waving our packlywanks when, on coming back homewards to Hyde Park Corner, to catch our bus, we found a tremendous crowd—Miss Becca (Stella) piloted us across to the gateway, through which the Queen was to pass, and which was lined with people—Just as we got across, there was a general rush and scramble—policemen waving their arms to clear the road, hats flying into the air—and four beautiful horses trotted past us—that was about as much as we saw—the crowd tumbled over us, and only showed one a glimpse of the Queens bonnet bobbing up and down, and her two Highlanders—After this excitement we had to recross the street—Poor Janet [Virginia] was almost crushed by the agitated ladies (they were almost all stout females from the country) who were also making for the pavement— The carriages and busses which had been held back, now poured down thicker than ever, and it was with the greatest relief my dear Herbert that I found myself stranded by St Georges Hospital—Then three or four gorgeous red and gold carriages with red and gold gentlemen inside, passed into the Park—and ladies in white and ostrich feathers from the drawing room, and the sight was over.

The most loyal of Her Majestys subjects stood in the road till she should return from her drive, but I regret to say that not even another sight of the top of the Queens bonnet was strong enough inducement to prevent Becca and me from hailing the nearest Hansom and driving home to tea—All the Green park was crowded, and all Hyde Park—The poor old lady is huzzaed whenever she appears, and crowds watch Buckingham Palace to have the opportunity—

That is all my Court News—now for 22 H P G.

Georgie came back yesterday, and brought a box of presents with him— for Stella a splendid fan—real lace, and real tortoiseshell, with her initials in diamonds; for Jack a medal which a young man always gives in France to his young lady—a picture on it of cupid and a pair of lovers receiving rings— for Gerald a machine with which you make your cigarettes and for father chocolates and French novels, for Nessa a fan, and for Adrian and me portfolios which French school boys use. Stella's fan cost £20 almost, and Nessa's a pound each (she has two) so you may imagine what your brother has been spending in Paris.

I do a few lessons with Stella every morning, but nothing very great.

Goodbye your loving,

King's

Goatus Esq

[14 May 1897]

My dear Thoby,

You do not say whether you consented to write an account of the Museum—but of course, my dear brother, you must do so—this will make your name known in Scientific circles—Talking of Entomology *etc*: I must tell you that our respected Aunt at Cambridge [Caroline Emelia Stephen] has entrapped a basket full of *wireworms* by putting sweet cake underground. She cheerfully proposed to present the Society [of Stephens] with this prize; however, I wrote a vehement letter (in shorthand) requesting her to put an end to the creatures at once, or at any rate to keep them for her own private enjoyment only. To which comes an answer (in vehement shorthand also) to say that they have been made way with long ago—how she does not state—

There is no more entomological news for you—except that the chrysalises are still in their maiden(?) state, and likely to remain so—

By the bye—yesterday, while conducting some evacuations in the back garden (for purposes which I will explain later on) we discovered a repulsive shiny brown chrysalis—kicking its tail with the greatest animation. After some discussion we (The President [Leslie Stephen] and I) decided that the pupa was only that of a beetle—and as such was exposed upon the garden wall, to take its chance—of death, by sparrows, or by the entomological investigations of the garden black cat—

The said evacuations have been organised by my revered father: he has presented me with a set of gardening tools—and commands me to convert the back garden—Already we have created a flower bed (minus the flowers it is true) and we propose to renew the grass—to have a border of lilies and other flowers—to rake the whole place clean—in short do not be surprised if you behold a miniature Kew when you are next here—Then, that we may not be wholly ornamental and wasteful—when the winter comes the flower beds are to be planted with cabbages—and one of these days we hope to install a cow or at least a sheep on the luxuriant pastures—

There mi' lord—this is a truly business like account of my occupations.

Today Stella went out for the first time in a bath chair[1]—she is much better I think—she really looks fairly well and plump. Dr Seton only comes every other day, and he is quite comfortable about her—one of her nurses has gone, and I think the other goes tomorrow or the day after. I spend most of my day over there—when Nessa is at her drawing—

My Dear Dr Seton says I must not do *any* lessons this term[2]; so I am

1. Since the end of April Stella Hills had been ill with peritonitis at her new home, 24 Hyde Park Gate, opposite No 22.
2. Virginia had been suffering from a slight nervousness which caused her family to fear a repetition of her mental breakdown after her mother's death in 1895.

cast upon the four winds—or whatever the proverb is—Nevertheless, my beloved Macaulay (with miserable eyesight *etc*—quoth JT.S [Thoby]) is most comforting—and Nessa and Adrian are terribly industrious. A. has just come in to say that he is going to *sing* in the School Concert!!! What is the world coming to? Now milord: this is a model letter: four closely packed sheets: go thou and do likewise!

Good bye—your loving,

Goat

King's

7: To Thoby Stephen   [22 *Hyde Park Gate, S.W.*]

Monday [24 May 1897]

My dear Thoby,

I have found out all the paints that Nessa wants[1], and their prices on the Store list—They are a good deal more expensive than I thought—Adrian is not saying how much money he has got—Stella keeps it for him—and so he cannot say exactly how much he will be able to give—but I expect not quite half. They altogether come to 9s. 4.½.—If you will look at the list, and then send it with a postal order to the stores, so that they may come before Sunday. I will write again, and say how much Adrian can give.

Mr [F. W.] Gibbs has given Nessa and me *three* tickets to see the Procession[2]—from St Thomas's Hospital—they are very good places he says. He does not know whether he can go with us himself but he told us to look out for a young man in want of a place who could look after us—So we are going to see him; and ask him whether you do not fulfil all the requirements!

Write to me directly if you think 9s. 4½ too much, and I will tell you of something else to get her.

Your loving,

Goat

Fill in the date at the top of the form. I am signing it.

King's

1. On 30 May Vanessa was 18, and the same day was Stella's 28th birthday.
2. Queen Victoria's Diamond Jubilee on 22 June.

Letters 8-41

With both her mother and half-sister Stella dead, Vanessa took over the running of Hyde Park Gate and the care of her increasingly morose father, while Virginia continued her education, partly by reading of her own choice, and partly under the tuition of Dr Warr of King's College and Clara Pater, who taught her Greek and Latin respectively. She became increasingly interested in literature and music, and Vanessa in painting. Their lives were not dull, for the four Stephen children had each other to console themselves for the tedium of entertaining their father's old friends and relations, and for their forced association with the army of Fisher and Stephen cousins. George and Gerald Duckworth still lived with them, and so for a time did Jack Hills, Stella's widower, with whom Vanessa was temporarily half in love. They amused themselves by bug-hunting and book-binding. They made frequent expeditions—to the New Forest, Brighton, Huntingdonshire, Lyme Regis, the Fens and Cambridge—and Virginia gradually began to make a new set of friends. Among her cousins were three whom she liked specially, the Vaughan sisters, Margaret (Marny) and Emma (Toad), and their sister-in-law Margaret (Madge). In 1900-1 she first met Thoby's Cambridge friends, Clive Bell and Lytton Strachey, with whom she had more in common than with the smart London society to which George Duckworth gallantly tried to introduce his half-sisters. Virginia had already begun to write intermittently a journal in which she practised narrative and descriptions of people and places. In 1902 she was 20.

8: To Thoby Stephen [Corby Castle, Carlisle]¹

Monday [27 September 1897]

My dear old Gribbs,

We are left to ourselves this afternoon, and, as some relief to my feelings, I will write to your Highness.

First of all, what a racoon—a wool-gathering racoon—you are to forget the bugs! Now I suppose you will not be able to go in for the prize unless *we* send them down in a Postal Box—what think you of that plan?

We got here on Saturday, at about 6, having started at 11.30. The house is a great red square country house—rather like the Park at Painswick. There is a great hall where you go in, and drawing rooms opening out of it. I have

---

1. Corby Castle, which lies just east of Carlisle on the River Eden, was the home of Herbert Hills, father of Jack. Stella Hills had died in London on 19 July, when she was expecting a baby.

never been in the midst of such gorgeosity in the whole of my long life. Nessa has a great room, and I have a small one next door. There are innumerable rooms and servants (four gents to wait on us at dinner!) and state rooms and a gallery, and smoking room—We have long long dinners—seven courses—and everything is very stately and uncomfortable. Susan Lushington is here, which is a blessing as she does all the talking, but she goes tomorrow. The river is quite near the house—a river quite different from our beloved Thames—it is most fiery and excitable—Jack has been fishing all this morning but has caught nothing. He is going to fish again this afternoon, and we are going to watch him. Yesterday we did nothing, as Mrs Hills is very religious, and disaproves of fishing and bugging on the Sabbath. Tonight however we are going to sugar.[1] Today we went for a long drive to an old Church [Lanercost Priory] where the Howards are buried, and we have just had luncheon.

It is very dismal and strange, and I wish to goodness I had the wishing gift, and could find myself—next minute—sitting in my armchair over my own beautiful fire at home. Perhaps we shall be able to get away on Friday— I hope so. This place is rather too much of a good thing.

How are you milord, and what are you about? I wish you were here, to wake them all up a little. Mrs Hills has a horrible pet dog, which is always getting ill—it was sick all over the carpet when we arrived on Saturday, and Jack has to hunt for it.

Oh dear oh dear—I wish we were on our native pavement (High St) at this moment—It is overpowering.

Nessa thinks you will never get through this letter, and I hae me doots—
Goodbye my Lord,
Your loving Goatus Esq

King's

9: TO THOBY STEPHEN   22 *Hyde Park Gate, S.W.*

Sunday, Oct. 24th [1897]

My dear old Thoby,
I have not written to you since that awful week at Corby—so methinks it is about time for me to approach your Highness again—

Shall I do any bug looking out? I have plenty of time for it, and I am very often in the [*illegible*] region—if it would be of any use I can easily do it.

I am beginning Greek at Kings College [London] and two history Lectures—We have got as far as the first verb in our Greek, and by the Christmas holidays you will have to take me in hand—Nessa goes on at her

1. To smear tree trunks with treacle to attract insects.

studio every other day, and I march down there to fetch her back generally. That is how we spend our days almost always. I have to write *essays* upon historical subjects for my history class, and on Tuesday I am going to have my first essay given back to me with the masters corrections.

Jack came back from Corby at 8 o'clock this morning. He is to stay here till his house in Victoria Grove is finished. He has brought a huge salmon, which he caught yesterday. Yesterday afternoon Georgie took Nessa and me to the Moore and Benson minstrels—they are very much the same kind of thing that goes on at Brighton, so you may imagine that dear Dorothea and Rosamond [Stephen] felt themselves rather above such an amusement— However, as a change they [*illegible*] amusing. I have been typewriting Dorothea's poems for the last fortnight, and I have grave fears lest her style should have infected me.

Jack brought back the catties [catkins]—he read in his book that to plant them was worse than useless.

Here are some of our Corby photographs—The dog is called Rap, and lives in a huge cart—I dont know to what species he belongs, but he is very well bred and a great beauty Jack says—

The man with the black dog is Taddenham the keeper—and I hope you can recognise Jack fishing in the river—

Goodbye my lord: I must now learn my Greek for tomorrow. My handwriting is rather illegible tonight—so I hope you will have got my drift safely.

Your loving Goatus Esq

King's

10: TO THOBY STEPHEN   22 *Hyde Park Gate, S.W.*

Sunday December 5th [1897]

My Dear Thoby,

Our correspondence has not flourished this term, the fault lying with *you* methinks? Now the holidays will soon come—thanks be to the Lord. On Friday dear Dobbythinga [Dorothea Stephen] arrived. She is to be here for a week, and already we feel quite swamped. She talks, in the voice you know, every minute of the day, wants no encouragement but goes on so, and will only be stopped by your going out of the room. Then last night as a relief to this, Georgie suggested that she should play to us. Thereupon she started forth to strum upon her mandolin. She sang to it in the most extraordinary voice that ever existed—very high and shrill, and absolutely out of tune from the very beginning. Oh dear what a wonderful creature she is! She has now—6.30—gone to church for the second time today. She refuses to take a cab on Sunday, and has carried off my watch so that she may be sure to be in time for supper.

Yesterday afternoon the Chief[1] came to see us. I only saw her for a moment, but I expect we shall see a lot of them as they have a house in Princes Gardens.

My studies end with an examination, which I shant go in for; Nessa only stops on Christmas Eve.

Oh milord, my fingers are so cold that my handwriting is sadly unlike itself—almost illegible one might say. It is freezing, and the Pond is covered with a thin piece of ice—certainly we ought to have skating by the time you are here. Then I shall have the joy of showing you my room—it is most choice—perfectly sweet, and the most artistic in the whole house.

The Mackenzies [neighbours] dog—a little pugnacious brown mongrel whom perhaps you know, met with an accident the other day—A cab slowly passed over its middle: we were watching and saw it get up and run about as though it was not hurt. But that night it became unconscious and died—I believe Nessas curse had something to do with it. She has a great hatred of the beast—it always fights strays, and a dog fight is her "abhorence" "I wish the little fiend were killed, she said, but I fear there is no such luck" I implored her as a touching and graceful act, to send a wreath to its funeral in token of forgiveness: this I think she would have done, had she not met Mrs [Enid] M[ackenzie] on her way to the Lost Dogs home to buy a new creature.

Gerald is at Eton for Sunday; I suppose you know about the great firm?[2]

Now milord, goodbye. You seem to have been altogether triumphant and glorious this term! Your report was enough to put father in a good humour for a week——

We shall soon meet, but if you feel kindly disposed you might write *me* a letter.

I am so penetrated with Dotty's [Dorothea's] style of conversation that I cant help writing exactly like her.

Your loving Goat

Have you heard anything of the bugs?

King's

11: To Emma Vaughan　　　　　　　　　22 *Hyde Park Gate, S.W.*

[January 1898]

My dearest Toad,

Your letter was a most delightful surprise—not that I ever expected you to write with such distractions around you!

1. Madge Symonds, daughter of John Addington Symonds, who married Virginia's cousin, William Wyamar Vaughan.
2. Gerald Duckworth founded the publishing firm of Duckworth & Co in January 1898.

Here it is so beastly that I envy you: it is freezing hard, and there is a horrible wind. Every morning begins with a deep yellow fog, and we have candles at 3.30.

This afternoon I went to Greek for the first time. There was only Miss Holland, tell Marny,[1] who said she worked two hours a day at her preparation and thought that too little! Dr. Warr[2] asked most tenderly after Marny and said that he should be very much pleased if she would do the exercises and send them to him to correct, and he will give them to me. Of course this is only if she means to come back this term—I said I thought she did. So will you tell her that the exercises for next time are Nos. 56 and 58? Make her do them.

Will [Fisher] has just been here. Hervey [Fisher] seems to have been rather bad, but the other Fishers sound very flourishing. Will you see them again?

Aunt Minna [Duckworth] has gone out suddenly to Monte Carlo and is going to Valescure on her way home. Gerald is also going there in a few days time. He comes back on the 27th.

Mr [F. W.] Gibbs is still living, but they say he must die soon, and Nun (father's sister) [Caroline Emelia Stephen] has been staying here to say goodbye to him. She caught cold and was ill for 10 days, which was rather idiotic but now, thank goodness, she has gone back to Cambridge.

Mia [Maria Macnamara] came on Sunday—Pat has been almost killed on his bicycle by a waggon, Maive has sprained her thumb, Dorothy is almost mad with earache, Bertie has been ordered to fight the "Bonerwals" and they mayn't be able to get home in time for the wedding.[3] The best man has had to go to sea, so it will have to be put off. There is all the Macnamara news!

How are you, and why on earth don't you practise? If you haven't learnt something new to play to me by the time you come home you know what to expect!

Give my love to Marny and impress upon her her Greek duties.
Goodbye now.

Your loving Virginia

Sussex

1. Margaret Vaughan, Emma's oldest sister.
2. George Warr (1845-1901), Professor of Classical Literature. In 1877 he had helped to found the Ladies Department of King's College at Kensington.
3. The wedding of Maive Macnamara, daughter of Charles and Mia Macnamara, to Frederick Goodenough, took place later this year.

5 Mills Terrace [Hove, Sussex]

[April 1898]

My dear old Bar,

I have been meaning to write to you ever since Sunday, but the post goes at 6, and I have always missed it. This morning your letter with the photograph came. You don't say what your address at Porto Fino is, so I shall have to send this after you to Rome. By the time you get it we shall be back in London again, which will be a mercy—We have quite come to an end of things to do and Nessa and I spend our time shopping in the Western Road! The Fishers are rather depressed—Uncle Herbert[1] looks very shaky, Emmie [Emmeline] insists upon rushing off to Lyme Regis to a wedding, and Boo [Cordelia] has been in bed with a chill. However last night they heard that Charles [Fisher] has got a first in Mods, and they are all very much pleased. Also your oranges came yesterday and they have stuck them up in the drawing room. It is fine but very windy, and bicycling is very hard work. Yesterday Charles and Nessa and Thoby and I went for a row. None of us could row, and we were almost swamped by Thoby—but we got back safely. In the evening we bicycled to Shoreham and back—and that is about all we have done.

Adeline [Vaughan Williams] and Will [Fisher] have just appeared—Adeline looks most flourishing, and Ralph [Vaughan Williams] is huge.

Thoby has managed father splendidly—Father dines with the Fishers almost every night, and spends the rest of the time lying flat on the sofa—He is extremely well, and says that he is going to set to work again when he gets back. Adrian is of course at 2nd Avenue [the Fisher's house] all day long. He and Tom [Edwin Fisher] shrimp and fish and hunt days together and I think he has got rather fatter. Nessa and I take walks in the evening when it is cool along the beach; and discuss the universe. We are both eating heaps, and I dine downstairs whenever father is away.

Rezia [Rasponi] does not look beautiful, though she is better than I expected.

Now Nessa and I are going to take some books back to the library. Father and Thoby are going to see the Bird Museum.

Gerald was here on Sunday, and very well and prosperous.

I hope you are enjoying yourself before you come back to your slums.[2] I am only thankful that I am not abroad—London is by far the best of places.

Your loving old Goat

Henry Duckworth

1. Herbert William Fisher (1825-1903).
2. George was assisting Charles Booth in the preparation of *Life and Labour of the People in London*, 1901-3.

9 *St Aubyns, Hove*
[*Sussex*]

Saturday April 23rd [1898]

My dear old Bar,

Nessa has just gone off to the private view at the New Gallery, where she is to meet Gerald. She looked extremely nice, with her Mrs [Sally] Young [dress] and her big hat on. We have just had Adeline and Ralph[1] here, to ask about nurses for Roland Vaughan Williams [Ralph's uncle] who is ill with peritonitis. But he is getting better now they said. Ralph of course was left outside.

I suppose Nessa told you about our journey: it was successful on the whole, and my bicycle which was left behind arrived yesterday. Father has begun work again; and is making poor old Thobs cram all the morning. Adrian had Macpherter here this morning and Nessa and I went to High Street. We met Kitty [Maxse] which was nice: she was just rushing off to stay with Margaret [Massingberd] at Gunby [Hall, Lincolnshire].

Nessa looks very well I think. The books and everything have been quite easy, and Thoby keeps father quiet. Gerald last night went to a party of spinsters which Miss May Balfour was giving. His two first books were out yesterday. All the trees are out, and the gardens are full of flowers. We have quite as blue a sky as you, I am sure; and altogether it is splendid to be back again. The servants are all well and seem to have enjoyed their holidays. The dining room carpet is a blow—it is much too small, and Gerald says of the worst lodginghouse colour and pattern—but it is going to be removed. Mrs Rowes is coming to lunch with us next Saturday, but you will just miss her!

You do seem to be having a busy time with all those people. I hope the Countess will be nice—Carnarvon I mean. Aunt Mary [Fisher] was so much delighted to hear that Nessa was asked to stay there[2] and says she must go next year.

Now I am going to develop our Frena [?] photographs as I am alone and have nothing else to do. Give Rezia [Rasponi] my love. We must see her some day. She sounds and looks charming.

Take care of yourself and come back fatter.

Your loving old Goat

Henry Duckworth

1. Adeline Fisher married Ralph Vaughan Williams on 10 October 1897.
2. In Rome, with the Rasponis.

Wednesday—May 25th [1898]

My dear Thoby,

Your letters have been pouring in upon us—*My* letter I was greatly pleased to get. I found it on Sunday night, when we came home from Godmanchester.[1] Perhaps Nessa has told you of our heroic determination to pay a one days visit there. We killed two lively rooks with one stone— Nun [Caroline Emelia], and Lady Stephen. Nun we had lunch with on Saturday, and we spent the afternoon sitting in her garden watching Leah [maid] planting flowers. Then at 4.30 we—Nessa and I—went on to Godmanchester. It is a much nicer place than one would think: very old and quiet and respectable. [*letter torn*] . . . have a comfortable house just . . . and we spent Saturday evening rowing about with Rosamond [Stephen]. Imagine our feelings!—just as we neared a lawnful of people Rosamond struck up "Farewell Manchester" at the top of her voice. It was most terrifying. However now that good work is done and we can rest quiet in our beds. I dont mean to leave London again in a hurry.

You heard about our burglars I suppose? They were and are very exciting. We all lie awake at night and imagine creepy crawly creatures stealing about downstairs. Nessa is most courageous, and only longs to have heard them as they got into the little room. She would then have rushed forth and engaged with them single handed. I, at the top of the house, feel tolerably [*letter torn*] . . . they would have to wade through . . . Sophia[2] before they hurt *me*. Poor Sophie locks her door carefully and vows that she will die on top of the silver chest—wh. is underneath her bed. By the way—she has been given by Isabel a box of South African butterflies—which box she has given to us. Would you like us to send them on to you? They are not much good, I am afraid. They are unset and most of their wings are off—however some of them are whole and in a good state. Only I dont see quite what we are to do with them. Nessa has been out to three or four dances, but she is still rather scornful of that amusement—poor old creature. I look forward to the time when "Mr. Stephen, the Senior Wrangler etc. etc. etc." shall escort her—I cant think how she has the courage to go through with it—Fancy sitting out a two hour long dinner, with two strange young men on either side of you! Such gaities [*sic*] are not in my line. What are you going to give her for her birthday? You know it is on Monday. I should think you had better buy something yourself at Clifton and send it to her [*letter torn*] . . . know at all what she wants . . . to do with drawing or painting comes in useful. You must trust to your wisdom.

1. Lady ('Aunt') Stephen's home-town just outside Huntingdon.
2. Sophia Farrell, the cook at 22 Hyde Park Gate, who stayed with the Stephens many years, and after Thoby's death went with Virginia and Adrian to 29 Fitzroy Square, and later to George Duckworth.

Georgie goes tomorrow to Aldershot for a week of camp. It sounds rather beastly. Will you ever have to do it? Our houses for the summer are as vague as ever. Father says he doesn't care and then insists upon impossible conditions. The [New] Forest though is almost done for: there seem to be no houses for let. Jack [Hills] knows of Rogers' house in Wiltshire, and Mrs Darwin has been telling Georgie of a large house 4 miles fr. Stroud. I dont hanker after that though.

Goodbye Milord. Remember Nessas birthday—

Your loving Goatus Esq

King's

15: TO THOBY STEPHEN   22 *Hyde Park Gate, S.W.*

Wednesday [15 June 1898]

My dear Thoby,

I doubt very much if you ever answered a long letter I wrote you— except by sending Nessa a birthday present. However tonight I am in solitary grandeur. Nessa and father have gone to dine with Jack, and Georgie and Gerald of course are out. Adrian I have just sent up to bed, after he has toiled through his algebra poor wretch.

Last night we went to the first of our four operas—it was rather long, but we managed to sit it out without a yawn. Adeline and Ralph went with us, and sat holding each others hands, and most enthusiastic. We go every Tuesday and Friday for a fortnight—Think—my dear Lord—you may have the honour of receiving *both* your dear sisters at your country house [Clifton College] on the 25th. We have both accepted, and if I can summon up courage to sit out a luncheon with the Bogey [Housemaster], and then to undergo a garden party I shall come. I have never really seen your residence —and this time next year you will be flitting. I will try to dress respectably, and behave in all respects as a good goat should. But the prospect is rather alarming.

I had a visit from Madge this morning. I dont know when she is going to Clifton but I think soon. There is no news to tell you and I am dead sleepy, after a day spent in writing Greek exercises and in trudging along the river bank with father from Hammersmith to Putney.

Houses for the summer are still mythical. Aunt Minna wishes us to take a small hotel—at about 20 guineas a week. You would have to act as head butler and Adrian would have to clean the boots. Father has a wild idea of Coniston (7 hours by train and a long drive) but we all sit all our weight on him.

Now Melord we shall meet soon—on Saturday week is it not!

Fond love,
Goatus

King's

[June/July 1898]

My dear Thoby,

    It has struck me that perhaps Madge and Will[1] would like a photograph of Nessa by Cousin Henry[2] for their present from us. Would you give it the thought of your great mind. I dont know what it would cost, but nothing very great, and I think it is the best present I can think of.

    Madge and Will both admire Nessa greatly, and Madge was asking me only the other day whether Nessa could not be made to have her photograph taken. Would your Highness let me know soon if you agree, as we should have to be seeing about it. It could be made a present both to Will and to Madge.

Your loving Goatus Esq

King's

17: To Emma Vaughan   [*The Manor House, Ringwood, Hampshire*]

Aug. 18th 98

> This stamp was left us by the Morants, but I
> have put it on crooked.

My dearest Toad,

    I have no notion where you may be at the present moment—You have made no sign, but remain dumb like others of your race—at any rate, I suppose you are not in London—We were all excited this morning by a letter from Herbert [H. A. L.] Fisher to Father announcing his engagement to Miss Lettice Ilbert—the daughter of Sir Courtenay Ilbert of Oxford. I wonder whether this is news to you, or whether you have heard before from Aunt Mary. At any rate, it is most exciting. Georgie says she is very pretty, and Father imagines her to have money, so it sounds satisfactory.

    This house is very nice—the garden is large and the house is comfortable though rather hideous—It has been so hot that we have hardly done anything. Nessa has been lent a horse and she and Georgie ride everywhere: I drive in a sedate pony carriage. We have not been free from visitors since we left London. First we had the three Italians [Rezia, Guido and Nerino Rasponi] for a fortnight, then Susan Lushington and now Aunt Minna. However, she is the last. I wonder what you and Marny are doing. What news have you of Will and Madge (as cousin Mia would say). We are quite in the dark about them—I have lost the address you gave me, and the others

---

    1. Madge Symonds and William Wyamar Vaughan were married on 28 July 1898.
    2. Henry Herschel Cameron, the youngest son of Julia Cameron, the photographer.

say that such a place as *Arolla* does not exist. But I think you said that that was the place? Are they well, and happy, and behaving in all ways as beseems? Everyone is marrying now—last year we were all single. It is a very sad thought—I am counting the weeks till the 22nd September when we return to our beloved city. I know you share my feelings. At the present moment a tremendous storm is raging. I write by the light of lightning—and rain drips on my head. It will I hope be cooler tomorrow. Nessa and I undo our dresses, pull our skirts over our knees and let down our stockings—but we still drip all over. These are improper details but there is nothing to tell you. I should visit Hanwell if I stay here much longer—is not that your opinion? Tell Marny that I am reading Homer! I can't do it in the least. I have to look out every word—but I have made out three lines unhelped this afternoon and I feel very wise—Xenophon is too dull to read much of—I fear that Marny has been much more industrious than I have—but looking out words in this kind of weather is too much of a good thing.

Nessa sends her best love and is particularly anxious to know anything about her young people (as she calls them now) that you can tell. Only do write soon, my dear Toad—You said you would write first—I do hope you are having as good a time as you can, but summer in the country is a loathsome thing—

> Your loving,
> Ginia

Sussex

18: To Emma Vaughan   *The Manor House, Ringwood*
                                                   [Hampshire]

Sept. 11th [1898]

This is a photograph of me
which I think is a very striking likeness!

My dearest Toad,

I have been meaning to write ever since I got your last letter, but writing in the country in this heat is very hard. We have had Charlie and Cordelia [Fisher] here for a week and Cordelia is a handful as you know. However, now they are gone. We have had a stream of visitors ever since we came here but no one interesting—unless Dermod O'Brien[1] interests you? Such a fat conceited young man never was. He had an attack in his inside when he was here, and had to go to bed the moment he reached London. It has been so baking that we have been able to do nothing. The only cool thing was to wade in the river over our knees with our garments huddled up in a most indecent fashion. We go back to London in 10 days now—on the 21st—It

1. Dermod O'Brien (1865-1945), who was later active in Irish affairs and a well-known amateur painter.

seems very near, and only the other day since we came here, but I rejoice at the thought of getting back. I have thoughts of learning *Latin* next term at King's College. Would you come too? You know some and I know a little, and it would be great fun going together. Besides you would make the acquaintance of dear old Warr. The term only begins on the 17th so you would be back in time. Do think of it.

I suppose the young people are now on their way home—Nessa's photographs have come, but I dont think them good.

Give my love to Marny, and tell her that I have done hardly any Greek. Xenophon is too dull to puzzle over.

Write soon.

Your loving Virginia

Aunt Anny[1] is about the same but has got to have another operation I am afraid.

Sussex

19: To Emma Vaughan   *22 Hyde Park Gate, S.W.*

Sept. 17th [1898]

My dearest Toad,

I find that my beloved Warr gives his Latin classes on a day which is impossible for me, so that I mean to go to Miss Paters Intermediate Latin class, on Tuesdays at 2. You only do reading—Virgil—with her—wont you come to that? I should think it was quite amusing.

Nessa says do you by chance know of any housemaid likely to suit us? Lizzy is going to be married on the 1st October, and we have not got anyone, or heard of anyone yet. Dont trouble—but if you should happen to hear of anyone you might tell us—I am much distressed about your jacket.

Yr loving

Ginia

Sussex

20: To Emma Vaughan   *22 Hyde Park Gate, S.W.*

Monday, March 13th [1899]

My Beloved Toad,

In case you have not read your Times this morning, I send you this extract—Goodenough—on the 11th inst. the wife [Maive Macnamara] of Frederick Goodenough Esq., of—Gladstone Road, of a son.

1. Anne Ritchie (1837-1919), elder daughter of W. M. Thackeray, and sister of Harriet, Leslie Stephen's first wife.

Does not that send you off your head? It cannot have been expected so soon. Think of Mia!

Nessa writes this morning that she does not come until 4.30 so I can give you no news of her visit.

I am now rushing off to dear old Warr. I shall give him Marny's love. Only one more lesson. You might write and say how the invalided creature gets on.

Your loving,

Sussex   Goat

21: TO GEORGE DUCKWORTH   9 *St Aubyns, Hove*
                                                       [*Sussex*]

[April 1899]

My dearest Georgie,

Our arrival has been rather disastrous. Thoby had a feverish cold as Nessa told you, but he came on here yesterday evening and seemed almost all right. He had a little fever this morning—101 and we got Dr Branfoot this afternoon. He says that Thoby has a little pneumonia in the right lung, but very slight. He says Thoby is in very good condition and is a very strong constitution. His words were "This is merely a little accident. Otherwise he is perfectly sound, and he will be right in two or three days". He has to be fed every two hours, and has poultices. We are getting a nurse for the night to feed him. We have not yet got one, but Dr. B. says he is certain of finding one before this night. He says there is no need for the slightest anxiety. Nessa is with him, but I get her out for walks, and I shall make her go to bed early. I think I have told you everything about him. It seems rather ridiculous—He talks away, and is perfectly comfortable now, and an excellent patient Nessa says. We have got everything we want. Father insisted upon having Dr B. again tonight, though Dr. B. said it was quite unnecessary. The Clifton doctor must have been idiotic. Thoby was in bed with fever the whole day on Tuesday, and had pains in his chest, and yet they let him travel the two journeys.

Gerald wrote this morning to say that he had a telegram from Mrs Graves at Davos, saying that she is dangerously ill and asking him to come at once. So he is going directly, and will be away for 10 days. The nurse has just arrived, so that is all right. Father is dining with the Fishers. He is quite cheerful now, and I really think everything is as satisfactory as possible. We went to Nun this evening. She is in good spirits, and comfortable. Rosamond [Stephen] arrives today at Sir Henry Cunningham's.[1]

We are all flourishing. Aunt Mary said she thought Nessa looked extremely well, which pleased me. We are most calm, and even amused—it is all so

1. Rosamond's maternal uncle, previously a High Court judge in Bengal.

idiotic. Dr. Branfoot is very nice and clever, and Thoby likes him. Nessa has not taken Thoby's temperature this evening but she thinks it is below 101 and he has no pain. Dr. B. says he is over the worst of it.

So you need not worry about us. I am telling you exactly all I know.

Yr loving,

Goat

8.30. The Doctor has just been—He says Thoby has less pain and is going on as well as possible, and that we have the best nurse in Brighton. Father says I am to send his love. Adrian is very much in want of money to pay debts for birthday presents and for extra reading lessons. Could you sign three cheques for him and send them as soon as you can—

Nessa says *you are on no account to come.*

Henry Duckworth

22: To Emma Vaughan   9 *St Aubyns, Hove*
                                                            [*Sussex*]

[April 1899]

My dearest Toad,

I have not forgotten your disgraceful behaviour on the platform which amused our fellow passengers highly. But I cannot send back "Madame" because the sheep dog has devoured it, along with a Cheddar cheese, a shoe of mine, a pudding and a bath bun. But our woes are many, nor do I know how to enter upon my discourse, dearly beloved Toad. But imagine our situation. Thoby arrived on Wednesday evening, apparently well save for a cold. He went to bed early, woke with slight fever—we sent for Dr Branfoot who said to our horror that there was Pneumonia in the right lung! We straightaway sent for a nurse for the night, and next day Aunt Mary insisted upon another for the day. Little Branfoot was most depressing—as he always is, the Fishers say; but after giving us all a scare he said it was a very slight case and that it would be gone in two or three days. However, Thoby is such a marvellous creature that he is already recovered, save for weakness. His temperature is normal, he is allowed solid food, and his lungs are alright. But you can conceive that this was not altogether the most cheerful way of beginning our holiday. We managed it all in the most businesslike fashion possible and they say that he could not have gone on better. But, my dear Toad, the aggravating and *damnable* (to put it briefly and forcibly) thing about it was that this need never have happened but for the "gross careless-ness', to quote Dr. Branfoot, of your blessed Clifton doctor. Thoby was ill in bed with fever and with a slight tendency to pneumonia the day before he started, and yet the doctor allowed him to take the two journeys all the same—it is only a wonder that things were not much worse than they have been, and if Thoby were not as strong as a horse, he would probably have been ill for weeks. So there! We are all furious about it: Father has written very strongly to the man himself, and Aunt Mary is dreading sending Edwin back to such a hole. Really it is rather maddening. We have had a curious time since Wednesday. Miss [Caroline Emelia] Stephen is here and the divine Rosamond. Rosamond came to tea the other day with Charlie and attacked us before him, whom she had never seen before, on our religious faith! It was amusing: then the day after she came at 10.30 and took us out on to the beach and discussed a future life at great length. I think she is a match for dear Aunt Hester. Lord, what a long letter this is—and you will never be able to read it—I purposely write to you and not to Marny so that her eyes may yet survive to tackle with Miss Pater's Greek.

It is a vile wet day, with a wind fit to blow the house down. This is just the hour when you and Marny ought to be sitting at tea with us in the drawing room at home. But this time next week we shall be nearer heaven. Brighton is a very good copy of the other place—what do you think? We have really done nothing—Thoby has upset all our plans so much. Nessa and I struggle out with the sheep dog—whose name is Gurth after the sheep herd in Ivanhoe—at our heels, to buy medicine and cotton wool in Church Road. I had a vision today, Jack [Hills] is here for Sunday—we were sitting in the drawing room after lunch. Suddenly I looked up and saw Nessa sitting writing *in her trousers*!!! My feelings you may imagine—She had forgotten her safety pin—and her skirt had all come undone and this was the result. I laughed so much that I could not say what was the matter. Jack discreetly looked the other way, and Nessa went behind a screen. This is the sort of thing that I have to write to you about. There is nothing else to do.

Oh my dear Toad, how I do love London! It is the most beautiful place on the face of the earth—

The Fishers are all well tho' I have seen very little of them. How are the Andante's? We long for news. And the divinity of the Roseate Nose and Aunt Hester, and Ellen, and Towler, and Marny, and the discreet reptile herself![1] I have a vague idea that your caution is thawed when you take a pen in your hand. Surely it is very different to write secrets than to speak them. I am quite sure that this is your weak point. Please forget your character and write to me as soon as you can. Are you in touch with a curate?

Goodbye at last. I must stop
Your loving,
AVS Goat

Sussex

1. The 'Andantes' were the Vaughans: the 'Roseate Nose', Lotta Leaf; Aunt Hester, the younger sister of Henry Halford Vaughan; Ellen and Towler, perhaps servants; Marny, Margaret Vaughan; and 'The discreet reptile', Emma Vaughan herself.

9 *St Aubyns, Hove*
[Sussex]

Thursday [20 April 1899]

My dearest Toad,

This is only to tell you that my dearly beloved brother is now convales-cent—indeed he is to sit up for a short time today, and is allowed mutton chops and beer, without stint.

We shall all return on Wednesday—oh, most blessed day—doubly blessed—though I regret to say that the anniversary was forgotten by us.

I have bought myself a box of nibs broad and vulgar, but more suited to the eyes of creatures that inhabit swamps. The garment in which Vanessa was left sitting was her TROUSERS: Τρουσερς: trousers: trousers now, does the obtuse beast understand?

Oh my dear Toad, tho' I love writing to you this handwriting is too heavy a cross. It is so devoid of imagination and character. Did you ever write about that Bus horse?

We had tea with Emmy [Emmeline Fisher] yesterday and she told us a piece of gossip which I am sure that you, my dear Toad, will guard from public knowledge despite your naturally expansive nature—

That an engagement will shortly be announced between Olivia Freshfield and Dermod O'Brien!!!![1]

This may be Emmy's invention, of course.

Give our affectionate love to dear Marny. Nessa and Adrian are at the present moment riding in du Ponts School, and now I must set forth to fetch them. Would that I beheld at my feet a humble creature indeed: but affectionate—The Toadus St. Albaniensis.
                    Adieu—Your loving Goat

The dog eat a choccolate (2 cs.?) cake yesterday and a cream cheese. This morning he was ill under Nessa's bed.

I think you might give me some Andante gossip in return for my engagement.

Sussex

24: To Emma Vaughan 9 *St Aubyns, Hove*
[Sussex]

[April 1899]

My dearest Toad,

This is the last letter I shall write, I promise, and it shall not be long.

It has been settled that we are to stay here till Friday which is sufficiently

1. Dermod O'Brien did not marry Olivia Freshfield, but Mabel Smyly in 1902.

ahemable. But it is raining steadily and there is a cold wind, and though Branfoot says that Thoby may travel on Wednesday, I expect we shall certainly have to stay till Friday, so that I shall not really be in London till Saturday and there will be no time to see about King's College. So, my dear Toad, I write to ask you to diverge into King's College one day when you are naturally in the neighbourhood and buy me a Syllabus, the biggest kind they have—Price 3d. You would be angelic if you would.

The weather is vile and my temper is akin to the weather.

Give our love to Marny: Nessa is going to write to her—

Your loving,

Sussex   Goatus

25: To Emma Vaughan   22 *Hyde Park Gate, S.W.*

Tuesday June 13th 1899

My dear and ancient Toad,

We transacted a small piece of business for you this morning; which I hope you will think satisfactory so far. We went to your friend Mr. Swendene (did you get St Albans Rd from him?) and asked further about the Sussex Villas house. It is practically let already, he says; but there is another, No. 6 Sussex Villas, a very nice *old* house, that is to be let in a month or two; for 75 per ann; and a *small* premium down. He says the people are open to any reasonable offer. He seemed to think that your not wanting it till the spring was quite a good thing—these people may take it on for another few months. At any rate he is going to write to Marny, and arrange a time for her to go over the place, which, as people are in it, is rather difficult. He said too, by the way, that people had been to him a short time ago asking if St. Albans was to let, or if it was going to be let; but he had said that Miss Vaughan had it—He said that Miss Vaughan would be exactly suited by this house in Sussex Villas, and might make a very valuable property of it if she chose! There—that is very long and explicit! though perhaps not readable to the naked eye of a Toad.

My dear Toad, I cannot write the multitude of questions that arise in my head when I sit down to write to thee—Especially when you are in such company I can only hope that you are noticing and treasuring every word, glance and gesture. You have been away a week today—when do you mean to come back again? Even now you may be seated in the house of my dear old friend Aunt Hester. Oh Toad, you are indeed a privileged animal to have such relations! Did Nessa tell you about Dorothea [Stephen]? We found two postcards from her one morning. On one she said "I intend to spend a week in London from the 24th of June. If my cousins wish, I will honour them by my company"!!!!!!!! The other said among other things—"We shall be very glad if you will spend the summer near us at Warboys—only we think that you will have to change the name to Peace Girls."!!!!! She is over-powering.

Our news does not run to much. The marriage[1] was rather dull—Emmy hysterical—swarms of Freshfields, Ritchies etc. Florence [Maitland, born Fisher] was there with the children. Aunt Mary almost crazy with delight. Our paper knife was quite successful—but they had 4 others! We have been to our Latin this afternoon; and yesterday was Greek. We had a most delightful lesson tell Marny. We read some of the Apologia and Miss Pater was perfectly delightful—she must come back again. We have practically taken the Huntingdon House.[2] The Parson will accept 9 gns and only minor details have to be settled.

> Would that I could utter
> The thoughts that arise in me.
> (as the poet says).

But I must wait till I see you. I have thought constantly of you—Why do you have all your meals in the garden? It sounds odd to us, we have almost had fires it has been so cold. What are Madge's household arrangements like and has she said anything about the room on the stairs—the cook's bedroom. I fear I wax illegible; my fingers cleave to each other—I have been using secotine, I can hardly form one letter different from another. Give my fond love to Aunt Hester—and to dear Marny.

Always your humble,

Sussex   *Capra*

26: To Emma Vaughan   *Warboys Rectory, Warboys,*
                             Huntingdonshire

12 August 1899   (this is all the address necessary)

Dearly beloved Toad,

This morning we heard from Susan Lushington that she arrives on Monday at Huntingdon about 12.30. Some of us must, I expect, meet her there, which means that we shall not be back here until 1.30—I do not know when you will arrive (if at all) but we *expect* you for luncheon: therefore, to be brief and at the same time explicit; if we are not *all* here to greet you on your arrival, shd. your arrival take place much before 1.30, we beg that you will in no way feel slighted, but that you will make yourself at home. Go on the Punt—feed the sea gull—visit the stables—examine the photographs — and take possession of our bedrooms and their appurtenances. I fear that Susan Lushington may in some way interrupt our afternoon, but she is sure to be unpacking, resting, and letter writing; besides she is a charming animal

1. Edmund Fisher to Jeanie Freshfield.
2. Warboys Rectory, Warboys, Huntingdonshire.

and can play the Spinet to perfection. *Some* other people—toads I should say—nasty slimy crawling things—*think* they can play—ahem!

You see, my dear toad, that the terrible depression of this climate has not yet affected my spirits. I suspect you and Marny of ulterior motives in thus blackening our minds, or perhaps you are too unimaginative and soulless to feel the beauty of the place. Take my word for it Todkins, I have never been in a house, garden, or county that I liked half so well, leaving St. Ives out of account. Yesterday we bicycled to Huntingdon—and paid a visit to our relatives [Lady Stephen]. Coming back we forgot all our cares— (and they were many—Nessa and I each had a large string bag full of melons which bumped against our knees at every movement) in gazing—absorbing —sinking into the Sky. You dont see the sky until you live here. We have ceased to be dwellers on the earth. We are really made of clouds. We are mystical and dreamy and perform Fugues on the Harmonium. Have you ever read your sister in laws Doges Farm?[1] Well that describes much the same sort of country that this is; and you see how she, a person of true artistic soul, revels in the land. I shall think it a test of friends for the future whether they can appreciate the Fen country. I want to read books about it, and to write sonnets about it all day long. It is the only place for rest of mind and body, and for contentment and creamy potatoes and all the joys of life. I am growing like a meditative Alderney cow. And there are people who think it dull and uninteresting!!!!

This all flowed from my lips without my desire or knowledge. I meant only to be short and businesslike. Poor Toad—when you come I shall say to you—Have you read my letter—And you will confess that you did try a bit on the road and you really do mean to have another shot on the way back. And you are only waiting for a rainy day to finish it altogether. Augusta[2] thinks it bad for your eyesight and Marny has telegraphed "Forbid you to read Virginias letters". I am a little cracky this afternoon, its the hottest day I have yet lived thro'. I have read a whole long novel through; beginning at breakfast this morning and ending at 4 p.m.

It is now tea time. (Thank Heavens, Toadus inquit)

I am very sorry to have written such a long letter, but I will write a digest in very black ink so as to make up.

Love to dear Marny and all my nieces and nephew.

Yr always,
Goatus

> Do find some news to tell us.
> We long for some.
> Oh October October
> I wish you were *ober*

---

1. Margaret Symonds' [Madge Vaughan] *Days Spent on a Doge's Farm*, 1893.
2. Emma's elder sister, Mrs Croft.

This letter only to say that we have to meet Susan Lushington on Monday morning so that we may be late for you, but shall be in for luncheon 1.30 anyhow and beg that you will Make Yourselves at Home—and not think yourselves slighted!

The rest all the better for keeping. News of a certain person and another *unknown* urgently required.

Do you see how much superior this paper is to yours?

Sussex

27: TO EMMA VAUGHAN

The Rectory, Warboys
[Huntingdonshire]

Monday 11th September 1899

1 Tuesday   12th
2 Wednesday 13th
3 Thursday   14th
4 Friday   15th
5 Saturday   16th
6 Sunday   17th
7 Monday   18th
8 Tuesday   19th
9 Wednesday 20th
THURSDAY 21

My dearest Todkins,

You see what a faithful creature I am! At the cost of many hours, and of much hard thought I have observed my promise to you. I have written a long account of our great accident;[1] and I expect a *very nice* letter to thank me. Do you see? You must read my work carefully—not missing my peculiar words—and then tell me your criticisms and humble thanks. Really I am an angel—no other word describes my character so well. You will find my handwriting a little crabbed perhaps; but this is owing to my enthusiasm in your cause. Yesterday was nipping cold and my hands were incapable of writing neatly; but I said *No* the Toad shall not have to wait any longer. I *will* finish this by tomorrow. Well, my dear Todkins—What have you been doing with yourself? Have you had any more attacks, or have you been a healthy toad? Do write me a letter full of *thoughts*: I like *thoughts* in a letter—not *facts* only. By the way, did Nessa tell you of her long letter from Madge—she said that—but I remember you think it wrong to repeat other people's

1. Virginia had written out for Emma Vaughan a mock-newspaper report describing the sinking of their punt on the Warboys pond. Emma was herself present on this occasion with Virginia and Adrian. Virginia's manuscript account of the accident is contained in the Warboys Journal (Berg Collection, New York Public Library, and another fair-copy is at Sussex University).

letters, so I certainly will not say any more about it. Only there were some *facts* in this letter of great interest.

Tomorrow, dear Marny comes. We had a wild idea of going to Ely and picking up Marny at Wilberton on our way back, but it is rather complicated, and I think we shall stay at home. There is nothing of great interest to tell you; and my hand is so sick of writing after the innumerable pages I have transcribed for you, that I will make my adieux.

Remember Discretion must be exercised. The work is strictly private.

The punt got full of water in the rain that we have had all last week and then Adrian pushed it off into the middle of the pond so that now it is drifting about there almost under water; and if it rains again, it must sink. But we are all too lazy to rescue it. A week on Thursday, my dear Toad! Oh, I shall be happy when I get back to London. All the same our time here has seemed extraordinarily short, and not so bad as usual. Indeed, I think this is a Place of great charms. Nessa and I went for a long walk alone this afternoon; along the road where we drove that evening and you were so frightened of the hay-cart. We walked and walked and walked for miles and never met a creature. Then we sat down by the wayside and gossiped; it was quite Divine. It is Autumn here; the leaves quite turned to gold etc. This is a photograph which you have not seen. I think it somewhat like an ancient beast of my acquaintance.

This is vilely written I admit; but I am writing against time, that is in a few minutes I shall have to light a candle and my arms ache all the way down and I am all bundled up in my chair with an old bit of cardboard to put my paper on. But the great work is written with an imaginative elegance which few can rival. Well, I will not utterly extinguish your eyes. When we next meet—I shall be tapping along Gloucester Road with a stick and a dog to lead me and a green shade over my eyes. You will give me a penny and say "Poor old creature, look Marny—she really is like that old goat we used to know". Give my love to Virginia and to John and to Millicent[1] and to Maryanne [?] and all my dear friends. Do send me some gossip. It would be like water to a fish.

Your loving Goat

Take *two* coos Taffy—take *two* coos (that is what the evening pigeons are saying all round at the present moment).

Sussex

1. Virginia and John were the children of Sir Vere Isham Bt., husband of Millicent Vaughan, Emma's older sister.

9 St Aubyns, Hove,
                                              Brighton

19th April [1900]
(Primrose Day)

Beloved Todkins,

I was most grateful for your letter, but for goodness sake do tell me the story of Madge and the telegram—I am longing to hear it and my desolute condition needs all the comfort possible. The ancient animal left for Paris yesterday morning at 8.15[1] and I expect she will be away one entire week. I am growing into my shell like a tortoise—I am so old and respectable and hardly human. Thoby is here today, but he goes tomorrow morning and then I shall be left alone with my Parent. However I have endless books and *Greek* (tell Marny—the greatest of comforts to me) and so the time moves along, though I could swear that at least a week has passed since I saw my poor dear old Sheep dog [Vanessa]. We had a telegram last night to say that she had arrived safely, but no letter as yet. She was buoyed up by the thought of seeing the Louvre but otherwise she was rather depressed. Do you know Paris my dear Toad, and what do you think of it? Her address is—Hotel St. Romain, Rue de Roch, Paris, in case you think of writing to her. Oh my dear Tods, what a vile place this is! It is baking hot, with no wind and not a sign of Spring—however that is preferable to a gale on the whole. The place is swarming with actresses and females of all descriptions; we go for walks along the Parade and moralise and look at the Niggers. All the old entertainments are going on, which I remember since I was a Babe in arms— I long for a ride on a donkey.

The Fishers overflow, but they are gradually dispersing—Adeline and Willy have gone and Lettice and Herbert at last. Lettice is looked upon with dislike by most of the Fishers now. They say she is much too talkative and pushing and without a sense of humour. They all adore Janie and Jo [Edmund Fisher], however—and the baby is a great cause of rejoicing. Poor Aunt Mary looks like a washed out ghost. She does everything—runs messages—looks after them all—and no one but Adeline thinks of helping her. Well—I suppose you two infants have been vaccinated and you will soon be flying for foreign parts. Jack [Hills] says that Italy is simply gorgeous now—hot and all the flowers out and the sky as blue as —my brain gives out —this ink will have to do for a simile. At the present moment, it is a most lovely and remarkable blue but I daresay when you get this, it will have turned muddy coloured.

We have no news I think. I hope you will be an angel and write to me soon again. I am as melancholy as Hamlet, and only long to sit alone and read or write to a reptile. I think sisters are too expensive luxuries: I mean to

1. George Duckworth, who had assumed the role of bringing out his half-sister, took Vanessa to Paris for a week.

tell mine so, but the worst of it is that there is no way of getting rid of them—

My dear, do you realise how many *months* it will be before we meet again? Will you have grown a beard, do you think, or shall I have sprouted horns?—

Give my dear love to Marny whom I think of constantly and with tears in my eyes. I do hope Vere [Isham] is reading Thackeray. There is no picture in my mind that gives me more pleasure than that of him reading and rereading Thackeray and playing a tune on the Cello between whiles. It takes me back to the days of my childhood. He ought to write letters like Edward Fitzgerald—The Omar Khayyam man you know—who had much the same tastes and was a man of genius into the bargain.

Thoby clamours for Tea—so goodbye, my dear little swampy reptile.

Always thine,
AVS

Sussex

29: TO GEORGE DUCKWORTH   9 *St Aubyns* [*Hove,*
                                           Sussex]

Sunday [22 April 1900]

My dear old Bar.

This is just a line, because it is time for post, to thank you for your long and most interesting letter—and also to say that there is no earthly reason why you should hurry back [from Paris] on Tuesday, if you want to stay. I am sure that Nessa is really enjoying herself thoroughly, and it is a chance not to be lost. Of course I want her; but a day more or less does not matter— and after all we see each other every day of our lives. So don't consider me— I am simply flourishing and so is father. We get on perfectly comfortably together. Aunt Mary has told him not to take me for long walks—and our life is most salubrious and comfortable.

Nessa's letters are frantic with excitement. My only fear is lest she should find it all too fascinating ever to leave it. Don't let her get engaged to a charming French Marquis—I am sure that they have not the constitution of good husbands. And don't let her see too many improper studios—The artist's temperament is such a difficult thing to manage and she has volcanoes underneath her sedate manner.

Father is stretched at full length snoring on the sofa, and this annoys me so much that I can't write sense. Thank goodness—he has now waked up (is that grammar?) and is going to play Patience. He *must* go to a dentist. Could you not write and tell him so?

Thoby's luggage has never turned up, Gerald says. Gerald and Jack have been here all today—Gerald is still very liverish and I am sure he ought to be resting.

Well let me know when you are coming—Will you both come here straight from Dover—or what? It is baking hot—no wind—quite unlike Brighton.

Yr loving,
Goat

Henry Duckworth

30: TO GEORGE DUCKWORTH

9 St Aubyns, Hove
[Sussex]

Thursday [26 April 1900]

My dear old Bar,

I was very much surprised to hear on Tuesday morning that Nessa was going to arrive in the evening. I had made up my mind not to see her till Wednesday or Thursday. But I was very joyful as you may imagine. She will have told you of her adventures—What a lucky chance it was to meet the Gibbs, but father was horrified at your having gone all the way to Calais with her. He said 'What extraordinary things he is always doing!'

Well—I think it has been a most successful expedition. She looks very well indeed, and seems quite intoxicated with all the things she has done and seen. We have talked hard ever since she came back, and we have not come to an end of it yet. She says she felt like a child, and enjoyed everything like a child. The pictures have got into her brain. She is always bursting forth into raptures about them and [*illegible*] and the other artist interested her enormously—Everything was interesting—and as for the eating! Words fail her when she tries to describe what that was like. She says she will never be able to go to a London place again. I am rejoicing now that she went. It sounds quite perfect—weather and all.

Your parasols were greatly appreciated. Aunt Mary really liked hers and Boo's [Cordelia Fisher] came at a most fortunate moment. Aunt Mary had been trying to make her use an old black one, but Boo said it was too ugly and refused. She was very much attracted by the thought of having a real Parisian one, unlike anyone elses. My green and white is the one I really adore. I met an old gentleman on the Parade with a huge one just like it, and I feel that it falls in with my character. The other one too is most elegant—only too elegant.

We shall talk and think of Paris for months to come I am sure. I had no idea that she would enjoy it all so much. You must have managed everything with the utmost skill and care and I am most grateful to you.

I wonder if this will reach you in time. It is cold and windy and horrible since yesterday.

Yr loving,
Goat

Henry Duckworth

[17 ? June 1900]

My beloved Todelkrancz,

Marny insinuates that I have planted the green Fiend in your heart—which makes me exceedingly glad—I wish though that the green Fiend or any other fiend would prompt you to write to me. I have had to make all the advances in this friendship, which is quite against my morals. Marny holds out visionary hopes of a letter—but the posts 'return the posts return and fall' and no letter falls on *me*. Ahem—Imagine whom I have seen within the last week! The very Margaret [Madge] Vaughan herself! and old Sym [Mrs. John Addington Symonds, her mother] into the bargain! I was sitting after breakfast waiting for Nessa to come in from her ride, when a hansom (naturally a hansom) drove up to the door, and the two remarkable females got out—I had to entertain them with my heart in my mouth for 10 minutes all alone—and I would sooner fight under Lord Methuen[1] than do it again! I barely had courage to look at the Arch Vaughan herself—but I thought she seemed very happy and as talkative as a jay. I really have an enormous crow to pluck with you—The first words Madge said were to ask me if I had heard about Will and Sedberg[2] (how do you spell it?) No said I—and then she explained what I suppose you and your fellow conspirator have been sitting on for the last 6 months—like two old mother birds on their eggs. Of course I do not *blame* you—oh no—but since you think discretion such an invaluable possession, I will try to exercise a little on my own account —Oh it is so interesting about—but I stop myself at once.

Well my dear Todkins—my encounters with the notorious family have been surprisingly frequent. Yesterday Thoby and I and father (Nessa is away for Saturday to Monday with the Normans, whom you and Marny know—at least you have seen young W. Norman) went to Emma Winkworth's garden party.[3] There we met both the Paters—dressed in the oddest fashions—like Botichelli angels—and as I stood talking to Clara there advanced upon me a tall and middle aged lady in Blue, with a little grocer like man beside her.[4] Good Heavens—who is this I thought, for she was evidently bent on shaking hands with me—Really and honestly, for the moment I did not recognise your beloved Lotta in this apparition! She is *enormous*. As for her body, I never saw such a shape save in those who are

1. Lord Methuen, then commanding the First Division in the South African war, was currently the target of much ill-informed criticism in London.
2. Will Vaughan may have been offered a position at Sedbergh School, Yorkshire.
3. Emma Winkworth, the daughter of Thomas Thomasson, the Lancashire cotton-spinner, owned a large house in Campden Hill, London, where she entertained her friends, among whom were Leslie Stephen and his family.
4. Walter and Charlotte Leaf. Charlotte and Madge were the daughters of John Addington Symonds. Walter Leaf was the scholar and banker.

doing business with Infants—and surely she can not already be advanced to such a degree. The waist was just under her armpits, and then she became vast—really noticeable. And her face too was quite changed—grown quite fat and rather dusky red. It is not a change for the better by any means, and I defy you and Marny, as members of the Church of England, to insist upon her Beauty any longer. Even her eyes, which used to be large and sad and mysterious are become commonplace—overwhelmed by the increase of her cheeks. It is most distressing. And she was so silent and stolid and staid and middle aged—save her voice nothing remained to tell of her kinship with the great and glorious Madge. Madge too told us that she had been over-hauling Lotta's wardrobe and—well—it *was* dull—so *respectable*—and Lotta thinks she *must* be middle aged and dress in black always. I think it *such* a mistake, and I *told* her so! Cant you imagine Madge's voice emphasising that? Since I wrote to Marny we have been to Cambridge for the May week, and I have danced at my first Ball. It was the Trinity ball, and the largest of all.[1] We got there late, and everyone was already full up, and Thoby knew very few people, so we did not dance much. Florence and Boo were there, and Alice Pollock and the Hugh Bells[2] (if you know them—M.A.P. calls them 'the most brilliant girl conversationalists in London'—and Thoby was much attracted by them, and them by him) and various other pretty young ladies of that description—no dear charming old fashioned quiet *lovely* Toads—but flaunting and frivolous and as garrulous as blackbirds. Boo [Cordelia Fisher] I was rather disappointed in as to looks. Florence had done her hair, in what she called a 'Roman' way, very smooth and low on the neck, and with a thick net stretched tight over it front and back. Some-how her face does not light up, as it should, and she refused to dance with 'horrible undergraduates' in a manner which reminded me slightly of you! So she and Florence and I sat on a kind of platform most of the time from which we could watch the dancing, without being disturbed. Florence I admire immensely. She is a true descendant of our beloved old French grandmothers and great grandmothers.[3] Nun (Miss Stephen) told me that Florence always reminded her of Aunt Julia [Cameron] in her way of talking; and she is really most beautiful and enough to charm your head off.

Heavens! what a long letter this is! But it is Sunday morning, and I am sitting solitary in my room with no dear sheep dog to talk to, and I cant help writing for the life of me, and you must be my receptacle. Talking of receptacles, I wonder if your *arrangements* in Switzerland are productive of

1. Thoby had gone from Clifton to Trinity College, Cambridge, in October 1899. Among the young men Virginia met at the Trinity Ball was Clive Bell.
2. Sir Hugh Bell Bt. His two daughters, by his second marriage, were Florence, who married Sir Herbert Richmond, and Mary Katharine, who married Sir Charles Trevelyan.
3. Virginia's great-grandmother was the daughter of Antoine, Chevalier de L'Etang, and Thérèse Blin de Grincourt.

amusement? Why on earth you should leave Italy—for good as Marny cheerfully says—for all the Alps in creation, I cannot understand. *Italy*, my dear Toad—only think of it. Aunt Mary writes that Emmy has been ill with dysentery in Florence—having parted with Fanny Noel in a burst of anger—Fanny—my dear Fanny—having so At. M[ary Fisher] says, refused to look after Emmeline, and altogether behaved in the most unkind manner. However Emmy is now recovering and is staying with an Aunt outside Florence. I confess I sympathise with Fanny. Emmy is a trial. Adeline I have not seen for ages, and my practising is now at a standstill. I am, however, feeling a little triumph over the Latin language as though I had stolen a march on it—great rough beast that it is! As for Greek, it is my daily bread, and a keen delight to me. For goodness sake prod Marny till she opens her Greek books again. It seems to me absurd when she has just climbed to the top of the mountain to let herself roll down again like a senseless stone. My metaphors are jangled out of tune by St Mary Abbotts bells, which insist upon calling for parishoners all the morning.

Now it is Monday morning—(I imitate Marny's habit of writing letters when the inspiration takes me—though I have not Marny's divine gift of losing the frenzy in the middle of a sentence and bolting off into the other side of the hemispheres—Her last letter was written in installments in this way). Last night we had Sally Norton and Professor Norton (her father)[1] to supper. Mr Norton talked to me about Greek (he is the most cultivated and wisest of men—so father says—and is over here now as Ruskins executor and told me emphatically to read Edward Fitzgeralds translations of Sophocles). Do hand this on to Marny—Nothing else, he says, gives the spirit so splendidly. We have just had a letter from Rezia, in which she says she has been to call on you, and found you gone. Aunt Mary also writes that Emmeline and Rezia have struck up a great friendship, and At. M. is very anxious that Rezia should travel back to England with Emmy, and come and stay at Second Avenue! Rezia promises to come, if only for 10 days.

This letter is apalling; when do you mean to come back my dear Toad, and what do you do then? St Albans is being decorated, and looks altogether dishevelled, with huge white boards up.

Do write to me and make Marny write too.

Give my love to her
Yr loving Goat

Marny's letter arrived this morning. Thank her a thousand times. Wednesday.

Sussex

1. Charles Eliot Norton, Professor of the History of Art at Harvard.

Fritham House, Lyndhurst
[Hampshire]

Monday Aug. 6th [1900]—only one week!!!!!!!!!!

Beloved Animals, and Cousins,

I must send you a word of welcome and greeting, now that you are Home again at last—at least I pray that you *are* home—you will have set off today (Monday) I suppose—and—Heavens—what a passage you will have tomorrow if our wind here is any relation to the Channel wind! I pity you from the bottom of my heart. However by the time you read this, you will want to forget all your woes, cast off your travelling-clothes, unpack your boxes, and sink into the ancestral arm chairs. I envy you, coming back to England with fresh eyes, and absorbing it all with double keenness. I adore the country now—at any rate *this* country—and so will you shortly—my dear cousins.

Dear Marny says nothing of *her* visit, which must take place soon after the Toads. We are breathlessly awaiting an answer from—Clara! We have actually asked her to stay here—and probably some of her visit (if she comes) will over lap the Toads!

Oh Lord—what Talk we shall have in our bedrooms—and wandering down the garden paths o'night, while the moon rises over the Forest and the lights of Southampton shine out in the distance. This place would turn a Grasshopper into a Poet—and we all come out with sudden spasms of sentiment.

I have a Pony and a respectable trap all to myself—the others ride and cycle all day—and in this I drive solitary miles and miles—through the forest and over the moor, and Heaven knows where—Soon they will be no longer solitary. A jewelled reptile will be by my side—"Oh Goat Goat—do take the reins—here's a Haycart coming!" Do you remember that! Oh my children how many things we shall remember, and what tales you will unfold! Six months almost isn't it? I shall drive down to the Station to meet you, Reptile, at whatever hour of night or morning you choose to arrive, and then we shall have a gorgeous 10 mile drive up here.

Now, you must go and wash, or have tea, or something, and I have, alas, to change for dinner—

Till the 13th,

Your expectant cousin,
Il Giotto

Do make some mark of your affection for me—Do write me a nice letter,— Here is Nessa just come in from a long ride. She has had tea with our neighbours Mr and Mrs Weston. Mrs Weston is a relation of yours—by all that's supernatural! and knows both of you well—She was a St John (is it true?) and a great niece of Mrs Pell—She asked tenderly after you. How odd —isn't it? According to Nessa, she is also the *ugliest* woman she has ever seen, which lends colour to the St. John story. They are the *ugliest* race under the sun—and their defects culminate in a certain sancta Johanna who shall be nameless (this is a libel entirely—you are both—ahem—I pine for a sight of Marny's profile, like a sensitive Madonna—or Whistler etching—and Toad—half of her our dear French great-grandmother—and half a little imp of wickedness.

Sussex

33: To Emma Vaughan   22 *Hyde Park Gate, S.W.*
27th Sept. [1900]

My dearest Toad,

Look at this precious scrap which fell at my feet this morning as I was turning out an old drawer full of odds and ends. Where the other half is, goodness knows but I am sure you will prize this as a relique.

Oh Lord, what a long time since Fritham! I have no time now for a long letter. Nessa has gone to stay with Kitty [Maxse] at Dunley till Saturday or Monday and so I am solitary—and you might write and tell me your reptilian doings. I want to know so much, and your news only oozes on to me in drops. What has dear Marny settled to do? Georgie strongly advises Weimar in every way but I am afraid this is too new an idea to be accepted at so late a date. But *you* are going to take the plunge—you most courageous of all reptiles! I do admire you for it, I can't say how much.

We saw Madge and Will the other day passing through, and like glimpses of morning sun (what metaphors!) the house echoed all through with shrieks and excitement. Old Lotta[1] came too, staid and matronly, and vague as ever. Shall we really meet at 6 Sussex Place? I know we shall laugh and shock Walter [Leaf]—Oh, how comic to think of!

I don't know where you are, but as Millicent [Isham] is at Brighton (I think) I suppose you are at Augusta's [Croft], or at any rate, she will forward to you. By the way, do you see that Warboys has been almost burnt to the ground? 16 cottages, a brewery and a cycle manufactory (Ingle Piggott— do you remember him?) I only fear that poor old Miss Noble has been burnt too—her dairy and cows and pigs all new, which she had just started. I have written for news but hear nothing—poor old Love.

Now I must really dis-robe and wash for dinner—Heavens, I shall have to sit at the head of the Table!

1. Charlotte Leaf.

Give my fondest love to dear Marny. We must meet often in London. How long do you stay?

Ask John [Isham] if he remembers me and tell him I am craving for a pillow fight.

Give my love to Augusta.

Your loving,
Goat

I wrote c/o on the first envelope—have to take another for all your scruples—Your aristocratic St. John?[1] another envelope wrong—have to take a 3rd!!

Sussex

34: TO EMMA VAUGHAN   22 *Hyde Park Gate, S.W.*
Tuesday, October 23rd [1900]

My dearest Reptile,

By this time you will be established, I suppose, though we have heard no news of you since Marny wrote and told us of your adventurous journey [to Germany]. I longed for a foreign Count *some* where in the story, and still believe in one, though the discreet Marny leaves him out altogether. Dear Marny has retired to Barton, as you know, and so our Vaughan news has almost come to an end. But I hope she will find lodgings before long, and then we shall be neighbours. Another house is to be let in Canning Place—do you think that quite impossible still?

Well our only news is the Symondsian wedding[2]—it was the comicest wedding I have ever been at, and I can hardly believe that they are lawfully wedded. It was at 11 o'clock, of all cold unhappy hours, and the day was grey and melancholy. Very few people had been invited too, save gloomy Symonds relations—However, Katharine was as merry as a Grig—laughed and talked to her bridesmaids before the wedding, and walked up the aisle actually nodding here and there as she went. I have never seen a bride so comfortable and composed. But alas—she wore an immense white collar, right up in peaks under her ears, and did *not* look her best. I am afraid this is the Furse influence. They raced through the service, had no address, and it was all over in a twinkling. Both of them made their answers loudly and in their ordinary voices. Katharine's veil came off as she walked down on Charles' arm, and Charles stopped and borrowed a pin and pinned it on again, to the great amusement of the congregation. And the organ played real dance music—which seemed quite appropriate to this peculiar wedding. Then we all went and had ices (of all things at 12 O'clock on an October

1. Emma St John Vaughan.
2. The marriage on 16 October between Charles Furse, the painter, and Katharine, youngest daughter of John Addington Symonds.

morning!) and cucumber sandwiches—in the Hotel. Old Sym [Mrs J. A. Symonds] came out quite lively and gracious—indeed I rather think that 'the last of my daughters married' is a relief to her—Katharine looked like a splendid nude statue with a Dantesque wreath round her forehead, and a kind of majestic monumental expression. Charles was in his element—talking hard the whole time—and oh Heavens—what creatures the female Furses are! Imagine all Charles' little ways in a woman! and his looks too—Madge [Vaughan] and Lotta [Leaf] undulated about—Lotta magnificent in dark crimson velvet—which now suits her *stately* form. Her nose too had lost that delicate blush rose tint which you and Marny used to admire so—like sunset over Mont Blanc. The Bridesmaids poor things were very cold, and only one of them [Vanessa] was beautiful, but she, as you can imagine, had looks enough to endow the whole lot, and leave a margin for herself. Madge gave me violets from her bouquet, and Katharine this sprig of I don't know what. I am sure you would like to add them to your collection—though I am afraid you treated my last contribution with scorn.

There, I think that will do for the Symondses, this time. Will and Madge looked both of them extremely well, and Will showed everyone photographs of the infant [Janet Vaughan]—If the Furses are as successful as that pair, they wont do badly. I am so in the dark as to all your proceedings, that I dont know what questions to ask you, but you must answer them as though I *had* asked. I hope you have got over your first lonely miseries—you poor strange little Welsh Toad! and I know that in time you will rave about Dresden, and discover some perfect Dresdenite—of the other sex.

The sheep dog [Vanessa] is staying away this Sunday with Georgie at the Craig Sellars, if you know who they are. I dont very well—but Mrs Craig Sellar is a charming elderly lady, who has lost her husband, and cant think of anything else, which makes her all the more charming. And there are two Miss Sellars and a W. Sellar—and they are all delightful and musical, according to Jack. I am going to my Queens Hall concert this afternoon, with a Miss Snowden[1], who works at the Academy and is rather an amusing little creature. But I cant help wishing for another little creature who shall be nameless.

We had a long visit from Adeline the other day, who discussed your character at great length, and said some things which I know you are too modest to wish to hear repeated—what do you think about an addition in that department! We thought there were possible signs, but I dont know. I wish there could be, she drifts about rather aimlessly with that great Ralph [Vaughan Williams], who goes on writing unpublished masterpieces, and grows his hair longer and longer.

Tottie Pater[2] is still ill, but gets better slowly. Tomorrow I am going to have my first class with Miss [Clara] Pater, she looks very white and shrivelled,

1. Margery Snowden, the artist, who became one of Vanessa's most intimate friends.
2. Walter Pater's sister.

39

poor Love—Dont you think those two old ladies most pathetic, growing old together, and one of them will drop off, and the other will be left. They seem so desolate with no young friends or relations. Angela James[1] is expecting a little James at any moment—so is Margaret Phillimore, and Helen is well on with the making of one mercifully.

It is beautiful, cold October weather, all the leaves coming off, and wonderful mists and sunsets. Dont you long for London, and St Pauls, and doesn't a foreign town seem clean and clear and unromantic after this wonderful town?

Now, my dearest Toad—the Swiss has come in to put out my clothes and she drives me mad with her boots which creak loud enough to be heard in Dresden.

So I must say Goodbye. You must answer this and then the sheepdog [Vanessa] will write next week, and so we shall keep our agreement.

Yr loving,
Goat

I hope you havent already heard the startling piece of news that dear old Mildred Massingberd is engaged to Major Leonard Darwin[2] a widower of 50 whose wife died two years ago!!! They are very happy, and are to be married at Gunby at the end of this month or next.

This letter was forgotten under a pile of papers on Nessa's writing table till today, Nov 11th, when Beloved Marny came to supper and took it away with her—so you are not as faithless as I thought. Write at once.

Sussex

35: To Emma Vaughan   22 *Hyde Park Gate, S.W.*

23rd April [1901]

These [*smudge*] are not dirty finger marks!!

My dearest Toad,

Have we quarrelled? But it takes two to make a quarrel and I never felt more kindly disposed to the whole of the reptile family in my life. Why don't we ever hear from each other then? *I* want to write, the sheepdog wants to write—but somehow the letters never get written, and I have not seen the Dresden postmark for six good months. It reminds me of the game we played at Fritham "Silence in the Pig Market. The first who speaks is the old sow." I am the old sow, I always was if you remember, but you must write and call me so.

1. A daughter of Lord Shuttleworth, she married Captain Bernard James.
2. Son of Charles Darwin, author of *On the Origin of Species*. Gunby Hall, Lincolnshire, had been the home of the Massingberds since 1700.

Sept 17th.

My dearest Toad

I find that my beloved Warr gives
his Latin classes on a day which
is impossible for me, so that I
mean to go to his Paters Intermediate
Latin class, on Tuesday at 2. You only
do reading - Virgil - with her — won't you
come to that? I should think it
was quite amusing

Nessa says do you by chance know
of any housemaid likely to suit us?
Lizzy is going to be married on the 1st
October, & we have not got any one, or
heard of any one yet. Don't trouble - but if
you should happen to hear of any you might
tell us — I am much distressed about your
Jacket

Yr loving Goat

Letter No. 19

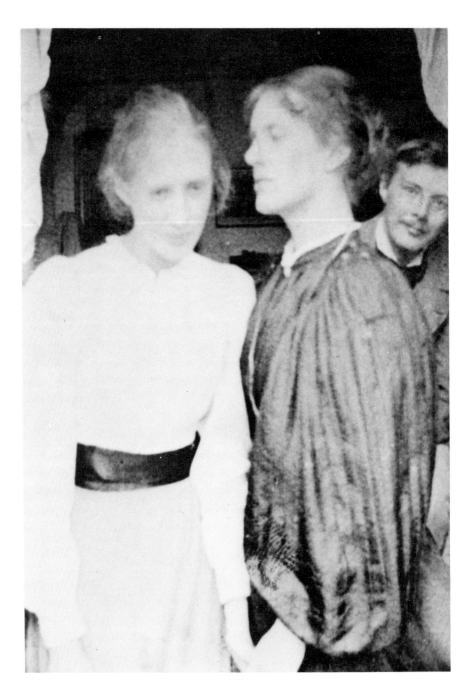

Virginia, Stella Duckworth and Gerald Duckworth in 1896

Well my dearest Toad, one disadvantage of writing so seldom is that it is so difficult to write when one *does* write. Do you know that we have been to Lyme Regis for a fortnight—that the sheepdog is going to try for the [Royal] Academy [Schools] in July—do you know anything of our movements or do you think us all dead and buried in the deep sea? Marny flies in for a cup of tea some afternoons when she is in London—in *Hoxton* rather, and so we hear a little gossip about you.

Will told me that you were getting rather tired of Dresden but he seemed vague. Madge said "Emma never writes to *me*. I hear nothing of her except from Marny". They were very well and almost too happy, one never found Madge without Will or Will without Madge. Old Sym loomed in the background, very massive, almost too massive for her aquiline nose and tragedy: she has grown mellower and grandmotherly too, and seemed to take a human and not vulturish view of life. She adores Will; Walter bores her and Lotta's children are so dull that she won't go to see them. I rather expect that the divine Lotta herself "the most beautiful woman in London" is not quite up to the Symondsian mark—rather county councilish—Walter will be Walter Leaf M.P., one of these days. What a good creature! Katharine and Charles [Furse] have just come back to London. Nessa met Charles at the New Gallery the other day. He asked her to come and stay with them in their new house, and she accepted.

Oh, you reptile, I do wonder what you do, and what you are going to do. What you think about all day. My old piano must be almost dumb by this time—you know it had a tendency that way—so few people play on it now.

Aunt Mary suddenly came here two days ago. It is all very tragic. Hervey [Fisher] seemed to get better for some weeks, and then suddenly went worse than ever—so bad that [Dr] Branfoot said he must be put in an asylum. So they brought him up to London and he is now in Bethlehem.[1] Just as this was settled, they heard that Arthur[2] was to arrive at Southampton, invalided home; they went to meet him and were met by a doctor who said they must not see him: he was in his cabin ill with a sunstroke. He was taken to Netley Hospital, where he will have to be a month or six weeks, and then I suppose it will take some time to get quite well as he had three sunstrokes on the top of each other. Oh dear, this sounds so like Cousin Mia [Maria Macnamara]! But if ever there were a Greek tragedy the Fisher family is one. Poor Aunt Mary looked worn out; she had all along refused to let Hervey be taken to an Asylum; and she will feel the want of him more than anyone, I suppose, yet it seems really better that he should be away from them all, and I think the cost is very little at Bethlehem.

The only thing in this world is music—music and books and one or two pictures. I am going to found a colony where there shall be no marrying—unless you happen to fall in love with a symphony of Beethoven—no human

1. The Hospital of St Mary of Bethlehem, an asylum in Lambeth.
2. Arthur Fisher, who died in 1902.

element at all, except what comes through Art—nothing but ideal peace and endless meditation. This world of human beings grows too complicated, my only wonder is that we don't fill more madhouses: the insane view of life has much to be said for it—perhaps its the sane one after all: and *we*, the sad sober respectable citizens really rave every moment of our lives and deserve to be shut up perpetually. My spring melancholy is developing in these hot days into summer madness.

We have had no going out—to return to the world as it is—since the Queen died [22 January 1901], or only very quiet parties. Nevertheless, we have bought dresses from Mrs [Sally] Young which deserve to be shown. Remember our great dinner party in your honour, my dear Toad; you will see them there. Do write soon—and let it be long. I have unlimited affection for you and admiration.

Goodbye dearest Toad, dear lovely charming gifted Toad!!

Sussex

36: TO THOBY STEPHEN   22 *Hyde Park Gate, S.W.*
Wednesday [July 1901]

My dear Thoby,

Your Bill was not in your room, but by one of my brilliant flights—half imagination half sober reasoning—I conceived that it was to be found on the writing table in the drawing room—where it *was* and here it *is*—Give my affectionate love and greetings to the White Ws.[1] Now we—that is you—have done our work for the year. I am very glad that you got these particular Bugs because our Hairstreaks are rather poor, and they always attract me as a family—Where and how did you get them? However I shant know till we meet at Fritham. I will tell Jack about it if he comes tonight.

I had meant on my own account to write to you. Father has begun to say "We must talk about what you are to read at Fritham". I have told him that you have promised to help me with a Greek Play or two—Sophocles I think. Father wants to get for me from the Library Jebbs Sophocles, only it is in seven volumes. So he says would you send a line with your invaluable advice—which play it had better be? I have read the Antigone—Edipus [*sic*] Coloneus—and I am in the middle of the Trachiniae. I should rather like to read the Antigone again—and any others you advise. I find to my immense pride that I really *enjoy* not only admire Sophocles. So after all there is hope for Shakespeare.

London grows steadily hotter and drier and browner; I long for Fritham and my apoplectic pony and my choice selection of books. I feel a maggot in my brain—I want to read myself blue in the nose—I never read a line in

1. The White W is a rare moth, one of the Hairstreak family (*Lycenidae*), and is so called from the white 'w's under its wing.

London—not a line that I like that is to say. Only Greek Histories and German novels—which is worst I dont know.

We are in the middle of the Examination [at the Royal Academy Schools]. So far it seems to have gone well, as far as we know. All the others are rather inferior, and she [Vanessa] has a good model and a good place, certainly if there is an Artist or a gentleman on the Council the result is certain. Privately I dont think anyhow there can be much doubt. The Schools are very empty, so they will let in bad people. We shall hear what has happened the day we go to the Forest probably.

Yr loving,
Goat

I have just had a tragic letter from Miss Noble [of Warboys, Huntingdon-shire]. Her Horse ran away and hurt himself so badly that he had to be shot, and her cow died. She says she would like to see you "When she has got over her great trouble".

King's

37: To Emma Vaughan   *Fritham House [Lyndhurst, Hampshire]*

Aug 8th [1901]

Dearest Todger,

How much longer are you going to live in Switzerland? You will be naturalised a Swiss subject before you know where you are, if you don't take care. Will you speak French or German and do you wear mourning for the Empress Frederick?[1] Enlighten me on all these points to-morrow when you look out your largest sheet of gray paper and your stoutest quill (only you don't write with quills) to answer this. What on earth can you find to do in Switzerland. For goodness sake, don't take to climbing mountains. Every newspaper almost, has a Matterhorn tragedy in it. Are you anywhere near the Matterhorn? I have the vaguest idea of your or anybodies geography. Our London season about which you ask, was of the dullest description. I only went to three dances—and I think nothing else. But the truth of it is, as we frequently tell each other, we are failures. Really, we can't shine in Society. I don't know how it's done. We aint popular—we sit in corners and look like mutes who are longing for a funeral. However, there are more important things in this life—from all I hear I shan't be asked to dance in the next, and that is one of the reasons why I hope to go there. This is the kind of thing I say to Dorothea [Stephen] and she glows like a sunset over Mont Blanc (can you see Mont Blanc from the window to disprove my metaphor?)

1. Empress Frederick, eldest sister of Edward VII, and wife of Frederick III of Germany, had died on 5 August 1901.

43

and says "Shut up!" One of the last things we did before coming away, was a quite unexpected one—we went to tea with Aunt Virginia.[1] This was led up to by something even more unexpected. One night we gave a small dinner party to which Bee Cameron[2] came and when we came up for dinner, we saw a large white form artistically grouped on the sofa by the open window. It was Aunt Virginia! So then she asked us to tea with her. She talked a great deal about you, my dear Toad and said how clever you were and how much she admired your spirit in going off to Dresden and wanted to know all about you, but as you hadn't written for so long, we couldn't tell her much. However, you see we got a compliment for you, which I know you will scoff at. I can never quite see Aunt V's surpassing charm or beauty. The charm at anyrate need not have vanished though the beauty has almost entirely. Save her great eyes, which *are* beautiful—and her enthusiasms and loud whispers and French manners, I think she was rather disappointing. But perhaps it wasn't a good day. Georgie met the Kay Shuttleworths just after they had come back from Mürren. They were full of both of your charms. "So very nice and agreeable—They made our stay so much more enjoyable than it would otherwise have been" Think of that my dear Toad! What a priviledge you must have felt it!

We are in the midst of London society here, though happily separated by a few miles of forest. The Lyulph Stanleys—the Richard Stracheys—the Freshfields[3]—lie all round us and occasionally ask us to tea parties. I won't say anything about the forest itself or the view from my window, which was the view from your window, because I remember a remark you made last year when we drove you through the most beautiful forest drive that exists. "Ugh, my dear Goat, smells like a *fried fish* shop!" I wonder what that diseased nose of yours smells in Switzerland—the nectar and Ambrosia of the Gods, I suppose. Fried fish I must say, has a great charm for me. Isn't this a fearful long letter? and my handwriting is apoplectic and paralytic. But I have a steel pen which writes like a rusty nail. How is dear Marny and her leg? and how are you?—write a long letter full of meat.

Your loving,
Goat

I defy anyone to prove which of these two letters was written first! [*other letter missing*]

Sussex

1. Virginia Pattle (1827-1910), who married the 3rd Earl Somers. She was Virginia's maternal great-aunt.
2. Beatrice Cameron, the daughter of Julia Cameron's son Eugene.
3. Edward Lyulph Stanley, later 4th Baron Stanley of Alderley; Sir Richard Strachey, father of Lytton Strachey; and Douglas Freshfield, the traveller and author, and later President of The Royal Geographical Society.

[October? 1901]

My dear Thoby,

    I dont know whether I imagined it, or whether you once did say really that you wanted a kitten for your rooms. Anyhow, if you do I could send you in a hamper a very nice black kitten with signs of distinguished birth about it—and a charming and lovable disposition (like mine!) I have been offered it by Miss Power,[1] but my room apparently would not suit it, as it ought to be able to get out of doors—which it could do in your rooms. However, I am afraid you will be able to get a Cambridge kitten (if you want one) without this bother of sending it. Only could you let me know as soon as you get this?

Yr. Goat

King's

Nov 5th [1901]

My dear Grim,

    Father has had a letter this morning to say that the degree [Hon. D. Litt., Oxford] is put off till the 26 Nov. and he wanted you to know, as you spoke of going there. We have been asked to stay the night by two separate lots of people—but I dont know—Oxford as you can imagine would draw me from my bestial comforts if any place would, but the bestial comforts (they come into Plato this morning, and seemed rather appropriate) are growing rampant. My real object in writing is to make a confession—which is to take back a whole cartload of *goatisms* which I used at Fritham and elsewhere in speaking of a certain great English writer—the greatest: I have been reading Marlow, and I was so much more impressed by him than I thought I should be, that I read Cymbeline just to see if there mightnt be more in the great William than I supposed. And I was quite upset! Really and truly I am now let in to [the] company of worshippers—though I still feel a little oppressed by his—greatness I suppose. I shall want a lecture when I see you; to clear up some points about the Plays. I mean about the characters. Why aren't they more human? Imogen and Posthumous and Cymbeline—I find them beyond me—Is this my feminine weakness in the upper region? But really they might have been cut out with a pair of scissors—as far as mere humanity goes—Of course they talk divinely. I have spotted the best lines in the play—almost in any play I should think—

    Imogen says—Think that you are upon a rock, and now throw me again! and Posthumous answers—Hang there like fruit, my Soul, till the

1. Miss Power was teaching Virginia bookbinding.

tree die [*Cymbeline:* V. v. 262-5]! Now if that doesn't send a shiver down your spine, even if you are in the middle of cold grouse and coffee—you are no true Shakespearian! Oh dear oh dear—just as I feel in the mood to talk about these things, you go and plant yourself in Cambridge.

Tomorrow I go on to Ben Jonson, but I shant like him as much as Marlow. I read Dr Faustus, and Edward II—I thought them very near the great man—with more humanity I should say—not all on such a grand tragic scale. Of course Shakespeares smaller characters are human; what I say is that superhuman ones *are* superhuman. Just explain this to me—and also why his plots are just cracky things—Marlows are flimsier; the whole thing is flimsier, but there are some very "booming" (Stracheys word[1]) lines and speeches and whole scenes—when Edward dies for instance—and then when Kent is taken away to be executed, and the little King wont have it done, and his mother tries to make him forget and asks him to ride with her in the Park, and he says "And will Uncle Edmund ride with us?" That is a human touch! What a dotard you will think me! but I thought I must just write and tell you—

I write even less connectedly and legibly than usual, because 3 or 400 years ago a wretched Italian tried to blow up the Houses of Parliament! So we English are celebrating the day at this moment—which would be all very well if the children in the muse (see how I spell it!) mews opposite didnt think it necessary to join in with horrible crackers and bonfires and shoutings and whoopings—It seems quite superfluous. Georgie came back last night; and his baggage—made up of Turkey carpets, and Rose leaf jam from the Sultans preserves—and Eastern embroideries and bags of precious stones uncut—and all kinds of extraordinary things—is bumping into the hall at this moment.

Did you go to Miss Noble [of Warboys]?

Yr. Goat

King's

40: TO THOBY STEPHEN   22 *Hyde Park Gate, S.W.*

29th Jan. [1902]

My dear Thoby,

Your book has come,[2] and delights me. These little Epigrams I think I appreciate most of all Greek—as the feminine mind would, according to my

1. This could be her first reference to Lytton Strachey, Thoby's great friend at Trinity, whom Virginia had already met in 1901; or possibly Sir Edward Strachey, who wrote extensively on the history of literature.
2. Thoby had given Virginia for her 20th birthday *Select Epigrams from the Greek Anthology*, edited by John William MacKail.

theory. And MacKail isnt so precious as I thought—and some—most that I know—of the epigrams are divine—I read them over and over again, for—[*torn*] . . . sound—when I dont know the [*torn*] . . . Nothing to my mind could be more Greek in [*torn*] . . . body—than these are. I [*torn*] . . . through them at my leisure, and the reading is made so easy by the crib at the bottom.

Thank you a thousand times, as old Ladies say. This is a real addition to my library—

Yr. Goat

King's

41: TO HENRY NEWBOLT   22 *Hyde Park Gate, S.W.*

[January 1902?]

Dear Mr. Newbolt,[1]

You must have been good enough to send me a post card with a little poem on it which gives me great pleasure and pride. I have spent Sunday at a house where the only book was your Admirals All—and now I come back to find this. Father is rehearsing Drakes Drum for Wednesday.

Thank you so much.

Yrs very sincerely,
Virginia Stephen

George Spater

1. Henry John Newbolt (1862-1938), the poet and man of letters. Leslie Stephen much admired his most famous poems, *Admirals All* and *Drake's Drum*, which he would declaim to his daughters as they walked through Kensington Gardens.

Letters 42-164

During the next two years Leslie Stephen was dying, and Virginia records his slow decline mainly in letters to her new intimate, Violet Dickinson. Leslie was suffering from an abdominal cancer, but only by degrees did he come to acknowledge that it was incurable, having survived an operation and more than one crisis that could have been fatal. He continued working until shortly before his death, and the Stephen children spent their usual summer holidays with him in the country, at Lyndhurst in 1902 and at Salisbury in 1903. Hyde Park Gate was filled by anxious relatives and friends, whose hypocrisy about Leslie's approaching death Virginia found increasingly intolerable. But she could claim that "We are really the cheerfullest family in Kensington". While Vanessa studied painting, Virginia read constantly, wrote her literary exercises, did book-binding, played the pianola, and studied Greek under Janet Case. Both sisters were induced by George Duckworth to attend occasional debutante parties, at which they felt themselves to be woefully inadequate. Thoby's and Adrian's Cambridge friends had not yet begun to make a great impact on their lives, and it was to Violet Dickinson, for whom Virginia felt an intense affection, that she sent her manuscripts for comment and almost daily bulletins on her father's decline. Her other friends at this period remained the Vaughan sisters and Beatrice Thynne. When her father died on 22 February 1904, Virginia was just 22.

42: To Violet Dickinson   22 *Hyde Park Gate, S.W.*

[Early 1902?]

My dear Miss Dickinson,

Nessa says that she told you that I have discovered your Scotts diary. I meant that in Scotts life [Lockhart's] there is his diary of a voyage to the lighthouses on the Scotch coast, but I dont know if that is what you want.

I do not think it is published separately—it is not very long. I have got the Life in several small volumes. Shall I send you the one with the diary? and if it is not right you can send it back.

Yours sincerely,
Virginia Stephen

Berg

[April 1902]

My dear Violet,

I should like to come and see you anytime—but may I write in a day or two? Father hasnt been well,[1] and the doctor here wants him to see a specialist, so we go to London tomorrow.

We are afraid there may have to be an operation, but I shall know more on Monday, and I will write then.

Anyhow I dont think I will come to dinner but to tea, as all 4 males [Leslie, Gerald, Thoby and Adrian] are at home and I cant very well be out for dinner. (You see, I write you very cool letters!)

Nessa sends me long letters—and I think she enjoys herself though she pretends Rome is above her.[2] I sent her to the protestant cemetry [*sic*] with red roses, and she found Shelleys grave, and enjoyed herself enormously. I believe the portrait [*unidentified*] is really beautiful, but I haven't seen it yet. This place where we are staying is a *sham* country cottage—all white paint and [William] Morris patterns, and green wood furniture. I cant bear the washy-artistic style and I long for something honestly ugly. Their taste was originally Early Victorian, because I find remains in corners, but now they have given up their souls. I haven't talked to an educated woman (except the cook) for a fortnight, and I dont feel fit for the drawing room—so you must make allowances.

I hope I shall be able to come one of the days you say, but at this moment I dont quite know whats going to happen.

Yrs aff'ly,

VS

Why cant we marry Peers for the day? and see Katie in her glory.[3]

Why is your knee delayed? You never seem to work properly all over.

Berg

1. It was during this visit to Hindhead Copse (Sir Frederick Pollock's house) that Leslie Stephen's cancer of the intestine was first diagnosed.
2. Vanessa had gone with George Duckworth to Rome and Florence for three weeks.
3. The coronation of Edward VII had been fixed for 26 June 1902, but owing to his illness it was postponed until 9 August. 'Katie' was Lady Katherine Thynne, who married Lord Cromer in 1901.

44: To Violet Dickinson   [22 *Hyde Park Gate, S.W.*]

[April? 1902]

My dear Violet,

I have offered your improper books to two men, and one said he'd give me one shilling and the other rose to nine, and would give more if the binding was better. Shall I close with this man, or try two others that I know of? They might be better—or not—write soon and say, because my 9s. man wont wait.

If one man thinks them worth nine times as much as another there's no reason why some other man shouldn't give nine times as much again. Are you ever coming here again? or does your first visit last you still?

This is vile paper, and viler pen, but we seem to have run out.

If you are in London do come here soon—if your legs will carry you (which is always doubtful).

Yr aff.,

AVS

Berg

45: To Violet Dickinson   22 *Hyde Park Gate, S.W.*

[April 1902]

My dear Violet,

There is to be an operation but it is slighter than we thought, and it can be done here. I dont quite know when it is to be, but not this week anyhow. I think Father is perfectly well now, and he doesn't mind the thought of it as much as I thought he would. It isnt a bad operation, but I'm afraid that he will always have to be very careful afterwards.[1]

I will come on Wednesday about 4.30. Unless I suddenly hear from Nessa that she is coming then,[2] which I hope I shant.

Yr. aff'ate,

VS

Berg

46: To Violet Dickinson   22 *Hyde Park Gate, S.W.*

[April 1902]

My dear Violet,

Allingham[3] cant come till Tuesday, so the operation cant be done till then. It is a great bother, and Nessa and Georgie might have stayed on as long as they had meant. They have come back very well and cheerful, though they didn't see much of Florence.

Yr. aff. AVS

1. The operation was not in fact carried out until December.
2. Vanessa and George were urgently recalled from Florence.
3. Herbert William Allingham, surgeon to the household of Edward VII.

I will write and say how he goes on. Of course I know you care about it—only I really think there need be no anxiety about the operation itself. Please get your knees well.

Berg

47: To Thoby Stephen   22 *Hyde Park Gate, S.W.*

[May 1902]

My dear Thoby,

Any of those Art books she [Vanessa] would like. She has the Fra Angelico—Rembrandt—Botticelli—and father is going to give her some-ones Life of Sir Joshua—But I know she wants to get as many of the series as she can, so any one of them she would like.

No. Bugs are out in either case, so I am afraid they must have overslept themselves—gone on a long journey as the woman said of the pony at Ringwood.

My mind is dazed with Sidney Lee.[1] He has come to consult about the Dictionary—(How I wish it at the bottom of the sea!) and his squeak sounds like a tormented Rat—

We shall meet before long. Mrs George[2] has now invited us—also Bessy Darwin[3]—either would be better than Nun, but it cant be helped.

Yr. loving,

Goat

What Books have you got? I am really rather a good binder.

King's

48: To Violet Dickinson   *Fritham [Lyndhurst, Hampshire]*

[early August 1902]

My dear Violet,

I'm afraid Nessa raised your hopes too high, and you will be very much disappointed—but the man hasnt sent the photographs yet—and they

1. [Sir] Sidney Lee (1859-1926) was Leslie Stephen's Assistant Editor of the *Dictionary of National Biography* from 1883, became joint Editor in 1890, and sole Editor from 1891 to 1901. He supervised the supplementary volumes until 1916.
2. Mrs George Darwin, wife of George Howard Darwin, later Sir George, the mathematician and astronomer. The Darwins, like Caroline Emelia Stephen (the Nun), lived at Cambridge.
3. Elizabeth Darwin, daughter of Charles Darwin.

mayn't do me justice—indeed I dont expect they will. If you are very kind to me, and spoil me thoroughly, and behave in every way tenderly you shall have one when you come here. (They belong to George.) *That* is something to look forward to?

I wish you were here now—only you are so fashionable you must stay in London for the Coronation. Look out for Adrian among the Westminster boys in the Abbey. Will you herd with the Peeresses—Katie [Cromer]? If you go, do tell us if she looked like a real Lady. She can—but she wants humanising—and there's no one to do it, unless you will. Nessa has asked Beatrice to come here. We went to lunch there one day, and Beatrice hobbled about the room in a dirty white flannel coat and enormous slippers. But Nessa will have told you about that lunch.

Katie has withdrawn from this world more and more I feel—soon she will be beyond human help or reach. But as a goddess she is divine.

I wish you were here (this is just what I said before, and if I say it again it will be true) but this is really something my idea of a Better World.

For one thing there is very little need of clothing, which I always think a great point about Heaven, and we do just what we like. Nessa and I trot about the forest together and look for foxes. Last year we saw two. By the way, the pony you are going to be driven about in, has an impediment, not in his speech, but his pace, and he suddenly stands still and kicks if you whip him. There is another pony which Nessa rides, but I am not allowed to drive him except with a man and *that* I don't think proper (I have very nice feeling on these points.) Nessa got this paper—isn't it vile? Half I say doesn't come out—which is such a pity.

Now I really do wish you were here. We are all alone—and I like Nessa very much, but she gets so bored with me (tho' she's very fond of me too).

Yrs. aff.,

AVS

Father is very well and cheerful. The dr. said he thought him extraordinarily well, and not getting worse.

Berg

49: To Violet Dickinson   [22 *Hyde Park Gate, S.W.*]

[20 September 1902]

Your [*sic*] a blessed old ——, I cant think of any way to begin because Aunt Maria wont do—so you'll have to do without. How could I write to you. What with feeling as shy as I do, and all my being got packed in the horse box. I was this moment pulling up my sleeves to paint my floor in a sudden fit of inspiration when Adrian brought up your letter.

Do tell me Katies messages—as water to one in a desert. I have only 10 minutes to write this in—and an Aunt and Cousin downstairs. We came back last night. It was glorious and gloriouser in the New Forest. We went out hunting at 6 one morning and my boots were like damp brown paper at the end. So tell me your mans name. You have made a lifelong friend of Georgie! What on earth did you and he say to each other? He is quite brisk and important. Gerald is very gloomy.

He passed over Westminster Bridge last night and a man ran in front of his cabhorse, and jumped into the river. "I jumped out too, said Gerald, and found myself ready to go after him. I never was so much surprised in my life. But providentially there was a boat in the distance." He begins the story by saying I almost earned the Royal Humane Societies' medal!

I tell you I hate writing letters, and Adrian stands over me. But do you go and write a long long letter about 6 pages to celebrate the Sabbath. I will write another, only I am so cracked today, and I can't find anything to write with. Tell us every thing you do.

Yr. AVS

I half sent you a telegram but Gerald thought me such a fool.

Berg

50: To Violet Dickinson   22 *Hyde Park Gate, S.W.*

[September 1902]

My Aunt,

Do be a woman of honour, and send me your bootmaker['s] name and place at once. Honestly, I have only one pair left, and my naked claws are heard tapping the pavement—which is so pathetic. Why the D—— cant you come up to London? Then I should be petted again perhaps, and mine is such a singularly loveable nature dont you think so?

I cant think how one writes to an intimate friend. Once I called Kitty darling in a telegram! and we have never been on good terms since. She wrote a long letter this morning, but she's freezing hard. Leo[1] will be the death of her.

The academy began this morning. Nessa is very happy, with a live head to paint, and [John Macallan] Swan to teach her. I don't know if he's much good. The picture is really first rate, and the heather too, which was rather like anchovies spread on bread and butter, or whatever that pink paste is. I always get it at teaparties and then I have to pocket it. Last night I went

1. Leopold Maxse, Editor of the *National Review*, married Katherine Lushington, the original of Mrs Dalloway.

out to dinner all glorious without—Sally Young etc. but a mass of festering corruption within—that is the string of a certain undergarment—not the one one talks about—broke, and the result was painful—in the middle of the drawing room too as I said good bye. I scattered gloves and fan and handkerchief, and plucked em all up together, and ran downstairs clutching my skirts under my arm. Then I came home and held them up in the drawing room, and Georgie was fearfully pained. But you have made a new man of him. He has been so lenient that I cant behave improper if I wanted to.

We have subscribed, and bought a Pianola! Father almost weeps over us, and all his ladies are tender and reproachfull.

I don't get any attention now. Nessa gets it all. She has so many intimates. Be a woman—write and tell me how all your Nellies [Lady Robert Cecil] and Katies and Beatrices are. Beatrice wrote "Dear Vanessa by Violets orders"!

Yr. loving,
Sparroy

Do remember the Boots—hellcat that you are. I am training for a curate and 11 children. Curate first children after *of course*.

Can you screw a set of teeth out of my dresses? As it is I spend most days having holes bored in me—and it really isnt worthwhile. Such an expense of temper.

Berg

51: TO VIOLET DICKINSON   [22 *Hyde Park Gate, S.W.*]
[September 1902?]

Woman,
    Is there a train about 1.30, from here? You said there was, but it doesn't come into Bradshaw. Make it plain. Do we go to Welwyn?
    You will be swarming with intimates.
    This fog is a nightmare of the soul as well as the body, and [Vanessa's] painting's impossible.

Sparroy

I bought a pair of boots.

Berg

52: To Violet Dickinson   22 *Hyde Park Gate, S.W.*

[September 1902]

My Woman,

Could you send me as quick as you can—as the matter is very important
—the number on the back of the 3 quarters face photograph of beloved
Sparroy, as I am getting some copies for a few of my intimates. I have risen
a step in the world since my motor drive.

Yr. Sp.

How did you toil up with all those parcels?

Berg

53: To Emma Vaughan   22 *Hyde Park Gate, S.W.*

[October 1902]

Darling Todger,

Come on Tuesday—to lunch, 1.30 or a little later—Do come to lunch—
then we can begin directly afterwards. I don't know what you want to learn
exactly—or whether I can teach you anything you dont know by the light of
nature, but if you will bring something to start upon we can see. I have been
making endless experiments and almost smelt my room out this afternoon
trying to do gold lettering. Tomorrow I shall experiment with gold on
cloth. I believe there is an immense field for this kind of thing. There seem
ever so many ways of making covers—of leather—linen—silk—parchment
—vellum—japanese paper etc. etc. etc. which the ordinary lidders never
think of. Dont go and give the show away to Glazebrook [?]—or make her
pay you handsome for your advice.

Marny showed me an account book you did for her—which I honestly
took for a professional job—I am sure all your finger exercises have made
you very nimble and neat—which is your nature too—and you will do a
roaring trade.

The thing I find so difficult is the lettering—that can only be done by
practice—still you can give more time to it in one week than I have done in
the whole of my career. I am a little hurt that the Rustic taste did not approve
of my Green linen dress—perhaps it was beyond them. I bought it of a little
man in Lyndhurst.

You are a dissolute woman—staying away till this time of year—Now
Parliament's sitting you may find London fashionable enough for you.
Otherwise, I suppose you would imitate Dukes and shoot pheasants till
January. I hear you charmed the notorious family [the Will Vaughans?] so
that the unborn sang for joy. (this is Marny's indecency, not mine) and they

asked you to stay on. The Pianola is flourishing, and plays after dinner till the other side (the Mackenzies,[1] who only do *hand* playing) are vanquished. Really it is a wonderful machine—beyond a machine in that it lets your own soul flow thro'. Even the carping Adeline was a little surprised. But I write to a still more carping Toad. Mrs William Darwin's[2] dead. Everyone seems to be dying—but I can still hope while Millicent [Isham] lives—She is like the sun through a fog—Adeline [Vaughan Williams] etc., are the fog. Give her my love.

AVS

Sussex

54: TO VIOLET DICKINSON   22 *Hyde Park Gate, S.W.*

[October/November 1902]

My woman,

Tuesday will do perfectly, about 5.

Father sees [Dr] Seton tomorrow, and something more may be settled, but Seton is such a woolgatherer. Jack and George and Gerald have all asked father to wait, or to see someone else, but he says it will save him pain if the operation is done now, before he is any worse. He wont believe that there is any chance of his getting better. However there is nothing more to be said now. I feel rather a brute, bothering you with all these things. Is that the way intimates are treated?

Kitty's [Maxse] very well, but planted at Hatfield with her Violet.[3]

Yr. Sparroy

What are you planting?

Berg

55: TO VIOLET DICKINSON   22 *Hyde Park Gate, S.W.*

[October/November 1902]

My woman,

I dont want a prize for coming to see you—however much it rains. I am very fond of you. But books do delight my soul. Your [*sic*] a blessed hell cat and an angel in one. What a squaling [*sic*] and a squeaking there must be inside you. I put it where I can look up and see it. It is so refined and pathetic. I am sure it has a past—like Gerald. How do you come by it, woman? I can

1. The Mackenzies were their next-door neighbours at Hyde Park Gate.
2. William Darwin was a son of Charles Darwin, the naturalist.
3. Violet Cecil was Leo Maxse's sister and married Lord Edward Cecil.

read the Greek pretty easily, not but what Case[1] says I'm a fool. Think of your poor Sparroy beginning the first page of the Greek grammar this morning! I go over it and over it, and nothing can I understand.

I think of you and your holy life on the mount.[2] I came home and raved about it—and then there was a letter from the man at Broomy[3] to say he's only got the house for the winter—and Georgie has written to ask if he can take it for a 'term of years'. It really looks like business—but the house wont be nearly as good as yours—and not much lonelier though we are 8 miles from a station. Dont chop any more paths, and dont make it too bald up round the house. When I come and stay I should like to have green shade in my windows. This you will consider I know. Still I dream of it—really I cant imagine anything better than the wood and the unexpected gardens, and the red tree. What I fear is that much digging will give your soul a peace such as no Sparroy will disturb. I feel the same thing with Greek. Time spent with dead Greeks is de-humanising—scraping about in the earth is de-humanising. Dont get too Holy.

The hedgerow[4] has had high praise from [Margery] Snow, who is thought rather a judge. Snow is come. Kitty [Maxse] is looming. Duff Baker is on the verge. So you see it is high time for you to have your fringe pulled. I'm afraid no one sees to it when I'm not there. Just count the words in this letter, and write me as many back, and I like them hot and affectionate. I am going to bed with your Greek book—under my pillow (not so improper as it looks). Tell me how your blessed wood gets on. Have the trees got yellow? Have you finished your hedging—or whatever you call it. How are my beloved Chalky Charlie and Quint.[5] Quint sounds like Dickens. Did you get your hatchet sharpened—hatchet sounds so mediaeval—you are a rum lot. I have one idea of you—at the station that pouring day which gives me fits whenever I think of it. Whenever N[essa] sees me laughing to myself, I say its only Violet.

Yr. lover,
Sparroy

Berg

1. Janet Case had been Virginia's private tutor in Greek since the beginning of 1902.
2. The cottage, Burnham Wood, which Violet was having built for herself in Welwyn.
3. Broomy Lodge, near Fritham, New Forest.
4. A picture painted by Vanessa.
5. Workmen engaged on the building of Burnham Wood.

[October/November 1902]

My dear Thoby,

Father is very cross because you have neither of you written to him this week. So do send a line, or we shall have resort to telegraphs.

Would *Wednesday* next week suit you and Adrian for a descent—that seems our only day. Nessa has just sent up her drawings and had one (out of three) returned—and the one is a painted head which she did carelessly, as it is always said that the Judges judge you by your antique work. So now she has three days a week with nothing to do—and Sargent[1] teaching her the other three. He is a splendid teacher, and very kind to her.

What has been happening to you, all this time? And Adrian? He writes very formal letters—but then the difficulties of writing to ones family are great I know. We seem to dribble along, with endless affectionate old ladies to tea, and admirers of fathers, who all come here now. Father has probably told you that he is going to see Treves[2] on Thursday. Seton says he had better, just to quiet his mind. Seton still is certain that he is better if anything, certainly not worse—Now we have heard that Nun is coming for two days—and Nessa is going to stay with the [Earl and Countess] Carnarvons—so I shall have only my one body between those two—(you appreciate the metaphor) I am helping Nessa to give Gurth a powder and to ointment his ear while I write—so you need only expect dull dutiful news—But I will write you a very nice letter soon. Has Byron come to a decent end? Lord preserve me from spending my fine brains over other peoples bones! and for goodness sake, dont you either. You are an Original Genius, my Lord.

Is there any news? Georgie has gone 5 hours in the train to hear Austen[3] make a speech tonight—his devotion is touching—but he has to work pretty hard. The Pianola is going strong. Broomy was a false alarm. Only Hayes Turner had underlet it to someone for 3 months. But if we wait 4 years we can have it. I saw a blue bird with a yellow chest and cheeks on my window sill, the other morning. What should you think *he* was. "My dear Goat—no woman knows how to describe a thing accurately!"

Yr. loving Goat

Answer about *Wednesday*.

King's

1. John Singer Sargent (1856-1925) was elected a Royal Academician in 1897.
2. Sir Frederick Treves, who had operated on Edward VII in June 1902. He had been Surgeon Extraordinary to Queen Victoria, 1900-1901.
3. George Duckworth was acting as unpaid secretary to Austen Chamberlain, who had just been appointed Postmaster General with a seat in the Cabinet.

[October/November 1902]

My Woman,

Why dont you come to London? Have you taken root in the soil—as I foretold lost to civilisation and all the graces. Really a cook more or less doesn't much matter. We lived on an old decrepit pious woman for a week the other day, when Sophy went for a holiday. The food was unexpected, but amusing, and added rather to the harmony of the household. But I know it isnt that that keeps you—its the slow effect of digging and planting all day long, which leaves you naked like Eve so that you dont dare show yourself in London—naked as to the spirit I mean, as we shall all be before the Lord. This evening for 2 hours I have tried to write sensible letters to old Aunts and family friends, and I haven't finished one of 'em—I cant write sensible letters, and you dont matter.

Nessa has got Sargent at the Academy now, and the Denty's daughter sitting to her tomorrow. Sargent is worth all the other teaching she's ever had. As far as I can make out, he likes her things but artists are so inarticulate. Anyhow she likes him—his voice—even his green eyes. He stands staring straight at the canvas for 10 minutes, and then says 'Youve got the right idea.' All the other scrubby creatures turn green with jealousy. What women are! I go and rummage in the London Library now. I got into the vaults where they keep the Times yesterday, and had to be fished out by a man. But too many books have been written already—its no use making more. Eleanor[1] is said to be a worse Prig acted than written—all talk. I'm going to write a great play which shall be all talk too—but so exciting you'll squirm in your seat. That is a plan of mine and Jacks—we are going to write it together— it could be done Im sure. Im going to have a man and a woman—show them growing up—never meeting—not knowing each other—but all the time you'll feel them come nearer and nearer. This will be the real exciting part (as you see)—but when they almost meet—only a door between—you see how they just miss—and go off at a tangent, and never come anywhere near again. There'll be oceans of talk and emotions without end. Im sure all this interests you so much!

I went to the zoo today and I want to get a nice green monkey.

Do write a good hot letter. Nessa going to stay with Ly. Carnarvon Friday to Monday so if yr in London you must come then.

Berg

1. A new play by Mrs Humphry Ward, then showing in London.

58: To Violet Dickinson   22 *Hyde Park Gate, S.W.*

[October/November 1902]

My woman,

Nessa is going away early on Friday till Monday so that we couldn't come to lunch. Friday week is a long time off. Couldn't you manage before that—anyhow stick to Friday week. I hope your grinders are all right, and the rest of your works well oiled. Father is seeing Treves tomorrow, and we are pestered with sentimental relations.

Yr. Sparroy

Father is seeing Treves only for his own peace of mind, because he wont believe that Seton is right in thinking him better. He says there is no chance of an operation—Seton I mean.

Berg

59: To Violet Dickinson   22 *Hyde Park Gate, S.W.*

[October/November 1902]

My woman,

Treves is rather worrying. He thinks father not so well, and says he will probably have to have the operation in about six weeks.

But Seton says just the opposite: he thinks Treves has forgotten how bad father was in the summer, and doesn't see that he is better now than he was then. Seton still is certain that father *is* better. But Seton cant say this to Treves, apparently. Last time Treves was here he said that he wouldn't do the operation unless there was actual pain—and there is none at all—because the operation itself is such a horrid thing, and doesnt of course cure him. This time he said nothing of that—but advised father to have it done as soon as he thought it worthwhile. I think that father has never realized how bad he will be afterwards—at least if what Seton and Treves himself said in the summer was true. He only wants to get rid of the present discomfort as quickly as possible—and thinks he will be all right afterwards. I hope we shall get Allingham to see him first anyhow, but then great doctors are so queer, and Seton wont say anything decided.

Of course if he were in pain it would be worthwhile—only from what everyone says, it isn't a cure or much of a relief—at any rate at first, and then any operation however slight—this one is perfectly easy they say—must be bad when you'r [*sic*] old. He is extraordinarily anxious to have it, and says he is going to make Seton settle a time on Monday, but I don't think Seton will let him. It would be idiotic to have it done before any of the things have happened which Treves says will happen, if there's the least chance that he really *is* getting better. Treves might easily have forgotten exactly how he was in the summer.

Its all d—— d—— He is such an attractive creature, and we get on so well when were alone, and lose our tempers and all the rest [*sic*].

Nessa went off cursing to the Carnarvons. I hope she'll like it once she's there. Wednesday we're going to Cambridge—come another day *Lover*.

Yr. wm. Sparroy

Berg

60: To Violet Dickinson   22 *Hyde Park Gate, S.W.*

[12 December 1902]

My child,

Everything seems to be going perfectly well.[1] Treves saw him again this evening and said he could not be better—his temperature normal, and he has no pain or sickness. He may see someone tomorrow if he likes. Treves evidently thinks very little of the operation itself. So I dont think there is any need to worry now. He was quite cheerful, and likes his room and the nurses.

We are all in roaring spirits, playing wedding marches. Nevertheless it wasn't cheerful this morning. First, just as we got ready to start, there came a telegram to the Irish parlourmaid to say her brother died yesterday, and so she and her sister, who's the slopper, started off for Ireland, for the funeral—which seems a consolation—and all the kitchen was in tears from sympathy.

Then it was terrible gloomy last night, and waiting this morning in a kind of Dentists waiting room, and a cold fog for Treves. Howsomever, Sparroy sings a Heathen song of praise tonight.

What a world it is! on the whole though I dont want to creep into my narrow bed—which is the grave—this very night.

Have you a real affection for the Sparroy? She folds you in her feathery arms, so that you may feel the Heart in her ribs. Rather mild, but these emotions are very upsetting.

With deep affection,
Yr. Sparroy

Berg

61: To Violet Dickinson   22 *Hyde Park Gate, S.W.*

[13 December 1902]

My woman,

We have just come back from seeing father!

He had a very good night—no pain—temperature normal—and the nurse told us he was quite unusually well.

1. Leslie Stephen was operated upon for abdominal cancer by Sir Frederick Treves on 12 December in a nursing home in Duchess Street, London, W.1.

We only stayed a minute, but he was quite cheerful, and like himself.

I have to keep up a conversation with a huge black female[1] while I write this—who wants disgusting details—but wont have 'em!

Settle a time for coming. Black female triumphs.

Sparroy

Berg

62: TO VIOLET DICKINSON   22 *Hyde Park Gate, S.W.*

[27 ? December 1902]

My woman,

Father is very well. He had two bad days this week when they were rather anxious, but the dr. this morning was delighted and said he had done wonderfully, and may get up on Thursday or Friday. I wish all your intimates weren't in such low water, I mean the Lytteltons,[2] and dragging the poor Hell Cat [Violet] down with them.

Christmas is the Devils own feast not the other way round, as generally supposed. Once when our singing mistress asked me why I hung up my stocking on Christmas Eve, I said it was to celebrate the crucifixtion (or however you spell it—not *fiction* I am sure—but the x looks so peculiar). We spent a very mild Christmas day. Nessa and I both forgot it was Christmas —a sign of age, and many lost illusions—Violet the latest. I am sure you cant be happy in a great strange house [Longleat?], with brilliant Ladies in diamonds, and no loveable Sparroy waiting to be attended to.

All that splendour must seem so *hollow* without the one true heart.

Georgie's away. We four have been playing Bridge all the evening!! not a very good game for the feeble minded. Nessa is an authority upon it. She and Adrian argued over a Bridge book till they both felt too much to speak. I went to *Two Dances* last week but I think Providence inscrutably decreed some other destiny for me. Adrian and I waltzed (to a Polka!), and Adrian says he can't conceive how anyone can be idiotic enough to find amusement in dancing, and I see how they do it but feel all the pretty young Ladies far removed into another sphere—which is so pathetic—and I woula give all my profound Greek to dance really well, and so would Adrian give anything he had. Nessa will talk to me all the time, so this letter is not written with that sense and sensibility to which you are accustomed.

Father thinks you a 'particularly nice woman' and would like to see you when next in London.

1. Leslie's sister, Caroline Emelia Stephen ("Nun").
2. Violet's friends were: Hester Lyttelton, and Margaret Lyttelton, Editor of the Women's Supplement of *The Guardian*.

Are you in good working order. Especially as to the seat of the affections, which is the heart. Dont let Beatrice [Thynne] behave too much like a Lady in a novel with her cigarettes and diamonds.

There are many very nice people in the world, but few of whom it can be said 'She has such a singularly loveable nature'.

Sparroy is very much attached to you. She blesses you.

Sparroy

Berg

63: TO EMMA VAUGHAN   22 *Hyde Park Gate, S.W.*

[Late December 1902]

Darling Todger,

You are a reprobate to remember my peculiarities as fruit eater—but the two pears were a bright spot in my day, and made me feel a new Goat. Also, I am almost convinced after much consideration, and personal experience, that Butts is the first Kensington fruiterer.

I hope you are regaining your wonted activity—and not imitating the ways of the Church—which seems utterly gone over to the bad.

Madge sent Nessa Halford's[1] photograph—which I gaze at with not a little foreboding. Some woman will suffer, mark my words, from that mouth and chin, one of these days. Clearly the Vaughan brew resists any adultera-tion from weak Symonds' stock—which may be a pleasure to you—but as I say, it seems to me anything but a comfortable look-out. I am let in for a 2/6d room (my share 2/6d—the rent 10/-) at the *other* end of Queen's Road. If I had a little black Vaughan blood in me—if I could sit and scowl and clench my teeth as that nephew of yours does—I shouldn't be landed in such undertakings. At this moment, instead of writing to you, I ought to tell Stebbing that I accept. But in the same way that I can't make up my mind to say no—I can't say yes, which is the most pitiable pass. The Somervells came to dine here the other night—there is something rather fishy about her, I don't know what—However I won't poison your mind. We sent Clara [Pater] a flower for Christmas; the old wretch hasn't answered. I expect she and Totty [Pater] are celebrating Christmas in bed—I believe a good dose of bed and doctor's visits is a real treat to them—and excitement—like going to the play or taking a drop too much, to *us*.

I saw Hester Ritchie[2] the other day, and she showed me a leather book she had bound—lettered though, by a shop. But it was unpleasantly well done. Are you reaping commissions? If I weren't the sweetest tempered old nanny-goat in the world, I should feel rather green at the thought of your gold letters and general promise. I am only a broken down failure at this art,

1. Halford, son of Madge and W. W. Vaughan, born in 1901.
2. Granddaughter of W. M. Thackeray, and Leslie's niece by his first marriage.

and have to grow old and see the younger generation shoot ahead of me. How are the family—or *is* the family—since so united and peaceable a family deserve a singular. I write nonsense, because the pianola is playing with extreme brilliance and precision in the next room.

Your loving,

Goat

Sussex

64: To Violet Dickinson   [22 *Hyde Park Gate, S.W.*]

[January 1903]

My woman,

If you come at 4.30 you can go and see father first. Then reserve your energies for the nieces [Virginia and Vanessa]. The other niece is splitting with desire to discuss the Studio, which is realized *tomorrow*.

Sparroy says its a question of D [eus] V [olens] whether shes in for tea tomorrow. Misery sits on her doorstep. Uncle dying—in fact dead[1] mourning for the flesh indispensable—dressmaker incompetent—Sparroy not what you call a strict woman of business. But Hell Cat rakes up the embers of my burnt heart—Why are you flirting with old [Aunt] Minna [Duckworth]? Does she tell you of the offer she had once. He went mad, so that if she had accepted her children might have inherited this, 'So lucky I didnt'. Such a strange businesslike Duckworth foresight.

Sparroy

Berg

65: To Violet Dickinson   [22 *Hyde Park Gate, S.W.*]

[25 January 1903]

My woman,

It sends real pangs through my heart to take things from your lean hands. Nessa produced your envelope this morning—and I said 'Dont tell me its more than a letter of affection'. But inside was a round hard substance, as might have been a heart of flesh, but turned out the same thing translated into gold and pearls. The blessings of friendship are indeed far beyond the gold and pearls of this planet—nevertheless Sparroy pins one outside and keeps the other close locked within. My dear woman, it is full of infinite tenderness and sentiment to me—it has a certain pathos, as though it had held the hair of long dead Sparroys and Violets—and now it shall descend to the illegitimates as a pledge that their mother had the friendship of very respectable women once. It is already doing a kind of Hester Lytteltons

1. Herbert Fisher died on 17 January 1903.

duty among the tangled overgrowth of my bosom, holding bunches of dirty lace and unexpected progeny of chemise etc.

I have had to confute the Christian religion tonight, and though that has been well done, my thoughts dont flow as easy as usual.

Will you name a day to meet the two Taylor children,[1] who are too strong taken pure, but mixed with V. D. will go down smooth. Really it is the kind of tea party one doesn't have often in this world, so screw yourself up, and come and Bless your love token on S[parroy]'s Bosom.

Please ask Hester L[yttelton] to supply me with a God *quick*—not the Christian God.

Yr Sp: Blessings.

Berg

66: TO THOBY STEPHEN   22 *Hyde Park Gate, S.W.*

[25? January 1903]

My dear Grim,

You are an angel to have routed out a Montaigne for me. I was getting quite desperate. I have hunted him 3 years. This one[2] is better than a Florio I think—I once had a chance of a 2nd Edition Florio [1613] in my penniless days—I may have told you the story—but it is a badly printed book, very black and close, and I dont think there is much to choose between the translations. I always read Montaigne in bed, and these books will do beautifully. The Bacon is one of my choicest works—especially the note on the title page.[3] I haven't got a copy, so I shall stick to these; it looks to me as though it had worn its corners round in some coat pocket. I shall carry it in my fur coat many a mile and many a mile—Yours are the only books I had given me. Gerald gave me a magnificent pearl necklace—which I smashed first thing, and all my other presents were jewels of some kind.

I have made myself thoroughly objectionable to Georgie about our money, and I think the wretched bankers are this moment dividing our shares, and paying mine and yours to our Banks. I haven't touched a penny of Gibbs yet[4]—Father went for a drive this morning and spends most of the day downstairs. Seton says he is first rate—He only comes every 2 or 3 days now.

I have routed out your grammar and Plato, and they shall be sent tomorrow. Plato was lost in the Nurses room, and I had some difficulty

1. Probably the children of Sir Henry Taylor, the dramatist.
2. An English translation of Montaigne's *Essays* was published in 1685 by Charles Cotton.
3. Francis Bacon dedicated his Essays to "My Deare Brother".
4. F. W. Gibbs had died on 18 February 1898. He left Virginia and Vanessa £1,000 each, and Thoby and Adrian £500 each.

in getting in. Also my whole existence seems to pass in doing up books. All fathers ladies send him books, which have to be returned. Would you ask David [bookseller] to try and get a Hollinshead[1], *not black letters*, for me some time? I could afford 2 or 3 pounds now—because I am already £50 in debt, and depending on my mythical accumulations to pay with.

Baccae is far and away the best play of Euripides I have read. When you come to London, I will give you tea in my shop—I wash up the tea things myself, and I have just bought 100 logs of ship wood for 6 shillings. I have invented a new way of bookbinding, which takes half the time, is just as strong etc. etc. etc.—I will write a long letter some day to tell you several interesting things.

Yr.
Goatus

King's

67: To Thoby Stephen   22 *Hyde Park Gate, S.W.*

[27? January 1903]

My dear Thoby,

Georgie has opened accounts at the Union of London and Smiths Banks for you and me and paid our money in. They want your signature. Would you send it to me. There will be about £40 odd of balance—but this isn't yet paid in.

Send your signature quick. Blow up Adrian for not thanking G.[eorge] for the wine, or telling him where the French picture books are.

Yr. Goat

We had a long visit from [Clive] Bell on Sunday. The Montaigne and Bacon are a continual delight to me.

King's

68: To Margaret and Emma Vaughan

22 *Hyde Park Gate, S.W.*

Jan. 27th [1903]

Dearest Marny and Toad,

You are wonderful people! I dont know if I have said it before—but I say it now—*nothing*—not the Equator itself—impresses me with such awe adoration and surprise as your power of posting letters! When I post them, they never arrive on the day they were meant to: no birthday letter

1. The (Raphael) Holinshed *Chronicles*, first published in 1557.

of mine reaches within a week of the proper time—and yours *always* do—
I wish you would tell me how you do it—for it is one of the gifts that give
most pleasure—my plate would have been empty, but for your genius—
you just rescued me from despair and made me feel young again, when a
birthday *was* a birthday. Marny is full of mysteries—which we cant solve—
I know it is something indecent—but Marny's hoary cheeks are beyond
blushes. *Please* remember how young and innocent we are, and how little
we know of the world and dont let your licentious passions run away with
you—Toad—restrain her! Of course, I overslept myself on Saturday till
St. Pauls was hopeless, so I didn't go at all, and now I curse myself for it—
At. Minna was here yesterday and rather discouraging, I'm afraid. She had
counted on letting her house for a large sum, but no one offers to take it and
so she says she doubts whether she can afford to pay any expenses at all,
in fact, she may give up all idea of a companion. She had decided that Ethel
Clifford anyhow wont do. However, we must wait and see. She is a stupid
old thing, and I feel very cross with her—I wonder how dear Marny is, and
what you do all day, and what has happened about Canning Place. I hope
you will walk in one day soon both of you, in good health, and invite us
to tea, at No. 8 C.P.

Sheep dog sends her love. I am yawning so that I cant write sense or
nonsense.

Yr loving,
Goat

I shouldn't quite give up hope of Sicily—But At. M. has got a fit of economy,
which may blow over, or it mayn't.

Sussex

69: To Thoby Stephen   22 *Hyde Park Gate, S.W.*

[January/February 1903]

My dear Grim,
    I suppose the Bank wants your signature not from mere curiosity or
for purposes of decoration—or to put in its autograph book—but simply
so that unscrupulous persons may not forge your cheques. Write your name
again as you will always write it on the back of cheques and send it to
    the Union of London and Smiths Bank Ltd.
        Charing Cross Branch,
        66 Charing Cross,
        S.W.

Yr. Goat

King's

[February 1903]

Dearest Toad,

I have had my interview which results thus: At. M[inna Duckworth] is willing to pay the hotel bills but not railway or steamboat, which to Naples would cost about £12—single fare—I don't know whether this puts it out of the question; but I went on and said how you had called and incidentally mentioned your wish to travel etc.—without explaining my share in the talk—Then would she like you for a companion? She said she had actually thought of asking you, but had not, because she knew you so little, and wasn't sure if you would be good to travel with—I said you were an excellent person—that I should much prefer you to Ethel Clifford—whom At. M. rather inclined to—that you were very cheerful talkative—independent—and able to look after yourself. She said the qualities she wanted were independence—conversation—good temper—and interest in general subjects—the thing she most disliked was boredom. I casually mentioned that you were a great patience player and hated doing sights and galleries—both of which points greatly took her fancy.

She said finally, that she had heard of a Miss Musgrove an old friend—who was going to Sicily quite independently at the same time—so that she was no longer so much in want of a companion—but that she should prefer one—and that there were one or two poor friends to whom she felt rather bound, but nothing yet was settled. I perjured myself, and said I had told you nothing of her plan—only thought it was worth mentioning to her—she said I had done quite right—and that she would certainly keep you in mind and asked me to sound you for your views later—but at present she said I was not to say a word of this to you! Her last words were—"Would Emma be in London and able to come and see me? We seem to have many points in common—but anyhow I cant settle yet". I don't know whether you will think this good enough—I wish it could be managed somehow—she particularly wanted to know if you were fond of reading, and well read? I said certainly—and had a great acquaintance with modern French and German authors!

Yr. loving Goat

Sussex

71: To Violet Dickinson   [22 *Hyde Park Gate, S.W.*]

[February? 1903]

Woman,

Come any day you can—everyday—if you come here you will see father who rampages for you—but whistle and Sparroy will come to you. Father is a fraud, only an invalid for the sake of his ladies. I wish I could be an invalid and have ladies. I am so susceptible to female charms, in fact

I offered my blistered heart to one in Paris, if not to two.[1] But first by a long way is that divine Venus who is Katie [Lady Cromer] and you and Nessa and all good and beautiful (which are you I wonder?) women—whom I adore. I weep tears of tenderness to think of that great heart of pity for Sparroy locked up in stone—never to throw her arms round me—as she would, if only she could—I know it and feel it. Honestly there was a look of Katie in her stupid beautiful head, and Katie in a bath towel would have what you call a bust just like hers, only Katie wont ever open her arms (which aren't of stone—the Venus hasn't got any by the way) for this poor Sparroy to enter. Then there was another, but the woman waits for the letters. Gerald insults me—says I drink whiskey—utterance so thick—*I* say mixture of Venus and Violet.

Yr. S.

Berg

72: TO VIOLET DICKINSON   22 *Hyde Park Gate, S.W.*

[1903?]

My woman,

I did not realize all the splendours of your book till I opened it—and it gave me shivers down my back with joy. I believe its an heirloom, and you ought to keep it. But I cant help saying that it gives *me*—though sinfully—great joy. Your soul will be warm (as with fur cloaks) in Paradise but how will your poor bones get through this world if you give away your substance like this? I curled up in my chair and read it all this evening.

Our little Swiss maid cant believe that the cloak is mine. She thinks its either lent or left by mistake, and so she hangs it over the back of a chair and wont put it away.

My woman—I am afraid your intimates are a darned troublesome lot, and you were trotted off your feet today and you will be in bed tomorrow. Were you very much exhausted?

The devotion of the Sparroy is not much to offer but such as it is——(a very tender passage).

Yr. Sparroy

[Ella] Crum[2] will tip you a pound tomorrow.

Berg

1. The surviving evidence, including the family photograph album, shows that Virginia had only once been to France, but not beyond Boulogne and Amiens. Perhaps she means a lady who lived in Paris.
2. Ella and Walter Crum were close friends of Violet. From this point onwards, for several years, the Crums are mentioned frequently in the Virginia-Violet correspondence, but Virginia seldom treated them seriously. They became butts for her wit.

73: To Violet Dickinson   [22 *Hyde Park Gate, S.W.*]
[1903?]

My child,

Sparroy will come on Thursday. If only the Duckworth family hadn't wool where the brain ought to be, her pockets would be lined with gold, and we would have drinks all round. I have tea on the housetop tomorrow. Crum coming.

Sp:

Berg

74: To Violet Dickinson   22 *Hyde Park Gate, S.W.*
[March 1903]

My Child,

Why do you confuse the infant mind with three addresses for two days? It makes me feel so nervous. However if this goes wrong it wont much matter —though it may pollute a maiden mind before the end, but Sparroy only flaps her warm blooded paw, and says she has tender memories of a long embrace, in a bedroom. Remember it is my turn for a moveable inside next. *Dont* go back to that wretched Cousin. Hell will hold no horrors for you if you exhaust all such things here. At this moment you are comforting the afflicted I know, and the heathen Sparroy reads Greek! I was alone all Sunday—Nessa went to the Watts[1]—and thought affectionately of that great intimacy which means so much to both of us. I sent you the Poetess. I wish Providence were a better judge of literature and then we should be spared Humphrey Wards,[2] or she might publish them in Paradise.

The new nurse has come, and creaks about, but I haven't seen her yet.

Dont be a bad woman. Say your prayers every night—if only for sake of Sparroys soul—which doesn't get many prayers to wash it.

Yr. AVS

Berg

75: To Violet Dickinson   22 *Hyde Park Gate, S.W.*
[early April 1903]

My Woman,

All your letters are only addresses. I read every word, damaging my eyesight, and only make out when your [*sic*] *not* in London. May is practically

1. G. F. Watts, the painter, a great friend of Julia, Virginia's mother. He died in 1904. Vanessa and George had been staying with him near Guildford.
2. Mrs Humphry (Mary Augusta) Ward, the novelist. In 1903 she published *Lady Rose's Daughter*.

here, and then you will be bedded out for good, and a whole vol: of our intimacy closed. These gaps are so disturbing, and letters are only fit for friendship.

Intimacy ought to take to telegraphs. Your letter-style is rather telegraphic. But now you can really be useful, and tell us where to get coffers cheap. We want a country house for Easter. Do you know anyone, near London, and comfortable who would let for a fortnight before 24th April? Father finds it more romantic on the whole not to go away, but if he can say "my children drag me' he will agree, only we've nowhere to go to, and it ought to be cheap.

The brilliant Sparroy, who really is a kind of female Kitchener has almost clawed two country houses, but they may fall through, though inspired by genius, anyhow, Violet is the family friend we all cling to when we're drowning.

A great flea jumped on to my Aeschylus as I read with [Janet] Case the other day—and now bites large holes in me. I was too polite to catch him with Cases eye on me.

Adrian and Thoby have come back [from Cambridge], and Thoby might really stand nude with Katie in the Louvre. He is a Greek God but rather too massive for the drawing room. We have endless arguments—about literature! Beatrice Chamberlain[1] is a real woman of genius, and a cut above literature. I wish I had half her brains to make books with. She talked a whole evening about Russia and Thackeray and all kinds of things, and everyone else went down like reeds in the wind. We had a twittering little Freshfield to meet her and Charles Trevelyan[2] who had to be kept quiet over art with Nessa in the back room—otherwise old Beatrice would have charged him.

Are the ceilings sticking, and does it look the kind of place to end one's days in, which is what one wants in the country.

Something pious and full of associations. Talking of associations, would you like the wardrobe in Nessas room, which is full of 'em, but . . . . . .

[last page missing]

Berg

76: To Violet Dickinson   22 *Hyde Park Gate, S.W.*

[10 April 1903]

My woman,

Sparroys blessing alights on the house, and breaks a bottle of champagne over it. Good Friday too. Do you feel that you have settled down to pass

1. Eldest daughter (1862-1918) of Joseph Chamberlain and sister of Austen Chamberlain.
2. Liberal Member of Parliament and later President of the Board of Education.

Julia and Leslie Stephen

Stella Duckworth

Caroline Emelia Stephen ('Nun')

George Duckworth

Vanessa and Thoby Stephen

your remaining days among cows and crocuses? Don't get too pious and simple minded—too pure to associate with the battered Sparroy. What does it feel like sleeping the first night in a house [Burnham Wood] one has built —solemn? Is the garden divine now? Even London streets are like gardens today—so you must be walking fields of amaranth and asphodel.

Do you see that there are 40 illegits: to every 1000 legal births? Doesn't it make you feel nervous. The risk of going wrong seems to be enormously increased, in fact inevitable practically, since I read that.

Plant a flower for Sparroy. Heartsease or Forgetmenot, or something that climbs and is evergreen, typical of much. Sparroy's tendril heart for instance. A fruitful vine for Katie [Cromer]—What a start in life that child will have.

Keep your own heart green and tender at least in that corner where Sparroy is planted.

An old Lady in Surrey is letting us her house [Blatchfield, Chilworth]. Where exactly I dont know. We probably go, if we come to terms, on 16th.

Tell me what you do, and if you feel a good woman. Spring in the country is like a clean bath. I get born anew into the bosom of my God once a year—a God half Katie and some rakish old Pagan, like you.

Blessings on the house, and my Violet, who is a kind of home for the orphaned and widows herself, flower grown too.

Yr. Sparroy

Berg

77: To Violet Dickinson

Blatchfield, Chilworth, Surrey

[mid-April 1903]

My woman,

It seems fated that theres no room for you, which is very depressing. I have got a double bed—some strange foresight made them give it me— I wish you could come, but I shall see you somehow in London, or your house.

Surrey is a sham country. This place isn't so bad as Hindhead, but its over run with Cockneys and Culture. Everyone artistic seems to retire here, and build a red brick house with sham Elizabethan white and black. However this house is better than that—three old cottages run together, and comfortable which is the main thing. The cold is still rather bad. Father likes the place, though, and has a very comfortable room and sitting room to himself. But he cant get out much, and I dont think he is better.

Shall you be in London anymore, or have you let your house, or what? The cottage is a delight to think of, if only you dont get it tainted with Deaths and sorrows, such as always cling to you, and make you a kind of walking hospital. Poor Sparroy will ask for a bed there soon.

Has your husband[1] heard about his exam:?

Thoby and Adrian are here. Adrian goes tomorrow, but Thoby stays till Sunday. He is a charming great inarticulate creature, with torrents of things shut up in him. Adrian babbles away, 15 years younger than all the rest of us. He grows too fast to think or feel, or do anything but eat. The excellent George, fresh from his Countess [Carnarvon] probably comes tomorrow—then I shall shock someone again which I haven't done for a fortnight. Gerald has taken up with an American millionaire and is cruising with him down the coast of Italy. He meant to go to Venice, but the yatcht [*sic*] was too tempting 'Everything is done in first rate style'. So Venice will have to be dropped. The honours of the family are many!

Write here and be a Kind Woman.

Yr. loving,
Sparroy

Berg

78: To Violet Dickinson   *Blatchfield, Chilworth,*
                                           Surrey

28th April [1903]

My woman,

We come home on Thursday. I haven't any notion where you are or are going to be, so I write. There is really no use in telling it you—my poor intimate—but since we have been here, the nurse has told us that she thinks Father weaker. Seton said so in London and wrote to Georgie and Jack. They know very little—only that the thing is getting worse—has got much worse quite lately. Seton expects some other complication, but they can tell nothing for certain. It may be 6 months or a year or even longer. Treves is the only person who could say more, and we think of having him if we can without frightening father. At present he seems to guess nothing; he goes by his nights, which have been good since we came here. I think you have really known all this. Apparently Treves expected it, only would not tell us, or told Georgie who did not understand. Anyhow theres nothing to be done, and sometimes I cant believe that it is true. Father is exactly as usual, to talk to; even writing, only he can not walk far, and gets tired. But everything goes on as usual, and I would not write to you, only writing is easier than talking, and perhaps I shant see you. Did the other nurse at the London Hospital tell you anything? He seemed to stay about the same, for a long time, and then suddenly to get much weaker. I think this nurse thinks him worse than he really is.

Anyhow I'm sure he doesn't yet notice anything. He told me today that

1. This is one of the Virginia-Violet running jokes. Violet never married. She is probably referring to Walter Crum or Ozzie Dickinson.

he thought he was getting slowly stronger. The fear is that his sister and other people will let him see it.

The world's a strange place. At this moment it none of it seems true, so I am callous and burden you with all these things.

Be a kind woman.

He is such a loveable creature.

Yr. Sparroy

Berg

79: To Violet Dickinson   22 *Hyde Park Gate, S.W.*

April 30th [1903]

My beloved Woman,

You are the only sympathetic person in the world. Thats why everybody comes to you with their troubles. I feel as though perhaps I oughtn't to have told you. Written down it sounds worse, for here seeing him, things go on as usual, and I cant help thinking that they are wrong. Of course theres really no chance of that, but I feel rather a brute to have told you all this without any need. If you saw him, you wouldn't see any difference I think. I sometimes wish everything would happen directly, and be done with. Theres nothing so bad as waiting and not knowing.

However that's what one *has* to do now.

Do come here, or I will come to you; but the great thing is that he should see people, especially just these next weeks, when he may begin to realise that he cant work.

Gerald is giving us his views upon Florence. You are the only person I ever do feel the least inclined to talk to—poor intimate. You dont talk damned theories, or expect sentiments.

Take care of yourself, and slaughter chickens by the farmyard full if they do your precious bones good.

Yr. Sp.

Write again.

Berg

80: To Violet Dickinson   [22 *Hyde Park Gate, S.W.*]

[4 May? 1903]

My Beloved Woman,

Your letters come like balm on the heart. I really think I must do what I never have done—try to keep them. I've never kept a single letter all my life—but this romantic friendship ought to be preserved. Very few people have any feelings to express—at least of affection or sympathy—

and if those that do feel dont express—the worlds so much more like a burnt out moon—cold living for the Sparroys and Violets. This is because you think, or say, you oughtn't to write nice hot letters. Kitty never pierces my tough hide, or tries to. She came to see father the other day, the first time since his illness, and asked him why he hadn't been to call on her, all this time, which was rather *too* fashionable, I thought. And didnt volunteer more than a fishy white glove to *me*—perhaps naturally—only this explains why in crises of emotion, Violet is the Sympathetic Sink, not Kitty.

All Stephen's are self centred by nature; taking more than giving—but if you once understand that, and it cant be helped you can get on all right with them. Indeed some of them are really rather loveable people.

You are a madwoman—why trudge all the way to Southwold to meet damp streets and stringy fowls. I wish you had sense about your own inside—if my pulse were weak, and sciatica in *my* joints you wouldn't hear of such things. You remind me, all along, of Mrs Carlyle. I am reading her too. Father says she's the most wonderful letter writer in the language. She certainly has a strong likeness to my Violet—she gets into just the same queer places as you do—and has to do with exactly your queer kind of people. She was a human woman too—only there you see your warning. How she drove in Hyde Park—and her heart stopped—so for Gods sake (you are so religious) take care of your bones—dont get anything more—feed and fatten. I shall take to talking about health.

Nothing has happened here. Nurse says father oughtn't even now, to go to the study, but he had better try, if he wants to. As yet he has stayed downstairs. Georgie is writing to Seton to say *we* are anxious for Treves, if it can be managed without worrying father. Seton apparently is really anxious for a thorough examination—and father refuses to let Seton touch him.

Come on Wed: 5.

Yr. Sparroy

Berg

81: To Thoby Stephen   [22 *Hyde Park Gate, S.W.*]

[May 1903]

My dear Cresty,

It seems about time that I should write to you, and that you should write to me—But there aint much news to tell you—We have just had Nun's visit—which, as you can imagine, was not cheerful. After half an hours talk one begins to wish that there were a way invented of stopping her. She seems to work round in a circle—But she is pathetic! Are you to write for Trevelyan?[1] Jack has a very strong opinion that you ought to go to the Bar—

1. George Macaulay Trevelyan, who had just become a Fellow of Trinity.

He says it wouldn't be so very expensive—and youre made for a Judge—
I wish you would—You would give judgments uninfluenced by emotion
I know—and if I had reason on my side, you should be my lawyer. Should
you like it better than Treasury or Colonial Office? I dont get anybody to
argue with me now, and feel the want. I have to delve from books, painfully
and all alone, what you get every evening sitting over your fire and smoking
your pipe with Strachey etc. No wonder my knowledge is but scant. Theres
nothing like talk as an educator I'm sure. Still I try my best with Shakespeare
—I read Sidney Lees Life—What do you think of his sonnet theory? It
seems to me a little too like Sidney Lee—all that about Shakespeare's eye
to the main chance—his flattery of Southampton etc.—But the Mr W. H. is
sensible—I must read the sonnets and find my own opinion. Sidney says
that Shakespeare *felt* none of it—I mean that not a word applies to him
personally—But it is a satisfactory book—doesn't pretend to make theories
—and only gives the most authentic facts.

The Season is beginning—not that that affects *me* much—but Georgie
and Gerald are out every night—balls and operas. Nessa and I grub along
in our own ways. She has nude models here 3 days a week—and the vigorous
[Janet] Case has swept down from Hampstead. Seton was here the other
day—He thought father a little weaker than when we went away—but says
theres no use in having Treves. It might bother father, and nothing more
can be done. Father is very cheerful, and talks away, but he doesn't get up
to the study—and cant do much work. He was very much pleased with
your letter—and handwriting! I think one of us might see Treves—without
telling father—even tho' he cant do anything, he might tell us more.

Dont work too hard—or do anything foolish—and take care of your
lovely crest—which must be sadly out of order now—

Yr. loving,
Goat

King's

82: To Violet Dickinson   22 *Hyde Park Gate, S.W.*

[19 May? 1903]

My woman,

Treves came suddenly today. He says that six months is the longest it
can last. There are complications which *may* happen before that; he cannot
say definitely whether they will happen, but he thinks it more likely than not.

He told us that when he saw Father last he did not expect him to live
six weeks. He thinks that at this moment he is better than he was then. I
cant understand what he means by this. I think he must have forgotten.
When he saw father last he was walking all round the gardens. But he
thought him today extraordinarily vigorous in mind and cheerful. It was a

specially good day, and the nurse says that Seton absolutely forgot to tell him some of father's symptoms, and made out that he was able to go for long walks. However I dont suppose it matters. Treves said there was nothing to be done. So now we seem to know everything there is to be known. Treves was decided that Father shd. do everything he felt he could do—walk and work and see people. He said we had certainly better go away in August as usual, though not to Fritham. He thought it was better to run some risks than to miss anything he liked doing.

He said he would grow slowly weaker, without pain, but it would be most merciful if he did not have to wait and know that it was coming. Georgie tries to make out that Treves is mistaken this time as he was before, and says he is certain father is getting better. However that is all part of the job, I suppose, and happily he is generally out.

I have had to write all this to the old sister [Caroline Emelia], and I think I put it rather brutally. Oh dear—what a queer world it is, and there doesn't seem to be anything more to say. Everybody comes in and says how much better he looks, and Heaven knows what the truth is, only one does know, but I cant think of it. Write if you ever come up—I suppose not till next week.

Yr. S.

Treves was absolutely decided and straightforward, and talked to Nessa and not to Georgie.

Berg

83: To Violet Dickinson   [22 *Hyde Park Gate, S.W.*]
[4 June? 1903]

My Violet,
    Would Friday 12th do instead of Thursday? If it collides with Katie, or is anyhow else inconvenient I will come on Thursday.

Beatrice is to be taken to Beresford [the photographer] on Thursday, which will be an entertainment. We had tea at Manchester Square, with Lady Bath behind the gorgeous teapot. Nessa tackled her and stopped her whispers (about distemper in dogs) with another Elderly Countess, and she woke up and pealed with laughter—and asked if we were at last settled in London? Her manners are a treat. Last night we had tickets given us for the opera and took Beatrice. She only wants hatching, that poor hardboiled creature, to make her heart beat. We stopped her shrieks, and made her talk like other people almost—not like Thynnes—for an hour. But she is pathetic I feel—grown into middle aged fast set womanhood without any caring for or sympathy, I am sure. And there was Katie in a box behind us, like some Justice or Victory with her calm brows, so majestic and tired, and more than ever like the Venus in the Louvre. But as far as I could see, she didn't look ill—only a little pale. We had a grim day, only unspeakably humourous too, yesterday—when the old Quaker Sister came again—begged us not to leave her alone with father, and then sat down solemnly and talked about the weather. Father was bored before the first five minutes were over, and could hardly sit in his chair. She saw it, and wanted to cry, and could only thump her old brains for commonplaces, which were worse than nothing. Finally she decided to catch an earlier train, 'I see it isnt safe to stay longer' she said. They had one flash up together and she finally collapsed in the hall—and said it had been very nice to see him—but very agitating—blowing her great nose louder than ever, and pouring tears down her pendulous cheeks. Oh Lord—we laughed—and yet it is damned pathetic —in a small way. I know she cried all the way home in the train.

Nessa has been lunching with Crum, and lunches there tomorrow too! Take care before you let loose savage intimates upon her again. The [John] Baileys are to be introduced. Madge Vaughan dines here tonight. We had six people to tea. I wish you were a Kangaroo and had a pouch for small Kangaroos to creep to.

Nothing much changes here.

Are you well, after those horrid Hospital operations?

Yr. Sp:

Berg

84: To Violet Dickinson   22 *Hyde Park Gate, S.W.*

8th June 1903

My Woman,

If I come Friday I shant clash with Katie shall I? If so, manage another day for me. I should feel like a soiled worldling, thick boots on, trampling the Elysian meadows.

Crum has asked me to dinner—I feel sure you have given me a *character* whereas I have—what you call *fallen* more than once—I dont mean precisely that I have done what the unfortunates do—but if my character and virtue consist in amusing the Crum dinner table, then I am an 'unfortunate' woman. I have sold my brains, which are my virtue. Never any lost woman felt so degraded as I do tonight. All relationdom safely out of the house, takes to writing letters. 'Darling, tell me if I can do anything—I will come at any moment.' The precise and only thing that anyone can do is to stay away and be silent. But thats past praying for. Friendship, relationship at anyrate, consists in talk, or letter writing of some sort. But the normal state of things now is a kind of grimness—and nothing much matters. I am sure the facts of life—the marryings and bearings and buryings are the least important and one acts one's drama under the hat—Lord—this is drivel—but Nessa and Jack talk on over their coffee. I think of Katie as Heaven and Peace—poor Love, probably a very hell if one were in her inside.

Father isnt so well I think—he had a giddy attack on Friday, and a rather bad symptom has come back, but not one that bothers him, so he is cheerful, and thats the main thing.

Georgie stays on at Pixton[1]—weighing the worth of a somewhat elderly, but quite untarnished, Coronet—would it be permanent, supposing he asked her? And could she go to Court. Those two questions give him sleepless nights, and will decide his life for him. Poor old creature—his virtues sink to the bottom I know, and I'm too lazy to fish them up, as I had ought. Katie must look like a Pagan goddess, sitting out in the grass—a Greek goddess before the fall of the world—you know they are in hiding somewhere —a practical idea—and one has an English Countess's Coronet on her head —(my mind runs on Coronets—) Athena married to Lord Cromer!

Yr. Sp.

Crum calls me "Sparroi".

Berg

85: To Violet Dickinson   22 *Hyde Park Gate, S.W.*

[June 1903]

My Violet,

Your letter makes me very unhappy, and I wish to the Lord it hadn't happened,[2] and that I knew you were all right. Ask Mrs. Crum to send me a line, dont bother yourself. You are such a poor boney old cab horse. Have you anybody respectable to look after you. I feel sure your worse than you say, and I shall probably come down and plant myself outside your door and whine till your well.

If you are still at Welwyn on Saturday we might come, but I expect you had better stay silent, my poor intimate you are a luckless Rake Cat.

I will write again, only send me word somehow.

No photograph even to cheer me, however I will have that out in another letter.

Take care of yrself.

Yr. Sparroy

Berg

---

1. Pixton Park, Dulverton, Somerset. George was staying there with the Dowager Countess Carnarvon.
2. Violet had injured her back.

[June 1903]

My Violet,

It is really too brutal that this should have happened. It makes me furious. And now you have to lie there in the heat, for 10 blessed days, my poor woman. I wish these things would happen to me and not to you. I could carry on my existence quite well flat on my back, but you are a toiler, and I know you hate it. Only do take care, and get quite cured.

One of us will come Monday or Tuesday. Probably the eternal Sparroy, who inflicts herself all round, but is always conscious of her peculiarities. We are inflicting ourselves on Katie today, which I feel to be rather an unnecessary thing to do—and Heaven knows it wont be an easy job. Kitty is evidently worshipped there—they all sit in her bedroom at night, and she spends the whole day talking 'theories' I suppose with Katie. I know Alice and Lady Bath and Katie and Beatrice[1] will all sit round like the magnificent aristocrats they are, and there wont be an opening for the nimble witted but entirely middle class literary Sparroy. However it cant be helped.

I cant express my feelings about your back. Fate is a brutal sledge hammer, missing all the people she might knock on the head, and crashing into the midst of such sensitive and exquisite creatures as my Violet. I wish I could shield you with my gross corpse.

I will write and tell you how we come through this afternoon, which makes me feel as though I were 11 and going to a childrens party.

Keep quiet and dont think of anyone but yourself, unless you like to turn over in your mind the tender affection which Sparroy bears for you.

Yr. Sp:

Berg

[June 1903]

My Violet,

I wish your letter had come before 8 last night—then we might have come to you on our way to or from St. Albans.[2] That was a pilgrimage— But are you really better? I dont much believe it—and I feel very unhappy about you—lying there alone poor beast, and we might have come in. Aren't there any Crums about?

Shall I come on Tuesday? only I know you will have swarms upon you then.

We got off easier than I thought yesterday. We had Katie and Beatrice

1. The Marchioness of Bath and her three daughters.
2. Where Lady Cromer had rented a house.

alone at first—Katie like a bit of a Greek temple lying in the grass—and Beatrice a gargoyle come to life! Lady Robert [Cecil] was there—such a little lady—but sitting apart deaf, unless some one shouted at her, which was rather hard to do. I told them about you—I wish *I* could hurt my back, and have all the beautiful ladies holding up their hands and saying Darling! You are the most popular woman in England—and much more than that— But you like your Sparroy? (you observe how thick the ink gets at this point—quite spontaneous) Katie has a splendid manner too—she waved everything about the way she wanted it to go—turned from one to another— but was just as simple and easy as ever—and I do like a Great Lady—when she's a goddess too. She isnt exactly easy—except in manner—but infinitely beautiful.

Shall I come Tuesday. Send a line or ask Mrs. Crum to—my Violet! I hope and hope your better.

Yr. Sp:

Berg

88: To Violet Dickinson   22 *Hyde Park Gate, S.W.*

[30 June? 1903]

My Violet,

You are too far off to write to—besides you have been carrying on a most improper clandestine correspondence, of which I dont at all approve. Really you ought never to have seen that literary effort.[1] It wasn't meant for anybody to read—not in that nude, really indecent state. I wrote it all by scraps when we were at Chilworth, and in a sentimental mood, which has leaked out damn it—and I haven't the patience to write it again. This is all to prove that if I had sat down solidly every morning and made it thoroughly substantial all through, it would have been a work of genius whereas, as it is—you have to pump up Compliments. Poor Violet. I think literary advice is a very ticklish thing. Of course I should be grateful for *criticism* as all writers are—the candider the better. I always think I might write so much better if I took time or trouble—or something else which I never do take. This is a very interesting subject—to you especially.

I only had one small scrawl from you. Buy some intimate notepaper— size of this.

I have been writing to try and patch up our quarrel with At. Minna— and all my ideas have been spent on that. Besides it is grilling hot.

We are going to a dance tonight. I cant imagine anyone less dance like

1. This has not survived. But Virginia was continuing her 'literary exercises', descriptions of people and events in her current life. During June, July and August she wrote a series of such exercises which she sent to Violet Dickinson (see letter 111).

than Tom. When are you coming back to your Sp's bosom? Kitty is eternal —cool and fashionable—white from tip to toe has little aristocratic stories without much point—which *is* the point. But, as you say, she is a good woman—and etc etc etc. I write half a sentence, very moral too, and forget how it was to end. Nessa has filched you I feel, and I only pick up the Crums that fall from her table (a joke failed, like a bad egg).

It is a toilsome world—I shall have earned my kangaroo nest before I die. The heat is rather bad for father—but he is extraordinarily cheerful, and writes and enjoys talking, and some days looks so well, and one cant believe that it is true. It is a strange pause with nothing much happening— and the world going on as usual.

Come here the moment you are in London. Friendship I say is the vine-prop of life. Many other pretty things I might say—only God has seen fit to withold them this afternoon. Nessa said your husband had passed— anyhow *thats* a mercy.

The Bath family have faded—as is their habit—gone out like fireworks. Beatrice made erratic efforts—spasmodic was the word I meant—(she *is* spasmodic) to come here, or to get us there—but once paper and pen gets between a Thynne and the world—the rest is silence. I think of you with tender longing. It would draw tears from your stony eyes to see little Wallaby nosing around with her soft wet snout for a letter—and none comes. Give my respectful remembrances to Hester [Lyttelton]—tell her I often think of the Goldfinch—and what it meant for both of us! Ah me! I met a very kind large shaggy Miss Talbot the other night. I only felt inclined to say—Be a Kangaroo to me! and she wouldn't have understood.

It's d——d hot. My wallaby paws stick to the paper as I write—and my letters are convulsive. Write to me, and tell me that you love me dearest. I wish no more. My food is affection!

Yr. Sp:

Berg

89: To Violet Dickinson   22 *Hyde Park Gate, S.W.*

[June/July 1903]

My child,

I will come with joy on Friday, but it grieves me to think that your works are rusty. I see they want a good licking by the devoted Sparroy—poor Beast.

I think £1 is about right for the Holy State. My copy is very chipped and part written by hand, so I got it cheap. I will bring it along with me, and the Booksellers list. I haven't got anything to say but I am going on just to show you I can spoil clean sheets, like a thorough Grubstreeter, which is what I shall come to.

You are a Carping Rake, to imitate your Sparroys little peculiarities.

Anybody can write half a sheet, but can anybody cram in the amount of pure hot affection that I do? And its not appreciated, only imitated and ridiculed, typical of so much in my life. I cant write a line because my head is smelt out with bundles of Mimosa, sent from New York by a Lady admirer of father's.

Crum is carrying on awful. She wont come *here*, which is so suspicious, but makes what you call assignations at her house.

Tell Beatrice that [William] Rothenstein has asked leave to make a drawing of father; and is coming here for sittings so we shall make conversation over her bones.

Have you any stays?

I tried to saw mine through this morning, but couldnt. What iron boned conventionality we live in—stays suggest many lively thoughts, but the letters are going.

But I've covered all sheets, and now you know what it is like you wont imitate Sparroy again.

I will lick you tenderly.

Yr. Sparroy

Berg

90: To Violet Dickinson   [22 *Hyde Park Gate, S.W.*]

[June/July 1903]

My Violet,

Will you give these to your husband. I think there are about 12. I would have got a postal order, but a shilling postal order must be such a horrible thing, and if I'd made it four and six it would have come back like Beatrices. Please thank him very much. I drove home like a duchess, and had 2d over for a treat, and also for the flowers, which not yet shed a petal.

Little Rothenstein has been here drawing father—he says Lady Beatrice Thynne is in some ways the most remarkable person I've ever known. When she comes into a room you feel expanded: in some lights her head is perfectly Greek etc. etc. etc. This isn't meant to be repeated, but half a compliment would do the old hard minded apple good.

Unholy chaos all round—my box is open at my side—waiting for something flat and very precious to lie on top. What'd you think it is? It is a source of unending joy to me. Really a wonderful photograph—

Father isnt quite so well these last 2 days. The discharge has come back which makes him tired, but not really bad. He is very cheerful.

Yr. Sp.

Berg

[7? July 1903]

My Violet,

I wish you would write and explain what you do. Are you coming to London ever? The summer is winding up, and then two months will separate our friendship. It is astonishing what depths—hot volcano depths—your finger has stirred in Sparroy—hitherto entirely quiescent. I know you are sitting by some bedside—either physical or mental. However thats your life—and the Almighty keeps you supplied.

The religious allusion on the last page drifted in, or was pounded in, by a fat religious cousin [Dorothea Stephen], very red in the face, who is arguing Christianity with Thoby. She is trying to prove that certain sections of her soul are alive and afloat while ours are 'atrophied.' She has now found a Bible, a sort of instinct (probably miraculous) leading her to the only Bible in the room, and has just read a psalm aloud, something about being saved from a Dog and her bowels. We try to look as though we are in church. Adrian entirely collapsed. She is now intoning through her nose, in an uplifted and sonorous voice. Oh my Violet, what a jumble the world is.

I dont know that things change much, but I feel somehow that father is a good deal weaker. He seems to feel weaker in himself, but he says nothing, and there's nothing to be said.

We go to various rather inharmonious parties. Sparroy isn't a social success. She stands in corners—never gets swept away into the whirlpool. Dorothea's metaphors affect my brain. She is expounding the mystery of sin—dictating from behind two very fat red hands—as though she were a prophetess behind a veil. I thank God that the underground is created, and her last train will soon be due.

Are you quite well my Violet, and wading through your sorrows? The only reason I have to believe in a God is that *some* life grows in one and out-grows most things. But otherwise—it seems to me he has a heavy hand.

I see Lord de Vesci[1] is dead.

Kitty was spending today at St. Albans.

Write me a good letter—if you dont come. You have the art of saying things.

                                                    Yr. Sparroy

Berg

1. The 4th Viscount de Vesci died on 6 July 1903.

[22 July 1903]

My woman,

This is practically the end of the week and no signs of you. Nessa and Adrian and I are going to spend Friday at Cambridge buying furniture for his new rooms,[1] and going for a picnic up the river. He begs humbly that you will come too. (The wonderful instinct this family has for clinging to you!) Really couldn't you? Or if that is too much of a job when will you come? our intimacy has been separated by more than a month, which is very trying.

Besides Kitty [Maxse] swoops down in a yellow bodied wasp like motor (Lady Alices) with Violet Cecil and Nessa disappears into their silklined maw, and I see nothing of her. My intimate I know is happy and engrossed with her plants and livestock, but she must cultivate this particular Sparroy plant.

Write and say when you'll come, or what arrangement for meeting we're to make.

We go [to Salisbury] on the 31st. When are you coming there? Georgie comes on the 18th for a fortnight.

Are we to ask [Lady] Beatrice [Thynne] this year, or is she better left with Katie?

Father is about the same. The nurse says he is rather more comfortable just now. [Dr] Seton hasn't been for a month.

We're just off to have tea on the terrace at Westminster. I hope the last of our amusements!

Yr. Warm Sparroy

Berg

[23 July 1903]

My Violet,

You sound rather depressed. I hope your not really—else whats to become of the creepers and clingers who make you their pole? The world aint worth a damn—of that I'm convinced. Come on Monday and make all our hearts glad. We are really the cheerfullest family in Kensington. Noise puts an end to everything else. Father has been extraordinarily well these last two days—and it seems entirely impossible that this thing should be going on getting worse all the time. Then sometimes he is so bad. Anyhow

---

1. Adrian had been at Trinity College, Cambridge, since October 1902.

its no use thinking about things, and mercifully the creator hasn't contrived us with that capability—at least not much.

Are you quite well—or are your bones feeling rusted—and the Crums.

I wish I had married Crum—for the cohabitation with you. You have at least ten husbands and wives (and children, only this isnt proper to be said —so skip) and *one Wallaby* (only one).

You will probably find the faithful [Margery] Snowden here on Monday. She is a commonplace tragic creature, going off to spend her life at Harrogate with a provincial family after three years in London. That is a kind of a tragedy—though not in this case romantic.

We are flourishing well—going off to Cambridge tomorrow morning— and it will be Paradise to get into the country. I imagine Salisbury to be ancient and dreamy, and no parties and no conversation. But the Fishers threaten to come—I think I told you—to a house lent them in the Close. Possibly they wont.

Anyhow you are going to come—the 12th is rather close on Georgies heels, who comes the 18th—but I'm no good at dates.

Take care of yourself, and keep happy, and be a good child.

Yr. Sparroy

Berg
Wallaby

94: To Emma Vaughan   *22 Hyde Park Gate, S.W.*

[24 July 1903]

Dearest Todger,

I hope your throat is smooth again—and that you can talk without shut doors and that blessed haloed Marn hasn't caught one too—else you will be a pair of Clara's [Pater]—We have spent the day at Cambridge, buying furniture for Adrian's new rooms in College and eating more ices than I remember in my Herbert and Jones days. I am waiting subsequent events now. We had a final burst of Dorothea [Stephen]—entirely triumphant as far as I am concerned. We have quarrelled happily! I had her and Pernel Strachey[1] to tea at the [bookbinding] workshop, and with some malice contrived to say "Lady Stephen"[2] in the course of conversation. This is a thing she [Dorothea] feels strongly about. She got purple like an apoplectic Alderman after dinner—took up a plate of hard biscuits which I had laid in for her rapacious and capacious maw—and pelted me viciously with each in turn, which was rather painful. And then the savage old beast threatened me with fat strawberries if I wouldn't unsay which I had said. Of course I wouldn't, so she deluged me with squashy strawberries and stained all my

1. Lytton's older sister, later Principal of Newnham College, Cambridge.
2. Dorothea's mother, widow of Sir James Fitzjames Stephen Bt. Virginia normally called her 'Aunt Stephen'.

white dress (tell Marny). She came to an end of missiles, so got up like the ponderous elephant she is, trumpeting loudly, and pounded round the room after me. I shrieked with laughter, which irritated her all the more, and she got me into a corner and pummelled me—till I told her she was too heavy to take such exercise in the heat and her behaviour was that of a infuriate cow. After that our relations were strained—we said not a word all dinner—and she said goodbye and went, probably we shan't meet again. England will be lighter when she is gone—*that* is undeniable. That is the way to treat relations—(nothing personal meant—you see I don't instinctively include you and Marn in the same species as F[isher]s. and Dorotheas)

Nothing more has been heard of the Fs. I am afraid their silence means that we're to meet later. Tell Marny we went to the Labalmondiers and didn't know a soul there—but Mrs L was like a charming old French picture. A fresh lot of tunes came today chosen by Adrian and a very mixed set—Bach and Schumann and the Washington Post, and the Dead March in Saul, and Pinafore and the Messiah. We find the difference in quality a very good thing because all our servants sit beneath the open drawing room window all the evening while we play—and by experiment we have discovered that if we play dance music all their crossnesses vanish and the whole room rings with their shrieks and then we tame them down so sentimentally with Saul or boredom with Schumann—on the whole their silence is the most desirable thing. This is the sort of letter—at least the sort of length, Dorothea writes about Christianity. Thoby and she are still arguing by letter. We hear that there is an unfortunate tendency among the Hindus at present—at least the better class—to imitate the English custom of taking only *one* wife. We thought Dorothea had fair chance of say fourth place, considering her handsome white hide. But the old buffalo has gone back to her native wilds, so there's no need to say anything more about her at present.

I have Marny's photograph on my shelf, like a madonna to which I pray. She makes my room refined, as lavender in my drawers—(!!)

I hope you are recovered and not needing [Dr] Smallfoot's attendance any more.

Your,

Sussex   Goat

95: To Violet Dickinson   22 *Hyde Park Gate, S.W.*

[end July 1903]

My woman,

I dont think the vile business of life will let us come down either day. I have to go and rout out books at the Library one day, which takes hours, and I must buy clothing of some sort, Damn it. Then we go Thursday. But you will have had a tender invitation to visit us, which you shall Accept, as you love your Sparroy (which you do, and cant deny it). Why didnt you call your house the Garden of Eden.[1] If you cast it over in your mind you will see the advantages it has. Pious to begin with, and then it somehow connects your maternal ancestry with the very respectable stork of Adam. But Adrian is grinding operas on the piano, and Nessa and Thoby are discussing God Almighty. I went to see Everyman last night, only it was wretchedly acted. God Almighty had goggles on *and* a beard.

Yr. Sp:

[Janet] Case ends "yours *affect'ly*". Lord, isn't that a triumph of mind over matter!
She sent me in her bill, added up wrong, so I wrote back and said "Corrections are useless. I can only put notes of exclamation"—which I did, all over the page.
Wasn't that witty?

Berg

96: To Violet Dickinson   *Netherhampton House, Salisbury*

[August 1903]

My Violet,

We are safe here—Father came in great luxury with the nurse. He is very tired today, and has been asleep most of the morning in his chair, but he seems to like the place. The nurse thinks his room and all the arrangements as good as possible.

It is a perfect house for us—roomy and comfortable—and the garden, if it would only get hot, looks delicious. I have a vast whitewashed attic to myself. Nessa has a magnificent room too. These people have good taste I think.

How are you my Violet—write and say. Your little notes are most refreshing—about the only person who writes as she talks. I will scrawl again soon—the effect of the open air upon me is to make me so sleepy I can hardly think a whole sentence.

George and Thoby come today—Susan [Lushington] tomorrow—and Violet when?

Yr photograph on my shelf—

AVS

Berg

1. Violet was a descendant of Emily Eden, daughter of the 1st Lord Auckland, and in 1919 edited Emily's *Letters* for publication.

97: To Violet Dickinson   [*Netherhampton House, Salisbury*]

Wednesday [August 1903]

My Violet,

Your telegram was an immense relief. Only take care, and run no risks, and do all your doctors tell you.

We are all the better, morally mentally and physically, for your visit. Such are the alleviations of our lot, I believe. Nurse says she is so glad Miss Dickinson is coming back—'it is an excellent plan' according to that sensible woman. I have had 2 long talks with her since you left—see what fruit your words have borne! and I think she liked it, and we talked of all kinds of things, and made a great advance. I shall go in to her every day now—and only wish I had begun before—

She told me, I dont know whether to comfort or because she believes it, that she is practically certain that the end will be this perforation. The haemorrhage going on all this time means that the growth is going that way —She says.

He is very weak today, and talks more about it now that only Nessa and I are here. He tried to walk with me, and when we got to the end of the garden he was so tired he had to go back—and he groaned and said he felt so bad—But nothing more has happened—I mean he has not asked us anything. I think he knows all but absolute facts really.

He said to me 'Does Violet Dickinson like me d'you think' and was pleased like a child, or Sparroy, when I said yes. I told him you had enjoyed your talk—and he said, voluntary, what a charming woman you were. It's a terrible flirtation.

Now we have just had a telegram to say that Ronnie Norman[1] is coming tomorrow. He is a good young man, and wont bother—so it dont much matter. Old Beatrice [Thynne] has written a laborious letter to put us off— she cant have Katie—but we try to make her come next week. No Fishers yet—I'm afraid everything points to a visit tomorrow, but my illegitimate Aunt [Violet Dickinson] is the happy background on these occasions as on all others. I turn to her when I am weary, and like the wicked cease from troubling. The Nurse is a find: it is marvellous what a blind ostrich Sparroy can be—do you remember the incident of her and her intimate in the early days? and now hasn't that blossomed (an afterthought you perceive.)

Yr. Sp:

Berg

1. Ronald Norman (b. 1873), a distant connection of the Camerons, later Chairman of the BBC.

Sunday, 30th August [1903]

My Violet,

You are a stinging reptile—one sheet to an intimate, and I told you to buy some large paper for me. Also you say nothing about your beast of a back—Nessa says its too elongated to be much practical use in this world. However, we hope it will come in in the next. When you next write put some affection in to your letters—like sugar in otherwise rather bitter tea. I always do. I suppose you are plunged in sadness—your Nelly [Cecil] will be taking up your attention. That strongheaded old Beatrice has put us off for good now—says she cant leave her mother [Lady Bath] and her Aunt. I cant help thinking she has shied at the last moment at the idea of the Stephen family. I cant imagine how she can possibly comfort Manchester Square—Beatrice is not the person I should turn to for comfort in the house at such moments. Her sympathy would be spasmodic—I mean *muscularly* spasmodic. However if we go so soon there really wouldn't be time for her here—and perhaps it's as well.

We have suffered from a plague of males since you left—Ronny Norman, an Indian cousin, besides Jack [Hills] and Gerald. Norman is a dry dog—theres no denying it. He has ruled out half the pleasures and beauties of life already, and will spend the rest of his days in very narrow limits. I speak like a prophetess. I have always foretold it.

Nessa has written to you about your plans. I tried to but my literary style was choked and strangled, and I have come to the conclusion that letters is a fraud, and what shall I do when I have to write to the trades-people—being the wife of a poor curate, and the mother of six children, born in 3 and ½ years? I shall go to the nearest post office and wire for Violet!!! That is practically what I spend my time in doing.

I have also now discovered that the nurse though only 29 years of age (I thought her 39) is a woman of great practical ability—and endless conversation. I go in regularly and sit on her bed—or she comes to our rooms, and we sit talking till next meal time. When I finish this interesting—very interesting letter—I am going down to see her. Nessa will have told you about father—I mean there isnt much change, though I daresay a fresh person would see that he is weaker. This haemorrhage hasn't stopped once the whole time—almost seems to get worse. He thinks about it I am sure—but says very little. Yesterday we went for a drive together to Bemerton and Wilton. He liked it I think and would get out and look for George Herberts monument, and walked for a few minutes in the gardens at Wilton[1]—but he is very weak. Heaven knows what we shall do when we get back—London empty, and he too weak to leave the house. But these things always come to pass in some mysterious way. It isn't lively—

1. The great house of the Earls of Pembroke near Salisbury.

We are very good about going out—we spend most of the day out, though it rains so that sitting in the garden is impossible. But I quite see that air now is very important—and I insist upon it, being a woman of much authority.

When you come, do stay a reasonable time. Those two days were a horrid scramble.

Yr. Sp:

Berg

99: To Emma Vaughan   *Netherhampton House, Salisbury*
                                       (our address)
30th Aug [1903]

Dearest Todger,

I dreamt of you last night which moves me to write today. We met in London and you said *"At last* the summer is over" which is what you will be saying under those conditions in a month's time. But the summer is a vain imagination of our hearts—it has rained I think every day since we came and we call it fine when a hurricane blows. It is doing both today, being a wretched Sunday. You have vanished into fine air—Marny said something about your going on a bicycle tour in which case I rather give up hope of ever seeing you again. I am going to keep to four walls when I get back to London—or I shall be disappearing too. I wonder if you have met Miss Hickman[1] on your wanderings. She is to be seen all over England at present. Our nurse is greatly excited about it. She knows the hospital and the Italian Quarter, and was once lost there herself. But by the time you get this, if you ever do, all that will have blown over.

The Fishers, now, are of permanent interest. They are a source of some amusement to us. I saw Adeline and Ralph [Vaughan Williams] at the station on the day they arrived, but Adeline stared so that I rushed past without a word. *I'm* not going to make advances Then we heard nothing whatever for 10 days when At. Mary wrote "am I *never* going to see you?" We called then[2]—Nessa and I—and had a most depressing interview. The Fishers would have made Eden un-inhabitable: At. Mary sat at a square table on a hard straight chair, writing—there is half a fire in the grate, which won't burn—it drizzles outside. There is one red cushionless sofa and in the middle of the room a draped table, like Fairbanks' waiting room, with books at intervals. No wonder when one looks out of the window to see Hervey lying flat on his face on a blanket in the middle of the lawn. Emmy was in a temper—hardly spoke—black goggles and weeds—Charles

1. A Dr Sophia Hickman had been reported as missing from 'the Italian quarter of London', Saffron Hill.
2. At the Fishers' rented house in the Close, Salisbury.

unwashed and unkempt, also black goggles—and so on and so on. They murmured something about tea but we fled and felt damp and depressed all the afternoon. They have been here twice. I saw them neither time and they go on the 10th.

We shall probably be back about the 18th—father hasn't been so well here and he is anxious to be at home. I wonder where on earth you are— this kind of weather is what you like I suppose. We tramp out along the road in the mud every evening and squat black toads come flopping under our feet—but for love of you we let them be (honestly, I shouldn't at all like squashing a toad—but it sounds better the other way) How is the haloed Marn? She seemed to be quite happy alone in London and having a thorough treat at Hoxton. I believe smallpox was all an excuse. Write and tell your news. How is Padstow[1] and is the world to be re-stocked yet by a fresh supply of Vaughans[2] and how is the [Millicent and Vere] Isham family and what are your plans?

Your loving,
AVS

Sussex

100: To Emma Vaughan   *Netherhampton House, Salisbury*

2nd Sept [1903]

Dearest Todger,

Some spirit surely connects us. As I sat writing to you on Sunday evening, I said to myself, or rather, as is the way with inspirations, had it said in to my ear—"The toad is at this moment writing to you". I almost put this in my letter—except that I knew if I did it wouldn't be so—to such depths of superstition have I come.

But really it is odd that after a silence of over six weeks, we should simultaneously think—with no particular reason—that we must that very moment write to each other. I had had a vague idea of writing to you, for several days, but it became imperative on Sunday—Heaven knows why. We have done this before too. I hope that frozen old Marn will write us a full and vivid account of Padstow. Are you going there? How is John [Isham]? I know who it is your going to ride with—another case of sympathy —and her name begins with a *W*!!

No signs of the Fishers—except Charles who came over the other day as though he had just got out of bed—that's the way they all look now. Excuse this illiterate and spasmodic letter. I think I am threatened with writer's cramp and palsy of the brain. Kiss the flags of Kensington for me— not that I in the least wish to see them again—I should think you might see

1. Cornwall, where Margaret Vaughan was staying.
2. Children of Will and Madge Vaughan.

Totty and Clara [Pater] in their red cloaks—they were coming back about now, their summer disorders generally drive them back to town and doctors about the first week in September. I suppose you are feeling thoroughly happy snuffing High Street airs. One might do that just as well as sit like I do and watch the rain on the pane. We have a Lady pony here, who is, I opine, long past child-bearing. She is a disappointed woman, and has no ambitions in life, and objects to hills, and nearly runs me into all the hay carts I meet. I go driving with Father, and when we meet anything else he seizes the reins, and I drop the whip and we are landed in the hedge to the vast amusement of the rustics! Don't disappear—whatever you do. Insanity seems to be coming over half the women in London.

I wonder if you're writing to *me* now, now that I've said that of course you won't.

Yours,
Goat

Sussex

101: To Violet Dickinson   22 *Hyde Park Gate, S.W.*

[19? September 1903]

My Violet,

Here we are back. Nurse says father is less tired than she expected—and he is certainly extraordinarily happy to be back. How things will settle down, I dont know. At present it feels rather grim, sitting here and waiting, and no escape—even of leaving this house. But I suppose we shall go back to our usual ways.

I wrote you a Collins—but forgot to send it—this is rather late in the day—but you will understand it as written—all very soft and secret. I didn't read your letter to Nessa, and we have made an agreement that your letters are to be included under the same rule as Snows—no one else is to read them. So dont hesitate to bare your boney bosom and that extinct volcanoe that calls itself a heart. How was Nelly?—how is your back?

My brain is dry of any thing today—for one thing it is so dull to be in London again, which is as though we had left yesterday and the house is a muddle and a chaos. Jack downstairs talking to Nessa—Sparroy scribbling at her blue table—a large family dinner party in half an hour. That is the state of things and has been for many years.

Kitty has suddenly realized that father is ill, and writes very affectionate letters to Nessa. She is a good woman and all that, and would do anything for Nessa I know, and as it is does a good deal—but the end of the long sentence is that she and Sparroy aren't what you call sympathetic—and her attitude on these matters makes me unreasonably irritated. But then her attitude is the worlds—and only my Violet says the right thing, and feels it too. George says nothing more, but asks every day almost how we think father is? like a pathetic dog—and yet he doesn't understand when we tell him. He is altogether well meaning though and would do anything to help—if he were more articulate. He trots up to father and asks how he feels, and father says much the same—and George comes over to us beaming. But he has given up his room—and all his little ornaments, and that means a good deal.

This letter is, what Kitty would call, a sign of the literary temperament d——d egotistic .. But I dont care a hang!! You've got to put up with it—my poor Violet.

Yr. Sp:

Yr letter just come—temperature *below* normal.

Berg

102: To Violet Dickinson   [22 *Hyde Park Gate, S.W.*]

[late September? 1903]

My Violet,

No time for a proper, or even improper, such as I usually write, letter. You must have these pens at once—because Sp: wants another communication. Yrs. are like the scent of profane Violets on my plate at breakfast, such as grow in the unhallowed part of a churchyard, where *I* shall be buried one day.

It is perfect hot sunshine here too, but there never was any time of the year so sad as this. Kitty says 'nonsense'. It always makes me think of death's and dyings.

Yr. Sp:

Berg

103: To Violet Dickinson   22 *Hyde Park Gate, S.W.*

[late September 1903]

My Violet,

Do write and get the slothful Crum to write to say how you are. I believe your d——d bad, and hiding it all this time. For Gods sake and Sparroys (two names not often joined) take care, and tell me what is the matter. This is sober truth.

You remember how my soft nose wrinkled in the carriage that day, well, its doing that now, only worse.

This is the important part of my letter.

We have had a debauch of the Thynne family. Katie [Cromer] and

Beatrice [Thynne] sprang up suddenly in the drawing room one afternoon. There was a crowd of other people, and the whole thing was overwhelming, but Katie fits in here somehow. She is tired but very beautiful—a pathetic look of weary motherhood already.

Then we lunched at Manchester Square today to meet Katie, but she never came—Lord knows why—no getting Beatrice to make a consecutive explanation.[1] We lunched silently with Lady Bath and Beatrice, three footmen, all silent but the dogs munching our chicken bones in the corner and the tick of Lady Bs Waterbury watch. 'Nobody praises me' said Beatrice once. She is enough to bring tears to the eyes sometimes. My Woman, are you a good happy woman, or a bony scratchy scrawly woman, and would you like to feel the Wallaby snout on your bosom? Say Come and I Come, Go and I Go, 'to the ends of the earth she followed her'. I wish I knew my Holy Bible better. That is a quotation (very apt) from Ruth you perceive.[2] The toils of the world are drawing round us. Case begins next week and the Academy, but shall I come down and see you? Say brutally no, I dont care a damn.

We are in most ways the same here. It is very slow, but comes nearer every day, I see. Well, I suppose we shall get through somehow, but it is a bad time, and nothing can stop it.

One thing is good: Gerald talked to Nessa and takes our view most strongly, says we must *of course* leave this house, and he wants to take rooms separate.[3] I believe he has wanted this a long time. He said he felt that he and Georgie were a generation older, and that we must make our own lives independently. He thought we ought to take a small house, Bloomsbury possibly, and be four together. He is going to urge this on Georgie.

Goodnight my Violet. Believe that I snuffle all over you, very soft and comforting, and only get well.

Yr. Sp.

Berg

104: TO VIOLET DICKINSON   22 *Hyde Park Gate, S.W.*

[end September 1903]

My Violet,

Here is your letter. Read it with a magnifying glass if you like, and send it back, and own that I was entirely right. What could poor Sparroy have

1. Lady Cromer gave birth to her only child, Evelyn Baring, later Lord Howick, on 29 September 1903.
2. Virginia is confusing the story of Ruth with Matthew VIII, ix: "I say to this man, go, and he goeth, and to another, come, and he cometh."
3. They were anticipating that Leslie Stephen would die within a few weeks or months.

done under the circumstances? Really I couldn't evolve the maid and the Tongue and the three pounds of gold, from these materials [*inexplicable*].

Yesterday was a great refreshment bodily and spiritual. If I lived in your Cottage [Burnham Wood] I should turn Saint.

Would you be careful to impress upon your husband not to talk a word to anybody about possible changes in our family [moving house]? If George or Gerald, even, were to hear anything of the kind they would be horrified, and make things much more difficult. Gerald was anxious that we should not talk to anyone, until he had settled things with George.

Of course it doesn't matter a bit your talking to your husband—and I know he wont repeat—only I am always in difficulties from indiscretions! (poor Sparroy!)

Yr. Sp.

Berg

105: To Violet Dickinson   22 *Hyde Park Gate, S.W.*

Friday, 2nd October [1903]

My Violet,

I wonder how you managed that journey. I think of your white cheeks— and the pain going on all the time, and the long travelling day and night. But you are there [Bordighera] now—that's something. As you love Sparroy come back very much better. I do hate you to be ill.

Its a brute of a world, and I'm in a damned bad temper. I hope you dont mind bad language and bad writing and bad everything. We have had endless affectionate sentimental visiting here, at their wits end what to say I suppose, and so saying the wrong thing. Why cant people be simple and straight-forward in this world—thats what I want to know. I always say what I mean, even if I say it with my Wallaby snout—with squeaks and grunts and pawings of the claw—but I say it—and *I'm* no Saint. Life would be so much simpler if we could flay the outside skin all the talk and pretences and sentiments one doesn't feel etc etc etc—Thats why I get on with you isn't it? (here you must show great emotion.)

But to business, my Violet. No news of Katie—except a line the evening I saw you from Beatrice. She says Katie and the Baby are well, and its nice to hear a child's voice. I never thought of it, but wont that—I mean the child—solve some of old Beatrice's knots? I believe it will. It will be some-thing spontaneous in that grim house—and thank God wont have learnt the Bath manner yet. D'you suppose two footmen will stand beside its cradle? Gerald passed you in Paris—no talking done yet—except that Nessa and Thoby sit together and plan his career—(two Es!) It is this kind of thing thats so damned pathetic. I do hate taking life seriously, and making plans and thinking about money and the future—but one must. Thoby wants to go to the Bar, and I am sure he will eventually. [Janet] Case is started again [Greek lessons]—so is the Academy [for Vanessa]. My poor Violet—what a lot of dry details you have thrust upon you. Tell me truly if you are worse or better or what. You remember there is a very fine instinct wireless telepathy nothing to it—in women—the darlings—which fizzles up pretences, and I know what you mean though you dont say it, and I hope its the same with you—'Cos I've written this letter without any effort to make it grammatical. John Bailey[1] wouldn't approve. Is Hester [Lyttelton] back? is Margaret Lyttelton back? George is full of Elsie [Elizabeth, Countess Carnarvon]—but merely filial. The Duckworth temperament I believe likes these temperate (John would scratch out this sentence) relationships. Sisters and mothers but not wives.

Nurse comes in to get a book—wants to know how you are 'Miss Dickinson would make a good nurse' she says—so strong minded, unselfish, and practical—those were her very words—and that is the last praise she reserves for the elect. Do you remember one day at Fritham in the spring of our relationship—how I said to you 'I should like to be nursed by you when I'm ill.' Wasn't that prophetic and instinctive? Typical of so much in our lives.

My Violet, how are you? I dont like letters which ask many silly questions, and repetition is a sign of weakness, but tell me true, I repeat again. It was I felt a melancholy last sight of you—that.

Does Cook find abroad satisfying? She must be a woman of great imagination.

The London hospital haunts me. I dream I'm a nurse there—which is of all likelihoods the least likely.

There isnt much change here—but it is extraordinarily pathetic somehow, to use an odd word. But there is nothing to be unhappy about.

My Violet—take care

Yr. Sp. AVS

Berg

106: To Violet Dickinson   22 *Hyde Park Gate, S.W.*

Sunday [early October 1903]

My Violet,

I am afraid you will have had to wait for letters, but I didnt grasp the difficulties of the post. But really there is nothing to be said. He gets steadily weaker, I think—less able to read or talk and more inclined to spend his day with his eyes shut or asleep. He asks to see people, for the sake of the change, I think, so Beatrice went in once, and Mr. Lushington [father of Kitty and Susan].

I hope as the weakness increases he will worry less about money and

1. John Cann Bailey (1864-1931), the critic and essayist.

his own helplessness. He has been very much depressed the last 2 or 3 days. Of course they still say 'no change'—but Nurse thinks him growing weaker; otherwise there is nothing they can tell us, so we dont ask questions.

Beatrice comes regularly—the faithful old thing. I dont know how much she does because she thinks she ought, but I think she is amused more than at Manchester Square, and she has certainly been a godsend all round, these long dull days. Thoby and Adrian like having her.

Kitty makes me angry and she hasn't been once, but writes sympathetic notes, and now she has gone North for a week. without coming here at all. Of course there are excuses, but it is silly to repeat as she does that she doesnt come because she can be no use. What can anybody do but come and see one, and talk? She is an odd fish, but I feel angry. I think Nessa is hurt by it.

However [Margery] Snowden comes in a few days, and she [Vanessa] really does enjoy seeing her—an incredible taste to me! and Jack also—and Beatrice is regular, and my Violet will come soon, who is the person I most want to see.

I cant write tonight—but I must tell you that we have had a certain amount of talk with G and G. about our prospects, and Gerald says he's going to leave us, and George says he's going to stay whatever happens—and they both agree that Bloomsbury is the best place. George has been so extraordinarily understanding and feeling about all this that one forgets his irritating ways, and I believe we shall all get on very well together.

This is a selfish letter!

We live such a queer mole like life: the outside world seems to have ceased—but you are in the thick of it.

Goodbye

Yr. AVS

Berg

107: To Violet Dickinson   22 *Hyde Park Gate, S.W.*

[11? October 1903]

My Violet,

I'm afraid you may object to this sheet of paper—but God wills it. You sent me one good letter. Such as it behoves an honest woman. Should you think that was pretty sound grammar? I tell you I write under great difficulties—because my electric light is seized with a sort of Vitus's dance—all because its wire is worn through—and poor Sparroy—never was a little Wallaby made to sweat so for her virtue—sweat, literally *sweat*. Today I put on combies, flannel trousers, sky blue—suspenders—all most hygenic—but so hot! My flesh is melting in streams of affection—and my skin is that irritable. Does one get used to it? And as if this weren't enough I was persuaded to buy a handsome black coat which I think was originally meant for lady *and* child—child contained within, you understand. Besides which the coat is inches thick—stands out stiff like armour, and weighs pounds and pounds. My combies are like sackcloth must have been, which one wore next to one's skin in penance.

My Violet, how is the spine? is it any better—any worse—or the same? Anyhow tell me *quite truly*; and for Gods sake and Sparroys take care. Do you feel pretty happy or pretty miserable, or a mix? Do you think of Sparroy with content and comfort? Do you love her much? You are to me a rock in the quicksand of Kitties and Snows.

We went and asked after Katie [Cromer] the other day 'Her Ladyship going on *very* well—and the baby'—that must be a load off their queer spasmodic minds. We must try and get hold of Beatrice [Thynne] before she ships off to Egypt. Kitty is in the very heart of the politix—at Birmingham with Joe [Chamberlain] and [George] Milner. Her head will spin right off with theories. George has moved to the treasury[1]—has a rise of salary and is head secretary. When we came to breakfast this morning there was a giant man in the hall. The treasury messenger with important letters from Cabinet ministers, which mustn't wait even the Sabbath. George touches his high water mark of worldly happiness at moments like these. But Sparroy has come to one mournful egoistical conclusion—she's a fool. I cant understand all these facts and figures for the life of me—and all the rest talk glibly. Do you understand? The British brain feeds on facts—flourishes on nothing else—but I cant reason. Do you mind—do you think it'll make me a foolish writer?

Nessa turns green to hear of your husband and Sargent. They have him next month at the Academy. [Janet] Case is as regular as a Clock. She's a nice woman really—and sometimes puts her arm round Sparroy!! As for the Nurse—she flourishes. When she buys flowers she gives us each a bunch. She runs here at all hours—when I'm in bed even—and spouts talk. I never heard anyone with such a lot to say (Sparroys letters are rather garrulous) She is so exquisitely clean and healthy and normal. I feel she bathes one all over—not with talk only.

Father gets weaker I suppose: he hasn't been out once since we were back—except that time he went half way up the street. He is finishing Hobbes.[2] There are some small things he can do afterwards. He said the other day, to the old Quaker sister, that he felt much weaker, but couldn't make out what was the matter and didn't like to ask Nurse. He enjoys seeing people for half an hour or so and talks away—but most of the day he is very tired. He said he didn't mind dying for himself, but he should like to see a little more of the children. He feels, I think, that we are just grown up, and

1. He was still secretary to Austen Chamberlain, who in 1903 was appointed Chancellor of the Exchequer.
2. *Hobbes*, Leslie Stephen's last book, was part of the *English Men of Letters* series.

able to talk to him—and he wants to see what becomes of us. In that way its hard—for him—but not really I think.

No talking to Georgie or Gerald; they are a marvelous pair. A dinner with them is something to laugh over ten days later. Character is what amuses me. Lord—they are comic—Gerald a little jealous and Georgie the good boy whose virtue has been rewarded. If ever I write a novel, those two shall go in large as life. "People always tell me George ought to have been a diplomat' says Gerald—'now I think I should have made a good diplomat'— and waits for our answer. Georgie explains very earnestly how one should always get up to open the door for a lady in a diplomatic household! Pixton [Countess Carnarvon's house] is the diplomatic household for him.

This is terrible garrulous—and not all of it exceedingly interesting. It rains all day—all night—I believe it would be very bad for you, so dont rush back like a homesick child. Is it very beastly—no one to talk to—and nothing to do? But if you can come home with a sound back for the winter, it'll be worth while. Tomorrow I am going to buy a gold pen—I go through miseries with my pens—all my paws black at the end too. Should you call this a pretty good hand? The truth is I want appreciation.

Why not see Nelly [Cecil]? She is an exquisite little creature—nothing like a woman of that kind and Violets kind in the world: they are all the things we poor writers try to write—and cant. Isn't that rather pretty? My Violet goodbye, and Bless you.

Yr. AVS

Berg

108: To Violet Dickinson   22 *Hyde Park Gate, S.W.*

[late October 1903]

My Violet,

We tramped Bond Street, missed our way, and then found that last Tuesday was the end lecture, and there is none tomorrow, and you are a foolish woman to imagine lectures where there are none!

Thoby thanks you very much, and would have come with joy. Fate has sent him a ticket for the opening of Parliament instead: he goes in dress suit and light trousers, more like a nigger on the Brighton Parade than anything else. Will you come and bring Miss Margaret Lyttelton to tea? It will be one of the ghastly times of life—half an hour of white agony talking to strange young ladies. Why do you insist upon it? She wont enjoy it either, and we shall look at each other like wild beasts caged.

Father is about the same. temp up again rather. Nurse thinks him not so well.

Yr. AVS

Berg

Wednesday [October/November 1903]

My Violet,

This is only a d——d. scrawl—like those you send me—nothing much to say. Affection? heaps of it. You are a star, a comet rather always wandering in our darkness. After I left you I had such a dose of concentrated relationism —a lecture 2 hours long from the little attitudinising woman [Adeline Vaughan Williams] you remember at Salisbury Station. She says we haven't shown any wish to see our relations, and they are hurt, and will give us up in future. Things *usen't* to be like this etc. etc. I'm no good at mending quarrels—being of a pugnacious disposition—so I left things rather worse than I found them. Sparroy among other things was accused of making a God of intellect, and shifting the burden of the world, which seems to consist of family affection, on to other shoulders! Well, I couldn't deny that could I? Such a nest of emotion we live in. Today the Quaker [Aunt Caroline Emelia, 'Nun'] has been again—tearful and always saying the one wrong thing. She comes again tomorrow. Everybody is told now not to stay more than 15 minutes, which is an excellent thing I think. He doesn't really enjoy people for longer, however fond he is of them. And the majority are easily despatched in 10 minutes.

Kitty back and going strong. Jack back tonight, so beloved Nessa has her cisterns full again—not a wholly apt metaphor. I write in such a tearing hurry—to catch the post as you would say.

Was the hat a success? Does the Boarding house still keep its character? (These two questions have nothing whatever to do with each other.)

Nurse stammers a little over 'love' wh. I propose to send to you from her, but asks when she shall see you again. Oh such lectures from her too. Sparroy thinks of nothing but self cultivation, never does a practical stroke for anyone else. Do you think thats true, my Violet. Dont say so, if you do.

We go to see Katie and the Baby on Sunday. I always wonder whether those ghastly expeditions are worthwhile.

Are you pretty cheerful my Violet, and good and affectionate, and loving Sparroy?

                                                            Yr. AVS

Berg

[October/November 1903]

My Violet,

What a wonderful woman you are for harbouring colds. Take the Sparroy to your breast instead! Father has had rather a bad tired day, after a restless night, but they dont seem to think anything of it.

Thoby wants me to ask you whether you would appoint a time for him to come and see you, and ask your advice about a tramp he is going to take on Sunday near Welwyn. Any time before Saturday. He says that your character interests him a good deal. He now examines everyone as though they were in the witness box and he a judge in ermine.[1] He is always telling me to explain myself clearly, and to say what I mean—the which is always beyond me, but I have a singular genius in saying all kinds of things I dont mean. Kitty has been here 1½ hours talking politics: I should feel more confidence in her schemes for setting the Empire on its legs again if they were ever exactly the *opposite* of 'what Leo thinks' (as she always begins her sentences.)

If you aren't well tomorrow, Sparroy will come in and see you—only you swarm with disolute Duchesses.

Did Margaret Lyttelton give you a chill last night? I should have rheumatism in all my bones if I sat next her at the play. Georgie wears white gloves at the play: 'a habit I picked up in Paris.' Paris is the home of diplomacy, so that it is distinguished to do what is the fashion there, though it has not yet been adopted in this benighted country.

I dont see any reason why this delightful letter should ever stop. I like drivelling away, as a Baby slobbers, to my Violet. By the way, talking of Babies I always feel impelled to mention a certain fact about Mrs. Crum when I am in any very public place, say in an omnibus, on Piccadilly Circus.

Goodbye my Violet. Send a boy messenger with a chain to fetch me whenever you want me. I am rather in request just now. I was asked to spend an evening in Montpelier Square [Kitty Maxse's house], but I said 'No I have other engagements' which I hadn't, but I thought it set a higher price on my head, and you know every Sparroy is numbered.

Yr. AVS

Remember about Thoby.
I got such a nice pen to write with I couldn't stop.

Berg

111: To Violet Dickinson   22 *Hyde Park Gate, S.W.*

[October/November 1903]

My child,
The letters came all right. I shall send you my manuscripts[2] to read, as you seem so tender.

1. Thoby, having come down from Cambridge, had decided to read for the Bar.
2. These may be the short descriptive essays (on such subjects as Wilton, Stonehenge, 'Country Reading', and 'The Talk of Sheep') which Virginia wrote before, during, and after her holiday at Salisbury. These manuscripts are now in the Berg Collection.

Are you recovered? You write in pencil which to the eye of affection may mean that yours is the couch of affliction. I sincerely trust not. Did the concert get into your Bronchials? George Eliot caught her death in St James Hall, but she had not a fur coated Sparroy hot of heart with a beautiful though incomplete pair of scissors to keep her warm. Think 'if you come to your coffin through coffin' [coughing] how mournful how pathetic and yet how divinely Greek! I must go to Sally Young [dressmaker], but I think you are too debilitated.

Yr. Sparroy

I have a great affection for you so on my account oil well those works of God and nature, lent you here for a brief space, but to be accounted for later on that day when the secrets of all souls, and the entrails of all Bodies shall stand before their Creator.

Berg

112: To Violet Dickinson   22 *Hyde Park Gate, S.W.*

[Autumn 1903]

My Violet,
    I only got in at 4.30 and found your letter, so I couldn't come. My poor old Animal—what sorrows do beset the flesh. I will come, I think, sometime tomorrow afternoon, as I have nothing to do, and so dont see me for an instant if you had better not, as I expect. I shall just ask about you. It is d——d—all your difficulties. Beatrice was here 2 hours, and saw father, which was successful, so was Nelly's visit, but I cant write a line.

Yr. AVS

Berg

113: To Violet Dickinson   22 *Hyde Park Gate, S.W.*

[Autumn 1903]

My Violet,
    May I come to lunch Thursday, 1:30, without being a bore—that modest I am! It is easier than coming in afterwards.
    Things the same here. I have no time to write, what with other necessary letters, so I must tell you anything there is to be said. What a universal receptacle you are!

Yr. AVS

Berg

[Autumn 1903]

My Violet,

Rigby[1] came this morning. He is *astonished* at father—says he could never have thought it possible that he could stay like this. He has not lost strength in 5 weeks: if anything he is more comfortable. He says he cant make any kind of guess at how long this will last. Of course he cant gain strength—but he may keep the same for some time longer. Oh what an odd world. Sometimes we are reprieved—and it is so queer, and almost hard to face the months that one may have to—and get a relief at the same time.

I am in such a hurry I cant write details, but he thinks we had better *try* one nurse as [Nurse] Traill is so anxious for it. [Nurse] McKechnie goes on 21st. We have more chance of getting her again when necessary if we let her go now, but I think it will be difficult.

What a dear Beast you are!

Yr. AVS

Berg

Sunday night [Autumn 1903]

My Violet,

I hate to write this letter to make you unhappy, but I know you want to hear. Father has some inflammation—it came on 2 days ago, and Nurse says tonight she thinks it is more serious than they thought and he may become unconscious at any moment. It may spread to the kidneys. Seton said at first that he thought it would go away, but it is no better, and they think that means that it is spreading. Rigby is coming tomorrow. We may know more then, and of course it is still quite possible that it will go down, but we have written to tell Adrian to come [from Cambridge], as it is not safe to wait. He has no pain, only discomfort, and a little fever. He is lying in his room reading, and he knows he is getting worse but he doesn't know that this inflammation is serious. He is quite cheerful. He may get over this of course, but I almost wish it could come now. He cant leave his room these last three days, and I think he wants to die.

I will telegraph at once what Rigby says—or if there is any change tomorrow. Dont think of coming *anyhow* till you have heard. If he doesn't get worse things will go on as usual, and we mustn't give up. If he does die

1. Hugh Rigby, consulting surgeon to London Hospital.

you are the only person who can help—and I will tell you to come. He would get unconscious, and could only live a few days without pain.

My Violet, it is very hard, but you are a comfort.

Yr. AVS

Berg

116: To Violet Dickinson   22 *Hyde Park Gate, S.W.*

Tuesday morning [Autumn 1903]

My Violet,

Rigby just gone. He says there's no immediate danger, but there may be a change at any moment. He thinks it more likely that he will live till Christmas, and get gradually weaker. He examined him, and found that the growth has increased very fast. He is to keep in bed as much as possible, and not to go downstairs again. We are to have a dr. every day, if not oftener, as he will have to be carefully watched. He cant come himself, so he is getting a friend [Dr Wilson] who lives in Kensington to come. He himself comes every 3 days. He is indignant with Seton, who ought to have been every day.

Yr. AVS

Adrian goes this evening as he cant stay, but it is very hard on him. Father saw him and was pleased, and not surprised. Rigby thinks he understands how ill he is, but he didn't ask.

Berg

117: To Violet Dickinson   22 *Hyde Park Gate, S.W.*

Wednesday [Autumn 1903]

My Violet,

Only a scrawl. Kitty here (11.30) talking her Trade, and a kind of Platonic dialogue, which has long ago ceased to be intelligible to me. Father is the same—he saw Romer[1] today—poor Romer hadn't known that he was ill; also At. Anny. The Quaker Aunt writes just now in great perturbation. Suddenly seized with a panic lest he should think her 'neglectful'—and so she comes up tomorrow afternoon. Mind you come. You will be badly wanted. She must only see Father for a second, if at all.

Yr. Sp:

Berg

1. Sir Robert Romer, a Lord Justice of Appeal.

[Autumn 1903]

My Violet,

I suppose the Horners[1] bagged you. Rigby came this morning and was delighted with fathers state—that is he has got rid of the inflammation, and there is now no complication. It was mainly Setons wrong medicines that caused it—the wretch. Of course they cant do anything to stop the weakness, but anyhow he has absolutely no pain, and he is much more cheerful, though so weak.

I suppose we shant see you till next week—a sad separation.

Kitty came again today—and the Quaker. Father said 'Dont go' to her half way through her visit, which she repeated, with tears in her eyes. 'Quite worth coming up for' she said—poor old creature. Kitty is unsatisfactory to me. I like something stronger tasting—like my Violet, or even the gawky old Beatrice. But she is entirely a good woman. Poor Wallaby has such cold paws, or he would write more fluent. How is Sarah? Nothing in this world but deaths and illnesses it seems.

I have to write six letters all about Father etc etc etc. You can't think how I hate it—cold paws and all.

What a comfort is friendship in this world. My Violet, how you do toil for other people—house hunting, all the rest of it. It is those things that count in the next world!—not going into picturesque Retreat in this.

Yr. Sp:

Berg

[Autumn 1903]

My Violet,

This is written under some difficulties—very cold, and pencil seems the only thing available. I ought to be dressing for dinner. Nothing changed here. One day is like another. I dont know what they expect. Send me your address, and I will write a real proper letter. Take care of the elongated back. Give Hester my affectionate respects. I go to the Greek play with Susan and Mr Lushington. It is an experiment: I have never spent 5 minutes alone with Susan in my life.

Goodbye my Violet—poor Sparroys claws are petrified cold.

Yr. AVS

Berg

1. Lady Horner lived at Mells, Somerset. She was a great friend of Burne-Jones and a leader of intellectual and political society.

[Autumn 1903]

My Violet,

Do come tomorrow if you can—I haven't seen you this 6 weeks.

Such a rush—of people to tea—all talking for 2 hours on end—now I must dress for dinner with Beatrice and the Ray [Lady Bath?]. Father seems rather better today, but his temp. is still above normal. Dr cant find anything wrong—thinks its poison from the growth—but it is, he thinks, going off now.

Yr. AVS

Berg

121: TO VIOLET DICKINSON   22 *Hyde Park Gate, S.W.*

[Autumn 1903]

My Violet,

I couldn't come that afternoon—Case stayed so late. When will you come? Only it seems brutal to drag you across London so often. Father had two bad days—Friday and Saturday—but today is better. He slept well and the doctor is satisfied. He says we must expect a great many ups and downs.

I suppose you are at Manchester St [Violet's London house] Monday morning—but in an absent minded moment I took your letter into the bathroom, where I wash my hands, and dropped it into scalding water—all sense washed out of it, therefore—affection remains indelible.

The Relations Swarm. I liken them to all kinds of parasitic animals etc etc: really I think they deserve no better. Three mornings have I spent having my hand held, and my emotions pumped out of me, quite unsuccessfully. They are good people, I know, but it would be merciful if they could keep their virtues and affections and all the rest of it to themselves. Why I like you is because your vicious. Entirely vicious.

George has been calling on the Talbots.[1] They sing your praises—though they are Bishops.

Nurse is mysterious: on Friday she sent for the doctor twice: we naturally thought something was wrong, but she refused to tell us. So Thoby saw him when he came, and it turned out that the haemorrhage had started again, nothing serious, but Nurse thought we should be alarmed. And yet think of all the alarms she has given us, more or less for nothing. I believe McKechnie makes her professional again, and we are going to be kept in the dark.

Yr. Sparroy

Berg

1. Edward Stuart Talbot, Bishop of Rochester.

Saturday [Friday] night [27 November 1903]

My Violet,

Such a cruel day for your journey—the careful Sparroy thinks. What a terrible thing motherhood, for instance, would be, if an intimacy increases the cares of daily life to this extent—but theres no immediate prospect of that. An afternoon indoors, by the fire, is a rare treat in this world. I began to write to you, and then Case knocked vigorously. She blushes like a maiden (I say nothing against her morals) when I say I am writing to you. She says 'Miss Dickinson (you'll be Violet soon) has such a sensible look in her eyes' but I wont listen to such stuff. Everyone sings your praises. Madge Vaughan has just been here—takes down your photograph from the mantelpiece—'Oh I have heard so much about her' aint it sickening? One thing I cant stand is *flattery*—Aunt Anny Ritchie says will you go to tea with her? Kitty says your a woman of genius—tells a long story of a party in some seaside village, which was made brilliant by your gifts. Then she produces some fine theory of genius to meet your case.

But this is a very dull letter. I never can write three lines without somebody coming in—never for any purpose. Madge has been here from 5 to 8— three whole hours, talking hard in my arm chair. She is a strange creature— half a child—but marriage is a heavy burden. She doesn't think much of John Bailey either. Those words will jump out writ in scarlet in the Lyttelton atmosphere.[1] We passed Diana R[ussell]. in the street the other day, tripping along with bright red cheeks, as though no evil doings were on her conscience—as there are, or ought to be. A Flora-George marriage[2] would not be unlike a Madge-Will Vaughan marriage—Madge tired out with brilliancies and speculating and home difficulties accepts finally the quite orthodox Will—and it is, as marriage goes (Sp: always a sceptic) a success. But I rather doubt. Flora will be settled into all her ways, and not willing to take the plunge soon. This letter anyhow, will have to be burnt as soon as read. I cant write happily with only skeleton initials.

I write this under some difficulty tonight. Susan L[ushington]. calls for me at 10 tomorrow—It will be, I know, rather a ponderous day—all that good behaviour, and white gloves like Beatrice. (However shabby her dress is she always wears tight, brilliant white gloves) But Adrian and his rooms are a cheerful sight. I feel a great affection for him, poor little boy.

Did you say goodbye to Katie? I suppose she is on the sea, or rocking in the rain tonight in all this wind, and Baby crying too.

I dont expect Hester [Lyttelton] has really such a loveable character as Sparroy—at least that is my guess. What should you think? This ink is

1. John Bailey married Sarah Lyttelton, daughter of the 4th Lord Lyttelton.
2. Flora and Diana Russell were nieces of the 9th Duke of Bedford. Flora, to whom George was briefly engaged, died unmarried.

diluted. Do you have much time for reading letters in the country—because I had thoughts of taking another sheet—Lord knows theres nothing to say. We have daily tea parties—oh so dull—distinguished old gentlemen for the most part, and a few sentimental Ladies. 'Your father looks *so* much better' etc etc. What d'you think they say it for? Well this business is a revelation of what human nature can be—in the way of sentimentality and uselessness—all save my Violet, who rises firm as a lighthouse above it all—what an apt simile. (Violet gets too many compliments)

Father is just about the same—and now it is the end of November—tomorrow his 71st birthday, and the day on which Minnie .[Harriet Thackeray], his wife, died, long ago [1875]. He asks no questions, sometimes says hes wondering what it means, but I believe he hardly thinks of death, or any future—or he would worry—The Nurse [Traill] has gone behind her mask again—the mysterious woman. She and McKechnie sit talking till 1.30 A.M. and drinking tea, but not a word is breathed to us. I cant help feeling that she is mentally tired of it all—almost bored. But she is a strange woman.

We have had no relations—at least missed them.

My Violet, are you good and well, and feeling pretty happy? Such a brilliant woman as you are (I cant get that word out of my head) ought to be happy—all her friends cawing with open beaks for her to feed them—Sparroy widest agape of all. Can you come next week—really I could come to you, if it is easier.

Yr. AVS

Berg

123: To Violet Dickinson   [22 *Hyde Park Gate, S.W.*]

[December? 1903]

My Woman,

A presentiment told me you wouldn't come today. We spend tomorrow at Cambridge—back in the evening. When are you up again. What Heavenly mercy that Lance is knocked on the head—but how? Is your husband all right? Things are rather bad here—at least one of the complications has come back, which makes him very tired, and very much depressed about himself. However he doesn't say much—

Seton says [Sir Frederick] Treves was *certain* that a complication would happen—but this wasn't what he said at the time.

What a damed [*sic*] mercy you haven't gone.

Write to Sparroy.

Yr. AVS

Berg

124: TO VIOLET DICKINSON   [22 *Hyde Park Gate, S.W.*]

[December? 1903]

My Violet,

Temp. has been 101 all day—this evening it has dropped to normal. He has slept most of the time; and it has been like other days. Beatrice was here. We went out with her. Remember you lunch tomorrow.

1.30 or rather later.

Yr. AVS

Berg

125: TO VIOLET DICKINSON   22 *Hyde Park Gate, S.W.*

[December? 1903]

My Violet,

He has had another very bad night, and he is very tired today. But except for this there is nothing much to be said. Haldane[1] comes this evening. Father wants to see him but says he is too tired to see anybody else.

Tearing wind, as I suppose with you, but otherwise rather a nice day, and we have been walking in the gardens.

Yr. AVS

Berg

126: TO VIOLET DICKINSON   22 *Hyde Park Gate, S.W.*

[December? 1903]

My Violet,

I meant to write yesterday, but there wasn't time. There is no change: he had a fair night, and the day is about the same. He is very tired and sleeps a great deal, but is quite cheerful when he wakes. He saw Romer today. He must see you tomorrow. Adrian is up today, much happier and more like himself I think. Last time it was all such a bad dream to him.

I have just been writing to Helen Holland[2] wh. makes me feel swimming in the head. Post going, joy to see you.

Case so excited about you. Thinks you charming and most original, and so honest, and wants to meet again, etc. etc. etc.

Yr. Sp.

Berg

1. Richard Burdon Haldane M.P., later Viscount Haldane.
2. A Duckworth relative, who married Bernard Holland.

Monday night [December? 1903]

My Violet,

There is really no change—if anything he is a little better, his temperature is lower.

But we know nothing, and we can only wait. Perhaps Rigby will tell us more.

I myself think that he will get through this. It would be best not, I know. He seems weaker today, but of course that is natural. He is lying in his room, reading a little. Adrian is here—poor little boy—he had guessed nothing, and he is terribly upset, though he says hardly anything.

Oh dear—if we only hadn't got to wait for weeks to come, but this is what I dread.

I will telegraph at once what Rigby says. He must know more.

Yr. AVS

I wish you weren't coming up earlier. If anybody can do anything you can—but I know we shall have just to keep on as usual.

Berg

Monday [December? 1903]

My Violet,

There is nothing much to say—his temp. stays 100, but I suppose will go higher tonight. He seems very weak and depressed, and not able to read much. His whole state seems to be a little worse than it was, with this continual fever. He saw Sir Alfred Lyall;[1] no one else—but I dont think he wanted more visitors.

Kitty suddenly turned up for dinner, and she and Nessa and Thoby and George are at this moment discussing politics in the drawing room—she is a good woman really! It is odd how she casts back to 10 years ago every now and then, and is more recognisable, and one likes her better. I believe if she ever stayed long she would wear off the other Maxse varnish.

This is the kind of letter the Quaker writes!

I will send a line tomorrow.

Yr. AVS

Berg

1. The historian and biographer.

[December? 1903]

My Violet,
   He seems very weak today, and has stayed in bed altogether. Nurse thinks he will hardly be able to get up again, so we have put a bed in the sitting room, and emptied it, and I expect he will be moved in there tomorrow. His temperature is below normal today. Nurse thinks he gets quickly weaker. Rigby is bringing his friend [Dr Wilson] tomorrow. I don't suppose there will be anything fresh. Father seems to like the idea of having a new doctor—not Seton, I mean. He is quite cheerful, but one can only stay with him a few minutes, and he cant talk much.
   He knows everything I am sure.
   Nessa is very anxious to see you. Possibly we might come tomorrow afternoon, but I don't know what time, or whether she can manage it— but she wants to. So dont stay in, if you are about, but I imagine you are in bed. How is your husband. My Violet, you are a comfort.

                                                                Yr. Sparroy
Berg

[December? 1903]

My Violet,
   Things are bad today. He had a sudden shivering fit this morning. and his temp. went up to 104. It went down again; and he has slept most of the day. Wilson doesn't know what it means, probably something to do with the bladder, but says theres no immediate danger. This evening he was very sick, and we sent for Wilson who has just gone: 11 PM. He says the sickness may be only indigestion—or it may be a symptom of other trouble. His temp. tonight is 104. pt 2. Nurse thinks him very ill. He is only to have a milk diet. Of course they may get this under—but they can tell nothing. They dont know whats happening. Wilson comes at 9 tomorrow morning. I will telegraph how he is.

                                                                Yr. AVS
Berg

[December? 1903]

My Violet,

I have got you two sponge bags.

We expect you tomorrow at 1.30.

Yr. AVS

A pot of flowers stands on my table, sent mysteriously, but I think by you. Thank you. You have done more than I ever deserved.

Berg

132: To Violet Dickinson   22 *Hyde Park Gate, S.W.*

[December? 1903]

My Violet,

Dont think me damned sentimental but its peace and balm to talk to you, and that is the only kind of good there is in the world. What all these tragedies are made for I believe. Otherwise it seems needless torture.

But you are a beloved creature—*that* is what I wanted to say—and it makes it all different to have you.

Yr. Sparroy

Berg

133: To Violet Dickinson   22 *Hyde Park Gate, S.W.*

[December? 1903]

My Violet,

Another very bad night, hardly any sleep at all, but his temp. is not very high. Wilson thinks that he has got weaker rather rapidly in the last few days, and says all the symptoms are more serious—but cant of course make any prophecy. He is really fairly cheerful and able to read a little—but doesn't get any sleep really. He is to have a sleeping draught tonight.

I am writing to Hester [Lyttelton] tonight—forgot to last night. I have searched the Times but cant find your lecture anywhere. Tomorrow I will go to Bond St—oh what a good Sparroy—on my tender Pads. It is soaking wet here. I only hope the Cottage has held together, and all your maternal ladies haven't suffered. Kitty dined here Friday. Came in after the meat was done, quite unexpected, and stayed till past 11. Really I shall have to revise my judgment. She is going back to her early ways again, and she is then charming.

Yr. AVS

Berg

22 Hyde Park Gate, S.W.

[December? 1903]

My Violet,

Father is about the same today. Wilson says he thinks the growth may be spreading to the bladder now, which is what they have always feared, or it may be only an irritation which will go away. They cant tell yet. He seems very weak today, so that Wilson is inclined to think the growth is spreading. We have had so many alarms though. Anyhow they cant say anything now. He is not very comfortable, and had a restless night.

I will write tomorrow. You must come on Sunday.

Yr. AVS

Berg

135: To Violet Dickinson   *22 Hyde Park Gate, S.W.*

10 P.M. [December? 1903]

My Violet,

Wilson has just been. He says there is no change since this morning. His temp. goes up and down every hour, but his pulse is about the same. He is perfectly comfortable; and talked naturally just now when we said good night.

Beatrice was here this evening. The Quaker [Caroline Emelia Stephen] has settled to stay, I hope only for tonight, at a Hotel near. She evidently wanted to, and she saw Father again and he knew her and she was pleased.

My Violet, you are a help.

Yr. AVS

Berg

136: To Violet Dickinson   *22 Hyde Park Gate, S.W.*

[December? 1903]

My Violet,

He is about the same—he had rather a restless night, but Wilson thinks him not changed and cant tell anything. He said to nurse 'We give him two months if all goes well'—but they have said so many things, one doesn't believe in them quite. Nurse herself says no one can tell anything. I am afraid Jack [Hills] may come to dine tomorrow night, but G[erald] and G[eorge] are away. Anyhow you come—You are a prop to this shaky Sparroy at any rate.

Yr. AVS

Berg

137: To Violet Dickinson   22 *Hyde Park Gate, S.W.*

[December? 1903]

My Violet,

Fathers temp. has gone down again. It is just under 101 tonight, but of course it may rise again. He has been asleep almost all day, and hasn't wanted to see any visitors. They cant explain it at all—Wilson thinks him weaker, and says he cant rally very much oftener, but thinks he will get through this, unless the temp. goes very high again, which he says is unlikely.

Take care, my Good Woman, and clear your pipes in the air.

Beatrice is more eccentric than fish flesh or good red herring!

Yr. AVS

Berg

138: To Violet Dickinson   22 *Hyde Park Gate, S.W.*

10 PM [December? 1903]

My Violet,

Wilson has been twice again, but says there is no change. His temp. is 103 pt 6. tonight. Wilson says the early hours of the morning are the critical ones, it is just a question of how often he can live through them. But he says his vitality is still great, and he does not expect any change tonight.

Kitty came this evening again. I spent the afternoon driving with Beatrice. She is really a good woman.

Yr. AVS

Come tomorrow, only dont if you feel too tired.

Berg

139: To Violet Dickinson   22 *Hyde Park Gate, S.W.*

Wednesday night [December? 1903]

My Violet,

His temp. is 100, but they say this doesnt count much. He is very weak, and Heaven knows what is going to happen. It cant go on like this much longer. But they dont really know what it is—and contradict themselves as usual. Stay till Saturday if they want you to—we are astonishingly sane, and go about our daily works as usual. It is much better so, and evidently there is no immediate danger.

Yr. AVS

Berg

Thursday [December? 1903]

My Violet,

I'm afraid your cold must be worse. Do take care, and stay in bed. No change here—his temp. stays 99—but nurse says it doesn't mean anything. Wilson is only coming every other day in future. He says his visits are useless, and they worry Father. He says he gets steadily weaker, but still has wonderful strength—terrible strength. There he lies all day, almost asleep, hardly able to read, but he does still enjoy seeing people. He had Romer and Will Vaughan today, Kitty yesterday.

Dont come tomorrow, *please*, if there is the least reason against it. Beatrice was here to lunch today. You will meet Nessa and George tomorrow.

Yr. Sp.

Berg

[December? 1903]

My Violet,

I'm afraid your cold must be worse—and Beatrice didnt come so we had no news.

Father has still some fever—just 100 all day, and it goes up at night, but Wilson doesn't seem to think it means anything. They really expect another violent attack like the first, I think—but he says he sees no signs of it yet. He is very tired today but saw two or three people. He has been asleep almost all day, till tea time, hardly reading at all.

I do hope you arent really bad. I know nothing about your colds—what they run to.

Kitty away—Jack back—Snow rampant. Beatrice deserted—various callers, infinitely dull.

Nessa begins Academy on Wed: probably, wh. seems the best thing to do, and I shall set to work steadily at my Greek. I suppose we shall come thru' somehow—but it is marvellously hard—I never thought to have to go through all this.

My Violet, take care.

Yr. AVS

Berg

[December? 1903]

Woman,

Why do you pitch on Tuesday? I cant get rid of Case, and Nessa has her life man that day, dam it. Couldn't we come some other time. Friday next is just possible, or Wednesday week after next which would do better. Rack your ruinous brains and find out a way, and send me some more trains. And write a still longer letter. You see what with trains and things one cant read there isnt very much left of your letter at the end.

Aunt Minna hasn't been written to yet. We are having a shot at a studio here.

Sparroy

How are your works? For goodness sake dont get married. Remember, Sparroy is an appendage if you do.

Berg

Christmas day [1903]

My Violet,

I can only write a scrawl tonight—and it wont reach [you] till goodness knows when. Father is just the same—but it is very hard work. He does want to have done with it all, so, and can hardly read or amuse himself, and yet must go on, day after day. He is comfortable, and happily sleeps a good deal. They seem as much in the dark as ever—dont know from day to day whats going to happen—and refuse to make any prophesy. If only it could be quicker!—but theres no use in writing all this—which only comes over me at times, and I daresay he forgets it too, sometimes.

Beatrice is a fixture here—dont tell her that—but I love her, and she may come as often as she likes, and stay all day if she will. We were out with her all yesterday afternoon—and she came to lunch today—and stayed till 7.30 and she comes to lunch tomorrow!

All the same she dont cut you out—I hope you are getting through with your Balls. Christmas went off here solidly, without much difference, and we are getting back to our old everyday ways, as tho' nothing had happened or were going to happen.

We must go abroad sometime—right away to Italy.

Goodnight my Violet. You have made yourself indispensable here.

Yr. AVS

Berg

Monday 28 [December 1903]

My Violet,

Father has been very tired all day, and tonight his temp. is up to 100 after all these days of normal. It may mean nothing—Nurse cant tell anything —but if there is any change tomorrow I will telegraph at once, and dont bother if you dont hear. He is so fearfully weak. Any small thing wd. make such a difference, and he has got weaker even the last few days I think.

Your letter is just in. It will be merciful to see you again. Beatrice took us driving today; she brings tears to my eyes sometimes. 'I like being stroked. No one strokes me' she says simply as a child.

But Violet is my woman. It is ages since you left—and months and months since all this began—a fortnight really, but there never was any time so long.

What has come to my wrist I dont know, but I cant make two consecutive letters, and the whole thing is laboursome.

Take care of your *back*—I am terrible sorry it is bad again. Do get well.

Yr. AVS

Berg

Thursday night [31 December 1903]

My Violet,

Wilson thought Father weaker this morning—his pulse not so good. His temp. has been 100 all day; at 2 AM. it goes up to 102. Wilson thinks the temp. may go down as it did before—but I dont know whether father will be able to live through the weakness which must come afterwards. He has been asleep most of today, very quietly. He sleeps more and more, but is perfectly conscious when he wakes. I think he gets weaker every day— and he takes nothing but a little milk and meatjuice, and that with difficulty. But in a way I feel happier about him—he is less able to think and to worry— and that is the worst thing. But however you look at it, it is a miserable time. If he had died at first it would have been easier, but now one has to give up more—I mean all these days he has been there, and able to talk a little, and one has had time to think—however, I know I shall be glad for him.

We have been tramping Bloomsbury this afternoon with Beatrice, and staring up at dingy houses. There are lots to be had—but Lord how dreary! It seems so far away, and so cold and gloomy—but that was due to the dark and the cold I expect. Really we shall never get a house we like so well as this, but it is better to go.

We are the sanest family in London and talk and laugh as though nothing were happening; Adrian and Thoby are going to sing the new year in! We should never get on without this kind of thing.

I write letters all about ourselves. Dont really hurry back because of us. It will make your husband angry, and there's no real reason except that we want you, which isnt sufficient.

The nurses are rather bothersome, but have now settled to dignity and silence, which is peaceful at anyrate. Traill is depressed, I think a little tired of it all.

Yr. AVS

Berg

146: TO VIOLET DICKINSON   22 *Hyde Park Gate, S.W.*

[January 1904]

My Violet,

This is written in a tearing hurry 11 P.M. We went over the house today.[1] The only thing is we think the rooms too small. It seems absurd, but Thoby and Adrian, possibly George do take up a lot of space, and I think that is a real objection. There isn't one big room, all through. Jack went with us, sensible but discouraging, showed us the neighbourhood which he thinks bad and says we should never get anybody to come and see us, or to dine. The walk to a cab is of course a drawback. He thinks we should have to spend a great deal in doing up, and doubts what we should get for this house. Altogether I think it is rather impossible. For two people, of course it would be perfect. The garden and steps and peace make my mouth water. If only there were more room, and they needed less doing up. Nothing settled yet—but I dont believe we shall take it—Oh Lord—what a bore it is, and my poor Violet took such a lot of trouble, and in some ways I know we shant get nothing near so nice.

Goodnight my Violet and Blessings for all you have done, and do for us.

Yr. Sp.

Berg

147: TO VIOLET DICKINSON   22 *Hyde Park Gate, S.W.*

[January 1904]

My Violet,

This evening he has had a bad attack of sickness again. Wilson doesn't know what it is, but thinks it may not mean anything. Anyhow Rigby comes

1. The Stephen children and George Duckworth continued their search for another house, in Bloomsbury. This particular house is now unidentifiable, and they did not take it.

tomorrow morning, so we shall know more. I believe we have got through the worst, and whatever happens now wont be long. But its a strange world to insist upon these things. You have been—but I find no words to express you!

Take great care of yourself, and come back fresh.

We will telegraph and send all news.

Yr. AVS

Berg

148: To Violet Dickinson   22 *Hyde Park Gate, S.W.*

Tuesday morning [January 1904]

My Violet,

Fathers temp. is still up—101 this morning and they think it may go higher. Wilson can say nothing, except that it is another attack like the first, but whether there will be another fall of temp. or whether he can live through this fever, he cant tell at all. He is fearfully weak, but of course he has still wonderful vitality. It is no use to make up one's mind again that this is to be the last attack; anyhow he will live some days at least. So we are just going about as usual, and trying not to think. Wilson says the whole thing is so mysterious that he would rather not say anything. There is no doubt of course that the bladder is perforated, but as they cant tell what gave that sudden relief, they dont know whether it will return or not.

I will write tonight, and telegraph if there is any sudden change.

Yr. AVS

Berg

149: To Violet Dickinson   22 *Hyde Park Gate, S.W.*

Wed: morning [January 1904]

My Violet,

He is very weak this morning, and can take nothing but milk, but the dr. says there is no real change. He thinks it bad. Temp: going up and down, and he is fearfully weak. It is the same as last time. He is very sick.

I will write again.

Yr. VS

Berg

150: To Violet Dickinson   22 *Hyde Park Gate, S.W.*

Thursday [January 1904]

My Violet,

Father is not so well today, his temp. has suddenly gone up to 102 pt 6—almost 103—and nurse expects it to go still higher tonight late. This is higher than it has been since the first attack, and Nessa evidently thinks it serious though she cant say anything. But of course it may go down again—its no use making up my mind to anything I feel. I think I had better not come to lunch tomorrow—as Wilson is coming in the morning, which may mean about 1. I will let you know what he says, but I dont suppose he will be able to tell anything.

Yr. AVS

I shall probably come round to you about 3 tomorrow, unless you stop me—probably I mayn't, but I shall try.

Berg

151: To Violet Dickinson   22 *Hyde Park Gate, S.W.*

[January 1904]

My Violet,

Just a line. He hasn't been quite so well today; his temperature has gone up a little—over 100, but he says he has no pain, and Nurse thinks it mayn't mean anything. He enjoyed seeing you immensely—and talked to me about you—said you were so charming, and he liked seeing you so much, and thought you were fond of him. He said you had talked of me—and did you talk of him? Wasn't that like Sparroy? I will write tomorrow.

Yr. Sp.

Berg

152: To Violet Dickinson   22 *Hyde Park Gate, S.W.*

[25 January 1904]

My Violet,

I wish I had time, as I have thought to write you a really pretty letter. Such as Sparroy can write. But why the Devil do you think or say that you *bore* me? You are a strange woman. Have you ever bored me or said anything but what was wise witty and delightful in the course of our long and tender intimacy? Modesty is attractive—but Lord preserve me from a fit of it! Your little Book lies by me, very fragrant.

I have had gorgeous presents today. Father gave me a ring—really a beautiful one, which I love—the first ring I have ever had. This time even, has compensations. It amazes me how much I get out of my Father, still—and he says I am a very good daughter! He is the most delightful of people—and Lord knows how we shall ever get along alone. But this is not what I want to say—but blessings on you, past future and present. Think we have asked Nelly [Cecil] to lunch and this coming. Oh Lord!

Yr. AVS

Berg

153: To Violet Dickinson   22 *Hyde Park Gate, S.W.*

Wednesday [February 1904]

My Violet,

Rigby agrees with Wilson. Says he can give us no idea of how long this can last. He thinks father will go on getting weaker and will become unconscious without pain—but I have no idea how long they expect.

It does seem very hard. Life, I am sure, is no pleasure to him—and he would have been glad to die a week ago—but theres no help for it. It is so hard to wait and see him get slowly weaker day by day. But these are the things one has to go through in this Brute of a world apparently.

We were out morning and afternoon, and Beatrice came to tea. She is extraordinarily honest and deep feeling and inarticulate. She lunches with us tomorrow, and brings her carriage.

I will write more another day.

Books are such a mercy.

Yr. AVS

Tell me all about your clothes, and triumphs.

Berg

154: To Violet Dickinson   22 *Hyde Park Gate, S.W.*

Sunday night [February 1904]

My Violet,

Father is worse today, and Wilson thinks he cant get over it. His temp. is 103 and his pulse is very bad. Wilson says he thinks it probable that he will not live a week. He is so much exhausted. Except for the weakness he has no pain, or even discomfort, and he speaks like himself, only he is so terribly weak. Wilson comes tomorrow at 9.30 and will be able to tell us more then, and what we ought to do about sending for Adrian. Nurse is much better; and of course now there can be no question of sending for a new one.

I know that death is what he wants, but oh Lord, it is hard my Violet.
I will telegraph after Wilson has been.

Yr. AVS

Berg

155: To Janet Case   22 *Hyde Park Gate, S.W.*

[February 1904]

Dear Miss Case,

Father is very weak, and has a great deal of fever, but he is without actual pain. He has so much vitality—but they can do nothing. He is quite conscious when you speak to him, and talks as he always did. He asked me today when you were coming, and what I was reading. But he is fearfully tired. Thank you for your letter. I dont think there is any good in going through these things—and it is all pure loss. But that one realises afterwards. You see I'm not in a pious frame of mind!

But we have all been so happy together and there never was anybody so loveable.

Yr. aff.
AVS

Sussex

156: To Janet Case   22 *Hyde Park Gate, S.W.*

[February 1904]

Dear Miss Case,

I suppose you are right, but it seems rather absurd—Your talk is as good as a lesson, and it was my choice too.

Please come sometime—only tell me when, so that I may give orders that they are to let you in.

Father is weaker, I think, but the doctors still say there is no change.

My hand is paralytic with virtuous letters—all so dull and dreary, six of them tonight—

Yr.
AVS

Sussex

[February 1904]

My Violet,

Wilson thinks he is getting quickly weaker, and does not expect him to rally, but cant say any more. He said at any rate he would live through the next few days. He is more comfortable and like himself, and is going to see Haldane today, as he wants to. His pulse is bad.

Yr. AVS

Berg

[February 1904]

My Violet,

Wilson says he is practically the same. He has no doubt that the growth or a clot of blood is preventing the poison from reaching the bladder as quick as it was doing, but he says this may break down at any moment.

Oh dear—it is very hard. He may live a week or so I suppose, or the end may come at any time! They cant tell, and we just have to sit here. But he has no pain, and the fever just now is less. I begin to wish for anything to end this. The waiting is intolerable—but Lord, these things have to be and we have to grin and bear them! The worst of it is he is so tired and worn out, and wants to die I think, and is just kept alive. I shall do my best to ruin my constitution before I get to his age, so as to die quicker!

Yr. AVS

Berg

[February 1904]

My Violet,

Wilson this evening thinks him rather worse. He said a week was the longest. but he may become unconscious at any moment. His temp. now is 103 pt. 4. It went up to 104 again this evening. He says it probably wont go down at all. He was wonderfully cheerful when we went up to say good night, and had asked to see the paper. Rigby comes tomorrow at 12.30. Wilson comes at 9.

It will be a comfort to have you.

Yr. AVS

Berg

160: To Janet Case   22 *Hyde Park Gate, S.W.*

[February 1904]

Dear Miss Case,
    Father is getting slowly weaker, and they say that he can only live two
or three days. But he has absolutely no pain, and still knows us and can
speak a little. There doesn't seem to be anything to say. It is so strange. You
will understand, I know.

                                                    Yr. aff.
                                                        AVS

                        I will write
                                        Wednesday night
Sussex

161: To Violet Dickinson   22 *Hyde Park Gate, S.W.*

[February 1904]

My Violet,
    Father is suddenly a good deal worse. He has had a shivering fit, and
they think the kidneys are affected. He is wandering. Wilson is away till
6.30 this evening. I will write tonight. This may go on some days, I suppose.
The nurses cant really tell one anything.

                                                        AVS
Berg

162: To Violet Dickinson   22 *Hyde Park Gate, S.W.*

[February 1904]

My Violet,
    Wilson says theres no change tonight. His pulse is a little stronger if
anything. He thinks he sees people in the room sometimes, but when we
said good night he was perfectly like himself.
    Kitty came this evening, and Nessa was pleased, also Jack. Kitty was
very nice, Nessa said. I didnt see her.

                                                        AVS
Berg

[February 1904]

My Violet,

Don't think me a crazy tempered Beast for the way I growl. With no one else shd. I dare to behave so badly. But this is devilish hard, and I believe he is very bad. Nurse thinks this may be the beginning of unconsciousness— he is wandering a little tonight. However, there's nothing to be said—but that at all times you are the comfort.

Yr. Sp.

Berg

164: To Violet Dickinson   22 *Hyde Park Gate, S.W.*

[21 February 1904]

My Violet,

Father has been becoming less conscious all the afternoon and evening. He now does not know us. Wilson says the poison must have reached the kidneys, and he does not think it possible for him to get any better. He says he may die tonight. It is 11.30 now, and he comes again later, so I will add anything. Father was very restless, talking to himself, but Wilson has given him morphia so that he now lies quite quietly.

11.30. Wilson just been. He says there is no change, and thinks he will probably get through the night. They give him morphia if he is at all restless, so he has no pain, and simply lies without moving most of the time. I will telegraph tomorrow morning. We are sending for Adrian.

Dont come, my Violet. Stay quiet, and get well. There is nothing to be done. I have been sitting with him—so have we all. It is quite peaceful. He doesn't take any notice. He seemed a little better this morning. and saw Kitty and talked away: it came on quite suddenly at 2.[1]

Yr. AVS

Berg

1. Sir Leslie Stephen died on 22 February 1904 at 7 a.m.

Letters 165-178

A few days after Leslie Stephen's funeral, Virginia went with her sister and brothers, and George Duckworth, to Manorbier on the Pembrokeshire coast, where she resumed her writing. At Easter the four Stephens, with Gerald Duckworth, went to Italy, Virginia's first journey abroad apart from a childhood trip to northern France. They stayed a few days in Venice and Florence, where Violet Dickinson joined them, and on their return through Paris they visited Rodin's studio and met Clive Bell at a dinner which was to prove a turning-point in Virginia's life. She had discovered the type of friend and conversation that she most enjoyed.

165: To JANET CASE   *22 Hyde Park Gate, S.W.*

Tuesday night [23 February 1904]

Dear Miss Case,

It [the funeral] is to be tomorrow at 3 at Golders Green. We shall go.

Father died very peacefully, as we sat by him. I know it was what he wanted most. Nothing now can hurt him, and that is what one has dreaded.

But how to go on without him, I dont know. All these years we have hardly been apart, and I want him every moment of the day. But we still have each other—Nessa and Thoby and Adrian and I, and when we are together he and Mother do not seem far off.

                                      Yr. aff.

Sussex   AVS

166: To JANET CASE   *22 Hyde Park Gate, S.W.*

[26? February 1904]

My dear Miss Case,

I send you these books which I hope you will like to have. I can hear his voice in every word of them, and that is what one wants more and more—I think of all the things one might have said and done, and never did.

Thank you so much for coming the other day. It was a real pleasure—though I feel a brute for talking of our bothers when you have so many of your own.

                                      Yr. aff.

Sussex   Virginia Stephen

Manorbier R.S.O.,
                                           Pembrokeshire

28 February 1904

My Violet,

I am happy about that ring. I dont mind how much foil they put so long
as I have it the same as when he [her father] gave it to me. I began to think
I might have spoilt it for ever.

We have come to the right place. Never were people so lucky as we are
in practical things. The house holds us perfectly, and is warm and comfortable,
and I havent seen such splendid wild country since St. Ives—indeed one
thinks of St. Ives in many ways. We have already spent an astonishing
amount of time walking about on the cliffs. Even lying in the sun. We live
almost under the shadow of a great feudal castle, which stands on a cliff
over the sea. Nessa and I have walked right along the coast already, never
meeting anyone.

There are about 3 houses here, and a wild queer Church on the hill.
It is cold, but very clear and bright, and no sound but wind and sea.

Thoby is wild with his Birds—there are all kinds here; and George
tramps about too with his glasses.

I dont want to think; I feel like a cow with her nose in the grass, but
I know that here in this quiet [*illegible*] it seems more natural and less terrible
than it did. The dreadful thing is that I never did enough for him all those
years. He was so lonely often, and I never helped him as I might have done.
This is the worst part of it now. If he had only lived we could have been so
happy. But it is all gone.

However, I wont write it; and generally I am in such an animal state
that I dont think it.

We are all very well, and this is the most resting of lives. It is a comfort
to write to you.

My Violet.

Yr. AVS

Berg

168: To Violet Dickinson   *Manorbier R.S.O.,*
                             Pembrokeshire

Friday [4 March 1904]

My Violet,

I have been a bad beast about writing, but mercifully that doesn't affect
you. The relations have been relieving their souls in pen and ink ever since
we came here—saying quantities of things which dont mean much, and
clamouring for letters. I saw the Pilot and some other newspapers, but not
one seems to me to have said a word that one cares to remember. I daresay

somebody who takes more trouble will write something in one of the Reviews, but it dont much matter. Father used to say that it would amuse him to read his own obituary notices, but I dont think he would have got through these. Stupid fools! I could have written them better. Aint it odd what very dull impressions people seem to have got of him.

What are your views about coming down? It is rather a delicate question, so that we had our doubts about writing. Your husband may think it bad for you, and you may have heaps of things to do—and you wont like to say so. There's nothing like simplicity in these matters, and I trust you somehow to say what you think. As you know by this time, you harmonise us wonderful well.

The only attractions we can offer are that the house is pretty warm and comfortable and our climate is much better than yours, so you could lead the quietest life—nothing agitating about us! Large tea and other meals and no more walking or talking than you like. Is this a good advertisement? We are entirely barbaric, do nothing all day long, and really there is some joy in the country.

This paper is like granite slabs to write upon, which affects my very brain.

We make queer little expeditions every other day with Georgie. He seems to think it helps to pass the time, as I daresay it does.

I begin to want my books again—and yet half dread them.

There are quantities of pictures for Nessa I should think, even from the windows.

I am priming myself to write to Nelly after this. Lord how I hate it!

All this stupid writing and reading about father seems to put him further away, only I know nothing can do that, and I have the curious feeling of living with him every day. I often wonder as we sit talking what it is I am waiting for, and then I know I want to hear what he thinks. It was a most exquisite feeling to be with him, even to touch his hand—he was so quick, and that one finds in no one else.

My Violet—I hope to see you—but if not—Sparroy is firmly planted in that cabbage patch you call yr heart.

Yr. AVS

Berg

169: To Lady Robert Cecil

Manorbier, R.S.O.,
Pembrokeshire

4th March [1904]

My dear Nelly,

We never thanked you for a carriage you send some time ago, which took us for a long drive. It was very good of you to think of it. I remember it came round just as we wanted an excuse to get out of the house, and escape relations!

This is a very strange wild place, something like the Cornish Coast. We live like barbarians, and never see anyone, but I hope Violet may come down. I dont know how long we are going to stay here, as there doesn't seem much object in anything. But I hope we shall see you, if we are in London together. You have been so good to us. Violet doesn't say how you are. I'm afraid weather like this is not encouraging, anyhow it cant be worse.

Vanessa sends our love. We have two Uncles with us here—one old and one young.

Your aff^{ate,}
Virginia Stephen

Hatfield

170: To Violet Dickinson   [*Manorbier, Pembrokeshire*]

8 March 1904

My Violet,

Should you mind being bothered with a horrid job? I must get some clothes. Could you buy for me anywhere stuff to make 2 blouses: one thin, sort of muslin or something: one thicker, black, and send the stuff to this address

E. Clarke
35, Green Street
Chelsea, S.W.

I think they might be spotted or striped or something not quite plain. Oh how I should swear if you were to ask me to do this kind of job! I dont know how many yards one wants. The shop would know. Would you pay out of this cheque?

George has gone back, which is, though I am a brute to say so, a relief. He never lets one alone a moment. Very well meant, but wearisome. I begin to dread our joint household, but it cant be helped. Nessa and Thoby and I get on very well together. It is so odd being alone, for the first time in our lives.

It poured all yesterday. Today Thoby has gone fox hunting on foot. His energy is marvellous.

My ring has come back, but it is very disappointing. The man says I have ruined the stone. It is rather a better colour, but full of odd cracks, and marks, as it was before. They must be in the emerald itself. I dont know what to do, as it isnt a bit like what it was when he gave it to me—and yet I dont like having a new stone put. I think I must though. Waters says he has done everything possible.

Yr. AVS

Berg

[March 1904]

My Violet,

You are a good woman. The stuff is perfectly right, much better than I could ever have got for myself.

Our plans are upset again. Gerald says he's going to Venice on the 1st and suggests taking us, which is I suppose sensible. Then we could meet you in Florence about the 7th—or whenever you chose. What a dream it sounds! I suppose it will turn out real though. I dont find the affairs of this world easy to realise. Much thinking would send me down bottomless pits I know.

I cant believe that all our life with Father is over and he dead. If one could only tell him how one cared, as I dreamt I did last night. You dont mind my filling my letters with egoistical complaining—very dull, but I cant help writing them to you. It is so hard to talk even to ones own brothers and sisters.

Since I wrote my ring has improved wonderfully. I cant think why, unless its being in the light that does it—but it has got much cleaner and a better colour. I shall certainly keep it. Of course it isnt right, but it is rather attractive looking.

I have had a long letter from [Nurse] Traill. She is in Edinburgh, but is going to the Barnardistons at York soon, which she seems to enjoy. No letter from Beatrice. I can see her biting her pen to the stump!

Why stay with Earle?[1] She is a rancorous woman. I never read such positive nonsense as her books are.

Yr. AVS

Berg

13th March 1904

My dear Mr Norton,[2]

You will of course have heard long ago of Father's death, but I should like to tell you that it was in every way the end that we wished for him. He was talking to us all on Sunday morning in his most vigorous and cheerful way—about books and people—and saying that he felt less tired than usual. He also saw a friend and she was amazed at his strength and interest in everything. Half an hour afterwards he became unconscious, at least he did not know us though he talked to himself constantly. This was on Sunday afternoon—All that evening he grew weaker, apparently without

1. Probably Mrs C. W. Earle, author of *Pot-Pourri from a Surrey Garden*.
2. Charles Eliot Norton was Professor of the History of Art at Harvard.

any pain—and he died at 7 on Monday morning so peacefully that one could only feel happy for him.

His dread always was lest he should lose his power of thinking, or should have to suffer pain. Of course all through this long illness he was often very tired and weak, but he had no actual pain, and his mind never seemed clearer or more brilliant. He was able to read on the last morning of his life, asking me to bring him an article on Shakespeare and a new poem by Thomas Hardy—and almost every day he saw two or three friends. Even though he was so ill I think this last year of his life was a happy one; he seemed so peaceful and glad—almost surprised—at the love of all his friends and the admiration which people have shown him more than ever before. I think there was no one so loveable. He often talked of you, and enjoyed every letter you sent him. Your letters, he told me, were some of the very few he cared to keep, and he gave me each as it came to add to the others. The last you wrote reached us after his death, and I have put it with the rest. I do not know if you have any photograph of him or would like to have one. We had several taken just before his operation in December 1902. They are, I think, as good as photographs can be, though he looks more ill than he did afterwards. I will send you one, in case you may like it.

> Your affectionate,
> Virginia Stephen

Houghton Library, Harvard University

173: To Violet Dickinson   [*Manorbier, Pembrokeshire*]

[March 1904]

My Violet,
    My plate would be empty without your letters. *Of course* come to lunch on Tuesday. I suppose we are to spend next week in a devils whirlpool of shops and dentists. I shut my eyes, and trust to luck to land me safe somehow and some time at Venice.
    Great travelling enthusiasm has seized us: we spend our evening following impossible routes with our fingers across the map—all wish to go different ways.
    The difficulty seems to be Gerald: however I let that slide with the rest. We are to travel through Good Friday. Somehow Geralds figure never did make part of the Venetian foreground I have in my mind!
    That scrap of Beatrice is characteristic: that is her great merit—never does or says anything quite as other people do. Did she mean that she couldn't write us banalities, or you?
    I never seemed to realise that you were still to let Manchester St.—shows what a egoist (as Kitty would say) I am. But for Gods sake dont get carried away to Chelsea or Kensington. Kitty already screams against

Bloomsbury. I dont think Nessa much minds—or thinks that distance from Montpelier [Kitty Maxse's house] is a drawback to her friendship. After all, I beseiged your icy heart in Manchester Street. That I always hold up as the type of an adventurous expedition—North Pole nothing to it!

I had a letter from Nelly too: but I shant make much of a job in that quarter. And now Hester is lost to us: who can you find me to flirt with?

I find the country a good place to work in.[1] I have really finished quite a lot. So has Nessa.

Now we have to look for rooms for Adrian [at Manorbier]: his landlady has just had a Baby, which will be a source of interest to him. He is domestic.

Oh dear, what a world it is! I keep thinking I shall find Father at home—and what I shall tell him—I wonder how we go on as we do, as merry as grigs all day long.

Yr. AVS

Berg

174: To Violet Dickinson   [*Manorbier, Pembrokeshire*]

[March 1904]

My Violet,

We come back late on Saturday. I suppose you will be at the cottage. Thoby has an exam: on Monday, I think. I must say I shall be rather glad to get back—why I dont know. This place is really beautiful, but the nature of the beast is perverse.

Adrian came down yesterday, and we have now decided that he can easily go with us for the first 3 weeks. He stays on here alone to work, and then we shall all go out [to Italy] together. I expect Gerald will find it more convenient on the whole to go alone. Five of us is too large a party to be luxurious.

Adrian is wildly excited already—talks of nothing but Venice and gondolas. This is the right spirit. You cant think how amicable we all are together—like husband and wives, more than anything else—and the odd thing is we dont get bored at all, but go our own ways, and meet fresh and cheerful.

I am reading and writing and have almost finished a Greek tragedy in the last few days—and that is what I call sensible!

Nessa has made a really good little picture of Thoby sitting by the window, and reading. It is very clever, and alive I think. Now we are all going out for 2 hours walk along the cliff to show Adrian the beauties of the place.

1. On 3 September 1922 Virginia recalled in her diary that she had for years been uncertain what book to write. "That vision came to me more clearly at Manorbier aged 21 [22], walking the down on the edge of the sea."

We saw Choughs and Ravens the other day, climbing up rocks to get at them, and rolling about in the maddest way.

Our only excitement has been the death of the washerwoman! As she stood at her tub. The village thought there ought to be an inquest, but didn't know how to begin; the doctor and policeman arrived separately from neighbouring villages, and refused to do anything without the other. So finally the village determined on its own account that death was due to natural causes, and have just buried her, going past the window in the oddest way. The first 6 rows of mourners held black edged handkerchiefs to their eyes, or mouths: they weren't crying; and the rest look fairly cheerful. Aint it barbaric? As you can imagine the whole village turned out to watch, and last night the young men who have nice soft voices sang a hymn under our windows.

My ring has certainly improved since it came back: it still has cracks and queer things if you look into it, but the general effect is rather beautiful, and I shant anyhow change it.

I had a beautiful letter from Fred Maitland[1] this morning: almost the only one I have had worth keeping.

Yr. AVS

Berg

175: To Violet Dickinson   22 *Hyde Park Gate, S.W.*

Thursday night [31 March 1904]

My Violet,

I must write you my last intelligible line, because I know it wont be possible in Venice—I only hope you are having a good rest, and that Crum doesn't worry you—as I do. I wish I didn't exhaust you over my affairs, but you cant think what a relief it is to have someone—that is you, because there isnt anyone else to talk to.

You mustnt think that I always feel as I do sometimes. I know that I wasn't really wrong: it had to be—but I cant bear to think of his loneliness, and that I might have helped, and didn't.

If he had only lived I could have made up. I think he just knew how much I cared, and the happy time was just beginning—and now it is all over. That is what seems so cruel. If I could only tell him once—but its no use writing it. But we have been very happy together. My Violet—it is a help even to write this to you.

1. Frederic William Maitland (1850-1906), the biographer of Leslie Stephen. He had known the family for many years, and married Florence Fisher, Virginia's cousin. Leslie Stephen had himself invited Maitland to write his 'Life'. It was published in 1906.

Keep well, and come out as soon as you can,[1] and dont worry about me, because I have a faculty for turning my mind on to other things, and I never stay long in one mood. Besides I know that Father was happy at the end, if only he could have lived. People dont believe it, but I know he wanted to go on living. Just as a young man does.

Goodbye my Violet

Write one of your beautiful little letters, all illegible tho' they be!

Yr. AVS

Berg

176: To Violet Dickinson   *Grand Hotel, Venice*

4 April [1904]

My Violet

This is the first possible chance of writing a letter. Think of this—when we arrived at midnight on Saturday we were told there were no rooms here or anywhere in Venice! Finally we got three very dingy little rooms—sleeping together in a dirty little place off the Piazza S Mark. We spent Sunday walking the streets—went to your rooms—all the rooms we had ever heard of—but all were full—and we had to go back for another night. Today we have got 3 rooms here. Nessa and I sleeping together: it is extravagant but it cant be helped. Of course we were fools not to settle beforehand.

However it dont much matter: we are quite happy lounging about and looking at things. There never was such an amusing and beautiful place. Gerald is bored to death, and very cross, and makes us take gondolas and doesn't like exploring back streets at all. Thoby and Adrian are rampant with excitement; A. wants to settle here for ever. They go about shouting with laughter and trying to speak Italian. We have a room here right at the top just at the side of the Grand Canal: beneath all the gondolas are moored, and the gondoliers make such a noise I cant think coherently. It was the strangest dream to step out into our gondola after those two days of train. But I cant be bothered to write about it! Nessa sits scribbling at the same table. It is rather cold today: yesterday was divine: only the place is crowded. We travelled with the Humphry Wards who, happily, have disappeared. It was an exciting journey, though it seemed endless—There was a snowstorm on the St. Gotthard: we came down into brilliant sun shine, and the lakes were pure blue. The mountains had snow all over them. Isnt this like a guide book? I wish we knew Italian. It is stupid to have to talk broken English and French—and, as I say, we get cheated everywhere. But they are a delightful people, and we—us four at least—are rapidly approaching their state of mind—general benevolence. I wish you would come out as soon as ever you

1. Violet was to join the Stephens in Florence.

can. I dont think Florence will come up to this. I cant quite believe it is a real place yet and I wander about open mouthed. We have had to go to so many rooms that we haven't done any sightseeing, except such as comes in every street. We walked all down the Schiavoni last night—where the buildings looked cut out of marble, and a great gondola hung with coloured lamps floated by. But I cant find words yet. Gerald probably goes on Thursday or Friday. I think he will be glad to get safe to Monte Carlo. Come as soon as you can.

Yr. AVS

Berg

177: TO EMMA VAUGHAN   *Palace Hotel, Florence*

25th April 1904

My dearest Toad,

We called at the Post Office the other day, providentially as it turned out, because your Post Card had just arrived. As you can imagine it is very precious to me—but how on earth did you come by it? Are you staying in Canterbury—have you run away with Canon [F. J.] Holland, are you married to the Sub Dean? Anyhow, how is it that you are in these sacred Precincts? There is no lovelier place in the world than Canterbury—that I say with my hand on my heart as I sit in Florence—and I have seen Venice too. Venice is a place to die in beautifully: but to live [in] I never felt more depressed—that is exaggerated, but still it does shut one in and make one feel like a Bird in a Cage after a time. We had a horrible big Hotel to stay in, which is not favourable to sentimental impressions. Still the pictures *are* pictures: till you have seen Tintoretto you don't know what paint can do. We floated in gondolas, eat ices at Florians, while the band played, and met more honeymooners than I like. All the world seems to be coupling itself. We are told that you never see Venice until you are just married; 2 is the right number—and we were 5!

We have been here a fortnight: it is a lovely place, just not lovelier than Canterbury, I think—but I dont know. The view from Fiesole—the country round Fiesole, San Servasio etc., is almost more beautiful than anything I have seen. I wont write a dissertation upon the Italian landscape because I know it would bore you. It is an amusing pretence to leave England by going to Florence (grammar all wrong). We find Prinseps,[1] Lytteltons, Humphry Wards, Cambridge Undergraduates, Carnarvons, and finally to make us feel quite at home, Aunt Minna [Duckworth] and Edith!!! We went to see them at their hotel, a gloomy lodging house near San Servasio. Aunt Minna looks more wrinkled and faded than ever, but she talks of people who

1. The children or grandchildren of Virginia's great-aunt Sarah Pattle, who married Thoby Prinsep.

are "much older and deafer than I am". May we all die like that!—she doesn't mean to die though.

Our next move is vague—our travelling is not so delightful that we wish more than is necessary. There never was a *beastlier* nation than this in its railways, its streets, its shops, its beggars, and many of its habits. My dear Toad, where is a decent woman to look sometimes? We went to Prato today and it poured all the time, and we saw the only thing worth seeing, and were set upon in the streets by innumerable small boys, and cripples. We walked faster than the cripples, but one devil of a small boy had the diabolic idea of following us wherever we went; and finally promised to leave us for 2 soldi. We didn't pay him, and he cursed us and went. Was there ever such a nation?

We have had a good offer for Hyde Park Gate; that makes us anxious to get back, as our new house must be got ready as soon as possible. We shall probably be in London again about the middle—14—of May. I think we shall stay in Paris for a week or so and leave here in two or three days. Violet D. is with us. Adrian has gone, and Thoby is walking among the Apennines.

Couldn't you write me a long letter as soon as you get this, addressed to me C/o Thomas Cook, 1 Place de l'Opera, Paris, I do want to hear everything: especially Fisher news, music news, any news. Everything English sounds clean and beautiful: we seldom see the papers, and to live in a degenerate tho' beautiful country is depressing. Thank God, I say, I was born an Englishwoman. Adrian and I sang paeans of thanksgiving on the top of San Miniato, one evening. Germans are brutes:—and there is a strange race that haunts Hotels—gnome like women, who are like creatures that come out in the dark. An hotel is a sort of black cave. This one is really very good of its kind.

Love to Marny. How are M[adge] and W[ill]?

Yr.
AVS

Sussex

178: To Violet Dickinson   [*Paris*]

[6? May 1904]

My Violet,

I discovered a letter written to you, but not sent. It was in my pocket all the time, when it should have been sending shocks and thrills through a maiden bosom in [Welwyn] Hertfordshire. We have had our Beatrice [Thynne] and she has flashed across us, and disappeared, leaving us rather gaping. She stayed exactly two days, in which she managed many more sights than you ever did, and preached like the valiant old Heathen she is.

She is as red and tough as a very fine apple; her face is positively muscular, with character which seems to have stiffened there. We took her to dine with Bell last night, a real Bohemian party, after her heart. Kelly[1] the painter was there, and we stayed talking of Art, Sculpture and Music till 11.30. This was all in the common cafe, while we smoked half a dozen cigarettes a piece. Kelly is an enthusiast, and Beatrice seeing this contradicted him. She expounded theories on Wagner which were, I know, made that moment. He actually shook his fist at her across the table, and at one moment I held her down—a stormy scene.

She left early this morning: to dine with some Cromer relations. She has originally meant to stay 6 weeks with us: I cant say, though I love her, that I think 6 weeks would have been successful. Now we go and see Rodins studio tomorrow morning, with Bell and Kelly—and that is our last expedition! Oh Lord, how cross I have been, how dull, how tempersome,—and am still. You had much to stand: I wish I could repay all the bad times with good times. There should be some system of repayment in this world—you believe in a next, I know, for that purpose. Oh my Violet if you could only find me a great solid bit of work to do when I get back that will make me forget my own stupidity I should be so grateful. I *must* work. We leave early on Monday. When will you come? Case says that Katharine [Horner] works hard, with a little pressure, but she gives no opinion of her brains. I would sell mine cheap at this moment. I cant write a word I want to, as I have forgotten everything.

Keep well. Both nieces will never forget all you did for them.

Yr. AVS

Berg

1. Later Sir Gerald Kelly, President of the Royal Academy.

Letters 179-188

The day after her return from Paris, Virginia suffered a severe mental breakdown, her second. "All that summer she was mad" (Quentin Bell, Vol. I, p. 90). Violet Dickinson took her to live in her house at Welwyn under the care of three nurses, and there Virginia attempted suicide by throwing herself from a window. In September she was sufficiently recovered to join her family on holiday in Nottinghamshire, and to resume her writing. Next month she stayed with her aunt Caroline Emelia in Cambridge, where she was in close touch with her brother Adrian, still at Trinity, while Vanessa and Thoby organised the move from Hyde Park Gate to a new house in Gordon Square, Bloomsbury. In September George Duckworth married. While at Cambridge, Virginia began to read through her parents' letters for F. W. Maitland's Life of her father.

179: To Violet Dickinson   *[The Manor House, Teversal, Nottinghamshire]*

[September 1904]

My Violet,
    Nessa said you wouldn't mind coming. I dont know how to write to you now, but if you didn't hate it too much I should like to see you. I haven't done a thing you told me to.

Yr. loving
AVS

Berg

180: To Violet Dickinson   *[The Manor House]* Teversal
[Nottinghamshire]

17 Sept. [1904]

My Violet,
    You are an angel to write. I think you have set us on our legs again. Really, I have been a good beast since you went—no grumblings—this is quite true. [Nurse] Traill and I and Thoby and Adrian begin the morning with an hours walk, directly after breakfast. From 10.30 to 12.30 I do Latin with Thoby. Then we play tennis, lunch, and go for a drive. After tea we play tennis, and have a walk when it is dark. I hope this interests you! At any rate it is some kind of a plan to go by.
    Nessa has got a model. You know we really get on very harmoniously

together, and I dont mean to have any more disgusting scenes over food.[1]

Savage[2] is away—drat him! You have heard that our last begging letter has been answered—and we are lent a Town house this time. I think we shall go there on Friday the 7th. Also we have had an estimate for moving wh. comes to £18.10. Also Colvin and Spielmann think that At. Virginia ought to fetch 200 or 250 if sold to the family.[3] The decorations at Gordon Square[4] are to be done in a fortnight. I cant think of any other businesslike facts.

Traill has been offered a case in Paris this winter, which has put her into a good temper. Altogether we are in better spirits than before you came. Isnt this a tribute to your beneficent powers? You cant think what a difference you made. Thoby and Adrian ask why you aren't coming here again?

Yr. AVS

Berg

181: TO VIOLET DICKINSON

*Manor House, Teversal,
Notts.*

[22? September 1904]

My Violet,

It is a great filip [*sic*] to get your letters—short though they be. You will be glad to hear that your Sparroy feels herself a recovered bird. I think the blood has really been getting into my brain at last. It is the oddest feeling, as though a dead part of me were coming to life. I cant tell you how delightful it is—and I dont mind how much I eat to keep it going. All the voices I used to hear telling me to do all kinds of wild things have gone—and Nessa says they were always only my imagination. They used to drive me nearly mad at Welwyn, and I thought they came from overeating—but they cant, as I still stuff and they are gone. [Dr.] Savage hasn't written, but I dont so much mind about that now.

I am glad cats are so prolific at Welwyn, and that my germs haven't killed them all. I wish you would convey to your husband how immensely

1. During her periods of madness, one recurrent symptom was her refusal to eat.
2. Dr George Savage (later Sir George), an old friend of the family, who treated Virginia during her illness. In the course of his career he was Physician-Superintendent of the Bethlehem Royal Hospital for the mentally disturbed, President of the Medico-Psychological Association of Great Britain, and Examiner in Mental Physiology, University of London.
3. A portrait of Virginia, Countess Somers, Virginia Stephen's maternal great-aunt, by Sir William Richmond.
4. 46 Gordon Square, Bloomsbury. During Virginia's illness the Stephens had taken a lease of this house. Gerald had decided to live on his own, and George had married on 10 September Lady Margaret Herbert, daughter of the 4th Earl of Carnarvon.

grateful we are to him—and I had no way of showing it or feeling it at Welwyn. I think of all the ferns I ought to have pulled up, and of the dining-room floor. Do give him any message that is proper, and make him understand our thanks.

Nessa looks really better, and we are very happy together. I really think she is happy with me now.[1] I am glad about Miss de Rhode [*unidentified*]. I am sure she has a character. What will happen to the Governess?

Bless you.

Yr. Sp:

Even this letter would have been beyond me before.

Berg

182: To Violet Dickinson
Manor House, Teversal
[Nottinghamshire]

26 Sept. [1904]

My Violet,

If we go up on the 8th we shant begin operations [on the move to Gordon Square] till the 10th—when your help will be badly needed by your nieces. I hope your Husband, and Mrs Lyttelton dont think that we are exacting too much—of course we *are*!

Oh my Violet, if there were a God I should bless him for having delivered me safe and sound from the miseries of the last six months! You cant think what an exquisite joy every minute of my life is to me now, and my only prayer is that I may live to be 70. I do think I may emerge less selfish and cocksure than I went in and with greater understanding of the troubles of others.

Sorrow, such as I feel now for Father, is soothing and natural, and makes life more worth having, if sadder. I can never tell you what you have been to me all this time—for one thing you wouldn't believe it—but if affection is worth anything you have, and always will have, mine.

It is queer now that I am better that I feel physically so much more. I am rather bothered with neuralgia, but that goes away with food and fresh air, and I hardly attempt to do more than bask and eat.

It will be nice to see you again. Nessa so happy.

Yr. loving,
AVS

I am longing to begin work.

Berg

1. During her illness Virginia had mistrusted Vanessa.

Manor House, Teversal
                                    [Nottinghamshire]

30 Sept. [1904]

My Violet,

All the things belong to us, the paper knife is my most valued possession!
—but could you keep them and bring them up with you to London, if it's
not too much bother. We leave so soon, that it doesn't seem worth while
having them here.

I am so happy that people are fond of me—you cant think. Beatrice
wrote me a letter which I shall treasure. I do love affection!

We have got [Margery] Snow[den] and [Clive] Bell here, both very easy
people, who can be left to their own devices.

We take immense walks, from 9.30 to 1. which are a balm and blessing
to my spirit.

I am longing to begin work. I know I can write, and one of these days
I mean to produce a good book. What do you think? Life interests me
intensely, and writing is I know my natural means of expression. I dont feel
up to much, as far as my brain goes. At least I soon get tired of reading, and
I haven't tried to write, more than letters. I have a headache at this moment,
so I wont go on.

I have taken to smoking a pipe, which the doctor thinks an excellent
thing, and I find it very soothing.

Oh my Violet, I do want Father so—and yet I am very happy in a way.

                                        Your loving,
                                                AVS

Take care of yourself. I am going to write to your husband and Mrs Crum.

Berg

The Porch, Cambridge

Saturday [22 October 1904]

My Violet,

Your letter just come, which keeps me in touch with the outer world.

This is an ideal retreat for me. I feel as though I were living in a Cathedral
Close, with the big bell of the Quakers [Caroline Emelia] voice tolling at
intervals. She is soporific, and leisurely to an excess, and my desire begins
to be to blow her up with gunpowder, and see what would happen! However,
as you say, she is a real Lady, and large minded, after her fashion, which
aint mine!

I slept this morning till 4.30, which is the best nights sleep I have had for a week, and sleep makes all the difference to me. I can sit alone by an open window for hours if I like, and hear only birds songs, and the rustle of leaves. The trees are pure gold and orange, and no place in the world can be lovelier than Cambridge. It is a very small world, I expect, as far as society goes, but what there is is amazing, and all well known to me.

Florence Maitland took me for a walk this morning. She is one of the most delightful, original, and beautiful people I know, and it is a real treat to see her. I am going this afternoon with her, and Adrian and the Quaker to hear Fred [Maitland] give the Sidgwick lecture at Newnham. Florence is most amusing: "Jane Harrison[1] has let herself go" she said to me. "Jane is a great admirer of Freds. I had to tell her she was positively indecent! She thinks Fred so beautiful that she would go anywhere to see him. Repulsive woman!" She is great fun, and is going to introduce me to the repulsive Jane, and all the other learned Ladies, which amuses me.

Oh my Violet, do you think I am going to stay 3 months at every house I visit, that you send me provisions for an army! However, the Quaker biscuits are always stale, and when I wake I eat yours always, and drink chocolate. That supports me till it is time to get up. You are a wretched spendthrift woman—who is going to feed *you* with biscuits when you are in the workhouse, I should like to know? Coffee too this morning: the stuff they give me is undrinkable. Tomorrow I am to have yours.

I heard from Nessa, very happy, in the arms of her Kitty [Maxse], who comes of course the moment my surly back is turned. But I am very glad.

I am going to see Fred Maitland on Monday, which I very much want to do. I feel as though I could write something worth adding or quoting, to the Life [of Leslie Stephen]. But he is perfectly capable of understanding everything.

I hear the Quaker trumpeting like an escaped elephant on the stairs, which means that it is near lunch time, and Quakers dont like to be kept waiting for their meals! I will introduce the subject of the book,[2] and your stay here. Copies abound, and she is as vain as most authors. I want Beatrice to come and stay too: else I shall hardly see her before she goes.

Adrian is delightful and glad to have me, I think. Really I feel better out of that whirlpool.

Yr. loving,
AVS

Berg

1. Lecturer in classical archaeology, Newnham College, Cambridge.
2. *Quaker Strongholds*, 1891, by Caroline Emelia Stephen.

24th Oct: [1904]

My Violet,

Your letter is a treat. I feel established in this minute Cambridge world already. Lord! how dull it would be to live here! There seem to be about 10 nice and interesting people, who circulate in each other's houses—Darwins, Maitlands, Newnham, etc. I went to see the Maitlands yesterday, and he is coming to talk to me this afternoon. I am going to offer to write down some of the things I remember—especially of this last year, when he was out of England. Nun wants me to very much. I see she is rather nervous of giving her own recollections, which weren't altogether happy or characteristic, and yet she seems to be the great authority. She has a very good hoard of diaries, of her own and her Mothers. Her Mothers are most amusing and interesting. She kept records of all her children said and did from the time they were born till 1873. Some of the child sayings are quite delightful, and extraordinarily characteristic of him as a man, and of the Quaker, who always makes haste to agree and to offer Lellie [Leslie] her best toy when he has broken his! I want Fred to get hold of some letters and publish them. Nun has a few, but they are excellent—beautifully natural and expressive like his talk. The difficulty is to find who has got, and kept, his letters. I have none.

I dont sleep much: otherwise I am very well, much less tired than I was in London. A bad night doesn't make the difference it did, and I have had no headaches since I came here—so I think the Quaker must be doing good.

I quite understand—only too well—Fathers point of view about her. I dont know what it is, but I can sometimes hardly sit still, she irritates me so. She is perpetually flowing with rather trivial talk, which nevertheless she takes great, and painful, care to express well, and pronounce exquisitely. Also I disagree entirely with her whole system of toleration and resignation, and general benignity, which does seem to me so woolly. I cant tell you how she maddens me when she begins to talk about Father. It is pathetic too—but oh such trash! She always manages to get hold of the wrong explanation of everything he ever said or did or wrote—at least so it seems to me. She always gives in to my opinion, and says "Oh of course you knew him much better than I did." It is a good deal to dispose of her theories that I want to write something for Fred, who must naturally be guided a good deal by her.

Now, my woman, to business. When could you come here, and should you really like to come? I am perfectly happy alone, so dont come out of charity. Of course, I want to see you, and so does the quacking Quaker, who says she feels much in common with you, and can never thank you sufficiently for all you have done for her dear ones! This week, I think Nessa is coming on Wednesday for 2 nights, and Nun has asked Dorothea Stephen for 1 night on Friday. So could you come on Monday, or early next week? and stay as long as you can. She was much touched by your wanting 'Quaker Strongholds' and I think wants to give it you herself, and inscribe it when you come. Nessa seems to have done most of Gordon Square housework, and to be dining with Kitty and various people. Make her understand that she is on no account to make an effort to come, if she is busy, because, tho' I want her naturally, I can subsist without her, and I am very well. I think she would be amused with 2 days here, and Adrian is very anxious that she should come—also the Quaker. Also Fred Maitland wants to see her, but I suppose that could wait. Dont let her come if she has other things to do.

I went to Meeting on Sunday, but as this is a devilish long letter, I wont say any more. It *will* be fun if you come!

Yr. loving,
A VS

Berg

186: To Violet Dickinson   *The Porch, Cambridge*

30th Oct: [1904]

My Violet,

I was very glad of your letter. Nessa's visit was delightful, and we talked the whole time, not on altogether soothing subjects though. I cant make her, or you, or anybody, see that it is a great hardship to me to have to spend two more long months wandering about in other peoples comfortless houses, when I have my own house [Gordon Square] waiting for me and rent paid regular on Quarter day. It is such a natural thing from an outsiders point of view, that I get only congratulations, and people say how lucky I am, and how glad I ought to be to be out of London. They dont realise that London means my own home, and books, and pictures, and music, from all of which I have been parted since February now,—and I have never spent such a wretched 8 months in my life. And yet that tyrannical, and as I think, shortsighted Savage insists upon another two. I told him when I saw him that the only place I can be quiet and free is in my home, with Nessa: she understands my moods, and lets me alone in them, whereas with strangers like Nun I have to explain every random word—and it *is* so exhausting. I long for a large room to myself, with books and nothing else, where I can shut myself up, and see no one, and read myself into peace. This would be possible at Gordon Sq: and nowhere else. I wonder why Savage doesn't see this. As a matter of fact my sleep hasn't improved a scrap since I have been here, and his sleeping draught gives me a headache, and nothing else. However I shall have a few days in London next week, which will be some relief, and meanwhile I can let off my irritation upon you! Nessa contrived to say that it didn't much matter to anyone, her included, I suppose, whether I was here or in London, which made me angry, but then she has a genius for stating unpleasant truths in her matter of fact voice!

I have written to ask Madge [Vaughan] to have me about the 16th, as Savage approves—really a doctor is worse than a husband! Oh how thankful I shall be to be my own mistress and throw their silly medicines down the slop pail! I never shall believe, or have believed, in anything any doctor says—I learnt their utter helplessness when Father was ill. They can guess at what's the matter, but they cant put it right.

This is a long and egoistical grumble, but I do get so sick of it all at times; this eternal resting and fussing, and being told not to do this and that. I wish I could cut off my leg at once and have done with it rather than go through the endless bothers and delays of a nervous breakdown.

However, I have had an amusing day with Beatrice, who is splendid fun. We lunched with Adrian, and went to a divinely beautiful service in Kings Chapel. Nothing comes up to the Church Service in these old Cathedrals; though I dont believe a word of it and never shall. Still the language and the sentiment of it all are dignified and grand above words. Beatrice's high voice is now going on down stairs, as she sits opposite the Quaker, and they discourse to each other till 7, when I get up—I am lying down, and descend. Beatrice leaves at 8. I think she has enjoyed herself, and I always feel that she is one of the pathetic people who do enjoy a happy day to the full.

I am getting through my copying—and now I have to go through 2 vols: of extracts from Father's and Mother's letters to each other. They are so private that Fred wont look at them himself, and I have to decide what he ought to see and possibly publish. I am very anxious to get on and write something, very short of course, which Fred can read and get a hint from or possibly quote from. I think I shall do this at Giggleswick[1] where I can be really quiet. But there is so much writing of different kinds to be got through while Fred is in England, that the other must wait.

The Quaker has stupidly asked a great dull Stephen cousin to stay here for 2 nights—Monday to Wednesday. You will be a great relief afterwards, and we will go to Meeting together. Would Mrs Lyttelton[2] like a description of a Q. Meeting from my gifted pen, d'you think. I dont know if I shall have time, but it might be amusing. G[eorge]. and Margaret [Duckworth] talk of coming down here one day—and I devoutly pray it may be when you are here. Otherwise I shall hardly see her till after Christmas—a hardship I can bear more philosophically than some! He will be buzzing round Gordon Sq: Indeed everyone is except one of its lawful owners!

Yr. AVS

Berg

1. Will Vaughan was appointed Headmaster of Giggleswick School, Yorkshire, in 1904.
2. Mrs Arthur Lyttelton, Editor of the Women's Supplement of the *Guardian*, a London weekly newspaper for clerical readers, and a friend of Violet Dickinson. This offer was Virginia's first tentative move toward journalism.

1st Nov: 1904

Dearest Todger,

To begin with, admire our new address[1]—not that it is a faithful guide, because I am at this moment staying with the Quaker Aunt at Cambridge. Do you remember a terrible afternoon last spring, the 10th May,[2] about when you came to call—and borrowed some letters! (wh. I hope you have safe) I was then hardly knowing what I did or said, and wondered if you noticed it. Well, for at least three months after that, I was more or less incapable of doing anything but eat and sleep, and had to be watched by three fiends of nurses. However, thank Heaven, that nightmare has dispersed at last: only Savage says I must live like Totty or Clara [Pater] the life of a valetudinarian for the next year. My main grievance at present is that I have to spend the next two months out of London—and as Gordon Square is ready and lovely, full of books and pictures, my language is not measured. When I tell you that I am going in about ten days to stay with your dear sister-in-law and brother, the Head Master, at Giggleswick, you will wish yourself in my place, I know!

This summary of the six and a half months that have passed since we met is necessary, though egoistical. Go then, and do likewise my dear Todger. As for you you have vanished in blue mist: where I ask Marny *repeatedly* in a letter, 'where is the Toad—is she eloped or married or what.' She pointedly ignores my questions and discourses of Hogsden [Hoxton] instead. However, with patience I have extracted the news that you are in Dresden, enjoying yourself hugely. How long are you going to enjoy yourself hugely in the middle of Europe, the oracle sayeth not—nor in what particular line your enjoyment lies. Do throw aside your toadish dumbness, which seems to have infected the Marn and give a brilliant account of yourself. Also say at what date your clammy feet will touch these shores—and come and pay your respects at Gordon first thing. We have had some interesting passages with the Fishers, of a highly diplomatic kind. I called at At. Mary the first thing during my ten days' visit to London—which ended in Exile here. She was immensely touched to see me, though I only stayed ten minutes. Then Nessa called and saw her, and took Tom [Edwin Fisher], who is nice, back to Gordon Sq. I have had several affectionate letters from her—but the amazing thing is that the ice cold Adeline [Vaughan Williams] has descended from her heights and has left a card on us—which happily found us out. After our heroics last winter when she practically said all was over between us, I was amused. The fact is, she is anxious to have a finger in the pie, and has now no legitimate excuse for a grievance. So it is more picturesque to be

1. She wrote this letter on stationery headed "46 Gordon Square, Bloomsbury", to which she added the Cambridge address.
2. The day when Virginia's mental illness began.

friends—however, she dont say nasty things for nothing—and *I* have climbed my heights and stay there at present, calmly indifferent. The great Ralph [Vaughan Williams], I hear, from Florence, is giving a concert at the Queen's Hall, composed *entirely* of his works: on the 2nd Dec: I think—when I shall be at Giggleswick, probably.

I must explain this big envelope, and the MS inside. The other day I turned out the accumulations of my writing case, and a sallow, Egyptian looking parchment caught my eye, covered with hieroglyphs. It was the MS of the famous account of our never to be forgotten (as your Germans would say) punt disaster,[1] which had stuck to me, humbly and dumbly, through all these years of neglect. So, having nothing better to do and *a pair of gold rimmed spectacles*—mark my age, I read it, and copied it as best I could in the largest and boldest hand—so that even your toad-dark eyes may read. I hope you will feel a little English when you read this account of the joys of an English summer. Oh how vividly that all comes back to me now!

I suppose you have heard the two tragedies which made last week one of the gloomiest I have known—The death of Charles Furse,[2] and the death of Margaret Hills,[3] Eustace's wife, in a bicycle accident. Of the two, Margaret's death is the sadder, I think; though they are both sad enough, but she had had fewer years of life, and her death seems merely aimless and cruel. Had she waited two minutes longer on the road—had her wheel not slipped—had it not rained the night before—she might be well and strong, and live to 90. Whereas, Charles' death was long thought of, I suppose, both by him and Katharine; and she must have known what a risk she was taking when she married him. But what a wrong thing it was of him to ask—and of her to accept, one sees now that she is left with two baby sons. She is to live at Netherhampton with Harry Furse and his sister.

I am going up to London on Monday for a week, to have my teeth mended and a dress made, and then I go down to Madge's for a week, I suppose: then back here to Cambridge till the 10th Dec: when Adrian's holidays begin and then we go together on a wild expedition by steamer to Edinburgh! Ain't that sporting! It is cheap, anyway—five days, there and back, for £2.10.0 and we love the sea. Then we all four hope to get lent At. Minna's cottage in the New Forest for Christmas—and then—*and then*—to settle down at home. That is the goal to which I look forward. You remember what your homeless vagrant days were like, without a picture or a book of your own, and only the houses of strangers. I have done that for seven months now—have to get through two months more—and never has a time been more miserable. Now, in answer to all this and in gratitude for the

---

1. See letter 27.
2. The artist, husband of Katharine Symonds, Madge's sister. He was 36 when he died of tuberculosis.
3. Jack Hill's sister-in-law.

MS, write me a long, long letter—46 Gordon Square will always find me, as I can't give exact addresses now.

Your loving,

AVS

Sussex

188: To Violet Dickinson   *The Porch [Cambridge]*

[November 1904]

My Violet,

I am dreadfully sorry you cant come—and so is the Quaker—but I suppose you are right, and anyhow I shall see you Monday or Tuesday.

As a matter of fact I ought to stick to me letter reading and copying so as to give Fred [Maitland] an important bundle before I leave. I thought it would take 2 days—and it has taken six!—but I hope to finish tomorrow. Then I have all Fathers and Mothers and Minny's [Harriet Thackeray] letters to read, select, and copy, which will be the hardest job of the lot. It is not made easier by the excellent Jack Hills: I told him casually that I was going to do this, whereupon he wrote an emphatic solicitorial letter beginning "Whatever you do, *dont* publish anything too intimate" etc etc etc. ending however, that he knew my views were totally wrong, and he should dislike whatever I did. So I wrote another and better explanation pointing out that I probably cared 10,000 times more for delicacy and reserve where my own Father and Mother are concerned than he could; and declaring that anyhow if I made a selection, it was to be final. Then comes a letter of 8 sheets; all abuse of my principles of selection; ridiculing the idea that *I* should set myself up to judge what it was good for the world to know etc etc etc. and repeating as usual that whatever I did, was sure to be wrong. Now, as I am doing what I dislike, against my will at Freds wish, and as the excellent Jack never knew nor understood Father, and has no more sense of what a book ought to be than the fat cow in the field opposite—I was considerably angry —and wrote him the letter which I am thinking of enclosing for your amusement. Burn it, and dont tell Nessa you have seen it. She substantially, in fact wholly, agrees with me, but I see from her letter this morning, that she cant stand up against the authoritative Jack. He deserved something a good deal sharper I think; and if I have to discuss the question any more, he shall get it. After all, it is not *I* that am writing the Life: My whole part in it is to copy and select from letters, and Fred Maitland has his own notion of what a life ought to be, and will carry it out without asking my opinion. If Jack wants to interfere, he ought to write to him direct, instead of pestering me with his thickskulled proprieties!!!

Jack always manages to put his great hoof down with a clatter on precisely the most delicate and difficult side of every question. He is legal and dry as dust to the back bone, poor little redtape tied parchment Solicitor! But I wont have him interfering where Father is concerned!

There—I let off the remains of my indignation upon you. Happily the Quaker has mounted her warhorse too, and strongly disapproves of the "very unintelligent behaviour" she calls it of Mr Jack Hills. Fred has, as I knew he would have, very clearset opinions of his own: if I wanted to, I could not alter them—but as it happens I entirely agree. It is a mercy that we have him to write it: else some one of the Hills variety might do it, and that would make me turn in my grave.

My life here is practically spent with old letters, and so my news is limited, Nessa was here for 2 nights, very cheerful and happy. The Quaker intones as usual. Adrian comes in like a vigorous daddy-long-leg's, and brings a breath of fresh air into the place. Otherwise it is a humdrum little society, which has but a small orbit or axel or whatever the thing is—to revolve upon. I am going with Florence Maitland this afternoon to interview a blue Persian Kitten which I think of buying for my room at Gordon Sq: I cant sleep a bit better, and I know as certainly as before, that Gordon Square is the *only* place where I can be quiet. However I dont expect any doctor to listen to reason.

I shall be glad to see you—and take care of yourself.

Yr. AVS

You see the degenerating effect of much writing upon my hand!

Berg

Letters 189-221

Virginia was soon well enough to embark on two new activities. The first (and less important) was to teach English Literature and History at Morley, an adult-education college in South London. The second was to write articles and reviews for the weekly and monthly press. Her first articles were published in the clerical journal The Guardian *in December* 1904, *and in the early months of* 1905 *she also began contributing to* The Times Literary Supplement, *the* National Review *and* The Academy. *She was to live at Gordon Square with Vanessa, Thoby and Adrian, and meanwhile paid visits to Madge Vaughan at Giggleswick, Yorkshire (where she wrote an article, her first for publication, on the Brontë Parsonage at Haworth), and to her Aunt in Cambridge. Christmas* 1904 *was spent by the Stephen family in the New Forest.*

189: TO VIOLET DICKINSON   *46 Gordon Square, Bloomsbury*

[8 November 1904]

My Violet,

As I came up in the train today, I thought to myself can I afford to buy a really nice china inkpot, for my walnut desk. And I came to the virtuous conclusion that I must put up with an ordinary glass one. This was virtue rewarded, because, when I came into my room, the first thing I saw was your lovely and most satisfactory and exactly what I had thought of inkpot, with all his holes, and a well for ink deep enough to write a dozen articles for the Guardian. But you know you've no right to make me presents, and your a bad beast. I'm going to get some real good black ink tomorrow, to christen it with. Gordon Sq: when I'm not there indulges in slate coloured water, like that I'm writing with.

I am feeling really quiet and happy and able to stretch my legs out on a sofa for the first time for 7 months. If only that pigheaded man Savage will see that this is sober truth and no excuse!—I know I shall sleep tonight as I haven't for a month. The house is a dream of loveliness after the Quaker brown paper. Nessa very very happy. We will pick you up tomorrow. The row with Jack has blown over. Violet's delicious.

Yr. AVS

Berg

Thursday [10 November 1904]

My Violet,

I came upon this kind of essay which I wrote at Manorbier. It aint up to much, as I was writing then to prove to myself that there was nothing wrong with me—which I was already beginning to fear there was. Also I wrote very quick and hasty—without thought, as they say, of publication. But the Quakers words bear fruit; and I think I may as well send this to Mrs Lyttelton to show her the kind of thing I do. Of course I dont for a moment expect her to take *this* which is probably too long or too short, or in some way utterly unsuitable. I only want to get some idea as to whether possibly she would like me to write something in the future—at Giggleswick for instance. Could you address this to her office address, which I dont know. I dont want her to think that she has got to show me the *least* favour, because of you!

Miss Case is very anxious that you should come with us up to Hampstead next Wednesday afternoon? Can you?

We are going.

Sleep no better—but I am *much* better here than anywhere else.

I do want to see you.

Yr. AVS

Berg

11th Nov: [1904]

My Violet,

What a bore about poor old Case—she was anxious to cultivate her friendship with you. Of course you and your husband must come to dinner. We had Florence Maitland here today, and she said that my diamond and ruby ring was supposed to be priceless, and originally belonged to our greatgreatgrandmother [Thérèse de l'Etang], the Frenchwoman whose portrait Nessa wears in her locket. She (Florence) has a sapphire brooch which belonged to her, for which she was offered £500!! She was a rich old Lady, and most of our things apparently descend from her, and are old French.

I dont in the least expect Mrs Lyttelton to take that article[1]—I stupidly didn't typewrite it—indeed wrote it myself rather hurriedly and illegibly as I hate copying—and forgot to give my address, or to enclose a stamped envelope for return. So I dont think my chances are good. I dont in the least want Mrs L's candid criticism; I want her cheque! I know all about my merits and failings better than she can from the sight of one article, but it

1. The article was not printed, and the manuscript has not survived.

would be a great relief to know that I could make a few pence easily in this way—as our passbooks came last night, and they are greatly overdrawn. It is all the result of this idiotic illness, and I should be glad to write something which would pay for small extras. I honestly think I can write better stuff than that wretched article you sent me. Why on earth does she take such trash?—But there is a knack of writing for newspapers which has to be learnt, and is quite independent of literary merits.

So I dont much care if she does say my writing wont do; except that I must try and get someone to take it. My hope is that she will say she would like to see other things. I could easily re-write some old things, or write new ones, if I have time, better than the Manorbier I sent her.

You will come to lunch on Tuesday.

My sleep is not better, except that I think I am less wide awake and get more rest, although I do lie awake from 4 onwards. I have a kind of feeling that I shall sleep when I go to bed, and that is half the battle. I am *miles* better than I was, and I cant see the sense of going away again. I am better and quieter here than at Cambridge.

Yr. AVS

I will try your prescription!

Berg

192: To Violet Dickinson   46 *Gordon Square, Bloomsbury*

Monday. 14th Nov: [1904]

My Violet,

Mrs Lyttelton must be a very sensible woman. Do bring her letter with you to lunch, as if I'm to try any other paper with the Manorbier article her criticisms however stringent will be worth attending to. Of course Manorbier was rough as hemp, under the circumstances—and I think anyhow, with a renewed brain I ought to do better now. But 1,500 words rather apalls me. I could write 3,000 twice as easily; 1500 is a very short article, and would have to be boiled down. However I am too delighted to have a chance of turning an honest penny to mind what I do for it—and she is very generous to allow me any subject—as that gives me a large field.

My precious MS. book, which would have given me hints for dozens of articles is lost in the move, so I shall have to write something new. At present I must toil at the [Leslie Stephen] letters, which are in four great bundles; besides I have 3 great bundles of [Charles Eliot] Norton letters to read through and mark, and Fred [Maitland] writes this morning that he cant get through all he hoped to do before sailing, and wants to leave a good deal for me to finish—references and copying I suppose, which takes time. Then I have to write something for him—however that can wait—and a cheque or two wouldn't come at all amiss. The family coffers are low—I sent my pass book to the Bank 10 days ago, and they have never sent it back, so I dont know the state of my private income. Still I want if possible, to pay rather more than my share this winter, to make up a little for those d——d nurses and doctors.

D'you think Mrs Lyttelton will let me write fairly often?—and what does she pay for these little articles? Not much, I suppose—indeed they aren't worth much—and I cant conceive why she has them. Would she let me review ever? I want to get the Cornhill or some magazine like that to take longer and better articles. Leo Maxse [Editor of the *National Review*] might!—however that must wait.

Fred sails on the 10th, so I shall have finished by then.

Sleep better rather last night. It will be a treat to see your elongated shanks again—and at dinner too. Pernel Strachey is lunching.

Yr. AVS

Berg

193: To Violet Dickinson   *Giggleswick School, Settle, Yorkshire*

21st Nov. [1904]

My Violet,

Here I am, sitting at my window under the moors, which are all white with snow and frost, and the temperature is below freezing. I keep warm with a fire, and a fur rug; and I might be in the heart of the Alps. The snow stays sometimes on the Hills till June or July, they say. The School is in a little hollow by itself, with great craggy moors on all four sides. I am longing to get a good walk out among them, but so far Madge has had bothersome little School duties to do, and I have not had a chance to get beyond the garden hardly. The country with its moors breaking into gray stone and gray stone walls instead of hedges and stone houses reminds me of Cornwall, and I always expect to find the Atlantic.

I have done my round of School duties—Lectures, Concerts, Chapel, Hall—and my word it is deadly. We have not had a meal alone so far—always either boys or masters. So I dont get much talk with Madge, and whenever we are alone for a minute in blunders Will, like George, and begs me not to let Madge talk morbidly. He is rather afraid that my influence upon her is not a good one, she says—and is always reminding her of her duties as the Headmasters wife. He *is* curiously like George: only with more solid brains; but he is conventional to the back bone, and loves all the small dignities and duties of his position. Madge only longs for amusing un-conventional people—artists and writers—and as she says—only Madge says many things without meaning them—Will is a Philistine and thinks there's something wrong in cleverness.[1] I cant help wondering whether she wouldn't have been happier unmarried—at least to Will. She does seem thrown away here. She loves the country of course, but the life is deadly, and she has no friends—there aren't any people for her to be friends with—except among the masters and one or two old Maids in the village. She is very charming, and artistic, and works away like a hero, and tries to take an interest in football and school contests but I cant conceive a drearier life for anyone— let alone Madge. She is probably planted here for life. Will is an excellent old Blunderbuss, very sterling and honest, but thickheaded and conventional till, as I say, he rivals his cousin George. He has none of George's tact, so that daily life is not made smooth by him. The children are delightful; very healthy independent little animals, not in the least shy of me; indeed I have just had to drive them all off my knee, and to refuse to tell them another long story about a Dog. I have already invented a great many wonderful facts about Wolves and Horses which they absorb very literally, and ask me all kinds of impossible questions. I was amused yesterday when in answer to Janets [Vaughan] demands I described the appearance and habits of the dragon—whose picture I wear in my watch chain. I had to make him as horrid as possible; and suddenly I found that Wills paternal eye was on me disapprovingly; he didn't like his children to be told fables, especially on Sunday. They have their Sunday books—but I must say, they dont seem to suffer in spirit. Madge is always trying to make them go their own way, and have their own ideas—and Will wants to "discipline" them in true pedagogic manner. However he is a most devoted Father, and husband for the matter of that—though somewhat a blind one, I think.

I think I sleep rather better—more soundly when I do sleep, and that makes a great difference.

Madge is longing to know you, and asks me always to describe you— which is difficult—except that you are 6 feet 2, and very comic looking!! She is very anxious to come and stay with us, as soon as she can get away from this infernal school, and she wants to meet people. She is like a starved bird up here, and it is quite pathetic how eager she is to talk, and how full of idea's and theories—which have to be silenced the moment Will comes in to the room—or he would call them "morbid".

Here a maid comes in to say that the gardener is taken very ill, and may she go for a doctor. Madge of course has to go off in the snow to the gardeners cottage—Will wont let her take brandy unless the doctor orders it. So here she comes back again; the doctor *does* order Brandy, as the man's heart is bad in the sudden cold; so she makes another journey, and then the maid tells her that she must have a Char in to help—and so it goes on—and the unfortunate novel which Madge is longing to write at, having the mood on

1. Yet Will Vaughan had a distinguished career as a schoolmaster. After leaving Giggleswick, he became Master of Wellington College (1910-1921) and Headmaster of Rugby (1921-1931).

her, wont get much done to it this morning I foresee. Will takes it all as part of the days work, and novel writing and everything else of an artistic kind must give way before it. I must say Madge takes it like an angel. It makes me rather angry though.

Mrs Lyttelton hasnt sent me any books yet, but as I haven't had a moment to write—except at the letters—I am rather glad. I expect they will turn up today. I hope she will say when she wants the reviews, and I will do my best to make a good impression.

I was to tell the truth, which need not be repeated, a little taken aback by [Lady] Margaret [Duckworth]. She is elderly[1] and dried up, and no mistake: I tried to be affectionate, but she evidently preferred to talk about the weather, so I didn't bother myself. She is clearly kind and good meaning, but there is nothing interesting or attractive about her—and never will be— that is the worst of it. If she were young, one could have hopes—but she will stay just as she is till she dies—dull and respectable and with beautiful manners. However they sound happy, and if they can manage that it dont matter what I say. Write again.

Yr. AVS

Berg

194: TO VIOLET DICKINSON

Giggleswick [Settle,
Yorkshire]

26th Nov. [1904]

My Violet,

I begin to loathe pen and ink after copying letters all the morning, and writing stupid articles for Mrs Lyttelton. She has sent me a book by Howells,[2] which she says is good; I haven't read it yet. I wish people wouldn't tell me what they think of books when I know I'm sure to disagree! However I must do my best. I have written her an article on Haworth,[3] so I wont go into details about that. I wrote it in less than 2 hours, so I dont suppose it is very good; but I never do know about my things, and Madge likes it.

Here we go on in the same way—endless teaparties of boys and masters and now the old ladies of Giggleswick have taken to asking us out—so we are rather sociable. I have had two good walks on the Moors though, alone, which I thoroughly enjoyed. The snow is as hard as ice, and not melted at all. It was 13 degrees below freezing last night, and except for the sun it aint much warmer today.

1. She was only 34.
2. William Dean Howells. The novel was *The Son of Royal Langbrith*. Virginia's review, in the *Guardian* of 14 December 1904, was her first published work.
3. Her article on Haworth Parsonage was published in the *Guardian* on 21 December 1904.

Madge is delightful, and we discuss literature and other things for hours on end. She is like a clever and loveable child, but not in the least mature. She and Will as I see more every day, are perfectly happy. She says herself that no life could suit her better, though she makes the most of her grumbles. She worships him, and refers to him in everything: and there is a great deal that is charming and clever about him besides all his solid good qualities. He is really the saving of her, and keeps her going in all kinds of ways. I cant imagine what she would do without him to decide things for her. They are a charming pair.

That silly old Nessa has been absorbing Savages theories as usual. I cant conceive how anybody can be fool enough to believe in a doctor. I know he will soon climb down and tell me what is the fact. That I am quicker and better in London than anywhere else—just as he had to give in about walking alone, and being isolated. My life is a constant fight against Doctors follies, it seems to me. Of course I dont sleep any better here, though I get quite a good amount and feel perfectly well. I think of my perfectly quiet room at home, where I need never talk or be disturbed with a pang. Lord what fools people are. I am coming up on Tuesday.

Yr. AVS

(here are some Brontë pictures for you) [postcards]

Berg

195: To Emma Vaughan   *Giggleswick School, Settle, Yorkshire*

Nov: 27th [1904]

Dearest Toadlebinks,

This is practically my last day here, and I know you would like a letter from the sacred precincts—(I wish to goodness Giggleswick Church Bells could be silenced, or rung in tune—my lack of harmony must be put down to them).

I have been here 10 days and go on Tuesday. Time enough to observe the Vaughan family and my conclusion is entirely favourable, your Brother, the Headmaster, is a most charming man; and his wife is very lucky in her husband—but then he is very lucky in his wife, they are equally blessed. Really they are delightful people to stay with; and for the first time in my life I have seen Madge perfectly happy and content with her lot. She doesn't rant—except against the world in general—and has developed a passion for paying calls, so if you walk with her down the main street, she stops and speaks to every other person, and she seems to enjoy it fully. Oh Lord those bells! The vicar seems determined that those who don't go to Church shall have their evening spoilt. It is deafening. I think the ringers are trying to keep themselves warm with hard arm-work. It is 13 degrees below freezing, snow fell a week ago and is now hard ice; the roads are glistening like glass; the boys spend their time tobogganing, and Madge as you can think, is in her element. At last she begins to respect our English climate.

Your nephew and nieces are most delightful children. I have at last found someone to understand me and that is Barbara, who can't yet speak but cuddles in my arms. Children are really the greatest fun in the world—the only happy people. Janet is very lively and handsome, but at this moment inclined to be uppish and pushing. That will wear off as Madge and Will snub her; Halford is much slower, but a darling fat sleepy little boy with lots of character and determination. A regular Vaughan in fact, whereas Janet is a Symonds.[1] We have endless boys and masters to tea, who are none of them very exciting, but they are nice—Madge gets on splendidly.

I have to go to Cambridge next till the 10th then we all go to Minna's cottage at Lyndhurst for Xmas, and we settle down I hope at Gordon for the New Year. I saw Marny the other day, who seemed very well and happy. When in the name of wonder are you coming back? Not till January I suppose. I have forgotten your address, so I must send this *via* Marny.

Yours,
AVS

By the way, I am reviewing novels and writing articles for the Guardian and so hope to make a little money—which was our old ambition.

Sussex

196: To Violet Dickinson   [46 *Gordon Square, Bloomsbury*]

29th [November 1904]

My Violet,

Why didn't you come round this afternoon? I arrived safe 2.15. Couldn't you lunch tomorrow, or tea or anytime. I have no engagements. I go to the Quaker on Saturday anyhow—also George and Margaret go (1st class) to the Darwins. It will be great fun, not but what I hate starting off again.

I have an article for you to criticise: I think I'll send it now and you can give it me with yr. remarks: I dont know if its any good or not.

Yr. AVS

Why is life "*Beastly*"?

Berg

1. The children of Will and Madge Vaughan were: Janet (b. 1899), later Dame Janet Vaughan; Halford (b. 1901); and Barbara (b. 1903, but she died in 1909). There was a second son, David, born in 1906.

30th Nov. [1904]

Dearest Mama Vaughan,

Your infant travelled quite safely, and changed at the right place, and didn't lose anything—except the precious stick, which I left at St Pancras and can easily get back. I finished my novel in the train, and wrote my review this morning in ½ an hour, and sent it off, so that was pretty quick, I wont say good, work. Here I find everything much as usual, the house very lovely, with certain improvements in furniture, which have been exciting Nessa's mind a good deal. Gerald *did* come to dinner, as I foretold; and is very anxious to stay with you, so do ask him. It would be very good for him to lead a healthy life, and he would be much touched to be asked. He said with great pathos "Dear Madge, I always liked her, but I thought she didn't care about me" I went out and got you 2 patterns of chinz; the green is the one I have: the blue is the same, save for the background. The price is on them. They come from Maples. I like the green up immensely, and I think it would do very well in your room. Also it doesn't Dirty soon. I also send Thoby's pamphlet[1] which will make you laugh, I think, and an article in the 19th Century about Palmistry in China, which amused and interested me. I will snuff round Covent Garden for vegetables in a day or two.

I am extremely well, and all the better morally and physically for my moor air; and the equally bracing fireside breezes. Now to what do you think that refers? I hope I taught you the rudiments of petting foster children, but you will have to stay here to be made perfect—do you hear—I walked to the zoo this afternoon, tell Brotherboy [Halford], and found it quite near, and heard all the Dragons lashing their tails and gnashing their teeth till the blue fire spurted from them—oh horrible! I have several more true and unhappy stories for them, as well as a few untrue and happy: how like life! Sophia is longing to make a big cake for Brother boys tea.

I find Nessa and Thoby in the whirl of fashionable dissipation—out every night, I think. All *my* invitations have been refused, so I sit over the fire alone, and long for a good talk with a Brazilian Ape [Madge], only she always got so sleepy. As I write these photographs arrived, and I send two of the best. Will you return them as I have to send them to Fred Maitland. If you wd. care to have them, I can easily get you copies. No news from that wretched man your husband, so I suppose his scruples or whatever they are have taken him to the St Pancras Hotel. I wish he would find my stick.

Kiss my beloved Carry [Barbara] for me, and Janet and Brother Boy— only he'll have forgotten Cousin Virginia as he threatened.

Yr. loving AVS

---

1. Thoby had written and circulated at Cambridge a pamphlet against compulsory chapel.

I must send the photograph tomorrow as they are too large for an envelope. Send me my George Eliot with an inscription.

Sussex

198: To Madge Vaughan   46 *Gordon Square, Bloomsbury*
1st Dec. [1904]

My dearest Madge,

I wish you would send your long rigmaroles—but in default I like your coherent letters very much too—too much. I do enjoy flattery! I never seriously meant to deny myself the pleasure of writing, however bad it be for the public morals!—As a matter of fact I am vain enough to think it had better read me than more popular authors. "Genius" is not a word to be used rashly; it gives me enormous pleasure, and something more than pleasure, that you should find anything of that kind in me. I am no judge; and honestly dont know from hour to hour whether my gifts are first—second or tenth rate. I go from one extreme to another; but when I am in my lowest depths I shall haul myself out of the water by reading your words of encouragement because, however extravagant, I know you mean them honestly. I cant help writing—so there's an end of it. I am very glad too, that in spite of my imperfections I did not seem to you finally intolerant and hard—which are two things I very much dislike. Your researches into my hand went to show that my heart was just as strong as my head, remember; and if I'm not sure of my brains power I am quite sure of my hearts power; and that I do care for certain people—you for example and those heavenly— (and earthly) Babies. Quite permanently. So let us strike a friendship! It came over me in the train that instead of staying with people in future, I should take two rooms by myself, next time. London gets too hot. This was not suggested by any discomforts at Giggleswick!!—but I thought that 2 rooms of my own, would give me greater freedom, and I could stay longer without the witness of a visitors book! So your suggestion of a room at Brookside is very timely. I will let you know when I feel inclined to come— and then I should be free, and we could see as much or as little of each other as we wanted. Dont forget the house for the summer.

I am just back from a tea with Lotta [Leaf, Madge's sister], who wished for news of you, which Will had already given her. I found Katharine [Furse, also Madge's sister] and Lina Waterfield[1] on the doorstep, and had a talk with Katharine which I very much enjoyed. She is very sad and splendid, and strikes one at once as full of a grave kind of courage—a reasoned courage

1. Lina Duff Gordon, with whom Madge had collaborated on *The Story of Perugia* (1898).

162

I mean, which will last her all through this terrible time I know. For however she takes it [Charles Furse's death], it *is* terrible, as one can see. I was amazed at the way she talked—so sweetly and naturally and she is coming to see us. She is one of the people I should like best to know. Lina was very beautiful, and softer than I expected but I did not talk to her. She seemed much more un-affected than I used to think—not that I ever knew her.

Your letter was a real treat; so write again.

Yr. AVS

Sussex

199: TO VIOLET DICKINSON   [*The Porch, Cambridge*]

Tuesday [6 December 1904]

My Violet,

Here I have been going on much as you left me. The Quaker is slightly more vegetable, without you to stir her up, and has begun to get out family annals which bore me to death, and reads them aloud after dinner. She reads as though she were intoning a prayer, and I have to call all my niecely duty to bear it.

I lunched with Adrian today, and met Mr Headlam,[1] whom I always like, though you think him a flirt. He is one of the people who really cared for Father and Mother—he has pictures of them both in his rooms—and besides he is a true artist in his way, which attracts me more than anything else in people. An artist is always so much more simple and sincere than anyone else, though he may be flirtatious too. Still there are flirts who aren't artists. It is pouring wet, for which reason perhaps I have had a pain in my back most of the day, though I had quite a good night, except for dreams. It is rather a bore, and I have to go out to tea with a great stupid school girl whom Nun wants me to befriend. However I daresay my tonic will take away the pain. It is such a bore to feel useless.

I am writing a comic life of Aunt [Mary] Fisher, as a pendant to the Life of Caroline Emelia.[2] I think it ought to be amusing, as she is a promising subject. Two novels[3] which look bad have come from Mrs Lyttelton. I haven't heard whether she will take my Haworth or what she thinks of it. Dont bother to read through the green book; those things are only essays and experiments and I dont think I want to print any of them—I had rather write fresh things than polish up the old—and they would want a lot of polishing. I think I have about finished the Letters for Fred, as the 2 last

1. Walter Headlam, the poet and scholar, was Lecturer in Classics at King's College, Cambridge.
2. These 'comic lives' of Caroline Stephen and Mary Fisher have not survived.
3. One of which was *Next-Door Neighbours*, by W. Pett Ridge (*Guardian*, 4 January 1905).

bundles have nothing worth copying in them. They are merely scraps about us, and other worries—of which they had many. The history of Laura[1] is really the most tragic thing in his life I think; and one that one can hardly describe in the life. The letters are full of her. If you see Mrs Lyttelton try to find out how often I may write for her with a chance of being accepted.

Your AVS

I got you and your husband (!) a Christmas present yesterday!

Berg

200: To Violet Dickinson   [*The Porch, Cambridge*]
8th Dec. [1904]

My Violet,
      Why should you trouble to write two letters, when one is quite good enough—too good—for me? Really I am surprised that you find that blessed green book any good at all. I remember hammering out those articles when I ought to have been doing Greek grammar—and having to stop writing of a sudden when Case came into the room. So I concluded that they couldn't be much good. I think you quite a first rate critic! and I'm not sure I shant appoint you Critic in Ordinary.
      I wrote a review this morning, and also an obituary notice of poor old Shag,[2] who was killed by a hansom, Nessa says. His was a most pathetic history, and I hope Mrs. L[yttelton] will print it, and make poor Sophies [Farrell the Cook] heart glad. She never could get reconciled to Gurth. But you will probably think it trash—and say so, if you do. Dont bother Mrs L: if she's busy. My proofs haven't come, but I dont want them. I want to get on with Mary Fisher while I am in the mood. These things amuse me, and if they make you grin, so much the better. Its the Quakers 70th birthday today; so I gave her two pots of flowers, and she gave me some frills such as she wears for my neck and wrists! which she sat up to make last night. They are really rather nice. I told her I wanted a treat to celebrate the day, so as she was going out, she stopped at a shop and bought me some chocolates, and herself some solid almond paste, and Adrian some chestnuts. We are going to eat as much as we can after dinner over the drawing room fire! Really the old Lady has a sense of humour; and I ventured to say that death on her 70th birthday from a surfeit of almond paste would not be a seemly end for the Light of the Quakers of Cambridge—at which she laughed.

1. Laura (b. 1870) was the only child of Leslie Stephen's first marriage, to Harriet Thackeray. As a young child she was seen to be mentally deficient and spent most of her life in asylums, where she died in 1945.
2. Shag was a dog. The article, 'On a faithful friend', appeared in the *Guardian* on 18 January 1905.

My back hasn't ached for 2 days, thanks to the tonic, though I had rather a bad night again last night. I dont feel so tired today though.

I shall come up on Saturday afternoon—and oh the peace of being at home again! This week *has* been long.

Yr. AVS

I saw Fred M[aitland] this afternoon for the last time. He wants me to write something of what I remember, for him—so that will give me something to do after Xmas. I want to do it as well as I can.

Berg

201: TO MADGE VAUGHAN   46 *Gordon Square, Bloomsbury*

11th Dec. [1904]

Dearest Foster Parent—if that is your proper title—

I am very glad that Brother boy [Halford Vaughan] likes his book and liked opening his parcel, which is the chief joy of getting presents. It is quite true that I still know all my beasts from their pictures in Bewick[1] which we were shown before we could listen to reading aloud. I should think Pennant[2] was not a great naturalist! I have been to Cambridge and come back, and now have no more visits to pay, thank the Lord!—isnt that polite! The Quaker was still quaking much as I had left her. Indeed she will still be there in her same gray dress and shawl 100 years hence. I dont think she will ever die. For one thing she spends so little vitality, of which she has originally a great fund—never walks, or goes out, and does nothing but talk mellifluously and eat great quantities of cake and almond paste. So I dont see why she should ever come to an end. I dont know why I discuss this cheerful subject! I hope, on the whole, you wont adopt Quaker principles—which do the human spirit cool—except the dress—But even that is too tolerant, and shapeless to be beautiful. I was rather bored with her discourse, except when I excited her to a religious discussion. You will say that I am criticising as usual—but after all it strikes me that *you* were the more critical of the two of us at Giggleswick! I mean you criticised me, certainly; which I dont mind, because I think criticism the only sound basis of appreciation—What a grand sentence—fit for the Guardian! The Quaker has the deepest horror of criticism and is always pulling herself up for it; but her tolerance is far more severe than any criticism—She is never enthusiastic.

Here I find that the world gets on pretty well without me: Nessa and

1. Thomas Bewick, the wood-engraver, whose best-known books were *Quadrupeds* (1790) and *British Birds* (1797 and 1804).
2. Thomas Pennant (1726-1798), the naturalist and traveller, whose books on animals also became classics.

165

Thoby dine out a great deal, and go to dances, where they distinguish themselves. And here comes Adrian, just arrived from Cambridge who must go and change into his dress clothes immediately for a grand dinner in Grosvenor Square! I foresee that I shall often be left by my fireside!

I have written 2 more reviews for Mrs Lyttleton, of silly novels; and worse than silly, being sensible; and she has taken my Haworth and likes it, and the other review, and you will see two of my works in Wednesdays Guardian I think.

I got sat upon as usual by the Quaker—(who thinks it right to criticise her relations, and *never* to praise them) for "journalism"—She thinks I am going to sell my soul for gold, which I should willingly do for gold enough, and wants me to write a solid historical work!! People do take themselves so seriously: she sits and twiddles her fingers all day long, but she exhorts me to realise the "beauty of hard work" as she says profoundly. Give my love to all the Babies, especially to Carrie, whose photograph I kiss. It is the most delightful photograph of you all. Love to the Headmaster. Write: AVS

Sussex

202: TO MADGE VAUGHAN   46 *Gordon Square, Bloomsbury*

[Mid-December 1904]

Dearest Foster Madge,

I got you the gloves, 6¼ size, because I find that these gloves stretch, and one's ordinary size is too big almost. They last indefinitely; the pair I had at Giggleswick I got in October, and it has had hard daily wear; and is shamefully black and dirty, but it is not otherwise in the least worn out. I wish I could meet you—but we go to Lyndhurst[1] on Wednesday for a fortnight, and I'm afraid you will be passing through one of those days. You may expect in a day or two a hamper of assorted vegetables, which I am going to try and get tomorrow in the Market. I shall pick out all the odd things I can see, as I know Brazilian Apes are accustomed to queer food! This may come in useful for the Old Boys.

My Haworth article has been taken, and comes out next week or the week after, I had a review in last week, and she has sent me others to do—so I dont fail for lack of scribbling—though not of an exalted kind! I wish you would hand me on Mr Maurice Hewlett,[2] or any body indeed whom you reject: I should like to [give] that affected Dandy his due! My real delight in

1. Minna Duckworth's house in the New Forest. All four Stephens went there for the Christmas holidays.
2. Maurice Hewlett (1861-1923), author of *The Forest Lovers* (1898) and other historical romances.

reviewing is to say nasty things; and hitherto I have had to [be] respectful. The worst of it is, I find, that very few people have the brains to write a really *bad* novel; whereas anyone can turn out a respectable dull one.

My family continue intensely sociable; and old Thoby spends every other night in waltzing with lovely young ladies. I can only hope for their sake that he knows a little more about it than he did when I last had the pleasure of dancing with him!

I wish you could see my room at this moment, on a dark winter's evening —all my beloved leather backed books standing up so handsome in their shelves, and a nice fire, and the electric light burning, and a huge mass of manuscripts and letters and proof-sheets and pens and inks over the floor and everywhere. Tomorrow week they will be bad enough for a general clearance; then I start tidy and gradually work myself up into a happy frenzy of litter. I wish I could write letters like John Baileys.[1] If I could find a French Memoir I would copy the first extract I came across for your benefit, but I am so illiterate! By the way, I am going to see Mrs Arthur Lyttelton tomorrow, my Editress. I hear that she thinks it an *honour* to publish John Baileys works. What then, must she feel it to publish mine, I ask you? But answer there is none!

Give my love to all the darling Babies. Are they going to have a Christmas tree? I must find a nice soft Beast for Carry.

Yr. loving AVS   *Write.*

Sussex

203: To Lady Robert Cecil

Lane End, Bank,
Lyndhurst [Hampshire]

22nd Dec. [1904]

My dear Nelly,

     (are you spelt like a bulldog or a human being?)

I meant to thank you before for your letter, which is the first letter I have ever had about my literary productions, and therefore very delightful! You cant think what vain beasts writers are—but Nessa will tell you. I dont think the artist is so much tempted that way, because all her or his, work is done in the open, and is therefore always criticised, whereas a poor wretch of an author keeps all his thoughts in a dark attic in his own brain, and when they come out in print they look so shivering and naked. So for other people to like them is a great encouragement. Not that a review deserves praise, it is necessarily rather dull work reviewing I think, and I hate the critical attitude of mind because all the time I know what a humbug I am, and ask myself what right I have to dictate whats good and bad, when I couldn't, probably, do as well myself!

1. His *Letters and Diaries* were published in 1935, after his death.

Please think over in your own mind some serious subject that wants writing about, and tell me when we next meet. I am a lady in search of a job at present—that is a good large ambitious subject to which to devote the next ten years of my life. I asked somebody who knows about such things, and he advised history of some kind, and added "When you'r 70 you will begin to put it on paper" Really I cant guarantee that I shall be in a fit state for putting it on paper, when I am 70; but these little considerations didn't seem to occurr to him (2 r's in occur?) where such a thing as history is concerned.

We came down here yesterday, after 10 days of fog in London. You see how delicately I tell you the news of the metropolis: were you picking roses and walking about under a Parasol all the time! Here we saw the sun for the first time—at any rate what was left of the sun, as it was just setting. However it rose all right this morning, as healthy as possible. It is the loveliest place. When you want to build another cottage, build one here. We have Beech trees practically poking their heads in at the front door—at least Adrian says he can smell them in the drawing room, and Forest ponies come when you call them—and Thoby saw a cow chasing a Fox in a field last night in the moonlight. This morning—I dont know that the fox has anything to do with it—he shaved off his moustache—in the hope of looking more like a lawyer. Nessa and I have hired bicycles: my front wheel went off like a pistol this afternoon, and has a great gash in its side. I dont know why I have written such a long letter when you didn't really particularly want it, but there are no books, and when I see a pen and ink, I cant help taking to it, as some people do to gin.

Your aff^{ate,}

AVS

Please say what you dont dare to say!

Hatfield

204: TO VIOLET DICKINSON   *Lane End, Bank,*
                                          Lyndhurst [Hampshire]
Xmas day [1904]

My Violet,

What is the use of my giving you our address before we went—as you know I did—when you go on amusing yourself by writing imaginary descriptions of a literary kind upon your envelopes. Only postmen with a taste for the higher kinds of literature will appreciate the task of making out your addresses. However the letters come right, which is a great tribute to their—the postmens—education. Now do remember what I have written at the top, and try and put it right next time.

It is Christmas evening, and we are all soporific from the effects of a

Christmas tea eaten on top of a Christmas turkey. Sophie never lets us off on Christmas day at all, and when this letter is finished, I shall have to go down and attack the turkeys legs which were left intact. Thoby had such a large helping that another plate had to receive the overflow, and he eat impartially from both. They spent the afternoon in making Rum Punch, which is made half of rum half of brandy, with sugar and lemon and hot water thrown in: the house smells like a public house in consequence, and we shall have a very merry evening. Isn't this better than your high and dry aristocrats? We all talk at once, and make such brilliant jokes as never were seen. Thoby and Adrian have hunted from 10.30 to 5 every day since we have been here, and propose to hunt every day till we leave—on their own hind legs, unless they can one day afford a horse. Old Gerald has sent us £2.10. each, and they are going to have horses out of this. There is a book I have long had my eye on which I shall now buy the first moment I am in London, and I am already rather excited about it. Nessa and I spend our days very harmoniously, a good deal out of doors, when we walk into the beech woods which come up to the house. Really old Minna showed some sense when she built this house, though she did make such a bad bargain of it. The house itself is really pretty and comfortable, and the position is divine. Tomorrow Nessa and I are going to hire a Bank Holiday pony and drive to the meet about 5 miles off, and have a picnic in the woods together. I shall probably make scrambled eggs. Lord! I wish you were with us!

I rather put my foot into it with Mrs Lyttelton, I am afraid; she wanted to cut out certain things in Shag [the dog article], and I wrote and said please do, and always alter my things as you like. I only meant—cut out if too long. I didn't mean in this cool way to ask her to do all the dirty work of correcting and polishing for me. I think I shall have to tell her so. I had 2 proofs of Reviews this morning, which were very badly printed, so I was in need of your proof correcting book, which I have left at home. I do nothing but read here, all day long, which is what I most enjoy, but I begin to feel the desire of the pen in my blood, and have hard work not to write. I dont want to be forever scribbling. I am just finishing the Life of B[urne-]. J[ones]. which begins to bore me slightly—not the Life, which is excellent, but the man. He seems rather a backboneless charming creature, and when one knows that he was *not* a great painter but only a glorified kind of decorator, all the anecdotes and letters etc. are rather too much of a good thing. I suppose he was a loveable sort of man, but not remarkable in any way. There's rather a nice page about our Prinsep relations. I always feel, though it is snobbish—only not really, because with the true great one doesn't feel it—that he *isnt* a gentleman—not in anything, not with the education or restraint or character of a gentleman. His letters I rather loathe.

Write, and address.

Yr. AVS

Berg

169

205: To Violet Dickinson   *Lane End, Bank*
                                                [Lyndhurst, Hampshire]
Friday [30 December 1904]

My Violet,

I cant think why you condemn me to suffer so needlessly. Mightn't you have saved me 2 *sleepless* nights—if not 3—by telling me straight out *what* Mr [Richard Burdon] Haldane said of Haworth? Anyhow, you needn't have told me he was very severe; now you *must* send me the whole letter without delay, and put me out of my agony. Really I think I shall give up writing, or at any rate showing my things to other people: I only get criticism and abuse, and no one thinks it necessary to be grateful. After all I didnt ask Haldane to criticise me—and yet he thinks he has a right to be very severe. Send it on, anyhow, now—severe or not.

Now, also, in your next letter written immediately on getting this, tell me if Mrs. Lyttelton thought me impertinent for telling her to do what she liked with my articles.

There was a third command I had to give, which I cant remember at this moment.

If Haldane is severe, I shall give up literature and take to art, I am already a draughtsman of great promise. I draw for 2 hours every evening after dinner, and make copies of all kinds of pictures, which *Nessa says* show a very remarkable feeling for line. Pictures are easier to understand than subtle literature, so I think I shall become an artist to the public, and keep my writing to myself. I am probably the only living person who can understand it. Bold politicians cant.

I am reading,   *Your Life in 15 Century*
                  Mrs J. R. Green.
                  Life of William Morris.
                  Layards *Nineveh*
                  History of Music
                  Not Wisely but too Well by
                  Miss Rhoda Broughton—also 2 bound

volumes of the Windsor Magazine, which I hire for 2d a week, a ridiculously cheap price. I have a whole bottle of amber coloured Barley Sugar which I bought for one shilling, and Thoby has another of raspberry coloured Barley Sugar, and Nessa and Adrian have tins of stuff called American Butter Toffee, and we all draw up round the fire, and suck long sticks, which gradually melt; now if this aint luxury I should like to know what is— especially when you have been tramping six miles through bog and dead leaves in the forest following a huntsman's horn. Thoby and Adrian rode for close on 12 hours yesterday, a hunting; and today they are so stiff they growl like tired dogs when ever they move. By the way I have just broken a tooth over a bit of barley sugar, which will rather spoil my looks.

Kitty writes very charming long letters—not to me, I'm sorry to say. *She* wouldn't tell me half a sentence in one letter and leave me to wait 3 days for it to be finished. But then I always did think Maxses a superior race of people. My tooth has just come out, and what remains feels like a ruined castle.

Why do I waste so much paper and good ink—let alone my time a laying of it on, as the man says in Punch—upon a quadruped—a longshanked reptile, who puts me off with half sheets left in the Ducal blotting book? I am using my very best paper too, which I reserve for the peerage, as a rule.

I have written an article here, and done up 3 old articles which you haven't seen, which ought to do for Mrs. L[yttelton]. I had some thoughts of sending them to you to see first, but I shant now. I hope you mind that, but I'm afraid its not likely. Shall I enclose the half of my tooth instead? It is an interesting relic of better days, and I think you might like to have it mounted as a pin or a brooch, with a suitable inscription. It had a large stopping in one side of it. You shall have this too when it comes out.

Georges hired motor has been burnt as it was being cleaned. I am afraid this will stint their generosity, which has not been strikingly shown yet.

I am corresponding with a woman called Sheepshanks[1]—what a good name for you—Violet Sheepshanks—who wishes me either to hold what she calls a 'social evening' or to teach *English grammar*!! I have had to tell her that I am not sociable, and I dont know any grammar. She lives in a Palace at Norwich, and I dont think my principles probably would suit.

I cant tell you what an inexpressibly bad woman I think you—so good bye, woman Sheepshanks.

Berg

206: TO VIOLET DICKINSON   *New Forest [Lane End,*
                                  Bank, Hampshire]

[early January 1905]

My Violet,

I am so cross today, crosser than ever—that fool of a man, the Cornhill editor [Reginald Smith], sends me back my Article—Boswells letters—without a word, but a printed slip. I never expected him to take it, since I found that it would only make 2 Cornhill pages which is impossibly short of course—but I thought he might say so. Also Haldane isnt exactly warm in his praise,[2] and altogether I feel, as you read in the Bible, despised and rejected of men. I was a fool not to find something suitable for the Cornhill,

1. Mary Sheepshanks, daughter of the Bishop of Norwich, and effective Principal of Morley College, South London, an evening institute for working people.
2. See preceding letter.

instead of sending an old and fragmentary bit—but I dont take this as an insult to my literary genius—only a d——d bore, because I want to make money—and I shant have time to write after we go back, except an occasional review. I had a letter from Fred Maitland saying that his materials come to an end in 1890, and will I try and rake some more letters up, and write as much as I can of all the last years myself—which will take me all my time—as it means going through letters which I had put away as useless—again. Also he wants me to try and make out a Bibliography, which is sure to be a tiresome and difficult job, also to collect articles which ought to be reprinted. And I had made a 1905 vow to keep myself in pocket money at least this year by my writing! However we have an extra £50, which will more than pay our bills and leave a little balance for the new year.

I have been writing 2 little articles for Mrs L:—I suppose she'll refuse them—one on Christchurch[1]—the other on the Forest—which I have tried to make good and careful. Then I have read a good deal, of many things, and reading makes me intensely happy, and culminates in a fit of writing always.

How are you, my Sheepshanks dear? The original [Mary] Sheepshanks wants me to go and see her, and talk over my views, which I aint none. She thinks I might combine amusement and instruction—a little gossip and sympathy, and then 'talks' about books and pictures. I'm sure I dont mind how much I talk, and I really dont see any limit to the things I might talk about. However as she is sure—the good Sheepshanks—that I shall be of the greatest use—I dont mind trying. I enclose some early works [drawings]—in fact the first I did when the divine inspiration seized me—and I am now improved, according to severe critics, and draw ponies out of my head, and domestic groups. We certainly *are* domestic: we all draw for 1 hour and ½ after dinner, and Nessa reads aloud, the silliest novel we can find, at which we all roar with laughter, and Thoby draws murderers escaping and criminals being hung—and once, I'm sorry to say, the back view of God Almighty—and Adrian draws foxes, as large as deer, running along with their tongues out, and a beautiful gent. on a horse, who's himself, galloping up in front of the hounds. They have just come in from their second and last hunt on horseback, which wasn't as good as the last, but they seem generally in good spirits. I never saw people eat as they do, and the result in Thoby's case is really rather alarming. He expands in his waistcoat, and rolls 2 double chins out of his collar.

I shall be rather—in fact very—glad to be home, in my own room, with my books, and I want to work like a steam engine, though editors wont take what I write. I must show you what I have done, when it is typed, and please be very kind. Mrs. L[yttelton] or Margaret L[yttelton] rather cobbled my poor Shag between them: I wish they would let me do it if it has to be done, and please dont say you want to alter heaps of things or I shall give up

1. Printed in the *Guardian*, 26 July 1905.

writing altogether and take to drink or society. When shall you be in London? Write a *long long* letter.

Yr. AVS

Berg

207: TO VIOLET DICKINSON   [46 *Gordon Square, Bloomsbury*]

[early January 1905]

My Violet,

Two good letters this morning, so you deserve a real treat—2 delightful manuscripts to read. I'm not sure whether they're worth sending to Mrs L. or not; only I took quite a lot of trouble over the New Forest one, and wrote it with sweat and toil, though it is so short.

You shall have heaps more when you come back. You are the person I can best stand criticism from—which aint saying much.

Yr. AVS

Berg

208: TO MADGE VAUGHAN   46 *Gordon Square, Bloomsbury*

[early January 1905]

Dearest Madge,

I hope the 16th, as you say on the flyleaf of your envelope, is the likely date, and not the 13th—and couldn't you make it the 17th—and stay more than 1 night? Adrian is here till the 17th, and we have no extra room: at least we could make an extra room, but we are without a bed, and washing things: so do come on the 17th and stay longer, and then we could do something really amusing.

Our last amusement is a silver point press, which prints off delightful little reddy brown drawings, and even my works of art, which are of the most primitive description being entirely a self taught genius—dont turn out so bad.

Lets have a dinner party for you, and introduce you to some Bohemian lights, after your own heart!

You will be amused to hear that I am going to teach a class of working women in the Waterloo Road [Morley College], upon English Literature! They begged me to give a course of lectures—which I feebly declined, and said I would rather get to know them personally than instruct them—but they are much too keen to let me off—and probably have the whole thing at their fingers ends.

We have just come back from the New Forest, where we spent the loneliest of Christmasses, which was very nice, and barbaric. Thoby and Adrian hunted regularly every day, and Nessa and I wandered about among dead leaves and bogs and forest ponies, and I never once changed for dinner, which is my height of bliss.

Please thank your son and daughter when you see them for their *extremely* interesting and confidential letters; Janets shows a really masterly grasp of—all kinds of things—and Halford imparted quantities of useful information. What a nice way to write a letter there's [*sic*] is! I think I shall correspond with my affectionate Aunts on the same principle. Wont Halford come up and meet his Mama here, and visit the Bears with Cousin Virginia? Just think what [a] thing that would be to look back upon, and how it would stay in his mind all his life!

We hope very much to see Katherine [Furse] one day, if she is in London again, but I suppose she has heaps to do. By the way, the Watts show is *atrocious*: my last illusion is gone. Nessa and I walked through the rooms, almost in tears. Some of his work indeed most of it—is quite childlike. Will you please express to Mrs Symonds [Madge's mother] my—I dont quite know what—she will probably have forgotten who I am—but explain that I am another kind of Foundling, like Margaret Down—or whatever you called her—and likely to prove quite as troublesome. Mrs Symonds, then, is some kind of Grand Mother! I wish *she* would ever come and see us. Now write a sensible description of your plans, with proper dates—

Yr. loving AVS

Sussex

209: To Violet Dickinson   *46 Gordon Square, Bloomsbury*
Sunday [early January 1905]

My Violet,

I will come and dine Monday, and not Tues, with pleasure. Here are two of my masterpieces—Nessa has bought a silver point press, and these are my first attempts; one is a Rose, which I use as a bookplate in Fitzgeralds books, the other is a copy of Shakespeare's death mask!—rather elongated you will see, but I have not yet mastered my medium, which is a very fascinating one. However I can tell you all about it when we meet. I am booked for Morley College!

Yr. AVS

Berg

210: To Violet Dickinson   [*46 Gordon Square, Bloomsbury*]
Postcard
[January 1905]

Please inscribe and send me another copy of Anthony Harte, as my copy is all wrongly bound, and numbered, and the same pages are repeated.

I think them *excellent* however in spite of this drawback, from which I hope the Hospital copies are free. I like the great sneeze! and I am sure my weary nights which aren't really weary, will be sweetened and made profitable. Dont cut a poor devil out whose trying to make a living by her pen.

AVS

Berg

211: TO VIOLET DICKINSON   46 *Gordon Square, Bloomsbury*

[14 January 1905]

My Violet,

I am discharged cured! Aint it a joke! Savage was quite satisfied, and said he wanted me to go back to my ordinary life in everything and to go out and see people, and work, and to forget my illness. He asked me to go and dine with him! He thinks me quite normally well now, and there need be no special care, which is such a mercy.

Morley College work is all right, but he wont say it mayn't *possibly* be too much. I have told Miss S[heepshanks] that I think there is no risk of illness, so I will start, if she likes now.

AVS

Berg

212: TO VIOLET DICKINSON   46 *Gordon Square, Bloomsbury*

[January 1905]

My Violet,

I am rushing off to my workers, so I cant write—which I wish to—my sentiments. Ask Nessa if I was cheerful last night! But what I want *immediate* is the address of Miss Burney who typewrites. I have to send some of Freds MS. to be done. I will write again.

Yr. AVS

Berg

213: TO VIOLET DICKINSON   46 *Gordon Square, Bloomsbury*

[January? 1905]

My Violet,

Of course come any time—dinner tea, lunch.

Mrs L: asks for articles. I hope you didn't drop a hint?

A mercy to see you in this weary world.

Just off to Morley.

Yr. AVS

Berg

214: TO LADY ROBERT CECIL   46 *Gordon Square, Bloomsbury*

[January? 1905]

Dear Nelly,

I was prevented from writing yesterday—I went out at 3 and did not get back till 12.30. You are a dreadful bane to authors; they *cant* withstand flattery, and though at present I know when I am being demoralised, I shall soon be too far gone for that: in which case I shall be more or less a responsibility to you for the rest of my life.

I didn't send you any works because for one thing I expect you have enough to do for your employers: and also from pure vanity—because so far what I have done is very experimental, and must all be rewritten. However here is the last production. I shall rewrite it in 5 years time; at present it is all disjointed.

Thank you very much for asking me to come some time. I shall be very glad to. I shall also like very much to come out on Wednesday. We can then talk shop as much as you like. I have a little book called The 'Authors Progress' which is the kind of thing we talk put into print. I have said that it is a most depressing and ugly book, and treats Literature like a trade.

Yr. aff.

AVS

Hatfield

215: TO VIOLET DICKINSON   [46 *Gordon Square, Bloomsbury*]

[January 1905]

My Violet,

What a mercy you approve! I really did get depressed about that thing, as I especially wanted it to be good.[1] You are an honest woman in what you say? Really that is a load off my mind if you like it, because I can trust your judgment in these matters.

Mrs Lyttleton has just been—she is a delightful big sensible woman. I wish she would pet me! I think she has possibilities that way! Just off to the Crums, where I know I shall be a howling failure.

When are we going to see you?

AVS

Berg

1. Probably Virginia's recollections of her father written for F. W. Maitland's *Life* of Leslie Stephen.

[February 1905]

My Violet,

I cant think where this odd bit of paper comes from, but it seems obviously meant for you, by reason of its *stripes*. Now do you see the joke? The whole of my reputation depends on it!

Nelly was like lavender and cream after Kitty: she made one or two corrections, which I had expected, but otherwise said she would like it [the memoir for Maitland] *printed* as it stands, and she does really like it, and thinks Kitty's point of view absurd. So you can imagine that I think her a woman of the finest critical judgement, and I am going to send the wretched thing off to Fred at once, without corrections. They can be made later if he wishes to print, but I shall make it clear that I *dont* wish it printed. Poor Violet—what it is to have a scribbling maniac among your dependents! I send you with this the miserable article[1] which I have screwed out with a view to Leo: say if it wont do. It is the last I shall do, as I have taken a plunge into tough Greek, and that has so much attraction for me—Heaven knows why—That I dont want to do anything else. I am really rather good at Greek.

We had Margaret L[yttleton] yesterday, who did her best to talk, but she is rather a stiff and starched young woman. I think she is really nice though, and asked us to go and see her. Tomorrow your blessed Katharine Horner[2] is coming to tea—so the young ladies are appeased—and then I shall shut myself up and translate Greek history, and nobody shall criticise me at all.

Tell Mrs Crum that I went to my women yesterday,[3] and had 4, as against 2 last week, and we discussed Venice, and I showed them pictures, and they were nice and friendly and full of interest, and told me about their Aunts who said that there was water in all the streets in Venice, and was it true, and the Clergyman at home (Yorkshire) had been to Rome, and shown them pictures of it. You will have to come down and talk to them one week—lots of jokes is what they like—and then they blossom out—and say how they have written poetry since the age of 11!

When am I going to see you again. This year—next year—now—or never! Aint it comic Nessa and [Nurse] Fardell having assignations at your house?

1. *Street Music*, which was published in the *National Review*, of which Leopold Maxse was editor.
2. Lady (Frances) Horner's younger daughter Katharine, who married Raymond Asquith, son of the Prime Minister.
3. Ella Crum had an unpaid post on the administrative staff of Morley College.

Nessa is sending her article[1] to the Saturday Review, I think, on Thoby's advice.

When will you come and dine!

Yr. AVS

Berg

217: To Violet Dickinson   46 *Gordon Square, Bloomsbury*

[mid-February 1905]

Wretched Woman,

Leo is *delighted* to accept my *charming* article [*Street Music*]—so there! After your croaks and groans I thought that little job was a failure anyhow. I think you must be too good a critic to see what will sell—that is my melancholy conclusion, and if my article had been really good, Leo wouldn't have taken it. But I want a little base popularity at this moment—I spend 5 days of precious time toiling through Henry James' subleties[2] for Mrs Lyttleton, and write a very hardworking review for her; then come orders to cut out quite half of it—*at once*, as it has to go into next weeks Guardian, and the Parsonesses, I suppose, prefer midwifery, to literature. So I gave up 10 minutes, all I had, to laying about me with a pair of scissors: literally I cut two sheets to pieces, wrote a scrawl to mend them together, and so sent the maimed thing off—with a curse. I never hope to see it again. It was quite good before the official eye fell upon it; now it is worthless, and doesn't in the least represent all the toil I put into it—and the book deserved a good, and careful review. However, to make up, the Times has sent me two trashy books, about Thackeray and Dickens and I may write 1500 words or so—Bruce Richmond[3] is generous—and this, with the Nat: give me a little cause for joy in the face of that righteous old Guardian. Really I never read such pedantic commonplace as the Guardianese: it takes up the line of a Governess, and maiden Lady, and high church Parson mixed; how they ever got such a black little goat into their fold, I cant conceive.

I spent all today reading Latin, out of pure virtue; so you needn't preach. What a bore about the Watts article! I think the Outlook and the Independent are the only possible two now—but I dont know that she wants to try elsewhere.

1. Vanessa had written an article on G. F. Watts, and sent it to the *Saturday Review*. It was rejected.
2. Virginia's review of *The Golden Bowl* appeared in *the Guardian* of 22 February 1905.
3. Editor of *The Times Literary Supplement*. Virginia's reviews of *The Thackeray Country*, by Lewis Melville, and *The Dickens Country*, by F. G. Kitton, appeared on 10 March 1905.

At [Dr] Savages dinner, which was more heavy and dreary than you can conceive, every person I talked to spoke almost with tears of the greatness and beauty of Watts—and wouldn't admit the possibility of criticism, and this, I suppose, is the sample British Public. Savage lives with an odd lot of people; a daughter who is not up to his level, and strange fossils.

I suppose we shant meet till the 1st when I hope to have the pleasure of shaking your hand on the staircase.

We are going to tea with the Horners tomorrow; a long letter from Katharine, insisting on Christian names!

Yr. AVS

Berg

218: To Emma Vaughan   46 *Gordon Square, Bloomsbury*
23rd Feb: [1905]

Dearest Toadlebinks,

I perambulate Long Acre, and Hatton Garden, and Young Street, and keep my tryst, which we made for the 13th Jan: if you remember, but the faithless Toad comes not—and news of her there is none. You know, I suppose, that there is only one possible construction to be put upon your conduct. By the way, Todger, it will soon be a whole *year* since we met, and if you can face that fact without emotion you are a heartless scoundrel! We saw the Marn the other day, and I thought she looked rather particularly well, so I don't think you need worry about her. She takes to Hoxton[1] a little more intemperately when you are not there to restrain her, but she seems happy and says she don't mind living alone. But I very much mind losing a sane first Cousin in the German Ocean.[2] How you can stand Dutchmen, when you might be living at the very hub of the universe, I can't imagine.

Now do you realise that the Stephen family are making their debut in the world next Wednesday as ever is—the 1st March, 9.30 P.M.—at home, house warming. If you have an ounce of warm blood in you, you will come back in time for this. Marn is coming, and half the notabilities of Kensington, and Bloomsbury. Our suite of apartments is to be flung open for the occasion, and four superb objects of art—the 4 Stephens in fact—are to be on view. It really ought to be great fun—only why the d——l aren't you there? The Fishers are coming in cabs and four-wheelers, and hackney coaches—a grand reconciliation scene is going to take place in the front drawing-room, when with one accord Vanessa and Adeline, Virginia and Emmie, At. Mary and Gerald, Tom [Edwin] and Thoby, Boo [Cordelia] and Adrian are going to fall upon each others necks, and then proceed to lobster and champagne.

1. Margaret Vaughan was still doing social work in north London.
2. Emma Vaughan had been in Dresden for several months studying music.

Clara [Pater], if health permits, is coming in a new Empire gown of scarlet plush, with amber beads, and a little old Lace: Totty [Pater], unfortunately, cannot, for obvious reasons [illness], go far from the house. Mia [Macnamara] is marching from Chorley Wood; and is said to have started already, with a selection of the Chicks—Even the Headmaster at Giggleswick [Will Vaughan] is said to have made arrangements with Mr Mott to take evening prayers—Lotta [Leaf] is—oh heavens, *Descending* upon us!

We have been rather gay—at least Nessa and Thoby dine out a good deal, and we see a certain amount of our dearly beloved and intensely respectable sister in law [Lady Margaret Duckworth]. I am realising the ambition of our youth, and actually making money—which, however, I spend long before I make. I am writing for—now for my boast—

The Times Lit. Supplement.

The Academy

The National Review

The Guardian—

Aint that respectable. My National Review article is about [Street] *Music* so you can imagine what a flutter is going through the musical world —it has probably reached Dresden. My remarks will revolutionise the whole future of music.

Now write, like a good amphibious little beast!

Yours,

AVS

Sussex

219: To Violet Dickinson   46 *Gordon Square, Bloomsbury*

[28 February 1905]

My Violet,

As I can make my boasts in public, I must send a line to say that I have heard from Fred Maitland, and he says my thing is "beautiful. Really it is beautiful, and if this were a proper occasion I would write a page of praise. But of course I know that this is not what you would like and I can only say that what you write is just what your Father would have wished you to write. Whether all of it will be printed I cannot yet say; but you well know that my inclination will be to print as much as possible."

So thats a mercy and now my mind is at ease and Kitty may pipe to the Devil. He is a really good judge. But I shall have to make it plain that none of it is to be printed—I dont think that would be possible.[1]

That wretched Academy![2] It sent me a proof, word for word as I had

1. Later she relented, and it was printed, but signed 'by one of his daughters'.
2. The journal *Academy and Literature*. Virginia's article appeared on 25 February 1905.

written my article, and now I buy a copy and find they have changed the title from "A plague of Essays" to "The decay of essay writing" which means nothing; cut out a good half—and altered words on their own account, without giving me a chance to protest. I shouldn't so much mind if they hadn't clapped on my name in full at the end—to which I do object.

Just sent off an article to Mrs. L: She is really angelic in comparison.

The household is working up for tomorrow night, and our spirits are rising!

Yr. AVS

Berg

220: To Violet Dickinson   *46 Gordon Square, Bloomsbury*
[early March 1905]

My Violet,

I cant come to lunch Thursday—d. it: 2 cousins are coming. and I have to go to a concert with them. Could I come to tea after it—rather late, 5.30?

A novel comes in from the Times; otherwise I havent any work, and I have spent the last fortnight reading Greek—lots of Greek, so I deserve a treat.

Just off to a dance!—where we shant know a soul. Does Lady Alice[1] expect me to lunch, or what?

Yr. AVS

Berg

221: To Violet Dickinson   *46 Gordon Square, Bloomsbury*
[11? March 1905]

My Violet,

I felt myself rather a selfish brute to talk so much of my own affairs—but that is the use I always seem to make of you.

I rather repent too, because I think I made too much of my being "driven"—only on that evening, happening to be depressed, I made the most of my grumble. Really I lead a very healthy life, and I dont think as a rule I do—or shall—go out very much—only things always come in a rush, and then I curse. Dont talk to Nessa, I really dont think talking does any good, and it really lies in my hands, and I shall make a stand if necessary. It is blowing and raining, and we have got to change and go and lunch with Lady Alice—which somehow seems rather a reasonless thing to do.

I have been toiling at a beast of a review[2] all the morning, which I cant

1. Daughter of the Marquess of Bath.
2. Either *Barham of Beltana*, by W. E. Norris (*TLS*, 17 March) or *The Fortunes of Farthings*, by A. J. Dawson (*TLS*, 31 March).

write and hate writing and write d——d badly. By the way I was in Fridays Times,[1] and Bruce Richmond thought it "admirable" and now sends me another great, fat book[2]—which I dont much want to do—as I know *nothing* of the subject.

I despair of my brains, which seem to be guttering like a tallow candle.

You are a really comforting woman, and where I should be without you, I dont know. That is the kind of testimonial that is worth having in this world.

Love to Nelly.

Yr. AVS

Berg

1. The review of *The Thackeray Country* and *The Dickens Country*.
2. Probably *Catherine de Medici*, by Edith Sichel. The review was not published.

Letters 222-285

At the end of March 1905 *Virginia went with Adrian by sea to Portugal, and from Lisbon they visited Seville and Granada in Spain. On her return to Gordon Square she busied herself with weekly reviews, and with descriptive writing (not for publication) when she went on holiday to Carbis Bay in Cornwall, to Giggleswick again, and to Blo' Norton Hall in Norfolk, which the Stephens leased for August* 1906. *She continued her weekly classes at Morley College. Slowly she made new friends. "Now we are free women", she wrote, meaning that she and Vanessa had rid themselves of the fashionable society which George Duckworth had considered suitable for them. Some of her aristocratic friends, like Beatrice Thynne, remained close to her, and she had made a new one, Lady Robert Cecil, who went with Violet Dickinson on a world-cruise in the autumn of this year. But for the first time Virginia was making close friends of young men who shared and stimulated her intellectual interests, the majority of whom had been at Cambridge with her two brothers. The 'Thursday Evenings' at Gordon Square began early in* 1906, *soon to be followed by Vanessa's Friday Club which discussed the arts. The membership of the two groups overlapped, and among the most frequent visitors to the house were Saxon Sydney-Turner, Clive Bell (who proposed to Vanessa and was turned down), Lytton Strachey, Walter Lamb and Desmond MacCarthy. At first Thoby's Cambridge friends appeared to Virginia "inanimate creatures", but when they began to join the Stephens on holiday, she discovered their merits, and the 'Bloomsbury Group' (though they never thought of themselves as that) came into existence.*

222: TO VIOLET DICKINSON   *Somewhere off the Coast of Spain*

April 5th [1905]

My Violet,

I may have a chance of posting this at Oporto this afternoon, so I write now. So far we have had a splendid journey, though at the end we begin to get a little bored, mainly owing to our fellow passengers. We stayed a day at Havre, and went to Rouen, and saw the 3 churches, and then set sail again. Unfortunately something went wrong with our engines, and we had to stop and drift with sails for about 7 hours, which was very dull. However this morning we woke to find the Coast of Spain in sight, and now we are passing along quite close beneath it, and the Captain expects to land at Oporto this afternoon. We have changed our plans a little; as we shall have to wait an extra long time to mend our engines we have settled to take train to Lisbon from Oporto, instead of going by sea. It is not a very long train journey, and it seems a waste of time to spend two days at Oporto. As far as I can make out our addresses and dates will be—

arrive Lisbon April 6th.
arrive Seville Hotel Madrid April 7th
arrive Granada Hotel Washington Irving April 11th.
arrive Lisbon Poste Restante April 17th.

leave in the [S.S.] Madeirensa, April 19th and get to Liverpool on the 22nd. So do write if you can. I am very hard up for letters. I feel as though I had been cut adrift from the world altogether; we lead such an odd dreamy existence. I am out of doors a good 8 hours a day, inhaling sea breezes enough to make the dead walk, and eating hugely, to pass the time, and I have had no pain the last 3 days, and sleep like a top. I am getting rather impatient to land, and see things—not but what the sea is beautiful to watch— but the ship is crowded, and one cant escape voices. There is one old bore of the worst type, who makes my life a burden. Happily we have discovered a place on the top of the engine room, to which an iron ladder leads, and we have taken our chairs there, and have escaped so far. We had the loveliest sight of Cornwall, and the Lands End, passing so close that we saw the houses and the people. I haven't seen Cornwall since we left St Ives. There are a great many Portuguese Jews on board, and other repulsive objects, but we keep clear of them. The only people we talk to are the Lloyds. She is a daughter of Alfred Booth,[1] the owner of the line and rather a useful acquaintance. There is also a man who knows all about Spanish hotels and travelling, and I think we shall manage all right. Everyone says that Granada and Seville are the two places best worth seeing in Spain, and this is just the right time of year. It is brilliantly fine, and so hot today that I can bask on deck without a rug.

You see, there aint much news; you cant think how bored everybody is, and how hard up for something to do or think about. They play the piano all day long, and eat sandwiches and drink soup.

I wonder what you are doing. I haven't heard a word from anyone since we left—a week ago today—and I dont know where Nessa is. We get back the day before Easter Sunday.

I wonder whether that wretched Sichel review came out in the Times, but I feel safe from editors, and even your criticism will lose its sting! In fact I feel completely demoralised, as though I were going through a second rest cure. My conscience is waking now that we are near shore, and if I am virtuous I shall write to the Quaker, but I think that can be left till after lunch!

Adrian is very happy, and takes great care of me, and does my hair at

1. Constance, who had recently married Godfrey Lloyd, later a professor at Toronto University.

night, and fastens my dress. When I got on board I found that I had brought no sponges or combs, and had to buy them from the ships barber. But otherwise I have not thrown myself on the mercies of Providence.

We sit at the Captains table, and I have to talk to him about twin screws. Would you like to marry a sailor? After all, I'm not sure that it isnt a better trade than letters.

Remember to write, and tell me how you are, and all your domestic affairs, as I shall get quite de-humanised.

Yr. AVS

Berg

223: TO VIOLET DICKINSON   *Seville, Hotel Roma*

10th April [1905]

My Violet,

We are now in Seville, as you may see. We came here on Saturday from Lisbon, and found rooms in this hotel, which isnt bad, and is cheap. It is a most attractive place—not that the Cathedral comes up to my hopes—but it is far and away the most Southern place I have seen—and the life is amusing for a time. Of course today it has rained as they say it hasn't rained all the winter, and we have had to spend most of our time exploring vague tombs in the Cathedral. If only the sun would come out it would be divine. The orange blossoms are out everywhere, and all kinds of trees; in fact an English August isn't more full summer. We went over the Alcazar this afternoon, in the rain. However, I am no good at guide books. We drove in the gardens yesterday—it is a queer deserted ramshackle place, like all Italian towns, and of course full of beggars, and guides. We shall only stay here over tomorrow, and then go on to the Washington Irving at Granada. I hope to get a letter from you somewhere—none here, or at Lisbon.

It is a great relief to be off the steamer at last. The people got intolerable, as they thought it necessary to be friendly and talkative. Our boat back only takes 3 days, so they wont have time to bore.

Lisbon is a splendid town, with at any rate one beautiful building, the Great Church at Belem.

We went up to the English Cemetry and saw [Henry] Fieldings tomb! The heat, until today, has been perfectly delicious. I wore my fur coat and sat wrapped in a rug all the voyage, but the moment we landed at Oporto the climate changed, and I longed for a cotton dress. Today we have gone back to an English April.

The people here are beginning to make ready for the festival. They have stood huge wax figures in the Cathedral—I cant conceive why—and they are building stands. Placards about the bull fight are up everywhere. I am glad we just miss it.

I have had 2 letters from Nessa—otherwise no English news at all—nor have we seen a newspaper. In fact we feel entirely adrift, and it seems 6 months since we left. I feel ready for all kinds of work, and most flourishing.

We have managed our journey quite successfully, though we discovered on the voyage out[1] that we ought to have booked passage on the return boat, which is very full, and we were told that it was doubtful if there would be room. If Adrians degree depends upon our getting back on the 22nd we were a little nervous; but the agent at Lisbon promises that it will be all right. I am afraid I shall have to sleep with a Portuguese Jew.

How are you—and what are you doing? I suppose you are now packing up for the summer.

I wish I could screw out an article for Mrs L[yttelton] but I doubt it. We are living as cheap as we can—but these journeys are expensive. I hope I shall get a lot of work to do this summer, so as to make both ends meet. I ought at this moment to be reading some English history for my women—I dont know a thing about it—but trust to luck.

Have the Crumbos [Walter and Ella Crum] ceased from troubling or what is happening; this time last year there was a general muddle.

We shall soon be back now, for which I shall be glad, though I have enjoyed myself, and so has Adrian.

Yr. AVS

Berg

224: TO VIOLET DICKINSON   46 *Gordon Square, Bloomsbury*

Bank Holiday [24 April 1905]

My Violet,

Thanks to our boat we only reached Liverpool last night late, and came up by the first train this morning, when I found your letter, which I now answer, after writing I dont know how many letters, so my hand is cramped, my brain barren, and Heaven knows what kind of letter you expect, as you live in a country cottage where the postman calls once a week, and not then if it rains, and which is a house, a prison rather, of unpleasant memories for one poor unfortunate at anyrate!![2] *That* is a sentence worthy of the Guardian at its best—might be printed just as it stands, without a single editorial comma—and would make the Church of England shiver in its vitals. The sea leaves my head in a state of swimmy swammy swampiness, so that I have

1. She uses the phrase inadvertently, but this sea-journey was in fact the source of her inspiration for the early chapters of her first novel, *The Voyage Out*.
2. Violet's house at Welwyn, where Virginia had stayed during her madness in the preceding summer.

sat the whole afternoon on Nessa's lap, in a maudlin condition. Didnt I say in one of my inspired writings, which you threw into the fire, that coming home was the best part of being away? It really is. Especially when you travel in Spain, where the trains stop to breathe every 5 minutes and then the idiotic boat is late at Lisbon. But to take up my pen again when we got to Granada—There we were very comfortable in the Washington Irving—I asked if anyone remembered an English Lady the length of seven fine males [Violet], travelling with a beautiful but haughty aristocrat [Hester Lyttelton], with their own bath in a waterproof jacket—but your fame has left Granada at anyrate.

It is far and away the best place we saw—almost have seen I think—I basked like a lizard in the gardens, and it was as hot as an English August, which conveys nothing to your mind but think of orange trees, with oranges, and every other kind of tree with large green leaves, and all the blossoms you can think of. The cottage garden is nothing to it. There my descriptive faculty is blasted.

Then we had to travel 24, or 48 hours to Lisbon, and slept one night at a little country wayside inn—where the fire burnt in the middle of the room, and the company of Spanish peasants sat round and drank and stared at us, and we expected to have knives in our throats every moment. Then we were given one room—the only sleeping room—with one bed—and a canvas door between us and the family who undressed outside, and we locked our door as best we could—and lay down delicately side by side in our clothes, and heard the old woman counting her money, and swearing and spitting, and by degrees we went to sleep, and at 9 they brought us goats milk, and told us to get up and be gone. This all happened on the edge of an arid desert, lit by stars, smelling of meadow sweet beneath the shadow of a Moorish Castle!

Next day we went on to Badajoz—and came on Tuesday to Lisbon, where we had baths, and that is the most delightful thing we did there. We had to wait 2 days for the ship, and sailed on Thursday. The ship was very small, very sea-smelly, and the moment we got out to sea it began to roll like an inebriate, and I sat down to dinner, and suddenly got up, and without words left the room. It was beastly cold and dreary—however next day was better and after all we had a fair voyage, and last night at eleven we got into the dock, and slept still in our berths.

So now our travels are over. Everything here is safe and clean and happy. Nessa looks very well, and says she liked [Margery] Snow[den] more the more she knew, and they were very intimate and shared the same room! Well that is more than I could have done. Here I come back to letters from Fred Maitland, among other people, and he is just back and wants to come and see me on Wednesday, and bring the rough sheets of the book. Then Bruce Richmond returns my Sichel review which is excellent, he says, but not what they want—that is a serious criticism from a historical point of view. I am really thankful to have the beastly thing in my waste paper basket, though I did waste time over it, as it was bad, and I knew it. However, he's sending me more books, and is polite.

Shall I come down and see you one afternoon—only I forgot that Mrs L. will be with you. I must break the evil spell some day.

Well, it is a mercy to be back, and within your range again.

Yr. AVS

Berg

225: To Violet Dickinson   46 *Gordon Square, Bloomsbury*

[April 1905]

My Violet,

I forgot to send these queer bits of stuff, which I found at Granada. I dont suppose you will like them, or find them in the least useful. But really you must take them.

I am getting famous at last, by reason of the article which I did *not* write. Bruce Richmond says the Times is an academic paper, and treats books in the academic spirit—whereas I do not. Do send me the review[1] if you have it. I suppose they praise learnedly: really it was a secondrate book.

We are now shivering over the New Gallery, which has its private view, and we dont know whether Nelly[2] is hung or not. I am going off at daybreak to buy a catalogue. I hope it will be there, though Nessa says she would rather not.

Fred Maitland has just been here for 2 hours, and is sending his ms. for us to read. He is evidently some way on with it. I like him more and more, and I know I shall like his writing.

People are beginning to hop in and out like rabbits. Beatrice I think, dines tonight; Madge and Will tomorrow. I wish you could meet her.

I am trying to write but my writing is so bad that I really think I must spend the summer reading stiff books; and making English History lectures for my women. I know this is what you want—only reviews, for the sake of money, and no silly articles.

Yr. AVS

We met Walter Crum in the street today, looking for a yeoman in a boarding house. He wants to tramp with Thoby.

Berg

1. Of the Sichel *Medici* book by another reviewer.
2. Vanessa's portrait of Lady Robert Cecil.

30th April [1905]

My Violet,

Great family rejoicings, the first commission! A Mrs Seton wants a life size portrait of her son, aged 4—or of her son and daughter. This is very immediate fruit. She liked the portrait of Lady Robert Cecil. So now one niece [Vanessa] at anyrate is launched—and the good Aunt ought to be proud, I think. Really it aint bad, as the woman is a perfect stranger, and the show has only been open 2 days.

We saw Beatrice on Friday—more tawny and unkempt than ever—*both* shoe laces untied, so I suppose marriage is quite out of the question. She chuckled and chattered like a mischievous bird, and we smoked cigarettes at 3.30 in the Bath drawing room!

[Nurse] Fardell was here today, but I sat in my room. She has been nursing Lord Edward Cecil.[1] Now Jack [Hills] sits downstairs, and I have 3 fat books about Spain to read for the Times[2]—a peace offering after the Sichel affair. You will be surprised to hear that I am an authority upon Spain —but so it is.

Nessa and I have been arguing the ethics of suicide all the morning, as we are alone, and what is an immoral act. You see how badly we need your chaste mind.

Yr. AVS

Berg

[May 1905]

My Violet,

You really have no right to scold—*you* dont write letters; an intoxicated fly might do what you do on a sheet of paper. Really next time send me news, and not all curses; besides which if our long and devoted friendship subsists on letters, dead it is by this time. Making a living, as I do, by the pen, it is indecent to use it for the purpose of friendship, so you would feel, if you had what we call a 'nice mind'.

I have been splashing about in racing society since I saw you—that is dined with George at Lady Carnarvons—*young* Lady C. this time, thank God. It was the night of the Kemptown races, and we talked about horses all night, which are probably more interesting than books. Then I have seen Margaret [Duckworth], who is a nice woman, and our acquaintance begins

1. Lord Robert Cecil's brother.
2. See Virginia's article, *Journeys in Spain* (*TLS*, 26 May 1905), reprinted in *Contemporary Writers*.

to grow promising. We shall have to know each other all our lives, so we can take time about it.

I have been reading Miss Robin's book[1] all the evening, till the last pages. It explains how you fall in love with your doctor, if you have a rest cure. She is a clever woman, if she weren't so brutal. By the way, I am going to write history one of these days. I always did love it; if I could find the bit I want. I have got a ticket for Dr Williams Library across the square, and describe myself as a 'journalist who wants to read history' and so I do feel a professional Lady. It is now time to apologise for my egoism, and ask you how you are. However, one more thing. Kitty writes that she has made great friends with the writer of Elizabeth's German Garden[2]; who says, what is the point of the story, that *my* article on *Music* interested her so much!!! By the way, what did Herbert Paul[3] say on the same subject? I have always meant to ask you.

Now, I have looked through several bookstalls for your flower book, but cant find it. It is more than ever borne in on me that the Quaker secretes one about her person; write, and make her disgorge.

I have been pouring my life blood into the grim bones of early English history all the morning[4]: they wont care for it. I cant screw up my courage to send anything to Mrs Lyttelton, or the Academy (I am back, I see, insensibly, on the old subject!) The Times sent me a proof of the Spanish books. I changed a little, to make my criticism less abrupt. Look in Friday's paper; or I'll send it you.

What news of the Lord Chancellor?[5] I see one of the Mackenzies[6] is to marry some one very grand. When do you come back again?

Write a good letter next time.

Yr. AVS

Berg

228: To Violet Dickinson   46 *Gordon Square, Bloomsbury*

[May 1905]

My Violet,

This morning comes a letter from Leo [Maxse] to say that my Music 'was very much appreciated' and he hopes I will send him something else— 'a paradox is always popular'! So I think I shall shoot my Spanish rubbish

1. Elizabeth Robins, *A Dark Lantern* (*Guardian*, 24 May 1905).
2. *Elizabeth and her German Garden* (1898), by 'Elizabeth' (Countess Russell).
3. The author and politician. In 1905 he published his *Life of Froude*.
4. A. S. Green. *Town Life in the Fifteenth Century*.
5. Lord Haldane, Violet's friend, who wished to be Lord Chancellor, but did not achieve the office until 1912.
6. The next-door neighbours in Hyde Park Gate.

[*The Andalusian Inn*] in *that* hole; and thank my stars that it hasn't already gone to the High Church parsonesses [the *Guardian*]. I am touching it up a little and adding a final chapter; do you really think it good enough to send—because I needn't? As a matter of fact, I didn't mean to write any articles this summer under my name, which is becoming rather thread bare.

Tomorrow at 1.30 I expect an addition to my family the Male Chinchilla. I go to meet him at the station. I read a story the other day about a woman who could only paint with a doll on her bed; here shall I satisfy maternal cravings with a kitten?

I am just off to my Morley; where I am to begin with Early Britain and Celts, and they will yawn I know.

Yr. AVS

What do you buy *turf* for; and how old is it:

Perhaps O.[1] will get his rise still. Has anything been said?

Berg

229: To Violet Dickinson   46 *Gordon Square, Bloomsbury*

[May 1905]

My Violet,
Tomorrow I have to spend in the dentists arm chair as usual—so think of me groaning whenever you feel particularly happy.

A letter from Ella [Crum] just came, in which she alludes to that *delightful* meeting which she did *so* enjoy a week ago!! Shant I broil in Hell one day? Tomorrow also is my working women, for whom I have been making out a vivid account of the battle of Hastings. I hope to make their flesh creep! Aint it ridiculous—teaching working women about the ancient Britons!

The cat was taken into the Square today, where it was drenched in a thunder shower, and had to be taken home, and my arms are scratched all over in consequence.

Why do I go on writing to you, when there are three serious and sober and very intelligent letters that I *must* write? It is because you are one of those dangerous women who exercise not at all the right kind of influence over young girls—and Virginia should be so careful whom she knows—I dont think Violet Dickinson is at all the friend I should like for my girls. No darling; she interfered with poor Mr Crum,[2] and made him marry a woman who might sit upon committees—etc etc etc. Ah if you could have

1. Oswald (Ozzie) Dickinson, Violet's brother, a barrister who later became Secretary to the Commissioners in Lunacy.
2. According to Violet, Aunt Mary Fisher had hoped that Walter Crum would marry one of her daughters.

seen his poor Mother as I did when she heard the news—No, I do *not* like Violet Dickinson.

Ask me another day, when Margaret Lyttelton's cease from troubling.

I suppose the holy rites of all the Bishops are now over, and the Lyttelton family more virtuous than ever.

Come up again, before we are all burnt to cinders. My skirt has just come off.

Yr. AVS

Berg

230: To Violet Dickinson   46 *Gordon Square*

Sunday [18 June 1905]

My Violet,

Think to what a pass things have come when I have to write for news of you to Ella [Crum]! And now it appears—as we say in the newspapers—that you have been in London all the time. Why do you say your journey is off? Just as I have worked myself into an unselfish frame of mind and tell everyone how glad I am you are going? Now must I show that the Devil is not dead in me and that my real feeling is purely selfish. But your utterances are so cryptic and epigrammatic that I really dont know what you mean, or why.

We went to our dance at Trinity, where we stayed till 5.30 and we had tea with Mr [Walter] Headlam, and sat with him in King's Gardens afterwards, which was well expounded to the Quaker, and we had a picnic up the river, and dropped our lunch basket into the water, and eat sandwiches soaked in the Cam, and I talked to Fred Maitland for 3 hours, and we dined with Adrian and we lunched with [Clive] Bell, and Nessa smoked cigarettes instead of dancing, and we came back on Thursday night, and we have been more or less dissolute ever since.

Such gaities make it impossible to sit down like a virtuous penny-a-liner, and Nessa and I have been arguing for six hours consecutively—which means generally that I lose my temper in some very remote cause—as for instance the Ethics of Empire (dont that sound grand). Old Thoby went off like the disreputable old ruffian he is to look for birds on the Norfolk broads. Poor Adrian was beginning to feel that his Cambridge was over, and we had to say goodbye to his rooms. It is rather sad to think that he must give up being taught—or rather amused—for ever, and earn his own living. He took a third—so at any rate he has his degree, though not a brilliant one.

Yesterday I did a very melancholy thing—which was to take my working women over the Abbey. Only one came!—and we solemnly went round the Chapel and the waxworks together, and saw the mummy of a 40 year old parrot—which makes history *so* interesting miss!

Ella asks me to meet Mr Buxton the Principal of Morley: so I am rising in philanthropic circles, as I sink in literary ones. No books whatever to review, and I grind at my history with a sense of utterly unrequited energy.

We also stayed at Oxford—this letter is what you might call a news sheet—and we were introduced to six new undergraduates at every meal, and in the intervals—it was a very wet day—the excellent Lettice [Fisher], expounded her theories, always proving them in her own person—how, for instance, the ideal life is the married life—the life of a worker—she teaches— the life of a philanthropist—she runs a slum. We had to confess that our lives were *not* after this pattern. Why is virtue so unattractive—only the utterly dissolute really appeals to me—Herbert [H. A. L. Fisher] writes his histories, and makes his jokes; and they combine intellect and humanity— and Lord, what a bore it all is! But she is really a nice woman.

I find a letter from Dorothea Stephen—that cumbersome square footed cousin—to say, as one might say it was hot weather—that "Christianity rests on a fact—the Resurrection. Believe this or be damned. Goodbye." Why these sudden pieces of news? They are startling in the middle of a dinner party of undergraduates. Now write a coherent letter, and explain what you mean, or what Nelly means. If she changes her plans now, she will prove herself an Aristocrat of the deepest dye. Quaker sends her love. She was quite amusing.

Yr. AVS

Berg

231: To Lady Robert Cecil   [46 *Gordon Square, Bloomsbury*]
[June 1905]

My dear Nelly,

I ought to have written yesterday, but many things prevented it—one of our young Uncles [Adrian] arrived suddenly with three sofas, several tables, and a ton of books from Cambridge.

I shall be delighted to come on Saturday[1]: though I am honestly afraid of boring you, and my habits are very untidy in the house.

Mrs Lyttelton wants me to write her a 'literary article' so I shall sit in a corner and wrestle with some melancholy minor poet. Can you suggest anybody?

I meant to write to you to demand an apology. It is a very bad look out for us if Violet is now found to be necessary to settle legal matters at the Antipodes. I am thinking of drawing up a set of regulations for the use of Violet: not to be taken out of the kingdom[2] etc. etc. etc. Besides which, I

1. To stay with the Cecils at Gale, Chelwood Gate, Sussex.
2. Lady Robert and Violet were planning to embark on a world-cruise to Vancouver and across the Pacific to Japan, returning home by the Suez Canal.

dont see that you have any right to go round the world. You owe duties in Gordon Square, for one thing. However, I will explain all this to you when we meet.

Yrs. affly,
Virginia Stephen

Hatfield

232: TO VIOLET DICKINSON   46 *Gordon Square, Bloomsbury*

[29 June 1905]

My Violet,

You will see in the Times that we have a Nephew [Henry Duckworth], born at 10 this morning, after some difficulty. However Margaret is extremely well, and her son is a true Herbert, with a hooked nose, and a light pink skin—poor little wretch. George sat up for two nights in misery, and hardly knows what he does today—so he took us all to eat ices at Gunters for a treat.

Oh Lord, what a fool I am? *I* go through 2 days of misery, thinking whether to stay with Nelly for a Sunday or not, and then I say yes, and now I hear she has her sister there; and I shall be in acute agony the whole time. Never will I accept any invitation again.

We have six people dining here. Beatrice among them. I have been doing entirely the wrong thing at Morley—Sheepshanks showed wolf's fangs.

Shall we ever find rest in this toilsome world?

Mrs Lyttelton never writes; so I sit and suck my pen.

I ran against Leo and Kitty last night, and rejected my editor this time.

Oh why did I ever accept Nelly? I might sit and read my book in peace, if only I had had the wisdom of a sucking child.

Yr. AVS

Berg

233: TO LADY ROBERT CECIL   46 *Gordon Sq.*

[3? July 1905]

My dear Nelly,

If you were not such a cynical woman you would believe me when I say how much I enjoyed myself with you. Really you made me very happy, in spite of my boring you etc. etc. etc. I think you are a very good person to stay with though I will not here give my reasons—my English being valuable—about a farthing, every 10 words, I should say.

Nessa was given a hot house bundle of exotics—double carnations, and strange unwholesome things grown under glass. My blue flowers beat them completely; and the Fresh fields[1] adorn the Hall. But you oughtn't to have spoilt that border. There are three distinct colours—light blue—dark blue, and purple.

I am now going to begin my Mrs Carlyle.[2] What a mercy it would be if one could write without reading—or read without writing, but a wretch of a journalist never can separate the two.

What a beautiful handwriting this is[3]—and how you can allow your visitors book to be bescrawled with a certain round and deceptive signature [Violet's?] I dont know.

We travelled up this morning with 2 nuns, and one of them said she was being asphyxiated, and must be taken out: but no one paid her any attention and so she recovered.

Now, do you understand that I wish to thank you?

Ever affate,
Virginia Stephen

Hatfield

234: TO LADY ROBERT CECIL   46 *Gordon Square, Bloomsbury*

[July? 1905]

Dear Nelly,

Thank you so much for writing. I didn't mean you to take so much trouble. It's the kind of letter you particularly hate writing too. The Old Maid was only meant for a joke, and a contrast; and if the flash didn't come in the right place she was a failure. And I think she was a failure. I like the old Home best myself and I dont care about the Professor at all—And as for sending my works to live professors—I get steadily further from it. The temptation to stick things into a great desk that I have, is increasing. I dont see why one should ever be read.

Do send me, however, something of yours to read. I think you owe me that.

I must rush and dress for the [Charles] Booths, and as Nessa is out my younger Uncle [Adrian] is going to act Lady's maid, or chief groom. This will explain the fact that my skirt was back to front, and my hooks undone— upon which you will probably be reflecting when you get this! Why does

1. The pun may be a reference to Virginia's and Vanessa's visit to the Freshfields at Forest Row, Sussex, where Lytton Strachey was another guest.
2. Virginia's article on the *Letters* of Jane Welsh Carlyle appeared in the *Guardian* on 2 August 1905.
3. All Virginia's early letters to Lady Robert Cecil were written much more clearly than to any other of her correspondents.

that Stephen girl go out at nights? It is such a pity for people who write to pretend they can behave in drawingrooms etc. etc. etc. This is the theme of a new story:

Send me your Manuscript:

Yr. aff.

Hatfield
AVS

235: TO LADY ROBERT CECIL   *46 Gordon Sq.*

[July 1905]

My dear Nelly,

Thank you very much for writing again. You cant think how delightful it is when people do like your writing; that makes it worth while to write— almost to print. But you are a spirited woman—and here is the address.

Miss Burney (or successor) [typist]
48 Bedford Row,
W.C.

There is a new woman, whose name I forget; but the address is right.

I will keep the conditions faithfully: I saw Violet, and never whispered a word [about Nelly's writings]!

I feel always that writing is an irreticent thing to be kept in the dark— like hysterics.

Yr. aff.
AVS

Send me the things very soon; and why not 4 chapters![1]

Hatfield

236: TO LADY ROBERT CECIL   *46 Gordon Square, Bloomsbury*

[July 1905]

My dear Nelly,

You are rather severe with me I think, to send two chapters out of a book, and not the beginning chapter.

But I have read them with great interest all the same. Does this seem to you the sort of humbug literary people generally write? Honestly you seem to me to have real gifts. In the first place, you can put great live men on the scene and move them about as they ought to move: 2ndly, you can talk without self consciousness: 3rdly you write what I call a pure and candid style. It is clear, without being prismatic; and nervous without being muscular, like Meredith for example. So with these gifts—and you know

1. Lady Robert was writing a novel, which was never published.

they are gifts, I dont see why you shouldn't write a really good novel—The faults that strike me—but I'm not quite sure because that is such a fragment to dogmatise upon—are a little tendency to write with your eye off the object; that is, you might concentrate a little more; and I am not sure that you should dwell so long upon a hero's parents. But that is a matter of proportion, and depends on the length of the book.

But do please go on with it: because I think you have a vein of rather refreshing humour in you: and you are so clean handed, and sensitive of touch. And I am sure you have the feeling of live people in you, and the way they act and react; I recognise it, because I am wholly without it.

This is written rather hurriedly, because I am coming to dine with you: so if I am late you are really responsible; and I mayn't plead this excuse before Nessa, or Sloper [the butler], I suppose.

"My mistress a horthur? What now!"

Your affate,
AVS

Send me the rest; and finish the book for the autumn Season. I will send the MS tomorrow.

Hatfield

237: To Violet Dickinson [46 *Gordon Square, Bloomsbury*]

[July 1905]

My Violet,

Tuesday will do just as well for me as Thursday, or any other day. But remember that you lunch here on Friday this week—and think on the seas that will soon divide us!

I have been trying to analyse Mrs Carlyle all the morning; and find I write such marvellous dry nonsense. I sometimes doubt the value of words, which is a terrible confession for a journalist to make. Proofs come of the Andalusian Inn, and a short review, which is a shade more scornful than I meant. But I dont suppose the most sensitive of authors cares what the Guardian says of him—preaching the charities of the parish in the next breath. Perhaps Mrs Lyttelton will have some sea sanity blown into her brains.

I went to a shop to look for little travelling books for you today—but they had only the usual Temple Classics. Here they are, in case you find them useful.

We take chairs and sit on our balcony after dinner, and watch the servant girls giggling with waiters in the shade of the trees. Really Gordon Square with the lamps lit and the light on the green is a romantic place—even

hangouts may be will o'the wisps. I say in my Carlyle article "Coruscations are more in letters"!! Such and so profound is my wisdom. Do you like my fluent rounded style, or my curt and mordant style the best?—or the better—as the [Edith] Sichels of this world have it.

I am dining with Savage tomorrow night, and I think I shall ask him what bee gets into my bonnet when I write to you. Sympathetic insanity, I expect it is. You know you must really be insane to leave England and think to widen your mind by knocking round the world. You will bring back photographs to show us! Here I state my firm refusal to look at one of them. I am treated with sympathy now, as one about to lose her solitary friend. Indeed I cant conceive a more pathetic case, and I shed secret and bitter tears over it. No one to ask me if my back aches, or if I have written anything lately—or to promise well for my future. Letters must come hot from the Equator with praise, or I shall give up literature and take to marriage. We saw Georges baby take his bottle the other day, looking more like a Christian now he can eat. His eyes are still shut, and squint; and he is supposed to be like his cousin, Lord Porchester![1]

But all this is profoundly uninteresting; and I begin to think that one sentence of my article at any rate is true. I am going to dine with the Buxtons to discuss my good—would be good at any rate—works—Letters are not literature! It is so odd to plunge into philanthropic society, living on the other side of the river of a sudden.

Now I must write 2 other letters.

Yr. AVS

Berg

238: To Emma Vaughan   46 *Gordon Square.*

[11 July 1905]

Dearest Todger,

You are a provoking reptile to sit tight in your hole when we come to see you. How could I know that Out meant In—you ought to have a voice in [the arrangements of] your hall now you are back. But it will take some time to wean Marny from her bachelor ways, and make her understand that Miss Vaughan has a sister.

Now concentrate your dusky jewel on the question how are we to meet? Do you realise that we are altogether new to you and therefore you must lunch here and be shown over the house, which is our favourite diversion nowadays. Will you come on *Wednesday next* at *1.30* to lunch—or suggest a day if that dont do.

I suppose Marny is taking the bankrupt ladies place by this time and is perpetually out, and really, as a matter of fact never finds it necessary to

1. A title of the Carnarvon family.

198

move that mendacious wooden [In and Out] statement—no word in the English language can I find to describe the instrument which flats keep in their halls.

There are *innumerable* things to talk about. Marny says "Toad and I have been talking wildly"—but it is nothing to the thunderstorms and lightning shafts which will break over your head once you set foot in this house. To begin with—we have a nephew—rather, more properly should I have begun—we have a sister-in-law—We have a new house, in which I own two rooms; one the loveliest Palace on earth; I have stayed with all your available relations, Lamport[1] is at last familiar to me and the loveliest of all its children, Virginia [Isham, b. 1898]: These drops prelude the shower.

Really, my chick, I think you might have called on your fond old cousins before this—my darling—here I am—if ever you want me—you have only to remember—*there she is*—a telegram—a post card—a boy messenger—and I shall be with you in a moment—Marny is so disrespectful about the Fishers; she comes here and stumps up and down the room by the hour with a poker, which she thumps, and talks of Herbert, and shuts one eye—till at last we have had to explain that we dont think such conduct *quite loyal*—

It is over a year since I saw you and how many such years do the scriptures allow us—one of them you willfully spend on fat German sausage eaters—never again do such a thing.

Now write and say you will come.

This lunacy is written waiting for dinner.

Yr. loving,

Sussex   AVS

239: To Emma Vaughan   [46 *Gordon Square, Bloomsbury*]

Friday [July? 1905]

My dearest Todger,

Marny threw out cryptic hints the other day that you are on the look out for a profession and might possibly take some work at Morley. I am dining with the Principal, Mr Buxton, on Monday, and if you liked, I could offer him your invaluable services. There is work of all kinds going, and they are perfectly *delighted* to find helpers. I am certain you would do it splendidly, and it is really interesting, I think—so much better than the poverty and crime in which Marny's lurid soul delights.

However, this may not be your wish at all. Send me a line; or, much better still, come here, and see us—which it is your duty to do. Come Saturday or Sunday at tea-time.

Your loving

Sussex   Goatus

1. Lamport Hall, Northamptonshire, the home of Millicent Isham, Emma's sister.

240: To Lady Robert Cecil   46 *Gordon Square, Bloomsbury*

[July 1905]

My dear Nelly,

You see what it is to have an author to stay with you—what torrents you bring down on your head. Please behave like the brutal and candid reader you are in your professional capacity. Of course I couldn't say all, or indeed half, what I wanted; it is too long even now I think. So I have had to cramp and cut short. She was a wonderful woman [Mrs Carlyle]—the more I think so the more I read her—I read your work the other day—and I couldn't see what was wrong with the grammar. Why mayn't one say "and which"? I always do. It seems to me yours is a harder job than mere reviewing: because people may act on your advice, and they certainly never do on mine!

Your aff.,

Hatfield   AVS

241: To Lady Robert Cecil   46 *Gordon Sq.*

[July 1905]

Dear Nelly,

Thank you very much for your criticisms which are so good that I have actually attended to them!

It is thankless work writing these horrible little snap shots—Six volumes of real genius boiled down into 1,500 words of solid prose! When I said that she [Mrs. Carlyle] wrote her letters with a particular object etc., I didn't mean that she wrote them to serve a useful purpose, so to speak; but she did write them with a distinct view of her correspondent—and with no thought of a possible biographer. However, I can't express myself this morning!

I am so sorry that you were made ill by my writing. That is really an unfortunate effect to have!

Your affate,

Hatfield   AVS

242: To Violet Dickinson   [46 *Gordon Square, Bloomsbury*]

[July 1905]

My Violet,

Here is Jane [Carlyle]—not much good I am afraid. Nelly doesn't feel enthusiastic; says its 'hard end' for the Guardian; and I have altered words to suit her. Bring it up tomorrow.

Yr. AVS

Berg

Virginia at 18

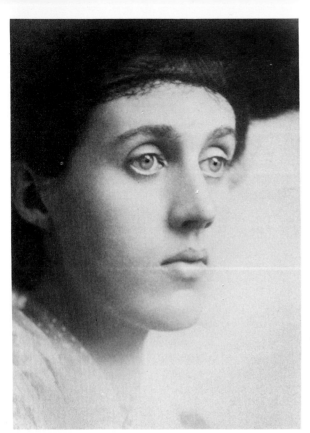

Vanessa Stephen in 1903

Thoby Stephen in 1906

[July 1905]

My Violet,

I will come next Thursday unless I am told not to—and I have a horror of inflicting myself on Welwyn again. For Gods sake dont have Thomas[1] to meet me. I feel that everything I do in that enchanted cottage has a spell over it!

We have got through our Sunday, which I cant help feeling a mercy, though it wasn't so bad. But there were 10 other people, mostly relations, and the river [Thames] swarms with paint and powder and brass bands all day long. Old Lady Young[2] is a fine old woman; really rather clever and wise, and amusing. Otherwise the people weren't amusing.

No other news can I think of tonight. Nessa had her Committee,[3] wh. sat for two hours on very few eggs: decided to take a room in S. Kensington, of all unearthly places. Nessa is Secretary, and will want all her diplomacy—one half of the committee shriek Whistler and French impressionists, and the other are stalwart British. George has been fluttering about, but I dont see him. All the Herbert family are to vouch for that baby's morals [as Godparents]—and Austen Chamberlain!

I had a long letter from Ella [Crum] to say did she ever tell me what a wonderful thing it is to have me at Morley. I do love flattery.

My cat is lost—out all day and night, and not back yet. I suppose some cat stealer has taken him, but I hope not. I am very fond of him; poor little beast.

No news from [Mrs] Lyttelton. I wish you could induce Nelly to like my writing.

Really it is better than that mild and mellifluous cant. If only I could attack the Church of England! Whenever I take up my pen for the Guardian Saxon[4] comes behind and suggests all sorts of proprieties.

Nessa is dining with Ronny Norman and his wife. Oh Lord the respectable stupidities of their world. George and he will govern us all one of these days, by sheer force of stupidity. One almost has to respect such a talent.

Yr. AVS

Berg

1. Dr Thomas had seen Virginia at Welwyn during her illness.
2. Sir George and Lady Young lived at Formosa Place, Cookham, which she made a centre of political and social life.
3. This committee was the origin of the Friday Club, founded for the discussion of the fine arts, which held its first meeting in October 1905.
4. Saxon Sydney-Turner, one of Thoby's Cambridge friends, was already a frequent visitor at Gordon Square.

[July 1905]

My Violet,

I sent off in great haste two wretched little attempts—say which is the least wretched, because I want to send the survivor to the Academy.[1]

I am going to make as much use of you as I can before you are beyond reach. O my Violet, why do you go when you have successfully trained me to climb round you? That is an image which should appeal to your feelings as a gardener.

We had a long argument last night about the friends who were to be invited to St Ives[2]; and it took rather an odd form, for we found that everybody wanted the others to ask *their* friends. And we each had to produce the names of two, and I had the greatest difficulty in finding even that number; and one of them was *decided* properly to belong to Nessa.[3] My trump card is no use this year. "Violet is *quite* an exceptional person" say both Thoby and Adrian.

I have been sent the proof of Mrs Carlyle. O Lord, it is bad—such an ugly angular piece of writing, all jagged edges.

Do you feel convinced I *can* write? I am going to produce a real historical work this summer; for which I have solidly read and annotated 4 volumes of medieval English.

Fred Maitland was here this afternoon. There is a man I respect. He would read 4 volumes to write two words, and think nothing of it.

The Baby, Henry Austen George Herbert de l'Etang [Duckworth], was christened this morning, and I hope sleeps the sounder for it; but his aunts weren't there.

Somehow manage to come when you are next in London.

Yr. AVS

Berg

245: TO LADY ROBERT CECIL   *46 Gordon Square, Bloomsbury*

[August 1905]

My dear Nelly,

Here are the ever youthful poets.[4] They are rather a melancholy company, I think. However the eldest cant be over 25. I read a real poem in the

1. Virginia published *Famous Women of Wit and Beauty* in the August issue of *Academy*.
2. The Stephens were planning a long summer holiday in Cornwall.
3. The other was Pernel Strachey.
4. *Euphrosyne*, privately printed in the summer of 1905, contained poems by Clive Bell, Lytton Strachey, Walter Lamb, Saxon Sydney-Turner, Leonard Woolf, and others. See Quentin Bell, Vol. I, Appendix C.

Daily Chronicle this morning, which had a right to be melancholy. It was written by a charwoman,[1] on a piece of paper in which sugar was wrapped, and she then went and hung herself.

> "Here lies a poor woman who always was tired
> She lived in a house where help was not hired.
> Her last words on earth were "Dear friend I am going
> Where washing aint done, nor sweeping nor sewing;
> But everything there is exact to my wishes,
> For where they dont eat theres no washing of dishes.
> I'll be where loud anthems will always be ringing:
> But having no voice I'll be clear of the singing:
> Dont mourn for me now, dont mourn for me never;
> I'm going to do nothing for ever and ever."

The jury said unanimously that she was mad, which proves once more what it is to be a poet in these days. However these seven poets have no such mania in them.

Why do I write all about suicide and mad people?—it is not a cheerful way of saying goodbye.

Please keep Violet in very good order, and *write long letters*. We are stationary: and a letter is bound to hit us. And remember that you are never to go round the world again.

Yr. aff.

AVS

Hatfield

246: TO VIOLET DICKINSON   [*Trevose View, Carbis Bay, Cornwall*]

[13? August 1905]

My Violet,

Here we are settled comfortably, and with the divinest view in Europe, I maintain. You wont find a better though you go round the world for it.

The house is at any rate separate from other houses, and there are plenty of windows. Nessa has been draping the chairs, which are blue plush with yellow patterns. We have linoleum carpets, and works of art thrown in. However, it really dont much matter. I look across the bay, and see the ships pass on the sky line, and think that yours will be one, which of course it wont.

It is a strange dream to come back here again. The first night we groped

---

1. In fact, traditional: 'An epitaph for a tired housewife.'

our way up to Talland House[1] in the dark, and just peeped at it from behind the Escalonia hedge. It was a ghostly thing to do: it all looked quite unchanged. Old people meet us and stop and talk to us, and remember us playing on the beach.

However, it is the loveliest country, whatever age you happen to be, and really not spoilt. We went for a walk this afternoon which we used to go every Sunday, and saw the Lizard and [St] Michaels Mount. I find it so difficult to write here, but I must set to work tomorrow. The Academy has sent me a book of famous women with a polite letter hoping I will write for them—and this is not to be despised—my balance is very light at the bank.

We seem to live in a perpetual love making, and giving in marriage.[2]

By the way, I read that the Japanese bathe always 3 times a day: Sometimes more often. So your sponges will probably do more for you than passports.

My friend, Pernel Strachey, has got diptheria, in a friends house, so she cant come here.

This is not a *valedictory* (a long word which I keep generally for the Guardian) letter. I mean I shall write or somehow say good bye again. Lord how I hate saying good bye!

This object must be pinched in the middle when it squirts you. I cant conceive anything more wholly useless, and unnecessary—however, you can leave it tactfully behind, and I will never ask whether it was a success.

AVS

The squirt wont get into the envelope; so you must imagine a most beautiful silver squirt, shaped like a watch, and fountains of nectar gushing from it at a touch.

Berg

247: To Violet Dickinson   [*Trevose View, Carbis Bay, Cornwall*]

[August 1905]

My Violet,
    There is nothing so abominable as saying goodbye in this world; and we have all been wound up for months to expect it which makes it still worse. You wont get this letter after all, so it dont very much matter. If you do, I want to charge you to take the very greatest care of every bone in your long

1. Talland House stood above St Ives Bay and was the scene of many summer holidays when the Stephen children were young. They had last been there in 1894.
2. Clive Bell had proposed to Vanessa, and was refused.

and attenuated body. Nelly has a husband; but your husbands are many and your family numerous, so your responsibility is all the greater.

It is a delicious calm sea today, so perhaps you will have the same at Liverpool.

Dont think anything uncharitable of me; and try to come back an unspoilt virgin in spite of your widened mind.

Yr. loving,
AVS

Berg

248: TO VIOLET DICKINSON   *[Trevose View, Carbis Bay Cornwall]*

27th Aug. [1905]

My Violet,

I feel entirely at sea where or when this will reach you, if it ever does. It is too late to make a shot at Vancouver. We have 6 separate lists of addresses, which are all ingeniously varied; in case we should get bored I suppose.

I find some difficulty in conceiving that the things we do at this moment here will interest you in some months time on the other side of the globe. Nothing *has* happened, however. We have had no visitors, as Elena Rathbone[1] and Pernel Strachey both fell through, and we have only Gerald to look forward to next week. So our life is one of pastoral simplicity: read and write all the morning, and walk in the afternoon, and play Bridge after dinner. And you are flying across continents!

But it isn't as dull as it sounds, and the country makes up for the society of *most* people. Most was underlined with a purpose, my Violet.

We watched the sea for the seven days we supposed that you were on it, and it was rough every one of the seven. I do wonder how you got through the voyage in your tiny cabin. Did Nelly and you share it; and were there delicacies innumerable? I can imagine vivid blushes, and shouted confidences. Thank God I was not in your place.

I suppose you have permanently attached to yourself at least six fellow passengers, and that all the steerage wives bore their babies under your guidance. [Nurse] Traill, by the way, is going through a course of maternity work. However that wont interest you. Have you bought any photographs yet? You dont go by Niagara, I hope. Lord, there are quantities of things I want answered at once. Not having a map here, you have now sailed entirely out of my ken. My mental geography ends at America. 'Where is Yokohama?' says Nessa!

---

1. Who married Bruce Richmond, editor of *The Times Literary Supplement*.

Thoby and Adrian are very nice, and easy going; they play piquet when they are not arguing points of law. Nessa produces 2 canvases a day; and is mad with the difficulties of the sea.

This is a divine place; none other like it in the world. I cant remember where your cottage is to be. We seriously think of buying a farm here for £10 a year; it would be an economical thing to do, I think.

I am writing for my own pleasure, which is rather a relief after my Guardian drudgery, and I can assail the sanctity of Love and Religion without care for the Parsons morals.

The Quaker has written a pamphlet about Christian Science, to confute Mrs Butler.[1] The Stephen family seems to think no controversy complete without their printed opinion. A wonderful race!

What a mercy it is, my good woman, that I can write to you, as old ladies say, with *perfect freedom*. Otherwise this letter would read a little incoherent.

Thoby has written to Bell to say he is very sorry;[2] Nessa told him, as she thought it better, and he says he long suspected it. Bell had confessed that he could even give up hunting if necessary in order to marry. No news from Bell. No one, I will here state, has yet asked me in marriage.

I am writing 2 large works; one upon the letters of the Paston family; the other upon the nature and characteristics of the county of Cornwall; I want to learn how to write descriptions without adjectives. Both works show remarkable promise—because they are still unwritten.

I dont suppose European weather can interest you, but try and imagine that it has been raining for 3 days running. Can you remember what rain looks like?

I imagine that I am going to address this letter to Singapore, or Yokohama. At any rate you will have crossed another sea; and your next step will be taken in my direction. At present I can only think of a long and attenuated form striding rapidly away from me across half the blue paper in the map. Take care of yourself my Violet. I have not left much room for emotion, which you must see in all the blank spaces. It is painfully borne in upon me that I have no right to be extravagant with my friends—lavishing them all over the world. I hope you feel vigorous and imperial spirited. Is the mind beginning to stretch? It is a painful process I expect. It will be terrible when you can only talk of our colonies, and blood and water. Give my love, if that conveys anything to you, to Nelly, and make it as hot as you can. I swear it leaves me alive and kicking. Write—and be a good woman. We want you badly.

AVS

Berg

1. Mrs Josephine Butler, social reformer (1828-1906).
2. About Vanessa's refusal to marry Clive.

Trevose View, Carbis Bay, Cornwall

17th Sept. 1905

Dearest Todger,

Your letter came just as we were wondering what had become of you. I cant say it set our minds at ease. Really for two virgins you do penetrate into the most impossible positions. Art, even in Suffolk, rouses the emotions and is besides such a veil for intimacy. Marny at a street corner beneath an umbrella, may conceal *much*. And Miss Harris I firmly believe to be a myth. Who the—what the, where the—is Miss Harris? Another umbrella, I think.

Here we have been living among the fields of paradise, among Gods. You can't think how people strip themselves of their coverings at the sea and appear as nature made them. The Stephen family disports almost—no, I will not finish that sentence. Two youths,[1] bachelors, will stay here shortly: and Cornwall is worse than any amount of sketching. Why do you go to Suffolk when you might come here? We have a little lodging house, of the most glaring description, but the divinest country all round. Moors, seas, hills, rocks, a land flowing not only with honey but with cream. Here Nessa paints all the afternoon; and I write all the morning: from 10 to 1. Thoby and Adrian discuss points of law; and then take to piquet. We all walk and wander like so many disembodied ghosts. We go to tea with the people who now own Talland. They are a delightful pair of artists, with a family of the age we used to be. Oh Lord it is Sunday morning, and the vapours distilled by innumerable congregations, of whom you are one, I hope reach me even in this unpolluted spot.

I am always put into clean clothes on Sunday which I do hate. No news of the Fishers, no news of anyone—but stay—as the villain says in the melodrama. We hear that Tisdale will give Lady Isham his best professional attention and Miss Sheepshanks writes that Miss Vaughan will help in the Library [at Morley] possibly twice a week. My night is Wednesday at 9. Dont translate Sheepshanks into Lamblegs; she is rather a watery kind of woman.

I heard from Madge this morning. The Moors are better than the Alps after all, and they have sold Davos[3]. What an odd end to all their agitations. Write and say what you do next. I wish you would visit *Paston* on the Norfolk Coast.[2] Love to the dissolute figure beneath the umbrella.

Your Goatus

Sussex

1. Saxon Sydney-Turner and possibly Ralph Hawtrey, the economist.
2. Where the Paston family lived in the 15th century.
3. The Symonds' house in Switzerland, where Madge and her sisters were brought up.

250: To Violet Dickinson   *Trevose View, Carbis Bay,*
                                  Cornwall

1st Oct: [1905]

My Violet,

We are already rather mixed by your systems of addresses. Kitty says you wont go to Singapore at all: however this must take its chance.

Writing to you at this distance is like talking to someone in the dark; and beggarly pen and ink though the staff of my life (just received a cheque for £5 from the Guardian) carry a very short way. Besides which when you have sat stationary a whole 8 weeks in the country it seems unnecessary to write letters about nothing. Our longest expedition was to the Lands End and just 15 miles; and meanwhile you whirl thousands I daresay. However to a person of imagination the Lands End is as impressive as the Equator.

We find some news of you in the papers; the Victorian went ashore after you left her. Perhaps you dont know it? What a chance for you! A real shipwreck, groaning victims, corpses perhaps; what a pity you were done out of it.

Oh Lord there are thousands of things I want to know and to ask. We have had visitors for the last 4 weeks; Kitty and Leo [Maxse] in lodgings; Gerald, Imogen Booth,[1] Sylvia Milman,[2] Jack [Hills], and now two Cambridge youths [Sydney-Turner and ? Hawtrey]. These last are a great trial. They sit silent, absolutely silent, all the time; occasionally they escape to a corner and chuckle over a Latin joke. Perhaps they are falling in love with Nessa; who knows? It would be a silent and very learned process. However I dont think they are robust enough to feel very much. Oh women are my line and not these inanimate creatures. The worst of it is that they have not the energy to go, and in all probability they will travel up to London with us on Thursday. It is now Sunday, and the first fire of the winter has been lit—It is rather exciting to get back and begin work again, although the country is so divine I hate to shut it out. It is quite deserted now, and the leaves falling; you are in full summer I suppose. Here I sit cold in my room, writing by candlelight though it is not much after six. Is there any place in the world—literally one may ask you that now—like Cornwall? All this morning I have tried to spin out words about it; so that the fine cream has been taken off my brain already. This is only skim milk for you. I have written quite a lot, always with your stern eye searching me out across the world. I wish I had you here to encourage. No one really takes very much interest, why should they, in my scribblings. Do you think I shall ever write a really good book? Anyhow I can manage rather better than I did though there

1. Daughter of Charles Booth, author of *Life and Labour of the People in London,* to whom George Duckworth had been temporarily a secretary.
2. The Milmans had been friends of the Stephen family for three generations. Sylvia was the daughter of Arthur Milman, a barrister.

are still awful bare and unprolific patches. Also I have read a good deal, mostly 18th century; that was my weak point. Writing is a divine art, and the more I write and read the more I love it. Nessa has done a lot of work, and far and away, I think, her best work. Some of it is really good; I want her to hire a room and have a small show this winter. Her [Friday] Club flourishes, and will begin immediately, I suppose. So we shall all get into swing again. I do wish you were in London; that is quite honest; I feel more than usually incompetent without you, and no one has quite your genius. Only the effervescent Crum remains; and Kitty who is to me as salt to a very sensitive snail. I liked her better this time, rather simplified in the country, but there is always Leo in every sentence she speaks. Oh damn Leo I say. She lives in an unreal Paradise; I am a kind of slug or snail there. By the way, Imogen Booth is a real find; very clever and broadminded, with a great deal of character. But she is off to America. Dont tell me you mean to stay away till February—or I shall take the pledge never to get on kissing terms with woman more—and think what that would mean to me. I am going to write to Nelly: though I think it is a case of bread on the waters, to be washed up perhaps six months hence in Grove End Road. How allegoric I am to-night! I feel that these words ought to be more durable than brass to travel all the way—where? Singapore, or Yokohama. That must be decided now; I think I shall toss. I hear that you are *everything* to Nelly; nothing left for me then. No news of your Lyttelton. I hope she will send more work. We are all flourishing, and as brown as your housemaid. I wish I could conceive of you at all. Thoby says you have all been received by the Mikado. Take care you dont get into Punch as an international joker. I can imagine you sprawling half across a cartoon.

Take great care of yourself, and consider that you only hold your shanks in trust. That sounds a Christian sentiment to end with. Come back soon, and we shall rejoice.

Yr. loving AVS

Berg

2 5 1: To Violet Dickinson   46 *Gordon Square*

Nov. 9th [1905][1]

My Violet,

It suddenly strikes me that I shall only just catch you as it is; so have you been flying through space. I did write to you the other day, but finding it all dusty and out of date I think I must try again.

It is odd to think that we were at St Ives when I wrote before; we seem rooted and settled here for ages. In fact I hardly know where in our manifold activities to begin. Should you think that was English? Heaven knows.

1. The Stephens had returned to London from St Ives on 5 October.

I have had such a run of work as is not remembered for I cant say how many years; books from the Times, the Academy, the Guardian—it must be confessed that I write great nonsense, but you will understand that I have to make money to pay my bills. The Quaker wont see it; and talks with deep significance of *serious* work, not *pot boilers*. Really I have almost more reviewing than I feel to be quite moral; but I manage some Greek and good English in between.

Then Nessa has fairly got her [Friday] Club started; and they are to have an Exhibition at once, and you will just be in time to go with me to see it. Really that gives me quite a thrill. I have been friendless so long that I shall suddenly feel respectable. Shall I buy a new hat to celebrate your return? I tell you an emphatic red line is drawn under Dec: 3rd in my calendar.

Nessa has written you so many sheets that I suppose I may be as foolish as I like here. Then we have our Thursdays[1]; your husband came to one, in the midst of discussion upon the birth place of Jesus Christ; the little poets[2] were rather afraid of his evening dress, and huddled together in corners like moping owls. But he was very good for them.

Then on Wednesdays I have my English Composition; 10 people: 4 men 6 women. It is I suppose the most useless class in the College; and so Sheep-shanks thinks. She sat through the whole lesson last night; and almost stamped with impatience. But what can I do? I have an old Socialist of 50, who thinks he must bring the Parasite (the Aristocrat, that is you and Nelly) into an essay upon Autumn; and a Dutchman who thinks—at the end of the class too—that I have been teaching him Arithmetic; and anaemic shop girls who say they would write more but they only get an hour for their dinner, and there doesn't seem much time for writing. Adrian started a Greek class; which lived for two lessons, and came to an end last night. Oh Morley College is a fine place and—can you end the quotation?

The other night I had such a desire for you that I took down and read through your Tract, which brought me great comfort. Oh thank God now you will have seen the world, and know all that is to be known; the mind of man, and the heart of woman. So stay at home and teach the young bears how to grow.

I have made tentative efforts to ingratiate myself with Margaret Lyttelton and Katharine Horner; but Katharine answers vaguely that she is in the country, and dear Margaret though a great force is rather oppressive in a drawing room. But I adore all young women. Kate Greenaways life[3] is just out. "Intimacy with Miss Violet Dickinson" has a paragraph to itself. "As

1. The 'Thursday Evenings' at Gordon Square.
2. See p. 202, note 4.
3. *The Life of Kate Greenaway* (the illustrator of children's books), by M. H. Spielmann and G. S. Layard, 1905. Violet had become a great friend of Kate Greenaway in 1894, and many of Kate's letters to her are printed in the biography.

Miss D. is particularly tall and slim etc etc etc" Anyhow you seem to have been a great comfort to her; you have had a past my Violet. It strikes me that you are really something of a celebrity—and not an improper one either. Aunt Anny [Ritchie] says that Mrs Lyttelton gives a "melancholy roar of laughter"; I went to tea with her, and she roared at me, like a shaggy old Lioness with wide jaws, and gave me 4 books to review; I am still stuck in the 4th.

I got two most charming letters from you and Nelly the other day; just as [Dr] Wilson had put some stuff in my eyes so that for nearly 3 days I couldn't read a word. It was really tantalising; and Adrian had to decipher Nelly's, as I couldn't wait for Nessa to come down and I didnt dare give him yours.

What fragment of your body will be thrown to me among the howling crowd of your friends? The widening of your mind has been a painful discipline. Dont buy me things: come back well and affectionate.

Yr. AVS

Berg

Nov. 10th [1905]

Dear Nelly,

Your letter of the other morning gave me great delight. It seems to me that you have a valuable talent which it is your duty to exercise, as my Quaker Aunt would say. I am an authority upon Japan now; I daresay I shall be given the Japanese books to do for the Times.

It seems absurd that we should still be in the same place where you left us. However I cant help it; and I really feel it difficult to find anything to tell you about the Capital—or Mother City of the Empire—as I suppose you now call it. Blood, you will begin when we next meet, is thicker etc. etc. We have just been having our Lord Mayor's Show. It was Dr Barnardo's homes, and the Entente Cordiale this time. I cannot say that I saw even the crowd. It is great fun to start the year again, and we are in full swing—painting, writing—Thursday evenings—and tonight we all go off with Beatrice Thynne to Nessa's Young Artists Club. They are very catholic in their tastes and call Thoby an artist because he doesn't paint—perhaps that is the long sought definition—and me one because? perhaps because I write reviews. Now would you like some Grub Street Shop? You are in the trade too. I have been scribbling all the time you have been sailing, and if all the sheets I have written were pasted together they would just catch you up— all but three feet 2 inches and $\frac{1}{4}$. It is the busy season, and I have never been without 3 books in hand since I came back. The Times sends me one novel every week; which has to be read on Sunday, written on Monday, and printed on Friday. In America, as you know, they make sausages like that. Mrs Lyttelton asked me to tea, and gave me a prize of 4 books afterwards; the Academy thinks I can write about Wilhelmina, Margravine of Bayreuth.[1]

Kitty distrusts the neighbourhood of the British Museum; Virginia might marry an *author* and they always talk about themselves! The Quaker writes "When I asked what you were doing I meant writing". Do you see the excessively subtle point of that sentence? Somehow she drew a distinction between reviewing and other kinds of literature. I wish you were back, and I could have tea with you in your country house. You will find it difficult at first to remember at what precise spot on the globe you are; and you may overshoot the mark occasionally and take the train to Cumberland instead of the Bus to Gordon Square. But I believe the brain recovers in a month or two. Anyhow a few hundred miles wont make much difference.

There is a rumour, I hope your friend lies, that you are going to stay in the Riviera when Violet comes back. I assure you that London is looking its best; Gordon Square in particular is full of a romantic and tender grace. The one quality lacking in Japan is what the Greeks (and the Cockneys) call Pathos. A bare tree visible in the Light of Human Suffering means more than all the Pagodas in Tokio. I am trying to evolve a theory for tonight: that is the inward and intimate meaning of the last few remarks. Tell me honestly what you think of my Style? Do you know I lecture on English Composition at Morley? "Is this an Arithmetic Class Miss?" a new Dutchman asked me last time when I had done. "It is clear that you must join the Elocution Class next door" I said.

Mrs Lyttelton told me terrible stories of her letter writing industry: how Violet will be snowed up with thick dispatches about Womens Interests and the Factory girls Morals etc. She writes once a week. Mrs Crum has found it necessary to contract her hand in order to let Violet share the difficulties of the adopted son. Should he be allowed cake—or only jam at tea—and which first—if either, as indeed she thinks herself—but Walter says—only you know Walter is so fussy—

Do write again: would red ink make that more emphatic? I have just written a very vivid account of the Desert myself: I confess I should have felt more at my ease in Japan. You and Violet seem to have explored each other with entirely satisfactory results; I wish you would now write an account of that journey for me; I dont so much care for Red Seas, and Rocky Mountains; but I love this Human Inside—

Come back soon. You cant think how crusty and forlorn I am getting, Nessa is just humanised by Kitty.

Yr. aff^{ate,}

AVS

Hatfield

1. By Edith Cuthall. Virginia's review appeared in the November issue.

[early December 1905]

My Violet,
   I dont know if you are really back. I am much excited to think you are. It is an immense pleasure—no English will do the work.
   Let me know whenever you are *not* in the arms of Crum, Lyttelton etc etc; and I recognise your husbands claims.
   Oh Lord—you are a good woman to have come home at last. I can come most times.
                                          Yr. loving AVS

Berg

Sunday [3 December 1905]

My Violet,
   It is a great and damnable disappointment that you aren't back. I had counted upon this Sunday. However, there is no more to be said; and I hope your brother is better, and that this will [not] be too late to catch you.
   You were badly wanted yesterday, at Nessa's Exhibition, it was successful, I think, except that the room was small and dingy and dark, and we had to carry round lamps when the light gave out. But I think people were interested in the pictures, and there were no very bad ones. Nessa's showed up well.
   The [Friday] Club flourishes, and begins to quarrel which is a healthy sign. You will be in the thick of it all soon, so I wont go into details. As a study of human nature I find it very amusing; but thank the Lord I am not responsible. Old Nessa goes ahead, and slashes about her, and manages all the business, and rejects all her friends pictures, and dont mind a bit. She is said to have a genius for organisation; and it all seems to interest her—it would bore me to death.
   On Friday Ella dines here and goes with us.
   But you will hear all these things yourself: what a mercy! I think I hate writing letters about facts, and I grow too stupid to write fiction.
   I had a most charming letter from Nelly: the only thing that palls is her praise of you. It isn't healthy to be so appreciative. A good quarrel—nasty sarcasm—and home truths—that is the right stuff for friendship. I think with pleasure of several edged words we have had together. The last on the platform of the underground railway!
   I am going to lunch with [Mrs] Lyttelton on Tuesday, asked a fortnight ago, so I suppose there is a literary party. I have written a lot for her lately; I enclose two proofs; they aren't really up to much; but one was a job that I

had to get through. I could wish that she had a finer literary taste sometimes; she sticks her broad thumb into the middle of my delicate sentences and improves the moral tone. If I could get enough work elsewhere I dont think I should bother about the Guardian. The Speaker happily wants me to write for them; and they have just sent 2 vols. of Aingers Essays[1] for me to review. This is more interesting than novels; and it is not a bad paper. You see, when you aren't here I have no one to talk to with perfectly unrestrained egoism.

Last night we dined with Savage; a party of 16, and my word, it was dull. You must make some orderly disposition of your corpse before you get back; I dont think Ella now that she has adopted a son is in the running at all. There are quantities of things I want to talk to you about; but I shant attempt to write.

Yr. loving,
AVS

I saw Katharine Horner the other day; with Lady Marjorie Manners, Cecily and someone else[2]; they all sat on the floor, and talked Hornerese.

Berg

255: TO LADY ROBERT CECIL   46 *Gordon Square, Bloomsbury*

[December 1905]

My dear Nelly,

Violet says you really are back, which I thought extremely unlikely, knowing your habits. I expect you wont want to see mere Europeans; but if you do etc. etc. This is written in a great hurry; we are having a dinner party, and I haven't begun to wash.

I lunched with Violet today: she looks extraordinarily well; I dont think I have ever seen her look better. And she seems to have enjoyed every moment of the journey; and is full of fresh views on life, and experiences, and friendship I suppose.

Shall we come and see you? Anyhow it is a great thing that you are back safe.

Your affate,
AVS

1. Alfred Ainger, *Lectures and Essays*, published posthumously in 1905. He was Chaplain to Queen Victoria and a friend of Leslie Stephen.
2. Lady Marjorie Manners was the daughter of the Duke of Rutland, later Marchioness of Anglesey. 'Cecily' was Cicely Horner, Katharine's elder sister, who later married George Lambton.

Have you many books to read? I have been reviewing one of your firms novels, "The Autobiography of a Red Haired Woman"[1] I expect you . . .
[*last page missing*]

Hatfield

256: TO VIOLET DICKINSON   46 *Gordon Square, Bloomsbury*

[3? January 1906]

My Violet,
    My letters are getting rare and few. We all grow old and bald and tooth-less—and this is one of my aged foibles. As a matter of fact nothing much has happened I think. Nessa and I have been going about, but Christmas is a dismal time. I have been writing all the mornings; not a word will ever be seen in print or by mortal eyes: except mine. Doesn't that excite you? Shall you be able to sleep tonight? This mystery is an exchange for your mystery. What great scheme can you and B[eatrice] possibly have made. Are we all to share bedrooms in some country cottage; or is Dickinson and Stephen started with a capital of £50,000? Your brain is such a boiling fizz of plots that any one may hatch at any moment. Why dont you say how your bronchitis is, or how you feel or anything about your vile body? I confess I do hate it, but these are the penalties of friendship.
    Nelly looked very ill and shrunk I thought—but I am no judge, and it may be temporary. It really is something to weep over when one sees her; I mean her deafness. She couldn't keep a diary abroad she said, because she liked to write what people said, and she had heard nothing! Aunt Minna and she seem both beyond the reach of human help; but At. Minna has had her day.
    I always feel talk bores Nelly too; so one doesn't know what to do for her. She said you had been an ideal companion; and I really think she meant it; always amused, and full of life etc etc.
    I am reading a Greek play, and Virgil and Shakespeare. By the way I bought my £5 worth. So really I feel virtuous, and no pot boiler.
    Nessa has done a picture of me, and a picture of 3 different reds. However she shall tell you. Oh Lord do come back, without any chitis this time. We are landed with Miss Forrest,[2] as you are landed with us. She sits vaguely in the drawing room for hours, and forgets whether she had tea or dinner last, whether children have meat or wine. My head spins with her stories; until I say sternly 'Miss Forrest take my advice and learn Greek' it is like a nightmare.

Yr. AVS

Berg

1. *The Red-haired Woman*, by Louise Kenney. It was published by John Murray, for whom Lady Robert acted as an occasional reader.
2. Nina Forrest, later Mrs Henry Lamb.

257: To Lady Robert Cecil   46 *Gordon Square, Bloomsbury*
[1906?]

Dear Nelly,

I will come on Monday next, about 4.30—unless your mind changes in the interval and you feel you cannot bear it. Dont insult your inferiors; you know a Reader is to a Reviewer what a Judge is to a struggling barrister.

Your aff^ate,

AVS

Hatfield

258: To Emma Vaughan   46 *Gordon Square, Bloomsbury*
[1906?]

Dearest Todger,

I hear you are going to do your duty by Ralph [Vaughan Williams], which fires me to come too. I see the concert is at 8.30 I am going to get myself a 2/- ticket. May I suggest myself to come and dine with you at 7.15, or thereabouts? Or we might pleasantly picnic in High St? The reason I suggest this is because I must be in Hampstead, and therefore on the underground, and therefore I could come to you with greater ease than you to me, and if we were to meet at the place we should miss—which is a Bull. (I always said I was a Celt at heart)

If this plan commends itself don't write; I shall turn up about 7 in time for 7.15 dinner or picnic. If you are adverse, say so, like an Englishwoman.

I warn you I shall descend like a Fury from the Hellenic Heights of Hampstead and you had better have my Hat ready for me. And what do I owe you (that is the tactful way of asking for a bill).

The corn plaster gave more pleasure than plasters are wont to do. I thought to myself, Toad will have forgotten—and behold, next morning there it was in its little box and I put it on, with profound relief, tho' Heaven knows why ones corn should budge an inch. It smells very vigorous.

Yr. loving,

Goatus

Sussex

259: To Violet Dickinson   46 *Gordon Square, Bloomsbury*
Tuesday [16 January 1906]

My Violet,

Are you back, or where are you? Would you like me to come and bore you one afternoon. I think [I] have seen the tip of your long tail only twice since you came back.

216

However, dont bother if you are overwhelmed. I am sorry that your brother[1] didn't get it. But politics make dry dogs; Jack has been here; gets on his legs before the fire and asks us if we think about the great questions of our time: Chinese Labour and Protection! and comes to the conclusion that the young generation is materialistic.

What news of Beatrice [Thynne] and the [Cromer] Baby?

Mrs Lyttelton came to tea the other day: with [Nurse] Traill!

I went to a dance last night, and found a dim corner where I sat and read In Memoriam. While Nessa danced every dance till 2.30. I had one argument about the Roman Empire—you see I am not successful.

Aunt Fisher was there also, in another corner; embracing old friends and shedding quiet tears. It was a lively evening altogether.

Have you disowned your Sp[arroy]?

A book—novel—from the Times this morning.

We had [Fanny] Fletcher last week; her looks are the origin of your story I believe; otherwise she seemed nice.

Yr. AVS

Berg

260: To Violet Dickinson   46 *Gordon Square, Bloomsbury*

[January 1906]

My Violet,

It doesn't matter when you come. But we have heard that [Desmond] MacCarthy has postponed his paper till the Friday after; Miss [Fanny] Fletcher is put off till then. But do come both times all the same, if it wont bore you. You had better make Lamb's[2] acquaintance in a friendly way before hearing the debate. I have a great deal to tell you about; about my paper knife, about a talk I had with Herbert Fisher—and various other things. Besides I have 2 printed articles to give you to add to your unique collection of the early works of Adeline V.S.

But I am racing to Morley. I have just written to J. W. Hills M.P.—it looks so natural he might have had it in the cradle. I cant imagine anyone better fitted to represent his country.

Really it is a great mercy he is in, and I hope it means that his luck will turn in other ways too.

The editor of the Guardian (*not* Mrs L:) has sent me 7 volumes of poetry and tragedy to review!

1. Ozzie Dickinson had stood as a candidate in the General Election on 13 January 1906. In the same Election Jack Hills was elected Conservative Member for Durham City.
2. Walter Lamb, who had just left Trinity and was lecturing in Classics at Newnham. In 1913 he became Secretary of the Royal Academy.

Dont tell the Quaker: but I can retaliate now with the Hilbert Journal. At least I never write for that. Paper knife sends his love, and says it is a hardworked place you've sent him to; and poets print on very woolly paper.

Yr. AVS

So glad about the Cromer baby. Is Beatrice coming back.

Berg

261: To Violet Dickinson   46 *Gordon Square, Bloomsbury*

[1906]

My Violet,
    I will come with great delight, as nature made me.
    It is sinful to see how old birds [Violet] peck their young ones [Virginia] from the nest when their season is over. I see Margaret Lyttelton and Katharine Horner, and [Elinor] Monsell and [Lucia] Creighton all poking their ugly beaks and chirping for more, where I used to snuggle in my baby days—We went to Court today and saw Leo tried for defaming a judge. It was very tame, and he merely apologised.
    Do try and pretend you have a vacant place for me, old Stepdame.

Yr. AVS

Berg

262: To Violet Dickinson   46 *Gordon Square, Bloomsbury*

[March? 1906]

My Violet
    Here is another work for you to sleep over. You see what a modest kind of author I am by that sentence. Dont bother to read it quick; I am in no hurry.
    We had Sarah [Mrs John] Bailey to tea; and Lucia Creighton and 2 Monsells: My God! We are beginning to follow your example.

Yr. AVS

Berg

263: To Violet Dickinson   46 *Gordon Square, Bloomsbury*

[end-March 1906]

My Violet,
    I will dine with you on Friday with pleasure and cut the Friday Club. Nessa's birthday isn't till 30th *May*: so you have plenty of time to feel

inspired. I have been driving with Nelly in the motor car all the afternoon; and writing marvellous Rot; and corresponding with Widow Green[1] and getting huge lumps of manuscript from Madge Vaughan which lies round me like a Learned Pig (make that sentence clear, as I say to my class, to which I go this instant.) and Eily Monsell is engaged to marry Bernard Darwin[2]; and [Henry] Lambs portrait is finished and it is bad.

And now I must go and catch my Bus.

Yr. AVS

264: To Violet Dickinson   46 *Gordon Square, Bloomsbury*

[April 1906]

My Violet,

I sent off the books; the Library had them all, for a wonder. Will your husband send them back to me when he has done with them. An art book got sent by mistake.

There is no news, so why should I write a letter? However—there are various things. One is this. Did you say you knew of a table with a desk— because I have smashed mine, or rather Maud [maid] sat down on it—and I want to get another. So if you know of one, as you said, how much is it, and whose is it?

I sent my H[umphry] Ward to the Speaker, but I see they have a review already, longer and even more vindictive than mine. They call her a snob, and a sentimentalist, with no knowledge of art, or humanity. So the honor of English literature is saved, and I can meet Mrs Ward unblushing. Lamb and Nina have finally drifted into marriage. At the Friday Club last week, we sat and listened to this kind of thing Nessa: "Well, Nina. Are you married". Nina: "Married? O no, I'm not married. That is I am married. I think I was married yesterday, and I was so hungry the whole time, and I had a new blouse, and a cake." Lamb was out. Aunt Minna says to me solemnly "You must have seen that he is a woman. I have no doubt she does it from the best motives, but it is really too obvious—poor girl."

Anyhow they are a stunted kind of nightmare, and I can't even take a psy. . . . igal interest in them.

By the way, *what* quality do I lack. Tell me this: I cant sleep at night for thinking that Nelly has found me out.

Nothing has happened, or is likely to happen, but my great brain goes on all the same, and that after all is the important thing. I am going to write a

1. Charlotte (née Symonds), widow of T. H. Green, the philosopher.
2. Grandson of the naturalist, he later became the pre-eminent writer on golf. Virginia knew both Bernard and his wife, Elinor Monsell, but Elinor was her closer friend.

review tomorrow of a book of letters,[1] garrulous silly old letters that ought to have been burnt when they were written. That gives me a horror of letter writing—for wh. reason I write to you, and you must write to me.

AVS

Berg

265: To Madge Vaughan   *46 Gordon Square, Bloomsbury*

[April 1906]

Dearest Madge,

I hope my sudden telegram didn't give you much bother. But after consulting with Marny and Emma who proposed to go with me somewhere, we found it impossible to combine, and the Giggleswick plan[2] was in the end the only one that had anything to say for itself. So I hope to arrive— somewhere—on the 12th. If you will send me the address I will make the woman understand. I promise not to bother you: you shant see me at all, except passing in the road, when we will bow, and go our ways. I feel rather an intrusive bore, stationing myself in your preserves when you probably want to be alone and quiet. I am bringing a great box of books, and I shall shut myself in my room and read.

I will bring with me the manuscripts [Madge's] which I have read with great interest and pleasure. Doesn't that sound a lie? but it isnt. Castle Stopping is on the whole I think the most successful. It is certainly most spirited and amusing, and so recognisable, in spite of the caricature. Then I liked next best the girl and the American where you seemed to me to have given a very vivid picture in a very short space. The Pity of It we have already. I think I see what Henry Sidgwick[3] meant, though I should have put it differently. You seem to have invoked very tremendous powers— love and death—for the sake of rather a superficial effect—and you have been content when you got your effect to go no further. That is my objection, put very roughly, and crudely. It remains all rather misty and intangible, though picturesque of course, as I think all you write is. It amazes me to see the date on these things—1889—when you were 20. When I was 20 I couldn't have written anything like that. You must have had a very mature mind. It strikes me that you might make a really good book out of that Diary. Suppose you went on day by day, writing out soberly and exactly, what you think, feel, see, hear and talk about, as you have done that one day, all things growing naturally out of each other as they do— wouldn't the result be something very true and remarkable? Because, without

1. *Poets' Letters, Speaker*, 21 April 1906.
2. Virginia returned to Giggleswick 12-25 April, and took lodgings with Mrs Turner near Madge and Will Vaughan.
3. Professor of Moral Philosophy at Cambridge. He had died in 1900.

counting your mind, your life is remarkable, and lived in a remarkable place. It is a book I should very much like to see, and I believe you could do it.

What other criticisms I have are just detail, so they will keep. Isn't this the letter of a miserable creature who writes reviews?

It suddenly seems to me quite possible that the woman wont have her rooms free for that time. However, I am very free, and can change at the last moment.

Yr. loving,

AVS

Sussex

266: To Violet Dickinson   *At Mrs Turners, Giggleswick,*
Settle, Yorkshire

Monday [16 April 1906]

My Violet,

When you write you only use a few oaths, and misaddress your letter, and make hieroglyphics—so what is the use of pretending that we can correspond? I have all the work to do; look at this sheet. You have never had such a one in the house, nor is there a single pen in Burnham whose constitution would last the strain of covering it.

This is how I write to the Quaker, which I did for an Easter Sunday penance.

I came here on Thursday: I am in lodgings, I am 10 minutes walk from the Vaughans. Nessa comes I think on Saturday: we shall both go back together probably on Wednesday, in order to be at Morley, d— the place.

I lead the life of a Solitary: read and write and eat my meal, and walk out upon the moor, and have tea with Madge, and talk to her, and then dine alone and read my book, which I might be doing now if I weren't writing to you.

There is a discreet elderly person called Mrs James who waits on me, and provides meals whenever I want them; I had sausages for dinner last night. But she is taciturn, and has a family somewhere downstairs. When I want my bath I stand in the hall and shout for it; and a man answers. Mrs Turner is *gone below* Miss. In the morning she brings a thing like a childs coffin to my room, which she calls 'it.' Coffins are neither sex, but strictly impersonal.

There is a Greek austerity about my life which is beautiful and might go straight into a bas relief. You can imagine that I never wash, or do my hair; but stride with gigantic strides over the wild moorside, shouting odes of Pindar, as I leap from crag to crag, and exulting in the air which buffets me, and caresses me, like a stern but affectionate parent! That is Stephen Brontëised; almost as good as the real thing.

Nessa has not written to day, and I am imagining a variety of horrors; motor car accidents and elopements with the Bishop of Stepney. I had one letter, in which she said it was her fate to meet Bisons,[1] but they seemed to her *tainted*; she hoped he hadn't noticed. But if she turns her face away, and holds her skirts about her feet, even a Bison will turn, I tell her. Otherwise she sounded happy; and had started the picture [of Lord Robert Cecil], and thinks he makes a splendid subject.

Otherwise I have not read a paper, or received any attention.

It is a very odd perpetually recurring society here; old creatures who are semi-official, and middle aged spinsters, who drop in for tea. Madge is a charming woman; full of theories and emotions, and innumerable questions, like a child of 2, but I like being with her, and somehow odd and unexpected though it is, we get on very well together.

She took me to see a Master and his wife today, who are the intellect of Giggleswick; raw Newnham let loose upon the moors; to grow crabbed and stiff, and call it originality. I know the kind! She offered to lend me her bicycle to bicycle 16 miles to see a River "green like a Cornish sea"; (or her carpet ha-ha!!) and then presented me with 2 volumes of a poetess who killed herself. However, I am what Madge calls "disloyal"; and Will calls something else to write horrid details to you.

I feel slightly melancholy and undomesticated; nor can I write well; and altogether mine is a case that needs affection and sympathy. Why did you steal way to Burnham, and never ask me to come and see you? Why does the viper woman Crum coil herself in the hot embers of your heart? And why dont you write me a letter in which all these things are explained. Then I will tell you all about the Moors.

Yr. AVS

Berg

267: To Lady Robert Cecil   *C/o Mrs Turner, Giggleswick,*
                             Settle, Yorkshire

Wednesday [18 April 1906]

Dear Nelly,

I was very glad to get your letter. From what Nessa says—and I dont see why she should lie—she has enjoyed her time with you immensely. I am almost unselfish enough to wish that it might have been longer. Indeed I did write to urge her not to come up here for such a short stay—at least not on my account. But I have no letter today. I have been amusing myself very much alone—I dont quite know how; except that I just do what pleases me—and only see people for 2 hours a day. It is the kind of country that makes me quite content: and I could wander about it till I was gray, I think. However, I shall be very glad if Nessa does come; I want to talk for 10 hours without stopping.

1. Vanessa's word for Bishops.

It is odd that you should have Landor to read; I am reading Pericles and Aspasia for the first time. It is almost the only thing of his I have read. Of course it is beautifully written; but just too much of a Greek copy to be quite the real thing, I think. But beautiful writing is like music often, the wrong notes, and discords and barbarities that one hears generally—and makes too. I am very glad that you liked my works—though you haven't said how much you disliked them at the same time. They were only half baked experiments, and I go on saying I shall do better. But really I feel rather hopeless about my writing—When it is done it is such a feeble thing. This is the salutary effect of the Moors and the Vaughans: and I'm *not* fishing for a compliment in Sussex waters!

I am going to get up at 6.30 tomorrow morning, and take my 2 small cousins [Halford and Janet Vaughan], aged 3 and 6 with their father to Manchester for the day. We are to see the zoo, and have all their hairs cut—and they have each got a shilling to spend. It will take us 2 hours in the train to get there. I must say it seems an heroic expedition; however I know it will be great fun—if it does end in tears.

If you look at this sheet of paper you will see a kind of inscription stamped upon it: that was where I was taught my alphabet this afternoon by the 6 year old cousin: the pencil broke in the middle: but I came out bottom.

I had a hieroglyph from Violet: the Crums seem to have collapsed somewhere on the East Coast. But the Crums leave me more than usual calm.

I must now go and try to trim a hat for tomorrow.

I hope we shall meet soon.

Yr. aff^{ate,}
AVS

Hatfield

268: To Emma Vaughan   *At Mrs Turners, Giggleswick*

21st April [1906]

Dearest Todger,

I was very glad to get your letter, although I feel guilty that I made you waste some beautiful days in London.

The weather is said to be breaking up here—After a week of summer, it is blowing and raining like a disreputable October.

I have enjoyed myself very much and I wish you would have come too. My life is simple and sedate, and is spent mostly alone. I have tea with Madge generally; or the children have tea with me here. They are a delightful happy family; I dont know which is most promising. Janet is growing into a very handsome and intelligent *woman*; and Halford is almost ready for school; and Carry [Barbara] is a very strong-willed affectionate creature, with a huge sense of humour; and no beauty.

Will was at Clifton when I got here; but he came home that day and has been here all the time. I think he is going to Oxford now, as he still has about a fortnight of holiday. I have been for one or two walks with him. He is extremely well, and vigorous, I think; and does the family great credit. Yesterday he and I, Janet and Halford and Nurse, had a long day of it. We started at 8 for Manchester, where the children had their hair cut, and we saw the zoo and got back at 5.30. They were all shouting about beasts when I left them, and Madge was screaming with laughter—as noisy as any family in England. I must say they are great fun, and Madge is really at her best as the mother of children. I see a good deal of her, at odd moments; and we have seen a little of the society of Giggleswick—The Motts, Bearcroft etc. There was a Committee of Ladies, also to consider the boarding out of workhouse children. Madge seems to be a power of some kind among all these people. Today she is giving an Easter Egg Hunt. I don't quite know what it means, but it is what my good Turner calls a "wild day".

I order my meals; at least say when I want them—have a sitting room, and a great bedroom; and all kinds of Yorkshire cakes and muffins. It is a splendid place to come to—but I have not yet had my bill. I go for long walks with Gurth, who has won old Turner's heart.

You see I am practically without news, and totally without ideas: but that is the effect of solitude. Tonight Nessa arrives. I am afraid we must go back on Wednesday, to be at that . . . . Morley. I suppose Shaxby [Morley's librarian?] will be at your desk. Sheep[shanks] is gone to Italy till Whitsuntide. Madge sings your praises: one morning you did wonders in entertaining etc.; and I sing accompaniment in the base. Write to me again—to London, I am afraid—and give my love to the Old 'Un; as Adrian calls Nessa. Marny is too respectable a name for the likes of her. My blood creeps at the thought of losing a L[ondon L[ibrary] book; it haunts me. I think I should jump off Waterloo Bridge if I ever did such a thing.

Loving
Goatus

Sussex

269: TO MADGE VAUGHAN   46 *Gordon Square, Bloomsbury*

[27 April 1906]

Dearest Madge,

I feel that I ought to write some kind of Collins to thank you for your great kindness and hospitality etc. etc. etc. However, you may understand all that. I have been rubbing shoulders with my kind all along Oxford St. this afternoon, and that leaves me singularly dissolute and debased. I think in what a noble spirit I ascended and descended your mountains. London is crowded and very brisk and cold. We have begun our Bohemian dissipations:

tonight Thoby is reading a paper to the Friday Club upon the Decadence of Modern Art. I am going to say that if all artists lived in Yorkshire they would be as healthy as—the Vaughan family. I often think of the children; and try to repeat their sayings and doings. Does Brother boy [Halford] call me that horrid tease?

This is only a brief and inadequate note: because I must dress, at least wash, and go off.

I shall send you a longer letter, some manuscripts, both of mine[1] and of yours. By the way, would you, when you think of it, return that Brontë book—as it belongs to the Times?

I did enjoy myself *immensely* with you; independently of the children, and of the country. And please understand this as written, because I cant analyse my feelings with any success.

Yr. loving,
AVS

Sussex

270: To Violet Dickinson   46 *Gordon Square, Bloomsbury*

[May 1906]

My Violet,

I met the table yesterday. She is a lady to her finger tips; and more splendid than any thing I conceived. She is just too high for my chair, so I shall have her side legs cut off. But my good woman—I *insist on paying her price.* That is the honest truth. Otherwise I shd. never have asked for her.

So send me the bill. She stands before my chair, ready to hold all the folios in the Brit. Mus.

Also her little pads for ink pots are cut; and she is so steady and discreet, and gives such an air to the room. I send for carpenter at once to make a ledge.

Send the bill.

Yr. AVS

Berg

1. Virginia had continued her practice of writing, as literary exercises, descriptions of the places she visited. Among those which survive (now in the Berg Collection, New York Public Library) are essays written at Giggleswick (April 1906), Blo' Norton Hall, Norfolk (August 1906), the New Forest (Christmas 1906), Playden, Sussex (August/September 1907), Wells, Somerset (August 1908), and Manorbier, Wales (August 1908). But she may also have begun writing at this period more imaginative works, of fiction perhaps. If so, they have not survived.

[early June 1906]

My Violet,

We shall be in to tea on Tuesday, whever you come. I have taken steps about the table, and it is to be done tomorrow. It has all kinds of complications internally, and Shaw says it is an excellent piece of work.

But please do tell me the price; because I dont think it right to take such gifts—and ask for them as I did. And it will last me till I die; and serve for all the books I shall ever write, and uphold the learning of the ages, and as my eyes fail, so the table raises itself. In fact there never was such a table. The little flaps appeal to me like human beings and Christians: something so natural and appealing and homely about them.

You never tell me what Nelly says *I lack*: until you set my mind at rest I cant think of going to tea with her; even when tempered with Miss Dickinson.

The good Times wants me to write 2 columns on the Lakes for them!!1 I have never been there—but the Imagination, as the poet says, has wings.

Give any version of my love to the Crum that you like: I feel deeply-honestly sympathetic. In fact I think she is some measure of a heroine.

Yr. AVS

At last my doubts about the t in Chestnut are set at rest.

Berg

[June? 1906]

My dearest Madge,

I feel rather guilty to have made you write so much and read so much in the midst of everything else. But I am *most grateful*, and that I hope you will believe.

I do agree with every word you say, and I think I understand your meaning.

My only defence is that I write of things as I see them; and I am quite conscious all the time that it is a very narrow, and rather bloodless point of view. I think—if I were Mr Gosse writing to Mrs Green!2 I could explain a little why this is so from *ex*ternal reasons; such as education, way of life etc.

1. *Wordsworth and the Lakes, TLS*, 15 June 1906.
2. Mrs T. H. Green, Madge's aunt.

And so perhaps I may get something better as I grow older. George Eliot was near 40 I think, when she wrote her first novel—the Scenes [*of Clerical Life*].

But my present feeling is that this vague and dream like world, without love, or heart, or passion, or sex, is the world I really care about, and find interesting. For, though they are dreams to you, and I cant express them at all adequately, these things are perfectly real to me.

But please dont think for a moment that I am satisfied, or think that my view takes in any whole. Only it seems to me better to write of the things I do feel, than to dabble in things I frankly dont understand in the least. That is the kind of blunder—in literature—which seems to me ghastly and unpardonable: people, I mean, who wallow in emotions without understanding them. Then they are merely animal and hideous. But, of course, any great writer treats them so that they are beautiful, and turns statues into men and women. I wonder if you understand my priggish and immature mind at all? The things I sent you were mere experiments; and I shall never try to put them forward as my finished work. They shall sit in a desk till they are burnt! But I am very glad that you were so frank; because I have had so very little criticism upon my work that I really dont know what kind of impression I make. But do please remember, that if I am heartless when I write, I am very sentimental really, only I dont know how to express it, and devoted to you and the babies; and I only want to be treated like a nice child. I do hope you are better.

Shall I send some vegetables? or what do you like out of this vast and wicked town? Please say,

Yr. loving AVS

Sussex

273: To Violet Dickinson   46 *Gordon Square, Bloomsbury*

[June? 1906]

My Violet,

Do come on Tuesday—though how you begin a journey to Cornwall with lunch here, I cant conceive.

We are preparing for a Thursday, having asked Margaret Lyttelton at the last moment. Last Thursday [Clive] Bell came!—he behaved with great self possession: looked and laughed and jerked his head: and in fact I think he must have made up his mind to think no more of it. Nessa is afraid of showing 'encouragement'—but I think it is much more sensible to get back on to easy terms; and he evidently wishes it.

These affairs of the heart are so perplexing! I shall never understand Bell's; unless he has them written red across his shirt front.

Nessa has done some really good pictures for the show; and Eily Monsell thinks them excellent. Lord Bob[1] came back this evening, and looks much better framed.

Madge tells me I have no heart—at least in my writing: really I begin to get alarmed. If marriage is necessary to one's style, I shall have to think about it. There is some truth in it, isn't there?—but not the whole truth. And there is something indecent, to my virgin mind, in a maiden having that kind of heart. "The air is full of it" says Madge: but I breathe something else. I have written such a lot: I think. You must read them now. Fred Maitland is sending MS: the Quaker's book is just coming out: I feel the Stephen family ought to refrain from the ink pot: but they cant. The table is a fresh temptation. Did you get the books, and were they right?

Yr. AVS

Berg

274: TO VIOLET DICKINSON   46 *Gordon Square, Bloomsbury*

[29 June 1906]

My Violet,

I am shocked to hear of your leg: which however being of the consistency of a daddy longlegs doesn't really matter. It is said that they dont notice how many they have, till they put on their stockings.

We have been to a wet garden party; where we had to protest the grass was dry: and now we are just off to the Friday Club, and tomorrow I go to the Quaker.

Is it true that you are coming to Greece: Clarke [?] told Nessa she has an Aunt, who may be made useful for the first time in her life. I make out that we can do the whole thing easily in 5 weeks: 1 week is ample for Noels [at Achmetaga, Euboea].

The cases are only to be had at Boots', and though I tramped Oxford St. in love and charity I couldn't find one. This may do, if so keep it. It is a handsome present. I wish you would come and see us. I dined out last night, and felt like a Hyena on a bank; never a drink for me. Is it, say I, because Hyena's are rare and fair; or because the stream dont want them?

I cannot write a letter at the best of times.

Margaret [Duckworth] sends a post card to say 'I quite understand. Shant expect you at Devonshire House or Osterley or anywhere" is that a snub? I think so—but we had to bring it upon us, and the sooner the better. And now we are free women! Any form of slavery is Degrading—and the damage done to the mind is worse than that done to the body!! Do come up soon. It is a dreary desert; and I howl and swear, and scribble away—but so

1. Vanessa's portrait of Lord Robert Cecil.

badly. I go to Nelly's for a Sunday: but O how I should like to be left alone; and I'm not a success there: tho' I love her: it is a stream that runs delicately up hill, and is very tortuous. If your husband has done his books will he send em back? The library is rather bothersome: but dont matter if he wants to keep them longer.

Yr. AVS

Berg

275: To Madge Vaughan   46 *Gordon Square, Bloomsbury*

[July 1906]

Dearest Madge,

I sent back today—at last—the Flaubert[1] which you lent me. I read it some time ago, and put off writing till I should have time to say how very much I was interested by it. It seemed to me one might write volumes upon all the questions it brought up. I think no letters I have read interest me more, or seem more beautiful and more suggestive. I know his novels but I know them much better now. She brings out all his peculiar qualities so finely that no autobiography could tell so much as he tells almost unconsciously. I have read none of her novels: but only the autobiography. It is an immense lucid kind of mind, something like a natural force—with no effort or consciousness about it. I think I understand his artistic creed better: I knew all his features and boundaries—but I sink into her and am engulphed! I wanted to endorse, and add to, your pencil marks; whole passages seemed to start up as though writ in old ink. They penetrate so far and sum up so much that is universal as well as individual, and they say things that almost can't be said.

Aren't letters of literary criticism dull? I have just come back from a Sunday with my Quaker Aunt—who is very like your Miss Clifford to look at, at any rate. We talked for some 9 hours; and she poured forth all her spiritual experiences, and then descended and became a very wise and witty old lady. I never knew anyone with such a collection of stories—which all have some odd twist in them—natural or supernatural. All her life she has been listening to inner voices, and talking with spirits: and she is like a person who sees ghosts, or rather disembodied souls, instead of bodies. She now sits in her garden, surrounded with roses, in voluminous shawls and draperies, and accumulates and pours forth wisdom upon all subjects. All the young Quakers go and see her, and she is a kind of modern prophetess. I think you would like her very much; and her grey dressing gowns. We have been watching the pairing season here, which is still noisy and brilliant, though by no means lovely. We dont do very much of it ourselves; but we

1. His correspondence with George Sand.

are now getting up a dance at the Friday Club! Also we have our Thursday evenings—and talk a great deal about Style, and various geniuses, whom we discover—but the world doesn't recognise them! I hope you are well—and the children. Am I to have another photograph? I want one.

Yr.
AVS

I dreamt of Giggleswick the other night—and its trees were quite bare!

Sussex

276: To Violet Dickinson   46 *Gordon Square, Bloomsbury*
Monday [2 July 1906]

My Violet,
    I am going to Nelly on Saturday, unfortunately. I cant pretend at this moment that I want to; as I dont succeed there; and my jokes are very thin and bald.

    I was very glad to get a letter at the Porch [the Quaker's house, Cambridge]; a voice from a live world into that remote part of it!

    But the Quaker was charming and wise and humane, and less of an inspired prophetess than usual. She is a remarkable woman I always feel when I see her; and a great deal better than her eloquence and her mastery of the language make one expect. We talked about 8 hours; and she dived into the ample recesses of her mind, and spun stories of her souls adventures and disasters; but she has swum through them all. I never saw anyone float through life as complacently and even gracefully as she does now, and the young Quakers and Quakeresses flourish beneath her shower. Death is what she wants, she says: because it will be so infinitely better than life. Meanwhile she cuts off dead roses, reads her philosophies, and talks and meditates. I should like to write [about] her later; but perhaps not in a letter!

    How bad is your leg? I didnt think that stumbling over a tree meant much—unless you were William of Orange—but I suppose your joints are weak. Let me come down some afternoon. What about Greece? The Quaker says she will think badly of us if we dont go.

Yr. loving,
AVS

Berg

[7 July 1906]

My Violet,

I forgot when you were here that we have promised to go to Eton on Tuesday for the Cornish wedding[1]—so I cant come to you, which is a great bore. But we have promised to go. And now the Quaker writes she is coming here from Wed. to Friday; and I dine out on Friday and we go to the play on Saturday—so it must be next week. Which day can you have me? I could come any day, I think, except Wednesday, 18th.

O what a bore these engagements are! not yours, I mean; which is a relief for the spirit, but here I sit before an empty box which must be ready in an hour; to start for Nelly. And I never get any work done. The dance was a great success, I think. What is Miss Clarkes version?

How is the knee?

Yr. AVS

Berg

278: To Lady Robert Cecil   *46 Gordon Square, Bloomsbury*

[July 1906]

My dear Nelly,

I got home safely, three or four days ago. The journey was very easy, and I did not lose my train or my temper or my luggage, and I have not been in the train ever since. But this Collins is a very formidable Collins; it has grown with waiting. Next time you will say you dont ask me to write Collinses. You will suggest that I had better send them to John Murray [the publisher]. Really when I think of Periwinkle I feel compunction. But dont bother when you read these—they cant wait; and dont write an answer—unless you like writing answers. Wasn't that put tactfully?

Now I shall say how much I enjoyed myself at Gale.[2] I really did: and if I had the pen of my Quaker Aunt I should say so in such a way that you would weep.

I think you are a very good person to stay with. Sloper [the butler] and I like belonging to you. You will have to send me ointment for my nose too. Compliments are best for my skin—the vet says.

When are you going to your next party? It was a brilliant success last night wasn't it?

Your aff.,

AVS

Hatfield

1. The wedding on 10 July of Desmond MacCarthy and Mary (Molly), daughter of Francis Warre-Cornish, vice-Provost of Eton College since 1893.
2. Gale Cottage, Chelwood Gate, Uckfield, the Cecils' house.

[22 July 1906]

My Violet,

I sent off some books yesterday, but not the right ones, I am afraid. The Butcher *Aspects of Greek Genius*[1], is rather good, I think; but you will have a mind like a bran pie after reading these odds and ends! Dont get Greece and Japan and the history of Welwyn all mixed; and tell us about Dr Young on the Acropolis—the man who wrote the Anthology—or Night Thoughts.[2]

I am so sneering because: well for various reasons; nature, and Jack [Hills] and the Sabbath, and the cheque for £9.7. which lies before me: or beneath me. This is the largest sum I have ever made at one blow; it is the gift of the Times.

But now to business:

George was here on Saturday; very earnest and eager to impress upon us the fact that women cant travel by themselves in Constantinople. Margaret went with a servant, and was insulted. He says also the heat in Greece is really bad; He thinks we ought to do Constantinople on the way back with Thoby and Adrian. Have you heard anything of the kind?

If it is true, it is worth thinking about. I went to Cooks, and found a stupid man who said that there was no tour to Constant: they cd. make out tickets. He is sending a list of routes and prices which I will forward.

Shall I come down again one day this week. Friday? But dont let me dislodge Mrs Lyttelton; or all my articles will be refused. But the Times appreciates me! Thoby made £1000. *one thousand pounds* by selling 10 pages of Thackerays Lord Bateman.[3] George sold it to Pierpont Morgan. So all Bar expenses and Greek expenses are more than paid for. I wish my manuscripts would sell for more than their meaning!

Yr. AVS

Berg

[July 1906]

My Violet,

I have heard from Cook: the whole thing with Constantinople works out at £37.5: first class. I think you stop as long as you like at places. I will come

1. S. H. Butcher, *Some Aspects of the Greek Genius* (1891).
2. She is referring to three Youngs: Dr Thomas Young, the 19th century scientist and Egyptologist; probably Francis Young, who edited *The Political Reader*, 1870; and Edward Young, who wrote the poem *Night Thoughts*, 1742-4.
3. *Lord Bateman* was an anonymous ballad, embellished by Charles Dickens and George Cruikshank, who published it in 1839. In that same year Thackeray wrote it out and illustrated it, and it was this manuscript which had descended to Thoby through his father.

Vanessa with Violet Dickinson in 1903

Madge Vaughan and her family at Giggleswick School

Lytton Strachey in 1911

Roger Fry in 1911

Vanessa Stephen painting Lady Robert Cecil in 19

down on Friday, with great joy: by the same train; only I must leave before dinner, as we have people here, and the Friday Club.

The Quaker arrived this afternoon: and has talked incessantly till this hour—10.45.

By the way, dont say anything about Thoby's sale of the MS. or his price. It is rather a secret, I think.

Yr. AVS

Berg

281: TO VIOLET DICKINSON   46 *Gordon Square, Bloomsbury*

[2 August 1906]

My Violet,

Here is Cooks letter. Keep it.

Your husband makes it clear that you can come, as far as fares are concerned. Do you want to come?

I think you must. I dream of it all night.

Really it is worth while to take a spirited view of the future. Things are bound to turn up.

Your husband seemed very anxious for you to go.

We are in a great mess and uproar; T. and A buying green spectacles and hammocks; and family agreements needing signatures, and Nina [Lamb] on top of it all!

We dined with Nelly and Ld. Bob last night, in the garden. It was great fun.

Yr. AVS

We go tomorrow.
Our address is

Blo' Norton Hall,
East Harling
Thetford
Norfolk.

Berg

282: TO VIOLET DICKINSON   *Blo' Norton Hall, East Harling, Norfolk*[1]

Saturday [4 August 1906]

My Violet,

The difficulties of writing in this place are many. However, I must tell you first that we can provide any surplus you want. Thoby has left special

---

1. Blo' Norton Hall, a moated Elizabethan manor house, lay on the Norfolk-Suffolk border between Thetford and Diss. Virginia and Vanessa took the house for four weeks, and were joined there at intervals by Thoby, Adrian and several friends.

233

instructions; at all costs you are to be brought. Besides Nessa and I are rolling like drunken sailors on the profits of our works. That blessed Lyttelton takes every word I write and corrects the spelling.

If only I had chosen a better moment to write to you, I would describe this place. Which now I shant do. It is 300 years old, striped with oak bars inside, old staircases, ancestral vats, and portraits; there is a garden; and a moat. You see people of taste can get houses cheap: the station is 6 miles off, and there is nothing to do. Nessa paints windmills in the afternoon, and I tramp the country for miles with a map, leap ditches, scale walls and desecrate churches, making out beautiful brilliant stories every step of the way. One is actually being—as we geniuses say—transferred to paper at this moment. That might mean that this letter was it: but it isn't.

Read your Guardian carefully, and see if you find anything about Henry James; the first words, like [a] coin with a head on it, will tell you who wrote it.

Nessa and I have to go now and call on the Parson and we haven't been inside the church, even to sight see. Really this is a charming country, and even beautiful, or rather quaint as we say of things that are long and attenuated and more grotesque than shapely—because their hearts are so good.

You will be off to Cornwall now. I do envy you that; because it is far the most Greek of any place in England. Thats how we shall talk, of noses and places.

Thoby and A. went yesterday, with 'hundreds of things left undone' They are at Milan now. We shall get post cards. Aunt Sophie,[1] the improper Monte Carlo Great Aunt, sends us a cutting all about English travellers and brigands and how no one must pay ransoms. We read Greek—Greek— all day long. I can shout oaths, of the classical period, and laments over unburied bodies. Do you think that will come in useful? Write you Tawny Devil.

This is the most important part of the letter. Will you come here after Cornwall? We have room: and house till 31st.

Berg

283: TO VIOLET DICKINSON   *Blo' Norton Hall, East Harling,*
                               Norfolk
Aug. 24th [1906]

My Violet,

Your letters are as scraggy as—well comparisons are odious. But if you weighed my words—independently of their meaning, you would find 6 3/5 in of your letters go to one of mine. We've measured it to the inch!

1. Lady Dalrymple, youngest daughter of James Pattle, and widow of Sir John Dalrymple Bt.

Nessa and I enjoy a kind of honeymoon, interrupted it is true with horrible guests. We have had 2 cousins; one [Hester Ritchie] is with us, and proposes not to leave us till we go—and there are moments when it seems best to go. However the poor thing only suffers from an empty head, in which whims go eddying all day long; and the Lord gave her a good heart; so she isn't as utterly damned as some of us.

I cannot write a letter here as the Quaker would tell you if you dropped on her now. To tell the truth, I *cant* read my grandfathers[1] letters; because I cant swallow her short cuts. (Lyttelton would correct that metaphor.) But the Quaker has a well worn semi religious vocabulary; left her by the late Sir James, I think; and when she talks of chaff and grain and gold and ore, and winnowing feelings, and upward tending lives, and yielding to the light, and bearings of fruit, I slip and slide and read *no more*.

We have had long letters from Thoby and Adrian. They have drifted down the coast, which is full of unknown towns and Roman ruins, and they landed at Cattaro, and were going to ride in Montenegro. They say it has been perfect; and the weather like a cool English June. They will ride for 10 days, and go to Corfu and Patras. I begin to chafe to be off. This is lovely old country, and I walk miles every afternoon, and leap ditches, and wade rivers. Still, it will be great fun to rush through Europe, and climb the Acropolis. I cant settle to read Greek history and Antiquities so I shall make the scenery—in fact the atmosphere and the colour my job: after all, I shall say, one doesn't come to Greece to look at ruins. And what answer will you have to that? And when you begin about the school of Pheidias, I shall look at the sunset, and make you feel a Vulgar Prig. However, I shant give away my secrets any more. I have written 40 pages of manuscript since I came here; that is about 3 a day, or rather more; because, of course, one must leave out Sundays.

George is coming here for Sunday; to impress upon us some last cautions, I think. He is a wonderful man. Aunt Mary says that Greece makes her think of Brigands and the dreadful story of the year 1856. And, is 'that Miss Dickinson' going with you? She didn't say that, but I felt it.

We haven't heard of Beatrice or of Nelly, or of anyone for 3 weeks. But it is great fun to dive beneath the sea as we do here, and find all the curates wives, and village post offices going on in spite of everything.

Here are some masterpieces. Do send them back if you remember; because I have a penance, which consists in reading my works over at intervals of 6 months.

Yr. AVS

Berg

1. Sir James Stephen (1789-1859).

[early September? 1906]

Dearest Madge,

Thank you so much for the berries. They are just the things I like, and make the whole room bright. I never saw such a splendid family![1] You should be a proud parent—you seem supported and protected on every side. They come just in the order we did.

I sent off some stuff to you today—I send tomorrow some nice sticky sweets for the children.

Do give them my love—only that conveys nothing!

Yr.

AVS

Sussex

284: To Lady Robert Cecil   *46 Gordon Square, Bloomsbury*

[early September 1906]

My dear Nelly,

Violet brought a great many pyjamas to dinner tonight. My underclothes are generally very simple, and I shall feel a real lady for almost the first time when I put these on in a Greek bedroom: or when I come in to the room suddenly and see them lying on the quilt—or rather the straw. I think few things show a more generous nature than the loan of ones own underclothes to strangers—not even blood relations.

I will take the greatest care—only that's not much really, I must own, and I wont pack my sponge in them, or use them to dry my feet on.

Dont you think this opens a very intimate and slightly bizarre chapter in our relationship. "The ladies were in the habit of lending each other their pyjamas". I am fizzing with excitement, and my temper is therefore very bad: so Nessa and Violet tell me all the evening. But think of Athens and Olympia and Delphi!!!

Only I feel that this should be the crown of a long life spent in teaching Greek verbs, to schoolgirls; instead of which I have done nothing whatever except write a cheque. That is the kind of thing that looks nice written down; as you are in the trade yourself, I will own that I never did think or feel anything like it till just now.

You will be romping along among all the books; I shall drop out; you will finish your novel; you will write Leaders for the Times; I cant help hungering a little for the 'book season' as my publisher brother [Gerald] calls it. Rather a good show this year he says; he had only 10 days holiday, because his authors are such a team to drive.

1. David Vaughan, Madge and Will's fourth child, was born on 15 July 1906.

You have got to have that Ms: ready to show me, 20,000 words complete, on 1st November. Do you hear? or I shall retain the pyjamas. That is our contract. Now any true author will sell his brains for pyjamas; Shakespeare did, as we know.

Please write, and they will forward. I will send you a card of the Acropolis. Love from Nessa.

Your aff^{ate},
AVS

Hatfield

Letters 286-326

On 8 September 1906 *Virginia, Vanessa and Violet Dickinson went to Greece where they joined Thoby and Adrian at Olympia. Together they visited Corinth, Athens, Nauplia and Mycenae, but Vanessa fell ill (apparently from appendicitis) on the return journey to Athens and remained there with Violet, while Virginia and her brothers visited the Noels in Euboea. Vanessa recovered sufficiently to continue to Constantinople, where she again fell ill, and the Stephens brought her back to London by train, arriving on 1 November, only to find that Thoby (who had returned home ahead) was also ill. None of Virginia's letters written during this Mediterranean journey survive. Her correspondence was resumed while she cared for her two invalid siblings. Vanessa recovered. Thoby did not: he died from typhoid fever on 20 November. Virginia's daily bulletins to Violet Dickinson (herself desperately sick with typhoid) tell the detail of their ordeal, and to spare Violet the anguish of Thoby's death, she suppressed the news for nearly a month. Two days after Thoby's death, Clive Bell again proposed to Vanessa, and this time was accepted.*

286: TO VIOLET DICKINSON   *46 Gordon Square, Bloomsbury*

[7? November 1906]

My Violet,

Nessa seems much happier and less tired this evening. She enjoyed Nelly and George and is certainly in better spirits. She says it would make all the difference to her to be at home, if it could be managed.

[Margery] Snow[den] telegraphs that she arrives tomorrow at 6. A.M. so Adrian meets her and brings her straight here. This has cheered Nessa.

Thoby has a temp. of 103 and is a great deal bothered with his inside but [Dr] Thompson is satisfied. Thoby thinks him very slow and Savage will be a blessing.

I cant help feeling rather more cheerful tonight. It will be such a mercy to have things settled.

You are an Angel with wings dipped in the skies (whatever your crooked old talons may be. They hold burning coals for little Wallabies soft snouts.)

Blankets and quilt arrived: Nessa delighted.

Yr. AVS

Berg

287: To Violet Dickinson   [46 *Gordon Square, Bloomsbury*]

[8? November 1906]

My Violet,

We have had a hard days work—but successful. Snow arrived at 6 AM and is staying here. Nessa is delighted, and she seems exactly right. Then Savage came at 2. rather hurried and determined that a home was necessary before he saw Nessa. She couldn't explain—he talked so hard and was so vague—thought she couldn't eat and had diarrhoea. Then he dashed off—saying that today was a bright day, but you were not an alarmist and therefore she must be very weak. So I felt rather in despair. Then [Dr] Thompson came—I had a long talk, and explained Vs views—he was very nice, and said that if she really minded fearfully he would consult Savage and tell me. Now he has just been again and had a talk with V herself. He says they will certainly allow her to be here; with [Nurse] Fardell, in her own room. Savage says it is *not* a case of nervous breakdown but merely general tiredness, and therefore the treatment need not be so strict. He says it will certainly not take 6 weeks, and he thinks we can perfectly well manage here, if she prefers it.

So I am going to London [Hospital] to get Fardell, and we shall start probably middle of next week.

Both Savage and Thompson think it will be a quick case, and say there is nothing serious the matter.

Nessa is very much cheered up, and says she can stand this quite well, and it makes all the difference being here.

Thompson was very nice, and very glad to discuss the whole thing, and to hear about her.

Thoby has taken a sudden turn for the better and his temp. is only 100. They think this is really the final drop now—so we go to bed cheerful. Perhaps I may come round tomorrow morning.

AVS

Berg

288: To Violet Dickinson   46 *Gordon Square, Bloomsbury*

[9? November 1906]

My Violet,

I am so sorry about the influenza. In case I dont see you I write this. Nessa is bright and not at all tired after a good night. She had [Clive] Bell yesterday, as he asked specially to come, but she was not tired, or says she feels happier for seeing him.

Thoby is kept back by the diarrhoea which is still severe and keeps his temp. up. I am asking Thompson to get a specialist, as the nurse has rather alarmed Nessa, and is alarmed herself. Thompson says it is quite unnecessary; that it is irritation caused by grape pips which he passes in great quantities. But the pain is bad, and I think it will be best to know everything that can be known.

Nessa and Snow are very happy together. I think that was a really good move. I am writing to Lückes[1] about Fardell.

Get well and dont bother.

It is such a mercy about Nessa. Savage and Thompson both say it is not a severe case, and they expect a quick recovery, as it is more physical exhaustion than nervous. Nessa says she feels she can get perfectly right here.

AVS

Berg

289: To Clive Bell   *46 Gordon Square, Bloomsbury*

[10? November 1906]

Dear Mr Bell,

I find that it would suit Vanessa better if you could come at 2 tomorrow instead of 5. Could you lunch here first at 1.30. Adrian will be in.

Thoby seems really better tonight; his temp is only 100 pt 8, and though he has some pain it is less, and he is far more like himself. The dr says he may see a friend for 2 minutes tomorrow, and I hope Mr Sydney Turner may be able to come.

Your very sincerely,
Virginia Stephen

Quentin Bell

290: To Violet Dickinson   *46 Gordon Square, Bloomsbury*

[11? November 1906]

My Violet,

I started out to come, and was stopped again. Fardell came, and we are trying to get round Lückes. Nessa seems well today and says she knows a rest cure is unnecessary. However I dont think she will worry if she is here.

Thoby's temp. is still up, and his inside is rather painful, but the dr. declares it is all accounted for; and says it wd. be waste to have another man. But we are prepared to have one at any moment.—I feel complete trust in Thompson. He is now alive to our anxiety.

Bell comes to lunch and sees Nessa afterwards. I think she enjoys it in an odd way. He is certainly very controlled.

1. The matron at London Hospital.

I wish I cd. manage to come round and see or hear how you are. But it is useless at present: something always stops me, and I sit with T. a good deal. Snow is excellent—as sensible as a Hen—if hens are sensible.

I will get a note to you tomorrow. *Dont bother, and dont write.*

AVS

Berg

291: TO VIOLET DICKINSON   46 *Gordon Square, Bloomsbury*

Tuesday [13 November 1906]

My Violet,

Ella [Crum] says I may write to you, so though it shall be short it shall be extremely affectionate. However you will want horrid details. The doctor says Nessa is decidedly better; she weighs nine stones naked, which is very little less than she ought to weigh—and I should like to know what you weigh—the weight of bones, I should think. I have got Mackechnie the nice Scotch nurse to come, and we are going to start massage and food tomorrow. But both Savage and Thompson agree that it is not necessary to isolate her, so she is going to see us as usual though no one else. Then we can get stricter if necessary; but they are very much pleased with her improvement. Thoby is just the same today, which is as they hoped. There are no complications, and he is doing as well as possible. Snow goes tomorrow.

Adrian and I flourish.

I dont know when you will be able to see me: and of course the doorstep will be crowded. However I wait my turn. Only do get well, and dont think of Stephens, or other horrors. We send our love. Wall[aby] wags his soft tail.

Yr. loving,
AVS

Dr. says Nessa is doing "wonderfully well" and looks miles better already. Weight satisfactory.

Berg

292: TO CLIVE BELL   [46 *Gordon Square, Bloomsbury*]

Postcard

Tuesday evening [13 November 1906]

Thoby had a good sleep this evening and the dr says he has had a better day altogether than yesterday. He is asleep now—Everything so far is satisfactory. The dr disapproves of reading—says talk is better.

AVS

Quentin Bell

[14 November 1906.]

Dearest Madge,

I meant to write before. The doctors are now certain that Thoby has Typhoid. The pneumonia was only part of it and is now almost gone. They hope he is through the worst of it,—he is certainly going on as well as possible. They think him better tonight. Of course it is a very long business, and the next week must be anxious, but his pulse is wonderfully good, and there are no complications.

The doctor is very anxious that Nessa should get completely strong after appendicitis,—advises keeping her in bed for the next week or two, with rubbing and feeding up. She is decidedly better, and they say that she will get perfectly right with rest and care in a short time. She has been rushing about ever since she had it. I will send a card to say how T. gets on.

Yr. AVS

Sussex

294: To Clive Bell   [46 *Gordon Square, Bloomsbury*]

Postcard
Wednesday, [14 November 1906]

The doctor says that Thoby has had a really satisfactory day, and thinks him better in every way.

I am sorry you couldn't see him today. Could you come tomorrow at 3.30? I am going out then, and possibly you could sit with him or read to him. The dr discourages reading, but doesn't mind a visit.

AVS

Quentin Bell

295: To Violet Dickinson   [46 *Gordon Square, Bloomsbury*]

Wednesday [14 November 1906]

My Violet,

I'm as hot—I can only think of one comparison, and I believe that aint proper. It isn't hell fire, so dont guess that. We are really merry grigs in this family, and any allusion to Greece is received with hysterical applause.

Visitors come and use their handkerchiefs a great deal; I begin now by saying my brother has typhoid my sister appendicitis—dont laugh. Thoby has had an excellent day and the doctor says we can be quite happy, his temp. is going down, and everything is satisfactory.

McKechnie came today, and the rest cure has begun—but it is a very jovial business, and Thompson says she has made excellent progress, and will be completely right in a very short time. He is surprised at the way she has picked up. So here I sit and think of many things: such as drains and boilers and carbolic and bedpans—why they always will come in I dont know. I think my heroic conduct in Greece has stayed in my mind. I discuss enemas at afternoon tea with Peter [Clive Bell]—whether you call them ènēma or enĕma—or enigma—what the difference between turpentine and glycerine may properly be thought to be. This is humanising him. Is this hot enough? old furry fleasome one? Beatrice [Thynne] comes as punctually as a piano tuner, and from the same excellent motives. But when she goes we kiss each other, and sometimes there is a tender passage on the chest in the hall, while she prods her umbrella on my toe.

Snow went this morning; and if she weren't so sensible and so nice and so proper and so like a lady I should be very fond of her. But she did a good days work; and I really am fond of her—and that is an egoistical way of putting it. Then I see Nelly, who is well—all that Nelly is you know better than I do—anyhow the surface is very exquisite and we talk about you, and the single spot.

I know you are a celebrated invalid; if I didn't love you, I should be so d——d bored. But remembering the passage from Ostende to Dover,[1] and the lady who had to be screened with the cover of Madame Bovary—and the white cliffs and George and the tea basket and the bed pan—you see how my mind runs—remembering all this, I feel myself curled up snugly in old mother wallabies pouch. My little claws nestle round my furry cheeks. Is mother wallaby soft and tender to her little one? He will come and lick her poor lean mangy face. When you are at your worst do you think of Mrs Lyttelton, Mrs Crum, or me. Think this out. When you wake in the night, I suppose you feel my arms round you.

Yr. loving,
AVS

Berg

296: To Violet Dickinson   46 *Gordon Sq.*

Thursday night [15 November 1906]

My Violet,

Your nephews and nieces do you credit. Thoby is as well as anyone can be who has typhoid, and his temp begins to come down, and all will go well. Old Nessa, jumping on to her weighing machine in a night gown, says the dr. with a blush, scales 9.4—so she has either put on 3 lbs since yesterday, or her weighing was wrong. The dr. says she may cut off a week of her rest, and 2 weeks will see her resurrection. I need not say—after all our chastening interludes—you will remember them—that I look upon her convalescence

1. On 1 November 1906.

but as another chance for defacing—or is it effacing—myself. So when you come to Gordon Square and eat the fatted pig you will just walk through a cold mist, a little sharp upon the skin—which will be me. Now what news is there to break the day upon? surmising that you have passed a sleepless night? Shall we say Love? If you could put your hand in that nest of fur where my heart beats you would feel the thump of the steadiest organ in London—all beating for my Violet. Sometimes, when I am ordering dinner, or emptying—a flower vase—a great tide runs from my toe to my crown, which is the thought of you.

I have been talking nurses for 24 hours, pure and simple; I only see Nessa twice a day for 10 minutes. She does not have visitors, or letters, but sits up in bed, and writes with a tender pencil to Snow. The family are all on a system, and have their hours.

Beatrice was somehow averted today: providence sent the rain instead. I get post cards from the Quaker about 'our' Violet. How many people share you? I wont go lots with Mrs. Lyttelton. The world is singularly purposeless without a friend to tell me how well I write; of course I might have made a prettier sentence, but I didn't. Now then will you believe that I am devoted to every hair, and every ridge and every hollow, and every spot upon your body? How many letters may I write to you? But they will pour, without any word from you. Remember that few people have so much responsibility as you do; it is all your habit of making friends. Wall[aby] wipes his tender nose, and nuzzles you.

AVS

Berg

297: To Clive Bell   [46 *Gordon Square, Bloomsbury*]
Postcard
Friday morning [16 November 1906]

Thoby is distinctly better this morning. He had a fair night and all his symptoms have improved, and the nurse thinks he is well over the worst. I couldn't write last night, as I had relations here. I think it possible T. might see you this afternoon, but it is a chance of course.

AVS

Quentin Bell

298: To Violet Dickinson   [46 *Gordon Square, Bloomsbury*]
Friday night [16 November 1906]

My Violet,
Consider the difficulties of writing a letter while Peter [Clive Bell] discusses modern verse, with a jerk and a twist. I look at him and think how

one day I shall look him in the eye and say your not good enough—and then he will kiss me, and Nessa will wipe a great tear, and say we shall always have a room for you.

I get such vague reports that I dont know which disease I am addressing. I need hardly say that I respect them all.

We have taken a decided turn in our household. Thoby has rounded the corner, and we think he will now go on straight, and Nessa is 'tons better' says the dr. He sits and talks to her, till I think I must interrupt. Then we have George and Gerald and Margaret, and old Aunts with pheasants and carnations, and many tears and embraces, and Kitty has gone off to the north and promised a dressing jacket which never comes—and Jack [Hills] has gone off shooting and lent us £100—but this is the kind of sentence which no human being with a temperature over 98 pt. 4. ought to read.

I went out this afternoon and saw Ella, and then I had a long call from Mrs [Charles] Booth, who has got enough wisdom to salt 20 dozen ordinary people, and it reminds me of you. But then you are a d——d practical woman, with a sharp edge to your tongue. Still take you all in all—at anyrate we celebrate you at lunch tea and dinner—and Aunt Fisher writes to enquire after 'poor Miss D" She has just driven up on a growler (10. P.M) to hear the last news, and driven off again, like an evil witch, before we could stop her. I heard a scrannel voice in the hall.

Now my beloved Violet, if there is a single thing in this world or the next, in the world beneath or the world above, that I can get for you or do for you—well there's no harm in promising—and Wallaby goes to bed with wet eyes thinking of his lean mother lying out in the brushwood with alien foxes round her, "alien" is a pretty word, aint it? If I could smooth a pillow, or boil a saucepan, or fetch a hot bottle, you know I would do it all wrong, with the best intentions possible. Wall rubs his soft nose on the quilt.

He is a dear little beast, and loves his mother.

Sp.

Berg

299: To Clive Bell   46 *Gordon Square, Bloomsbury*

[17 November 1906]

Dear Mr Bell,

Thoby is worse this morning, and the dr. thinks that there is some perforation. They advise an operation at once—at 12 this morning—and will then sew up the ulcer in order to prevent the poison from leaking. It is a serious risk, but they give us hope as his pulse is good.

Vanessa thought you would like to know.

Yrs.

Quentin Bell   AVS

Monday [19 November 1906]

My Violet,

I dont know what variety of spots yours are. Thoby swears he beats your temperature, and we are a little scornful of the Dickinson typhoid compared to the Stephen typhoid. However we are improving; and Nessa's recovery is a little too rapid for my liking. The dr. goes in a stern sad man and come out a little weak round the lips: "Your sister is so remarkably sensible. We had better leave it to her." However, belief in her own power of taming doctors is really bracing, and she has the weighing machine to bear witness. She weighs 9.4: I dont; you dont; nurse dont; Gerald with a latch key and a watch chain and £2 10 in his pocket weights 14—or is it 15? yes 15. We all looked the other way.

Old Thoby says "I must be bad indeed before I shall forget you" to his nurse. So between the two—typhoid and appendicitis—all emotions seem to be germinating. It is dull to be a healthy happy Wallaby, with no heart and no inside. But then, I begin to see that every bed made for others, and every saucepan washed for others opens a new window into the soul. So I am all windows and no Wallaby. It is rather like being in a lighthouse.

Now I have dear Peter Bell to talk to. He thinks there never was a family like ours; never was a sister like ours. So I agree and we hint at love and marriage and what will be good for a woman who has had appendicitis, and a proposal, a woman of very scrupulous mind and unselfish nature.

Then I jumped in and said you are all sensitive appreciations, Mr Bell; you have no character. You want bottom.

He blushed like a sunset over Mont Blanc, blinked like a windmill, and said You are quite right Miss Stephen: it is very painful.

Then I said, "but many good qualities are dormant. You need family life".

'I do' he sighed, with such significance, that I said 'you must really be one of our family" So we approach and recede—and if he dont call me Virginia and kiss me on the doorstep before the days out—I dont love my Violet. And that is the oath to swear by. I feel all my heart drawn to you. Upon that I cuddle on my mat, and roll over and let you look for fleas. Wall kisses you.

                                                                          AVS

Berg

Tuesday [20 November 1906]

My Violet,

How you can trust any nurse to write down your vocabulary I dont know. My patient [Vanessa] is only allowed to write a very occasional letter to Miss Snowden—thats the drs. orders. He thinks you agitate—any woman that size must be eccentric—whereas he saw Snow for himself, and diagnosed her case.

We are going on well through our stages. It's a long business, but there's no need to be anxious. I must get out my pen again, and make that do its business. I reviewed 2 silly novels; no 3—and a 4th remains. My aim now is to pour out 500 chaste words in order, symmetry and taste—no matter what they mean.

Why dont you read the Creevey Papers through? I cant stop imbibing disreputable gossip; I begin to see what it is to have a taste for memoirs—like Lady Hilton, and Margaret. Is this conceited? but take the leavings of my brains when they have spent themselves on appendicitis and they stick like a leech to Creevey. I think I shall write an article for the Academy. But this dont interest you. What you like is oaths and scandal. So mark then, my weazened pimpernel, I shall have a niece in February.

Susie Grosvenor is engaged to John Buchan;[1] and the wise—that is Jack—predict tragedy. How is she to live with a clever man all the days of her life? She is pretty and flaxen and brainless (this is Jacks voice) must have a man to hold her handkerchief—but her heart is excellent—He has a brain, edits the Spectator and thinks of politics. Now make a story out of this as you lie in bed, and think of me.

Weighing day tomorrow I think, if the machine aint broke by Gerald. Goodnight and God—have I a right to a God? send you sleep.

Wall nuzzles in and wants love.[2]

Yr. AVS

Berg

302: To Lytton Strachey   46 *Gordon Square*

Thursday [22 November 1906]

Dear Mr Strachey,

We should like so much to see you, if you could come one day. I wonder if this next Sunday would suit you, about 6 o'clock in the evening? Vanessa is much better, and would like to talk to you.

Yours very sincerely,
Virginia Stephen

Frances Hooper

1. The novelist, later Lord Tweedsmuir. He married Susan, a grand-daughter of Lord Ebury, in July 1907.
2. Thoby Stephen had died that morning, 20 November 1906.

248

Thursday [22 November 1906]

My Violet,

I'm in a tearing hurry—Beatrice and Peter [Clive Bell] talking behind me. It is a mercy you are doing so well; a temperate life the dr. says is the specific for typhoid. You are as fussy as a hen—how d'you know my back aches? The dr. makes me share Nessa's rest cure, and I have milk and tonics and for the last 3 days I have had no more pain than a Caryatid.

Leo wants me to write an article for the National—not criticism but anything else.

Nessa gained 2 1/2 lbs this week, on half rations; she really is a wonderful old thing; and the dr. thinks her a credit to the race; says her nerves are 'beautiful'—one of the few people who have a sound body—and rest for a week or two more will set her quite straight. He is a very good kind of man, and he has set himself to understand Nessa now, and spends hours with her— talking mostly about football and electric light. Thoby is well as possible. We aren't anxious. His nurses really are nice women; and full of fight and energy—and so far there have been no quarrels. Indeed I had the greatest compliment I have had yet—"you really are more sensible than other people, Miss Stephen"—and she didn't know that I am also more inspired than most people—Aint I?

I feel I write like an eccentric typewriter; but I have to scrawl 'lines' on postcards to all the d——d relations, who think it so much to their credit to ask for news. Aunt Fisher limps in by the back door—why—no one knows.

Margaret offers me underclothes. Really the different departments of the Sparroy are being undertaken by different people—but none like you—Oh how pretty.

Yr. loving,
AVS

Berg

[23? November 1906]

My Violet,

There isnt much change. His temp. is up to 104 again this afternoon, but otherwise his pulse is good, and he takes milk well. The nurse is nice and quiet. The dr. hasn't been yet, but I write to catch the post. I dont think he will say anything.

Nessa had a rather tiring morning, as Kitty stayed an hour and I am afraid was rather full of agitating talk. But Nessa was set on having her. She has seen no one this afternoon, and though she looks tired she seems cheerful—reading illustrated papers.

I must go and give her tea.

You do her good I am certain, and I think Kitty *will* be good after the first interview wh. was bound to excite. Jack like an idiot told her to stay as long as she liked, and I had gone out with George.

Yr. AVS

Berg

305: TO MADGE VAUGHAN   *46 Gordon Square, Bloomsbury*

[24 November 1906]

Dearest Madge,

Nessa wants me to tell you that she is engaged to marry Mr Clive Bell. It happened 2 days ago: he was a great friend of Thobys and Adrians at College—and we have seen a good deal of him.

She is wonderfully happy, and it is beautiful to see her.

Yr. loving,
AVS

Sussex

306: TO VIOLET DICKINSON   *46 Gordon Square, Bloomsbury*

25th [November 1906]

My Violet,

You should have had a letter from Nessa before this. She wrote, and I suppose I put it down somewhere, as my habit still is.

You cant think what feats I have done with Snows telegrams and letters.

Thoby is going on splendidly.[1] He is very cross with his nurses, because they wont give him mutton chops and beer; and he asks why he cant go for a ride with Bell, and look for wild geese. Then nurse says "wont tame ones do" at which we laugh.

Nessa also increases steadily. Really I think we are through our troubles —but it has been the devil of a time. I have tried to write—but perpetual sense has consolidated my brains. Thoby has been reading reviews of the Life [of Leslie Stephen], and wants to know if you are up to that? The dr. says his brain is the strongest he knows; and his heart is fit to do the work of two men. Still, it is a long job, as you have to be so careful with food—and then as his lungs were bad there is the danger of cold—and he is like a child. We hope he will get away in 3 weeks, with Bell; and Nessa will be more than ready to go before that. She is to get up and come down if she likes this week

1. He had been dead five days.

—but I have made her promise to stay more or less in her room till she goes away—at least to make that her headquarters. She really is a wonderful woman. She sat down solidly to get well, confronted all the doctors, and has proved that she was right all the time. She saw Kitty one day, but as a rule she only sees us. They let her do as she thinks fit now; I feel happier about her than I have done for months. She does seem to me rested all through—brain and body—and ready to begin again as fresh as paint.

And now that Thoby is out of danger things will go swimmingly: only my dear old furry one must heal up—and come to a festal dinner. This is perhaps the dullest letter that *my* pen ever wrote; of course if Snow had written it, or Ella, or Herbert Paul—one would have thought differently of them. I went to the zoo this morning with Adrian; and a Kingajou[*sic*] hung on to my hand: O Kingajou, I said—if I were you! You will understand that that is exclamatory, and it is a poem too. And I saw the kangaroo, with its baby in its pouch, and it licked its nose, and wiped its eyes. That is Violet I cried.

Yr. AVS

Berg

307: To Lady Robert Cecil   46 *Gordon Square, Bloomsbury*

[November 1906]

Dearest Nelly,

I will come to lunch on Friday if that does. I feel it rather wrong to inflict myself upon other people just now—but I suppose that is morbid. Anyhow Nessa is divinely happy, and looks like a beautiful wise child. I only see her twice a day as Mr Bell is there the rest of the time—but I am trying to work.

Yr.
AVS

Hatfield

308: To Violet Dickinson   46 *Gordon Square, Bloomsbury*

Monday [26? November 1906]

My Violet,

The Doctor says that Nessa will be able to go away today fortnight—as near as he can tell. She is to keep to the rest cure for another 5 or 6 days, and she wont really come down much before she goes. Adrian's friend Cole[1] has offered us his house in Wiltshire—or Berkshire—It is large and comfortable—the dr. thinks it just right—and Thoby would join us there when he could come, or go for a little to the sea first with Bell. Bell comes everyday

1. Horace Cole, the hoaxer, Adrian's friend at Cambridge.

to see him and read to him—which is really the best possible arrangement—though one door is shut! Sydney-Turner came back from Copenhagen on hearing of Thoby's illness—giving up 2 out of his years 6 weeks holiday; really Thoby is spoilt by his friends. Kitty comes. Nelly sends him carnations. Of course he is fearfully weak after all his fever—he did have it high really till last week—but he is all right.

I dont feel as though I had any grip of a pen left—common sense does dry the intellect. The nurses get a little bored when there is nothing to do but feed up; but on the whole the menagerie behaves itself, and I stand in the center with a long whip. Really all your talk of housekeeping was a fraud; I do the bills, and the rates and the costs and it only wants 2 minutes and I spend 20 balancing a sentence. I try to hammer out an article for Leo; something fantastic about Greece, but it wont come smooth.

I had a walk on the Embankment with Katharine Furse the other day: it was like walking with a steam engine, and her mind never stops going. Still, it is a healthy kind of machine—and I suppose she has to get through her life somehow.

Also I saw Kitty; and as usual I recant a great deal that I said, though I think the main lines hold good. She seems fairly happy—well, its an odd world.

Thoby sends his love. So does Nessa—but Wallabie love is the nicest kind to get.

Yr. AVS

Berg

309: To Violet Dickinson   46 *Gordon Sq.*

[28? November 1906]

My Violet,

Your husband is a very forgetful man; but in spite of that failing—O how unlike us, Miss Beale and Miss Buss[1]—we get on very well. And is that an improper and impertinent remark? Well: now for business.

The old fraud (so we call Nessa now—yes, I know she was exhausted by years of unselfish labour on behalf of a sister)—sits hung with variegated gems, by a large vase of roses, and a fire of hot coals. She neither writes, reads, nor in any way toils or spins; but just exhales a great bounteous

---

1. *Miss Buss and Miss Beale,*
   Cupid's darts do not feel.
   How different from us,
   Miss Beale and Miss Buss.   *Anon,* 19th c.

Miss Beale became Principal of the Ladies' College, Cheltenham; and Miss Buss Headmistress of the North London Collegiate School.

atmosphere—the essence of amethyst and amber. Cant you imagine it?—well, it does want imagination. Thoby doesn't sleep very much, but otherwise he is all right, and is having whey, and chicken broth—chicken pounded to dust. Next week they talk of jelly, which makes his mouth water. He doesn't read much, but likes to be read to, and Peter is willing. One of these days I shall have to thank him. Nelly has just been; at least I find pheasants in the hall—and she rains pheasants.

I read in the Brit. Mus. all the morning, and sermons on the death of Christina Rossetti. Do you know she was about as good as poetesses are made, since Sappho jumped. Why where and when did Sappho jump? Dont excite the patient.

At Christmas time perhaps we shall all take up our beds: while you are quiescent I wish you would write down in your mind a list of friends; not in alphabetical but in sentimental order: L. [for Lyttelton] comes first in that alphabet doesn't it. V. is A in mine!! Now that was crabby; and little Walls can be ignorant, selfish, and arrogant little walls, if they can only spell like that.

Are you reading the Iliad? Do you remember Mycenae? How I wish I'd written something there.

I must wash, and give Adrian his dinner. He says he L. L. L. *likes* you! Why did he stammer so?

Yr. AVS

Berg

310: To Violet Dickinson   46 *Gordon Square, Bloomsbury*

Thursday [29 November 1906]

My Violet,

Here is the morning's post, like the morning's milk—20 letters for Miss Dickinson. Which will she open first? The fat one, with the large hand and the hand and the coronet and the sealing wax: so my genius tells me.

Well, my Violet, did you sleep, and did you dream—and did you dream of me? You see I ask and ask, but answer there is none.

Nessa has gained another 2 lbs: the dr. says it is about time to stop—and she may get up on Sunday. She does get up every day—and puts roses behind her ear, and wears the pink opera cloak we bought at Constantinople to sit by her fire in, while she eats her pheasant and drinks her milk. Is that a sentence? no, it is a disjointed alligator.

Dear old Thoby is still on his back—but manages to be about as full of life in that position as most people are on their hind legs. He asks daily after you, and whether you have sloughed yet, and how many spots you had, and what your temp. is. Shall he come and see you, or will you come and see him first? Peter is an angel—I always forget whether I kiss him or not. Altogether, the hospital is satisfactory; and so far I have not let out my true character. You cant think what a triumph it is to be asked to buy waterproof sheeting, as though one understood; and had never written a line in ones life.

I have afternoon tea with the dr. sometimes, and he is going to send me a pamphlet on the state endowment of hospitals. I picked up some hints from Ozzy [Dickinson] about that—only unfortunately Thompson thinks the other way round—and though I was able to agree, I cant argue.

When the dr. feels your pulse next, I wish you would ask him from a friend who wishes to be nameless but is interested in the question whether he thinks your heart a good one, and if he can discover any particular tendernesses in it—and if there is one for —— But the secret would be out. Give my love discreetly all round.

Yr. loving,
Wall

Berg

311: To Violet Dickinson   *46 Gordon Square, Bloomsbury*

[30? November 1906]

My Violet,
This can only be a scrawl, as Beatrice is dining here and Sydney Turner and Peter—and Heaven knows how we're to feed off a pheasant. I saw Kitty this morning. She tells me to dress better and I may marry—she aint sanguine. Still she is the best of women, with a heart of gold. O dear, that I should ever come to say that of her.

Nessa flourishes, and still sits by her fire. Savage came today, and says she has a splendid constitution and we need never feel any anguish about her health. He says she was quite right: and no rest cure was really necessary.

Thoby slept better. He still isn't allowed to move, but next week the feeding stage will begin.

This is dull and dreary. But the talk of nurses is like opium to the brain—only it dont soothe.

Your AVS

Berg

312: To Violet Dickinson   *46 Gordon Square, Bloomsbury*

[1? December 1906]

My Violet,
I hear you are doing as well as possible. That is the usual phrase. So are we here—but doing as well as possible still takes time. Nessa has beaten you all—She really is renovated all through—and you should see her with a rose

in her hair by her fire! Thoby has little ups and downs; last night he slept badly, indeed that has been the difficulty with him all along, only the dr. doesn't seem to think it matters much. Otherwise he is getting on, and we begin to scent the country in the distance. I have no idea how long these diseases take. He sends his love.

Adrian has gone off to Cambridge for Sunday, so I am sitting over my solitary fire and reading Dean Swift. If you want to limit and define your own miseries, compare them with his. However I daresay you are glad to take them as they are.

I lunched with Nelly today, and we talked our literary shop. If I were Edmund Gosse, I should enjoy it better—and my puzzle is that she cant really be amused. But then you see her great melancholy eyes—and O Lord what a mercy it is to have something to talk about!

Katharine Furse is a fine woman as you know; only I dont think she is a woman at all, but a great virgin tomboy with a life time of sorrow set down in her suddenly. She doesn't know what to make of it; it is all crude and uncomfortable. You know only very rich soft natures like Nessa's absorb their experiences.

O how I wish I could write English. I have been reading Shelley all the evening, till George came in and thought me lonely, and asked me to go and dine with them. So I made an excuse. Did you ever read Shelley? It is about as good as most things—as walking or running or talking or writing to Violet.

Well—I must put out the lights, and take this to the post. It is a lovely night—but I hope you will sleep through it.

Yr. AVS

Berg

313: To Violet Dickinson   *46 Gordon Square, Bloomsbury*

Sunday [2 December 1906]

My Violet,

If only the British public would not celebrate their makers praise—or if only their maker would provide adequate voices, and Broadwood pianos. O God! how I suffer. You will tell me it is nothing to typhoid fever—but the injury to the mind is greater than the injury to the body. Read your Plato.

Well—I am so sick of writing bulletins—and I know yours is the kind of mind that is really happiest in a sick room. Ah ha—you cant call me a healthy happy Wallaby!

But I must waste this sheet of paper. Which is perhaps the most sacred of Gods handiwork. I must sully it with this kind of stuff—when really I might inscribe words of fire and flame. What is the difference between a word of fire and a word of flame?

Ask Swinburne or Ella, if she is in the room.

Nessa is so well I cant think of any sickroom details about her—except that she said she was having indigestion yesterday and so they are giving up her milk. Thompson comes to see her tomorrow for the last time. He says she is "splendid"—you will give me a prod in the ribs of course and tell me to efface myself—efface myself and efface myself—but when you see me next you will regret the loss of my nose. Some people thought it was my finest feature: others hinted that a little pumice stone applied to the tip, or as they called it 'the point' might be as well: only one, Miss Violet Dickinson, said "Rub it off altogether: pain on earth is ease in Heaven. The noseless enter where the nosy are denied." Aint that the kind of thing you write and have found in red?

Now, after this respite, about Thoby. He is going on slowly but satisfactorily. Everything is healing, but he is not to eat anything solid yet, and he is not to sit up. He draws birds in bed, and Peter reads Milton to him. He cant write much, and he dont get letters. He is wonderfully good, and Simon, his lawyer, has written a charming letter returning his fee, and hoping he will come back as soon as he can. I suppose you and he are about at the same stage now, only I think he has had a much sharper attack. Still Thompson is quite satisfied.

Adrian has gone for a walk with George [Macaulay] Trevelyan today, or he would send his love; indeed he does send his love—it is a permanent article. I can take as much of it as I like. Now are you fond of me?

Yr. AVS

Berg

314: To Lady Robert Cecil   46 *Gordon Square, Bloomsbury*

Sunday [2? December 1906]

Dear Nelly,

The tea gown was a great success—she is having the blue one copied. Thank Heaven I didn't have to choose for myself. She is coming down to dinner tonight, and when I pass her door, I hear not only perpetual voices but laughter. I ask what they [Vanessa and Clive] talk about, they say art. Do you believe it? Well, you may mix art with many things.

Please dont keep any one out of Gale on our account. I feel January is a vague term—and there are the relations in law [Clive's parents] to visit. But as you know, or ought to know, we should like to come.

I cant help feeling though that the more I work and the less I talk the better—at least the less bad—for the world at present.

This is not a remark that calls for a compliment.

Yr. aff.
AVS

Hatfield

[4? December 1906]

My Violet,

The nurse says you are not to read for more than 5 minutes which I take to be a hint as polite as the obtuse race can make them. So you must swallow news in pills: Nessa has been sitting up for about 2 hours with no ill effects.

Thoby is more hungry but healthy and rather better they say. I suppose he cant get stronger till he eats. These dreary details you will supply for yourself. They say his attack must have been worse than yours as his temp. was so high, but its a thing that leaves no ill effects—indeed it recoats your inside—so you can look forward to a double life in purity and cleanliness.

Now is 5 minutes up?

Yes Miss: and your handwriting takes double time.

Sydney Turner is talking and drinking and smoking and purring all at once.

Love from Adrian.

AVS

Berg

Wednesday [5 December 1906]

My Violet,

Here's your five minutes worth.

All is going as well as—what is the metaphor? ask Ella. Nessa gained 2 lbs. again this week. She will soon scale 10 stone as nature made her—and that without isolation—and with no excess of food. She sits up for 2 or 3 hours in the evening over her dinner, and smokes a cigarette and doubtless thinks of Peter—though we skirt that subject. Thoby goes on slowly, but there's only one pace in typhoid they say, and you must stick to that. He likes being read to, and Peter drones on by the hour—Peacock and William Morris—and Gibbon.

We begin to flirt with our nurses, and call them 'my woman' and they knit pale blue ties which they promise him, if he's good—so he takes his medicine, and chocolate instead of food. He says he's been worse than you— and much worse than Nessa. He had drs. 3 times a day.

And now aint it time for poor little Wall to make his mew? Who thinks of him now, or licks his under fur. There are many who can grate their tongues over his outer fur; but it needs a subtle lip to find his down.

I lunched with Gerald at the Savoy today. We had—5 minutes up—all right nurse—dont tell my patient about solid food. O damn these women! I shall never fight my way through the threefold barrier: Ozzy, Mrs Lyttelton, Ella. But suppose I do, and come bleeding into your room will you cherish me, and entertain me comfortably. Aint that in the Bible? O my Violet, get well, and stay well, and think of nothing but a holy future life.

Yr. AVS

Berg

317: TO VIOLET DICKINSON   *46 Gordon Square, Bloomsbury*
Sat. [8 December 1906]

My Violet,

Nessa got off safely,[1] wrapped in innumerable petticoats. I heard this morning that she is well and safe, and the country is lovely, and the house is comfortable, and Snow is placid, and they sit with their feet on the fender, and take a walk in the sun. It is the life that suits her though I should ask for the nearest pond. She is going to paint. Thompson says she has a constitution to be proud of; I always said so, in spite of sisters.

Thoby wont get away for Xmas; I shouldn't think; but they think he will be up—We can go away afterwards. At. Minna has offered us her house [Bank, New Forest], and Nessa could come and join us there. He is going on well, and the faithful Peter comes with his book under his arm, though the house must have lost its jewel.

Well, it rains outside, and the only comfort is a book and a fire; and these you can have too I hope, besides which you may think of your hall table with its flowers and its coronets; and of your husband, and of your Kathleen[2] —I dont know what is missing in your Heaven; except a small animal that burrows with its snout.

I have been writing at my article; but it is vile bad, and I sometimes think incessant sense, (sense is almost chronic with me now) has paralysed my genius.

Still, I can invent new puddings!

I want to write about Christina Rossetti; so if you can find out what she thought about Christianity and what effect religion had upon her poetry, and will write it on a post card you will do more for me than if you looked out a train, and bought a new hat.

So goodbye, my dear treasure; do you think anybody in the world is quite as nice as you are? Are you modest or are you vain? I think the Christian soul can make a retreat of illness.

Yr. AVS

Berg

1. To stay with Margery Snowden at Horace Cole's house at Newbury, Berkshire.
2. Sarah Kathleen Bailey, the daughter of the 4th Lord Lyttelton, and the wife of John Bailey.

Monday [10 December 1906]

My Violet,

Nessa is very happy and well. So Snow writes. I get close letters, all detail that I hate. And you want more of it! Well—Thoby is going on well; he has chicken broth of a kind, and will be up by Christmas. The dr. approves of his trip with Peter, but wont say yet when that will be. I suppose early in January. He has a great many flowers and attentions, and is very good and delights his nurses. The dr. says he has a remarkable mind. Now, are the invalids disposed of? And is it right to end a sentence with a preposition?

We will turn to more interesting subjects—as, Walter Headlam and my manuscripts. Now Violet raises herself in bed, and calls to the nurse to draw the blind a little higher, and bids them tell Mrs Crum not to come in yet awhile.

I am to send him all my unpublished works; and he will write me a sober criticism. Doesn't that do you good, and make you believe that life holds possibilities? Further, he wishes to dedicate his translation of the Agamennon[1] to me, instead of to Swinburne; in gratitude for 3 pages of the finest criticism known to him which I wrote and despatched 4 years ago! How many of my letters will thus rise up and bear fruit? I may be incubating heaven knows what glories.

Then I saw Fred Maitland, whom I love. He gets more meaning into 10 words than I do into 100 and than Snow does into a 1000—we will not go on with the calculation which might be painful. Anyhow, he brought me a packet of letters from distinguished people about the book, and 2 of them say that my part of it was 'beautifully done'. I cant keep off the Sacred Subject; my nose will have to be tapped when you come out. May I make your Mellins[2] for you in future? He (this is F.M.) is really satisfied, I think, and goes out happy to Teneriffe.[3]

Are you in what state of body or mind? My plan is to treat you as detached spirit; maybe your body has typhoid; that is immaterial (you will be glad to hear) I address the immortal part, and shoot words of fire into the upper aer [*sic*] which spirits inhabit. They pierce you like lightning, and quicken your soul; whereas, if I said How have you slept, and what food are you taking, you would sink into your nerves and arteries and your gross pads of flesh, and perhaps your flame might snuff and die there. Who knows?

Yr. AVS

Berg

1. Walter Headlam's *The Agamemnon of Aeschylus* was published in 1910, two years after his death.
2. A children's bedtime drink.
3. On his voyage to Teneriffe, F. W. Maitland developed pneumonia, and died in Las Palmas on 19 December.

Wednesday [12 December 1906]

My Violet,

For a woman who writes tracts you are singularly untractable. I swear that joke swelled on my pen, like a drop of perspiration—or did I mean inspiration?

O why do you dwell upon the material point of view—what are chills, what are hot water bottles, when the Xtian faith is celebrating (beneath my window) its 1906th anniversary?

Well; Thoby is going strong—at least the dr. is satisfied, and the nurses are pleased: he begins to curse a good deal, and points out the virtues of a mutton chop. Are you allowed solids yet, he wants to know. The dr. promises to get him up by Christmas. He means to go first to Bournemouth and then to Wiltshire when he is quite cured to hunt with Peter. Snow sends me an occasional line; but she has a Harrogate sense of humour. However, I gather that Nessa is extremely well, and very happy; they walk every afternoon. I dont hear from Nessa. The address is:

> West Woodhay House
> Newbury
> Berks.

So now we may listen to our carols again. What a strange religion—and to think that you and Christina Rossetti and the boarding houses of Bloomsbury all worship at the same shrine. Now supposing I went and danced chaste Bacchic dances beneath the plane trees, and chanted the odes of Sappho, the next policeman would put me in an ambulance. Do come out from your sickroom a Buddhist.

I dined with George and Margaret last night, and we had some very exquisite conversation; I do like refined home life—connubial maternal and civic affections all sound and serious. If Plato were alive I should take him to Charles Street; Margaret would entertain him, as George says. Really she is a good woman; in 10 years I shall love her. I look at the germ sometimes, and it is a healthy growth, but some what stunted.

I am so sorry about your husband. Nor do I know what degree of affection one may offer through the post.

Yr. AVS

Berg

[13? December 1906]

My Violet,

I hope your husband is all right. I check your stage by Thobys; he is very cheerful today, and saw Peter. Nelly sent him some flowers; and next week visitors are to be admitted.

Snow sends her daily report; it is always excellent, and rather soporific. They find each other's company satisfactory at all points: I do think that is like a taste for oysters—or shall we say clams? But it comes in useful now. It is plain to me that I am a very inefficient sister; but I also perceive that I can housekeep. You should hear my morning dialogues—what invention and resource, skill and courage I show! Books too high!! What is this price of veal cutlets a lb? Where is the second leg of yesterday's chicken? O my eye—why should it be confined to the drawing room, or style to the study?

I am going to see Kitty tomorrow, a curious woman with a soul the colour of an opal. Now I like wrapping up profound little sentences like that for you to unroll as you lie and look at your counterpane. I—well, what about I? too much about I. Dont I remember the crossing from Ostende, and the yellow lover, and the tame gold finch, and the voice that went on, like the voice of judgment, solemn and insatiable at my ear—while the sea blew grey?

So now about V: well, V. does equally for I and for Vanessa—but I am surfeited with Vanessa; and therefore I will talk about Violet. Is she a good happy resigned woman? Christina Rossetti positively liked being ill she said; it reminded her of her narrow bed, and of the chance of hell fire, and the probability of eternal torment. And to a Christian this is about the most cheerful thought in the world. I think that is enough about the next world. You see I did try and be unselfish.

I think it must be bad for your moral soul to inhale quite so much incense as the morning post offers up punctually at your bedside; "Darlings" from Kathleen "Beloveds" from Ella—and all kinds of significant silent things (I got that in a novel) from Haldanes and Horners.

You will gather there is no news.

I wish we could put our pens in the fire, and take to the material embrace.

Yr. AVS

My MSS went to Headlam today.

Berg

[14? December 1906]

My Violet,

Well, my good woman; as sure as the sun rises, here am I. Wonderful is the force of pen and ink. I like finding a pencil twitter on my plate at breakfast—old Mum Wallabys feeble voice, querulous with love (and chiding) for her offspring. I do hope the other orphan convalesces too; there are rumours floating down Piccadilly, and out of the Club windows, that Miss Dickinson eat a fish, and one has it that it was a sole, and another says plaice.

Thoby is going on too, and will have some minced chicken tomorrow; anything solid to bite he says. They give him chocolate mean while. Snow didn't write today; because, I suppose, I leave her letters mostly unanswered. The kind of reflection you get of Nessa through Snow through the post, is watery and virtuous but somewhat vaccuous (does that mean cowlike?) They eat and sleep, and do little sketches, and I daresay talk more about Peter than about art.

My sweet nose is held to the grindstone of real life; (you will be glad to hear) I had a visit from Thena Clough[1] today and Mrs Prothero.[2] Thena is like a plump brown thrush, as she certainly sings a wise song. I liked her—though why I take it for granted that I know her, I cannot say. She seems to be included somehow in my knowledge of human nature; not precisely specified.

Well, I saw Kitty too; and you malign her. She is ever human, and capable of understanding that I differ, and yet live, and am perhaps human and perfectable. She will never believe that I write; but you are one of the few people who will believe it.

Gerald has gone off to Egypt, for a month. He wants to feel warm, and the Club fire wont do. Really, I love Gerald: he has been very sympathetic and useful all this time.

Now, my Violet; take your medicine and think of me.

Shall we ever meet again?

Yr. AVS

Berg

1. Athena Clough, tutor at Newnham College, Cambridge, of which she became Principal in 1920-1923, succeeding Katharine Stephen, Virginia's cousin.
2. Wife of George Walter Prothero, the historian, fellow of King's College, Cambridge.

[15? December 1906]

My Violet,

If there is one book that I want more than another—no, its *not* the Bible—it is the Poems of John Keats, in a brand new edition complete in one vol. published by the Clarendon Press at Oxford. Give me that and I shall dream all day beneath leafless trees.

Do you think that intelligent nurse could carry out this prescription, and see that the book is brown, with a white label—not unlike a fine posset?

Adrian says what may I send Violet as a token of my affection?

Your Love, sez I.

But she has that already, sez he.

"I would rather be near Violet than anyone else in London" is another literal quotation.

I felt peace drop upon my soul this afternoon, and my temper is excellent this evening. You know, there is nothing like friendship in this world! Do sleep and dream sweetly.

Yr. AVS

Berg

Sunday [16 December 1906]

My Violet,

I am sorry about your husband, but I dont see that I can *do* anything, as the Aunts all say. You know my beautifully spiritual theory, that friendship is entirely a thing of the mind, and a thought is worth perhaps twenty dozen deeds. A profound truth is hid beneath that seemingly smooth surface. Break it, and dive beneath.

Thoby has a Buffon[1] already, but, acting again on my system, he thanks you as much, no more, for the thought than the deed. He is really getting on well, and we talk of getting up, and going away, and the future. Old Nessa, hybernating like a sleepy bear sends inarticulate messages through the literal Snow: Nessa sends her best love, and says it's a fine day. What is to be done with a mind like that I ask you? If I had it I should first try the power of affliction, then of religion, then of education; I should wreak it and furnish it and stamp it and pinch it till it bore some resemblance to human nature. However she says that Nessa "Looks extraordinarily well already." I copy words because you wont believe mine.

I have been having a debauch of music and hearing certain notes to which I could be wed—pure simple notes—smooth from all passion and frailty,

1. *Epoques de la Nature* (1779), by George-Louis Leclerc, Comte de Buffon.

and flawless as gems. That means so much to me, and so little to you! Now do you know that sound has shape and colour and texture as well?

A London Sunday affords no topics for letters, unless it be the singular and by no means edifying topic of the Christian religion. A church bell—they ring them for 2 hours daily—says something to me hardly to be translated: there again it is sound that wraps up the meaning and colours it and translates it and keeps it mystic and unexpressed meanwhile. Should you think there was any sense in that? A letter should be flawless as a gem, continuous as an eggshell, and lucid as glass. I give you that for your next tract. I am going to be Librarian at Morley. Miss Sheep[shanks] says that she thinks my gift is rather influence than direct intellectual teaching.

Do get well, beloved Violet.

AVS

Berg

324: To Violet Dickinson   46 *Gordon Square, Bloomsbury*

[17 December 1906]

My Violet,

This must be an inarticulate scrawl, like the twitter of some frozen sparrow in the graveyard behind your house.

[Dr] Thompson suddenly proposes to move Thoby at the end of the week—Friday or Saturday—to the New Forest. He sat up out of bed today, and the great thing is to get away as soon as possible. It seems rather marvellous, as this is the first time he has been up—but it will be a mercy if we can do it.

Aunt Minna will let us have her house, and if all goes well and Adrian and I, Thoby and a nurse move there on Friday I expect to avoid the crowd.

He is decidedly better, and gains every day something.

Very good news of Nessa through the usual illiterate medium.

I wish you could get away at the same time and Ozzy too.

I hope he is better.

Yr. in haste but in love,

AVS

Berg

325: To Madge Vaughan   46 *Gordon Square, Bloomsbury*

Monday [17 December 1906]

My dearest Madge,

I know I ought to have written, but took it that you would understand. Your plans are not to be realised; Nessa and Clive are to live in a separate house, probably in Bloomsbury. Adrian and I must turn out and find a smaller one, perhaps up here too. I think it would be a real mistake to live together; I think the same square or the same street would be dangerous—ten minutes walk is what we propose.

This does not mean that I expect to quarrel; I like him very much—and you know what Nessa is—but the only chance for us is to start fresh again—They must have their life, if we are to get any good from it—and I mean to—and we must have ours, if we are to profit.

But leaving theories—I hate them—Nessa is wonderfully well, and went off last Thursday with Clive to stay with his family in Wiltshire.[1] They are good country people, and certainly very kind and considerate of her. She sounds as happy—well—as happy as she can be; and that, as I always suspected, is a large order. When you ask me what I think of her engagement you ask more than I can say, because I dont think very much yet. I know I like him, and I like him most when I see him with her. He is very honest, and unselfish and scrupulous; he is clever, and cultivated—more taste, I think, than genius; but he has a gift for making other people shine, and he is very affectionate. You must make a character out of these hints—I write in the middle of a tea party—They are a most reasonable pair of lovers, and tell me that they discuss art as much when they are alone as when they are with us; but there is a good deal else. They are devoted.

Vanessa's illness was not really serious, and the dr. is surprised and delighted at the way she picked up. She will be away with Clive till the beginning of January: and they mean to marry later in February. Adrian and I go to the New Forest for Xmas week—then stay with the Bells for 2 or 3 days, and then back here. I hope we may see you sometime. It was a most happy chance that you asked Thoby for a photograph: he was taken by Beresford [facing p. 201] the week he left England. I will send you one when they come; they are good—but not very much when you think of him. There is nothing I can say about that that you dont know. Adrian is well and so am I, and we must 'make the best of things' as father would have said. I stayed with Katherine [Furse] yesterday; she is a wholesome person to see; I begin to realise what her loneliness must be. Love to the children.

Yr. loving AVS

I got some flame coloured stuff in Constantinople which reminded me of you. I will send it off, in case you like to have it. It will cover a chair anyhow!

Sussex

1. Cleeve House, Seend, Wiltshire.

[18 December 1906]

Beloved Violet,

Do you hate me for telling so many lies?[1] You know we had to do it. You must think that Nessa is *radiantly happy* and Thoby was splendid to the end.

These great things are not terrible, and I know we can still make a good job of it—and we want you more and more. I never knew till this happened how I should turn to you and want you with me when no one else could help.

This is quite true, my beloved Violet, and I must write it down for once. I think of you as one of the people—Adrian is the other—who make it worth while to live and be happy. You are part of all that is best, and happiest in our lives. Thoby was always asking me about you. I know you loved him, and he loved you.

The only thing I feel I could not bear would be to think that this news should make you worse. It would not be right. I can feel happy about him; he was so brave and strong, and his life was perfect.

Now we must be more to each other than ever; and there will be all Nessa's life to look forward to. She is wonderfully well.

"I think on the whole I get happier every day—though it's difficult to think that I can ever be much happier than I have often been at moments during the last few weeks." That is what she writes today.

Beloved, get well and come back to your Wall who loves you.

Yr. AVS

Berg

1. Virginia had kept the news of Thoby's death from Violet for nearly a month. Violet found it out by accident. In the December issue of the *National Review* she read a review of Maitland's *Life* of Leslie Stephen. The reviewer wrote: "This book appeared almost on the very day of the untimely death of Sir Leslie Stephen's eldest son, Mr Thoby Stephen, at the age of 25".

Letters 327-388

The original Hyde Park Gate family of ten had now been whittled down to two, Virginia and Adrian. Julia, Stella, Leslie and Thoby were dead, George married, Gerald an independent publisher, Laura locked up mad, Vanessa engaged. To Virginia, Adrian was still "a poor little boy" aged 23, and she felt responsible for him, arranging that they would give up Gordon Square to Vanessa and Clive, and move to a new house which she found in Fitzroy Square, only a few blocks away. She and Adrian spent Christmas in the New Forest, and in March 1907, shortly after Vanessa's marriage, she took him on a short visit to Paris with her sister and brother-in-law. At first Virginia found it difficult to accept Clive as a worthy husband for Vanessa, but their relationship improved with correspondence and frequent meetings, when she could not fail to observe the happiness of their marriage. In London she was occupied with Morley College and almost weekly reviews for The Times Literary Supplement. *Visits to Cambridge led to her first mild flirtation with a man, the scholar Walter Headlam, 16 years her senior, who died in the following year. Everyone expected her to marry someone, but none of the Thursday Evening young men yet made that sort of appeal to her. The summer holidays were spent by the Bells and Stephens at Rye in Sussex, where Virginia met Henry James. A new note of literary exaltation enters her correspondence, as if literature was the only true consolation for the loss of her brother and (as she first imagined) her sister too. She was now 25.*

327: To Violet Dickinson   *46 Gordon Square, Bloomsbury*

Tuesday [18 December 1906]

Beloved Violet,

Here is a line to wish you good night—whereas it will wish you good morning. And you must imagine the most compassionable and soft of Baby Walls just climbing on to your bed—one claw catches in the quilt and nurse raps his behind. If I were given to prayer I should pray that you might have slept well, and woken peacefully. I know all good people think very much the same about dying and being born; and there is nothing dreadful is there? —in what comes so naturally.

But I dont need to preach—you know it all better than I do. I shall come to you very soon for—well, not for consolation, but for all the things that make life worth having.

And if that is not what one would choose to have written on one's tombstone I can think of nothing else.

Nessa became engaged 2 days after Thoby died; but she was really engaged I think the moment she saw Clive, (as I call him!) She could never let him go back. So she went through those days in a kind of dream. I feel *perfectly happy* about her. When you see them together you realise that he does understand every side, and all that is best in her. I never saw anything so beautiful as she was. He is very considerate and unselfish, and he is really interesting and clever besides.

You know what she has in her, and all that seems now called out; she is a splendid creature, and makes me hope all kinds of things.

She will write and tell you all this herself. It seems so natural and right that she should marry Clive that I can really imagine nothing else—or wish for anyone but him.

Adrian and I go down to the Forest on Friday.

I will write. I will do anything as you know that would help you—but I am a very incompetent person, specially at boiling milk.

Good night: beloved creature.

Yr. AVS

Berg

328: To Clive Bell   46 *Gordon Square, Bloomsbury*

Thursday [20 December 1906]

My dear Clive,

I can quite believe that you are very happy with Vanessa—but as she also seems to be very happy with you, I dont see that my sisterly solicitude has any right to complain. My friends take very good care that I shant be lonely. I never knew that Lady Pollock[1] came under that head till this afternoon. Jack is so fond of you, and she believes you have a very pretty sister, and she supposes we shall get a house in this neighbourhood to be near the British Museum.

I wish you would write a description of yourself—your features your gifts your prospects your parents—that I might know exactly who you are and what you are and above all whether you are worthy of Vanessa. The general opinion seems to be that no one can be worthy of her; but as you are unknown this is no reflection upon you. Only it will show you the kind of reputation she has; perhaps you know it already. I begin to wish she were a little more various—but I do homage all day long prostrate and acquiescent, before her shrine. And I suppose incense rises in the fields of Wiltshire also; the last worshipper was Pippa Strachey[2] who lunched with me today. She has

1. Wife of Sir Frederick Pollock, Professor of Jurisprudence at Oxford. She visited Gordon Square with her son John (Jack).
2. Philippa Strachey, Lytton's older sister, who was later prominent in the movement for broadening women's education.

an imm*ense* admiration—you can put the accents on——for Vanessa—and thinks *no* man good enough. This letter can be divided into equal parts if necessary; but I have an instinct that one word does for the two of you.

I am writing to your mother to suggest that Adrian and I should come on the Monday after Christmas—I suppose it has a date.

I gather from Vanessa's letter—she doesn't say so in so many words—that I shall be treated to some of the purest commonsense—the commonsense of lovers that is perched on the peak of the world—if I dont appreciate your family. Really I dont see the terrible gulf that divides one from the Bell family and the human race.

Here is a house agents list: the Queen Square house is all panels and old oak.

Please add a word to Nessa's letters now and then to say that she is well in your eyes besides her own. I can read for myself that she is happy.

> Your aff.
> AVS

Quentin Bell

329: To Violet Dickinson

Lane End, Bank,
Lyndhurst [*Hampshire*]

Saturday [22 December 1906]

My Violet,

Your parcels come dropping in by every post. I really have very little morality about giving and receiving; only I doubt that you should be so excessively blessed. Adrian has been turning over the question of the cheque all day; finally I made him promise to use so much as will provide a horse for 5 days. There never was a happier present; he had only funds for one hunt—and there is nothing he cares for more. And it will keep him out all day, and make him think of other things—poor little boy.[1] So you see, as usual you simplified and adorned our lifes; lying on your sick bed, and groaning I daresay—At least that improves the picture.

Now for a list of my presents; there was the Keats which I cut solemnly and savouringly (as Mrs H. Ward has it) with the carving knife after tea; there was the paper and there were the skins. So, if there was only a little pen and ink thrown in, we should have our great book complete! It is odd what funny unorthodox tastes we share together—for handmade paper, and strange tawny skins. Further, my benefactress, there was your letter, which should rightly head the list of your charities. Really it was a pious searching letter such as Mother Abbesses might write to their nuns, in spiritual crises. For while it poured balm, it also pointed a higher way, and that is the kind of encouragement I value. You inspired a very affectionate

1. Adrian Stephen was now 23.

269

letter to the old happy gipsy—and you so smoothed all the edges of my torn feelings that I have thought of her easily and without bitterness. I think I had felt rather harshly; and perhaps I had said something too sharp to be pleasant, though it was true. Now you have made 2 people—3 people counting Adrian—happy today; because I know very well that my feelings still have power to affect Nessa, whatever I may say. And I have the natural feeling now that any happiness is so rare that it must be treated tenderly at all costs. I think that is why she is so completely happy; it is a kind of economy, because it mayn't last. But, with my usual confidence, I am pretty sure that it will last, to her dying day.

It is as beautiful as it can be here, clear and sharp and all the trees are full of colour and line. We have been walking in the forest and meeting deer. How I wish you could be out, knocking about in the bogs and tearing through holly bushes! I feel a sort of animal desire to breathe and move and do nothing that needs intelligence.

But I have a good many books, and I do vaguely wish to work too. Indeed I have read rather a lot, sitting over the fire with Adrian. Only I think less than is conceivable, and hear words droning through my mind without troubling to attend.

Adrian and I talk a great deal of our future; and it really begins to look quite vigorous and healthy. He drew plans of phantom dinner parties that are to be given in the new house in March: and a certain V. D. comes at the corner, in the middle, sometimes she even carries the joint, to make the sexes equal!

How are you I wonder?

Yr. AVS

Berg

330: TO VIOLET DICKINSON   *Lane End* [*Bank,*
                                  Lyndhurst, Hampshire]

Sunday [23 December 1906]

My Violet,
     Your letter gave me the first news of Freds [Maitland] death. Then Adrian went and read it in a paper. O dear—the earth seems swept very bare—and the amount of pain that accumulates for some one to feel grows every day. I dont know that he would have minded dying, he was already so refined away that the body seems to be a small part of him. But he was very human and loveable—and everything to her and the children. I hate to think that they should begin to suffer. I was thinking that I should see him often, and perhaps he would come and dine with us—and anyhow he would be there always.

He was one of the few, the very very few, who wrote me something about Thoby which seemed true and inspiring. He was a real genius; father always said so. He made everybody else seem clumsy and verbose. But these things are only the odd thoughts that come through my mind. I do admire so few people—none I think as I admired him—and somehow the loss is very great.

There is nothing to tell you today—but that we walked in the forest. It was a beautiful day, and quite sunny. Then I have just finished a Life of York Powell[1]—and I heard from Nessa that she is still happy, and means to be married in a mauve dress with a red rose; and they are discussing what hat Clive shall wear.

Now I must write to Kitty. Adrian is brewing whisky toddy over the fire, and shouting out stories of father when he was an undergraduate. It is a blessing we have that book. I think Fred knew that.

This is a d——d dull letter. I hope you will eat Turkey for your dinner, and drink a glass of champagne.

Yr. AVS

Berg

331: To Violet Dickinson

[Lane End] *Bank,*
Lyndhurst [*Hampshire*]

[25 December 1906]

My Violet,

It has been quite an absurd Christmas day—think—I was woken by sunlight dancing on my nose, and cursed, and woke and saw the whole pane blue, and then the whole field white, and little birds and modest cottages, and blue smoke, and peaceful trees: I should have saluted the happy morn had I been a Christian. As it was I went and knocked up Adrian and we came down to our letters and parcels. Then in the intervals of eating turkey we have tramped in the forest, which is as a painted wood, all clear sharp tints, and delicate lines, and crisp white spaces. If Clive were here to sum up the scene, as is his way, he would call it 'obvious' I suppose; it is convenient to have a mouthpiece for one's own cynicism anyhow.

We lost ourselves thoroughly, or rather, for Adrian will never admit that he can lose himself, the road took us wrong, and we had a very long walk, till it was dusk. And then we sat and read. I am reading now a book by Renan called his Memories of Childhood [*Cahiers de Jeunesse*, 1906]: O my word it is beautiful—like the chime of silver bells; and when his old peasant mother writes it is the same thing, so that I think it a virtue in the French language that it submits to prose, whereas English curls and knots and breaks off in short spasms of rage. Also I am reading my dear Christina

1. Oliver Elton's *Life* (1906) of Frederick York Powell, Regius Professor of Modern History at Oxford, who died in 1904.

Rossetti with her kind voice and her prominent eyes, and her acquiescent piety: but all the same she sings like a robin and sometimes like a nightingale —the first of our English poetesses. She doesn't think, I imagine; but just throws up her head and sends forth her song, and never listens, but makes another. O you Christians have much to answer for! She died surrounded by all the horrors of the Church, poor woman. Then I am reading your Keats, with the pleasure of one handling great luminous stones. I rise and shout in ecstasy, and my eyes brim with such pleasure that I must drop the book and gaze from the window. It is a beautiful edition.

Yr. AVS

Berg

332: To Violet Dickinson   [*Lane End, Bank,*
                                             Lyndhurst, Hampshire]
[28? December 1906]

My Violet,

I am glad you have been up. It is freezing cold here so that Adrian couldn't hunt and we went for a walk instead. Yesterday I lost myself, and got home so sleepy that I couldn't write—but, my word, trees are better than people. I have a long letter from Clive, pompous and polished as usual, but not amusing. He is a careful youth, and realises his own luck which is something. He says his family is "tiresome"—to which I always feel inclined to say a family is always as good as you deserve. Nobody is ever too good for their own flesh and blood. But he takes pains to show that he sees their limitations.

Why on earth does Nelly say I have a 'steady head!? and what do you know about the way I have come through these months? I wonder. I am amused by the indiscriminate praise I get; however Walter Headlam will tell me the truth.

I think housekeeping is what I do best, and I mean to run our house on very remarkable lines. Does housekeeping interest you at all? I think it really ought to be just as good as writing, and I never see—as I argued the other day with Nessa—where the separation between the two comes in. At least if you must put books on one side and life on t' other, each is a poor and bloodless thing. But my theory is that they mix indistinguishably.

I had a letter from Katharine Furse asking me to go and stay with her, but I shant, though I think she is a good person to be with. She has a real thread of courage running through her, which is better than genius, and better than virtue; indeed I put it first of all qualities. She makes herself go on, and never says a word about it, though every day is hard work, like some one cutting steps in the ice. Kitty [Maxse] also writes, and [Janet] Case and Jack [Hills] and various relations. I suppose you are swamped too.

I have 5 volumes of poetry to review for the Guardian—and one takes for hero the Almighty, and Jesus Christ, and the villain is Satan. How I am to discuss the character drawing without losing my place I dont know.

No letter from Nessa today.

I met an old man on the village green yesterday, lame and frost bitten and ruddy and white haired who told me he had had goose for dinner and "really thought he was the happiest old man in the world" He looked so convinced of it and so stealthy as though happiness was not altogether respectable that I told him he was a credit to the race and upon wh. he shambled off to the public house, and I nearly followed.

Get well; read, and flourish.

We go on Monday.

Yr. AVS

Berg

333: To Violet Dickinson

[*Lane End, Bank, Lyndhurst, Hampshire*]

[30? December 1906]

My Violet,

There is but little news, and my mind misgives me that I wrote you a very acid letter the other day—but I had a d——d pain in my head which made me snarl. However it is quite gone, you will be glad to hear—poor Violet, you have enough pains of your own to think about, and I am as sweet as usual.

I shall want all my sweetness to gild Nessa's happiness. It does seem strange and intolerable sometimes. When I think of father and Thoby and then see that funny little creature twitching his pink skin and jerking out his little spasm of laughter I wonder what odd freak there is in Nessa's eyesight. But I dont say this, and I wont say it, except to you. Tell me if it bores you; I dont want to make things worse for you, and I know my letters aren't soothing.

It is so cold that we can hardly leave the fire. Adrian comes down in his gaiters every morning and prods the earth with his stick; and it rings like iron, and then there is no hunt. So we walk in the afternoon, along drives that are frozen into ridges, and laid with ice. It is very lovely and silent; we meet no one, but a deer now and then. Then the sunsets and all the trees look as though their tips had been dyed red, and they are combed out against the sky, and we wonder whether nature is not a little gaudy sometimes. The forest always disappoints me—it is too orderly and picturesque.

I have been reading Keats most of the day. I think he is about the greatest of all—and no d——d humanity. I like cool Greek Gods, and amber skies, and shadow like running water, and all his great palpable words—symbols for immaterial things. O isn't this nonsense? Adrian plays patience at my side. I have done my 5 reviews also, and my mind feels as though a torrent of weak tea had been poured over it. I do think all good and evil comes from words. I have to tune myself into a good temper with something musical, and I run to a book as a child to its mother. Dont you think the flesh is a cumbersome illustration, and the text is all written or spoken in half a dozen words? I am so stupid I cant follow out what I meant to say.

Get well do; however Ozzy is the best argument for that, and Kathleen, and Ella. Where do I stand in the hierarchy? Anyhow, you are a game old thing and that is what I like about you. Write—or dont if it tires you.

AVS

Berg

334: To Violet Dickinson

Lane End [Bank,
Lyndhurst, Hampshire]

[31 December 1906]

My Violet,
   This is only a line as I have to write various dull letters before going.
   Nessa sounds happier and happier but wants to see us. I have long letters fr. Kitty and George.
   The world is full of kindness and stupidity, I wish everyone didn't tell me to marry. Is it crude human nature breaking out? I call it disgusting. It is thawing now, and the snow is all dirty. I shall be glad to go, and I only wish I was coming back to London and cd. sit with you in the fire light.
   I wish I knew how you are. Sleep is the very devil, and drugs are worst of all. I read your Keats all day. O divine!
   I will write again.

Yr. AVS

Berg

335: To Violet Dickinson

Cleeve House, Melksham,
Wilts.

Wednesday [2 January 1907]

My Violet,
   The thickness of this nib and the luxury of this paper will show you that I am in a rich and illiterate house, set in its own grounds, gothic, barbaric. I dip my pen into the hoof of an old hunter.
   But to business. We came here late on Monday, and were greeted by Vanessa and Clive, standing like husband and wife before a great log fire. It was a symbolic attitude. Vanessa—you see how pompous I am—certainly looks well. I thought her thinner, but her weight has gone up slightly. I wont talk of her health, because I am always prejudiced, and you know it.

Besides it is a subject upon wh. I cannot speak without a quickened pulse. It was strange and rather strained, but by no means alarming. A little rabbit faced woman, craning forward and attenuated, with wisps of white hair, delicate creases in her face, and eager abstract blue eyes: that is Mrs Bell; then Mr Bell is light and simple—not as solid as I expected—a very cheerful cordial and obvious country gentleman who has probably *not* been at college. The daughters are so exactly what one would have guessed; it is absurd to write it out. They play hockey and beagle, and laugh at Adrians jokes, and come down to dinner in pale blue satin with satin bows in their hair.

Neither of us had a moments shyness, indeed I made soliloquies, vague and rather fantastic, and Mrs Bell looks as though she thought us a parcel of clever children, who have yet to learn the meaning of things.

Yesterday I rather lost my temper and went out to trample it into the mud. But since that I have been very nice and sweet tempered, and I feel calm and domestic. Clive certainly is an interesting person, and I really feel happier, and get some glimpse of what Nessa means by marrying him. She is as happy as anyone can be; and more like herself than she was. She seems to have taken her bearings, and to see her life ahead of her in her own clear and reasonable way.

I dont think marriage will make any difference, because the best of us survives though it is d——d painful to cut away the inferior parts. They talk of 7th Feb. and will be away almost 3 months. Also they take on Gordon Sq:[1] so we are free to choose our house at once.

Are you well today—how is Ozzy [Dickinson]? I could write a good deal about you but I daresay you would be bored. We sleep Thursday night in London and go on to Booths Friday morning—A[drian] hunting.

AVS

Berg

336: TO VIOLET DICKINSON   46 *Gordon Square, Bloomsbury*

Thursday [3 January 1907]

My Violet,

Here we are for the night, passing through. We spent the day at Bath—a Meredithian expedition—so far as Nessa and Clive were concerned. They swung along the streets arm in arm; she had a gauze streamer, red as blood flying over her shoulder, a purple scarf, a shooting cap, tweed skirt and great brown boots. Then her hair swept across her forehead, and she was tawny and jubilant and lusty as a young God. I never saw her look better. Indeed our two days were more of a treat than I expected; I am not unselfish,

1. Clive and Vanessa were to live at 46 Gordon Square, and Virginia and Adrian were about to search for a new house.

as you know; but selfishly I do enjoy life and beauty and audacity, and all that freedom and generosity which seem to bathe her like her own proper atmosphere. And Clive as I think I said, is perfectly fit to receive all this; I think he has a very sweet and sincere nature, and capable brains and great artistic sensibility of every kind. What you miss is inspiration of any kind, but then old Nessa is no genius, though she has all the human gifts; and genius is an accident. They are the most honest couple I ever saw; a little more imagination and they would be less scrupulous—but on the whole, I doubt that man and woman are made much better in the world. I did not see Nessa alone, but I realise that that is all over, and I shall never see her alone any more; and Clive is a new part of her, which I must learn to accept.

Still—O this is a selfish letter—I can make a living out of what is left; and it is the purest of all earthly affections; so even you must admit I think.

If either you or Kitty ever speak of my marriage again I shall write you such a lecture upon the carnal sins as will make you fall into each others arms; but you shall never come near me any more. Ever since Thoby died women have hinted at this, till I could almost turn against my own sex! But this will make no impression upon either of you.

Tomorrow I spend at the dentist till we go to the [Charles] Booths: they are jovial and domestic and rather beautiful as far as they go—a sort of harmony of affection which is pleasant at a distance.

I am so confused and egoistical tonight that I cant write a sympathetic letter; but you always have Ozzy as I reflect with some satisfaction. Do get well and enjoy your life. So few people have as much cause for happiness as you have. Beloved Violet—you have a pure fount of sweet water in you —miraculous to me.

Yr. AVS

Berg

337: To Violet Dickinson   [*Gracedieu Manor, Whitwick, Leicestershire*]

Saturday [5 January 1907]

My Violet,

Here I am again in a luxurious country house¹, with butler and footman, and the whole place flowing with cheerful domestic life, and kindness and sweetness—but I dont feel myself a part of it. Still, it is really worth seeing, because they are none of them extraordinary and yet set in motion like this the whole effect is harmonious like a comfortable family picture by a Dutch painter (shall we say?) I feel devilish stupid, and only half in my right

1. Belonging to Charles Booth, the writer on social questions.

senses. I cant talk good sense for long, and I had to sit by a great fire and discuss the state of the church in France.

Adrian has gone off shooting, and I spent the morning decorating a Christmas tree, hanging long chains of silver balls across it and funny little candles to all the twigs. This reminded me of my own youth. Then we sprinkled the whole thing with stuff like fishes scales, and wrapped the pot in scarlet cloth.

Then I stuck a lump of toffee and an orange into a green muslin bag. Then I was shown the kitchen and the family dinner. O dear how odd and simple all this is—and I suppose it is as good a way of spending ones life as another. It is very melodious, as I say to Nessa and Clive when I want to be laughed at.

It is a large family, and they marry, and produce children, and come and settle near, and you feel that the prolific power of the race is boundless. Moreover they mix with great smoothness and sweetness, and circle round Mr and Mrs Booth like so many humming tops. Mrs Booth is charming; she sits upright and talks admirable sense in a clear high voice—takes broad views of the church in France, quotes [Jacques-Bénigne] Bossuet, discusses politics, and meanwhile sympathises and advises with each daughter and son and baby, and keeps them all depended from her middle finger.

Now I must go and light my candles, which I have perched in a way of my own; I have also to show them how you fasten a sponge to a stick. I shall be given a yellow bag of toffee when it is all over, and we end with snap dragons.

I am so sorry (O read it how you like!) that Ozzie is so bad. It is damnable for you. I suppose you will wait to go away till he is better. I am glad that you can hop round the room; only do take care. You are an impetuous woman. Another very happy and charitable letter from Nessa. I think our visit really was a success.

Yr. AVS

Berg

338: To Lady Robert Cecil   46 *Gordon Square, Bloomsbury*

Monday [January 1907]

My dear Nelly,

The worst of waiting to write to you is that meanwhile the benefits accumulate—pheasants and furs—I daresay flowers and fruits—And it is only by scrutiny that I charge you with half your sins: "We think it was Lady Robert" or Kitty mumbles something about Nelly, and jumps into her cab, and leaves a great box in the hall.

Now the pheasants are long since gone, and I think they were specially nice pheasants, and I gave my solitary wing some special attention—considering it as a piece of tender meat, critically. Why is there nothing written about food—only so much thought? I think a new school might arise, with new adjectives and new epithets, and a strange beautiful sensation, all new to print. How generous I am! I might have kept this all to myself. But the fur is another matter. It is a very subtle and serious matter, wrapped round the most secret fibres of our consciousness; you dont know what a lot might be said and felt and thought—what reams, therefore might be written —about such a gift; and here am I going to squeeze all this in to the usual Thank you. I think I ought to be hurt, and then angry, and then apologetic, and then generous, and then sentimental and then philosophical, and then merely friendly. Whereas I am none of these things; only I think I am grateful—because, if I have none of the finer feelings, I am yet fitted with a marvellous simplicity of nature so that to buy a fur is impossible to me, but to accept a fur is quite easy and pleasant. O well—this is the way we writers write—when we wish not to say something. As you are a novelist yourself you need no further explanation.

I think you ought to write novels: you can write letters which is far harder. I never say what I mean to say; because I seem to have told you that I didn't want to come to Gale. What I meant I think was that there are times when my company seems an infliction to myself, and therefore a curse to others; but whereas I can drug *it* (that is me) in a book, or an ink pot, you would have the creature crude and naked, and therefore it would be best to keep within reach of drugs for the present. And it is also true as you say, that I have to talk a great many words, from a very shallow mind at present; Is this about enough about myself? I have 10—no 12 letters to write in an hours time; and I mustn't stay chattering here all day.

Nessa drives morning and afternoon in a carriage and pair with her husband (what is the word?) and finds her family [the Bells] honest and kind: now you can make a picture of all that, from the topmost twig to the profoundest root.

Yr.
AVS

Hatfield

339: TO VIOLET DICKINSON   46 *Gordon Square, Bloomsbury*
[6 February 1907]

My Violet,

This is written in the midst of our last night.[1] We have all been to Fidelio.

These days seem very turbulent but tomorrow it will be all over. Really marriage makes very little difference—Tho' I hate her going away. But I

1. Vanessa and Clive were married at St Pancras Registry Office on 7 February.

really have been quite good tempered. I say not at home to everyone. Margaret Lyttelton is coming one day, and Katharine Furse.

I hope you really are well and comfortable, and dwelling upon a cheerful future. Your present is lovely. Settlements signed and done.

I will write again.

AVS

Berg

340: To Violet Dickinson   [46 *Gordon Square, Bloomsbury*]
Postcard
[8 February 1907]

Wedding successful,—very quick and simple. But Nessa and I got lost going in the Pentonville Rd. and the motor took a short cut so that they missed their train—and had to wait till 12.40. Nessa sent in a line, much amused.

AVS

Berg

341: To Violet Dickinson   46 *Gordon Square, Bloomsbury*
[February 1907]

My Violet,

I know I have behaved very lazily and selfishly, and not cheerfully as Ozzy would have me.

I feel numb and dumb, and unable to lay hands on any words. It is quite calm and pleasant today, and I feel elderly and prosaic, and much as though I were 50.

Nessa hasn't written yet, but I suppose they arrived.[1] George and his motor were bound to upset everything. There is no news I think; I saw some houses this afternoon, and I think we shall get one at our leisure. There are so many, and people are so anxious to let.

How are you—and what do you do I wonder?

Dont write letters about me or my feelings; but about yourself.

Adrian is perfectly charming, and I do want to make a cheerful place for him. It is terrible that he should have no brother.

But we go along—and I wrote this morning—rather well I think.

Margaret L[yttelton] comes tomorrow. I like her, but it is like making Pyramids when you talk to her.

Take care.

Yr. AVS

Berg
1. They went to Manorbier for their honeymoon.

279

Tuesday [February 1907]

My Violet,

You do make me feel penitent. When I hear of your worries and wishes —I dont know if a pen is as fatal to you as it is to me—I feel positively fraudulent—like one who gets sympathy on false pretences. Remember my dear delightful exquisite and eccentric—how shall we end it?—perhaps Giraffe, that I hate writing letters. I would rather send telegrams, save that my style is too expensive.

But I am perfectly well: aren't I the healthiest woman in London? I do regret that I expressed myself so forcibly that day: it was only a passing melancholy. I dont think I can do very good work just yet, but I take infinite delight in exploring my own mind. I am going to write something serious, needing work; and I am stumbling through Lucretius. I hope also, but this I must whisper, that I have found a house, in Fitzroy Square. Bernard Shaw and his mother lived there for many years. There are the usual intricacies; but Adrian is rather eager—and I dont think we shall do much better. Still this is only a phantom so far.

Then every morning I come down to a great sheet signed Vanessa Bell. "Put in as many superlatives as you like in your account of me. You cant say too much. You cant think how delicious it is here. It's simply divine, warm and sunny. We lead the most healthy existence—early to bed and late to rise, a walk on the beach in the morning—and by the fissures in the afternoon. Clive thinks me looking remarkably well, he says. O I am d——d d——d happy. I am doing a sketch of my husband reading. I find it most exciting beginning again."

So you can read many chapters there. It really does make me less cynical to read her letters.

I had 6 invitations yesterday: one from Ly. Young[1], to stay with her 'for weeks' as a great kindness. I have had this proof sent: I wrote it in the summer: it is only a dutiful exercise. Margaret L. and I kissed on the door-step. I think she is a very nice woman. I like kissing people: handshakes are abhorrent. Now I will write: but for Gods sake dont think of me. Do SLEEP.

Yr. AVS

I spent Sunday motoring with Katharine Furse. Who is much like a Greek statue draped.

The old Times sends me a novel every week.

Berg

1. Wife of Sir George Young Bt., a friend of Leslie Stephen. They lived at Formosa Place, Cookham, Berkshire.

343: To Lady Robert Cecil   *46 Gordon Square, Bloomsbury*

[February 1907]

My dear Nelly,

Your chauffeur left 2 bunches of tulips on me. Will you thank him—
Is it proper? You must settle this for me. Anyhow I thought it a very
pleasant attention.

Mrs Bell is struggling with the English language: there aren't enough
words for happiness—besides hers is a special kind of happiness. Husband
too: there should be accents or inflexions. Finally I have written out a code,
which can be used in telegrams: there are 4 ds.[1] She uses 6.

I have been teaching a Milkman [at Morley College] to write English
for 2 hours; and the effect is so singular that I had better say no more. It
is like floating your brains in cold mist.

Yr. aff.
AVS

Hatfield

344: To Violet Dickinson   *46 Gordon Square, Bloomsbury*

[February 1907]

My Violet,

I couldn't come later, but I will try and come at 4.15 tomorrow.

O dear what endless pain there is for someone to feel—poor Margaret.
Now we hear that Moorsom[2] a friend of Thoby's and Adrians has killed
himself. He was dining here the other day.

I saw a very likely house in Upper Montagu St. today. Adrian wants
me to say that he has lost your cheque. Aint it like the family!

Yr. AVS

Berg

345: To Clive Bell   *46 Gordon Square, Bloomsbury*

[February 1907]

My dear Clive,

Your letter surely craves a premeditated answer; yet how did the
correspondents of Gibbon achieve their share of the task? did they perambulate the study table too, casting periods as the angler casts his line
or did they commend themselves to the sheet as simply as the child betakes

1. Possibly Virginia's ration of d—d's.
2. Kenneth Moorsom, formerly at King's College, Cambridge, and a clerk at the
House of Commons 1901-7.

itself to the Lords Prayer? I have a fancy that the great man was content with little eloquence in his friends if their attitude was pious.

A true letter, so my theory runs, should be as a film of wax pressed close to the graving in the mind; but if I followed my own prescription this sheet would be scored with some very tortuous and angular incisions. Let me explain that I began some minutes since to review a novel and made its faults, by a process common among minds of a certain order or disorder, the text for a soliloquy upon many matters of importance; the sky and the breeze were part of my theme. A telegram however, with its necessary knock and its flagrant yellow, and its curt phrase of vicious English—I know not which sense was most offended—hit me in the wing and I fell a heaped corpse upon the earth. The sense, if that can be said to have sense which had so little sound, was to discredit the respectability of a house in Fitzroy Square. And there you see me in the mud. Shall I argue that a mind that knows not Gibbon knows not morality? or shall I affirm that bad English and respectability are twin sisters, dear to the telegram and odious to the artist? I state the question and leave it; for it will ramify if I mistake not through all the limbs of my soul and clasp the very Judgment seat of God. So then let us turn—and where? First, I think, to Vanessa; and I am almost inclined to let her name stand alone upon the page.[1] It contains all the beauty of the sky, and the melancholy of the sea, and the laughter of the Dolphins in its circumference, first in the mystic Van, spread like a mirror of grey glass to Heaven. Next in the swishing tail of its successive esses, and finally in the grave pause and suspension of the ultimate A breathing peace like the respiration of Earth itself.

If I write of books you will understand that I continue the theme though in another key; for are not all Arts her tributaries, all sciences her continents and the globe itself but a painted ball in the enclosure of her arms? But you dwell in the Temple, and I am a worshipper without. It behoves me then to speak of common things, that are and cease to be; of people and of houses, of Empires and of governments.

I read then, and feel beauty swell like ripe fruit within my palm: I hear music woven from the azure skeins of air; and gazing into deep pools skimmed with the Italian veil I see youth and melancholy walking hand in hand. Yet why separate and distinguish when all are pressed to your ardent lips in one clear draught?

Let us then have make [*sic*] an ending: for in truth I must copy out this sheet.

Yours ever,

AVS

Quentin Bell

1. cf. The dedication to *Night and Day:* 'To Vanessa Bell but, looking for a phrase, I found none to stand beside your name'.

15th Feb [1907]

Dearest Madge,

I am returning your basket with some vegetables. I hope you are cut off from spinach still! I think the railway will either send them up to you, or tell you where they are. They should arrive tomorrow (Sat.) morning.

I found the other day a manuscript belonging to you. I will send it—and I hope you wont think that I am never to be trusted again. We had a very sensible and businesslike wedding in the registry office behind St Pancras workhouse. Nessa and I lost our way in a motor, they were married and paid 7/6—and finally they lost their train at Paddington. But they are happy enough to be quite beyond the reach of accidents, and Nessa wrote her first letter to me sitting in the waiting room, very much amused. They sound so happy that they make noises like children instead of writing. It is very strange to watch—or rather not to watch—It does seem all a dream still.

Adrian and I try to get a house, and I hope I have found one now in Fitzroy Square—but they always fall through at the last.

You and your 4 children are just by my inkstand. They give me great pleasure—so does their mother. Thoby used to say that you were the most beautiful person he had ever seen.

It is very hard not to have him here—I cant get reconciled—but we have to go on. Adrian is well—but I cant be a brother to him!

Yr. loving,

Sussex   AVS

Friday [15 February 1907]

My Violet,

You will be glad or sorry or mostly indifferent to hear that George has another son[1]—born this morning at 9.30—both well. I feel some kind of affection, though our kinship is much diluted—Herberts and Duckworths!

But now to business. I really do want your advice about this house [Fitzroy Square]. Will you listen to the facts and give me your verdict?

Sophia [Farrell] approves of it in every particular; Shaw [the builder] tells me it is in a sound state, well built can be decorated for £150—most of wh. is outer paint, supplied by our landlord. They will put in a bath. There is electric light. All things about the place are satisfactory; and the Agents believe that we shall get it for £120.

1. Auberon Duckworth.

Beatrice comes round, inarticulate with meaning, and begs me *not* to take the house because of the neighbourhood. You say something about that this evening. Well—how am I to judge—or what importance ought I to attach to respectability? There is a Boys College on one side: a dr. [doctor] on the other: there are hospitals and institutions at intervals, nursing homes. Bernard Shaw, or his mother, was the last tenant. The streets surrounding are dingy, but no worse than they are here I should say.

Anyhow you see my predicament. If I hint at any question of respectability to George Gerald or Jack, they will refuse to let me take it—and yet I have spent every day for a month looking for houses, and I feel—desperate I should say if you would let me exaggerate—when I think of beginning all over again. The only alternative is the Upper Montagu Street house, which I saw today with Sophia. She says it is 'not a patch on Fitzroy Square and very dirty, but we could manage there.' I dont want to take a house which would be unpleasantly disreputable. I dont want to be frightened off a house by a vague phantom, probably unnoticeable. Can you discriminate between all these interests? Such are the trials of affection. Your word would settle my mind either way. I do begin to feel that we must make up our minds; and the last week or two have produced no possible houses.

Thank the Lord, that discourse is over. Do you want to see me or dont you? I made some kind of tentative proposal to come down for a night which like so many sensitive ideas of mine died of silence. I could always come for a night. I dont realise your plan.

Walter Headlam came to tea today, with Lytton Strachey. I hate pouring out tea, and talking like a lady, and realise my own inadequacy without Nessa. However it has to be faced.

I wonder—you wouldn't think it!—how you are, and whether you sleep at night, and when I may expect to find your body and soul harmonious again. Your soul was floating like a captive balloon last time I saw you; a white globe, transparent and ethereal, veined with fire. O isn't that pretty? I am spending all my hoarded garrulity upon you because Adrian is dining out, and I should be reading a novel called "Temptation" for the Times. But such is my prudery, that when temptation is written out in plain English, I throw the book under the sofa, and take to my virgin sheet. Living much alone as I do I find it necessary to think of pleasant things: Lucretius and Violet.

Tomorrow we go down to the Quaker: I dont look forward to it—to her—but I suppose we shall do some gymnastic feat of the emotions, some crisis, or reconciliation. All my friends are silent, like frogs when the moon rises; or house sparrows at sunset. Katharine Furse is too erratic to count upon. Beatrice almost too energetic. I love them both: I love them when they are not there—they leave beautiful spaces behind them. Now some people I love in the flesh.

I am trying every morning to finish a long drawn out piece of writing, which dwindles on like some elongated misshapen—tallow candle?—and then I shall plunge into the depths of some soporific work, needing green spectacles. I cant write—but I suppose it doesn't matter. Why did you show Walter Crum that proof? It was really only a dutiful exercise. But any praise is welcome.

Nessa still writes very inarticulate letters. I dont much realise what has happened. Still it would have been unbearable if she hadn't married. I dont get reconciled to anything.

The thought of you makes a considerable difference: do you see that written out letter for letter?

Write one line: dont bother.

Yr. AVS

Berg

348: To Violet Dickinson   *The Porch [Cambridge]*

[17 February 1907]

My Violet,
    I feel rather repentant when I think what a very long letter I wrote you, long and vehement and egoistical, and all about that d———d house. Somehow I got in rather a state of mind about it. I think we have settled to take it now: I hope I shant find that you disagree.

But the advantages seem to me to be solid; and the disadvantages are mythical; and Adrian approves, and Sophie urges with all the force at her command, and it is considerable: she promises health and happiness, low books, and no repairs.

We are doing what I seem to have done very often before—spending a quiet Sunday here. The Quaker is like some glossy evergreen; I feel she will rustle her leaves over all our graves. She thinks we both look extremely well—whereas she had expected—hoped rather—that after all we had gone through we might be morbid in some way. However she is predicting a very curious death for old Aunt [Lady] Stephen: "indeed one cant wish her to live". She is a little melancholy about you: you say you are better, but she hears you dont sleep.

Do you sleep? Say so: if you do. I know few things more weary and pale and ashen than a sleepless night.

I have had one moderate bout of argument—it always begins with the question of my literary career—very tentative and significant and eager for hints though cautious; and we always end with our old argument: had father an imagination or not? She has just produced some documents from a portfolio to prove her side, and vanishes, to rest.

But with all her faults—and who am I to call my family perfect?—she

285

is about as tough an old heathen as they make; we shant develop such thews and sinews not if we live 80 years. She never alters, but she is thoroughly well seasoned, and if you wish to—Well, anyhow, I shall talk till 11 tonight, I suppose Adrian is dining out.

We go back early tomorrow; and I hope to have the question of the house finally knocked on the head. O what a mercy! Then I shall work.

Write sometimes—not if it tires you. How is Ozzy?

Yr. AVS

Berg

349: To Violet Dickinson   46 *Gordon Square, Bloomsbury*

[February 1907]

My Violet,

I am sorry for your disapproval [of Fitzroy Square], but I dont think I take Mrs Crums verdict. After all, I was strongly warned against Manchester St.[1] as most disreputable by our agent. I have written to Jack to ask him to find out at once, and let me know. I discussed it with the Quaker; and she says that unless the house itself was in disreputable hands she thinks it would be a pity to go by what people say of the neighbourhood. If the house had a bad name it might be unpleasant, but I cant believe it has.

But of course, when one asks for advice it means agreement, and I come to a pass where I must settle for myself. Please dont bother, or write to [G. B.] Shaw, or do anything.

These things dont matter a 2d. damn, except that I swear.

I will write again. Upper Montagu St. has fallen through, as the woman wont take off her premium.

I am a troublesome scratching fleasome and fretful beast—but eternally grateful. How shall I ever say that loud enough? Shall I come down to Aldeburgh [Suffolk] for the night?

Yr. AVS

Berg

350: To Violet Dickinson   46 *Gordon Square, Bloomsbury*

[February 1907]

My Violet,

We *have* waited: I cant go into all our reasons and emotions. Anyhow the thing isn't settled, and we try to come to a clear judgment. Only it is about as difficult as it can be: Jack writes it is he believes 'perfectly respectable.' Shaw the builder says he wd. send his own wife there: the Sq. itself

1. Where Violet's own London house was situated.

is all right but he has gone to ask at the Police Station. I shall hear the result tomorrow. It's no use writing; of course it is damnably disappointing—

The worst of it is that it seems so impossible to make a good decision; supposing things are as Mrs Shaw[1] says wd. they really be so unpleasant as to make the house untenable?

Really it is an excellent house: we shant get a better, and Shaw agrees.

AVS

I will come on Friday 4. and I will come down to the cott. on Sat. but its no good my coming if I have to start house hunting again. Wd. it be easier if I came for Sunday—early and went late—save a bed?

Berg

351: TO VIOLET DICKINSON   46 *Gordon Square, Bloomsbury*
[February 1907]
My Violet,
    No letter from Jack or from Mr Shaw: so we have made an offer for the house, and I think we have probably got it. I am sure this is right. Here is a card from the Quaker.
    I am sorry I bothered you. I dont think I have asked in a hurry, and I dont mean to repent. I have still to interview lawyers.
    I cant dine on Friday, as Gerald is coming here to go to the Friday Club—but I will come to tea—4.30—or 4—

Yr. AVS

Adrian and Sophia are both unhesitating.

Berg

352: TO VIOLET DICKINSON   46 *Gordon Square, Bloomsbury*
[26? February 1907]
My Violet,
    I had time to ponder your merits on the platform this morning—a gracious occupation—you can believe as much as you like.
    It was the easiest journey [from Suffolk]; I read my Balzac, and got home in time to call Adrian, and found hot coffee waiting me.
    I hear that our terms are accepted—the lease is being made out. So God be thanked!

1. Two Shaws are involved: George Bernard Shaw, who had lived in the Fitzroy Square house before his marriage in 1898; and Shaw the builder, who was to put it in order. Violet had consulted Mrs G. B. Shaw, or his mother.

287

Adrian's plan for next Sunday has fallen through: he asks if he might come to you? He would get down later, as he is drilling; and he would take a walk on Sunday, and he would enjoy it very much. But say if you dont find it convenient. I cherish your wisdom, which is the sweetest and sometimes the bitterest known to me.

Now I must take the brush to my head, and try and dine out like a Lady.

Yr. AVS

Dont think I purposely withhold your cover coat: I try to remember it.

Berg

353: To Violet Dickinson   46 *Gordon Square, Bloomsbury*
[2? March 1907]

My Violet,

I couldn't manage today, as I had rather a rush, and a German lesson to end it. Sophie and I and Shaw tramped the house, and smelt into corners, and it is all highly satisfactory, and I am supposed to have a nose for a house, and I hope we start work next week.

I dont know how to make plans, but I somehow think that Life or Fate or Providence (as the Quaker would say wishing to spin out a sentence) will cast us together somehow somewhere and somewhen.

Adrian and I are just off to a party at the Trevelyans, for which I feel singularly unfit—but we must take to the water again.

Yr. AVS

Berg

354: To Violet Dickinson   46 *Gordon Square, Bloomsbury*
[March 1907]

My Violet,

We are going to a concert on Tuesday, or we would have come. Shall I come to tea on Monday?

I have a favour—a very great one—to ask: could we possibly spend Sat. to Mon: the 23rd at Manchester St.? We would have all meals out of course: it is only a question of a bed while the move goes on. But dont hesitate—as the old ladies say—to refuse.

Nothing in the Times this week is mine, so dont praise the wrong people.[1]

1. All articles in *The Times Literary Supplement* were anonymous.

I wrote to Nelly and sent her my Greek book.[1] O the vanity of Authors!

I had a serious interview with [Walter] Headlam: he said he was miserable that I didnt marry, but sat alone and moped. What am I to do! Am I such a d——d failure. We talked for 2 hours.

Yr. AVS

Berg

355: To Clive Bell   *46 Gordon Square, Bloomsbury*

Friday [22 March 1907]

My dear Clive,

I can conceive no possible circumstance less suited to writing a letter, or even an address, than those in which I am at this moment.[2] Still you know, for you have discussed my theory I hear, that there is a kind of sting in such grotesqueness. And besides, if I dont write to you now, I shall never write to you again. Honestly, I withdraw into a strange upper world when I sit down before a table; very soon it will be withdrawn beyond sight, and belief. O God, the world it frets and rages: little chopped waves have surged to the very roof of the house. My room is a bare island in the midst. After luncheon I shall be swamped too.

Well then, how am I to write a letter? But perhaps you have observed that this is a favourite device with letter writers, they are always in haste, or in discomfort, or in a temper, so that you only get the dregs of their genius, and you can speculate what a letter it would have been—seeing there are six careful sheets already—had he had time or temper, or so on. And I put 'he' because a woman, dear Creature, is always naked of artifice; and that is why she generally lives so well, and writes so badly.

I had another argument with Walter Headlam yesterday, and I was triumphant. It didn't, even, come to argument, because a week at Cambridge gave him leisure to reflect that he knew little of humanity, and very little of Stephen humanity; and he met me in a gentler acquiescent mood, ready to learn and believe, and tentative in his theories. He destroyed his own argument by some ghastly blunders in my own proper science: the theory of Vanessa. He said of her that she was sweet and gentle and good, but neither interested in people—nor—but this is malice on my part—could he see her beauty! And then he had to own that he really knew nothing about us.

I have been reading a book which I should tell you to read, but that I

1. Probably the journal of her Greek tour in September and October 1906. The present whereabouts of this manuscript is unknown, but Sussex University has a typescript copy. So does the Berg Collection.
2. Virginia and Adrian were leaving Gordon Square the next week for their new house.

dont want a snub: "my dear good Virginia, when I was a boy of 20," and so on. At any rate, it is the Life of Sidney by Greville[1], and it has some passages of the ripest melody, like plaited columns of marble, if I may mix my metaphors and confuse my sense. And if there are such books in the world, I shall continue to live and read.

Well, well, there are many things to talk about, for as the weather warms so do my ideas kindle. I think you suffer from the same complaint, which is Gods own malady. Give my love to my sister, and, if you like, kiss her left eye, with the eyelid smoothed over the curve, and just blue on the crest.

Yr.
AVS

Quentin Bell

356: To Madge Vaughan

Hotel Rastadt, 4 Rue Daunou, Paris

2nd April [1907]

Dearest Madge,

I got your letter when I was sitting on a cupboard in the drawing room, directing painters. We fled after 3 nights without sheets in bleak rooms; but it was all very amusing. In a week we shall be back—the 12th that is. I wonder if you will come?

It makes me shudder when my own words come back to me, written or spoken. When I said 'happy', I was using a short cut; for I dont know what I mean by happy—except when I see Nessa, and she doesn't explain. I think in your case I meant wise, and mellow, and permanent; as though you had found a dwelling place after all, from which to deliver judgments. I think it may be rather a melancholy position; only it is true and lasting. That is a paradox if you are also like a bird. Did I say that? I think I meant again that your eye glanced and flitted, fetching food for your soul; but I maintain that the spirit is stationary. That is what your children give you, and life I suppose. Anyhow it seems to me delightful. What a racy old woman you will make, and what a mother for Janet!

Now have I been saying rash things that will require explanation? It is quite likely, because I write in a hotel bedroom, and in a minute I must get ready for dinner in some eccentric tavern in Montmartre with Nessa and Clive.

They are in another hotel but we see a good deal of them, and they are really a pleasure, if only to look at. I cant believe that Nessa wasn't born married, because it seems so natural and appropriate. She sings to herself

---

1. *Life of the Renowned Sir Philip Sidney* (1652; ed. Nowell Smith 1907), by Fulke Greville.

as she walks, and buys strange plumes and draperies in the Louvre; but as we decided at lunch, she looks best undressed. We talk a great deal about beauty and Art, and meet various old bachelors who have known Whistler, and play the violin, and cant paint.

I am longing to be in my own house, and start work. We are having bright green carpets and I want to buy old furniture.

Violet Dickinson came in 2 minutes after we left that day. But it is just as well to begin with her drawing room.[1]

I hope we shall meet.

Yr. loving,
AVS

Sussex

357: TO VIOLET DICKINSON   29 *Fitzroy Square, W.*

12th April [1907]

My Violet,

You have made a monstrosity of our address—29 *Gordon Square*. However, your letter did come at last. What with your Homers and your Jekylls,[2] your new puppies and your budding trees—was there ever such a good gardener as Ozzy?—I am melted into an indistinguishable mass; pearl grey, and vaporous.

Well, God knows where one should begin a letter, seeing that I have been to Paris and back, changed my house, entered a new study all in the interval.

Now I am learning to write to the tune of twenty railway vans, which grind rough music beneath my window; but the grey houses opposite and the trees which are just beginning to grow green, are expected to heal the damage to my style.

The house isn't nearly ready; but we are waiting for carpets and book cases. Your little man is very good and intelligent, and he is now turning a French bed into a sofa. Nessa and Clive bought one in Paris.

I haven't seen Nessa alone once since she was married; and you know the kind of image one gets of her, coloured by Clive—It is very beautiful and happy and all that; but it is rather tantalising. But it is clear to the most prejudiced eye that God made her for marriage; and she basks there like an old seal on a rock. I dont think we shall see very much of them; as all our habits seem to be rather different.

I had 3 letters from Walter Headlam while I was in Paris; the last

1. Madge and Violet had never met, and Virginia was planning to bring them together in Violet's house.
2. Gertrude Jekyll, the gardener. 'Homer' unidentified.

sending me love 'as to a sister.' I know the cynical, even I will say the Kittylike, attitude with which you receive these confidences!

I am trying to write 3 articles for the Times: I begin in the linen cupboard, and work my way up to the top of the house. Today I am sitting in my own room for the first time.

Do you see I have curtailed my correspondence to a half sheet? But you also see that on some occasions I increase the measure: it is a very great compliment. But then I am such an interesting person to write about.

Now do send a whole letter—you strange sensitive creature with horns flickering like a snail. How is Ella? O damn Morley. I spent 2 hours there on Wed: and no class came.

Yr. AVS

Berg

358: To Madge Vaughan   29 *Fitzroy Square, W.*

[April 1907]

Dearest Madge,

Your flowers were—and still are—delicious. I think I see that the children have been picking them, perhaps in the wood where we played Bears once, last Easter. I wish you would bring them to London: they will forget their Elderly Cousin, or think her a horrible Myth—such as I think some of my relations. Will saw us when we were barely in: I am still arranging books, and we have practically no furniture. There are a great number of empty sitting rooms. Nessa and Clive are also established [at 46 Gordon Square], and I think their house is rather beautiful. But then they had wedding presents to lay out—they bought beds and chairs in Paris, and old silver and unbleached linen in London. He is writing and she is painting, and we all seem very busy.

Shall you come down ever? I think you will grow into a Northern Moor one of these days; I shall climb your heights. That is meant for a compliment. I wish I could play with the children, and have you to treat me as a child—a very nice child.

Yr.

King's   VS

359: To Violet Dickinson   29 *Fitzroy Square, W.*

[23? April 1907]

My Violet,

Why dont you lunch here on Thursday or Friday, or at any rate come to see me. Then I can tell you all about the house—if that is what you want to know, though God knows other peoples houses dont interest me.

You are very polite about my writing; I think that is the best thing I have written; and Headlam thinks—many things too subtle to be said here—about my style.

Yr. AVS

Berg

360: TO VIOLET DICKINSON   29 *Fitzroy Square, W.*

[3 May 1907]

My Violet,

I cant come on Monday or Wednesday as we go to the Opera both nights. Couldn't I come some other day?

I have this moment used your name in a lie, invented to excuse my lunching with Margaret today. So remember: you are lunching with me today—Friday 3rd May, on your way through London.

We have made another £70 this morning by selling 3 tea pots and a mug. So if I want double windows I shall get them; but my carpet is now down, and the noise is only like a melancholy Atlantic sea, and not really bothersome. I think I shall get rather fond of it.

I will send you some writing; but I have frittered away my time talking to plumbers and sewing women.

Write me a nice letter. I want Affection. I dont get None. I sing your praises.

Yr. AVS

Berg

361: TO VIOLET DICKINSON   29 *Fitzroy Square, W.*

[May 1907]

My Violet,

You told me—so Nessa and I thought—that you were going to send a line to say whether I was to come on Thursday or Friday. So I waited, and never heard, and supposed it was today. O Lord, what a nuisance all dates are—they never come right. I wish I had gone, as I did almost, on the chance it was Thursday.

Here is some bread for your tea.

Shall I come another day—all next week, except Monday, is free.

Yr. AVS

Berg

29 Fitzroy Square, W.

[May 1907]

My dear Nelly,

Thank you very much for asking me; I wish I could have come in for my share of Ponds Extract and Ellimans Embrocation, and I love shut windows. But we are going to the Meistersinger tonight, and to more music tomorrow and I couldn't very well come away.

Will you tell Violet that she has a singular view of life, and that I am very anxious to contradict all she says. We bought a dog [Hans] at the dog Home the other day: it is perhaps the most witty, and also cynical person I have ever known. When I talk of the domestic virtues, and in particular of tolerance and love it howls. Its father was a sheep dog, and though it must have had a mother no one knows who she was.

Are you reading that very . . . book by Kitty's friend[1]—yours?

Yr. aff.

Hatfield AVS

29 Fitzroy Square, W.

[May 1907]

My Violet,

I can be free all day on Thursday—lunch or tea?—let me know. It isnt the Opera after all on Monday. However, I am having Walter Headlam, and I think that should be a private interview. I saw him at Cambridge last week, and found him 'changed and altered' as Mary Cholomly[2] would say: he had never got my letter and thought me fickle and cold and treacherous. But we made it up—a subtle phrase secret and ambiguous. How d'you think we made it up?

I have just begun to do the drawing room books, but it needs immense determination. All the volumes are lost, or upstairs or downstairs, and they must be herded and separated, like the sparrows whom God counts.

O it is a hot afternoon, and I wish I were basking on the back seat of the carriage, driving to Eleusis. I heard a mystic story about Eleusis from Miss Case the other day: how all the fields are covered with flowers in the evening, as you drive back, and there are none at midday.

I think I shall have double windows, as a luxury, as I cant quite get used to the carts.

1. Elizabeth Mary, Countess von Arnim ('Elizabeth', later Countess Russell), whose latest novel was *Princess Priscilla's Fortnight*.
2. Mary Cholmondeley, novelist (1859-1925). Her most famous novel was *Red Pottage*, 1899.

Here is a review, which was originally long and vigorous; the Times have cut it down and tamed it. I wanted to scourge that Fine Lady the Baroness—Kitties friend: it is chatter and trash. I have reviewed a novel called The Glen O' Weeping[1]; damned it, and now all the other reviewers are exclaiming, and there is a 2nd edition.

How did you enjoy the Bells?

Yr. AVS

Berg

364: To Violet Dickinson   29 *Fitzroy Square, W.*

[May 1907]

My Violet,

Do come to lunch on Monday. We shall be just back from Hampton Court, rasped and corrugated, I suppose, but you like rough skins.

O why do I ever let any one read what I write! Every time I have to go through a breakfast with a letter of criticism I swear I will write for my own praise and blame in future. It is a misery.

The Quaker is really a woman with a stupendous belief in her qualities: I must have a bed and a washstand, turn the drawing room into bed room, and grant interviews all day long—to hear mild optimism and weak interest —and criticism too—why dont I work harder?—Is it worth it, I ask you?

We are trying to choose curtains, and I have ordered myself some double windows. But whats the use of windows when there's no plant to foster?

Snow is staying at Gordon Square; everybodies pictures have been accepted for the Friday Club. Even Mary Creighton is to illumine the world with four separate panes of glass.

There is no more news than this, except that the other night at the opera I looked up and saw Katie [Cromer] in the middle of the Royal Box; and all the house looked pale and stunted, and she blossomed like a Rose—you will know the kind; but whether it was imagination or truth, I never saw such a gigantic woman, flowing over regal arm chairs; and rearing herself like some Matron on the Parthenon; the style of thing you dont appreciate. Now had she been a ragged beggar at a street corner, with a string of onions and a patch work shawl, you would have crowed and chuckled. I am going to write a book upon the Aesthetic Sense in Violet and Nelly.

You see, I want affection! And think of Creightons tomorrow: intelligent questions when I ask for love, and a high standard of family life! But Walter Headlam has just sent me a Poem.

Yr. AVS

Berg

1. By Marjorie Bowen, reviewed *TLS* (24 May 1907).

365: To Violet Dickinson   29 *Fitzroy Square, W.*

[1907]

My Violet,
    It doesn't in the least matter. I dont think I should have sat out the
Horners anyhow. They terrify me.
    I will come to tea tomorrow. 5.
    So sorry you have troubles.

                                                        Yr. V.

Berg

366: To Violet Dickinson   29 *Fitzroy Square, W.*

[1907?]

My Violet,
    I will come Thursday at 5.
    I enclose a letter from Margaret. I think Nessa told me that you had
heard Hort[1] well spoken of.
    I have not told Nessa. It seems to me quite unnecessary to upset her
mind again about this, unless there is really good reason.

                                                        Yr. AVS

Berg

367: To Lady Robert Cecil   29 *Fitzroy Square, W.*

[May? 1907]

Dear Nelly,
    Do come on Wednesday—at 5 I shall be in—and as I have never before
or since that visit of yours—thank God—had so many people to tea at
once—and never shall if I spend 20 years in this house, you will have no
fashion to be afraid of. You keep a cup of acid on your writing table, I
observe, and sometimes dip your pen in that: it is said to colour the ink
better. I believe there is some other version of what Violet's friend said
the other day about Lady Roberts values; anyhow you dont have to con-
tend with obscene old women, and young women too with beaks dripping
gore, who advise you to marry. That is my daily penance, and has been
these six months. "I think you should keep a maid Virginia—to do your
hair—it makes such a difference—Men notice these things—not of course"
—and so on and so on. Well, one of these days they shall have their paragraph—That is a terrible threat!

1. Possibly Dr Edward Hort, a specialist in internal disorders, whom Virginia
    may have consulted.

I had an exquisite niece[1] of yours today to lunch—and we talked of Aunts, how some are dull, and some bore their nieces. She is like—what shall I say—down off a swan's neck. Well, I will tell you all these things on Wed.

Yr.
AVS

Hatfield

368: To Violet Dickinson   *29 Fitzroy Square, W.*

June 3rd [1907]

My Violet,

This is rather a nice letter, isn't it? You see I turn to you as the natural echo of my praises. Send it back, because I want to flaunt it in the Quakers face.

We had a dulcet visit; at least she writes that she is thankful for my love and friendship.

Are you coming up again and if so—well! I wont ask for more. I realise how many Halls are open, footmen waiting, and Ladies and Empire builders expectant.

Dodd,[2] a little New English Club artist, half drunk, and ecstatic, wishes to paint my portrait—and I am to sit in the afternoon from 2 to 4.30. Alone?

Nelly and I have had a spirited correspondence: "Violet says you think me vulgar." "O you damned Woman of title and fashion! So on, and so on. I am going to tea with her. I told her you and she and Kitty terrify me, as beings moving in a higher world, with voices like the ripple of Arcadian streams.

I had a happy day yesterday, talking to Nessa, now that Snow has gone. After all, she might marry 20 Clives and still be the most delightful creature in the world. And I like him better too; I think he unfolds, and they are beginning to accept invitations, and give little parties. She overflows in all ways.

Here is a nice letter, 2 whole sheets. So write.

Yr. AVS

Adrian has passed his final, and is called to the Bar tomorrow.

Berg

1. Lady Gwendolen Godolphin Osborne.
2. Francis Dodd, painter and etcher, to whom Virginia sat several times between October 1907 and July 1908. His drawing of her is in the National Portrait Gallery, London.

Sunday [7 July 1907]

My Violet,

If you knew the misery it is to me to sit down to a writing table and begin a letter!—I do it once a week, with the groans of a martyr tied to the stake, while a vulture pecks my back. And there is the Quaker who doesn't like to be kept waiting, because if I have anything to say, I can barely say it on one precise day.

Well—I have been alone this Sunday, Nessa Clive and Adrian have taken lodgings at Cambridge, which I refused to do—as I meant to read, or write, or somehow enjoy myself—and 4 people in lodgings is no better than a prolonged Bank Holiday. I should have lost my temper, and had to waste hours recovering it, as on the Acropolis [September/October 1906]— do you remember. So the consequence was I had down all the books I want to read, French and Latin and English and Greek—and then all the Square filled with volunteers; however I read on and on, and never was so happy in my life—a little beast in a green forest, with all its fruit and nuts. But this morning I knew I must see Life; so I went in the Tube to Golders Green, and walked through some dusty fields to Hampstead; and I sat down in one, where there was a corner empty, and eat my sandwiches, and a cake with sugar on the top which I had with me in a piece of gray paper. Then I found a farm, with a stuffed jay in the window, where the people were having Sunday dinner; then I climbed the top of the Hill, and saw St Pauls on one side and Harrow on the other. This is a beautiful story— such as I shall tell Nessas children; and they will say here "Do go on, Aunt Virginia; what happened next?" "An Ogre" I shall say: and they will know and believe; but Violet who has lived all her life among sophisticated people so that thick white scales, like those that drop off dried fish hung in the sun, grow on her eyes—Violet shant hear anymore of this story.

Well then I came home—and you cant guess what I did—I slept in my chair—and I washed—and put on a skirt which has lately been cleaned. And I went and called on Margaret [Duckworth]! Now there was a loosely built fresh coloured gentleman there in a frock coat, who might have come out of a novel; he was a Racing man, and he said the country was going to the Dogs—German's [*sic*] invading us. Charlie Beresford[1] says we have no fleet—and Trades Unions at the bottom of it all! Free thinking is all very well in itself, but free thinkers must be kept silent. Let the people hear, and theres a kettle of fish.

And I saw George and Margaret, and felt as I always feel 10 years old, with Aunts and Uncles and nice manners: and I always expect George to give me half a crown and Margaret to open a cupboard and bring out a box and take off the lid very slowly, and give me a large, rather nasty

1. Admiral Lord Charles Beresford, Commander-in-Chief Mediterranean, 1906-8.

sweet, with almond or fruit, or something I dont like, which I shall drop in the gutter on the way home. I think old George is a little hurt, because he counted the weeks since we had met, and said he never saw his 'family' now. I see he is too much hurt to speak naturally even of Nessa and Clive.

But what my position among them all is, I dont know; I see what you call their kindness, and Margarets good feelings; and Georges odd relics of what was once affection—and then there is Nessa, like a wasteful child pulling the heads off flowers—beautiful as a Goddess (at which you always smile) and Clive with his nice tastes, and kindness to me, and his slightness and acidity—well, I might pour out the English language without making a coherent story of it.

Anyhow, I've written such a letter as it is not decent to receive at breakfast time, when you have guests. It looks too intimate. Now I am going to get out all my books again, after I have written to the Quaker, and I am going to write in my head, where I always write immortal works, an article upon Lady Fanshawe,[1] and I am going to walk round my desk and then take out certain manuscripts which lie there like wine, sweetening as they grow old. I shall be miserable, or happy; a wordy sentimental creature, or a writer of such English as shall one day burn the pages.

All the lights in the Square are lighting, and it is turning silver gray, and there are beautiful young women still playing tennis on the grass.

Shall you be in London, and shall you come and see me?

Yr. AVS

Berg

370: TO VIOLET DICKINSON   29 *Fitzroy Square, W.*

[July 1907]

My Violet,

I was at the point of writing you a long letter—20 sheets—all numbered, perhaps transfixed with tape—when yours came. I was going to ask whether I could come down and see you.

I cant come on Wednesday unluckily, as Nelly is coming here. I can come on Thursday, Friday or Saturday.

I have been spending Sunday at Cambridge with Nessa and Clive *not* with the Quaker.

Yr. AVS

Berg

1. Review of *The Memoirs of Ann, Lady Fanshawe*, 1600-72. (*TLS*, 26 July 1907).

Saturday [20 July 1907]

My Violet,

Here is a nice pleasant tawny old book, which I daresay you have got already, or wont read anyhow. If so, do send it me back. I got it from an old Jew, who always spends an hour or so in discourse with me; and we stroke all the venerable books, and discuss title pages, which he can read, whatever the language, and print, and the degeneracy of people who buy new books, and all sorts of interesting subjects, even Tristram Shandy 'no one would wish for a complete set—I myself have never read it through, though I take it up often'—So it dont matter that the book is without a title page, and 3 sheets of introduction: it is white as driven snow within, and outside like a ripe fiddle. "Have you a friend with a garden, he said; who likes sullets—sullads you understand" That is the amount of his learning. So my good woman,—this is a specimen of my narrative style, which is far from good, seeing that I am forever knotting it and twisting it in conformity with the coils in my own brain, and a narrative should be as straight and flexible as the line you stretch between pear trees, with your linen on drying—I felt in my pocket and counted out minute silver pieces, and gross coppers, which fell short, as I piled them in a row on the table. So he forgave me the rest, magnanimously, as between scholars. Now after some conversation between us, I have never read the book, but I like snatches, it is going down to Welwyn, where it shall live among trees.

I have finished this beautiful discourse; and I dont think I have another to begin on. Last night I dined out in Chelsea, and mauled the dead and rotten carcases of several works written by my friends; how I hate intellect! There were several brilliant young men, whose lights had been kindled at Cambridge, and burnt all of them precisely in the same way; and some said they were artificial, supplied by the county loan at so much the cube. You turn them off, when company isnt there, to prevent waste; and you know what you have spent, to a penny. An elderly man who had somehow got my name right, said to me "In the course of your life Miss Stephen, you must have known many distinguished people. Stevenson, I suppose?" Yes and George Eliot, and Tennyson before he grew a beard I said. But the astonishing thing is that these great people always talked much as you and I talk; Tennyson, for instance, would say to me, "Pass the salt" or Thank you for the butter. "Ah indeed; you should write your memoirs; one gets paid for that kind of thing" he said; being a dealer in pictures.

At this moment I should be cobbling a terrific passage in my article on Lady Fanshawe; which begins reptile and turns quadruped in the middle. If only my flights were longer, and less variable I should make solid blocks of sentences, carven and wrought from pure marble; or the Greek marble which absorbs colours. One of my disasters is that I have lost that green book in which I used to write when the Bug hit me. But as I was telling you, Lady Fanshawe is rather disappointing; only a thread of a story, and some nameless descendant has tied a volume of dry little notes to her tail; and the Times say they must have my article at once, and that flurries me—so instead of writing it I write to you.

All the money I earned last month I threw away in one handful to Katharine Horner; who will sniff and turn aside to the last ducal spray of diamonds. I got her a nice old lookingglass, with Lady dolphins naked to the waist clasping arms round it. She is something of a sea green mermaid herself, so I gave it her; half of her lives beneath a sliding tide—O damn the i's in this English language!—remote and half dim.

On Monday Lady Gwendolen Godolphin Osborne[1] comes to lunch. "Miss Dickinson told me I might call; but I didn't dare. Now I may come, invited, I shall *love* it." Are these human or mermaid manners? "Lady Gwendolen, I shall say, how was the Queen looking at the Ball the other night?" I passed through ranks of carriages driving home from Chelsea; and tried to imagine splendours, but all the coachmen were smoking pipes and reading pink papers; and I could rise no higher than Mr and Lady Margaret Duckworth, who were there; Margaret under the Ladies—George under the Mrs.

Isn't this a nice long happy unselfish letter, for me to have written on a hot summer morning, standing at my desk, looking at ancient grey stone, and a cat that clasps her paws upon a white butterfly, and then rolls over and sleeps again: When shall you have the pleasure, as Ly G[wendolen] G[odolphin] O[sborne] would say, of seeing me?

Yr. AVS

Berg

372: TO LADY ROBERT CECIL   29 *Fitzroy Square, W.*

[August 1907]

My dear Nelly,
These were found in the hall when you had gone, and they dont—the pencil naturally wouldn't—fit our door.

Do you think you will come and see us at Rye?[2] That would be a great pleasure—indeed if I had your nieces manner I could tell you how very much I enjoyed your visit yesterday. It was time anyhow.

Your aff.
AVS

Hatfield

1. Daughter of the Duke of Leeds, and niece of Lady Robert Cecil.
2. Virginia and Adrian took a house for August at Playden, Rye, Sussex.

[early August 1907]

My Violet,

I was only for a Sunday at Cleeve [the Bells]—came back first thing Monday to make room for the sister, nurses and doctors.[1] Nessa seemed very well—very happy. Sitting all day with Clive.

I am alone here till I go on Thursday, as Adrian has gone down to Camp.

Shall I see you?

What the D—l you mean by your allusions to Fanshawe [Virginia's review] I dont know. I am corresponding with the editor [H. C. Fanshawe] who writes 12 sheets to the Times pointing out his virtues. The Times says it read my review with the greatest pleasure. Such is the gossip in the literary world!

Write.

                                               AVS

Berg

[August 1907]

My dear Nelly,

My brother would like in some way to convey to you that he does not frighten you; and that we hope very much for the honour—O for the style of Lady Gwendolen Godolphin-Osborne. Any day between the days you mention does us. You will be given a chair beneath an Apple tree, and left there. Such are the manners of—a certain class of English society.

I have been writing for 2 hours: I had 12 sheets from Mr Fanshawe this morning, who says I did no justice to the gravestone, with a correct inscription, lately put up to his ancestress; or to several new facts; and how can I say "Lady F. it seems is still a grandmother" when no grandson of hers is alive.

But the Times tell me they read my remarks with the greatest enjoyment.

                                          Yr. aff.

                                               AVS

Hatfield

1. This refers to an illness of Clive's sister Dorothy.

375: To Violet Dickinson 29 *Fitzroy Square, W.*

[August 1907]

My Violet,

Here is this work, very hastily polished off this morning. Indeed it is a hasty job altogether; however you and Nelly are to be the only readers.

I heard from Nessa this morning that she feels extremely well, and the sickness is quite stopped. This rejoices me; and, as you say "your affection is wholly selfish" O woman with a tongue dropping livid poison!

Yr. AVS

Berg

376: To Violet Dickinson 29 *Fitzroy Square, W.*

[8 August 1907]

My Violet,

It was very tender and kind of you to write. One feels so ossified; things go on and have to go on, and the pain [of Thoby's death] is always the same, I think. It is so odd the way you remember that.

However, my great religion is to be happy—I really care very much that Adrian should be happy—selfish as I am.

I am sitting among shrouded chairs, smoking a cigarette, before I go to catch my train. The country will be a delight. Our address is

The Steps
Playden
Sussex.

I think B[eatrice Thynne] comes tomorrow, with Adrian. Shall you write to me?

Yr. AVS

Berg

377: To Lady Robert Cecil *The Steps, Playden, Sussex*

Friday [16 August 1907]

My dear Nelly,

The effort it is to write,[1] not to you, I mean; for I have written to no one. But I feel like one rolled at the bottom of a green flood, smoothed, obliterated, how should my pockets still be full of words? This comes of sitting all day, before a tremendous view, flat as sand; the sea once came

1. Virginia continued to write her literary exercises. At Playden she wrote, among others, essays on a fair at Rye and an expedition to Winchelsea.

right up to the foot of the Cliff on which this house is built; now it has withdrawn, and instead of bleached bones, and the ribs of ships hung with weed, there are sheep, and cottages, and cornfields. But you dont like descriptions of places—a needless extravagance you call it.

Are you coming here? I am like the Syren who stretches her arm through the water to pull the sailors on top down to her. If you keep The Life,[1] or Myth, dont quote it—see my vanity! and dont show it: I cant remember now how bad it is; but I know it will have to be re-written in six months; and I shant do it; and I dont want immaturities, things torn out of time, preserved, unless in some strong casket, with one key only.

What are you doing? I am embalmed in a book of Henry James: The American Scene: like a fly in amber. I dont expect to get out; but it is very quiet and luminous.

Yr. aff.

Hatfield   AVS

378: To Clive Bell   *The Steps, Playden,*
                                                       Sussex
[18 August 1907]

My dear Clive,

As there is a tremendous downpour which will last some 3 hours—we can foretell about how long it takes to empty a sky's landscape full of clouds upon us—I will answer you first: go on with Mistress Dolphin [Vanessa]; then despatch some transactions. I did get and read Le Ferment,[2] the other day; and thought it a remarkable work; so that I shall try to snatch the others too from your grasp. But the L[ondon] L[ibrary] politely hint that 25 books exceeds the orthodox 15—by—how many? I wont count. Mérimée I read on that occasion which I have so graphically described. The long season of 'boiling, boiling—boiling'. The Athenian goats boil over with far greater effervescence than other goats; so that often the end of a sentence recalled me to—what some call life. I even wrote an ingenious essay on the Inconnue[3]; one page has the blood of a mosquitoe on it, like a flying red comet.

I have read the Maria Tellier,[4] and the Rouge et le Noir [Stendhal]— but as for the rest, you know I plod consistently behind the times, in the worn rut of convention, deserted of all the gamesome young dogs, and it will be a gymnastic exercise for me to undertake Prévost and Barrès. But I am very glad of the list.

1. Probably the comic Life of Violet Dickinson.
2. Unidentified. Possibly Alphonse Daudet's *Fromont jeune*.
3. Prosper Mérimée, *Lettres à une inconnue*, 1873. Her essay is in her 'Greek Diary'.
4. Guy de Maupassant, *La Maison Tellier*, 1881.

Well—all my news seems to live in Wiltshire. I am reading Henry James on America; and feel myself as one embalmed in a block of smooth amber: it is not unpleasant, very tranquil, as a twilight shore—but such is not the stuff of genius: no, it should be a swift stream. I am reading Flaubert's letters and the Christian Morals of Sir T[homas] B[rowne] which seems to me to include some splendid things, among many hints and exquisite adumbrations.

How is my —— I dont know what degree of reticence should be between us; but you can fill up the blank with any figure you like; my balance is boundless. Ah, I often think—was thinking but yesterday, how the best thing one can say of this world is that such a creature can grow there. How she contrives it, how she draws honey and not poison through all the black veins which spout their malevolence into our eyes is proof of her—I hesitate for a word, because I wont attribute such qualities to Heaven. Heaven made Sunday: and on Sunday theres no letter for me— There's Roast Beef—a downpour. Moreover in the course of this garrulous letter I have tramped 2 miles and lost my amethyst brooch. But we had Bath Buns for tea, and I have made a tie of purple silk for Adrian. Both eyes are to be kissed, the tip of the right ear, and the snout if its wet.

Yr.
AVS

Quentin Bell

379: To Lady Robert Cecil   *The Steps, Playden,*
                              Sussex

[August 1907]

My dear Nelly,

It was charming of you to repeat the compliments of my editor. They fell like sweet rain on an Earth cracked with drought; I feel as though I should never write a decent word, whatever editors say.

You dont say whether you will come here—I hope you may. We are, I think, empty—our bedroom is—till about the 3rd Sept. If any day happened to suit you it would be, as you know and as I, no Lady Gwendolen Godolphin, cant say, great fun for us if you could come.

Nessa comes to her house on the 25th.

I hope you are protecting literature: did you recommend [John] Murray to print Landor on Fox?[1]

Yr. very aff.
AVS

Hatfield

1. W. H. Wheeler's 1907 edition of W. S. Landor's *Commentary on Memoirs of Charles James Fox*, 1812.

Sunday [25 August 1907]

My Violet,

You drive me to write. O melancholy creature why do you see specialists? I wish to god you wouldnt. What you want, probably, is air and food and good society; here you should have a couch beneath an Apple tree, and sometimes I would sing to you, and sometimes I would leap from branch to branch, and sometimes I would recite, my own works, to the Zither.

There comes a time, you see, when condolences are no use; I cant figure to myself any fate so miserable as yours—except that I daresay you prefer it to paying visits; and your house is your own house, and there are books, and all the things that you like I suppose. You see how tame I'm getting. Nelly wrote and told me: all I can say is, why do you see doctors? They are a profoundly untrustworthy race; either they lie, or they mistake.

Still, you will say, what the d—— does she know what it is to have a pain in the back—the worst thing about that little black devil is that she cant sympathise, once you get off her paper or her own spirits she feels nothing. Now, dirty devil (for your language is hot and strong—comes bubbling from the deep natural spring) amuse me. Well then, we went and had tea with Henry James[1] today, and Mr and Mrs [George] Prothero, at the golf club; and Henry James fixed me with his staring blank eye—it is like a childs marble—and said "My dear Virginia, they tell me—they tell me—they tell me—that you—as indeed being your fathers daughter nay your grandfathers grandchild—the descendant I may say of a century —of a century—of quill pens and ink—ink—ink pots, yes, yes, yes, they tell me—ahm m m—that you, that you, that you *write* in short." This went on in the public street, while we all waited, as farmers wait for the hen to lay an egg—do they?—nervous, polite, and now on this foot now on that. I felt like a condemned person, who sees the knife drop and stick and drop again. Never did any woman hate 'writing' as much as I do. But when I am old and famous I shall discourse like Henry James. We had to stop periodically to let him shake himself free of the thing; he made phrases over the bread and butter 'rude and rapid' it was, and told us all the scandal of Rye. "Mr Jones has eloped, I regret to say, to Tasmania; leaving 12 little Jones, and a possible 13th to Mrs Jones; most regrettable, most unfortunate, and yet not wholly an action to which one has no private key of ones own so to speak."

Well—this ceases now to interest you: great Barking Sultan; if you could see how painfully I drive a pen, which confesses itself a martyr to the sleepy staggers, you might pity me. But I dont think you would; for

---

1. Henry James lived at Lamb House, Rye, from 1898 until his death in 1915.

you have a maxim about the enjoyment of our gifts, how it is a trust, with income payable to so and so and so and so.

Some doubt is felt, by those who read your last letters, and unfurled the curling tendrils, as to whether you wished for a picture post card of Rye, or such rude figure as I can make with words. For one moment I thought you wished me to draw, which indeed I can do, having already designed many triangles surmounted by oblong boxes, which are ornamented with Christian crosses, on my blotting paper.

From our garden we look over a dead marsh; flat as the sea, and the simile has the more truth in that the sea was once where the marsh is now. But at night a whole flower bed of fitful lighthouses blooms—O what a sentence!—but irritants are good I am told—along the edge; indeed you can follow the sea all round the cliff on which we stand, till you perceive Rye floating out to meet it, getting stranded halfway on the shingle, like— nothing so much as a red brick town. But then "red brick towns dont float; and these semi metaphors of yours are a proof that you dip hastily into a pocket full of words, and fling out the first come; and that is why your writing is so . . ." Anyhow, we have a real country cottage—white walls, and bright pictures, and cheerful manly books, Stevenson and Thoreau, and a garden, and an orchard; I dont really enjoy any of these things; it bores me dreadfully to cut the flowers, and I am determined that Mrs Dew Smith is a vague weak shallow kind of person; who has realised all her dreams in this house, and will be told forever, how charming it is, and how clever she is.

Gerald [Duckworth] has been here today; my spirits spring like fire now that he is gone; Adrian and I had the heaviest work; for we ran out of our talk on the way up from the station, and then we each took turns with a question, till when it came to mine I could only say "What do you usually have for lunch on Sunday Gerald?" Which however was best of all, for he remembered the lunches of 20 years ago. "O those puffs! not short pastry, but puff pastry—There was one dish, my dear, just black at the bottom, all flaky, done with more butter than she uses now—which I shall remember till my dying day." Then we talked about beef; and at last he fell asleep; as a prize pig, well entertained might sleep. This is brutal, because he took a great deal of trouble to come; and I should be affectionate. Nessa comes tomorrow—what one calls Nessa; but it means husband and baby, and of sister there is less than there used to be. But perhaps it is better; so the sanguine say. We are having Katharine Stephen for 2 nights, and then [Walter] Lamb and [Saxon] Sydney Turner; but I shall read and write, and only occasionally expose myself to their wisdom. I have 7 volumes of poetic drama to review for the Guardian, and a novel for the Times, and I want to write out many small chapters that form in my head; and to read Pindar, and a mass of other books; I know I shant. I begin to understand that I never shall.

You will probably suffer from many long, and diffuse, egoistical, ill written, disconnected, delightful letters, because solitary as I am, and fertile as a tea pot, it becomes necessary to empty the brew on someone; and there you are recumbent at Welwyn—what more can you expect, my good woman. "Those tiresome Stephens!" Ella's epigram. Ellas only epigram.

Yr. AVS

Berg

381: TO VIOLET DICKINSON   *The Steps, Playden*
                                            [Sussex]
Sunday [1 September 1907]

My Violet,
    I think few acts more deserve admiration than this which I now under-take of my own accord; for I have sent you I dont know how many sheets the other day, and I have had no answer but a growling letter asking nay, demanding, a post card. If you would do me a favour, you Bio—or mytho—grapher, tell me why you want letters, what you get from them, what you miss without them—in short, explain the whole situation; because I may be feeding an impure hunger. God, I wish I could make this pen wed this paper; I bought them both, for love of you, in Rye; and the discord is painful at every step.
    I consider now what there is to tell you, if that is what you want; how I haven't moved from Rye since I came here, how the French are still on the other side of the channel, how certain stars still hang above me at night, and the moon is steady. But you dont care a b——y d——n (My Violet, what language—even disembowelled thus!) for generalities however literary and picturesque; and if I could so fashion the globe and my own dent on it as to pack it harmoniously within this sheet you would think it out of place at breakfast, ask Ozzie to put it behind the bookshelf, and talk about something else.
    Nessa and Clive are here, and Snow is with them, and we meet every day, to walk, or smoke, and talk together; once we took a drive to a Church on a hill—that was on Thursday when we had Katharine Stephen with us; once we had the Prothero's and Henry James to tea on the verandah here; and there was such talk—as you might have this very afternoon in Welwyn. Now I have sketched the situation; placing all my pieces in position, and a woman of imagination can surely put them in motion for herself.
    Further, I write in the morning and read Pindar, in a room which over-looks the Marsh; beneath Adrian takes notes on English History, and spells out Wagner on the piano. Once more, I have a letter from B[ruce] Richmond asking me to review a novel by Marten Maartens at once, at some length,

for Fridays Times; and a letter from Leo [Maxse] in which he says that he is 'constantly trying to think of subjects what would be likely to appeal to you" and is open to any suggestions.

Now my authors vanity is appeased; shall we hint that it was the pricking of this that made me write to you! O no, it was affection, boiling, like that goats milk used to boil in Athens.

You really dont give me a chance to be unselfish; I cant—literary sense forbids—fill the page with questions, do you sleep, eat, suffer pain? and you wont write, and I must write to you, and the only thing there is to write about is—well it aint neuter anyhow.

Katharine Stephen stayed 2 nights; and it was like sleeping on the bosom of a maternal cow, cool, wholesome, not too soft, but fragrant. She has a smoother surface than the rest of her race, as though rubbed down by the attrition of countless human bodies; but her milk lies in deep places, and so issues fresh and sweet, like something kept in a shaded cavern, packed in ice. She asked me to stay with her; and used at odd moments of the day, to remark that she felt happy.

Margaret Lyttelton cant come; but that was not unexpected; [Walter] Lamb comes on Friday, and then [Saxon] Sydney Turner.

Nessa is like a great child, more happy and serene than ever; sketching with Snow, draped in a long robe of crimson, or raspberry coloured silk, with clear drops of amethyst and things she calls 'cairngorm' about it, and old yellow lace.

To be with her is to sit in autumn sunlight; but then there is Clive! Snow dined here last night, and says they are completely suited—completely happy. It bears in upon me more and more that we are all so much dry or green wood, thrown on her flame; and it dont much matter to that portent what it feeds on: it "transmutes".

Now I must set myself down to my novel [review], and then to my 7 poetic dramas; shall I ever bear a child I wonder?

Adrian and I think of letting Fitzroy Square, and living in rooms, to escape the burden of a household.

How am I, in this half inch of paper, to assure you of all my devotions, and enquiries—how you are, what you do, and the rest of it? It cant be done. So, kiss your dog on its tender snout, and think him me. In fact make him into an idol of me and I will so worship the hall clock.

Berg

382: To Elinor Monsell [Mrs Bernard Darwin]

The Steps, Playden
[Sussex]

Sunday, [22 September 1907]

Dear Eily,

If you knew how much I enjoy getting a letter I dont deserve you would write oftener—all about yourself and God, or Art, and the chickens and the Darwins—Ah what dumb creatures we are! There was an age when I went about exhorting people to write and talk and run bodkins through their veins, but they wouldn't, and wont; but go like sealed casks through life, musty and mildewed before any one tastes a drop of them. I am in the middle of Flaubert's letters; and your wail is exactly in sympathy with his, which was absolutely continuous—Really it gives one a physical headache to listen to him—And such it is to know what a prose style should be, or to have an image of Gods or costermongers in ones brain. I think your misery is a healthy one; I hope so, because I share it. Still, these are glimpses, such as never visit the Dobbins and the Thompsons; and all our [*illegible*] are a form of incense at the altar.

Nessa is here,[1] and we talk—when her husband is gone for a walk alone and that is seldom—of art and life, and marriage and motherhood, and she always comes back to it—being the richest and ripest old creature under the sun—that Art is the only thing; the lasting thing, though the others are splendid. It is an agony though, but the mercy is to suffer and seethe, and not live as the —— I wont use proper names again as you will tweak my tail for it—the animals do. But by the time you get this you will be coaxing some work of genius out of you, and what I say will be morbid garrulity.

I like your poem; indeed it is a theory of mine that happiness and sorrow are equally good, and beautiful, if you can only find the form for them, because that tickles, supplies, the sense which is above the reach of these accidents. If you had a young man [Saxon Sydney-Turner] exquisitely cultivated, almost omniescient, pale as a lily and dusky as a cedar, picking out hymn tunes in the room beneath you, you wouldn't write sense either.

Nessa is very well and beautiful and happy as some rich flower drawing nourishment tranquilly all day long. It is a game of mine to find figures for her; but they always perish before her. Did you do a drawing for me? That was divine charity: was it the one I saw? I should honestly like to have it, if I may. You know I like your drawings: some of them particularly. This is curious, charming country: I dont feel so sure of Mrs Dew Smiths taste as you do; dont you think she has lapses. But it is a perfect house for us; and Adrian and I begin to feel responsible people. I hope you will

1. Vanessa and Clive stayed in Rye itself.

310

write again; I am very fond of you, and you seem to me one of the quickest of women; quivering your feet like a moth on the wing. We have great Hawkmoths here, over the tobacco plants, at night.

Yr. AVS

Lady Darwin

383: TO VIOLET DICKINSON *The Steps, Playden*
[Sussex]

Sunday [22 September 1907]

My Violet,

I wish sometimes the unpremeditated desire to write to me would come over you. Every word I must earn before I have it. And yet you are a good, generous, woman too; and would give me pounds or blood if I asked it.

Where are you, how are you, and do you love me—or have you found some choicer specimen somewhere! O no—I wont believe it.

I have been talking to young men for the last fortnight—Lamb and Sidney-Turner, but they remain so disinterested that I see how I shall spend my days a virgin, an Aunt, an authoress. S. T. is now downstairs with Adrian, making out a chess problem, or fingering his own opera on the piano. For they can write music, as well as Latin and Greek and all the rest of it. [Lytton] Strachey is with Nessa and Clive. My God, they are a happy couple! I used to think it might be intermittent, but now I see with pulse serene the very heart of the machine—how for weeks together they seem to hover over the same flower. We have gone on, having picnics and walks and so forth, you will tell me how fortunate and happy I am.

We go back on Thursday, and I want to write for six months unceasingly —about the pace I go now—ink pots drying beneath me—paper withering, as beneath the blast of some Tropic wind.

On Monday I go to Morley and lecture on Keats. Adrian is going to the Working Men to teach them History; he has found a man to read with. My letters are horribly egoistic—but whats an Aunt for?

I think you might tell me when you will come and see me. Have you heard from Nelly? I was talking today—singing rather—the praises of that exquisite constellation—Nelly and Violet and Ly. G. God: Osborne. Like a hot goat, I am pining for my garden of beautiful women.

No news of Kitty.

Yr. AVS

Berg

[29 September 1907]

Dearest Todger,

You are a good faithful little beast to write; I daresay damp, marshy, island places develop your virtues. There was a great toad at Rye, who used to climb on to my knee and exhibit his jewel, and I kissed him. We got back two days ago: and I received a summons from Morley to attend on Mondays! I blasphemed Sheep [shanks] on a post card, and got a curt reply to say I had chosen Monday myself and alterations are now very difficult. However, nothing will induce me to sacrifice my Richter[1]: I go tomorrow and tackle the egg eater.

There is a certain smugness about Sussex, and I envy you your Highlands, in spite of the Scotch. Didn't you know that my Scotch blood had mixed long ago with the French and English, so that the finest conoisseur, tasting it, can detect only a peculiar sweetness, neither French nor English but like the essence or soul of something long since dead? That is why— but you know what the effect has been.

I found yesterday a man who cures corns, called Lenfestry—wealthy, though undistinguished. Will he be Marn's father-in-law?[2] I don't like to write to her. I heard from Aunt Mary the other day; and the ten children are all either coming to-day for the night, going to balls, staying at Seaford, hearing R[alph Vaughan Williams]s piece at Cardiff, producing children— while Aunt M. sits at home, praying that Emmie's next attack may seize her on a visit. Do you know of anyone who wants, not a secretary or a journalist, or a nurserymaid or a governess, or a cook, but a—Cordelia [Fisher] in short?

I suppose you will now be in the train or on the boat. So I will send this to the flat.

Yours,
AVS

Sussex

1. Hans Richter, the Hungarian conductor, particularly of Wagner, who often performed in London.
2. Margaret Vaughan never married.

385: To R. C. Trevelyan   29 *Fitzroy Square, W.*

[Autumn 1907?]

Dear Mr Trevelyan,

Thank you for sending me the notice of Mr Binyon's[1] lectures, which I had not seen. I am afraid I cannot go myself, but I will certainly tell others.

Yours sincerely,
Virginia Stephen

Trinity College, Cambridge

386: To Violet Dickinson   29 *Fitzroy Square, W.*

Tuesday [1 October 1907]

My Violet,

God knows where you may be at this moment, and as you dont write I see no way of beginning or going on with this letter. I cant tell you for instance how I sat to [Francis] Dodd today—or saw someone like Katie —only overgrown as a ripe mulberry tree—at the concert the other night.

I gave a lecture to 4 working men yesterday: one stutters on his ms— and another is an Italian and reads English as though it were mediaeval Latin—and another is my degenerate poet, who rants and blushes, and almost seizes my hand when we happen to like the same lines. But I dont have any notes—I can tell you the first sentence of my lecture: "The poet Keats died when he was 25: and he wrote all his works before that." Indeed —how very interesting, Miss Stephen.

By the way. You are a d——d bad woman: I asked you *not* to show my writing, and you read it to the Crums. Do send it back here at once. Please never read, or quote or show—it puts me in a misery only to imagine it.

We are all driving our pens like so many ploughs: Clive is starting his reviews and articles and novels; Nessa is getting models; Adrian analyses old ladies wills; I—as usual. To punish you, you shant know what it is that I'm doing—and yet,—well it needs reading in the British Museum, and a special ticket.

I am beginning to like this house; and to wish to make—a little money and buy furniture.

Now write, or telegraph: I will pay you 6d.

Yr. AVS

Berg

1. Laurence Binyon, the poet, who lectured on Oriental painting.

387: To Violet Dickinson   29 *Fitzroy Square, W.*

[Autumn 1907?]

My Violet,
    I dont think I can afford a dress at this moment.
    Will you send me back the copy of my Life of you? I always forget it, and I want to have it, great work as it is!

                                                                Yr. AVS

Berg

388: To Lady Robert Cecil   29 *Fitzroy Square, W.*

[October? 1907]

My dear Nelly,
    It will be delightful if you will come to tea. Would Tuesday or Wednesday next week suit you?
    Why should I be angry—or is the temper of the beast such that you must always take precautions? Of course I was angry—that you didn't come and stay with us. Now you see my manners are aping those of Ly G. God[olphin]-O[sborne]—but there is always this unfortunate drawback to a perfect success—that I cant, nor if I die for it, tell a lie.
    Are you condemning authors as usual?

                                                                Yr. affate
                                                                        VS

Hatfield

Letters 389-447

In London Virginia was occupied with reviewing, the opera, learning German, sitting for her portrait, and (until the end of 1907) teaching at Morley College. Three societies formed the basis of her social life: Thursday Evenings, the Friday Club, and now the Play Reading Society, their membership being more or less interchangeable, and their meetings alternated between Gordon and Fitzroy Squares. For a time Virginia was diverted by two flirtations: with Hilton Young, from whom she half expected a proposal and turned it down when, in 1909, it came; and, more important, with her brother-in-law Clive Bell, to whom she became closely allied during their holiday at St Ives in April 1908 by common resentment of the demands made upon family life by Vanessa's baby, Julian. In August she went alone to Wells in Somerset, and then to Manorbier in Wales, seeking solitude but escaping it by writing and demanding a flood of letters. During her long absence from London she was engaged in writing Melymbrosia (The Voyage Out), *and completed seven chapters of it in the intervals of reviewing and going for long walks. Clive had become her confidant, both literary and personal; and to a lesser extent, Lytton Strachey. Violet Dickinson and the Vaughans were beginning to fade.*

389: To Violet Dickinson   29 Fitzroy Square, W.

Tuesday [15? October 1907]

My Violet,

I wrote you a long letter, and lost it. When I got back my heart leapt up to see the flowers, until I checked myself and supposed that they were a present from the gardener to Sophy—you know my modest way! Then it was explained how a maid had brought them, with Miss Dickinsons or Miss Lytteltons love. A van outside confounded the two. I didn't think Lyttelton was likely.

My writing makes me tremble; it seems so likely that it will be d——d bad—or only slight—after the manner of Vernon Lee.[1] This isn't a catch for compliments. I will send you something when I have written it, but I have wasted all my time trying to begin things and taking up different

1. Perhaps the first record that Virginia had begun to write a novel. She called it *Melymbrosia*, but it was published seven-and-a-half years later as *The Voyage Out*. Vernon Lee was the pseudonym of Violet Paget, who wrote some thirty volumes of history, travel, fiction and philosophy. Virginia's opinion of her books was qualified—see Letter 397.

points of view, and dropping them, and grinding out the dullest stuff, which makes my blood run thick. However, I shall begin again now: I have 4 books of white paper waiting me.

When shall you come through London. I think I might somehow insinuate myself inside a cab; or wait on the top of a box, or roll into a rug somewhere. Why do you stay at Aldeburgh, there are east winds there, both of God and man.

Nessa and Clive came back yesterday—but I cant now go into his character; it will really be some time before I can separate him from her. I dont think I have spoken to him alone since they married.

Adrian is going off to his new man on Thursday. Altogether, as you are a woman of discrimination you can picture us, as Aunt Fisher says: she has just written to beg us to dine with her—any night—any time— any clothes. I am sitting to Dodd once more tomorrow. I have got to review a book on Marie Antoinette.

Now shall you write and tell me—your letters aren't letters—but as though the Chow had got his tail in the ink. Beatrice has sent Nessa some gigantic 3 pronged forks.

AVS

Berg

390: TO VANESSA BELL   [29 *Fitzroy Square, W.*]

[October? 1907]

Beloved,

We missed you today. Here is a cheque. Harry [Stephen][1] writes that as he only spends 2 days in London he wants to meet you and Clive at dinner on Tuesday if possible. Could you dine here, at 8?

I have Dodd tomorrow, so God knows if I shall see you. O misery. But why should I intrude upon your circle of bliss? Especially when I can think of nothing but my novel.

Yr. B.[2]

I hear that you have sent some venison. It is very convenient—we shall make a pasty.

Berg

1. The third son of Sir James Fitzjames Stephen, who succeeded his elder brother Herbert in the baronetcy in 1932. He was a Judge of the High Court, Calcutta, 1901-14.
2. In writing to Vanessa, Virginia usually signed herself 'B' for 'Billy Goat'.

[November 1907]

My Violet,

Here is the Review. Well, going through it again, I think it is fairly clear that the whole of Nelly's objection to Miss Sinclair[1] is a moral one. She thinks that Miss S. holds up a bad man to our admiration. She makes one or two purely artistic criticisms, as to likeness to life and so on, that I cant judge, as I havent read the book.

I think her position is quite tenable *if* she could explain her reason for thinking that morality is essential to art—But this she refuses to do. By Miss S's *insincerity* I think she means "bad morality" or that she knows such conduct to be wrong, and advocates it, for the sake of unconventionality. But I dont think she proves either that such conduct is wrong; or that Miss S. advocates it; or that, supposing both those things are so, that they damage the book as a work of art. I have made some more remarks in the margin—as I went along rather hastily—so dont show them to Nelly.

Yr. AVS

Berg

392: To Violet Dickinson   [*29 Fitzroy Square, W.*]

Postcard
[4 November 1907]

Dont say a word to Nelly of my criticisms, as they are hasty, and probably some of them unsound.

AVS

Berg

393: To Lady Robert Cecil   *29 Fitzroy Square, W.*

[November 1907]

Dear Nelly,

Dont you think 'Our book box' is *not* the right name?[2] R. Smith suggests it this morning. Personally I should like something simpler, and not jocular. I dont know what you feel. 'A monthly review' 'The book of the month' 'Our Review' 'The Reviewers Choice'—'The Book on the

1. In 1907 May Sinclair published *The Helpmate*. Her hero is a man who is unfaithful to his conventionally good wife and is made to seem morally superior to her.
2. Virginia and Nelly Cecil were planning to write together a new review section for *The Cornhill*, which was edited by Reginald Smith.

Table'—Lord how bad they all are. 'A book! The Monthly Book' and that
suggests nurse—Only I think it should be something formal and not trivial
and chatty. But you will make your own suggestion—I am writing to
him too.

Yrs.

Hatfield   AVS

394: TO LADY ROBERT CECIL   *29 Fitzroy Square, W.*

[November 1907]

My dear Nelly,

Would you and Lord Robert dine with us on the 12th at 8? It will be
a really disreputable dinner—not even a party, and not much of a dinner.
If we dress, we dress in soft old time stained clothes.

I have been writing to Reginald [Smith]—Really, you know it will be
great fun! Of course I talk of Lady Rs [Robert's] modesty, and we shake
our heads over it together.

Yr.

Hatfield   AVS

395: TO MADGE VAUGHAN   *29 Fitzroy Square, W.*

Nov. 6th [1907]

Dearest Madge,

Dont you think it disgraceful the way you neglect your foster child?
I should have a case against you in any law court—not one letter since—
last Christmas I should think.

I want to know what each of your sons and daughters is like—in face
and character: what their mother does and thinks—is she writing a great
work—on the lines I once laid down [in Letter 265]?

We spent the summer, which seems a long time ago, in Rye, and saw
a great deal of Henry James, who talked about you, and made a dreadful
picture of a young woman forced by circumstance to spend her life among
high places in the midst of perpetual winters. I have not seen any of your
relations—not even Marny, who stayed with you, I think.

Adrian and I have settled down for the winter; and I begin to feel that
we are staying in this house, not merely passing through, as I did. I am
trying to beautify it; but as I cant buy priceless looking glasses, and we
want to keep free from arm chairs, there is not much to be done. Think
how near to the Zoo we are!—and Adrian means to become a member.
He is working away, and enjoying his Law.

Nessa and Clive live, as I think, much like great ladies in a French salon;

they have all the wits and the poets; and Nessa sits among them like a Goddess. I think you know that we also are going to have our Janets and Halfords—It is exciting: I shall spend most of my time in the nursery, I foresee; and leave the wits downstairs.

Have you been writing in the Times lately; do tell me when anything comes out.

I wonder how Miss Perfect and Mr Birkbeck are [teachers at Giggleswick]. Dont you think one evening, when Will has gone to dine with the gentleman who doesn't ask you, that you might write me an account of all these things? Are you coming to London? Would you like some Vegetables? Give the Children my love—only it wont mean anything to them. I hear you saw Adeline [Vaughan Williams], and went to Ralphs music.

Your loving,

Sussex   AVS

396: To Lady Robert Cecil   29 *Fitzroy Square, W.*

[November? 1907]

Dear Nelly,

I am sorry I did not let you know, but I never thought of it—why didn't you ask?

I can't see that it matters if all the books are autobiography—as the understanding was that we were to choose what we thought interesting. I don't see that R. Smith can complain if we make a good choice.

Of course I can easily send you a line to say what I am going to do— but I always leave it to the last minute, and at this moment have no ideas at all.

Yr. aff.

Hatfield   AVS

397: To Violet Dickinson   29 *Fitzroy Square, W.*

[December 1907]

My Violet,

Thank you very much for your letter.

Am I not to come and see you?

Well—of course if it bores you and distresses you, I suppose I must refrain. But you might consider my feelings rather more than you do I think.

I have been staying at Oxford, and stretching my brains with trained Arabs, with not an ounce of flesh on them. The atmosphere of Oxford is quite the chilliest and least human known to me; you see brains floating like so many sea anemonies, nor have they shape or colour. They are bloodless, with great veins on them. (This reads like a school childs exercise —so precise and true is it.) Of course Herbert Fisher[1] has his merits; but what can you do with a brain so competent that nothing resists it—because after all, it attempts only solid things—histories, and triumphant little text books. Now my brain I will confess, for I dont like to talk of it, floats in blue air; where there are circling clouds, soft sunbeams of elastic gold, and fairy gossamers—things that cant be cut—that must be tenderly enclosed, and expressed in a globe of exquisitely coloured words. At the mere prick of steel they vanish.

I wish you could tell me of some book to write about. I am sobbing with misery over Vernon Lee,[2] who really turns all good writing to vapour, with her fluency and insipidity—the plausible woman! I put her on my black list, with Mrs. Humphry Ward. But though this is true as truth, as the Sage said in the fairy tale, still it can't be said in print; anymore than I can sit to Dodd naked. Though Heaven knows the verdict of my glass is—Damn modesty.

The Quaker has written me a 'spout of pure joy, from my entrails' O Childhood! O Motherhood! O Lamb of Light! O Babe of Purity! O! O! O! Tell me my darling, how you feel this wondrous blessing? Ah God, I would as soon tell the butcher which was my jugular artery, or the thief which was my diamond ring. She hopes to suck blood and bread from me.

Well—you see the advantage of writing to you is that I needn't see when you yawn, and look like a restive mare at Ella's clock. All chattering, hurrying, inarticulate, importunate, busy bees come from Ella in this world: that reminds me I must at once write to Sheepshanks and say that I will teach no more.[3] 'O no more—darkness has vanquished Light.' I dined out last night, but I have only as usual to damn my kind and the poisoned world where I live.

Yr. AVS

Berg

398: To Lady Robert Cecil   29 *Fitzroy Square, W.*

[December 1907]

Dear Nelly,

I ought to have thanked you before this for the poem which came some days ago. She wrote some things I have read elsewhere, and remembered. They have great charm—but I think H. Newbolt has printed too

1. H. A. L. Fisher had been a Fellow of New College since 1888, and lectured on history. Virginia was staying with him.
2. Review of *The Sentimental Traveller*, by Vernon Lee (*TLS*, 9 January 1908).
3. Virginia gave up teaching at Morley College at the end of 1907.

many fragments dont you?[1] Some read like rash experiments. But they are very interesting. I am asked by the Friday Club to 'approach' Lord Robert. If he would consent to speak for 10 minutes, on any Friday night, on any subject, except politics, they would be delighted. I daresay however his own mind is in no doubt whatever. But it would be splendid if he would. And I want also to bother you with my good working man [from Morley College]—who is a socialist, of a kind, and a poet; but also very clever and enthusiastic, and he can write short hand, and is a good man at accounts, and has a testimonial. His name is Cyril Zeldwyn, 29 Montagu St.—But I'm afraid there is no chance that you will want him—and dont bother—

Yr.

AVS

Hatfield

399: To Lady Robert Cecil   29 *Fitzroy Square, W.*

[December 1907]

My dear Nelly,

I am very grateful to Lord Robert for offering to see Mr Zeldwyn. I will certainly tell him. I dont know what job he is after now—I dont think he is really very exciting; but what you call a deserving case.

Will you and Lord Robert dine with us on Thursday 16th? We will try and be disreputable, but I am afraid we are more likely to be respectable middle class, which is so dull. Anyhow, will you dress as little as is consistent with your part—We will have Herrings and Tripe.

We dine—if you can call it dinner—at 8.

Yr. aff.

AVS

Hatfield

400: To Lady Robert Cecil   29 *Fitzroy Square, W.*

[1908?]

My dear Nelly,

I am so sorry about Lord Robert, I hope he is better now. I had a card from Violet to say 'Don't go to Grove End Road'[2] which was peremptory.

I wish it wasn't part of Violet's charm to be cryptic, and inaccurate; I wish she didn't select what she thinks amusing. I wish you both weren't

1. In December Henry Newbolt published a posthumous edition of *Poems, New and Old*, by his friend Mary Coleridge, who had died in August 1907.
2. Lord Robert Cecil's house in London.

so modest, so sharp of tongue. 'South Kensington Venus of Milo' is excellent, from one who has studied Keats for '20 years or so'. What is there left for me to say? or is it any use for me to unsay what I never said? Vulgarity is a word I never thought about you; but your education is no excuse; it sounds better than mine. After all, what have you to excuse? Really I don't know what its all about; (my Aunt stays in the house, and confuses my mind). I can't help wishing that there was some simpler way of expression between reasonable people; less charm and less modesty. However, it is the creed of all good women.

These are the preachings of that Venus, I suppose; and you will run away, or feel crushed—or quote Milton. If you knew how alarming you and Kitty, and Violet are! I won't quote though; when shall I come and see you? Only you must promise not to laugh at me.

Your affte.

AVS

I have forgotten to thank you for the 19th Century[1] which I enjoyed very much.

Hatfield

401: To Violet Dickinson   29 *Fitzroy Square, W.*

[26? January 1908]

My Violet,

Your wishes are very kind—I suppose.[2] What does one say on these occasions? I am speculating about a book; I enjoy this more even than buying one. It flatters my vanity. Why? Now this is a subtle psychological question, and perhaps you will decide it.

Nessa and Clive dined here last night; she had a long visit from Katie [Cromer], which she said was like the descent of Artemis or Aphrodite. Did Nessa ever say anything so literary? No—but Aphrodite pushing through fields of Amaranth, and plucking berries of amber, while jays twittered on her shoulder. If Katie should ever attain to that rank where a Court Poet or fool is needed—there is one—I need say no more.

Yr. AVS

Berg

1. The monthly journal of politics and the arts.
2. Virginia was 26 on 25 January.

402: To Madge Vaughan

[February 1908]

My dear Madge,

I thought I had written to you. All is as well as possible with both of them—the baby[1] flourishes, and Nessa has got on steadily from the first. She is to get up today, and next week will begin going out the Doctor says.

I find it hard to describe Julian, save that he is healthy and fair, with large blue eyes. Nessa takes great pleasure in him, though she is also very critical.

Well—it is a mercy that is over, and I go about congratulating myself all day long.

I hope you have lost your cold. Everyone here, except ourselves, has influenza. That wont interest you! but I write in haste.

Yr.

King's   AVS

403: To Violet Dickinson

[February 1908]

My Violet,

Now I shall have to get you a postal order. I have my eye on a beautiful Molière, for which I shall appropriate 10/- and that is altogether too much. But flesh is weak.

We had Miss Daniel[2]. She seems quick and merry and I think will do very well. Nessa flourishes—the doctor has given up daily visits.

I shall like my book.

Yr. AVS

Berg

404: To Lady Robert Cecil

[early March 1908]

Dear Nelly,

I am afraid I cant come to lunch, as I have my German lesson on Tuesday which I had forgotten. But my sister is bringing me to pay you a visit—unasked—Well, I daresay I shall be in the way, but I like poignant situations.

Here is your review. I think it tenderer than the woman deserves, though if I were she I should gather some meanings between the lines; of course it is quite fair, and plain and reasonable: good criticism I call it —because while it gives an opinion it also shows what the stuff is like.

1. Julian Heward Bell was born on 4 February 1908.
2. Virginia and Adrian had begun taking German lessons with her.

Do you say 'By comparison' or 'from comparison'—I say 'from'—only for the sound, I think. Legouis is a man who writes on Wordsworth's youth[1], I think: we have his books—unread. Well well—what are we coming to when the aristocracy can write literary criticism! I must tell my friend—brother—citizen—[Francis] Dodd.

Yr. AVS

I like that last sentence—applied to others.

Hatfield

405: TO LADY ROBERT CECIL   29 *Fitzroy Square, W.*
[April 1908]

My dear Nelly,

I ought to have thanked you before for the National Review. I will send it back. B[ernard] Holland writes a good deal beside the point; but he quotes some lovely little poems, which I had not read. I think she[2] has a curious magic for 2 or 3 lines, or even more; but it seems to fade very easily. I don't suppose she could have managed a long poem—but some of these are perfect.

By the way, [Reginald] Smith, the good grocer, wants me to write about Delanes life[3]; and I find it is all politics. I will try, but if I fail, as seems likely, I will write about Mr Abercrombies poems.[4] I expect to spend my holiday wrestling with them on the moors. They *may* be works of genius: I haven't read them!

I hope De Morgan[5] is done to your liking. I am so sick of writing at this moment!

Yr. VS

Hatfield

406: TO CLIVE BELL   [29 *Fitzroy Square, W.*]
Wednesday [15 April 1908]

My dear Clive,

I have been reading your letter aloud to Adrian and Saxon, who is dining with us. I wonder how much you contribute to these conversations

1. *The Early Life of Wordsworth*, by E. Legouis, 1897.
2. Mary Coleridge.
3. Review of *The Life and Letters of John Thaddeus Delane* by Arthur Irwin Dasent (*Cornhill Magazine*, 1908, N.S. Vol. XXIV). John Delane was editor of *The Times* 1841-77.
4. Lascelles Abercrombie, *Interludes and Poems*, 1908.
5. William DeMorgan, whose novel *Somehow Good* was published in 1908.

of yours. I never hear them; nor does Saxon. Once in a German railway station he met an American who seemed to him a sensible man. He, Saxon, is very considerate and even caressing tonight, and asks me what preparations I have made for St Ives. Have I ever read Apuleius? No—but I have heard of the Golden Ass—and such is his charity that he thinks this creditable. I had Janet Vaughan and Hester Ritchie to tea with me, and I find myself rather good with children. But I take it for granted that they have only reached a certain stage, which I invent for them; and now and then I imagine that they have their suspicions.

You see, I am dull, and uninformed. Delane is infinitely depressing, because he managed to live a substantial life without once disarranging anything. I cant get at him at all. Imagine a gigantic George, with all George's palpable illusions, as to the value of coronets, and the authority of white waistcoats come true. For I cant believe in wars and politics. I think I shall write about Abercrombie after all, but to do that I must read him.

I dreamt last night that I was showing father the manuscript of my novel; and he snorted, and dropped it on to a table, and I was very melancholy, and read it this morning, and thought it bad. You dont realise the depth of modesty in to which I fall.

Thanks to Nessa's warning, we have prevented our landlord from robbing us of £4.5/- I told him we could reclaim the tax; and he said I was quite right.

I have been writing Nessa's life; and I am going to send you 2 chapters in a day or two. It might have been so good! As it is, I am too near, and too far; and it seems to be blurred, and I ask myself why write it at all? seeing I never shall recapture what you have, by your side this minute. I should like to write a very subtle work on the proper writing of lives. What it is that you can write—and what writing is. It comes over me that I know nothing of the art; but blunder in a rash way after motive, and human character; and that I suppose is the uncritical British method; for I should choose my writing to be judged as a chiselled block, unconnected with my hand entirely.

I gather that you are going to a dance; and I believe you go because you think your wife the most beautiful woman in England, and she goes because she thinks so too. Kiss her, most passionately, in all my private places—neck—, and arm, and eyeball, and tell her—what new thing is there to tell her? how fond I am of her husband?

Your AVS

My address at St Ives will be,
  Trevose House,
  Draycot Terrace.

Quentin Bell

Monday [20 April 1908]

Dear Clive,

What an inquisitor you are! Such gifts surely are ill spent upon the placid fortunes of your sister in law; you should create a young lady to deserve them. But if silence whets your appetite, I can always be discreet.

Mercifully Bank Holiday is over, and the wind is sinking. No fishing boat could venture out today, so my landladies daughter told me at breakfast, and the family depend upon the sale of mackerel—and its lodgers. There are two here, upstairs; a 'confidential man', and his wife, and child; and not one of the three has had a bath in the 7 weeks they have been here. So Mrs Rouncefield told me, with a suspicion of pride. I had a very strenuous walk against a 40 mile wind this afternoon, but I found some gorse bushes, which smelt of nuts, as George Meredith says they do; and I took shelter beneath a grey rock, hollowed by Druids, I suppose. Also I observed the singular beauty of leafless but budding trees against a deep blue sea. The sea is a miracle—more congenial to me than any human being. Yes, you talk of average men and women—and I am glad, though you wont allow it, to believe that the average woman has her superior. But —how am I to account for George, and Hugo, and Walter Headlam? No, the eternal puzzle still forbids me to accept your enviable decisions. There are moods when I doubt that we even are as extraordinary as you would have us. At least if we are extraordinary—cheepers and chirpers and child-bearers and scribblers as we are—What must the rest be! The human race seems to drop down a bottomless pit. My mood is embittered by the Life of Delane, which I have been reading all day. I must write about it tomorrow —and it closes me round with depression. How people can live that life, and why they should write about it, or why in the last instance I should spend one moment or one drop of ink over it—is all a chain of rusty iron to me. I am the slave at the end.

Your dog [Gurth] happily was induced to sit in a trough today, under the belief that he was going the best way to drink it; and so matters are improved.

Tell Nessa to bring all her thick clothes. It is very cold, but divinely beautiful. Tomorrow I am going to Tren Crom.

Yr. aff.

AVS

Quentin Bell

Trevose House, Draycott Terrace, St Ives, Cornwall

Wednesday [22 April 1908]

Dear Lytton,

The only notepaper to be had in the county of Cornwall is this—what they call commercial. Indeed, if you could see under what circumstances I write a letter you would think me something of a moralist. I have a sitting room, which is the dining room, and it has a side-board, with a cruet and a silver biscuit box. I write at the dining table, having lifted a corner of the table cloth, and pushed away several small silver pots of flowers. This might be the beginning of a novel by Mr Galsworthy. My landlady, though a woman of 50, has nine children, and once had 11; and the youngest is able to cry all day long. When you consider that the family sitting room is next mine, and we are parted by folding doors only—what kind of sentence do you call this?—you will understand that I find it hard to write of Delane "the *Man*". I have had a long letter of instruction from [Reginald] Smith. He bids me bring out the human side, "his unswerving loyalty, alike to subordinates and chief,—in a word the high qualities of head and heart which" etc. etc. "Nay, my dear Miss Stephen, there is no comparison, for the real human interest, which the Cornhill seeks, between Delane and Mr Abercrombie." "I really believe, dear Miss Stephen, that if you will put heart and head into it, you will make a mark in reviewing." Did you ever have a compliment like that?

I spend most of my time, however, alone with my God, on the moors. I sat for an hour (perhaps it was 10 minutes) on a rock this afternoon, and considered how I should describe the colour of the Atlantic. It has strange shivers of purple and green, but if you call them blushes, you introduce unpleasant associations of red flesh. I am afraid you have little feeling for nature. I have seen innumerable things since I came here that would be worth writing down—"yellow gorse, and sea—" trees against the sea— but I should no doubt use so many words wrongly that it would be necessary to write this letter over again—like Clive. I have read a good many books, it seems to me. Your Pascal is looked at suspiciously by the servant. I picked a branch of white blossom yesterday, and asked her what it was. She said it was May. Somehow I thought that May was pink.

It will be a charity if you will write an answer. I am amazingly garrulous, because I have not spoken since I saw you, except to discuss the joints of animals.

Yr. Ever,

VS

Frances Hooper

Trevose House, Draycott Terrace, St Ives, Cornwall

Tuesday [28 April 1908]

Dear Lytton,

Your letter was a great solace to me. I had begun to doubt my own identity—and imagined I was part of a sea-gull, and dreamt at night of deep pools of blue water, full of eels. However, Adrian came suddenly that very day, like some grim figure out of a Northern Saga—so I imagine —some ice bound captain, travelling for centuries with a frozen beard. He had been snowed upon, and hailed upon and rained upon, and when he descended towards evening upon some lonely farm, the good women cowered behind the door, and bethought them of their honour. Sometimes, such was their modesty, he had to walk 4 miles at the end of the day's journey. However, he had had a very good time, and had met many worthies, and had many stories to tell. Then Nessa and Clive and the Baby and the Nurse all came, and we have been so domestic that I have not read, or wrote. My article upon Delane is left in the middle of a page thus—"But what of the Man?"—To answer that question, it will be necessary to come back— Saturday—but you will have time to write here, and to notice that my "b" is like that and my "v" is like that. A child is the very devil—calling out, as I believe, all the worst and least explicable passions of the parents—and the Aunts. When we talk of marriage, friendship or prose, we are suddenly held up by Nessa, who has heard a cry, and then we must all distinguish whether it is Julian's cry, or the cry of the 2 year old, who has an abscess, and uses therefore a different scale.

Adrian went back last night, to have tea with S: T: [Saxon Sydney-Turner] dine with S. T. and discuss the opera with S. T. I sent him a large pot of cream, and I expect a letter in Ciceronian Latin. "Did you approve of my use of *cur* with the Dative, or do you think it too Tacitean?" You terrify me with your congregations of intellect upon Salisbury plain.[1] My reverence for clever young men affects me with a kind of mental palsy. I really cannot conceive what the united minds of all those you name produced in the way of talk. Did you—but I can't begin to consider it even. I saw Rupert Brooke once, leaning over the gallery at Newnham, in midst of Miss [Amber] Reeves and the Fabians.[2]

We are going to a place called the Gurnard's Head this afternoon— and now I look up and behold it pours! So we shall sit over the fire instead, and I shall say some very sharp things, and Clive and Nessa will treat

1. Lytton had been staying in a small hotel on Salisbury Plain with James Strachey (his younger brother), Maynard Keynes, R. C. Trevelyan, G. E. Moore (the Cambridge philosopher), R. G. Hawtrey (the economist), Rupert Brooke, and Charles Sanger (the lawyer).
2. Rupert Brooke was President of the Cambridge Fabian Society.

me like a spoilt monkey, and the Baby will cry. However, I daresay Hampstead is under snow. How is your cold? I got a stiff neck on the rocks—but it went.

Yr. ever,
AVS

Frances Hooper

410: TO CLIVE BELL   [29 *Fitzroy Square, W.*]

Wednesday [6 May 1908]

My dear Clive,.

I have taken this great sheet, but I dont know whether I shall fill it, or whether loosing my garrulous tongue, I shall reach the uttermost corner, and crawl even into the crevices. Now there are 3 hard cs already; they dog me, and pepper my page with their brazen rings. I saw Saxon last night—did we not see the dawn rise, and the milk carts begin? A merry humour came over us, after a 'fairly satisfactory—yes, I think I may say, very fairly satisfactory' performance of the Gotterdammerung and we sat here, over our galantine, till three thirty. He read us 2 letters—one from Nessa, with—'very affectionate' at the end, exquisitely soft and just, like the fall of a cat's paw; and one from you—you brought a tear to my eye, and a blush to my cheek, by speaking of bandaged hands and crippled knees.[1] A little forethought over night would have saved it; but my train came upon me so suddenly. Before I had arranged my pose as woman of action I was called away; you know the results of disturbing the pen inchoate. But I should apologise; a subtle sense of what is due, however, makes me think that Nessa is the injured party. God knows it may be a punishment that I have no letter today. Perhaps you are in bed, for gravel may have got into the wound. Well, how am I to make you understand my contrition!

Why do you torment me with half uttered and ambiguous sentences? my presence is 'vivid and strange and bewildering'. I read your letter again and again, and wonder whether you have found me out, or, more likely, determined that there is nothing but an incomprehensible and quite negligible femininity to find out. I was certainly of opinion, though we did not kiss —(I was willing and offered once—but let that be)—I think we 'achieved the heights' as you put it. But did you realise how profoundly I was moved, and at the same time, restricted, by the sight of your daily life. Ah—such

1. When Virginia left St Ives, she forgot to take with her Delane's *Life*. Clive rushed back to fetch it, and handed the book to Virginia as the train was leaving the station. He slipped and injured himself. This formed the excuse for a renewal of Clive's and Virginia's reciprocal solicitude for each other, which was gradually turning into a flirtation.

beauty—grandeur—and freedom—as of panthers treading in their wilds—
I never saw in any other pair. When Nessa is bumbling about the world,
and making each thorn blossom, what room is there for me? Seriously
nature has done so much more for her than for me. I shrank to my narrowest
limits, and you found me more than usually complex, and contained.
Chivalrous as you are, however, you took infinite pains with me, and I
am very grateful. There are various matters I should like to talk to you
about; for, with my loose pen I am always afraid of inflicting gashes on
your ears. I have been reading Lamb and Landor—and set beside them a
page of my own prose. Lord! what vapid stuff! If you could have seen my
misery as I was at this exercise you might have believed in my modesty.
I see all you say of my looseness—great gaps are in all my sentences,
stitched across with conjunctions—and verbosity—and emphasis. If I had
had a good grounding in Greek, I might have done better.

I have been writing Delane, and now I must face my novel. I think
you will laugh at the natural trend of this letter; I have read it over, and
half think to burn it; but if I do I shall have no answer, and no—truth.

I had no notion what an exquisite writer Lamb is; and thus I have a
juster opinion of Miss V. S: and God knows how I shall have the courage
to dip my pen tomorrow.

Yr. aff.
AVS

Quentin Bell

411: To Lady Robert Cecil   29 *Fitzroy Square, W.*

[May 1908]

My dear Nelly,

I was very sorry not to come that day, but our opera began at 4.30.
I don't know whether you are in London or away, your letters have the
charm of mystery. You hint at politics, and strange summonses, and forget
that we plebeians know nothing of these matters.

I have not heard from Violet, and Ozzy, and I do not correspond.

I have written a commonplace article about the solid virtues of Mr
Delane, which, when compressed into 5 pages, lose all their meaning.
However—it is an ill omen—Reginald approves. What is your next? I
must send back your Nat. Rev.

Yr. aff. AVS

Hatfield

May 13th [1908]

My Violet,

I dont know whether this will catch you anywhere, since I have no notion when boats sail, or how long they take. I made an attempt to follow the course of the Trent, but I have mixed Barbadoes and Bermuda in my mind. As you can imagine my chief curiosity is not about Barbadoes but simply: how do you and Beatrice get on? I try to imagine long hot days on deck, and meals, and odd little middle aged women, who will confide their histories to you, and Beatrice will scowl at them, but get a great deal of information from stewards and captains.

These are my speculations; and I should also ask you how you are, but you will have forgotten all about that I hope: anyhow you may tell me when you write.

I had a fortnight at St Ives; Adrian and Nessa and Clive came for the last week. I doubt that I shall ever have a baby. Its voice is too terrible, a senseless scream, like an ill omened cat. Nobody could wish to comfort it, or pretend that it was a human being. Now, thank God, it sleeps with its nurse. Now and then it smiled at Nessa, and it has a very nice back; but the amount of business that has to be got through before you can enjoy it, is dismaying. Clive and I went for some long walks; but I felt that we were deserters, but then I was quite useless, as a nurse, and Clive will not even hold it.

Now I am at work again, and in a state of acute misery: I have had to write an article upon Delane, which Smith likes, and it is therefore bad. I have refused to review any more novels for the Times; and they send me Philosophy. I am struggling with my work of the Fancy and the Affections [*Melymbrosia*].

In your tropic sea, with green palm trees blowing on the shore, and naked boys fishing sponges from the rocks, or Beatrices half pence, none of these matters affect you at all. The Quaker has just published, and sent me, a book called "The Arising Light; Some Thoughts on The Central Radiance."[1] It is a gloomy work I know, all gray abstractions, and tremulous ecstasies, and shows a beautiful spirit.

We go almost nightly to the opera, and in the afternoon we have our German [with Miss Daniel]. Yesterday we came to a passage about maidens and the perils of war, at which she blushed and said to me, as one woman to another, "We will not read this, as It is not nice." She has, as the young poets say "an incomparable virginity." Sheer virtue as love alone could drive me, on this hot afternoon with a hand all tremulous with pen driving, to fill this great white sheet; no one has asked me to marry them, and I have had no more illicit kisses. In short, we are as you can imagine us; I

1. Caroline Emilia Stephen, *Light Arising: Thoughts on the Central Radiance*, 1908.

saw George in the Strand, and ran, and caught a Bus—the wrong one—
but he never saw me. John Bailey has been cross examined by Eustace
Hills, and it is said that the Times have been shamefully treated; and that
Murray has triumphed unjustly.[1]

The desolation of London when Manchester St. and Square are empty
is apalling; I must write to B[2]; I try to call forth her laugh, as of a startled
jay, and to imagine her figure, in the striped coat, in New York. Keep the
interviews for me. If she sticks anyone in the eye with a bonnet pin she
will undoubtly be taken for the Indiana murderess.

I hope you sleep all day, and dream of me; writing is the very devil;
I sit over a fireless grate with my head in my hands. Are you happy?

AVS

Berg

413: To Lady Robert Cecil   29 *Fitzroy Square, W.*

[May 1908]

My dear Nelly,
Thank you very much for sending Violets letter, I had one later, just
before they reached New York. It was hot, and she longed to be home!—
but I daresay boredom is a healthy sign. I am sure she is bored—but so
should we all be.

The National Review is here, polluting my room with its abuse of the
late Sir Henry C[ampbell] B[annerman]. I think politicians and journalists
must be the lowest of Gods creatures, creeping perpetually in the mud,
and biting with one end and stinging with the other, in spite of your con-
nections. Mary Coleridge[3] is in odd company. You are sarcastic, but I shall
certainly come to see you, if only I saw my way to cover my head and my
back. Half my life is blighted by the necessity of dressing; all my friendships suffer; some die. Have you an affection for me? old and bitter as I
am! and, to end this egoistical sheet, Smith has added words to my sentences,
cut out others, till I threaten to resign. I am furious.

Yr. AVS

Hatfield

1. John Murray, the publisher, had brought an action for libel against *The Times*,
   which had printed a letter accusing Murray of making an unjustifiable profit from
   his publication of the Letters of Queen Victoria. Murray won his case.
2. Beatrice Thynne, who lived with her mother, Lady Bath, in Manchester Square.
   Violet's own house was in Manchester Street.
3. Some of Mary Coleridge's poems had been printed in the *National Review*.

Monday [18 May 1908]

Dear Lytton,

Could you come to tea with me on Thursday? I have got so miserably
involved in opera and the German language that that seems to be the only free
afternoon, but it would be delightful if you could come then. I have been
getting my books in order, you will be glad to hear: the gaps are awful.

Yours ever,

Frances Hooper   VS

415: To Lady Robert Cecil   29 *Fitzroy Square, W.*

[May? 1908]

My dear Nelly,

I am going to another opera on Tuesday, so, unless I could come early,
I am afraid that afternoon is useless.

I am so bewildered with operas—we go regularly—that I cant make
sensible engagements. Shall I come down one day and see you, and return
by the night train?

I dont know how to settle these matters.

Why dont you stay in London?

When is Violet coming back!

Yr. AVS

Hatfield

416: To Clive Bell   29 *Fitzroy Square, W.*

[May 1908]

My dear Clive,

It was charming to get your letter this morning. I also consider the
subject, conscious of great warmth, and at the same time of a wish to make
things clear. (I choose a bad moment—carts roaring, dogs barking, the
cock calling for his hen) But it would be comfortable to reach a simple
state in which we could feel easy, which might last too. Are explanations
any use, I wonder? If I could make you see the state in which half my days
are spent you might realise many things. When you and Adrian are talking
I plunge about in a phantom world, and wonder who the people are in
hansoms, and what is going on in a certain place in the New Forest. But I
dont see that these matters are very exalted, or any better than your manly
talk. Nevertheless I am sometimes (to be candid) bored by general conversation, and usually very much excited by what I am thinking myself.

Then you come with your singular gift, and tell me that what I think is the thing; and my head spins—I feel above the Gods.

But is it really the thing? Isn't there a kind of talk which we could all talk, without these mystic reservations? That is what I grope after, and believe we ought to find. As it is, I bid fair to become a prophetess, with only one worshipper. Saxon, Adrian and the rest accept my lowest estimate of myself, and think it handsome. These are all contrary blasts, as you will perceive, and whirl me to those extremes which we both regret. And you are partly responsible! Honestly I find it very hard, when I am not with you, to realise what you say. When I am with you, I realise my limitations distinctly. Nessa has all that I should like to have, and you, besides your own charms and exquisite fine sweetnesses (which I always appreciate somehow) have her. Thus I seem often to be only an erratic external force, capable of shocks, but without any lodging in your lives. But the main point of all this is that we are very fond of each other; and I expect we shall make out a compromise in time. I suppose we shall see more clearly what is what; and if we do our best to realise that, I cant see that much else matters. As for the value I put upon the truth of all these theories, my feeling, I mean, for you and Nessa, that is unspeakable. A miserable shifting, grey day, like today, is made tolerable only when I think of you.

I have been slashing at Melymbrosia!

This might go on for ever; but my hands are cold, and the light fades, wire by wire. Are you in the dark too, I wonder? My answer always is that you are happy whatever anybody else may be. Think of old Nessa in her armchair, with her red petticoat showing, and the Westminster [Gazette] on her knee!

Why dont you come to lunch with me on Thursday, 1.30? That seems the only time. Will you and your wife also dine with us on Thursday?

This letter has just come. Imagine the fields of Paradise and father and [Nun] Aunt!

Yr. AVS

Quentin Bell

417: To John Waller Hills   29 *Fitzroy, W.*

[May 1908]

Dearest Jack,

I am very sorry. I am afraid it must have been a great shock to you.[1]

Your aff'ate

VS

Nessa comes back on Sunday.

Berg

1. Jack's mother, Anna Hills, had just died.

29 *Fitzroy Square, W.*

[June 1908]

My Violet,
   What a wonder that you are really back again. I have no trust in ships, and didn't expect anything so definite. You dont say how you are. I will come on Wednesday, but I must go back by the 6 something, because we are going to the opera. I will come by the 3.9. and find my way up. We all flourish—Julian vaccinated—I am rushing off to Hampstead.

AVS

Berg

419: To Lady Robert Cecil 29 *Fitzroy Square, W.*

[June 1908]

My dear Nelly,
   Could I come down to you on Wednesday, 17th! I have lost your letter, in which I think you told me about trains. There must be one in the morning however, and another in the evening—which would bring me back at bed time. It would be a great treat, as a railway journey is a great excitement.
   We went to Hampton Court yesterday, and to Kew the other day, and to Hampstead, and Dulwich, coming home at night—and the romance of the suburbs almost astounds me. There are enormous trees, and great lakes of water, and profound solitudes. This is what Adrian calls 'phrase making'. I went down to Welwyn and had tea with Violet; she says she's no better. I believe Welwyn will do more than the tropics.

Yr. VS

Hatfield

420: To Madge Vaughan 29 *Fitzroy Square, W.*

Sunday [28 June 1908]

Dearest Madge,
   I waited to answer your letter, so that I might hear something more about Walter Headlam—I had only seen the paper. I hear, from Mr Sanger, that he came up from Cambridge on Friday, and was perfectly well; he went to a hotel, and was taken ill on Friday night, and moved to a hospital, where he died on Saturday [20 June]. No one knew what was the matter, nor was there any operation. He could tell me no more than this, and it seems very strange. He was supposed to have recovered entirely from his illness—indeed it was thought to be very much his own imagination. Anyhow, it is tragic, for he always seemed disappointed and aggrieved with

the world. Last time I saw him he complained as usual, but thought that he was becoming known, and he had almost finished some edition of Aeschylus.[1] I think there was something very charming about him, but he was difficult and I think he had quarrelled with most of the people at Cambridge.

I met your friend, Mr Norton, the other night. The guess was quite right—he was travelling with an Aunt, and knew that Will was a school-master, and lived at Giggleswick, but did not know his name.

Are you coming to London at all? I think it is time.

It is impossible in a letter to describe our habits—I dont know that you asked me to describe them. As you know, I write, like some city clerk, and after all, it is quite harmless. Adrian is learning about wills. We have parties, and discuss the arts—I expect you would descend upon us like a prophetess with streaming black hair, and eyes of coal, and denounce us. However, I should welcome it, and refuse to be cowed.

Give my love to the children.

AVS

Sussex

421: To Clive Bell   29 *Fitzroy Square, W.*

[Summer 1908?]

My dear Clive,

Here is another of my works,[2] written last summer. It is rather thin and hasty, and as you will see, I have had to refrain and conventionalise where I might have been pointed. Even so, Violet thinks it a little harsh—such is the vanity of the modest. It has been copied by a Professional; and the other writings which I find are in such a horrid state that I cant read them myself even—and you know how I love my own works. Indeed that revelation of the passionate maiden heart is no longer concealed from you—but I still have some decency. I still think I will find other things to talk about, the Prime Minister, or Poetry.

Kiss my sister. "Clive whats that letter about? O these Authoresses!"

Yr AVS

Quentin Bell

422: To Violet Dickinson   29 *Fitzroy Square, W.*

[July 1908]

My Violet,

I wont stay with you for Sunday, because I want to write a long review, and that is my best day. But, if you will have me, I will come on Saturday,

1. A prose translation of his complete works, published posthumously in 1909.
2. The 'Life' of Violet Dickinson.

336

11th, and stay to dinner, and go back late. If you are asking some one else to come down, I will come another day—most days suit me.

I have got 2 huge volumes of Ly Bury's Diaries[1] to read and write about. Was she a relation or friend of yours? She lived in the time of the Regency, with which I always connect you. That reminds me that I have thrown away your envelope flap and cant remember the name of the book you want. Tell me, and I will bring it down. I have also been writing about President Roosevelt,[2] for Smith, at his command. The sublety [*sic*] of the insinuations is so serpentine that no Smith in Europe will see how I jeer the President to derision, seeming to approve the while. I have also—you like to hear literary gossip!—entered into a long correspondence with Prothero,[3] and we decide that I am probably to write about Ly. May Montagu.[4] Will you give me some address in Wells to write to, as the time draws near, and Wells [Somerset] seems the most likely place.

We have a party tonight; at which a young lady, not V. S., is to meet her lover.

What are you doing, lying beneath your trees?

Case and I correspond with enthusiasm, and discuss you; Daniel sings your praises.

Yr. AVS

I have to spend tomorrow in a pilgrimage to Godmanchester [Lady Stephen]. 3 hours in train 3 hours there!

Berg

423: To Violet Dickinson   29 *Fitzroy Square, W.*

[July 1908]

My Violet,

Thank you very much for all your singular goodness about my rooms. I have got them in the Vicars Close [Wells] for a week, and then I shall look about. Ought I to thank Mr Tudway? if that is his name?

This is the first letter of friendship that I have written for 6 weeks. Nothing happens here, except that I write and write, and curse and burn. It is regular as the seasons. I missed a visit from B. Richmond the day I came to you; however, nothing would alarm me more than to give him tea.

1. *The Diary of a Lady in Waiting*, by Lady Charlotte Bury (*TLS*, 23 July 1908.)
2. *A Week in the White House with Theodore Roosevelt*, by William Bayard Hale (*Cornhill Magazine*, 1908, N.S. Vol XXV).
3. Sir George Prothero, editor of the *Quarterly Review* 1899-1922.
4. Lady Mary Wortley Montagu (1689-1762) the traveller and letter-writer.

Lady Gwendolen [Godolphin Osborne] hopes I will go and see her at Windsor, if I'm not too much bored, or have her here. I sit every afternoon, in low neck, to Dodd, who is etching a picture, like George Eliot meditating the Spanish Gipsey [*sic*]. I am going to review a German book for the Times,[1] and Daniel is giving me special lessons on it.

Shall I see you again?

Or are you off?

AVS

Berg

424: TO VIOLET DICKINSON   29 *Fitzroy Square, W.*

[July? 1908]

My Violet,

Do tell me how I write to a Duchess:

1. My dear Duchess, (too familiar?)
2. Dear Duchess of Leeds, (too formal?)
3. Dear Duchess, nondescript?

Leeds has asked us to dine to meet Mr Ponsonby, but we cant go, or wont go.

I counted the hours I spent with you yesterday on my watch—3 or 4 they were—very serene for me—but how did you sleep, I wonder, after the sudden revelations I made you—of my genius, and charm, and melancholy, and love and beauty, and misunderstandings. I think with joy of certain exquisite moments when Rupert [the chow] and I lick your forhead [*sic*] with a red tongue and a purple tongue; and twine your hairs round our noses.

Yr. AVS

Berg

425: TO LYTTON STRACHEY   29 *Fitzroy Square, W.*

[28 July 1908]

Dear Lytton,

I shall be in on Thursday at 4.30, and delighted if you will come. Why are you a suppliant—why was your name once Lytton?

I go to spend a month at the theological college at Wells on Saturday.

Yours ever,

Frances Hooper   AVS

1. *Londoner Skizzenbuch*, by Von A. Rutari (*TLS*, 30 July 1908).

Vicars Close, Wells
[Somerset]

Monday [3 August 1908]

My dear Clive,

First, let me implore you to tell me what I should have seen had I looked out of the window at Slough? was it a naked Goddess or a Wesleyan Chapel? I mixed Slough with Swindon.

I am in the midst of ecclesiasticism here, bells, tolling for prayer; clerics sauntering past, ladies with wreaths, choir boys—Above me is a theological student, and last night Mrs Wall [landlady] came to ask whether I would receive a visit from him. I hesitated—upon which she said that he was a perfect gentleman, named Dallas, and it did seem a pity as two people should meet on the stairs and not know each other. I should have been an outcast had I refused, so I sent a message to say that I should be delighted. I hastily disposed my books—and hid my cigarette, and made out that I was studying a map of Somersetshire. He came in a minute, and we were both horribly shy, and he took a shiny armchair, and I another, with a lamp between us. In three months he will be ordained, and become one of 10 curates at St Mary Abbotts. I asked him whether he liked preaching and visiting—but he said he had done nothing but read so far. "Have you read both sides?" I ventured, at which he grew uncomfortable, suspected I meant Roman Catholicism—and said he had done all that at Oxford. "But of course, one has to read what the laymen are reading, in order to keep in touch." His Bishop, also, liked him to hunt in order to keep in touch with the hunting men, and his ambition was to have a parish, in a good hunting centre, not too far from a town. Then we talked about winter sports, the different sets at Wells Cathedral, town and county, all very dull and set on tennis parties. "They ask you when they've only met you once"— and Miss Margaret Cowper, the Music Hall singer. In the midst of these matters—I think I kept my end up pretty well, by pretending that I hunted in the New Forest—he told me that Raphael was the greatest painter, and he would go anywhere to see his works. I am afraid he saw through me, at the end, because he asked me if I was the Miss Stephens who wrote for the Tatler. "I spell my name without an s" I said, and so we got on to names, and he went at last; I asked him to look in again, as meanly as I could—but God knows what we should find to say. I was driven to this kind of thing "Do you know some people called Lawrence? I think they went to the winter sports once."

I must thank you for your exquisite allegory, which, if I play the part of Waterfall, seems to me pitched in your usual strains of aetherial flattery, I cant protest, because so much of what I must praise in you is included in the praise of myself. But—if you could see me under the influence of Lytton, Saxon and Miss Sheepshanks—"Miss Stephen do you ever think!"

you would liken me rather to some swaying reed which swings with the stream. But enough of this—Shall I venture a 2nd sheet and delay my walk on the Mendips a few moments. The afternoon sun is still hot, and both the dogs [Gurth and Hans] show an apoplectic tendency. Indeed the rustic humour is entirely occupied with the dogs. "What a fat dog! D'you think he can see?" and so on.

I am climbing Moore[1] like some industrious insect, who is determined to build a nest on the top of a Cathedral spire. One sentence, a string of "desires" makes my head spin with the infinite meaning of words unadorned; otherwise I have gone happily.

The Cathedral noises are more disturbing than good horse waggons; in this hot weather, old ladies chatter their gossip across the Close, and love making begins with the rise of the moon. But passion is proper to the season: and I shake my head, but resign myself. I screwed out a page of Melymbrosia—did you know that was the name?—this morning, but with such rage, such interruptions, that I must bargain for an upper room. Ah, but the rapture of being once more among my loves!

I read a considerable amount—St Simon, and Les Oberlé[2] and so on: but I should soon tire of acquiring knowledge—(and I here beg pardon for my cacophonies), and feel ripe for a debouch of speech. Perhaps I shall enjoy an ecstasy upon the summit of the downs, from which Mrs Wall once, some 40 years ago, saw the sea. I am tempted to rush up to Manorbier for 10 days after this in order to look at some waves and cliffs; I am almost drowned in earth and antiquity here. Kiss your wife and whisper to her that if I were to write all that I think of Julian, you would draw a long sigh—keep silence, but meditate in your brain thoughts not to be uttered to women. If Adrian were there, a glance would pass between you. I will let you know my train[3] when Bank Holiday is over.

Yr. AVS

Quentin Bell

427: To Vanessa Bell   *The Close, Wells*
                                                        [Somerset]
Tuesday [4 August 1908]

Beloved,
    As you do not praise my blue paper you shall have a bit of white, albeit the edge is dusty. Pray thank your husband for his letter; I will be

1. G. E. Moore, *Principia Ethica*, the bible of the young Cambridge intelligentsia.
2. René Bazin, *Les Oberlé*, 1901.
3. Virginia was meeting Vanessa and Clive in Bath.

at the station at the time he says; he is a demon to tantalise me with his "small post". Perhaps you will explain. An honest mind has no secrets.

I woke from a terrible dream, in which Jack [Hills] was breaking to me the news of your fatal injury from an omnibus, and found your letter; well, my good beast, things sound better. Julian good, a studio, and somewhere to sit in. I am hopelessly confused about my visit; but I had taken no steps.

This morning I had a letter from Hilton Young,[1] sending me an address at a farm house, and asking when I should be in Marlborough, so that he might come and have tea with me. Olive Ilbert[2] wrote by the same post, begging for news of our Thursday Evenings—who had come and what had been said. I am rather pleased with the idea of Manorbier; so I shall tell H. Y. that I shant be at Marlborough. I shall write with friendliness— but I have no discretion—no kind of instinct in me, such as most women have, in affairs of sex. Is it a fancy, a truth? But what should I say to Olive if he did propose to me? There would be a situation fit for the stage. She begs that you will write to her; and means to write me a long letter on landing, so I think she means to keep her eye on me.

I have been to Glastonbury[3] by train this afternoon—the kind of expedition you hate—and it wasn't one of my best. It was dark and windy; I missed the ruins, and found them, and thought them not half as good as the Glastonbury I have had in my head. They are too clean, and too dilapidated; besides new scaffolding is all over them, and there are benches at the proper views, notices about the sacred building; and middle class bicyclists resting their ugly bodies all over the place. A man was digging and throwing up bits of pottery, which was like Greece; but who wants to discover more stone pillars of mutilated Early English architecture! So let us hear no more about them, my good Ape.

I cant get on with my writing, and I sit in an upper room and look into a glass case of black theology; and Cynthia[4] will not speak, and my ship is like to sink.

However, it is always so when I take it up again, and it is worse than usual in a lodging, so perhaps it will come in time. Have you any news of Eily? I only see the Daily Mail; and I suppose you have a Times. Nun also writes, in fine feather; "The lads of Martineau Hall at Oxford" have asked her to discourse to them upon Quakerism and Free Thought; she has agreed, all in a tremor.

Aren't you amazed at the superstition still alive for picturesque old

1. Edward Hilton Young, later Lord Kennet. In 1908 he was 29 and the assistant editor of *The Economist*. He was a regular participant in Thursday Evenings, and for a time was much attracted by Virginia.
2. The sister-in-law of George Young, Hilton's older brother.
3. The ruins of the Benedictine Abbey, six miles from Wells.
4. The character who became Rachel Vinrace in *The Voyage Out*.

Ladies, fluttering about the inner mysteries! There is here a book called "The Preachers Promptuary of Anecdote", and I find the originals of all our Cabbin Boys in it. Amazing—"The lying woman of Devizes" who was struck dead in the marketplace—the little boy who dug holes on the sea shore, to hold the sea—the little boy who said an Alphabet because he did not know the Lord's Prayer!

My student [Dallas] greets me curtly; I believe he has discovered that I am one of a blasted race.

O what joy to see you! I should rather like to see Julian, ripening like a nectarine in the sun, but I daresay it is better not. But kiss him, and just shiver his head with your finger tops. I catch myself comparing him with other babies, and when I see small boys of 8 or 10 I marvel to think that we shall have one going about the world with us, and asking information. "Who was Cousin Mia? Dont you like Uncle George? Why has Aunt Goat never married? I think you very beautiful Mama!"

Yr. B.

Husband writes a charming letter; dont believe him if he ever feels old again; he has the clown in him still.

Berg

428: To Vanessa Bell   [*The Close, Wells, Somerset*]

Friday [7 August 1908]

Beloved,

I managed my journey [from Bath] with consummate skill, walking from one end of Shepton Mallet to the other, and avoiding the wrong train. I always ask everything—owing to certain adventures which I have no time to relate, and I find an astounding humanity in the race.

But I was fretful and peevish all the evening, because I had had my delight taken from me. For the first time, I could neither write nor read, but got out my calendar, and calculated the days to Saturday.

I did not have a letter from you this morning, but a solemn letter from Dorothea, saying that Helen[1] is very seriously ill, has been growing weaker for the last ten days, and Herbert and Katharine[2] are with her. She is conscious, and has no pain. It sounds desperate—but I dont know what to do. I must write an affectionate letter. They are all solidly devoted, of course, but I dont remember Helen much—except once, when we asked if she could play, and she strummed through a Beethoven Sonata, with the tramp

1. Helen Stephen (1862-1908), Virginia's cousin. She died on 9 August.
2. Sir Herbert Stephen, 2nd Bt., and his older sister.

of a regiment of dragoons. Nun also writes, to tell me the same thing, with a sigh of relief.

I wonder if you talked about me, as you went home, or thought of me when the moon rose, and the rabbits who nibble the carnations came out to play. How should I know about the rabbits and the carnations, unless I had read Clive's letters? I like to have a little scene, in which I am the leading lady; when I marry I shall never be quite so eminent. Indeed, I never am eminent, as it is, except when you and Clive are there to hint at catastrophes, and last times.

O I have been so peevish all day! I balanced one table on another, and put my writing book on top, and stood on a mound of cushions and tried to write Melymbrosia. But a violin began 2 doors off, and all the tradesmen called, and they came and bashed the floor over my head. Then I went out and bought my Daily Telegraph, which I hand over to Mrs Wall, when I have done with it. 'I do like a bit of news'—and I bought a note book. I have bought a note book in every country town in England, I believe—and tried to evolve an article for the Cornhill, upon Mlle. de la Vallière.[1] It is a choice between her and Miss Beale[2]—but will the Cornhill call a prostitute a prostitute, or a mistress a mistress? However, I shall write it, at Manorbier, post it, so that R[eginald] S[mith] gets it when I am out of England. Do not understand by this that Miss Beale was a prostitute.

You will say I know, that it is well to keep me hungry, and one treat a week is enough for me. I believe I could manage whole fortnights, with outspread wings, at a great altitude, with no descent. Has it ever struck you that the way we take our pleasures is very unlike? Does it strike you that this letter is neatly written, in a hand that would do no discredit to Margaret, and that the sentences, though dull, are much of a size, and finish neatly? That is because you told me that I wrote you careless letters. But the truth is we are too intimate for letter writing; style dissolves as though in a furnace; all the blood and bones come through; now, to write well there should be a perfect balance; and I believe (o another sheet, one of the sheets I ruined for H. Young) that if I ever find a form that does suit you, I shall produce some of my finest work. As it is, I am either too formal, or too feverish. There, Mistress!

By the way, all the names will have to be changed again—Cynthia dont do. All fine ladies, ingenuous young ladies, with Meredithian blood in them, are called Cynthia; do find me another.

I spent a whole hour reading my 100 pages, and came to the conclusion that there is something of a structure in it; I did mean something; though there are such lapses that I almost fall wide awake—feel as old Sheep feels,

1. *Louise de la Vallière*, by J. Lair (*Cornhill Magazine*, 1908, N.S., Vol. XXV). She was the mistress of Louis XIV.
2. *Dorothea Beale of Cheltenham*, by E. Raikes, 1908.

as she goes about her world. However, the effect of reading is to make me very anxious to finish what I have to say. Sometimes I felt like a happy animal in its own burrow—weather tight and safe; and of course I think it can be improved. I made out various matters on a walk today. I sat on a hill and observed the Champaign, which is very noble, like a background in Velasquez. Ah well, I wont venture anymore. Why dont you write to me about pictures?

I must now write to Nelly, Violet, Dorothea, Nun, Aunt Mary, and I should write to Olive [Ilbert].

Her address is,

> British Embassy
> c/o G. Young.
> Manchester on Sea
> Mass. U.S.A.

Yr. B.

My caramels are very nasty—a sad disappointment—I eat your chocolate, and wish I always took your advice—My lip is bleeding. I bit it.

(Tomorrow it will be, Mrs Oram, Cathedral Green)

Berg

429: To Clive Bell

5 *Cathedral Green, Wells*
[*Somerset*]

Sunday [9 August 1908]

My dear Clive,

If you could have seen how often I read and reread your letter, deciphering every word, feeling every comma, and deciding in my own mind why some words had been rejected and others chosen, you would not accuse me of neglect. I then turned to Lytton's poems—a pretty occupation for a virgin on the Sabbath! Yes, they are exquisite, and a little anthology I have here of minor Victorian verse shows none better. But (you will expect that but, and relish it) there is something of ingenuity that prevents me from approving as warmly as I should; do you know what I mean when I talk of his verbal felicities, which somehow evade, when a true poet, I think, would have committed himself? "Enormous mouth", "unimaginable repose", "mysterious ease", "incomparably dim"; when I come upon these I hesitate; I roll them upon my tongue; I do not feel that I am breasting fresh streams. But then I am a contemporary, a jealous contemporary, and I see perhaps the marks of the tool where Julian will see the entire shape. I sometimes think that Lytton's mind is too pliant and supple ever to make anything lasting; his resources are infinite. Jealousy—no doubt!

I have had the luck to pitch on the single house in Wells, I believe, where there are two children, between 3 and 5, who play all day long beneath my windows, and shriek incessantly. They tease the dogs and make them growl; they open the door and let them in; they peep in shyly, and ask to look at my ink pot. Their parents come after them, to apologise, and stay half an hour, telling me stories of their health and intelligence. The man has an impediment, which makes him repeat all he says twice over, and the woman is deaf, so that I have to repeat all I say twice over. However—she can make a salad and fry potatoes, and that amounts to genius in a landlady.

I think of Nessa with Julian! A page of Melymbrosia was strangled in the birth this morning. I look on the tombstones for a name for Cynthia, and found one lady called "Trideswide". Belinda[1] is perhaps a little too dainty for my woman, and what I conceive of her destiny. But I talk grandly, feeling in my heart some doubt that she will ever have a destiny.

Dorothea—to turn to business—writes that Helen [Stephen] may die at any moment; it is hopeless; and thinks that Katharine might possibly like to see her. I must offer, very tentatively, to go to Bristol, but I cant think that she will wish it—I hope not. If I go to Bath on Saturday, and to Wales on Monday, I ought to despatch Gurth on Friday. Will you send directions? I have not heard from Wales; could you possibly send me the exact name of someone who might have information?

Kiss my yellow honey Bee; you cant think how I look for letters and long for Saturday. I could write another sheet on that theme and make you blush—but—I am really shy of expressing my affection for you. Why? Do you know women? I had a walk yesterday after tea, between the downs, that almost crazed me with a desire to express it; I gave up at last, and lay with tremulous wings. I wish for nothing better—unless it were a kiss to crown all.

Quentin Bell

430: To Violet Dickinson

Sunday [9 August 1908]

(All the bells ringing, and the fashion of Wells parading before me. It is a lovely place, and the country round is as good as it can be. 5 *Cathedral Green, Wells*)

My Violet,

I have no notion where you are, but I have promised to ask you whether you remember Mrs Wall, the widow of a railway guard, who was at your mothers wedding, knew your grandfather, and knows you by sight. 'A very

1. Clive had suggested this name for the heroine of *Melymbrosia*.

tall lady.' I couldn't say that you had mentioned her, but I was sure you would remember. She burst into tears when your brother was defeated [at the Election], and damns all liberals and non-conformists for his sake. Indeed I am in a hot bed of family traditions and generally pass for Bishop Aucklands great niece.[1] I am urged to find his tomb, and I pretend to all kinds of knowledge—how sad it was when Miss Tudway went on the stage, how sorry I am that Mrs Tudway dont get on with her daughter in law, and how we shall all miss the old lady 'when the day comes for her to go.'

I spent a week in the Close, and then the theological students turned me out. But I hover beneath the sacred shade, living now in a vergers house, called Oram; they come in to tell me I must dine early, in order to go to service.

I had lunch with Nessa and Clive in Bath the other day, and Nessa said she was finding this summer more tolerable than last. She has a barn where she paints the village children, and sees very little of her family except Julian. Her nurse has now gone on a weeks holiday, so she sees nothing but Julian. Lord! What it must be to have a child!

I tramp the downs, and goad myself till I foam at the lips with all the bad qualities I possess—selfish and shallow as I am. What are you about— and how are you?

I think of going on to Manorbier in a week, as Nessa and Clive go to Scotland, and there writing an article about Miss Beale as a prostitute. I am sick of the whole thing, and yet it is very difficult to sit down after breakfast in a lodging parlour, opposite a portrait of Prince Albert, without a desk, or a table that stands, and conceive scenes in a novel.

Helen Stephen, Katharines sister, has suddenly been taken desperately ill at Bristol; she is dying, and possibly I may go to Bristol to see Katharine, but I dont want to. I dont see that it ever does any good. Poor old Aunt Stephen is also helpless, and the Quaker forebodes tragedy everywhere.

I read a number of things, think sometimes of your good qualities, and wonder whether you are fond of me. Are you a fine character now? What is your cardinal point, by which one might pick you out in Heaven? Where do you place yourself in the scale of humanity? Now if, as I imagine, you are sitting in some ancestral garden beneath a white umbrella you will have time to answer my question, and to assure me of your affection.

Yr. Sp.

Berg

---

1. Violet was herself the granddaughter of the 3rd Lord Auckland, Bishop of Bath and Wells 1854-69.

5 *Cathedral Green, Wells,*
Somerset

Aug. 10th [1908]

My dear Saxon,

I was very glad to hear from you. Adrian confirms what you say of the beauties of Rothenburg, and adds that the German temperament is sympathetic to him. The little boys don't laugh. I wish I could say as much for the population of Somerset, but my appearance, when I have been on the downs in a shower, and jumped a ditch on the way home, delights the people of Wells—draws a smile even from their Bishop. You will see that I have moved into the very shadow of the Cathedral. My windows are said to look at the West Front (perhaps it is the East) but as a matter of fact they are obscured by a gigantic and probably primeval oak.

As for news, I am entirely without it. I am even driven to fabricate it. I told Adrian that Clive was meditating a small 'post'—on re-reading his letter, in a less sanguine frame of mind, I see it is 'past'—to make my meaning clear, I will call it 'the irrevocable'. I met Nessa and Clive in Bath the other day, and over our buns at Forts we read your letters. We then strolled round the Circus* where a band of white haired gentlemen played selections from Glück and Handel. Once I clapped, and all the eyeglasses were raised in astonishment. The fashion paraded past us, at a foots pace; and Clive and Nessa vowed that they had never felt more perfectly content. Clive quoted Landor.

I have been reading an immense number of books, and look forward to my nightly 10 pages of [G. E.] Moore, when the bells have done tolling and my landladies children are in bed, with something like excitement. Well—there are numbers of things in the world which I don't know— numbers I shall never understand. I sent myself to sleep last night by thinking what I feel at the prospect of eating an ice; and woke this morning convinced that Moore is right. He calls it a glass of port wine, but I suppose that makes no difference? Will you tell Adrian that Helen Stephen is dying —may be dead at this moment. She had a habit of always talking to dogs, when people were in the room. I think of going to Manorbier on Monday, but I cannot hear of rooms. My future, therefore, is quite vague, and I study the map continually, to see upon what coasts the different lines debouch. Hans jumped into the moat yesterday, (Sunday) and chased all the episcopal swans and ducks, to the consternation of the inhabitants; there is one swan which rings a bell, and the birds are blessed annually. My theological student never came again, and was very curt when we met.

I hope you will write and describe the operas—unworthy as I am to hear. Will you dine with me on the 1st Sept: 8 o'clock.

Yr. AVS

* and the Crescent, and sat in some gardens

Sussex

Monday [10 August 1908]

Beloved,

By some miracle a 2nd letter has just arrived from you, it being 5.30. Does that mean I shant get one tomorrow? Ah, woe's me. I will observe all your directions; but for Gods sake, do let us meet somehow. As for Manorbier, I am still without an answer. Either my letter has gone to the wrong person, or they have no rooms. Could you give me an exact address? I dont want to stay on here, Marlborough is impossible, and I am taken with a passionate desire for Manorbier. Besides, I must write Smith's article.

Well, what news is there? No news, and if I were to write my heart out, as sometimes seems to me possible, I must set about it seriously. I gather you dont think much of Hilton Young. Am I to have no proposal then? If I had had the chance, and determined against it, I could settle to virginity with greater composure than I can, when my womanhood is at question. I should flaunt it in Snows face. I should be respectable at all parties, and look wise when Imogen [Booth] talked of lovers. But the truth is I dont think he will do; and whenever we meet we feel the incongruity, so instead of proposing he may withdraw.

At this season we should be walking together; I am in just the mood to discuss winter plans. Leaves are falling, and there is a soft gusty wind, not too cold though; I should make you stay out till dinner time, and I have found the perfect evening walk, with such a view for the home coming, which was wont to be the best time. We had got excited, then, and were saying what we really thought, of our gifts and futures; and sometimes you said such delicious things, and I walked like a peacock, all aglow. I wonder if I ever said such things to you. Did you ever feel neglected? Well, your daughter will know one day more than I ever shall.

By the way, I have imagined precisely what it is like to have a child. I woke up, and understood, as in a revelation, the precise nature of the pain. Now, if I could only see my novel like that—I have being [*sic*] trying to arrange a method of imagining scenes, and writing them, and wrote rather better this morning. I heard from Violet, who sounds in her most dashing and successful mood, staying with some aristocrat who is mad but delightful —says rather improper things, and fills her house with 16 visitors when there are only 11 beds. You can imagine the jokes! Then Dodd writes that he is much pleased with his print of me, and will send me a copy; it looked rather too stout, so he added flounces to the dress. The only good part was the line of the skirt—so my vanity once more will be shocked. My lip is probably a chronic blemish; I always forget to anoint it—and how do you account for that, considering my vanity? By this mornings post, too, I got a card, with musical hieroglyphs; halfway through breakfast, I sang my song to keep myself in spirits, and saw it, as though in a mirror before me —mocking me. I at once changed my tune, and sang the second song, which no one knows. Tell the Chipmonk [Clive] his malice is thwarted; I sang for half an hour, and all the house crouched on the step to listen.

I dont think I can offer to go to Bristol[1]; what should I do? I shall write and say that I am near.

I have been polishing my periods, and sending a letter to Saxon—I did mean to end 'affectionately' but was crowded out. If Saxon could read the meaning of such an ending, from a virgin to a bachelor, he would know that it was passions knell.

Find me a name for Cynthia, good Beast, with all speed; and if it could have the same number of syllables, so much the better. I read every birth and death, shop sign, and tombstone, without success. Lettice[2] is almost Kitty [Maxse] verbatim; what would happen if she guessed? Never was there such an improvident author—Flaubert would turn in his grave.

You see I am in the predicament of a shy caller, a shy adorer rather; I have nothing to say, and I cant go. I have everything to say. The children here bring me their dolls to mend, and I am planning a sentimental expedition; I shall take them to the sweet shop, and let them choose. The slavy here sleeps in a hole in the wall, with a window the size of a slate, and a basin like a pudding bowl. A candle burns perpetually in a corner of the stair case, and there are banisters of carved oak, and great halls on the landings. The womans husband says that there is a good deal more of the gentleman about Gurth than about Hans: two small boys with white heads stopped me on the road today and asked if I had a Bear?

Well, goodbye, my honeybee; Tell me Julians witticisms. You have a touch in letter writing that is beyond me. Something unexpected, like coming round a corner in a rose garden and finding it still daylight.

B.

Berg

433: To Vanessa Bell [5 *Cathedral Green, Wells, Somerset*]

Tuesday [11 August 1908]

Beloved,

I have had an immense number of letters today.

Helen in the first place, died on Sunday night, very peacefully. Nun writes that Lady Stephen's [Helen's mother] life will be shortened, but that Helen herself could not wish to live, which makes her death all the sadder. So she, at least, is satisfied. Rosamond [Helen's sister] says that Lady S. is well, though tired. I pity her, poor old creature, and, Katharine too, who

1. Where Helen Stephen was dying.
2. An earlier name for Clarissa Dalloway, who first appears in *The Voyage Out*.

thought Helen the most congenial and gifted of them all—so she told me the other day.

Then I have this letter from H[ilton] Y[oung] which I enclose, that you may be witness to all my actions.

I shall say that I go away on Saturday, but that if he likes to come before then, I shall be delighted to give him lunch. He is still jocose, and if he wishes to propose, he may as well get it over; but I think he only means a friendly talk; and in either case, I think there is no use in avoiding him.

But I cant walk all the way to Cheddar with him.

Saxon and Adrian both write; they have heard Parsifal, and I cant pretend that I have yet mastered Saxons reasons for not finding it so exciting at the first time of hearing as some others; or Adrians reasons for feeling just the opposite. I imagine some tart scenes between them. However, Adrian is delighted with the Germans, has paid calls, and finds his German better than Saxons 'who is always at a loss." Nelly writes that she wishes to treat Miss Beale, the book I had half marked for myself. Miss Beale educated Miss [May]Sinclair—"of course I shall draw attention to the fact with appropriate comments."

Eily writes, 2 quarto sheets; wishes to know in particular what I think of Clive? Is he a genius? She knows he is interesting to talk to, and sees he has had good effects on your art—but would like, if it is not impertinent, to know more. Is Clive a genius? What is Clive like? An exquisite, fastidious little Chipmonk, with the liveliest affections, and the most tender instincts —a man of parts, and sensibilities—a man of character and judgment—a man with a style, who writes some of the best letters in the English tongue, and meditates a phrase as other men meditate an action—But a man of genius? This long paragraph is too long to rewrite; but you will see that it is inadequate even as prose; and as the truth—well, you sit yourself on his knee. Ah, I'm so excited about my novel! I read 2 pages, and thought them good. I dont rhapsodise anymore, but believe that the best novels are deposited, carefully, bit by bit; and in the end, perhaps they live in all their parts. 'Perhaps'—I write as Julian sucks his bottle; a necessary occupation, but not of intense interest to you perhaps. Write a sonnet to his eyelashes.

No news from Manorbier. Yr. B.

Berg

434: To Vanessa Bell   5 *Cathedral Green* [*Wells,*
                                        Somerset]
Wednesday [12 August 1908]

Beloved,
    To my great melancholy, I have had no letter from you today, but a

card from your husband. I wont disparage his card—still a letter would have been pleasant.

If I were to hint at all the miseries which steal out when you dont lull them to sleep, I should only be chidden. I suppose all the blame rests with the post, and there is nothing to fear.

I have been attacked by toothache; Heaven knows why; but it has suddenly gone again, so I only tell you in order to get pity.

I heard from Manorbier at last; Mrs John knows of a small cottage, which wouldn't suit me she thinks, but it is the only place to be had. Apparently, it is very humble, and the woman cant provide hot baths—but I dont see that that matters. At the same time, Sheep[shanks] writes and asks whether I will join her at some Devon village, where are to be found Mr and Mrs Gilbert Murray, Mr and Mrs Bertie Russell, Jane Harrison and [Francis] Cornford! Too much elderly brilliance for my taste; besides Sheep: might sit down on me by mistake, and I should never recover. However, I have no doubt I am missing lifelong friendships, and all for the sake of lonely walks along the sea shore, with an occasional leap over a fissure. I wish we could meet for more than our 3 hours on Saturday; they leave me melancholy, but I look forward to them with impossible hopes. One of these days, I am determined, you shall have a country house, with stone balls on its terrace, and a lawn; and a little cottage in the trees at the bottom of the garden. There I shall have a room, a great table, some books, and a looking glass, besides a curious cabinet, full of small drawers, in which your children shall search for secrets. I am pleased to find that the children here find me rather amusing. What shall I tell you? I wish, someday, you would write down what you need in a letter; some facts I know; but as for the padding, the reflections and affections, I never know your taste. About my novel, for example—does it bore you? As you cant answer, I will tell you that I wrote rather well this morning, in spite of my tooth, and in spite of my habit which I can never outgrow, of hiding my manuscript when anyone who does not know my trade comes into the room and pretending that I am reading letters. The woman says she never had such a busy lodger. I like her, and her name is Dorothy, but that wont do for Cynthia. No answer from H[ilton] Y[oung] I begin to feel nervous, and wish I had your approbation. But then you wont post your letters in time. I walked to the top of a hill today, imagining that I was Christ ascending Calvary, and cheered myself so that I laughed aloud, and proceeded to think of Dobbins and Sheeps[1]; and various quips of my own; but the weather is cold.

I will send your dog. I should be glad to keep him, for he is really rather an engaging beast, but I suppose he will be better with W. L. [Walter Lamb]

1. The daughters of two bishops—'Dobbins' Creighton, daughter of the Bishop of London, and Mary Sheepshanks, daughter of the Bishop of Norwich.

O God! I must write my mortuary letters [about Helen Stephen?]; and I have only 10 minutes before post. Still they are better done in hot blood. Saxon is only 'aff^ate" to me.

Yr. B.

Berg

435: To Saxon Sydney-Turner   5 *Cathedral Green, Wells,*
[14 August 1908]   *Somerset*

My dear Saxon,

A postcard has just been brought to me from you, with a picture of Hans Sachs[1] on it. He looks very much what he does upon the stage, which is always a satisfaction.

I have been horribly disabused by visiting Glastonbury and Cheddar; Cheddar is exactly like the scenic railway at the Exhibition, and I was not in the least anxious to be reminded of that; besides there was no switch back, and the populace was disgusting as usual. In my absence,—this was yesterday—(you must put up with small beer) Hans and Gurth were taken for a walk by the slavy; they both escaped, raced round the town, and were taken in charge by a policeman, who put them into prison. Mr Oram, a verger, and my landlord, had released them, but I found the household almost hysterical, and I had a solemn interview with Mr Oram, who begged me not to be agitated, and assured me that I was not, strictly speaking, a criminal. Gurth had no name on his collar, and the law etc., etc., Mr Oram has an impediment in his speech, which makes him repeat everything twice over. He also insists upon calling Hans 'Miss Hans' and was very arch about 'His Lordship' (Gurth) running after 'this young lady'. "You know how it is with gentlemen, Miss Stephens—pardon me the liberty' I had to pretend that I was deeply moved. Do you think all the lower classes are naturally idiotic? I can't conceive how this man who is the father of two children, gets through his life, or for the matter of that, buttons his waistcoat in the morning. His youngest, or as Clive would have it, younger, daughter, has just declared her wish that I should be her stepmother.

I go to Manorbier on Monday, and I think my address will be Sea View, but post office would find me. Letters are a great treat, but I have not yet begun to feel bored; and I think a change of scene will just carry me through—especially as I have to write an article upon Mlle de la Vallière, and to contrive some decent way of alluding to her relations with Louis. I think R. Smith will strike out the word 'mistress' and substitute 'unfortunate attachment'.

I have been reading a good deal, and make some way with Moore, though I have to crawl over the same page a number of times, till I almost

1. The 16th-century German dramatist, and a main character in Wagner's *Die Meistersinger von Nürnberg*.

see my own tracks. I shall ask you to enlighten me, but I doubt that I can even ask an intelligible question.

The Daily Telegraph is discussing the sanctity of marriage, and Haynes[1] is giving tongue, and all the deserted wives and husbands in the country are wondering [how] far the marriage service represents the true word of God. Such a display of imbecility is hardly credible; it is like stirring a muddy pool, and waking innumerable newts.

What do you think of Adrian's German?

Your affate VS

Sussex

436: To Lady Robert Cecil   *5 Cathedral Green, Wells,*
                                   Somerset
Aug. 14th [1908]

My dear Nelly,

I am once more sunk into a state of complete indolence, when I love getting letters, but hate answering them. I wish providence would let me lie on my back, and send flights of Nellys over me, with letters in their bills, and I should only have to gape and swallow them. But the laws of nature forbid. I wish, too, that you didn't keep my letters in the china cupboard; because then you are liable at any moment to confront me with some rash judgment, meant only for the morning fire. Did I say that Mary Coleridges poems would fade?[2] I meant only that they are very slight; some seem to me first rate, in that line; they say exactly what she meant. I dont know what happens to such things, but I expect one or two manage to go on, for hundreds of years, like those anonymous poems, which are so charming, in the Anthologies.

I have been drowsing here in the most ancient and most respectable of cities for a fortnight till I feel that I must get onto a cliff and scream at the Atlantic. Is it the Atlantic at South Wales? I dont know, but I think of going to a place called Manorbier on Monday, for another fortnight. It is as lovely as the Hebrides, with a ruined Castle in every bay.

I am going to write an article for *"our Good Grocer"* [Reginald Smith] upon Mademoiselle de la Valliere; I dare not tell him, lest he insists upon a study of Sir Henry Campbell Bannerman; and I dont know how I am to allude to the fact that she was Louis 14th ——. Shall I simply leave it out? and merely hint at an unfortunate attachment. I expect that's the phrase. If I were going to write upon Miss Beale[3] I should point out how easy it is to be a good schoolmistress, and spread awe in the hearts of tremulous,

1. Edmund Haynes, the expert on matrimonial law and morals.
2. See letter 405.
3. See p. 343, note 2. Nelly had been asked to review the book.

half educated, earnest women. I have just been looking at the book. It is a type of the official biography: all committees and organisations—and what an ugly woman! She always allowed 2 hours to catch any train, and brushed away her breadcrumbs herself. In these matters she always had the good of her school at heart! O what inflictions people are with their dreary phrases! I sometimes think no crime is so bad—the suffocation of life—But it is authorised, on the contrary, and if you had to bring up a child you could not avoid the Miss Beales and Miss Busses. But to explain what I mean would take too long, and I never can explain it.

Dont you think you might write me a long letter, within the next fortnight? My address will be, Sea View, Manorbier, R.S.O. Pembrokeshire, S.Wales.

I expect to be horribly uncomfortable. What are you doing? I haven't seen you for 6 months and missed your exquisite incredible niece the other day.

Yr. aff. AVS

Hatfield

437: To Vanessa Bell   [5 *Cathedral Green, Wells, Somerset*]

Friday [14 August 1908]

Beloved,

Have you been having the Devil of a time with Julian? I gather that you have, and all my peaceful hours are made to blush for their ease. What with milk and washing, crying and grumbling, you must have spent a miserable week. Poor woman! I adore you.

I have heard nothing from H. Y. [Hilton Young]: and it strikes me that I probably led him to think that I should be here till Saturday week. He said something about being away. However, I may have been too cold, or too hot, or he may have thought better of it. Anyhow, my chance of a proposal dwindles, and I feel complacent. I shall see you tomorrow! Indeed, if I were wiser I should hoard my sweetness, and spend it like a king. I shall probably weep when I leave you tomorrow evening, for more than a fortnight.

I went to Cheddar, found it a wretched place, like the scenery beside a switch back, crowded, and full of grottoes and caves, into which I could not bother to look.

A drunk man terrified a little girl in the carriage next mine, so that the train had to be stopped, she taken out, and put in with me. She was like a frightened rabbit, and crouched in her corner.

When I got home I was solemnly waited on by Mr Oram, who begged me not to be agitated, but said he had a painful story to tell me. The slavy

354

had taken the dogs for a walk, they had escaped; they had 'cruised about the town', till a policeman found them, and put them in prison, finding that Gurth had no address on his collar.

Mr Oram had fetched them back; but the policeman wished to see me. All this he repeated over and over again, adding his theory: that "Miss Hans had run away, and his Lordship (Gurth) followed after. O she's a sprightly little lady. But dont be agitated ma'am: my advice to you is this; say that the address is now being engraved. I would not recommend anybody to trifle with their conscience in an ordinary way, but a young lady, travelling alone—its very awkward. Do not consider, ma'am, that you are, in the eye of the law, a criminal. We will sit down, if I may take the liberty, and consider what is best to be done.' I should think this lasted a good hour.

I met the policeman this morning, as I took Gurth to the station, and he merely suggested that some day I had better get a new collar. Gurth was very good, and the guard promised to see to him. Hans has just been violently sick.

Such is my news.

Do you see that Dodo has a daughter?[1] Well, the rabbits of the field multiply, and replenish the earth with their bones.

Shall you kiss me tomorrow? Yes, Yes, Yes. Ah, I cannot bear being without you. I was thinking today of my greatest happiness, a walk along a cliff by the sea, and you at the end of it. I am determined to burn all my life of you, and begin another; for I have made out a pleasant scheme of you.

Bruce Richmond writes that he wants to send me a book on famous Scotchwomen.[2] So I suppose the autumn season has begun. I wish Prothero would write. Saxon sends me the information, on a card, that the back of Hans Sachs house is more beautiful than the front. Clives theory is right I am sure; the younger Pliny.

O tomorrow!

Yr. B.

Berg

438: To Clive Bell   *Sea View, Manorbier*
                                                [Pembrokeshire]
Aug. 19th [1908]

My dear Clive,
    There is no doubt but that I was well advised in telling you to come here for your honeymoon. I am surprised to find how beautiful it all is—

1. Dodo was Antonia, the eldest daughter of Charles Booth. She married Malcolm Macnaghten.
2. *A Group of Scottish Women*, by Harry Graham (*TLS*, 3 September 1908).

more than I remembered—how lovely, and how primitive. I have not been on the cliffs yet, my business yesterday keeping me on the trot, but directly this letter is done, I am off to Proud Giltar.

Ah, it is the sea that does it! perpetual movement, and a border of mystery, solving the limits of fields, and silencing their prose. I am now writing in the private room and at the desk of a gentleman farmer called Barkley; he is about thirty, and has a face like the present Duke of Devonshire. He has just been in to ask me to use his books, if I find any to my taste. I find odd volumes of Scott, some standard novels, others that are not standard and the 'Popular Educator' in a leather binding. After I wrote yesterday, Mrs Lewis had the brilliant idea that the house just behind hers, on the hill, was furnished, but unlet. She sent for Mr Barkley, the owner, who agreed to let me one room, with a great bow window facing the sea, several deep arm chairs, and a desk. So I am in luxury; I have brought my books up, come and go when I like—it is but a minute from the cottage, and begin to write tomorrow. Nobody disturbs me, they light a lamp for me after dinner, and the only noises I can detect, with my window open, are distant sounds of cows, a bluebottle outside on the cistern and at the moment the flapping of a red admiral who has come in and like all insects, cant get out.

Well, what shall we discourse about? If I begin upon literature, and slip by easy stages to a certain work; and I may as well ask you what you think of a Spanish name for the lady [Rachel Vinrace]. Cintra? Andalusia? Her father touched at many ports and sailors like sentimental names: he may have had other reasons too, not to be defined.

Smith has written to me again, repeating with mild compliments that he would like me to write a series of articles upon Men and Women, as I see them in their biographies. I must repeat what I said before. Professor Sully, and Mr Stebbing[1] both 'say nice things' of my writing. I believe I shall become a popular lady biographist, safe for—graceful portrait, and such a lady!

I think a great deal of my future, and settle what book I am to write—how I shall re-form the novel and capture multitudes of things at present fugitive, enclose the whole, and shape infinite strange shapes. I take a good look at woods in the sunset, and fix men who are breaking stones with an intense gaze, meant to sever them from the past and the future—all these excitements last out my walk, but tomorrow I know, I shall be sitting down to the inanimate old phrases. As a matter of fact, Mlle de la Valliere ought to make into something graceful at least; and I am going to contrive a scheme as I walk.

Poor Clive! What a sister-in-law! But if you were not so polite you

1. James Sully, Professor of Philosophy at University College, London, and a writer on psychology; William Stebbing, for thirty years a leader writer of *The Times*.

would have none of it. There was a day when I never talked of my writing to you. I have passed your house, and imagined numbers of things. There is a certain road, with shadows across it, leading to the sea where Nessa and I walked, and she declared that Romance was not a thing of the past, as she had thought, but was going on all round us. The Bensons have never let, and there are three other houses unlet, and not one is building. Next year we might come here.

I split my head over [G. E.] Moore every night, feeling ideas travelling to the remotest part of my brain, and setting up a feeble disturbance, hardly to be called thought. It is almost a physical feeling, as though some little coil of brain unvisited by any blood so far, and pale as wax, had got a little life into it at last; but had not strength to keep it. I have a very clear notion which parts of my brain think. Enough, however; Nessa is horribly bored, and says I take too much pains when I write to you. But this letter is not well written. Did I tell you that I went to Evening Service on Sunday— a bat was in the church, all the women frightened for their hair—and I walked off with the Cathedral hymn book?

Yr. AVS

Kiss my old Tawny, on all her private places—kiss her eyes, and her neck socket.

Quentin Bell

439: To Vanessa Bell   *Manorbier [Pembrokeshire]*
Thursday [20 August 1908]
Beloved,

Why did my letter give you the impression of such gloom, I wonder? I cant remember any plaints; but I see that you attribute it to H[ilton] Y[oung]. I dont think that whatever he could do would bother me much —might of course make shiver my vanity—but I expect the real cause was that lodgings are vile, and children shriek.

I am quite happy here, in my big room with a comfortable chair, and no one ever disturbs me.

It pours, beneath a drifting mist, and I have been writing the first pages of Mlle de la Valliere, and snapping my fingers at all the storms and all the lovers (who wont love me) in the world. I always want you; but save for that, I haven't been lonely yet, and I have been away for 20 days.

You dont give me your address, and your punishment will be a severe one. 'No letters? Clive.' 'Yes, my honey jar; one from Snow, from Kitty, from Walter Lamb.' 'Oh I dont count them. No letter from my Apekin I mean?' "No; not a line." 'Oh how I hate Scotch moors.'

I have another letter from good Mary Sheep; the [Bertrand] Russells telegraphed on Monday to ask me to stay with them for four days, but as I had gone the telegram was returned. Ought I to write to Mrs Russell? I have never seen her. Sheep: ends 'The life of the senses is more within my reach than the life of the mind'. Well, it depends what she means by the senses.

I walked along the Cliff yesterday, and found myself slipping on a little ridge just at the edge of a red fissure. I did not remember that they came so near the path; I have no wish to perish. I can imagine sticking out ones arms on the way down, and feeling them tear, and finally whirling over, and cracking ones head. I think I should feel as though I saw a china vase fall from the table; a useless thing to happen—and without any reason or good in it. But numbers of people do fall over; my good landlady tells me stories. Her son in law was found dead in the road, his horses coming home before him, and no one knew how it happened. She is full of saws, and wisdom about making the best of things, and 'here we are, and we must grin and bear it'. She offered me a horn cup, made from an ancestral cow, which I had to refuse as well as I could; and then said that I was like the gentleman she had just had—a true lady.

I dont think the Cliffs are as fine as Cornish cliffs, and the land is certainly tamer, but then Manorbier is practically in the 4oties; there was a school treat on the beach yesterday, and for some reason it seemed to me exactly the kind of thing that happened in the year 1845. They drove off in a two horse waggon, with little bonnets, and side whiskers.

Well—if I am to go out, and I get bitchy if I stay in, I must tramp now, in my great boots and water proof.

Were you sorry to leave Julian? Tell me what Scotland is like.

My book for the Times about Scottish women has just come—a fat dull work, I expect. Write an immense long letter. I pine if they dont come. Kiss your hand.

B.

Berg

440: TO EMMA VAUGHAN   *Manorbier [Pembrokeshire]*

[August 1908]

Dearest Toad,

Yes, it is all very well for you to be indiscreet—but what if you knew what I know? Have you heard that—No, I won't reveal other people's secrets.[1] Still, she shouldn't go to a lecture if she can't control herself; or

1. The family jokes and scandals referred to in this manic letter are not now recoverable, since Virginia was building her fantasies on a letter just received from Emma Vaughan, which has not survived.

the Committee should put locks on the doors. Why she did it then, instead of waiting till—I can't make out; but for the last month or two I have suspected—from the colour and shape and so on—well, she signs her name now with a hyphen.

Poor cousin Mia! is it out at last? I was afraid that last meeting at the Jolly Miller would do for her. Can you imagine? She drove up, in the village omnibus (which takes the Coroner about) at 6 o'clock—not more than a shawl over her shoulder, and her right leg bare. She asked if she were a flower-bed that they raked her so?, and sang and sang about geraniums and roses. "Monty's in the cupboard!" she cried at last, and fell into the cistern, afishing for black beetles. But that's the beginning—Aunt Mary heard, and set off at once, in a veil with cupid in the border, chasing butter-flies, and reached Rickmansworth just as Charlie was talking to the beadle. She sat with him beneath the plum tree in the garden till the sun went down and at night cried "I'm only a little bag of bones—And the bed is so big!". . .

At the same time, poor Aunt Minna who has been brooding constantly over her disappointment with Marny in the summer, set out for Rickmans-worth, to find the bluebell walk. She got to Richmond and asked everyone she met whether bluebottles weren't very late this year? "Have you any bluebottles? Is this the Star and Garter? Then I must be at Greenwich after all. But why did naughty Margaret Vaughan tell me B. stood for bug?" Well, well; I could run on, if you could call it running, when every sentence draws a tear. So poor Will has followed John Bailey's example after all—with the exception of the bedroom poker, I hope. We call it poker—though it has another name. It's worse, though, when the quakers run amok: here's a letter from Cambridge just come—'Can you not persuade your Aunt that at her age *more clothing* is needed? and the neighbours complain of the noise.' What am I to do? Margaret on my hands too, with her visions of a world where they neither marry nor wear wedding rings. Happily, though the earth spins round me, and it is rumoured in Hoxton that Marny had a hand in the last butchers bill at the hospital (Yes—*she* knows what I mean—) I keep calm and virtuous here by the sea shore. I don't agree that your native country surpasses any I have ever seen (for we must now talk moralities, so that Hilda, who stays with you, shan't blush) but it is passable—a good country for toads. Rain all day, storms at night, and such a croaking in the swamp as sends all the dreams away, if you sleep with your window open. However, they believe in the virtues of toadskin here, laid upon burns, or upon the brows of guilty women. It brings vice to the surface, they say, in a yellow patch. Many of the village women are disfigured. I lodge in one cottage, but have my sitting-room in another. The room belongs to a young farmer, Mr Barclay, who let it me on condition that I would write neither fiction nor poetry at his table. I said my time was mostly taken up in cor-responding with my cousins, two maiden ladies, the name of Vaughan. "What, Vaughan of Upton Castle?" he said. "The oldest name in the kingdom—but not one of the most respectable. Old blood will have its humours. Your cousins now are they virtuous young women?" I then told him the story of Marny and the Bishop's chaplain. We laughed till the spiders waltzed in the corners, and were strangled in their own webs. I am to drink a glass of port with him tonight.

Yours,
G.

Sussex

441: To Vanessa Bell   *Manorbier [Pembrokeshire]*

Wednesday [26 August 1908]

Beloved,

I had a piteous disappointment yesterday. I kept your letter till tea time, and went for a long walk planning a surprise at the end. I lost my way, sat on a hedge and directed myself all wrong by the map, and had to tramp till 6. The one thing that quickened my step was the thought of your letter—and when I got home, rushed to my room looked on the table. There was nothing there!

Nor is there any letter this morning. Damn these posts! But lamentations are dull. Reginald Smith bandies compliments with me, wont entirely give up the idea, and says that if I had read more I shouldn't think and write with that originality which the Cornhill loves! Of course, I had been posing as an illiterate woman, who had twice as much difficulty in writing an article as other people.

Nelly's latest has been sent me also—upon Galsworthy. She means to be honest, and to blurt out the truth without thought for style—but the result is mere rant. I cant even make out this time what her grievance is, but she is denouncing somebody—I think it is the people who call her an aristocrat. I had better send it to you.

O dear O dear! The second and last post has come, and there is no letter again. Are you ill, have you been shot, or is it merely some trick of the posts? I cant make out how it can take 3 days to get a letter here—I have tried to walk myself into a philosophic mood, in the churchyard, but I cant help feeling melancholy. It rains and blows—and here I must sit and wait till tomorrow morning—and perhaps even then—

However, I must take a book and read, and try to forget all about you. There are poisonous gnats (in North London) I read; perhaps you have been stung—or do you remember that young lady of title last year, whom Violet felt for so much, whose husband shot her by mistake for a rabbit.

A woman [Mrs Luard]—colonels wife—has been murdered in Kent— All the consolation I get is a card from the London Library to say that I can have Saxons book on astrology [recommended by him] if I want it.

I am inclined to stay here till Monday now; my tooth has stopped aching, and I see I shant have done my writing till Sunday, and I am much happier here than I should be in London. Much happier!—that is mere optimism. I dont see how I am to stagger to the end of this sheet when I dont know whether you are in a state to read it. I turn to your letter and try to make out that you have no post out on Sunday, and only one early in the morning on week days, so that, if you missed this, I should not get a letter till tomorrow morning. I sink to the lowest depths of acquiescence, and consider that after all we are mere lumps of flesh, propelled about the world for a season, and our sufferings are shocks leading nowhere. I am myself a worm, with a spade cutting through it.

It is now thundering out at sea, and some silly women, out for a holiday, are bathing. It is too fantastic of them—but they wont drown. Monster that you are—I adore you.

Yr. B.

Berg

442: To Clive Bell   *Manorbier [Pembrokeshire]*

Friday [28 August 1908]

My dear Clive,

I must answer you today, though I have not much time to do it properly. I am going to Tenby, for the sake of having my tea in a shop, and making choice of buns, and also because it is alternately raining and shining.

Ah well!—I am in a mood today to care very little what anybody says about Melymbrosia. The mood has lasted indeed seven days. I cant see what you have to 'up-blow' me for, since in my eyes the changing of names is the most trivial of occupations, and I am aware that the only thing that matters is a thing that you cant control, nor I neither. (I think it should be 'either') Whether my conception is solid is a vastly important matter to me, but at the same time, almost impersonal. I mean to stand at my desk this autumn and work doggedly, in the dark, without lifting the lid off the pot, more than I can help, or inviting people to come and have a sniff. But as you know, I count immensely on your encouragement. How is all this to be reconciled? Well, let us turn to another matter. You ask me whether I like your letters. In what sense do you mean, I wonder? That is the worst of being in Wales; I can't wait to get an answer, and so must hazard some kind of criticism that mayn't be at all what you want. Anyhow, I reread them all this morning, and found only one sentence improperly understood before. They are very pleasant letters—there can be no doubt that I like them. For one thing, they are very affectionate—show a spirit exquisitely poised, so far as I am concerned. They are deliberate, a trifle 'reminiscent', but for all that personal in the best sense. I expect that we differ a little in our view of what a letter should be, for I expect (as I read them) that you think more pains are needed than I do. But I dont imagine that you want literary criticism from me; so the only view I will put forward is that you might put your style at the gallop rather more than you do. After all, the only way of expanding it is to try to grasp things that you dont quite grasp: and a slight tone of monotony, which I detect sometimes, seems to me to come from the fact that you are content to do things that you can do very well. But I tremble as I write! After all, you may have meant me to answer quite a different question. I often think that we are most unlike in the values we attach to things; you will take seriously what is frivolous to me and vice versa. If I had time I would explain more fully —Anyhow, dont write differently, and the [more] often you write the better I should like it—and I keep your letters. Kiss Dolphins nose—if it isnt too wet—and tap pony smartly on the snout. Whisper into your wife's ear that I love her. I expect she will scold you for tickling her (when she hears the message)

Yr. affate

Quentin Bell   AVS

443: To Saxon Sydney-Turner   *Manorbier, South Wales*

Aug. 28th [1908]

My dear Saxon,

I suppose you are back again, and I note what you say about the concert. I am pining for music. Could you, if you think it necessary, get me a ticket for Tuesday night? where ever you choose. I will order dinner at 7. to give us time. I shall only get back on Monday evening, but if I find a card saying that you had no time to get a ticket, I will try for one on Tuesday. How I hate making arrangements!

The weather here is quite hysterical—passionate storms for no reason, and then brilliant sun. It has been doing this for a week, and my good landlady says that it will soon have her windows in. She faces the sea. So I expect to spend the night soon in the fowl house.

I have had no news from Adrian since you left him, and only letters every 3 days from Nessa and Clive. They have nothing but abuse for highland scenery, and Nessa is much distressed because Clive will shoot rabbits. I also heard from Lytton the other day, about a small literary job,[1] and he sounds in great spirits, adoring the lochs and burns and all the rest

1. Lytton Strachey was staying in a cottage near Aviemore in Scotland. He had been asked by Frank Sidgwick to write an introduction to the *Letters of James Boswell to the Rev W. J. Temple* (ed. T. Secombe, 1908). He refused, and suggested to Sidgwick that he should offer the commission to Virginia. This proposal came to nothing, but Virginia reviewed the book when it was published.

of it. The country here isn't nearly up to Cornwall, though I prefer it to the floridity (is there such a word?) of Somerset. I am always glad to find that Cornwall remains unapproached.

I have just had a card from the London Library to say that Lilly's astrology[1] is at my service. Are you still pursuing that science?

I much look forward to seeing you and hearing your adventures.

Yr. aff.

Sussex AVS

444: To Vanessa Bell   *Manorbier [Pembrokeshire]*

Saturday [29 August 1908]

Beloved,

I had your charming letter this morning—for your letters do charm and you know it; and if you pretend to fear our sense of style, it is only because you despise it. Besides no one can say that my letters are well written; I am much too vain to think it.

I had my tea in Tenby yesterday, but chanced on a dull dirty shop, where I was charged a shilling for a stale bun, and thus the great object of my journey failed. But it is very difficult to walk here, because when it isnt raining it is blowing so hard that I can hardly see my way along the Cliff. I end upon the beach generally,—find a corner where I can sit and invent images from the shapes of the waves. A child of 12, a pretty little girl, does the same thing also, and will always sit me out; but I daren't ask her what she is thinking, though I want to know. How ridiculous it all is! I sometimes feel surprised when I realise that we are all set out on our journey, as human beings, with all our ceremonies, and marriages.

I had a letter from poor old Case yesterday; she inverts her address 'Virginia, dear', which is a sign of tenderness, I think; and tells me how she has been nursing a friend in London who died on the same day that Helen Stephen died, but will be more missed. She is full of tender humanities, and a kind of cultured Christianity, though she is too well educated to be a Christian.

This time next week we shall be at Siena! Divine! If I weren't to be with you, I should be rather sorry to end my solitude. It is amazingly comfortable to stretch ones legs and have one's read out, and not to be interrupted at half past six, and spend the evening at the opera, or in talk about it. I never knew I had such a desire to read; and in London it is always fretted and stinted, and always will be. I wish one could sweep ones days clean; say not at home, and refuse ever to go out. But dont understand— or understand with discretion—that I grumble at Adrian, or at anyone; the

1. William Lilly, the 17th-century astrologer. His *Introduction to Astrology* was reissued in 1835.

great gain of here is really, I believe, that one can see such beautiful pleasant things, and smell, and be at peace; and if I live in London, I must, I suppose, see people.

Do you call this well written? careful, and rhythmical? if so, my good beast, your ear is stuffed with feathery down. I am also sunk into such a simple inarticulate mood, that I doubt whether you will understand my bleatings. The only words I have spoken for four weeks, except when I saw you, have been very loud and hearty. "Fine day! No, he wont bite. I should like a fowl tonight.' One has to be so cheerful with the lower classes, or they think one diseased.

I ordered two pounds of tea from the Stores and gave them to Mrs Lewis today. She was greatly moved, and has been fluttering about me, asking whether there isn't anything I should like to take away with me. I have suggested a bunch of flowers (which I am certain to leave in the train) but I dread the horn mug. Now, you dont suffer from the desire to be liked so much that you would write a letter to the Stores; I expect I shall leave all my fortune to a home for stray pug dogs, having become entirely maudlin in my old age.

I finished Moore last night; he has a fine flare of arrogance at the end—and no wonder. I am not so dumb foundered as I was; but the more I understand, the more I admire. He is so humane in spite of his desire to know the truth; and I believe I can disagree with him, over one matter.

I am sending you the Cornhill, in case it arrives just in time for your journey, you may like to see Nelly.

It is far more vexatious to understand her meaning than Moores; there are some sentences which seem to graze two different meanings, and then to be draped in an alien metaphor; it makes one's head spin, as in a nightmare.

Have you any theory about the Leward [*sic*] murder—or was it suicide?[1]

If you leave on Tuesday, and it takes 2 days to reach you, I shall only write one more letter, I suppose. As I am discharging pale soliloquies without a grain of fact in them, it is about time I said no more—but embraced you!

Yr. B.

Berg

445: To Lytton Strachey   *Manorbier, South Wales*

Sunday [30 August 1908]

Dear Lytton,

I haven't heard from Frank Sidgwick, so I expect he must have found some one else to write for him. It would be a charming book [Boswell's

1. Mrs Luard, wife of General C. E. Luard, was found dead in her summer-house near Sevenoaks on 24 August. The autopsy later revealed that she had first been struck from behind, and then shot twice.

Letters] to do, but I don't see how I could manage it in the time. I shall be knocking about in Italian Inns, without an inkpot or a scrap of blotting paper, and I suppose, one French novel.

Well—I have been spending a delightful holiday, given up to reflection and the beauties of nature. I hardly know how I shall emerge again, or whether I shan't speak in words of one syllable. I live in the greatest discomfort, but have hired a room in another house, where I retire to mumble over Moore, and to exclaim "My wig! What a man!" when I read Racine.

Adventures I have none—unless you can count a sage correspondence with Saxon, something after the manner of the Dutch school of painting. He sends me an inventory of his bedroom furniture, and I answer—it's my only defence—with the most dissolute of metaphors. I was also invited to spend a week with the [Bertrand] Russells, and meet Mr and Mrs Gilbert Murray, Jane Harrison and [Francis] Cornford and Miss Sheepshanks. It was a little too elderly: I couldn't face it. Yes Clive spoke very highly of your poems, and I got them out of Nessa at last. They lie on the table before me, and I read them when I happen to be feeling pure. Compliments I know mean nothing to you; nor my green blushes, nor any other form of adulation. If you think of me as a woman of sound common sense, I have a vivid picture of you—an oriental potentate, in a flowered dressing gown.

Nessa and Clive seem horribly bored in the Highlands—and no wonder. The Scotch are an amazing people. I spent this morning toiling over a number of Scotch women, your relative Mrs Grant of Laggan[1] among them; and had to draw largely upon my imagination.

O what a mercy to write no more, but to lie on one's back in a vineyard, and let grapes drop down one's throat—But I must go and pack—I go to London tomorrow.

Yrs. ever,

Frances Hooper   VS

446: To Vanessa Bell   [*Manorbier, Pembrokeshire*]

[30 August 1908]

Beloved,

I dont know whether this will get to you, and I have only time for a scrawl, being perplexed with innumerable small jobs. All my things have to be carted down, boxes packed; bills paid; and I tremble at the thought of tomorrow.

I sometimes think I will never travel again. My articles are all unfinished and hideous, and the Times say they must have them by Tuesday.

1. Anne Grant (1755-1838), the poet and essayist. Lytton's mother, Jane Grant was remotely related to her family.

Ah what pleasure to see you again—and with God be the rest—or at rest, I cant remember which. In spite of my complacency yesterday, I feel rather wild, and in need of domestication.

Perhaps we shall have a tremendous shower of talk; but you are in no need, and I fear you will be very practical. 'Now make haste. Have you packed your hair oil' and so on.

I have had no letters, and so I have no news; but if I waited till I had been for a walk and filled my brain, that might do instead; unfortunately the post goes at 5.30. I have been writing to Lytton and to Case; I feel somehow that Lytton is a trifle Blasé, and our friendship is strictly and even cynically Platonic. He says that Clive thinks his poems almost as good as Catullus (after some others). Where are my works then? I shall have to alter my standard for judging Clive's praise—sad, oh sad. But I feel so full of ideas at this moment, for a book I am going to write; and I believe I shall carry through Melymbrosia, and I believe I care less than ever before for what people say.

This is gibberish tho'; and if I were a vain woman, vain of my letters that is, I would never let this go: I wish you would consider what I say about burning letters. I admit that it flatters me to think they are kept; but it also hampers me in the least literary of my intercourse. Did you ever read the beautiful poem in which Browning (now in what tone of voice do you deliver that, I wonder?) explained how one writes to one, 'and one only'?

I fancy you stumbling through these words—sometimes coming to a stop altogether, and muttering 'well, if she will write such balderdash' and then there will be half a minutes interruption while Clive makes you repeat your next word.

I dreamt of Clarissa[1] last night; she was new born, and had a fine row of teeth, which were without roots; and she could say 'no objection' which I thought proved something out of Moore.

Yr. B.

Berg

447: TO VIOLET DICKINSON   *Manorbier* [*Pembrokeshire*]

30th Aug. 08

My Violet,

I write in the most horrid Chaos, on the verge of going up to London. Still, as you wont write to me, I must write to you. But what with writing for Smith and writing for the Times, and writing to Nessa, and writing cheques, post cards and love letters, my pen is worn to the stump. Besides,

1. Invented name for Vanessa's next child.

to keep a correspondence warm it should be constant; and you may be on the seas, or in bed, for anything I know.

I have enjoyed myself very much here. Wells became rather too venerable and hot, towards the end of the time; but I got onto the Mendips once, and saw the place where my great uncle the Bishop eat his Lambs tails. That track had an immense success in Wells; 'Yes, my uncle was very fond of Lambs tails; I fancy them myself.' It was so homely, and familiar. But happily it wasn't the season for Lambs or I should have eaten nothing else, but their tails.

Then I came on here; and found myself lodged in the cottage of a stone mason, with no conveniences of any kind. But I take my cold tub like an Englishman, and I hired a room in the house of a gentleman farmer and there I sat and read, and wrote those brilliant articles which I speak of. Read your Times with attention for the next two or three weeks, and see if you can spot me. Bruce Richmond and I keep up a mildly humorous correspondence. But I have had no adventures, to speak of. Often I get no letters for 3 days at a time, Nessa being in Scotland, and Adrian in Germany, and Violet estranged, and I rarely open my lips. I talk a little to my landlady about the rheumatics, and which is the best way of cooking eggs. We have just had an affecting scene. I asked her for her bill, and she scratched her head and said 'I shall charge you for one egg a day. Fires cost nothing, fowls cost nothing. It has been a pleasure to serve you.' And then you call me an egoist—a woman who doesn't love her kind! I think of becoming a philanthropist this winter, and perfecting that side of my character, which some judge defective. Where will you be then—when Nelly asks me to her bedside, and I take Kitty to the surgeon, and Hester[1] has her next baby in my house, and Beatrice confides to me the tragedy of her life!

We go to Italy on Thursday, and if you were a woman of any vitality you would write me a long letter, and try to explain yourself. Supposing we drift entirely apart, in the next 3 years, so that we blush when we meet and remember our ancient correspondence. Will it be your fault or mine? Yours, I think; because you are always so unselfish. When you write to me, you talk of other people, so that I begin to forget what you are like. I can conjure up one or two grimaces.

I have been writing at my work of imagination [*Melymbrosia*]; and have now done one hundred pages. I begin to ask, whether I shall ever dare to print them? I shall work hard at it this winter, and see at any rate whether I can finish it.

Nessa is in her shooting box, alone, with three men. She says the Highlands are like Christmas cards, and she will be very glad to get to Italy. Her son takes up a great deal of her mind, and she is beginning to boast

1. Hester Lyttelton had married, in April 1904, Cyril Alington, later Headmaster of Eton.

not only of his beauty, but of his character and wit. I am rather fond of him too; he has changed completely since I last saw him.

I suppose you are staying in some great house, where they dress for dinner, and drive about in brakes. I suppose you are very witty at dinner, and all the old generals confide in you. When the ladies go to bed, Lady Cynthia or Mildred comes to your room, and asks your advice. You are rather random and free spoken, which however, she finds the greatest refreshment: and says she never met anyone like you (Lord, what a long letter this is. I meant to contain myself in one sheet, but all my books are packed, and I like writing to you, once I get started). You kiss each other, and next time I come to Manchester St Rose will tell me you are engaged with a young lady in the drawing room. O if you would only write your life!—much better than editing your great grandmother.[1]

I heard from Nelly the other day, from the Highlands. She will make jokes. I spend my time deciphering them. But you think me unjust to Nelly; and I believe she gets irritated with me, and does her best to flout all my prejudices. Still, she is a very charming woman!

Do you like my writing? Have you changed your opinion of it?

I begin to believe that I shall write rather well one of these days.

The Quaker is rejoicing over Helen Stephen's death, and meditating an address to an Oxford College in November. What the difference is between her inspiration and my journalism I dont know.

Are you fond of me?

Yr. AVS

Berg

1. Virginia means Violet's ancestress, Emily Eden, whose letters Violet eventually edited for publication in 1919.

Letters 448-498

In September 1908 Virginia went with the Bells to Tuscany, returning through Paris, but if she wrote any letters during this journey, none has survived. There was another visit to Cornwall in November, with Lytton Strachey, and Virginia spent Christmas with Adrian in London. 1909 contained no significant landmarks in Virginia's life, unless one counts Lytton's proposal of marriage to her in February (a proposal which was immediately withdrawn by mutual consent), and the death of the Quaker aunt in April. She continued to write Melymbrosia *slowly, gratefully submitting her manuscript to Clive for criticism. In late April she went with Vanessa and Clive to Florence and Milan, but the expedition was not a success, and Virginia, emotionally exhausted, returned alone.*

448: To Clive Bell   29 *Fitzroy Square, W.*

[1? October 1908]

Dear Clive,

There is nothing much in this, but I send it partly to show my sense of gratitude for your services with my box and to supplicate that the novel I left behind may be sent, and to thank also for my entertainment at your hands, and those of my great mistress. I was very happy . . . [in Italy and Paris]

Yr. AVS

Quentin Bell

449: To Lytton Strachey   29 *Fitzroy Square, W.*

Sunday [4 October 1908]

Dear Lytton,

It was charming to get a letter from you in Paris. We came back two or three days ago—Adrian is just back[1]—there are concerts and reviews and Saxon till 3 o'clock in the morning—it's all begun again: We had very successful travels however, and ended with a week in Paris and mild Bohemian society. We drank an immense amount of coffee and sat out under the electric light talking about art. I wish we were 10 years younger, or 20 years older, and could settle to our brandy and cultivate the senses. As it was, I sometimes thought of other things—novels and adventures.

1. He had been in Bayreuth with Saxon Sydney-Turner.

Why don't you bring off your novel? You must. Plots don't matter, and as for passion and style and immorality, what more do you want? Have you been attending to English literature all this time? I must buy the Spectator.[1] I feel as though I wanted to read through whole libraries—but of course I shan't. There are books all round my chair, and I can't bother to pick them up. Adrian has just told me a dream of his—how he travelled for 40 years with the Hermit of the Dead Sea—It was Saxon.

Yr. ever,
AVS

Frances Hooper

450: TO VIOLET DICKINSON   [29 *Fitzroy Square, W.*]
Sunday [4 October 1908]

My Violet,

It was very pleasing to find your letter waiting me—among a rubbish heap of bills. We got back on Thursday, and Adrian came on Friday, so we are all started again. We had a very successful journey, Clive is an admirable man, and I never did a thing or wrote a line.[2] We lounged about in Siena and Perugia and Paris. I liked Italy much better this time, except for the people. But the country was beautiful—all the grapes ripe, and the earth warm. We met Elsie, Ly Carnarvon, at Perugia, who asked us about George, and I haven't seen him for six months.

It is very thick and hot here, and I cant make up my mind to put anything straight, but the dear old Times wants me to set to work. I bought a chair and a sofa in Paris. Do you realise that you have never been inside this house?

Julian looks about 2 years old, and is quite responsible now. Nessa will probably make a very nice child of him. He has beautiful eyes, and a great big head.

I have a petition to make; although I packed with the utmost discretion, I left behind me the 2 things I love best—and thus leave out to the last— my fur slippers. I have to go to my bath now on naked soles, and when the cold weather comes I shall get chillblains. Can you tell me where you get them, or would you like to give me my Christmas present now—or, if I got some small beasts skins would you sew them up, as you did before?

Where is Nelly? I heard from Beatrice—like the growl of a dog with a bone.

Yr. AVS

Berg

1. To which Lytton was now a regular contributor.
2. In fact she kept one of her 'literary diaries', a copy of which is in Sussex University, and another in the Berg Collection.

[October? 1908]

My dear Clive,

Will you think me a great bore if I turn to the dreary subject again, and ask you whether you have anything to say about that unfortunate work?[1] I have a feeling at this moment that it is all a mistake, and I believe you could tell me.

At any rate I put myself in your hands with great confidence; I dont really think you will be bored by my demands, and I believe you do speak the truth.

At the same time, I groan over my egoism that wont let me or anyone else think of better things.

Yr. affate,

AVS

Dont bother to write at length—in fact, dont write if you had rather not.

Quentin Bell

452: To Lady Robert Cecil   [29 *Fitzroy Square, W.*]

Postcard
[26 October 1908]

Your Miss Beale[2] is admirable. You find much more to be said for her than I saw—indeed she becomes impressive. But she was ugly too, with her horrid Gothic brick all round her.

AVS

Hatfield

453: To Violet Dickinson   29 *Fitzroy Square, W.*

Thursday [29 October 1908]

My Violet,

It is too touching that you should send me shoes. I did not mean that you should keep my wardrobe supplied. I thought you had a great hecatomb of Somersetshire lambs, offered up to the shade of your Grandfather (and my Great Uncle) the Bishop [Lord Auckland].

1. Virginia had given Clive the one hundred pages of *Melymbrosia* which she had completed in Wales. His reaction to the book is contained in letters published by Quentin Bell, Vol I, Appendix D.
2. Nelly's review of *Dorothea Beale of Cheltenham* for the *Cornhill.*

I went out to get you a book in thanks; but found nothing, and now I have written for some elegies which will come in a day or two.

I met Bruce Richmond last night at a concert, and we had an awkward moment. He has shrunk, and become a lively little old man—I thought he was younger and bigger. I want to ask him to dinner—but do I dare? I also saw the benignant goddess, Katie [Cromer], and helped her into her jacket, which was all inside out. Could I ask her to tea, do you think? I am writing all day long about Ly. Holland.[1] I think Nelly is much better on Miss Beale. I told her so—but I think she suspects me.

Yr. Sp.

The shoes fit excellently, and I go to my bath in them. The shape is wonderful, like coal scuttles.

Berg

454: TO MADGE VAUGHAN   29 *Fitzroy Square, W.*

Nov. 1st [1908]

Dearest Madge,

I was very glad to get your letter. How am I to protest that I don't forget any of you? You, or the children or the moors. I met a young man who admires you the other night—Arthur Daykins, and if you had heard me describe you—you would have felt quite secure about me. But to sit down and write a letter is such a misery. I always want to find a larger sheet and I don't keep any. We are all back and very industrious as usual. How any woman lives who has 4 children, I can't imagine; I stagger along, like a washerwoman with a basket on her head—and yet I am single.

Julian is quite grown up—I dont see why we treat children as Babies at all. He is perfectly rational; and very busy with his own business; I think he is rather quick and practical—very sweet tempered, and I suppose he will be beautiful.

Are you writing? I always ask that question, and you always tell me it is better to be married. Arthur Daykins, who seemed a very cultivated young man, was anxious that you should publish a novel. I have read Mr Forsters book[2]—but it repeats what he has said already—However, it is very amusing.

I hoped to see you the other day. We shall be here I suppose for Christmas. I am often imagining myself on the moors. I think about you

1. Review of *The Journal of Elizabeth Lady Holland*, edited by the Earl of Ilchester, and *The Holland House Circle*, by Lloyd Sanders (*Cornhill*, 1908, N.S., Vol. XXV).
2. E. M. Forster, *A Room with a View*, 1908.

and the children too. I always believe that I know all about them—but Janet is older than I thought possible. Do write again. I was very happy to get your letter.

Yr. AVS

I have just routed out your letter, which had got beneath bills, and you ask about Italy. We had a splendid time. I never saw such a beautiful country. All the vines were ripe, and we wandered about in the evening and came upon odd little farm houses and women picking maize—Is that likely? I thought of you there too—for we went to Perugia, and stayed at your hotel, and all the visitors were reading Miss Symonds,[1] and saying how it was the best guide book in Italy. We made a great stir by saying that we knew you. People used to take us with them for walks on the strength of it. We went to Siena—which I liked better than Perugia, partly because there were fewer English. Then we spent a week in Paris. But London is really more beautiful than Paris—This is all very fragmentary! I find it so difficult to see how a letter ought to be written—Show me.

Sussex

455: To Madge Vaughan   29 *Fitzroy Square, W.*

19th Nov. 08

Dearest Madge,

I have been disgracefully long in thanking you. Your book[2] arrived just as I was plunging off by the Cornish Express to spend a week at the Lizard![3] I have read the introduction, and I think it is very good indeed. It is more restrained than usual; more direct, I think, and somehow mature and wise. You seem to speak with experience. You get a great deal of colour into your writing, and she must have been a great character. I have read the book; but I shall read it again. I should like to 'review' it—but the only work I do is for The Times, and I don't think they care about reprints at this season—I asked the other day about another book. If you could suggest a place to write in, I would gladly do it. I am deep in Venetian history[4] at this moment—fascinated, like a Lizard in the sun.

I remember that you want a drawing by Thoby. Nessa has them, and she promised to bring one, but I shall write now, and send it later. It is

1. Madge's guidebook, *The Story of Perugia*, written in collaboration with Lina Duff Gordon, was published in 1908.
2. *Days Spent on a Doge's Farm*, reissued with a new biographical preface, 1908.
3. Virginia, Adrian, and Lytton Strachey had been staying for a few days in Penmenner House, in the Lizard peninsula, Cornwall.
4. Review of *Venice*, by Pompeo Molmenti (*TLS*, 7 January 1909).

just two years since he died, and I feel immensely old, and as though the best in us had gone. But what use is it to write? It is such an odd life without him.

Give my love to the Children. Janet will be out before I turn round. When shall I see them—and you?

Thank you very much for the book. I am glad to have it.

Yr. AVS

Sussex

456: TO LYTTON STRACHEY   29 *Fitzroy Square, W.*

20th Nov. [1908]

Dear Lytton,

The Lizard is but a dream to me now. I really can't believe in you at all. The Daily Telegraph talks of "forget-me-nots, primroses and apple blossom" flowering in profusion on the coast. So I think of you as a kind of Venetian prince, in sky blue tights, lying on your back in an orchard, or balancing an exquisite leg in the air while I—It wasn't actually foggy, but worse, a dun coloured mist, through which all the poor and the meat and the gas jets were visible. I had a number of letters, mostly bills, but a scattering of invitations, from Lady Pollock, Trevelyans, and Protheros. I accept them all of course. Last night we had Duncan Grant[1] who thinks your address is Penzance; and tonight we dine at the Friday Club, off a 2 shilling dinner. It sounds a little pandemoniac; in the intervals I try to read Romeo and Juliet! I have a dread lest my St Simon, about which I was so parsimonious, should be castrated, and when I get where you are, I shall find stars.[2] But it will be a long time before that happens. I want a fire and an arm chair silence, and hours of solitude. You enjoy all these things, in your island. Do you think much?—have you written more poems? I had cut my [review] novel, and thought it ghastly dull. When shall you come back?

By the way, if Esther [maid?] should approach you with two pairs of scissors, will you stick to them. For some reason I was sent off with two, and came back with none. Adrian meant to leave a map, but packed it, but if you want it he will send it. He has invented a sister taken ill at the Lizard, staying in a friend's house, with appendicitis—crisis lasted 48 hours, but operation avoided (for the present). She had a touch of it in Athens.

Yours,

Frances Hooper   AVS

1. The painter who had been studying in Paris and at the Slade School. He was a cousin of Lytton Strachey.
2. Lytton was reading Virginia's copy of St Simon, which she had left behind with him in Cornwall. Hers was an abridged edition. Lytton's was in 16 volumes.

[24 November 1908]

My Violet,

I behaved with great stupidity and tore up the card with your book's name on it. If you would repeat it, I would go and get it. As for your compliments—they fall like dew. Shall I make you understand that I am greatly refreshed by seeing you, and boring you, and talking of unwritten works?

O if you could see me struggle with my novel—it is a most agitating work—and probably a will o' the wisp. My reviews dont count at all.

I am just off to Godmanchester [Lady Stephen]. Lady Gwendolen [Godolphin Osborne] came yesterday, and stayed 2 hours. She was charming, and really more human. I liked her. We discussed our views of the world, and how she lived and how I lived.

Yr. AVS

Berg

458: To Lytton Strachey   29 *Fitzroy Square, W.*

[1 December 1908]

Dear Lytton,

I was being suffocated in Lady Pollock's drawing room this afternoon—you never saw such a sight.

I shall be in on Thursday if you could come then.

O how those old women spoil my life. Think of the embraces of Mrs Clifford[1] and Aunt Anny![2]

Yrs. AVS

Frances Hooper

459: To Violet Dickinson   29 *Fitzroy Square, W.*

[December 1908]

My Violet,

I have been at Newnham [College, Cambridge], cold and ill-tempered. Do give me the Oxford Book of French Verse. Edited by St John Lucas. I have never got it, and want it.

Now you must tell me also what you shall have.

Yr. AVS

Berg

1. Mrs W. K. Clifford, the novelist and dramatist, and widow of W. K. Clifford, the mathematician and philosopher, who had been a close friend of Leslie Stephen.
2. Lady Ritchie, Thackeray's daughter, and herself a novelist.

[17? December 1908]

My Violet,
    Why didnt you come up? I was merely walking round and round my room and looking at the backs of books. You might have jogged my ideas.
    Well—how am I to make any engagement? Nessa says you are going to France: I stay here till Easter. I have no particular engagements. Couldn't I come and see you one day or will you lunch? On Monday I have Ottoline[1] and Miss Case, who wish to discuss the morality of Baroness de Mayer. I have just written an immense dull article upon Venetian history for the Times, rather in the style of Herbert Fisher and Miss [Edith] Sichel.

                                                    Yr. AVS
Berg

460: To Lytton Strachey   29 Fitzroy Square, W.
[25 December 1908]

Dear Lytton,
    We have asked the [H. A. L.] Fishers to come on the 7th—a Thursday. Will you come then—I suppose we must dress. I imagine that you are now leading your Aunt into dinner. We are comatose—ham divine, but turkey oppressive, and we shall lie before the fire, speechless, till bed time.

                                                    Yrs

Frances Hooper   VS

462: To Clive Bell   29 Fitzroy Square, W.
Christmas Day [1908]

My dear Clive,
    How am I to thank you for your present? The chairs were laden with it this morning. I have seldom enjoyed a happier breakfast. First I saw that it was Byron—a poet I have never read, for lack of an edition to read him in. Then I saw the margins, and the binding, and the print. The magnificence was overwhelming—We carried them like a train of ants into the study. I have been fingering them all day. I have written all this without a word of thanks—but you know your sister-in-laws temper by this time. She is a good garrulous creature, who says many things, and feels intensities, but seldom manages to say them right. Your wife gave me such a talking to the other day; she will deny it, but dont believe her. She said I never gave, but always took. In this case, as she must own, I have been forced to take.

1. Lady Ottoline Morrell, who then lived at Peppard Cottage and in Bedford Square.

I have to leap over ramparts of books in order to leave the study. All you get from me is a discreet Brass tray. Will you employ some dingy afternoon in finding or framing (that would be better) an inscription for the title page. Really they are magnificent. Besides Don Juan and the rest, I think also of 'the thought' as people say. I find it very comforting.

Well—as for news, you deserve a letter, and not Nessa this time. She must be thanked however. She sent me a beautiful skewer. The Apes [Virginia, though plural] thought it was a rod at first, but being satisfied by their nurse, they are now sucking at it in a row, something like Julian and the sugar tongs, save that they turn it over now and then, put their noses through the loop, and make a little odd chuckling noise. It keeps them happy by the hour.

We had Lytton last night; you will be glad to hear that I am not in love with him, nor is there any sign that he is in love with me. Then Duncan Grant came; we had very desultory talk. D. G. is difficult, but charming. He said he was alone, so we asked him to lunch today. He was difficult again; I think he has too many ideas, and no way to get rid of them. I daresay Adrian and I aren't particularly sympathetic—but, again, I think him charming. Lytton told me the whole story of Adrian's love affair the other day—how he had wept in Boswells rooms, and yet had never spoken to the man. This is all my news.

It has been perfectly grey from daybreak (I imagine) and the view only became tolerable when the lamps on the other side of the square were lit. We have dozed over the fire.

It will be a great relief when you are back [from Clive's parents].

Yr. aff.

Quentin Bell   VS

463: To Violet Dickinson   29 *Fitzroy Square, W.*

[late December 1908]

My Violet,

I found that Sophie [Farrell] was hoarding a parcel, with a great variety of things in it. My book and my knocker are both very charming; your power of finding presents is remarkable. It is the result of a generous nature, which never forgets, but buys in June, if it sees something; whereas all my presents are bought on Christmas Eve, and never fit. Yours, by the way, is for New Year.

Will you come to tea with me?—when?—Dont drop me; as Mary Sheepshanks says. These new years are dreadful trials. Isn't it creditable that we still—have some affection!

Yr. VS

Berg

[4 January 1909]

Dear Lytton,

I had heard vaguely of your flight to Rye. Isn't the Mermaid [Inn] rather dismal—like a battleship in the time of Nelson—I remember creeping into it one day, and an old woman chased me out. I am sorry you have been ill. Was it Christmas? We sat over the fire and watched the snow, in an odd white glare. Now Adrian is down in Wiltshire, tramping in the mud, I suppose; and I don't know what I have been doing—seeing Mary Sheepshanks, I think. She deluged me till 1.30 in the morning with the most vapid and melancholy revelations—Imagine 17 Sheepshanks in a Liverpool slum, and Mary (so she says) the brightest of the lot—and then she told stories of women betrayed and love rejected, and cold and poverty and old age with the creeping paralysis—and the upshot of it all was that one should reform the divorce laws. That is what I find so depressing about her—She comes to a dead stop in front of some sordid matter of fact. Like the French she has no outlets. "At the age of 20", she said, "I ought to have married a curate." Was that her delicate way of putting it?

You are going to meet the Fishers on Thursday—You and Herbert must talk about Voltaire, and I shall say how I have just been seeing his waxwork at Madame Tussaud's. I can't help thinking he is rather a fraud (H. F. I mean). He is impossibly enlightened and humane. She is a bright woman.

I read the letters to the unknown [Mérimée] when I was supposed to be boiling goats milk in Athens, and I remember that I found them rather comforting in the circumstances. They seemed so cynical—an arid elderly couple, with all their wits about them. I hate their precise ways.

I am sitting over my fire towards midnight, having put the dog to bed, and have just finished the Ajax [Sophocles]. The ancients puzzle me—they are either so profound or so elementary, and when one has to spell out every word one can't tell which. However, there is at least one passage of great beauty although I find that it can be read 20 different ways. Yesterday I saw Henry Lamb with his evil goat's eyes—and Saxon was there too, and Nessa and Clive. Clive seemed to me depressed, but I think one must ignore it. The Freshfields have asked us to stay: Sidney Lee is coming to tea with me—that is all my news. I have also been asked to write 'impressions' of Walter Headlam, for his Life.[1] But they would have to be lies.

Now I must go to bed, and read some of my exquisite Cowper.

Yr.

VS

Frances Hooper

1. The Memoir by his brother, Cecil Headlam, 1910.

Monday [4 January 1909]

My Violet,

It was no good trying to answer a letter dated motor car somewhere on the Road to Avignon. If you had given me a proper address you should have had a letter on new years day precisely, with a sentimental retrospect,—melancholy anticipation (I have just been writing that phrase somewhere; and I never can get the sound of my own writing out of my head. That's what comes of being as selfish as I am. I shouldn't wonder if God struck me deaf and blasted me blind and set my own tunes grinding perpetually through my brain, as penance).

Well—when are you coming back? It is already next year. How was your party? I never envisaged (as the French have it) anything so ghastly. Think of the long white roads, and the dusky inns at night, and the intelligent American with her guide Henry James, and Violet with her practical instincts all alive, for fleas and smelly water.

How is Ozzy—and how is your spine, with all its delicate tendrils. Whenever we have Herring for dinner, I think of you.

Nothing has happened to me, except that I have ground out two long articles, for the Times.[1] One upon Boswell I think rather good. As for the work of imagination I turn hot and cold over it, and all my friends tell me its no good for *me* to write a novel. They say my creatures are all cold blooded, like those same Herrings. But you dont, my Violet, do you? Ever since we trod the groves together you have seen that my passion was for love and humanity; though it has had to kindle through depths of green water.

Julian has cut a tooth. Nessa and Clive are very flourishing—so happy, that I think of marriage.

Write to me.

                                        AVS

Berg

Thursday [14 January 1909]

My Violet,

I am distressed at the accounts of your [motor] accident, but Thank God that France grows stout trees. You really are too complicated to keep in motion. Perhaps you were an air animal, born before your time; or perhaps you are some curious but inconvenient survival. Once you swam over the

1. Review of *Venice*, by Pompeo Molmenti (*TLS*, 7 January 1909); review of *Letters of James Boswell to the Rev W. J. Temple* (*TLS*, 21 January 1909).

Houses of Parliament, and Westminster Bridge Road, when they were under water. But as for walking on dry land—Providence never made you for that. Throw this theory at your doctor.

I meant to explain that if you skip Greece, with all its painful memories, you will come to Italy last autumn.[1] It isn't amusing at all—as your housemaid asked (with a fine critical taste) that it should be. But I have written nothing whatever that she would pass. What glory it would be to amuse your housemaid!

I have just come back from the Freshfields, where I talked for long stretches about Tolstoy. Mrs F: has lost the use of her right arm; and has a good deal of pain, but she seems to me a valiant woman, who keeps afloat. and strews her bed with the last French review, and the last English memoir.

'So convenient for my daughters that I can read: they can leave me alone.' Old people are either tragic or very happy. That sounds deep—dont think too much what it means. It is not really meant for a concussed brain. I was forgetting.

What are my shoes?

Yr. VS

Berg

467: TO VIOLET DICKINSON   29 *Fitzroy Square, W.*

[26? January 1909]

My Violet,
    You are much too generous. It should have been 5 and not 15 [shillings]. What book shall I get you? You said you would tell me.

I am considering which book I shall get—a very pleasant situation. Especially as I have been very economical in that line lately.

I feel immensely old—old[2] as a hoary grey tortoise, who only comes out in the sun.

How are you?

Yr. AVS

Berg

1. Virginia had lent Violet the journals of her visits to Greece in 1906 and to Italy in September 1908.
2. Virginia was 27 on 25 January.

468: To Lady Ottoline Morrell   29 *Fitzroy Square, W.*

Jan. 16th [1909]

Dearest Ottoline,[1]

What a pleasure to get your letter! It made me very happy. Thank you for writing. If you will have me for a friend, it will be a great joy for me. Shyness, I suppose, makes it difficult to say that it is delightful to know you and like you as I do. I wish I could tell you how much pleasure your letter gave me.

                                        Your affectionate,
Texas   V.S.

469: To Lytton Strachey   29 *Fitzroy Square, W.*

Thursday [28 January 1909]

Here are the papers.[2] I hope you will see the whole thing—I can't say I do at this moment. Caroline is the most alive to me, with her dead husband Sir Julius, who wore a white slip beneath his waistcoat I imagine, and waxed his moustache. Nessa and Humphry Maitland are discharging their views already. I think you ought to begin at once.

Oh what a day! It clings to the fingers and creeps beneath the nails: Why do you tantalise me with stories of your novel?[3] I wish you would confine your genius to one department, it's too bad to have you dancing like some (oh well—I'll drop the metaphor) over all departments of literature —poetry, criticism (both scientific & humane) art—belles lettres—and now fiction. A painstaking woman who wishes to treat of life as she finds it, and to give voice to some of the perplexities of her sex, in plain English, has no chance at all.

My glove was a disreputable object.[4]

Here I sit, waiting for Adrian and Saxon to stagger in from the opera, and bury their noses in a pie. Life surely should mean more than this. And yet, it all seems very reasonable. I will ask Saxon.

                                        Yrs.
Frances Hooper   VS

1. Virginia had first met Lady Ottoline Morrell late in 1908.
2. This was a short-lived experiment in creating a 'novel' by an imaginary correspondence, in which each person adopted a fictional character. Caroline (Lady Eastnor) was Lady Ottoline Morrell, Sir Julius was Philip Morrell, Humphry Maitland was Walter Lamb. Virginia took the name of Eleanor Hadyng, and Lytton of Vane Hatherly.
3. Lytton may have been contemplating a political novel, but none was published, and the whole idea may have been a fantasy by which Virginia was temporarily taken in.
4. Virginia had left it behind in Lytton's house in Hampstead.

Feb. 1st [1909]

Dear Mr Hatherly,

I shall be happy to give you tea tomorrow. If there's one thing a Yorkshire woman can cook, it's a muffin.

I missed you by 10 minutes at the Philips'[1] the other day.

So you've noticed it then? How clever you are, and how unkind! For don't you think that these "extraordinary conclusions"[2] you like so much may be rather uncomfortable for me and perhaps (though I really won't admit it) a little uncomfortable for Clarissa? We were not happy—no—and yet I know its dangerous to imagine people in love with one, and so I told myself all the time. But James is really—sometimes a woman feels so much older than a man. There! that's worthy of Lady Eastnor [Ottoline]. I am thinking of his face, as he helped me on with my cloak, and said good night. I don't admit for a moment that you have any real ground for your "extraordinary conclusions", and I suppose I should do better to say no more about them. You always tempt me to run on, and justify myself and explain myself, with your hints and subtleties and suggestive catlike ways. Could you come early tomorrow—by the bye? Mr Ilchester [Saxon] has sent me a ticket for the Wagner opera—what d'you call it—and I don't want to miss the overture.

Your very sincerely,

Frances Hooper   Eleanor Hadyng

Sunday [7? February 1909]

My dear Clive,

You are really angelic to take so much pains to give reasons and advice.[3] They seem to me excellent; for you have laid your finger on spots already suspected by me. I will only offer some explanation of the wretched first volume. Those bare passages of biography were not meant to remain in the text. They are notes to solidify my own conception of the peoples characters. I thought it a good plan to write them down; but having served their purpose, they shall go. Helen's letter also was an experiment. When I read the thing over (one very grey evening) I thought it so flat and monotonous that I

1. James and Clarissa Philips, in the letter-game, were Clive and Vanessa.
2. Lytton (Mr Hatherly) suspected a love affair between Virginia and Clive, and was able to voice his suspicions more frankly through the medium of the letter-game and its pseudonyms.
3. Clive's criticism of the further chapters of *Melymbrosia* (*The Voyage Out*) which Virginia had sent him is printed by Quentin Bell, Vol. I, Appendix D.

did not even feel 'the atmosphere': certainly there was no character in it. Next morning I proceeded to slash and rewrite, in the hope of animating it; and (as I suspect for I have not re-read it) destroyed the one virtue it had—a kind of continuity; for I wrote it originally in a dream like state, which was at any rate, unbroken. My intention now is to write straight on, and finish the book; and then, if that day ever comes, to catch if possible the first imagination and go over the beginning again with broad touches, keeping much of the original draft, and trying to deepen the atmosphere—Giving the feel of running water, and not much else. I have kept all the pages I cut out; so the thing can be reconstructed precisely as it was. Your objection, that my prejudice against men makes me didactic 'not to say priggish', has not quite the same force with me; I dont remember what I said that suggests the remark; I daresay it came out without my knowledge, but I will bear it in mind. I never meant to preach, and agree that like God, one shouldn't. Possibly, for psychological reasons which seem to me very interesting, a man, in the present state of the world, is not a very good judge of his sex; and a 'creation' may seem to him 'didactic'. I admit the justice of your hint that sometimes I have had an inkling of the way the book might be written by other people. It is very difficult to fight against it; as difficult as to ignore the opinion of one's probable readers—I think I gather courage as I go on. The only possible reason for writing down all this, is that it represents roughly a view of one's own. My boldness terrifies me. I feel I have so few of the gifts that make novels amusing.

I expect your praise is immensely exaggerated: you (I guess) have so much more of the dramatic instinct than I have that you see it into my scenes. But I take praise very gratefully; long for some assurance that all my words aren't vapour. They accumulate behind one in such masses—dreadful, if they are nothing but muddy water. I think myself that the last part is really the best; at least I have written it with far greater relish, and with the sense of having the thing before me. What vanity these sheets will seem, one of these days, when Melymbrosia is a dusty book on your shelves, which Julian tries to read, but cant! However, there are numbers of things that I should be interested to say about the book; and we need not always be thinking of posterity. I too write in haste, just before dressing to go out. I will only add here I have blind faith in my power of making sentences presentable, so that I leave bald patches gaily, to furbish up next winter.

I was a little afraid that you would accuse me of compromise; but I was also quite sure that, made as I am, that sequel was the only one possible. I want to bring out a stir of live men and women, against a background. I think I am quite right to attempt it, but it is immensely difficult to do. Ah, how you encourage me! It makes all the difference. Are you really interested? I suppose so, since you say it; but you have no notion how pale and transparent it reads to me sometimes—though I write with heat enough. That will do, for one evening!

I have also a number of things to say of your Peacocks, but doubt that you care much to hear them. They are not merely polite; they are questions, for the most part, that I should like to ask you. If I can be interested in Miss Warmington (a delightful woman) why cant I be interested in you? After all, you have a point of view. I will suggest no more, at present, as Nessa says you are depressed, and my talk might drive you mad. Praise too, I suppose you dont care about.

You said something about Clarissa [Vanessa]; if you meant seriously that you wished me to go away with her I am very willing. I am sure a few days away would be an excellent thing; 10 days in bed must leave a weakness in the joints. However, she seems very truculent.

Yr. aff^{ate},

VS

Quentin Bell

472: To Lytton Strachey   29 *Fitzroy Square, W.*

[9 February 1909]

I shall be in to tea tomorrow.

We are just back half dazed from the opera—six solid hours of it— and if it were properly edited one might get through in 30 minutes.

VS

I laid out 6d upon the Spectator and was rewarded—only it means I must read another book now.[1]

Frances Hooper

473: To Lytton Strachey   29 *Fitzroy Square, W.*

[16 February 1909]

Dear Lytton,

Thank you for the shilling—I believe it was only sixpence though— so one day I will give you six coppers. I am sorry you have a cold—you would have died at Oxford. Our marrow was frozen, and our spirit chilled to death. There was [K.L.][2]—a weak man, I am glad to find, though plausible, and Humphrey Paul[3]—and endless others.

1. Lytton's review of *Hudibras* had appeared on 6 February in the *Spectator*.
2. Initials inserted by Leonard Woolf and James Strachey in their edition of the L.S.–V.W. correspondence (1956). This letter was not microfilmed with the others, and the original is not available for inspection. 'K.L.' was possibly H. A. L. Fisher.
3. Son of the historian and politician, Herbert Woodfield Paul.

Herbert [Fisher] gave voice to one profound remark—"G. L. Strachey must be related to Sir Frederick Pollock".[1]

Yr.

VS

Frances Hooper

474: To Clive Bell   *29 Fitzroy Square, W.*

Feb. 19th [1909]

My dear James [Philips],

I ought to have written before, and you must lay the blame on Mrs Harley Sebright [H. A. L. Fisher] that I didn't. I took pen and paper to Oxford and calculated upon one of those warm confidential hours, when one has slipped one's silk dress off, and huddled one's dressing gown on, when the fire blazes, and all the brilliant talk is over. No wonder that this hour has been dedicated by generations of women to the prosecution of their friendships. The intimate, emotional, and (it must be confessed) often irrational, though entirely delightful nature of their relationships is to be fixed on it. One cant write epigrams, or talk politics or housekeeping in one's dressing gown, with the hair about one's shoulders; one cant part without a kiss.

These reflections are superfluous though, seeing that I had no fire, no conversation and no friend. I couldn't even write you a letter.

The Sebrights have a new red villa, standing in its own grounds. Cabbages tap at the dining room windows; great white fowls run across the lawn. I wonder how many conversations that room has heard about hen keeping and vegetable produce—how often Mr Sebright has said to the lady next him 'We never buy an egg', and Mrs Sebright has flushed with pleasure and called across to him 'Next year we shall have our own potatoes' You can imagine how the talk goes after that. This is the groundwork of the establishment, but the rarest culture flowers on top of it. There were Regius Professors at dinner, and undergraduates who had won prizes without number, and were consequently unable to talk—as though they sucked their prizes, as babies suck their corals. Why is it that women of 18 and young men of 21 have less to say to each other than any other of God's creatures? They terrify me; I know, as I have sometimes been terrified by the critical gaze of your son Peter [Julian], who cant talk yet, and is so innocent.

The poor woman has no children, and therefore all the matrons are very tolerant of her cats. I was scratched, but Lady M said to me, in such a voice

1. On the next day, 17 February, Lytton proposed to Virginia, who accepted him. Both immediately realised their mistake, and the matter was not carried any further.

'That is Molly's [Lettice] favourite puss' that I couldn't complain. Her chickens, her cabbages, and her philanthropy are humoured for the same reason. Mr Sebright is an excellent specimen—really, I dont mean to sneer, the one fault is that he *is* a specimen—He is like a bunch of perfect blossoms, or a basket of picked strawberries; and for my part I like the varieties better. If you were to take the normal Englishman of culture and put him under a magnifying glass you would have Harley Sebright.

I should like to turn Oxford into a Cathedral city and people it with Deans and widow ladies. The profession of learning should be carried on in a manufacturing town. Perhaps in your 18th century they managed things better, I detest the modern way of it. I detest pale scholars with their questioning about life, and the message of the classics, and the bearing of Greek thought upon modern problems. [Richard] Porson was always drunk; [Richard] Bentley was notorious—for something disreputable; and the only true scholar I ever knew ended his days in a madhouse. My week, on the whole, has been rather a busy one. I dined with my publisher [Bruce Richmond], and felt like a cannibal because the dinner was so good, and I knew what went to make it—the blood of respectable young men and women like myself and my neighbour. I am afraid that one cant believe nowadays in starving genius, frozen in a garret.

We were a dreadful set of harpies; Middle aged writers of mild distinction are singularly unpleasant to my taste. They remind me of those bald-necked vultures at the zoo, with their drooping blood-shot eyes, who are always on the look out for a lump of raw meat. You should have heard the chattering and squabbling that went on among them, and the soft complacent coo of those that had been fed. That great goose Lady G[regory?] was the loudest in her squawking; the rest of us sat round and twittered, half in envy and half in derision.

For some reason I am tormented this morning by the image of a great brown woolly bear, which comes crawling across my page, and curls up into a ball when I touch it with my pen[1]. It is deliciously soft, and rolls about in the palm of my hand. I think it has something to do with Clarissa [Vanessa]. We used to be told when we were children that woolly bears could sting. I must now change my tone, and write to the consumptive daughter of a literary Duchess.[2] How little letters say!

Yours ever,
Eleanor Hadyng

Quentin Bell

1. A caterpillar, possibly of the Tiger Moth.
2. Lady Gwendolyn Godolphin Osborne, daughter of the Duchess of Leeds, or even a wholly fictitious character in the letter-game.

Thursday [11 March 1909]

My dear Ottoline,

Adrian and I shall come if possible—if we dont have to see an Aunt [Caroline Emelia] who is very melancholy about our morals—with great pleasure on Sunday. We were so dirty and ill-tempered on Tuesday, after travelling all day[1], that we thought we should disgrace your drawing room. You would have had to take us into corners, and draw screens round us. But however dirty you may be tonight, we insist upon your coming to us.

Although there wasn't a bath, we were very happy in Cornwall. I wish one could manage so that Bloomsbury was on the sea shore; and all your company sat among sandhills. Think of Eddie Marsh smoothing down the bristles for all his ladies! Then one could roll occasionally, which would be such an advantage.

> Your aff.ate,
> V.S.

Texas

[mid-March 1909]

My Violet,

I was beginning to wonder whether some saying, blasphemous and obscene, overheard in the underground, in which your name occurred, had been repeated to you by—God knows who—Ella Crum—who is never guilty of indiscretion besides—is out of London. Adrian has been in bed with a bad cold, and is now tolerably recovered. The Quaker is very bad. She has to have a nurse, and I cant understand what's the matter, but I think it sounds rather serious. I saw her two weeks ago, we were to have stayed this week, but she puts us off indefinitely. I cant have you to tea on Wednesday—because I am having a tea party that day, at which Beatrice is going to meet Lady Ottoline I hope. Could you come next Monday or Tuesday? I would try to get Nessa—but I dont know whether Julian could be brought too.

I have been writing—oh—a d——d dull review of a book by a woman who had a child before she married—Mrs Henry Cust[2]—and atones for it by studying mediaeval Germany profoundly. My review is going to deal with the subject of the illicit passions in a masterly way—and to suggest

1. From Cornwall, where Virginia had been staying with the Bells at the Lizard.
2. *Gentlemen Errant* (*TLS*, 15 April 1909).

better means of penitence. Then, I am going to write about the Carlyle love letters.[1] The Times, you see, gives me all the subtle and doubtful passions to discuss.

I would come and see you if you liked.

Yr. AVS

Berg

477: To Madge Vaughan   29 *Fitzroy Square, W.*

21st March [1909]

My dearest Madge,

I saw Emma the other day, and she says you are still at Bournemouth. I didn't know it; and I am so sorry. You have been having a very bad time, I am afraid[2]; I do hope you are happier now.

It is months and months since I heard from you or saw you. I think the only plan will be to set up a spare bed in the linen cupboard, and lock you in there when you are passing through.

Things seem to go on here much in the same way. As a matter of fact I suppose there are all kinds of changes, as life is certainly very exciting, but one would have to be a novelist to describe them. Oh how I wish I could write a novel! People and their passions, or even their lives without passions, are the things to write about. Have you finished your book? Anyhow, the stuff of infinite novels must be in you. Children seem to me so queer—so much that is definite in them from the first moment. Julian is a miracle; but I dont pretend to understand them. Nessa and Clive are going off to Italy after Easter; my plans are vague. I hope very much that somehow I may see you.

Dont write if you are busy; I shall hear about you from the Vaughans.
Give the children my love.
Your loving,

Sussex VS

478: To Violet Dickinson   29 *Fitzroy Square, W.*

[March 1909]

My Violet,

Thank you for sending the book.

Shall I come and see you again? I imagine that you are too busy.

---

1. *The Love Letters of Thomas Carlyle and Jane Welsh* (*TLS*, 1 April 1909).
2. This refers to the serious illness (smallpox or tuberculosis) of Barbara, Madge's third child.

Adrian and I think of taking a steamer in the middle of the night and landing at St Malo, as the First Cock rises to crow on Easter day. There is a night when the Bird of Dawning croweth all night long. I have been a craven, and left my gentleman[1] to go to his concert alone. He sent me a ticket for tonight.

The Quaker sounds very bad; but there is a great reticence in naming internal complaints, so I know nothing definite.

Well—I wish I ever saw you: a fine spirit, like some pale taper in a gale —Do you see yourself—flowing all night long—the flame streaming like a river.

VS

Berg

479: To Violet Dickinson   29 *Fitzroy Square, W.*

[9? April 1909]

My Violet,
The Quaker died on Wednesday night.[2] I heard this morning. I suppose it was much best that she should die—but it seems rather melancholy now. She was so remote, and yet full of life too.

We didn't go to St Malo after all: it suddenly occurred to us both that we could afford something more exciting. Adrian went off to Venice this morning. I shall wait till the 23rd and go to Florence, with Nessa, which will be divine.

How are you? Dont bother to write.

You were very exquisite the other night, and I suppose I was very egoistical.

Perhaps I shall see you again. Anyhow, I have your address.

Yr. AVS

Berg

480: To Lady Robert Cecil   29 *Fitzroy Square, W.*

Tuesday April 13th [Monday, 12 April 1909]

My dear Nelly,
When you wrote to me you did not think I should answer on a great sheet like this—however, it is very doubtful whether I shall finish it.

The effect of this ghastly [bank] holiday which leaves me alone in London, and shuts all the shops, and gives all the postmen a day off, is to make me turn to my friends. There should be threads floating in the air,

1. A stranger, who had sat near her at a concert, and sent her tickets for another.
2. Caroline Emelia Stephen died at Cambridge on 7 April 1909.

which would merely have to be taken hold of, in order to talk. You would walk about the world like a spider in the middle of a web. In 100 years time, I daresay these psychical people will have made all this apparent—now seen only by the eye of genius. As it is—how I hate writing!

Yesterday I met your friend Miss [May] Sinclair. I confess, I rather sympathised with you! She seemed to me a woman of obtrusive, and medicinal morality; and prodded it home with little round eyes bright as steel—talked very seriously of her 'work'; and ecstatic moods in which she swings (like a spider again) half way to Heaven, detached from earth. This was at Mrs Protheros.

My brother and I spent six hours the other day walking the streets of London, and trying to decide where we should spend Easter. This was on Good Friday Eve. At last, just as the clock struck 5, he bought a ticket for Venice, and started at day break; and I bought one for Florence. I am going with Vanessa and her husband in a weeks time. I believe there will be roses and wisterias hanging over yellow walls, and their golden river—immense bare hills all round, and little pink villas scattered like egg shells about them. I never get used to the bareness of Italy, the grass is so mangy. Oh how I should like to—discover how to write!

Now Swinburne is dead, Meredith dumb, and Henry James inarticulate, things are in a bad way. The Cornhill seems to me singularly dull; Nelly wont publish her novel; and Virginia Stephen knows nothing about humanity. I have been writing an obituary all the morning of an Aunt who died. She was a quaker and this article is written for the Guardian. If one could only say what one thinks, some good might come of it; but I can't see the need for respectful lamentations. When you die, I shall tell the truth about you. It would be a very interesting article—something like a Japanese watercolour, with an angular ivory face. I wish I could understand where the puritan strain comes in: the Lambtons[1] were jolly country squires, weren't they? with curious manners at table.

I saw Violet the other day. She was just going to take to her bed, at a friend's house. She looked very tired; and then there was Ozzy. Do you think his manner is a disease?

Do write to me or come and have tea. My drawing room mourns, like the sea, in flowing purple. It is new since you were here; as for my sitting room, there are great pyramids of books, with trailing mists between them; partly dust, and partly cigarette smoke.

I hope yoù are well, and fond of me.

Yr. aff.

VS

Hatfield

1. The family name of the Earls of Durham. Nelly Cecil was the daughter of the 2nd Earl.

Tuesday [13 April 1909]

My dear Clive,

Your first letter was so delightful, and so unexpected that it should have had an answer directly. Why should I excite you? Why should you be glad to hear that I and my bundle of tempers come with you to Italy? Ah, how pleasant a world, where such facts do exist! how exquisite that you should recognise them. When I have melted down the whole of my illusions, one or two things remain, bright as gold, or diamond. One is—well, that you care for me, and that we are likely to spend many years in the same neighbourhood. I have spent such a sepulchral day! Where am I to begin, in describing it? First, as to the [Quaker's] Will. It is very disappointing. Nessa and Adrian each have £100: I have £2,500. The rest goes in legacies, to the other Stephens. Katharine [Stephen] has about £3,000—including the Porch and the Public House—It is miserable for Nessa; still worse for Adrian; I am determined to make him share mine—but there's no need to talk of that act of feminine weakness.

George came here, and we went to Golders Green [Crematorium], in profuse, watery rain. He is almost circular with flesh, soft as a babies, infinitely respectable, and more clearly in the wrong than I ever saw him— full of solicitude about Aunt Stephens health, and slipping in phrases used by the Archbishop of Canterbury—a very good humoured philanthropic creature, but, I thought, a mere lump of flesh, veined with sentiment. There were perhaps six people in the Chapel; two of whom, Albert [Venn] Dicey and Alice the maid, wept audibly; Sir Herbert [Stephen] was there, upright as a dragoon, and Dorothea [Stephen] in a pork pie hat. I was much puzzled by the burial service; but the whole ceremony was very thin and prosaic—it ended by my having Dorothea, Leah [servant], and Alice to lunch. George considerately hinted that it was the proper thing to do.

I have spent the afternoon hearing curious medical details and superstitions—how the last time Nun stood up was to watch Ruby's [dog] funeral— how she read a particular hymn on a particular morning—Oh and loathsome details without end from Leah and Dorothea—and then Albert Dicey came to tea, and I have just packed them all off in a fourwheeler. A bonfire in the back garden would have done equally well. We might have danced round it.

As for Lytton, I haven't seen him; feeling out of the mood at present, and I suppose he thinks I went to France. Do you see that R. K. Gaye has been found shot? Killed himself, I suppose.[1] I wonder why.

I hear that Miss Una Birch thinks you the most fascinating man she ever met. This is not to repay your compliments.

---

1. It was later confirmed that he had committed suicide. He was a tutor in Classics at Trinity.

Oh, you should see my Obituary![1] It is a pity to curtail a pen which floats and flies to the step of a funeral horse, with a tight black tail—but it had to be.

I wish I could write on; but I want this to catch the country post. I shall dine with you tomorrow. Kiss my Dol—phin.

Yr. VS

Quentin Bell

482: TO VIOLET DICKINSON   29 *Fitzroy Square, W.*

[13 April 1909]

My Violet,

I was sorry I couldn't come the other day. Will you ask me—or tell Miss Dodge to ask me—(not necessarily to a meat meal) sometime before the 23rd. Unless you ought to see no one.[2]

I have been attending the Quakers cremation today; a dreary business. Leah came home to lunch, and Dorothea; they wept and told curious anecdotes all the afternoon, and at one point Leah and I fell on each others necks—an experience never to be repeated, I suppose. There was something very gloomy in the picture of dying alone with Leah to sustain one. "She called me Bearkin" said Leah.

Look out in the Times for an article upon the opera. I had a visit from Bruce Richmond the other day. We had a strange tea party, and talked shop. I hope to write an occasional essay.

Take care of yourself.

Yr. VS

Berg

483: TO VIOLET DICKINSON   29 *Fitzroy Square, W.*

[15? April 1909]

My Violet,

I cant dine, but might I come to tea tomorrow? 5.

Please dont dwell upon my exaggerated account of love; as a matter of fact I am a woman with very little sexual charm. Warming to the task, I often represent myself as irresistible.

The ashes do go to a Quaker cemetery. It was very chill at Golders Green. I have been describing her—in the Guardian!

Yr. VS

Berg

1. Virginia's obituary of the Quaker was published in *The Guardian* on 21 April 1909.
2. Violet was ill at Miss Dodge's house.

484: TO CLIVE BELL   29 *Fitzroy Square, W.*

[April 1909]

My dear Clive,

Friday would be best, and very charming, I need not say. Old Case comes on Monday. Perhaps we shall meet at the Freshfields music tonight. We have endless documents to sign on your behalf.[1] I hope you are touching a large amount of capital.

Yr. AVS

Quentin Bell

485: TO MADGE VAUGHAN   *Hotel Manin, Milan*

[8 May 1909]

Dearest Madge,

I meant to write from Florence, but now I am on my way back, spending a few hours at Milan. (This pen is impossible). I hope you are happy again about the children. We spent a fortnight in Florence, and Nessa and Clive are staying on till the end of the month. We had a tremendous tea party one day with Mrs Ross.[2] She was inclined to be fierce, until we explained that we knew you, when she at once knew all about us—our grandparents and great uncles on both sides. She certainly looks remarkable, and had type written manuscripts scattered about the room. I suppose she writes books. There were numbers of weak young men, and old ladies kept arriving in four wheelers; she sent them out to look at her garden. Is she a great friend of yours? I imagine she has had a past—but old ladies, when they are distinguished, become so imperious. Lina Waterfield[3] also came in for a moment, but I hardly spoke to her. She has beautiful eyes. The garden; though it rained, was wonderful; I could fancy you wandering about it, and eating un-ripe oranges. Florence was lovely—more lovely than seems possible. We used to wander about along the river at all hours; or sit and bask on the hills. We talked a great deal—such talk as you and I might have in the small hours. I wish that ever did happen now.

I must now try to find my way to the station, and then discover the right train. I know not a word of Italian, and seldom go right even in England, so that this letter is something like a farewell. Last night I sat up with a party of nuns; who looked extremely contented and aloof, but would

1. Possibly the legacies from Caroline Emelia Stephen, or Vanessa's marriage settlement.
2. Janet Ross (1842-1927), the author of several books about Italy, particularly the arts of Florence, where she had lived since 1867.
3. Caroline Lucie Waterfield, formerly Duff Gordon, who lived at Aulla, north Italy, and had collaborated with Madge Vaughan on *The Story of Perugia* (1898).

393

not stop whispering—whether about their souls or their neighbours I dont know. The Italians are a charming people—I dont see how they can help it, with so much air, and so few slums.

Do write, if you ever have time; but I shall hear of you from Marny. Give all your children my love. Elsie[1] often talks of them.

Yr. loving,

VS

Sussex

486: To Violet Dickinson   29 *Fitzroy Square, W.*

Thursday [13? May 1909]

My Violet,

Why dont you write to me? I might be buried in Messina, or bugeaten in Florence, or vanished, or prostitute, or in love, or pregnant, and you would not know or care. It is always the part of the older woman to write. However, I feel amazingly old. What have you been doing? How are you? Last time we met was in that sumptuous Jewesses [Miss Schreiner] room, when everything was like an illusion. Do you remember that curious episode on the empire sofa, when she played Brahms or Schumann to us, and all her boots?

We had a very lazy time in Florence. There were squalls at the street corner—squalls of weather I mean. We saw Rezia [Corsini][2] and Mrs Ross; and they both disappointed me. It is very difficult to take up a friendship again. I am now writing about Mrs Carlyle; wish you would write and encourage me. Every other night, I look into the middle box on the pit tier, and see Beatrice [Thynne], black and red, resting an imperious fist on the ledge. She looks as though she were ruling modern society; like a Roman Empress, with a drop of hot Tartar blood.

I often think of you; twice shot through Welwyn lately, and seen your yellow road. Can I do anything for you? as Aunt Mary would say.

Ottoline is slowly growing rather fond of me. It is like sitting beneath an Arum lily; with a thick golden bar in the middle, dropping pollen, or whatever that is which seduces the male bee.

Nessa has a picture in the New English [Art Club], and all her friends are envious.

Do write, my Violet. You would scarcely believe how fond I am of you. How are you?

Yr. Sp.

Berg

1. Possibly an ex-domestic of Madge, passed on to Virginia.
2. Lucrezia Rasponi had married Filippo Corsini in 1901.

[May 1909]

Dearest Madge,

I was very glad to get your letter. I wish you sounded happier about Barbara. Lady Cromer's little boy[1] has just had the same operation, and is getting on well. I wish we could take a house near you this summer. Adrian and I are going to Bayreuth in August, but I shall come back before the end. I should very much like to come up sometime—about then. I could always get rooms with my friend Mrs Turner, if it were convenient. Nessa has to spend some weeks with her family in law; and I expect they will stay down in the West. I sat next Walter Leaf[2] at dinner the other night; but he would not tell me much about you. They seemed to me a middle aged pair. We go to a few dinner parties; they are very solemn, and as unlike life as can be. I think you get the better of us there. Do you remember the Miss Perfects tea party? Then we have people here on Thursdays, and go to innumerable operas. We have just got to know a wonderful Lady Ottoline Morrell, who has the head of a Medusa; but she is very simple and innocent in spite of it, and worships the arts. I gave your message to Elsie. She seems very happy, and always talks about you and the children. It would be much nicer to talk to you than to write to you. I want to get Barbara a toy; or whatever she likes. Do send me one line on a card to say. Julian is fascinating.

                                                                    Yr. VS

Sussex

Tuesday [18 May 1909]

Beloved,

This is the last letter, thank God, written to the tune of the pianola. You haven't written today—The Singes [Virginia herself] in consequence are all hooting and copulating. When I was in my bath this morning Maud [maid] came and rattled, and said that Mrs [Madge] Vaughan was in my bedroom. I went down, and found that she had rushed up to London last night, hearing that Barbara was worse, and was on her way to the station. I dressed, and we had a long conversation. She was in a wild state, as you can imagine. She seemed to think that Barbara was dying, and that it was the doctors fault, or hers for having a new nurse. It was mixed up with rhapsodies about fate, and God, and religion: she made swoops all the time, in her usual way, to explain things—and lay down the law. I think it has been ghastly. But I found it hard to say anything. Her mind goes off at such

1. Evelyn Baring (later Lord Howick), b. 1903.
2. Married to Madge's sister Charlotte.

a tangent. She picked up a novel of Aunt Annys [Ritchie], and insisted upon my reading the first paragraph. "It *is* true—whatever you may say." As it was a mild disquisition upon a spinsters old age, I couldn't see the force of it. All the old torments about Emma [Vaughan]. "I who only thinks of the cost of bananas and Lady Somers tea parties" and Marny, and Will's stoicism came up. She said she was certain the Vaughans were scrofulous "one has only to look at Marny's face."; whereas the doctors said that the Symonds were consumptive.

She is like an excitable child, working itself into a passion. I think there is something very loveable about her in spite of her incoherencies.

The unfortunate child [Barbara], anyhow, has been so scarred that her looks will be spoilt for life.

I went round to Gordon Square yesterday, and saw your cook; who wished me to tell you that Gurth is in excellent health. We have accepted the Frankfurts and rejected the Creightons for next Sunday; so you will be free of me till Monday afternoon probably.

You may not know that George Meredith is dead[1]: how I wish the Quarterly would ask me to explain him, once and for all! Adrian thinks of pointing out that 1909 is as disastrous as 1809 was prolific—

We are now going to hear a play by Somerset Maugham, as Armide has been put off.[2] You will have it next week, I suppose.

I hear the bell!

Beloved, I adore you, more than I can say.

Yr. B.

Berg

489: To John Maynard Keynes   29 *Fitzroy Square, W.*

[May 1909?][3]

Dear Mr Keynes,

Will you dine with me next Thursday—the 27th. at 8. I hope you may be in London.

Yours sincerely,
Virginia Stephen

King's

1. Meredith had died that day, 18 May 1909.
2. The Maugham play was *The Explorer*, showing at the Lyric. *Armide*, the opera by Gluck, had been running at Covent Garden.
3. This date is given with some reservation. Virginia had known Maynard Keynes since at least 1907, but not well. In 1909 Thursday falls on the 27th only in May, but the letter might have been written in February 1908. After 1909, Virginia's friendship with Keynes grew so rapidly that she would not have addressed him so formally.

490: To Violet Dickinson

29 *Fitzroy Square, W.*

[May? 1909]

My Violet,

Do come to tea on Wednesday.

We are just going to the funeral of Madges child [Barbara]—a melancholy thing to do.

Yr. VS

Berg

491: To Lady Robert Cecil

29 *Fitzroy Square*

Sunday [30 May 1909]

My dear Nelly,

I am abominable to sit in silence all this time when you were so kind as to write to me, and praise me (which I loved). I want to know too, why I am a strange woman; and now, to punish me, I daresay you won't explain. I shall come up one evening, and take possession of your arm chair and sit there till you give me a reason for your remarks.

I have been staying with the Freshfields. I have been writing, like a Bank Clerk, and I don't think that I have any news whatever. So what does one write letters about? You know, I imagine. But then you live in the world. You have a garden too, with trees against the sky, and a bonfire in the middle distance. I could make an exquisite story out of you—so don't imagine that all the insight is on your side. I can imagine you, from the moment you wake in the morning till you go to bed again, without leaving my chair.

I am going to see Violet tomorrow. These accidents, I believe, are in the nature of spiritual retreats; she has much of the mystic in her, and she gets no time for it when she's up. I hear she looks very well, and is very cheerful—so that I am probably right.

What are you writing? Why don't you ever take a great sheet (like this one) and scribble on your knee (as I am doing) and send it to me? I do nothing but read Mrs Carlyle and Thomas Hardy; about whom I am going to write perhaps—only not in the same article. I am also promoted to dine with Reginald; and to have the Brontë manuscripts shown me.[1]

Yours affly,

VS

Hatfield

---

1. Reginald Smith, editor of the *Cornhill*, was the son-in-law of George Smith of Smith, Elder & Co, the publishers of the Brontë novels.

June 4th [1909]

Dear Lytton,

I hear that we missed you at Cambridge the other day. We had an exquisite vision of the place. There was a wonderful young man in a shooting jacket and black trousers, with the head of a Faun—who was he? I daresay you know.

The whirl of the London season is upon us. We are entertaining Jack Pollock. Lady Ottoline. I am penetrating into the most mysterious places. There is a Jewess who spends 50 guineas on a hat, and wishes to meet me, not that we may exchange views on that subject, I imagine. We see her at the opera, where she displays a wonderful arm upon the ledge of her box. Then, upstairs we meet Charlie Sanger, and Saxon and the great Mr Loeb[1] who has the finest collection of operatic photographs and autographs in Europe. Saxon—however that subject is beaten red. We are taking him to a Fancy Dress Ball, he is appearing in the character of Gunnar.

I am absorbed in Michelet.[2] Is it really a vile book? It is thus that I should write the history of the Restoration if I were a man.

We stayed with the Freshfields a week ago. Nature and art did their best; it was sumptuous; but they were like wax-works, slightly running in the sun, except for Gussie [Mrs Douglas Freshfield], who has the spirit of a Roman Empress. I daresay she is a hard woman. We sat in a little summer house and discussed the immortality of the soul, and mid-Victorian scandal. I never saw anything so remote as she and poor Douglas. He seems to have stiffened all over, and is now practically jointless. This is only by way of conversation; and you must not answer, if writing is a bore, as I daresay it is.

Heaven knows what address I am to put.

Yours ever,

Frances Hooper   VS

6th June 09

My dear Nelly,

The other day I was sitting on that superb terrace and overlooking your woods. However, they said you were away. I talked a great deal about you, and pretended to have an insight into your heart which the Almighty might envy. Your praises were sounded, and from the hoards of my knowledge

1. James Loeb (1867–1933), the American banker, who founded the Institute of Musical Art in New York and the Loeb Classical Library.
2. Jules Michelet, the 19th-century French historian; perhaps his *Histoire de France*.

I added a piercing note. This went on in a very hot little summer house, I having been excused lawn tennis on the ground of general incompetency. It is dreadful to come down to breakfast with great coils of hair, sticking feebly with pins, touching ones shoulders. How do young women manage? They were very kind and said nothing, but over their fires at night—oh I tremble to think of it!

Italy was really beyond words—even a trifle melodramatic—not unlike a Meredith novel—too brilliant to be quite natural. This refers to the sight of Florence in sunset from the hills above. There were gruff old ladies in villas, with whom we had tea. I find England far more mysterious. Your Sussex really overcomes one—with laughter sometimes. It is a little ridiculous. All the cocks crowing, and the cottage gardens and Priests touching their hats to us.

I almost went to see the British horses yesterday with Violet. But every ticket was sold—it would have been a sight, and Violet's knowledge of horseflesh is profound I expect. Besides, she would have known half the country squires. There is something very racy about her.

If I knew where you were, I should write a more coherent letter; but it is like shooting into the air. I wish you would write to me. How are you— what are you about?

Your affate,

Hatfield

VS

494: TO LYTTON STRACHEY   29 *Fitzroy Square, W.*

Friday [25 June 1909]

Dear Lytton,

Why don't you come and see me—or am I a brazen hussy to ask you— however I'll risk it. I shall be in today, or Tuesday for tea, and it would be charming to see you.

Society is very hollow. I am going to write about Sterne[1]. Would [you] lend me a book called the Princesse de Cleves?[2] The L.L. [London Library] has lost it.

Yours ever,

VS

Such a night last night—[Francis] Dodd feeling compelled, as a Blacksmith's grandson,[3] to tell Lady Ottoline that he was—constipated!

Frances Hooper

1. Review of *The Life and Times of Laurence Sterne*, by Wilbur L. Cross (*TLS*, 12 August 1909).
2. By Madame de la Fayette (1678).
3. Dodd was in fact the son of a Wesleyan minister who had once been a blacksmith.

[early July 1909]

My Violet,

I go to Cambridge on the 10th—and both Thursday and Friday are taken up with opera.

Couldn't I come one day by that train which gets in after lunch, and then I can go back in time for dinner, or bed.

My head spins with Vernon Lee, whom I have to review.[1] What a woman! Like a garrulous baby. However, I suppose she has a sense of beauty, in a vague way—but such a watery mind.

Thank you for asking me!

           Yr. VS

Berg

496: To Violet Dickinson   29 *Fitzroy Square, W.*

[July 1909]

My Violet,

If you could have me another day next week, it would be easier—as I only come up from Cambridge on Monday morning, and we are going to the opera in the evening. I am free most days; but if Monday is your only day, we had much better stick to it.

I have a good deal of work to do—and cant do it!

You are an absurd woman to pretend that you think I *hate* coming.

I am probably fonder of you than most people are. My nature is so pure. Let me have a line.

           VS

Berg

497: To Violet Dickinson   29 *Fitzroy Square, W.*

[July 1909]

My Violet,

This is not a Collins (though I enjoyed myself very much)—but to ask if there is any chance that the cottage you had in Cornwall would be to let for a month from Sept: 10th? Nessa thinks Cornwall wd. be much nicer than Northumberland.

They want 5 bedrooms, and to be near a beach for Julian.

If you could give me the address of the man, I would write.

           Yr. VS

Berg

1. *Laurus Nobilis* (*TLS*, 5 August 1909).

Tuesday [July 1909]

My dear Clive,

Here is Marjorie Strachey[1] who wants to come and see me. Shall I be acting with my usual lack of consideration if I ask you to come on Thursday? A rare compliment is implied. Of course, I could have you both together; but what pleasure would that be?—mixing my champagne with ginger beer. And yet, as the poor woman is going North eternally, I hardly like to refuse; and if I have her to lunch, I must sacrifice those four volumes of Sterne. Thursday or Friday suit me. Then you shall hear how the fragment of a compliment has been paid me. You and Nessa would tread it under heel. If you come on Thursday you shall have the money I owe you; a manuscript, and the conversation of a charming young woman.

I am not really inconsiderate am I? If so, it is because love is blind.

How pretty!

VS

Quentin Bell

1. Lytton's younger sister.

Letters 499-515

In August 1909 Virginia went with Adrian and Saxon Sydney-Turner to Bayreuth, for the opera, and then to Dresden for more opera and pictures. Finding their company faintly uncongenial, perhaps because she failed to match their musical enthusiasm to the full, she consoled herself by writing letters to Vanessa which were among her most affectionate. She saw much of her sister in Dorset in late September, but at Christmas she took a sudden decision to go alone to Cornwall, which still meant more to her than any other place.

499: To Vanessa Bell   *Bayreuth*

Saturday [7 August 1909]

Beloved,

We arrived yesterday without adventure. Adrian did most of the management, but it seemed very simple.

The crossing was like floating down an Indian river; we lay and smoked for hours in the sun, and it was perfectly calm. Holland looked a very charming country. There was a fair going on and all the women wore great white caps, with gold balls over their ears. However, you know all about that.

Our lodgings here are much better than I expected. They are clean and bare, without carpets, and almost without ornaments. We have a little sitting room too. Our house is in a street of villas with small gardens, where the family spend their time, talking, and there is a kind of partition where the children play. There is a small boy of Julians age, who sits there alone, and makes sand heaps quite happily. We wandered about Bayreuth after we arrived. It is like an English market town—with a great many ironmongers, and a broad street with a fountain in the middle, and an 18th Century mayors house. Unfortunately the shops are full of cards and Holy Grails. The cards interest Saxon profoundly, as they show the singers in different parts, and thus lead to a good many comparisons. We are very minute in our ways already. We sat and watched the people in the park for an hour. My God, they are hideous! The women have a strap round their waists, a green hunting cap, with a feather, and short skirts. They are never fashionable. I dont cause any horror. We dined at the foreigners restaurant, and even there they are incredibly stout and garish. Every young woman, too, brings an old housekeeper, less smart than Sophie [Farrell], to look after her. They eat enormously, off great joints, covered with fat.

This is a very dull letter, but I haven't collected my wits yet. Saxon is very amiable, but almost stone dumb—or whatever the phrase is. He upset the ink at breakfast, and tried to clean his chair with the end of a handkerchief dipped in milk. It was like an ineffectual old cat. Then he cleaned a pair of scissors on a piece of bread. He says that he may have to spend some time at the dentist, as a stopping has come out. He slightly prefers travelling with his back to the engine. He is gentle, and full of consideration, and ineffective ways. Adrian grows a little tart with him.

Now we are going to read Parsifal, and then lunch, and then we shall hear the immortal work.

It is the hottest day we have had this summer. I suppose it is the same with you.

Yr. B.

Berg

500: To Vanessa Bell   *Bayreuth*

Sunday [8 August 1909]

Beloved,

No letter has yet come from you. I hope this heat has not turned you apoplectic: it is roasting like Hell here. We heard Parsifal yesterday—a very mysterious emotional work, unlike any of the others I thought. There is no love in it; it is more religious than anything. People dress in half mourning, and you are hissed if you try to clap. As the emotions are all abstract—I mean not between men and women—the effect is very much diffused; and peaceful on the whole. However, Saxon and Adrian say that it was not a good performance, and that I shant know anything about it until I have heard it 4 times. Between the acts, one goes and sits in a field, and watches a man hoeing turnips. The audience is very dowdy, and the look of the house is drab; one has hardly any room for ones knees, and it is very intense. I think earnest people only go—Germans for the most part, in sacks, with symbolical braid. Everything is new art—the restaurants have single lines drawn up the walls, with triangles suddenly bursting out—the kind of thing one sees in the Studio [the art magazine]. The grossness of the race is astonishing—but they seem very clean and kind. They suit Saxon very well. He thinks them so sensible.

So far, we have got on without more than a temporary tartness. Saxon cant decide anything—even what he wants to eat—but Adrian is very prompt and business like. I am haunted by the thought that I can never know what anyone is feeling, but I suppose at my age it cant be helped. It is like trying to jump my shadow.

We have been discussing obscure points in Parsifal all the morning. It seems to me weak vague stuff, with the usual enormities, but I can only read the German with great difficulty.

The time seems to go in preparing for the opera, listening to it, and discussing it afterwards—but tomorrow I must begin to write—you will laugh.

I left behind a good many necessary things, and brought impossible precautions.

I dreamt all night that I was arguing with you; and you showed a peculiar bright malice, which I sometimes see in you. I wish I had that picture of you.

How does Sophie do?

Give her my love.

Yr. B.

Berg

501: To VANESSA BELL   [*Bayreuth*]

Tuesday [10 August 1909]

Beloved,

I believe Saxon sent you a long and erudite letter this morning. He has been composing it at meal times, and humming it all day. Some of it 'rather pleased' him.

We have got into our stride, I think, and it is really rather an amusing life. I spend the morning writing, and the others go for a walk; we meet for lunch, and this afternoon, as it is an off day, we walked out to the Hermitage. This is a place built in imitation of Versailles; and it is all over-grown and deserted, with little French Temples, and ruins, and courtyards. Wherever one goes, one finds a garden set with tables, where monster men and women drink great jugs of beer and eat meat—although it is a blazing hot day. The weather tends to break up. The colours are very beautiful— yellow and leaden. We walked home through the fields. I dont much admire the country, because it is very florid and without shadow; and one feels wedged into the earth, with no sea anywhere. However the town is charming; most of it built in the 18th century; there are very wide streets, with solid grey houses, like Cambridge houses, only somehow rather rustic. Last night we walked about after dinner, and all the people were singing over their beer. As there was very little light, and a few people peeping out of windows, and virgins tripping by in cloaks, and a great yellow coach standing in the middle of the road, one might have been in the year 1750. Saxon is dormant all day, and rather peevish if you interrupt him. He hops along, before or behind, swinging his ugly stick, and humming, like a stridulous grasshopper. He reminds me a little of father. He clenches his fists, and scowls in the same way; and stops at once if you look at him. Adrian and I wink at each other, and get caught sometimes. About 11 o'clock at night, when we begin to yawn, he brightens up, and comes out with some very acute and rather acid question. We argued till 1.30 this morning. It was about something Adrian had said two or possibly three Thursdays ago, which Saxon had not under-

405

stood. He hoards things, like a dormouse. His mind is marvellously accurate, but I am rather surprised by his intellect. He sometimes seems quite fresh and about 26, and manly. I think he suspects that we think him obsolete, and wants to assert himself. I dont know what Adrian has told you, but I am surprised at our good temper, so far. We are rather austere, like monks and nuns, speak little, and—oh I long for you! There are bullocks here, with eyes like yours, and beautiful trembling nostrils.

Adrian has just brought me your letter, for which I thank God; I was fretting the drought. You are a tawny devil to talk of your letters being dull! My conclusion was that the way to get life into letters was to be interested in other people. You have an atmosphere. Ah! there's no doubt I love you better than anyone in the world! I dont think I am selfish about you. I wish you were out of London; and I am seriously alarmed to think that you contemplate another [baby] Bunting. Do wait another year, if you fill her veins with salt, she may take after her aunt; but a watered child would very likely be a true woman. I dont in the least mind your showing Clive my letters; because I dont make much difference between you; only they are dull. He mustn't criticise. As for 'genius', even I have done with that. Pernel [Strachey] thought Olive [Ilbert] a great bore, and rather disagreeable. The lodgings sound exactly right. Are you boiled alive?

B.

Would you keep me a copy of the [*Times*] supplement with my Sterne in it? It comes out on Thursday: also wd. you keep my Holmes[1] on the 26th. I paste them in a book.

Berg

502: To Vanessa Bell   *Bayreuth*

Thursday [12 August 1909]

Beloved,

I suppose you are toiling to God[manchester] in the heat. It is cooler here, though hot enough; and I dont see that I can get any sympathy in that way. A great bug stung me on the second joint of the third finger yesterday; it swelled at once to a bright red mound, and if I had been a married woman with a sentimental affection to removing the wedding ring, a blacksmith might have been needed. As it is, though still 'itching' (as Saxon says) I am comparatively calm. We heard Parsifal yesterday; it was much better done, and I felt within a space of tears. I expect it is the most remarkable of the operas; it slides from music to words almost imperceptibly. However, I have been

1. Review of *Oliver Wendell Holmes*, by Lewis W. Townsend (*TLS*, 26 August 1909).

niggling at the effect all the morning, without much success. It is very hard to write in ones bedroom, without any books to look at, or my especial rabbit path, into the next room. I have balanced my box on my commode, and made a shaky desk.

Saxon seems rather more shrivelled every day. I believe you would find him more trying to travel with than—the great B.[1] (which some interpret Bore). He is a dead weight. Nevertheless, we are all cool and pure. I always have to scribble to you after lunch, before changing for the opera. They make me read the libretto in German, which troubles me a good deal.

Is Sophie as dear as Mirtilla [servant]? I expect she is lazier.

I have had no news or letters, except yours last night. Aunt Stephen seems to me a good deal rubbed out. Do you like your portrait of Kate [Katharine Stephen]?

Oh my God, I must change now: it is very hot, and a great many fashionable women have arrived, who stare at me between the acts, and, as my head was washed yesterday, my hair is unusually free.

I haven't seen one German woman who has a face; they are puddings of red dough, and they dress in high art colours, with symbolical embroideries, rather like old Irish jewels, in their backs. I am beginning to make winter plans. Shall you kiss me ever? I cant imagine why Clive wants to read these letters; perhaps he dont! They are dull, but affectionate.

I adore you.

Yr. B.

Berg

503: To Vanessa Bell   *Bayreuth*

Monday [16 August 1909]

Beloved,

No letter today. As it is hotter than ever here, I'm afraid you may be burnt up, or possibly country letters take longer to come. I write in haste—this is no device, to excuse my dulness—but I am scrambling through my article, which has got into a fix, and the opera at 4 cuts the day short.

They dont do the thing as well as we do it, I think: our seats are very near, and the ugly creatures look still uglier. I can never quite get over the florid Teuton spirit, with its gross symbolism—and its flaxen tresses. Imagine a heroine in a nightgown, with a pig tail on each shoulder, and watery eyes ogling heaven. Saxon says nothing; Adrian prods him for an opinion. He reclines on his hip between the acts, and pulls at a weed. There is a great crowd, and we get stared at, not for our beauty. Yesterday, a lean woman

1. Billy Goat

with a face like a ferret bowed to me, and looked familiar, but I cant think who she is—a Coltman, or a Bonham Carter, perhaps. The Meinertzhagens run into us sometimes, but we dont meet other wise. Adrian seems quite indifferent, and so is she, as far as I can judge.

Saxon spent the morning writing a letter; I asked him who to?—and he said 'no one'. It has just occurred to him that he will send it to Clive. Last night he burst out into a very quick shrill sing song, in German: it meant come come come and be killed, Nicholas, my goose! He had made it up at dinner, he told us, which accounted for his absorption; Adrian and I talk to each other. He sneezes a great deal, like a dog, and he always says that he can see nothing funny in it.

These are the humours, sweet honeybee; writing seems to me a queer thing. It does make a difference. I should never talk to you like this. For one thing, I dont know what mood you are in, and then—but the subtleties are infinite. The truth is, I am always trying to get behind words; and they flop down upon me suddenly. When I write to Ottoline or Lytton, I honour all the conventions, and love them. And then, you are much simpler than I am. I thought about that at the opera last night. How do you manage to see only one thing at a time? Without any of those reflections that distract me so much, and make people call me bad names. I suppose you are, as Lytton once said, the most complete human being of us all; and your simplicity is really that you take in much more than I do, who intensify atoms. I have been thinking a great deal about father too, and discussing him with Adrian. I believe he was really very modest; he was certainly not selfconscious in his work; nor was he an egoist, as I am. He had very few sympathies though; and practically no imagination. You might give your view; this is much at random. God! how happy to be with you again! and then these letters will seem absurd. Do you want me too? It would be rather nice if I slipped in now? I have got a great many plans in my head.

Yr. B.

The Apes kiss you.

We go on Saturday to Dresden—address, c/o. Fraulein Meincke, Prager Strasse, 38. Dresden. A.

Berg

504: To Vanessa Bell   *Bayreuth*

Thursday [19 August 1909]

Beloved,

To my joy I had a letter from you this morning. I had made up my mind to some catastrophe, and suspected that Clives letter to Saxon was a tactful way of hinting that you were in bed with appendicitis, or nursing Julian through convulsions.

You will be glad to hear that I decided that if you died, my life would be worthless, and went on of course, to enjoy the picture. We spent a lazy day yesterday, indoors most of the time, as it rained, and there was no opera. We talked amicably, and kept ourselves quite happy. Saxon says he is feeling distinctly better, and he is almost sprightly. His conversation is still odd.

"What did you mean, Virginia, when you said, about three years ago, that your view of life was that of a Henry James novel, and mine of a George Meredith?." I had to invent a meaning, and he actually told me that he thought me a very clever young woman—which is the highest praise I have ever had from him.

Olives [Ilbert] letter was most irritating. She begins by saying that she fears she has offended me—but that I am so much above her etc. She goes on to make some arid jokes, and ends up with what I take to be pinprick—how she knows me better now than she did a year ago, and hopes I am not breaking hearts.

I cant think why she wants to keep in touch with me; her letter is full of hints, but I shall write—if I write—like a superb Elephant.

We certainly shant be back by the 28th. I begin to see that Adrian will stay in Dresden. Have you heard anything about Hyde Park Gate?[1]

We have got to have tea with old [Francis Warre] Cornish and the Meinertzhagens [daughters of Georgina and Daniel] this afternoon, between the acts. They seem to me like pink dish clothes, which have hung out all night in the rain. Adrian is brotherly to them—cuffs them with his paw like a big dog.

Did Sophie discover what happened to your milk?

I have been writing at Holmes all the morning; it keeps my temper very sweet. We have not quarelled once, and I believe we are rather more friendly than when we started. There is certainly something very attractive—not physically—about Saxon. His purity of mind is such. Also Adrian is for the most part, not only clever but even affectionate. For Gods sake, dont tell him so! This year has made a great difference in him—as Aunt Mary might say.

We are now going out to Lohengrin—a very dull opera, and this is, I expect, a damnably dull letter, but the quickest Ape brain always flags after dinner. It is thought that it is partly a recollection of struggle for food, when in a wild state. I should point out to you, that it is very dangerous to allow these animals to go long uncared for: they are apt to return to their savage ways. At present, I must confess, I never saw a more engaging troop: their

1. There was a plan for modernising Hyde Park Gate in order to let or sell it more advantageously.

fur is in excellent condition—teeth white, and lips inviting. They gibber if I only say 'Maria' [Vanessa] to them. I think you would be touched. No one kisses them here.

When do you go to Poole? Is there a house for me?

VS

Berg

505: To Vanessa Bell   [*Prager Strasse* 38] *Dresden*

Tuesday [24 August 1909]

Beloved,

There is no letter from you today, and Adrian curses you. However, I gather you are run off your feet; how ghastly to go on, after London, with a week of being nurse! I see no end to your toils. Moreover, you have twice as long to send as usual. What a world—what a world!

Saxon is happily better today; and he has made one or two remarks at meals to Fraulein Meinke. As they were lamenting the badness of servants, he said that the Athenian ladies 2,000 years ago, made the same complaint. They understood him to say 200, and old Meinke explained that she had read the Life of Johnson. Meanwhile, the Singer tells us how she has a contract for 5 years at the opera here lying on her table; but she cant make up her mind to sign it. The strain is such that the old mother has gone to bed with neuralgia. We have heard all the rights and wrongs of the case at least 10 times over. They like best to talk about food, and really know nothing about music. Muffins make them quite lyrical "with a whole pat of butter on top, for breakfast."

We went to Salome, (Strauss, as you may know) last night. I was much excited, and believe that it is a new discovery. He gets great emotion into his music, without any beauty. However, Saxon thought we were encroaching upon Wagner, and we had a long and rather acid discussion. He has an amazing knowledge of detail—I cant think why he doesn't say something more interesting. It is like reading a dictionary. We went to the pictures this morning. Saxon of course made straight for the Van Eyk; Adrian and I did the Italians. It is a very poor show; there are 4 good Veroneses, one genuine Titian—but they have scraped it to the bone—and the Rafaels. They are smooth works, beautiful in colour, but insipid. Saxon discovered a painter called Van Dreft[1]—who has one picture. It is very beautiful—Saxon says "painted with such tenderness". But we couldn't see the Dutch. This will bore you.

I got my Holmes article done in time, and sent it, so I didn't think I need write to Bruce Richmond.

1. It was Vermeer: see next letter.

A thoughtless bird has performed upon my straw hat. Surely there were thousands of hats that would have done, and women are so little able to cope with such disasters. I have also spilt the ink over my clean skirt—and, trying to make a dash with my combs, one fell, dragging the side locks with it.

Oh my beloved creature, how little use I am in the world! Selfish, vain, egoistical, and incompetent. Will you think out a training to make me less selfish? It is pathetic to see Adrian developing virtues, as my faults grow. He and Saxon discuss how to mend my plaquet hole.

I must start for the opera.

Yr. B.

Write me a nice letter; you are rather cold.

Berg

506: To Vanessa Bell   [*Prager Strasse* 38] *Dresden*

Wednesday [25 August 1909]

Beloved,

I am very glad you are going earlier to Studland [Dorset]. Do you think you could take me a bedroom and a sitting room there for a fortnight from the 16th—and say that I may want another bedroom part of the time? If I had the address I would write myself.

Adrian had a letter this morning from his clerk here to say that he sent him a brief to Fitzroy Square on the 13th. Waller[1] has written to ask why it has not been done. We have not heard anything about it. Did Sophie show it to you, or say she had a letter for Adrian? Probably she thought it not worth forwarding; and the idiotic clerk must have forgotten to say that it was to be sent on. Adrian is rather perturbed, naturally; as Waller will be annoyed. We have telegraphed to the clerk.

We went to the pictures again this morning, and discovered several Italians. Vermeer is the man I meant. I love it and Palma Vecchio's 3 Sisters. I have been talking to Saxon for 2 hours about art—you would have laughed. Van Eyk is the greatest of all he says. Every picture is different—such work in it. Italians dont see.

Here is Adrian and I must rush. Adrian has been closeted for 2 hours with the Singer, discussing a private legal affair. She almost wept on his shoulder.

He wont say what.

Yr. B.

Berg

1. John Waller Hills, now a solicitor.

507: To Violet Dickinson [*The Cottage, Studland, Dorset*]

21st Sept. 09

My Violet,

I took your letter to Bayreuth and meant to answer it. But the opera was always interrupting. Now, having waited goodness knows how long, you may be dead. After all, the last thing was that you had overthrown a market gardener. If you were dead, how would you be buried. I have often gone over in my mind, the habits of the Cowper family. What odd people you know!—there was the lady [Miss Sandeman] who fed the Toads and married an Italian Marquis also. Has that turned out well—are there many children?

We went to Dresden, where we became intimate with an American opera singer, who was on the verge of a lawsuit, and conferred with Adrian every afternoon in her bedroom and now wishes me to buy her a marabout boa with chenille trimming. Then we came back to London, and now I have rented a small cottage for a fortnight, near Nessa.

Julian rushes straight into the sea, and falls flat on his face. Nessa tucks her skirts up, and wades about with him. Clive meanwhile dives from a boat, in a tight black suit. Yesterday, I hired a gentlemans or ladies—it was bi-sexual—bathing dress, and swam far out, until the seagulls played over my head, mistaking me for a drifting sea anemone. Today, however, it is raining; and so you have the joy of this letter. I make my own breakfast, every morning, and take in the eggs and milk, in my nightgown. Milk goes sour very quickly, and turns to a smooth kind of custard. Butter and bacon, on the other hand, will keep, with luck, a week. Do write, and tell me how you are; and remember me to Miss Schreiner, of whom I have such happy recollections. Do you remember when she played to us in the empire drawing room, with all the objects?

Yr. VS

Berg

508: To Lytton Strachey 29 *F.S.*

Wednesday [6 October 1909]

Dear Lytton,

I am told that you came here the other day, when I was away. I was just writing to ask you to dine with us when I hear from Nessa that you have disappeared to some seaside Inn, dragging with you Mr Norton,[1] whom I dare not call by any other name, who was to have taken Ottoline off our hands tomorrow. God knows what will happen now. She will languish like

1. Harry Norton, the mathematician, to whom Lytton dedicated *Eminent Victorians*. They were staying together at Brighton.

a sick and yellow alligator. To make up, you must write and say what you're after. Our summer has been strange—scarcely credible indeed, what with American prima donnas needing advice in their bedrooms, and asking questions about Saxon, in private, and young men from Cook's, and pure English maidens, among whom I have no right to class myself. Anyhow, we have seen what people call life.

Now we are back again, living on culture chiefly, the [Charles] Sangers, and King Lear, and the memory—alas it fades!—of conversations with Walter Lamb. I wish (as usual) that earth would open her womb and let some new creature out. They are grown very stale, and one will have to go back to nature I foresee.

How are you? I hope you got some good in your retreat—did you have adventures?

Nessa and Clive come back tomorrow.

Yr. ever,

VS

Frances Hooper

509: To Violet Dickinson   29 *Fitzroy Square, W.*

Monday [11 October 1909]

My Violet,
    Are you in London?
    Shall I come and see you? We are all back now.
    How are you? Adrian says he thinks he met you today, but couldn't make up his mind. The lady smiled—was it you, or a prostitute?

Yr. VS

Berg

510: To Clive Bell   29 *F.S.*

Thursday [28 October 1909]

My dear Clive,
    I will answer your letter though I hope to see you this evening. As for that article,[1] I am very glad that you thought it imaginative—because of course that matters more than mere cleverness, and makes me hopeful about the future of the series (as I suggest to Smith that it shall become) However—

1. *Memoirs of a Novelist.* Purporting to be a review of the *Life* of a Victorian novelist, both biographer and novelist were creatures of Virginia's invention. It was an important development in Virginia's imaginative writing, but it was rejected by Reginald Smith, and Virginia never wrote for the *Cornhill* again. See Quentin Bell, Vol. I, Ch. 8.

it was the last sentence in your letter that I wanted to answer, and even to contradict. On the whole, I think our interview was successful. Considering how rusty we have grown in each other's company of late I was surprised to find how naturally I could talk to you, and how very nice it was. I suppose, as usual, I didn't see what you felt, but it wasn't spilt milk to me. If we are formal at first, isn't that because we have got out of the habit of talking? I open these difficult questions with trembling, feeling always that you and Nessa may find me morbid (as is the nature of spinsters, living alone)— However, if you don't think the habit a bad one, I am quite sure that I enjoy seeing you. But I shall leave it to you, because I have proved myself hopelessly incompetent in the past!

Your affectionate,

Quentin Bell   VS

511: To Violet Dickinson   29 *Fitzroy Square, W.*

Postcard
[6 December 1909]

Friday would be delightful. I think Adrian arrives from America on Tuesday, if the Mauretania isn't late.

I suppose dinner is 8, and trust God that ones natural beauty will suffice.

VS

Berg

512: To Vanessa Bell   *Lelant Hotel, Lelant R.S.O.,*
                                        Cornwall

Christmas Day [1909]

Beloved,

I went for a walk in Regents Park yesterday morning, and it suddenly struck me how absurd it was to stay in London, with Cornwall going on all the time. I bought an A.B.C. and found there was a train at 1. It was then 12.30. However, I caught it, and arrived at 10.30 last night.

Adrian simultaneously made up his mind to go to Brockenhurst [New Forest]. At breakfast we had both decided to stay in London. Sophie was hysterical, and I have no pocket handkerchief, watch key, notepaper, spectacles, cheque book, looking glass, or coat. However, it is a hot spring day. I have been walking along the sands, and sitting in the sun, and when I have done this, I am going to Trick Robbin[1]. Lytton came to tea on Thurs-

---

1. Virginia's phonetic rendering of 'Trecrobben', the older name for Trencrom, a flat-topped hill behind Lelant.

day, and we were very intimate and easy and I have no doubts of his charm. But Duncan Grant also arrived, which was a little difficult. He went in ten minutes.

At seven o'clock Desmond MacCarthy appeared, wanting tea. I suppose the scandal will be spread now. He told me how much he disliked going to South Africa, and how his novel was becoming ridiculous. He seemed whimsical, but slightly tragic. He gave me a small humming bird—dead—which he had bought near the British Museum. Then Castle[1] came to dinner, and I was very much bored. He has a dull fluent mind, tinged with romanticism—but I daresay Irene[2] would never find it out. I doubt though that he would master her sufficiently for her respect.

Then there came Lytton and James [Strachey] and Frankie Birrell[3], Duncan Grant, Keynes, Norton, and [Horace] Cole. They sat round mostly silent, and I wished for any woman—and you would have been a miracle. I talked to Frankie and Keynes most of the time. But it was desperate work. However Frankie (if that is his name) told me how he had an idiot brother, and we discussed sex and illegal rites. Cole, of course, was disastrous. He began to tell stories about shooting policemen and challenging Hugh Lane[4] which I had to answer, across the room, and everyone sat silent. Then he stayed till 2 talking about Mildred and the Pasolinis.

Everyone left—even Norton couldn't sit him out. I told Norton that you were asking him to dinner on Thursday; if you aren't he is going to dine with us. I saw him blush at your name—but all the intimacies were impossible.

It was like climbing a wall perpetually. I am so drugged with fresh air that I cant write, and now my ink fails. As for the beauty of this place, it surpasses every other season. I have the hotel to myself—and get a very nice sitting room for nothing. It is very comfortable and humble, and infinitely better than the Lizard or St Ives. The subtleties of the landscape—they must wait. How I wish you were coming out with me now—it is very warm, bright blue sky and sea, and no wind and smells heavenly. What a mercy about H.P.G. [Hyde Park Gate].

Yr. B.

Berg

1. Tudor Castle, who worked in The Admiralty, and died young.
2. Irene Noel, daughter of Frank Noel of Achmetaga, Euboea, Greece. She later married Philip Baker (Noel-Baker).
3. Francis Birrell, son of Augustine Birrell, had been at King's. He later became a journalist and dramatic critic, and after the First War, ran a bookshop with David Garnett.
4. The art collector and critic.

Lelant Hotel, Lelant
[Cornwall]

26th Dec [1909]

My dear Clive,

It is past nine o'clock, and the people still sing carols beneath my window, which is open, owing to the clemency of the night. I am at the crossroads, and at the centre of the gossip of the village. The young men spend most of the day leaning against the wall, and sometimes spitting. Innumerable hymns and carols issue from barns and doorsteps. Several windows, behind which matrons sit, are red and yellow, and a number of couples are wandering up and down the roads, which shine dimly. Then there is the [Godrevy] lighthouse, seen as through steamy glass, and a grey flat where the sea is. There is no moon, or stars, but the air is soft as down, and one can see trees on the ridge of the road, and the shapes of everything without any detail. No one seems to have any wish to go to bed. They circle aimlessly. Is this going on in all the villages of England now? After dinner is a very pleasant time. One feels in the mood for phrases, as one sits by the fire, thinking how one staggered up Tren Crom in the mist this afternoon, and sat on a granite tomb on the top, and surveyed the land, with the rain dripping against one's skin. There are—as you may remember—rocks comparable to couchant camels, and granite gate posts, with a smooth turf road between them. Thinking it over is the pleasant thing. By writing to you I am sparing the 20 last pages of La Terre qui Meurt [René Bazin], for bedtime. Is it a good book? I suspect not very. It is accomplished, but not moving. But I suspend judgement—Then I have run through a great part of Lady Hester Stanhopes[1] memoirs, and curse my folly in not bringing the six volumes. One reads like an express train—from tea to bedtime. It makes me rock with delight—thinking what a number of wonderful things I shall dig out of it in my article. One gradually sees shapes and thinks oneself in the middle of a world.

The life I lead is very nearly perfect. A horrid tone of egoistic joy pervades this sheet I know. What with the silence, and the possibility of walking out, at any moment, over long wonderfully coloured roads to cliffs with the sea beneath, and coming back past lighted windows to one's tea and fire and book—and then one has thoughts and a conception of the world and moments like a dragon fly in air—with all this I am kept very lively in my head. For conversation there are the maid and the landlady, who tell me about the moon and the chickens and the wreck. A ferryman this morning told me about trawling and angling and drowned sailors. I pick up a certain amount of gossip by stretching my head out of the window and listening to the leaning men beneath. Now, suddenly at half past nine, the carols have

1. Virginia reviewed *Lady Hester Stanhope*, by Mrs Charles Roundell, in the *TLS* for 20 January 1910.

stopped, and there is only one man walking quickly, and whistling. A strange affair is life! However, one might run on and on, covering sheets, with mysticism, ridiculous in the daylight. My Lady Hester got into the habit of talking so that she could never read, and must dictate letters, and took herself for the Messiah. Suppose I stayed here, and thought myself an early virgin, and danced on May nights, in the British camp!—a scandalous Aunt for Julian, and yet rather pleasant, when he was older, like Norton, and wished for eccentric relations. Can't you imagine how airily he would produce her, on Thursday nights. "I have an Aunt who copulates in a tree, and thinks herself with child by a grasshopper—charming isn't it? She dresses in green, and my mother sends her nuts from the Stores". But Norton will become a politician, and cease to woo the arts with hairy arms. Spite toils in me, you see, even by the side of the green ocean.

I forgot to tell you how I travelled down with a youth who had had brain fever three times, and was bound to become excited as the lights of Truro appeared (his sister explained, and he grinned at her) Happily he took to running in the corridor, and showing people the moon. His sister said that she often feared for his life, especially on moonlight nights—did he take the stars for the lights of Truro?—but was herself sailing for South Africa, where a brother kept an Inn. Then there was a woman with eyes like those bunches of frosted grapes one sees in grocers shops—who divides her time between Spain and Penzance, thinking that they have much in common, owing to the Armada. Then there was a virgin, who only thought of her own hat, which, with its dead seagull, would lop sideways—and in the midst of them all sat an aged couple, growing colder and colder, on a polytechnic tour.

But I must now go to bed.

Yr. VS

Quentin Bell

514: To Violet Dickinson

Lelant Hotel, Lelant,
Cornwall

Dec. 27th [1909]

My Violet,

I meant to stay in London, but rushed off here on the spur of the moment. The idea came to me at 12.30—and the train left at 1. Accordingly I am less competent, as regards underclothes and shoes, than usual. Maud packs old amethyst necklaces, but forgets pocket handkerchiefs. The landladies husband had to lend me his watch key, and I borrow pencils and stamps. However it has been quite worth it. There is no one else in the hotel, and all the festivals have passed over my head without a trace. I have been tramping about the country, and dabbling in the Atlantic. It is as soft as Spring, and at ten o'clock at night I sit with my window open; old farmers are saying good night, and calling the weather dirty beneath me.

How any one, with an immortal soul can live inland, I cant imagine; only clods and animals should be able to endure it. As for news, I have none —only Saturdays paper, with lists of preachers in London.

Was Lady Hester Stanhope an Aunt of yours, or a friend of your Aunts? I have to write about her, and spend my time, reading, not a silly new book by a woman called Roundell, but the old diaries written by her doctor, which keep me entirely happy. She seems to have been an insolent noble aristocrat, not unlike Beatrice, only crazed about the Messiah, and the stars; with a passion for conversation. She was a niece of Pitts', and talks of Miss [Eleanor] Eden, who was to have married him, and how she peeped at her at church, and she was beautiful as an angel. Families lose their features terribly.

What have you been doing? I meant to buy you a Christmas present, but forgot; the truth is, I was on my way to buy it, when I had the idea of coming to Cornwall, and that took all my money. It shall be now for the new year. I did get you a card, only sent it to Sophie instead. It was of waves, breaking on a promontory.

I start early tomorrow, and leave all this. It is very melancholy to be shut up in London again. Only the delights of human intercourse reconcile me to it. Are you coming to tea—or are you staying in great houses? I suppose you see many sides of life.

Yr. VS

Berg

515: TO CLIVE BELL   29 *Fitzroy Square, W.*

[31? December 1909]

My dear Clive,

I deserve your taunt and I am stung by it. But why do I always feel self-conscious when I write to you? I wish you would think that out and tell me. In Cornwall it was worse than ever, because I had talked my tongue sore, and my brain was full of the ghosts of phrases. I am speechless now, but I should very much like to pour out my discontent upon you. Unhappily, the post goes, I have been talking incessantly since 4.30 yesterday afternoon, when I had Pernel, Lytton and Irene [Noel] in a heap—We went on with the usual selection and we discussed love and sex and filth and Sir Joshua's pictures and ethics—Nessa I suppose has told you the new facts—which already seem stable and fly blown—about Adrian[1], and Irene's affections.

1. Adrian had decided to give up the law and become an actor, but the idea was short-lived. Later he became a psychoanalyst.

My conclusion is that one's world must be smashed to atoms. We are merely treading old ground. You should have heard Norton upon his soul and beauty. One thing pleases me—a poem.[1] Did I ever tell you so? I suppose not. I meant to, in Cornwall, but the d——d smugness overcame me. I am still very shy of saying what I feel. It is a very great pleasure though.

Will you come to tea, and let me rave?

Your very affectionate,

VS

Quentin Bell

1. At Christmas 1917 Clive Bell distributed to his friends a 30-page booklet entitled *Ad Familiares*. In it is a poem *To V.S. with a book*, dated December 1909.

Letters 516-548

The year 1910 *began and ended with two significant events. In January she joined the Women's Suffrage Movement, and in December she discovered, at Firle in Sussex, the first house which she could call her own. In the early part of the year, weakened perhaps by overwork and the fiasco of the* Dreadnought *hoax in February (explained in the relevant footnotes), she seemed once again to be on the verge of insanity, and successive visits to Cornwall, Dorset and a rented house near Canterbury failed to restore her. In late June she re-entered the mental nursing-home at Twickenham for six weeks, but her condition was not serious enough to prevent her from writing letters, and in them she ridiculed her situation more than she craved sympathy. Work on* Melymbrosia *was postponed until her full recovery. She spent two convalescent holidays, again in Cornwall and Dorset, and by the autumn was well enough to resume her work for Women's Suffrage, and was involved, from the side-lines, in the controversy created by Roger Fry's first Post-Impressionist exhibition. She spent Christmas with Adrian in Lewes, and it was then that she found the villa at Firle which she named Little Talland House, in the neighbourhood which was to remain her country base for the rest of her life.*

516: To JANET CASE   29 *Fitzroy Square, W.*

1st Jan. [1910]

Dear Miss Case,

Would it be any use if I spent an afternoon or two weekly in addressing envelopes for the Adult Suffragists?[1]

I dont know anything about the question. Perhaps you could send me a pamphlet, or give me the address of the office. I could neither do sums or argue, or speak, but I could do the humbler work if that is any good. You impressed me so much the other night with the wrongness of the present state of affairs that I feel that action is necessary. Your position seemed to me intolerable. The only way to better it is to do some thing I suppose. How melancholy it is that conversation isn't enough!

                                                          Your aff.

Sussex   VS

1. This was Virginia's first active involvement in politics. The campaign for women's votes, led by Mrs Pankhurst, had been gaining popular support for years, but the Prime Minister, Asquith, was a strong opponent of the cause, and his refusal to grant the vote to women led to increasing protest and violence between 1910 and the outbreak of war.

Monday [14 February 1910]

My Violet,

Why didn't you come in the other day? Your modesty is too great. Scarcely an inch of flesh was showing. I could then have told you about our visit to the Dreadnought.[1] It is now a dull story. Two interviewers have been today, and one wishes for my portrait in evening dress! Also what age, and creed am I?

Do come in; or let me come.

Yr. VS

Berg

Sunday [27 February 1910]

My Violet,

I find that the 1st is a Tuesday, and on that day I have to go to my Adult Suffrage; so that I should have to leave you as soon as I had eaten. Our meeting seems like the marriage of mountains. Does this put you out? Could you have me another day? It is damnable. Life becomes more and more complex. But pages are occasionally added to the work of fancy.

How fond should you think you were of me now?

I saw a bookseller the other day who says that first editions of Miss Austen are very valuable. Have you sold yours?

I spend hours writing names like Cowgill on envelopes. People say that Adult Suffrage is a bad thing; but they will never get it owing to my efforts. The office, with its ardent but educated young women, and brotherly clerks, is just like a Wells novel.

Beatrice came here the other day, with a funeral horses headdress nodding over her rich red face. For some time, I used a kindly but subdued manner, for, as I never read the morning Post, I thought that Lady Bath might be somewhere beneath a tomb. However, it was a spinster aunt.

I wish you would enlighten me upon human nature. The deeper one gets, the muddier it is.

Will you ask me another day?

Yr. VS

Berg

1. This famous hoax, stage-managed by Horace Cole, had taken place on 10 February. Virginia and five friends visited H.M.S. *Dreadnought* at Weymouth in the disguise of the Emperor of Abyssinia and his suite, and were received with dignity. Cole then leaked the story to the Press.

519: To Violet Dickinson

[8? March 1910]

My Violet,
    I dashed off here, and forgot to write. The whole [Dreadnought] affair is at an end; and without a scratch. Adrian and Mr [Duncan] Grant saw McKenna.[1] He merely laughed at them, and supposed they had come to save themselves. When they said that they wished to apologise in order to get the officers out of the scrape, he was amazed. He said that it was ridiculous to suppose that anyone on board could be blamed for an instant. In fact, he seemed to think the suggestion impertinent, and said that an apology was not to be thought of. He advised us not to do it again; but it is certain that it has had no bad results for anyone. The story about the Admiral must be pure fiction.[2]
    We came here suddenly—Nessa and I and Clive. We have had one beautiful day, and now it pours. I will try to come to tea on Wednesday, but I mayn't be able to.

Yr. VS

Berg

520: To Saxon Sydney-Turner
29 *Fitzroy Square, W.*

[9 March 1910]

Dear Saxon,
    I have a card from Dr. Williams's Library to say that they cant renew vols 1 and 3 of Pausanias.
    Would you bring them here on Thursday, or could you send them to Dr. Ws., Gordon Square.
    Bernard Shaw kept us on the rack for 3 hours last night; his mind is that of a disgustingly precocious child of 2—a sad and improper spectacle to my thinking.

Yr very aff.
VS

Sussex

---

1. Reginald McKenna, First Lord of the Admiralty.
2. The *Dreadnought* was the flag-ship of the Commander-in-Chief Home Fleet, Admiral Sir William May, and his flag-commander was William Fisher, Virginia's first cousin. Both officers had received the party. It was alleged in Parliament that the 'Emperor' had conferred the Royal Abyssinian Order on Admiral May, who applied to the King for permission to wear it, but Mr McKenna denied the story.

423

521: To Violet Dickinson   29 *Fitzroy Square, W.*

Monday [25 April 1910]

My Violet,

I didn't know you had gone already. We got back 10 days ago.[1] I stupidly made my head bad again, and have been doing nothing. However, [Dr] Savage thinks that it will get quite right if I keep quiet. I feel a good deal better, only cant do any work, which is a great bore.

Write and say what you're doing. Is there any chance that you will be in London?

We had 2 splendid weeks at Studland, and the third was pretty good.

Yr. VS

Berg

522: To Vanessa Bell   29 *Fitzroy Square, W.*

[1? May 1910]

Beloved,

I had a very good night—slept like a top from 12 till 8.30 without pain.

I had Marjorie [Strachey] to dine. She was calm, expecting to be sick, but very nice. As she wished to be sick into her own basin, she went early.

Today we went for a motor car drive to Hendon. Then Olive[2] came to tea. She plunged into Hilton after hinting for some time. She evidently thinks that I am wavering, and taking up Adult Suffrage with a view to my future.[3] I was reticent. She looks rather melancholy and dry eyed, and has some internal complaint.

I shall see you at dinner. I hope the Ws.[4] do.

Yr. B.

I have a long letter from Walter Lamb, enquiring about me, who says that Lytton is much broken in mind and health and is looking for lodgings for the term. Perhaps this is the result of the letter.

Quentin Bell

1. From Studland, Dorset, where Clive and Vanessa had taken her to recover from an illness which threatened to develop into a new attack of insanity.
2. Olive Ilbert, the sister-in-law of Hilton Young's older brother. In May 1909 Hilton had proposed to Virginia at Cambridge who turned him down, saying as an excuse that she could marry no one but Lytton.
3. Hilton Young was Assistant Editor of *The Economist* in 1910, but had political ambitions.
4. Perhaps Sydney and Alice Waterlow, whom the Bells were visiting in Rye.

Virginia Stephen in 1903

Virginia at Studland in March 1910

Virginia with Clive Bell at Studland in 1911

Virginia with Leonard Woolf at Asheham in 19

Little Talland House, Firle, Sussex

Postcard
[16 May 1910.]

It is possible that there will be tickets for Tristan at the opera itself: if not, Adrian advises the tobacconist, and there is a Keith Prowse in Langham Place who is often surprisingly good.

A garden tonight would be Heaven.

D [Duncan or 'Dolphin'] is here.

VS

Quentin Bell

524: To Clive Bell   *Canterbury*

Monday [6 June 1910]

My dear Clive,

It is very doubtful whether a woman of my defective taste should write a letter of affection. It wont reach you either, till I'm with you.[1] Then we may quarrel, and the thought of what I have said will eat into my brain. All I wanted to say was—how very much attached to you I am, and how much pleasure you give me. I see that I never did understand so much as I thought: perhaps I didnt have the chance. The future will be made much more pleasant by being more appreciative of you. I cant go on to say in what directions I am more appreciative, being stupid with paying bills, but I think that if you saw what I meant you would be pleased. I expect that what I mean will wear through in time.

For Gods sake, dont say that this is 'being nice' to you!

Yr. aff^ate,

VS

Quentin Bell

525: To Lady Robert Cecil   [*The Moat House, Blean,*
                                      nr. Canterbury]

June 13th [1910]

Dear Nelly,

What a ghastly apparition you have just made! After an absence of ten years, you come to the surface again, beside our moat, spouting horrid blasphemies. Are you much changed by contact with the world? Is it any use for me to write, I wonder?

1. Virginia was to join the Bells on the next day at The Moat House, Blean, near Canterbury.

Really, I remember you quite well, and was trying to draw you only last night. When shown to the company it was pronounced 'head of a male, unknown'. Dont you think you might sit in your tiled room, on the chintz sofa, by the low table, covered with books, where the Chow (what was his name?) still scratches—I remember everything, as though it were yesterday, instead of ten years ago,—and write to me?

Where have you been all this time? and has your view of the world changed? Are you still an aristocrat? are you exquisite or shabby? Are you a friend of Kitty's—or—? How painful these questions are: People oughtn't to go away for ten years.

I had the great pleasure of seeing your exquisite but not altogether incredible niece the other day. It was like watching a white moth quiver over a flower. One couldn't call it conversation. If my shadow had fallen she would have been out of the window.

Dont you think that Miss [Edith] Sichel, that talented Jewess, has trampled Mary Coleridge a little flat?[1] But I didn't know her. From her poems, one expected something—I dont know what.

Is Violet still alive! This is like shouting through a fog horn, and you may never hear me.

But a letter would be a great delight, even if dictated by a heart in which the flame of affection has long ceased to flare. For 3 months I have lived like a tame Rabbit. Are books still reviewed, I wonder? Is Reginald [Smith] writing letters?

By the way, are you an Adult Suffragist? This is a real question.

Yrs. ever,

VS

Hatfield

526: To Saxon Sydney-Turner   *Moat House, Blean,*
                                            nr. Canterbury
Monday [13 June 1910]

My dear Saxon,

I write, more to mitigate my own lot than to please you. The rain falls, and the birds never give over singing, and hot sulphur fumes rise from the valleys, and the red cow in the field roars for her calf. In these circumstances you would address yourself to Chaucer, and master his habits before tea. I have tried, but cant persist—I pick chocolates out of a box, and worry my sister. Shortly before the rain began, three days ago, we had our windows prized open by a Smith. The decay of centuries had sealed them. No human force can now shut them. Thus we sit exposed to wind and wet by day; and by

1. In her Preface to Mary Coleridge's *Gathered Leaves*, a posthumous volume of her stories, essays, letters and diaries.

night, we are invaded by flocks of white moths. They frizzle in the candles, and crawl up my skirts to die, in the hollow of my knee. There is something unspeakably repugnant in the feel of creatures who have lost their legs.

However, Nessa has done her best for us. She has invented an old woman, who comes before anyone asks her, to stop the chimbleys smoking, and finds eggs, by looking for them, on the common. Then Nessa said at breakfast, "What a very large family Mr Lefevre must have!" and pointed to a photograph of gospel preachers since the time of Wiclif. The poor old man who owns this house, Mr Lefevre, called here the other day; and said that his happiest hours had been spent here, but times were changed. He alluded to the death of his prolific wife, which happened in sad circumstances which I will explain one day. At this, Nessa and Clive suddenly lost their tempers and showed their intolerant brutality in such a way that the old man was led out by his daughter (herself much moved) in tears.

If you should write to me, in one of the living languages, preferably Romance, I should have one happy breakfast. Hitherto, they have been dependent on Nessa's charity. She is having a long correspondence upon illegitimacy with Snow [Margery Snowden].

Shall you come and stay here one Sunday? The weather is changing as I write. It would be dry by the time you came.

Yr. very aff.,
VS

As this was not posted, owing to an expedition to Whitstable, your letter has arrived, with its strange, sad, and utterly unexpected, but unmistakable, signs of inebriety. But this shall go no further.

Barbara Bagenal

527: To Saxon Sydney-Turner   [*The Moat House, Blean, nr. Canterbury*]

Tuesday [June 1910]

Dear Saxon,

It was like your malice to profit by the ignorance of a poor creature; however, you show your parts very well in French.[1] You appear more like an exquisite black Cat, tipped with white at the paws, than ever. You should have lived in an age when fencing was part of the learning of a gentleman.

This morning I was put in a high position by the arrival of a parcel for me, and no one else had anything. The envious couple [the Bells] have hardly yet done making their allusions. What shall I send in return? Oh yes—this

1. In response to Virginia's request in her previous letter. He was in the habit of writing to his friends in Latin.

is the treat for you, the policemen are performing at Maidstone tomorrow. I got you four tickets, in case you should like to take three friends.

The serious part of this letter, I may say, is now to come. Will you spend next Sunday here—accurately speaking part of Saturday, and part of Monday, with the whole of Sunday?

I shall probably be alone. But I dont know what operas there may be.

Julian has just raised a blush on the face of the parlourmaid by calling his mother a ———! When she said "Hush!" he replied —— ——! Did you ever? He has been burning his mouth with peppermints.

Your very aff.

Sussex VS

528: To Violet Dickinson

Moat House, Blean,
nr. Canterbury

Tuesday [21 June 1910]

My Violet,

We have been here for a fortnight, and your letter was sent on. I'm afraid I cant come, because I shall stay here another 10 days. Savage thought I had better go away for a bit, as I couldn't do much in London.

Nessa and Clive and Julian have been here; Nessa goes back today.

We have a circular lawn and a moat. We get walks through the woods— not, so far, discovered by Helen Holland, who is a mile off. Do write.

It takes a long time to get ones faculties to work again. I wish I could have come.

Yr. VS

Berg

529: To Vanessa Bell

[*The Moat House, Blean,*
nr. Canterbury]

Friday [24 June 1910]

Beloved,

Savages decision is of course, rather depressing[1]; but not unexpected. I only feel cross that he didn't insist at once.

I suppose you didn't ask about the cost. I'm afraid it will be great. Also I should like to begin without delay, and not stay on here till Thursday. I suppose Savage will tell me as soon as he knows.

I've no doubt it will be damnable, and the thought of the nurses and the food and the boredom is disgusting; but I also imagine the delights of being sane again. He says he wont insist on complete isolation, so I suppose I shant be as badly off as I was before.

1. Dr Savage, on being told by Vanessa of Virginia's still depressed condition, advised that she should enter the nursing home at Twickenham.

There isnt much news to tell you. Sophie [Farrell] seemed on the point of collapse at first, and has to sit while I order dinner. But she is as mild as milk, and Georges guinea makes her almost weep. I think we ought to start a sinking fund for her.

When I heard the cocks crow last night, I thought she was gurgling her last. With great cunning, I told her how Jessie had complained of the range; she at once became very magnanimous, and said that Jessie hadn't had *her* experience; and that as a matter of fact, the range here is a very good range as ranges go. The one at St Ives *was* a bad range, but she often cooked for 30 people on that. However, her system of stoking produces warm drinking water, which almost makes Clive sick.

She was carrying on a lively badinage with the boy when I was in the W.C. just now. The Reginald Smiths have written to ask me and Adrian to join a small "Cornhill party" on Thursday night; when someone is going to recite "The Contributors Dream". I rather wish I could go. The glimpse I get of society in your and Adrian's letters makes me, of course, long to be in the thick of it.

Did you have any intercourse with Dorothea, or Hilton? George has written two very repulsive letters, oozing with patronage, and semi-lunacy. He thinks apparently that I must be smoking too much, in order to ward off mosquitoes from the moat. I rather expect a patent head net, of the newest pattern, such as the peasants wear on the campagna. He wants us to go to the Pollards again. I think I shall say that I expect to be confined next month, and let him muddle it out for himself. He will suspect Saxon, and take immediate steps to have him promoted. He will also run down to Brighton, and negotiate a settlement with Saxon père. How tactful he would be with the lunatics at lunch! bringing down a basket of plovers eggs, I expect.

Did Clive tell you of our melancholy discussion yesterday, in the intervals of a thunder storm? I fear you abuse me a good deal in private, and it is very galling to think of it. I begin to appreciate Clives position under Lyttons treatment. However, I daresay you feel something, too, that Lytton doesn't. Only, as I never abuse you, I feel it rather hard; and possibly I ought to consider a scheme for the future.

But I daresay this is all great nonsense; and if it isn't, there may be no use in saying it. Of course, I adore you!

I wonder what you make of Adrian.

Saxon has written to say that he cannot get leave for Monday, or he would have come. I suppose he would have to go up on Sunday night, which certainly would kill him.

Would you let me know what the rent of Lingfield Road is.[1] Clive is doing my income tax, and has lost his note.

1. A house in Wimbledon, which had belonged to Leslie Stephen and was inherited by his children.

Your letters are a source of great joy. I'm afraid you had a dismal time here, and that I have altogether been the devil of a bore. Your husband is extraordinarily sympathetic and charming.

Yr. VS

Will you thank Adrian for his letters. I will write.

Berg

530: To Violet Dickinson   *29 Fitzroy Square, W.*
Tuesday [28 June 1910]

My Violet,
    I return the stamps which I got on false pretences. I'm cursing my luck. Savage now insists on a rest cure, and I'm to retreat to a woman at Twickenham for a month.
    It's a great bore, and I suppose my niece[1] will arrive without me.
    Nor shall I see you again for some months, and you will have forgotten the very charming cast of my nature.
    Do write from the top of your alp.

Yr. VS

Berg

531: To Vanessa Bell   *Burley, Cambridge Park,*
                                        Twickenham
July 28th [1910]

Beloved, or rather, Dark Devil,
    I meant to write several days ago, although you do say you dont care a damn. But in that too I was hoodwinked by Miss Thomas.[2] I gather that some great conspiracy is going on behind my back. What a mercy we cant have at each other! or we should quarrel till midnight, and Clarissas [the coming 'niece'] deformities, inherited from generations of hard drinking Bells, would be laid at my door. She—(Miss T.) wont read me or quote your letters. But I gather that you want me to stay on here.
    She is in a highly wrought state, as the lunatic upstairs has somehow brought her case into court; and I cant make her speak calmly. Do write and explain. Having read your last letter at least 10 times—so that Miss Bradbury [nurse] is sure it is a love letter and looks very arch—I cant find a word about my future. I had agreed to come up on *Monday*; which would leave time for walking. Savage wanted me to stay in bed more or less this week. As I must

1. Vanessa was expecting a baby, 'Clarissa', in July, but Quentin was not born until 19 August.
2. Jean Thomas, the proprietor of 'Burley', the mental nursing home.

see him again, I suppose I must wait over Monday. But I really dont think I can stand much more of this.

Miss T. is charming, and Miss Bradbury is a good woman, but you cant conceive how I want intelligent conversation—even yours. Religion seems to me to have ruined them all. Miss T. is always culminating in silent prayer. Miss Somerville [patient], the absent minded one with the deaf dog, wears two crucifixes. Miss B. says Church Bells are the sweetest sound on earth. She also says that the old Queen the Queen Mother and the present Queen represent the highest womanhood. They reverence my gifts, although God has left me in the dark. They are always wondering what God is up to. The religious mind is quite amazing.

However, what I mean is that I shall soon have to jump out of a window. The ugliness of the house is almost inexplicable—having white, and mottled green and red. Then there is all the eating and drinking and being shut up in the dark.

My God! What a mercy to be done with it!

Now, my sweet Honey Bee, you know how you would feel if you had stayed in bed alone here for 4 weeks. But I wont argue, as I dont know what you have said. Anyhow, I will abide by Savage.

Miss T. and I have long conversations. She has a charming nature; rather whimsical, and even sensual. But there again, religion comes in; and she leads a spotless life. Apparently she is well off, and takes patients more or less as a spiritual work. She has harboured innumerable young women in love difficulties. They are always turning up to lunch, and I creep out of bed and look at them. At present there is one upstairs, and a barren wife across the passage. The utmost tact is shown with regard to our complaints; and I make Miss T. blush by asking if they're mad.

Miss Somerville has periods of excitement, when she pulls up all the roses, and goes to church. Then she is silent for weeks. She is now being silent; and is made very nervous by the sight of me. As I went out into the garden yesterday in a blanket with bare legs, she has some reason. Miss Bradbury is the woman you saw out of the window and said was homicidial [sic]. I was very kind with her at dinner, but she then put me to bed, and is a trained nurse.

Miss T. talks about you with awe. How you smile, and say such quaint things—how your eyes fill with tears—how beautiful your soul is—and your hands. She also thinks you write such beautiful English! Your language is so apt and so expressive. Julian is the most remarkable child she ever saw. The worst of her is that she is a little too emotional.

I have been out in the garden for 2 hours; and feel quite normal. I feel my brains, like a pear, to see if its ripe; it will be exquisite by September.

Will you tell Duncan that I was told he had called, and that I am furious that they didn't let me see him. Miss T. thought him an extremely nice young man.

Do write, today. I long to see you. Its damned dull being here alone. Write sheets. Give Clive my love. His visits are my brightest spots. He must come again.

I will be very reasonable.

Yr. B.

Berg

532: To Clive Bell

*Burley, Cambridge Park,
Twickenham*

Postcard
[2 August 1910]

Can you possibly come down tomorrow (Wednesday) afternoon? Savage is ill and cant come. It would be a great joy to see you—Could you wire if you cant come.

VS

(as early as possible)   3.30 from Waterloo.

Quentin Bell

533: To Saxon Sydney-Turner

*The Wharncliffe Hotel, Tintagel,
Cornwall*

Monday [August 1910]

My dear Saxon,

I meant to ask you the name of the hotel in the Scillies, but forgot. Could you send me a card? We[1] think of going there on Thursday.

Really, there is no place quite so beautiful as Cornwall—in spite of the inconvenience caused by several passionate lovers. You come upon them on the cliffs. If I am ever a lover, I shall try to convey to the world my great amiability. Even when clasped round the neck, I shall try to encourage timid maiden ladies to approach.

Last night we crept under the windows of the grand hotel, and saw Miss Mickle and Mr Thomas Dunhill playing Brahms to a great drawing room full of dowagers and athletes.

Yr. aff.
VS

I hope you have had no more fits.

Sussex

1. Virginia had gone to Cornwall with Jean Thomas.

Berrymans Farm, Gurnards Head
[Cornwall]

Sunday [4 September 1910]

Dearest Clive,

I should have written long ago, to thank you for your letters, which were a great delight. You cant imagine, though, how little human I have become. One is a very nice animal, apart from books and culture, but almost dumb.

I begin to wish now to talk to you, at an inopportune moment, partly because I am so happy. I have had to borrow a long-necked ink pot from Mrs Berryman. One dips, like a sparrow, and how to blot is a problem, when I turn over.

Our travels I suppose Nessa has told you about; yesterday we walked along the coast from St Just. We walked till 5 in the afternoon, through a perfect September day, along little paths in the turf, looking into deep sea. We tried for tea at this farm house, and were told we could sleep as well. As the one lodging at Zennor was filled 10 times over, virgins sleeping with matrons in one feather bed, we were much relieved.

We have had no adventures to tell you about; it seems likely that two large steamers are going to collide in three minutes. The pigs and geese are making the farmer, a stout man, with a bad leg, hobble across the yard. From what Mrs Berryman says, the great dispute, which parts husband and wife, is whether the geese shall feed on the fields or the moor. She has practically told us that life is full of trouble; and as she is a great black woman, there must be truth in it. The one interesting letter I have had, is from Madge, who also finds life a handful. She is moved, hearing that I have had a rest cure, to look in the looking glass. There she sees a face scarred with care and passion. Rest cures (though urgently advised) would do her no good: besides, to fight on is the only remedy for some. Then she hints that her heart is gnawn by sorrow, that the people of Surrey[1] are fat, and cannot understand lean spirits who have been in Arcady. "But, thank God, I *have* been in Arcady—no rest cure for me, in this world, but Arcady, denied to ——" Apparently denied to Will, and me and the ladies at the next table in the hotel at Mürren [Switzerland]. She ends, "I wish to get to know Clive. I feel drawn to him". She is really a very attractive woman.

This letter is taken up, after sitting on the Gurnards Head, watching a 3 masted sailing ship fetching a compass, as Wattie [Walter Lamb] would say, which makes me glad he isn't here, but mumbling his tragedy beneath yew trees, with moping James [Strachey]. It appears that the geese, in taking flight from the tail of the wain, grazed 3 inches of skin off the smallest brats leg. Mrs B., bringing in jam tarts, an apple pasty, and cream for tea, remarks that one's always in *some* trouble. So I was right.

1. William Wyamar Vaughan left Giggleswick in May 1910 to become Master of Wellington College.

I remember that you asked me some searching questions about my health. I feel that this fortnight has done a great deal of good, and brought back that kind of spring which has been lost all this time. But a bad night certainly is able to make me incapable again, and it seems very easy at present to make a bad night. My resolution is to be cautious at Studland,[1] not walking too far, or exciting the emotions, and taking great care to circumvent headaches. Will you try not to irritate the beast, for amusement? As to my being recovered, I think there is no doubt. You will find me scarlet and brown and I believe, fatter.

With regard to happiness—what an interesting topic that is! Walking about here, with Jean [Thomas] for a companion, I feel a great mastery over the world. My conclusion upon marriage might interest you. So happy I am it seems a pity not to be happier; and yet when I imagine the man to whom I shall say certain things, it isn't my dear Lytton, or Hilton either. Its strange how much one is occupied in imagining the delights of sympathy. The future, as usual with these sanguine apes, seems full of wonder.

It is pure—affection, I suppose—that makes me run on, because I doubt that you will have time to answer. I have been thinking of Thoby all the time here; I suppose it is the birds. Tomorrow we walk over to Lelant, where we sleep, and go to London on Tuesday. By this post I am writing to Mr Child[2] (on my last sheet of paper) and I hope to work on Women every morning at Studland. I have only one book here—a small Pope. I fumble the words, awkwardly, with a kind of awe, like a rustic. That world becomes astonishingly far away. How odd—that one writes oneself!

Your verdict upon Mr Wedgewood has set my mind at rest—but have you tried Miss Murray? You see, she has 9 years in which to catch me up, if she isn't level already.

We have been walking among the most remarkable moors, among barrows, British villages, stone maidens, and beehive huts. If it weren't for the excitability of geese at night, this would be the place I should like to live in.

It will be very nice to see you.

Yr. aff.

Quentin Bell   VS

535: To Clive Bell   29 *Fitzroy Square, W.*
Thursday [8 September 1910]
Dearest Clive,
    I'm very sorry that I didn't write before, but I thought that you saw all my letters to Nessa; and I was purposely very lazy. But I did write, as a

1. Virginia was to join the Bells at Studland within a few days.
2. Harold Child, a close associate of Bruce Richmond, and frequent contributor to the *TLS*. At Studland Virginia wrote a review of *Mrs Gaskell: Haunts, Homes, and Stories*, by Mrs Ellis H. Chadwick (*TLS*, 29 September 1910).

matter of fact; and didn't send it, when Nessa's letter came, as I thought it looked like asking for Lytton's letter. However, waiting didn't do any good apparently; and I suppose I have made you angry. I half meant to put an explanation at the end, to assure you that I wrote without that object; but only managed to say that I didn't want an answer. Well—it doesn't much matter either way.

I've had a good many small incidents—a very strange conversation with Mr [Harold] Child, upon sexual relations, a certain number of delightful compliments and I'm now pledged to do a good deal of work.

Also Wattie has written—insinuating, as I think, that Miss C.[1] has refused him. His tragedy promises well.

I lay awake till 5 this morning, for some unknown reason, and in consequence I am so heavy lidded that I can hardly see. But it hasn't made my head ache—stupid though it is. I drove with Nessa today.

Yr.
VS

The cheque is for the pound you gave me.

Quentin Bell

536: To John Waller Hills   *The Cottage, Studland,*
                                   Dorset

5 October [1910]

Dearest Jack,

I ought to have thanked you long ago for the partridges. They were delicious, and came in very handy.

I suppose you will be at Highhead until Parliament meets. It's so gorgeous here, that it seems a pity ever to go back.

Nessa is here with her two sons. They are very happy, and Julian is now most attractive. Claudian [Quentin]—the baby—is too small to count much yet.

What an excitement about Eustace and Nina Kay-Shuttleworth![2] I wonder if you expected it. I hope he is very happy.

Your aff'ate,
VS

Berg

1. Perhaps Annie Cole, who in 1911 married Neville Chamberlain.
2. Jack's brother Eustace married Nina, daughter of Lord Shuttleworth, on 21 December 1910.

537: To Violet Dickinson   *Court Place, Iffley,*
                                            Oxford
17th Oct. [1910]

My Violet,

I should have written before to thank you for the charming pouch, which looks as though gold were shovelled into it—But laziness is a great curse. Are you in London? I go there tomorrow, for good, I hope. Savage has still to decide my future, but I now feel very well again.

Nessa's son is better, and Julian is now a strapping schoolboy, very domineering, but attractive.

What are you doing? Vapours seem to hang between us. You might be (as you will be one day) chanting in Heaven. I am staying here with a remarkable family—Costelloes and Pearsall Smiths.[1] Mrs Pearsall Smith is a very spruce and practical edition of the Quaker, without any mysticism about her, though she too is a great light! I imagine they might have been rivals, for Mrs P. S. also writes books upon the soul, and hers are translated into Chinese. She unmasks all the hypocrisies—how the Friends prophecy at dinner, out of malice, so as to cheat someone of a hot dish. Religion would be amusing if one could get priests to be honest.

Are you in London?

I met Katie [Cromer] in the street the other day—in straight American clothes, and rather lined. I remember her as one of the beauties of her age—now some decades ago. Aunt Minna [Duckworth], however, still lives, and makes one feel young.

                                                            Yrs. VS
Berg

538: To Madge Vaughan   29 *Fitzroy Square, W.*
[Autumn 1910?]

Dearest Madge,

We caught our train, in spite of Robin's predictions. Now we are back again, and crouching over our fire, which isn't as splendid as yours.

It was a wonderful sight—the School [Wellington] I mean, and all the different people—the Canon, and Mr. [R. St. C] Talboys—I keep thinking of it all. I wish I had seen more of you, but if talking is bad for you, perhaps

1. Mrs Robert Pearsall Smith, her son Logan, and her granddaughters, Rachel and Karin Costelloe. The Pearsall Smith family came from Philadelphia. Logan had already collaborated with his sister Mary Costelloe (who had married Bernard Berenson in 1900) on the periodical *Golden Urn*. Some of Logan's contributions to it formed the basis of his masterpiece, *Trivia* (1918).

it was better not. I did enjoy talking to you. It was a great treat to see you, and Janet and David. I've been telling Nessa all about it.

I most stupidly left my spectacles in my bedroom. Could you be very kind and send them—or perhaps Janet would. Give her my love. The toads are in excellent condition tell her; so she must make haste and come and see them.

Adrian sends his love.

Yr. loving,

VS

Sussex

539: TO CLIVE BELL   29 *Fitzroy Square, W.*

[Autumn 1910?]

Dear Mr Bell,

There was great excitement in the singeries[1] last night when a tall black man, muffled in an overcoat, left a box at the door. There was straw in it. We opened it—Wombat got the straw for his litter. The pot is a beautiful pot. May we hope Mr Bell that you and Mistress will baptise it one of these days? The smaller monkeys we dont allow to touch it—young beasts are so quisitive and their fingers is so many claws. We shant allow them to drink out of it, as they might be drownded, all out of curiosity too. Mango always looks for his reflection in tea pots, what he is [is] a Vain Rake, and one day God will punish him. If you please sir, kiss our mistress when she's not looking and tell her its Us.

Your obedient singes and Wombatts

Quentin Bell

540: TO VIOLET DICKINSON   29 *Fitzroy Sq., W.*

Monday [14 November 1910]

My Violet,

Why didn't you tell me that you had influenza before? I would have sat by your bedside. Perhaps it struck you that that wasn't my gift. I would have read aloud to you from my own works. Can I come to tea, and stay for as long as you like, on Friday? I suppose you wouldn't be well enough to come on to the Friday Club and hear Helen Verrall[2] read a paper upon

1. Virginia's habit of inventing animal names and characteristics for her friends and family is well illustrated in this letter. The *singeries* undoubtedly refers to 'the apes', the plural name by which Virginia often called herself ('singes'); the 'smaller monkeys' could be Julian and Quentin; 'Mango' is perhaps Adrian; and 'Wombat', the dog Hans.

2. Daughter of A. W. Verrall, the Cambridge classical scholar.

ghosts? They have found out something about the soul, which one ought to know.

My time has been wasted a good deal upon Suffrage. We went to two meetings, at which about a dozen people spoke, like the tollings of a bell. If they spoke faster all their words went into one. It was at the Albert Hall. The only amusement was that a baby cried incessantly, and this was taken by some as a bitter sarcasm against woman having a vote.

George turned up yesterday, with a kind of white frill under his waistcoat, and a gigantic diamond, set in green enamel, which is chipping off. He looked like a valet; and I do not think that my bitter remarks about him were wrong. He supposes that we all feel honoured by Lords calling, and that exasperates one. He has bought a country house,[1] on the advice of some Irish peer. It has to be large enough to hold Lady Vera,[2] who never travels without a maid and a man. I passed her the other day in Grosvenor Square, walking with Elsie [Dowager Countess Carnarvon]. As she wore crimson velvet, up to her knees, and her knees had grey stockings on, while Elsie was smothered in good black cloth, and brown fur, I took them for a good woman rescuing a prostitute, and exercising her in the afternoon.

Do you take Sanatogen? I find it very warming to the brain.

I have to write a review about the Duke of Newcastle[3] this week; and next week I begin my work of imagination.[4] You will then hear a good deal about it. When you were ill, did you think at all about the chances of liking me better? I refrained from writing to you, though wishing to, because of the sad revelations made at our last meeting. Would you inform me?

I hear that Margaret Lyttelton continues to sit silent, though people explode gunpowder beneath her. She has been made a Younger Suffragist, but they say that she is fit for the grandmothers. I went down to Twickenham, (Miss Thomas) last week, and had a most interesting time, trying to ignore the oddities of several not altogether like other people women. One of them leapt with fright when one looked at her, and shook her fork in one's face. The thing was to keep on talking. Are you thinking of sending Beatrice there?

Are you really better? Can I send you anything?

Yr. VS

Berg

1. Dalingridge Place, near Forest Row, Sussex.
2. Lady Victoria Herbert, sister of Lady Margaret Duckworth.
3. Review of *The First Duke and Duchess of Newcastle-upon-Tyne*, by Thomas Longueville (*TLS*, 2 February 1911).
4. Virginia was resuming the writing of *Melymbrosia* (*The Voyage Out*), which had been interrupted by her illness.

Monday [14? November 1910]

Dearest Clive,

How complicated life is! Suppose I were to come to tea with you, and Mr Rendel[1] were to call, and Vanessa were to tell him you were in (Adrian met the Sheep on the stairs) would you send down to say you were engaged —or would you not let him up, and trust that I should stay on, and that he would take the hint and go? That was what I hoped you would do. It never occurred to me that I could stop her. As for its being a choice between her and you, I merely pitied myself (with my usual egoism) for losing my pleasure, and having to undergo an infliction. If one of us was going to lose a temper, I thought it should be me. She [Mary Sheepshanks] stayed for two hours, flopping like some debauched and battered moth, round her own discontent. She was as ugly as a dirty rain drop—a swollen one, that has run down a window, and got all the smuts in to it.

Contrasting this with what it might have been—its too damnable. Next time (which I dont dare to suggest) I will make the proper arrangements, but I'm certain that I shall never have the courage to turn people out when they're on the stairs—not if I'm in my lovers arms!

Yr.
VS

No, I dont see why you should be furious—with me, at least.

My sister threw me over this afternoon, because it was fine—but *I* wasn't angry—I've been trained.

Quentin Bell

541: To Violet Dickinson   29 *Fitzroy Square*

Sunday [27 November 1910]

My Violet,

You should have had the decency to write from your retirement. Dont you see that, having cast this umbrage upon your emotion for me, you put me in a very delicate position—so far as being inoportunate [*sic*] with letters is concerned? Suppose you just sniff 'Oh that tiresome chit, again' and roll a ball for your dog to gnaw out of my sentiments, how can I proceed without caution?

How are you? Where are you? If in London, would you like to see me? I cant help hoping that you're alone at Welwyn, and that it is pouring as it

1. Possibly J. M. Rendel, who married Lytton's oldest sister Elinor, and was an expert on Poor Law administration.

is here, so that you cant go out for fear of the rheumatics, and the leaves are sticking to the window panes. You will then have time to think over your wasted youth, and friendships thrown away.

We are so much oppressed by this election,[1] and the rain, that we have to dine out in a little restaurant off Soho, where prostitutes lure young men. The wickedness of London on a day like this is inconceivable; one imagines vice smelling in stuffy rooms.

I suppose you have been going everywhere—to the Grafton Galleries,[2] and the Bernard Shaw play [*Misalliance*]. Now that Clive is in the van of aesthetic opinion, I hear a great deal about pictures. I dont think them so good as books. But why all the Duchesses are insulted by the post-impressionists, a modest sample set of painters, innocent even of indecency, I cant conceive. However, one mustn't say that they are like other pictures, only better, because that makes everyone angry.

You will be glad to hear that I am seething with fragments of love, morals, ethics, comedy tragedy, and so on; and every morning pour them out into a manuscript book [*Melymbrosia?*]. Never shall I write a review again. Do you think it would be indecent to put Aunt Minna upon the stage, and Aunt Fisher, and the Quaker? Such riches as we have in our relations it seems a pity to neglect.

One of Miss Thomas's most excitable lunatics—the one who leapt when she saw me—has been almost dying, but is now better again. Miss Thomas says that these excitements are the wine of life. This bears out my theory, based on Aunt Fisher, and all the other sepulchral women, that what people like is feeling—it dont matter what. Last Sunday I stayed with the Cornishes at Eton, and heard the most singular conversations carried on by old Mrs C. alone, over everybodies head. What is love? What is vice? What is religion? "Oh, d'you know that Virginia has the most lovely little sins?" She has now written to congratulate me upon an article by John Bailey upon Tolstoy "No one but you, Virginia, could have written it." When the old talk they are very alarming. Old Mr Cornish talked too.

Write, even a post card, to say how you are, and whether I shall send you anything—a hot water bottle, or a bit of binding?

Yr. VS

Berg

1. Parliament was dissolved on 28 November.
2. The First Post-Impressionist Exhibition, which was mounted by Roger Fry, and caused an explosion of public indignation, opened at the Grafton Galleries in November 1910. Desmond MacCarthy was Secretary of the Exhibition, and Clive, Vanessa, and Duncan Grant were whole-hearted in their support of Fry's initiative.

543: To Violet Dickinson   29 *Fitzroy Square, W.*

[December? 1910]

My Violet,

I will come on Saturday with great pleasure—no clothes—not very clean. Just back from a political meeting, and sat on the platform (for the sake of my Christian blood) next Portuguese Jews, whose sweat ran into powder, caked, and blew off.

                                                                    Yr. VS

Berg

544: To Violet Dickinson   [29 *Fitzroy Square, W.*]

[December 1910]

My Violet,

It is a great pity that I am a prose writing and not a poetic animal. Then I could express my feelings, gratitude, contentment, spiritual joy, physical comfort, friendship, appreciation—all these you should take and shake, and make rhyme. There are many others.

When they all come together, one is really very enviable.

I was very happy in my comfortable bed; also at meals; also sitting over the fire.

Of course, I had to wrestle with my stout devil selfishness. Did you notice it? Sometimes it takes an hour before breakfast to subdue him. But then, what a glorious victory! What a snowy soul! What a delightful creature, in short!

This must stop (though it could go on) in order to catch the post.

Besides, you have a dozen sheets to read I know. With great affection.

                                                                    Yr. Sp.

Berg

545: To Janet Case   29 *Fitzroy Square, W.*

[December? 1910]

Dear Miss Case,

I am dining out on Tuesday, so I dont expect we shall meet till May or June. But we can always hope. Do you ever take that side of politics into account—the inhuman side, and how all the best feelings are shrivelled? It is just the same with philanthropy, and that is why it attracts the bloodless women who dont care for their own relations. Miss Emphie Case [Janet's sister] will see my point. I know 2 Duchesses, so I am still one up—if a

Dowager counts. Is yours Sutherland or Rutland or neither? I saw Miss LL. Davies[1] at a lighted window in Barton St with all the conspirators round her, and cursed under my breath.

Yr. aff.

Sussex
VS

546: To Vanessa Bell
Pelham Arms, St Anns,
Lewes [Sussex]

Christmas Day [1910]

Beloved;

Breakfast was as bleak as a workhouse today; not one letter, not one parcel; the postman actually passed the door.

Miraculously, he returned, with your short, but expressive, curse. As for forgetting you, the poor Ape was preparing for a day of stoic endurance upon the downs. Adrian saying that Claudian [Quentin] was probably in convulsions.

My only other letter was from Jean [Thomas], enclosing 'What I believe' by Tolstoy. She sent a long serious letter with it, exhorting me to Christianity, which will save me from insanity. How we are persecuted! The self conceit of Christians is really unendurable. But the poor woman has got into one of her phrases, which lasts a whole letter, about something lacking in your life, which alone will bring etc. etc. Then it all comes over the other way round.

The weather has been surprising; we walked on the downs this morning, explored the town this afternoon, and are now going to church.

The eccentricity of our appearance is magnificent. Adrians hair flows like a crazy poets; then we bought him a Harvest hat for a shilling, a strawberry roan colour, suited for an August afternoon.

I wear a bright purple cloak, over my red dress, with a smart black toque.

Asking about church just now, Mrs Mears said "There is a Roman Catholic church two doors down" evidently placing us among the foreign Christians. Yesterday by the way (Adrian will tell the story) I got past the ticket inspector with a dog ticket. Hans had mine. I was given a packet by Sophie, inscribed "For dear Hans", and asked to give it him on Christmas day. It was a bar of milk chocolate. Clearly, something softens in servants brains.

We have just discovered that one can telephone from here; Duncan can be talked to for two pence. Adrian comes up beaming, from Love, I suppose. I withdrew discreetly. He says talking is much more satisfactory than writing.

1. Margaret Llewelyn Davies, who was closely involved in the Women's Suffrage movement, and was Secretary of the Women's Cooperative Guild.

Last night before dinner we wandered in the streets, and spent about ten shillings upon various small objects, calculated to make us cheerful—a flying bird, now whizzing round, a pencil, a cooks knife to cut the pencil, an earthenware pot, a jar of Aspenalls black enamel, a walking stick—in short a great many small objects.

Have you had any excitements? Letters? Confidences? Compliments?

As usual, I am violently in favour of a country life. I like walking and coming back for tea, and finding letters (oh what a sarcasm.) and having tea, and then writing over the fire, or reading a book about the poor. (a safety pin for the bird to hang to has now been stuck into the ceiling)

I like looking out places on the map; already I have bought two guides, and planned several expeditions.

The country is very beautiful; we jest, pithily, about greens and purples and how you would say "What a wonderful red that green moss is!" One becomes so simple in the country—running out at all hours.

Why did you go to a pottery at Bristol?

Yr. B.

Berg

547: To Vanessa Bell   *Pelham Arms [Lewes,*
                              Sussex]
Tuesday [27 December 1910]

Beloved,

No letter from you today, which is rather mean, I think, considering how long mine are, and written under such difficulties.

I have just come back from my visit to Brighton. It was the bleakest thing I ever did.

A strong wind was blowing on the downs, but I had a beautiful walk until I sighted a white tower on the race course. Then I descended into the suburbs of Brighton, which are dusty and windbitten, and got a tram to the Pavilion. A little red-nosed clerk [Saxon] appeared, so much like other people that I didn't know him. Far from lunching out in some queer angle of the Pavilion, as I expected, he told me that we were to lunch with his family. We drove to the far end of Hove. He lives in a street of small villas. The house has a great air of poverty. It is too bare to be ugly—linoleum carpets, and only very low fires. A Miss Charlotte, practically bald and very lean and cold, was crouching in the dining room.

Then Mrs Turner appeared and took me to her room, which reminded me of Aunt Marys. The brushes were so mangy in bristles, and the combs yellow and broken. She is as attenuated as a field mouse—but you have seen her. Then we lunched, and old Turner, called 'the doctor', a Mr Stafford, who is afflicted in every way,—can hardly speak—Ravenscroft and Saxon

443

came in. We had the remains of several hearts, which would hardly go round; and portions were sent up on plates for people in their rooms. Your picture of Saxon hangs over the sideboard on a dull red paper, and looks oddly out of place.

I kept up a feeble conversation about the beauties of Lewes with Mr and Mrs Turner; Saxon did not say a word; but smiled at me once. They were all very lean and uncomfortable. After lunch I was taken to the drawing room, where they had lighted a fire in my honour. It is a bright yellow room stuffed with very cheap objects. Mrs Turner began to talk about Saxon. He appeared and murmured "Shall I go up to Mr Palmer?" "He's gone to sit with one of my patients" she said "so that I may talk to you. Now, isn't that wonderful of the boy? Not many sons would do that." She told me how he had learnt his letters before he could talk, how he had had the whooping cough when he was nine months old, and often turned as black as the poker "for a child of that age couldn't understand about coughing the phlegm up", how he had never given her a moments anxiety; except about his food. His sciatica chiefly comes from eating the wrong things; and going without dinner. She only wished he could find a good wife! but he showed no signs of it. I'm sure she thought that I was after him, and had come over to pursue him. Then she told me all about Cuthbert, who is six feet 1 and looks every inch of it; very different from Saxon; very handsome; and would die if he had to sit in an office like Saxon; he has shot 3 elephants; one cant imagine Saxon shooting an elephant!—but still, if he chose there's nothing he couldn't do. He has the sweetest nature of any living creature. Then we talked about his dinners again, and she asked me to speak to him seriously; and about his landlady, and about his constitution, which is naturally very tough, for though small-boned, he has a great deal of strength in him, more than Cuthbert; though people always think *Saxon* the weaker of the two.

Then we got on to Julian, and the nameless one,[1] who ought to be called Vivian, or Fabian or Virginius, according to her.

At last I said I must go; and she evidently had many patients waiting for her. Miss Charlotte is a patient. Evidently, they are very poor patients.

Saxon took me to the station; and we hardly spoke. It was very gritty and windy, and as there were no shops open, rather dull; there was no sunset, so that the glass didn't burn; and it reminded me of many dismal hours; and the Fishers.

I feel that one ought to think very kindly of Saxon. It is such a poverty-stricken middle class family, and if I were as distinguished and nice as Saxon, I should be much more arrogant. Think of Ottoline, in comparison!—how one might boast of having risen to know her. But of course he is completely placid and sincere, and always remembers his mother's hard lot. It was amazingly without colour.

1. Vanessa had grown displeased with the name 'Claudian', which she had chosen for her second son, and later called him Quentin.

444

Adrian is spending the day with Duncan. He did manage to catch his train last night.

Yr. B.

Berg

548: To Clive Bell   *The Pelham Arms, Lewes*
                                       [Sussex]
Thursday [29 December 1910]

Dearest Clive,

I didn't deserve another letter from you because that old Bitch left off suckling her whelps and wrote—However, I did deserve one, because of the quantity that goes into mine. I didn't neglect you; it seemed to me as though I were vociferating to a stone wall. So please write again—Nessa has a chow hand—three words, with all the fur on them, take up a line. With Adrian and Duncan swarming on the floor, making it like the bottom of an alligators tank, one gets no chance of reading. But I read your review with great pleasure—here you snort; partly derived from comparing it with what I should have written (this sounds natural) partly, from its own merits. You are much sturdier on your legs than you were; you stride over the ground, and plant words firmly, in a way I admire. My tendency would be to insinuate. But I'm glad that I need no longer pay compliments to Mr Buxton Forman[1]; it seems a pity that one's writing should be loaded with that kind of weight. I think you're good enough now to fly straight. I dont think I feel as warmly as you do about Trelawny's letters, which I've just finished. The imagination is often very watery, and the strength the strength of a man of action, whose brain is a simple machine divorced from his body. The quotation I liked was about the fleas: "he piqued himself upon being as dirty; having as much vermin, and letting them loose from his fingers in the same dignified manner, as if sparing a conquered enemy". Isn't that what Cole would do, supposing he caught a large bug in company? But I like the later letters, harping upon Shelley.

Here comes an eccentric post, with a letter from Madge, about her soul, which now, clothed in flesh, floats among the "elemental feelings which are *the Best,*" and scorns the "panoply of existence". Her pen has a way of squeaking like a slate pencil; I always make it squeak now. But at the same time dear Ott[oline]: asks me to stay with her: and Molly MacCarthy asks me to lunch; these small attentions are very comforting.

I probably go back on Sunday night, so as to start fresh on Monday; Jean comes tomorrow for the night; Adrian has just gone. As for my writing—you will have to wait for Mel[ymbrosia]. to see what has become

1. Henry Buxton Forman, who edited in 1910 *The Letters of Edward John Trelawny.*

of it. The Lit. Sup^t. doesn't print my single review; and the [*Guardian's*] Womans Sup^t. I take to be dead, and giving off odours. I should say that my great change was in the way of courage, or conceit; and that I had given up adventuring after other people's forms, as I used. But I expect that I am really less sensitive to style than you are, and so seem more steadfast. I'm not particularly conceited at this moment. No compliments come my way!

Will you really come and stay with me, if I buy this cottage?[1] Will the old Butcher's dog [Vanessa]—or will she always make excuses? If I were sure of that, I shouldn't hesitate; as it is, I think I'm going to risk it. For one thing, the charges at this Inn are so exorbitant that one couldn't come often; and then another side of life reveals itself in the country, which I cant help thinking of amazing interest. It is precisely as though one clapped on a solid half-globe to one's London life, and had hitherto always walked upon a strip of pavement. But I will do nothing without taking advice. Adrian wont share for a year anyhow, as he is going abroad for his holidays.

Your buns have just come—a great delight.

Yr.

VS

Running on like this, I have missed the post.

Quentin Bell

1. During this holiday Virginia found a semi-detached house in the village street of Firle, near Lewes, and decided to rent it. She named it Little Talland House in recollection of her childhood at St Ives.

Letters 549-570

Virginia settled in at Little Talland House, enjoyed walks on the Downs, wrote her novel, and entertained her friends, who entertained her with their love problems. Among them was Katherine (Ka) Cox, whom she had met staying at the Bertrand Russells, and they planned to go on holiday together to France. But hearing that Vanessa, now pregnant for the third time, had fallen ill in Turkey where she had gone with Clive, Roger Fry and H. T. J. Norton, Virginia hurried to join her at Broussa. There she found that Vanessa had had a miscarriage, and they returned by train to England. A further complication was that Vanessa and Roger Fry had fallen in love during this Turkish expedition, and the Bell marriage was henceforward slowly transformed into what Quentin Bell has called "a union of friendship".

549: To Violet Dickinson

Pelham Arms, Lewes
[Sussex]

New Years Day [1911]

My Violet,

Many happy returns of the day. The only present I have got for you is a picture of some cattle, which will interest you when you hear that the same people use them as used them when the Domesday Book was written. So the guide book says. In fact, it is altogether an interesting picture, when you think that your Sp: may be going to take a cottage in the neighborhood. It is a very ugly villa; but underneath the downs, in a charming village [Firle].

We have been spending Christmas here, with an extremely considerate landlady, who is so much struck by my incompetence to face life, that she always offers to lace my boots, and give me my bath. Miss Thomas came down for a night, in an interval between discharging a woman who wished to commit murder, and taking one, who wants to kill herself. Can you imagine living like that?—always watching the knives, and expecting to find bedroom doors locked, or a corpse in the bath? I said I thought it was too great a strain—but, upheld by Christianity, I believe she will do it.

What have you been doing? I forgot to tell you that Sophia cherishes a passion for celery, and devoured your roots by herself. Would you give your blessing to my cottage? I am very much tempted to take it, for £19.10 a year.

Nessa is with the old Bells, who talk of nothing but hockey and dill water. However, as it is Christmas, they have champagne for dinner, and she

447

manages to get slightly tipsy every night, so as to think it all a dream. They want to call the baby a new name, as everyone dislikes Claudian.

I'm very much excited by the thought of going back and writing the work of imagination. What a good thing the Quaker wont be shocked by it—she wanted me to write a life of Henry the 8th! One doesn't really think about her much now; that's what comes of being a mystic, I believe. They fade. But perhaps in Heaven they are as solid as brick.

A great attack was made upon my faith this Christmas, and I am led to think that Atheists are still persecuted. For instance, wishing to read just now, I was dinned crazy by a cracked church bell, which didn't peal, but merely hammered, like an arrogant and bigoted street seller. Then the congregation sings without understanding, and as for the psalms, which all the little news boys and errand boys, sing, I never heard anything so sense-less in my life. However, I suppose it would be too rash to burn them all. They must have imaginations. I am more charitable about them than they are about me.

This new year is not sanguine. It has been raining all the morning, and is now so dark—partly because the blinds wont pull up—that I am writing at 3 by firelight. In an hour it will be pitch dark. A summer night with stars is brighter. If you are at Longleat [Marquess of Bath], perhaps you have electric light, gramophones, telephones, and forget the seasons. If Beatrice is there give her my love, and tell her to write to me; if she wont do that, to come and see me. What is the price of the matting you have at the cottage? expensive?

I saw Aunt Minna, who was starting for Teneriffe, for winter sketching. Colours have to be very bright for her to see them; what with moss, lichens and sea birds, the rock is green, vermilion and Chinese white. She is taking glasses, like the window panes in country public houses; and with these she can see stationary objects that are not too near and not too far. She is a valiant old woman.

Yr. VS

How is Mrs Crum? Is there any news of Walter?

I go back tonight.

Berg

550: TO LADY OTTOLINE MORRELL   *The Pelham Arms,*
                                     Lewes
Sunday [1 January 1911]

Dearest Ottoline,
    It must be delightful [for Philip Morrell] to be in [Parliament], so trium-phantly—and what a mercy to have it over—only aren't you worked to the bone? We went to one meeting only, and that, what with cheering and

stamping and emotions of all kinds, was very exhausting. The candidate was a loathsome Portuguese Jew. But the crowd is far more exciting than anything else, and makes it almost impossible to sit down and read in ones room again.

Here I am sitting over an inn fire, and listening to the creaking of an enormous sign, painted with your family arms. They look rather beautiful, and I hope they wont be done away with when the Lords go. I wish I'd heard you upon morals in high life! But there are merits in the aristocracy which dont appear to you—and manners, and freedom.

I am very much tempted to buy a house here. One has the most lovely downs at one's door, and there are beautiful 18th century houses, with Corinthian pillars inside, oak panels, and marble mantelpieces. Are country cottages very expensive? Do the roofs leak? One misses such a lot in London. Even now, when it is about to rain, there are wonderful colours.

I suppose you have heard of the terrible ructions which have split our world in two since you went away[1]. The plan is now to give a fancy dress ball, where Clive shall be a Guardsman, and Lytton a ballet girl, and they will embrace before they discover, and make it up. But quarrels are really rather exciting.

Is our world very small compared with yours? I am now going out to walk for miles and miles. I wish you were here.

Do let me come down for the day some time. I should love it.

Your aff.ate,
V.S.

Texas

551: To Clive Bell   *Bagley Wood, Oxford*

[23 January 1911]

Dearest Clive,

Tuesday would be best and, I need hardly say, delightful. On Friday I dont really get back till 5.30. Here I am in the heart (or perhaps that isnt the typical feature) of young womanhood. I like clever young women, in spite of my brother in law (That was said to tease).

Gumbo [Marjorie Strachey] is seated at the piano, dressed in a tight green jersey, which makes her resemble the lean cat in the advertisement, singing O Dolche Amor, to her own accompaniment. The accompaniment ends: she flings her hands up, and gives vent to a passionate shriek; crashes her hands down again and goes on. A dry yellow skin has formed round her lips, owing to her having a fried egg for breakfast. Save that her songs are passionate,

1. The quarrel between Clive Bell and Lytton Strachey. Clive had become jealous of Lytton's intimacy with Virginia and Vanessa, and thought himself excluded. He told Lytton that he would no longer be welcome at Gordon Square.

we have not mentioned the subject. But Roger [Fry] is discussed perpetually, and she has a letter from him, about her Friday Club paper, which he takes to be a direct attack upon himself. Beginning my dear Marjorie: it ends Yrs. very sincerely. I have not seen her alone, as I went first to Court Place[1], and was there made to play Scramble patience for some hours. We had an icy motor drive over to Bagley.[2] The motor broke down on the slope of a steep muddy hill; and Gumbo was seized with hysterics, imagining that a dog would run between her legs. I said that she need fear nothing of the kind, but did not give my reasons: and the baying of a hound in a far away farm made her fling herself upon Ray. Last night Gumbo gave us a long disquisition upon her character, talents, passions, and so forth; and told us that she would give all the praise she has for brilliance, if one person (preferably a man) would say she was lovely. No one rose. She has improved; and we get on better. No one makes me laugh more. She is a real figure.

Thus far I got; and then Ray's Miss Cox[3] arrived. Miss Cox is one of the younger Newnhamites, and it is said that she will marry either a Keynes or a Brook. She has a superficial resemblance to a far younger and prettier Sheepshanks. She is a bright, intelligent, nice creature; who has, she says, very few emotions, but thinks so highly of Gwen [Darwin] that she even copies her way of speech. I am writing this in the waiting room at Oxford, having caught an unexpected omnibus on the high road, and thus arrived ½ an hour early. We played patience to an early hour this morning; and became very frank and indecent. Gumbo told us how her period affected her entrails, and finally destroyed her voice, upon which we all asked (she had been singing Brahms) whether she was now indisposed. It appeared that she was suffering from diarrhoea—all this pleased me very much, and I repeat that I like clever young women. Also I had a compliment on my beauty. This was a little dashed by hearing that Gumbo had felt a distinct emotion of love upon last seeing Nessa.

Yrs.

Quentin Bell   V.S.

552: To Violet Dickinson   29 *Fitzroy Square, W.*

24th Jan [1911]

My Violet,
    You couldn't have given me a more useful or delightful present. I've just had to throw away my old book stand. This one comes like a miracle to replace it. You are a wonderful woman! Are you in London? Shall I come and

1. Where the Pearsall Smiths lived.
2. Bertrand Russell's house. Mrs Russell (Alys) was an aunt of Ray and Karin.
3. Katherine ('Ka') Cox, who later married Will Arnold-Forster. She was a close friend of the Costelloe sisters, Rupert Brooke and Gwen Darwin.

see you? I'm very much excited—furnishing my cottage, and staining the floors the colour of the Atlantic in a storm. Are you well?

With great affection,

Yr. Sp:

Berg

553: To Lady Ottoline Morrell   29 *Fitzroy Square, W.*

[end-January 1911]

Dearest Ottoline,

I wish I could come next Sunday. It would be enchanting (perhaps not for your maid though!) and we could leave Desmond [MacCarthy], as one leaves a kettle on the hob.

But, alas, I've got to go down [to Firle] and make curtains and move beds at the cottage, having been so rash as to ask 5 people to stay the week after. Nessa is bringing a sewing machine; and in the intervals, I shall spur her to bouts of talk. Then we shall become very intimate, and matronly, and discuss the past and the future. Will you let me come some other time, for the night, as before? That visit remains so clear in my mind, as a thing I enjoyed immensely. You give your friends great happiness. Desmond was purring all over.

It was very good of you to write to Mr Pearsall Smith. It isn't an audience to be afraid of—mostly eager gulls.

I suppose Harry Lamb is back again, with all his whims. He was seen in London. Marjorie [Strachey], I think, has cooled down. I spent a Sunday there; and she seemed switched off on another tack. She has taken to painting pictures. I cant help wishing (its a thing I dont often notice) that she wouldnt wear drawers of shiny black alpaca, like a chemists coat.

Yr. aff.ate,

Texas   V.S.

554: To Violet Dickinson   29 *Fitzroy Square, W.*

Sunday [29 January? 1911]

My Violet,

I will come to lunch on Thursday with pleasure.

I spent yesterday finishing off the cottage. Its right underneath the downs, and though itself an eyesore, still that dont matter when one's inside. I have one gooseberry bush; 3 mongrels, thought by some to grow currants. Shall you ever come and stay there? There is a Bath, and a W. C.

Yr. VS

We shall be on the telephone on Tuesday—797 Mayfair.

Berg

555: To James Strachey   29 *Fitzroy Sq.*

Postcard
[3rd March 1911]

Dear James,
     Will you come and stay at Firle on the 18th? I warn you it won't be comfortable; there will only be the pleasures of the soul—Nessa, Norton (perhaps) and me. I hope you will brave it.
                                                                          Yrs.
Strachey Trust   VS

556: To James Strachey   29 *Fitzroy Sq.*

[10 March 1911]

Dear James,
     Do come [to Firle] on Friday, leave, if you must, and come again. There are many trains; not extravagant—weekend tickets etc.
     I think Nessa will be all right; though we have reasons for wishing otherwise.
     Chaperones I know we must have; my heart being inflammable.
     But couldn't you really burke your function; and stay on—it would be much better.
                                                                          Yrs.
Strachey Trust   VS

557: To Saxon Sydney-Turner   29 *Fitzroy Square, W.*

[11 March 1911]

My Dear Saxon,
     I went to the library about your quotation. They had only got the volumes up to 1907. I looked through them (from 1902) and could not find any paper by Gaye [?]. Shall I look in the British Museum? The Library would get in the later volumes for me, but it would take time—and I think you are in a hurry.
     I'll look in Dr Williams [Library]—in case he has them.
     By the way, I saw Ottoline the other night, who talked of you with her usual mixture of awe and affection; and read me a letter from Harry Lamb, describing your 'supremacy' not daring to ask you to tea. She wanted me to explain that she is at home now for 3 Thursdays. Then we discussed Harry Lamb at great length—then I saw Walter and heard the story of his corres-

pondence with Dr somebody or other about Christianity. Dr —— says "How I wish I had a man like you on my staff!" Walter is making himself exceedingly agreeable to the young things at Newnham.[1] His stone is melting.

Yr. very aff.,

Barbara Bagenal

VS

558: To Clive Bell

Little Talland House, Firle

Saturday [March 1911]

Dearest Clive,

Your wife having given me a good snubbing, I was too proud to ask you to come down, though much tempted to. I cant help thinking that you have missed more than Roger Fry will replace—not conversation, no—but a starlight walk upon the downs, a horse nibbling and taking one for a great white sheep, a flock ringing bells, startled birds and the sea too. All these things I have had to myself—remembering certain strictures, I will keep them to myself. Only, as I've seen no one but the woman Nessa calls Widow Simpson (wife Stephens—she gave me a bunch of her own early violets) I cant be garrulous on those lines. The only event has been a telegram from Adrian, to say that [Horace] Cole has made him miss his train; and he's motoring down. This almost threatens Cole himself. Anyhow I shall hear the last gossip of that sordid, gas-lit Piccadilly circus affair.[2] As both Cole and Irene are upon the downward path, sampling human nature and spitting it out, why not marry them together? I cant help thinking that he has more heroic qualities than her other samples.

In default of company (a rusty sneer intended!) I have done nothing but read. Meals take 10 minutes to prepare, if one is sagacious enough to begin one's potatoes after breakfast. Owing to this foresight, I had a potatoe so cooked that its skin rose in crackling bubbles, on the surface, and it was soft to the heart. Also a tapioca pudding.

I have just upon finished Desmonds Santayana, with amazement— whether at his powers or my own, or at the thoughts in the world, I cannot say. I think it is really astonishment at the number of disembodied things of great importance shut up in books. Having lived an active talkative life so long, prying into people through their sayings, I had rather forgotten how much thinking is done outside my own head. And yet, reading is like shutting the doors of a Cathedral, one becomes so pure. This would not apply to works of imagination, I suppose. Are you still a reader?

Active life again encroaches—Widow Hughes, this time, who can cook, and feels terrible lonesome at home, would like to be my cook, just to have

1. Walter Lamb lectured on classics at Cambridge from 1905-7 and 1909-13.
2. See the penultimate paragraph of this letter.

something to do. Now that her lodger, a gamekeeper, is gone to better himself, and her eleven children are placed in the world (all except the little girl who's not quite like other people) she often stands outside her door of a morning and says "Which way shall I go?" Being very fond of the hills, she goes up there sometimes at dawn, and picks mushrooms in the Summer. But then theres the day, and the long evenings—and so on. The question is, how to dispose of Widow Stephens, who is favoured by the Vicar, and given the Church to clean, though she's going through her funny time of life, when women often feel too queer to clean their own houses, let alone other peoples—

(Sunday)

Adrian arrived at nine. The Cole affair has broken out again. Lilian has disappeared. Adrian was whirled about until 6 o'clock—Various brothels were visited. One of the men left Paris yesterday, the theory is that she killed her illegitimate child: and the Jew, knowing this, does what he likes with her. She had had a mysterious letter. But killing an illegitimate child would surely be a slight crime; and she cant care for her character. Yet she has got no money out of Cole, so that it does not seem politic to bolt just yet.[1]

However this was all washed out of my head by a tremendous walk which we've just come back from. We found the churchyard [at Bishopstone, near Lewes] where Rutherford[2] is buried, and Saxon stood bareheaded. It was a divine Spring day. Not only the Parliament,[3] but several singing birds have been at it. Adrian is now occupied, like a wizard brewing potions in a cell, peeling onions, with his great horn spectacles on, and a pipe in his mouth. The hotch potch is being prepared. I, you see, escape to the drawing room. My head feels like a gently bubbling kettle—an ideal state; though perhaps you wont see the virtues of it reflected here. By the way, I'm told that I said that Duncan *dis*liked R.Fs [Roger Fry] picture: I think I said that he thought it nice but weak. O these misunderstandings.

Quentin Bell

1. The details and characters of this 'sordid affair' are not now recoverable.
2. William Gunion Rutherford (1853-1907), Headmaster of Westminster School, and a classical scholar.
3. Between February and May 1911 the House of Commons was vociferously debating the Parliament Bill.

559: To Molly MacCarthy   29 *Fitzroy Square, W.*

[March 1911]

Dear Molly,

I shall be delighted to come to lunch on Thursday, only I'm afraid I must go sooner than I generally do go, when I come to see you, as I have to dress up again as a South Sea Savage, to figure in a picture. Its an awful bore! How angelic of you to have sent those things! They hadn't come on Monday, but we left very early, and I expect they are there now.

Will you tell Desmond that I am sending back his Santayana, which I enjoyed immensely, and read straight off in amazement at the number of ideas in the world. I am sending, too, the old book which he lent father years ago not to forget it.

Here, at last, is what we owe for the tickets.

I met Miss Ponsonby the other day: and shall like very much to meet her again.

I hope the dance didn't exhaust you. Was I less alarming as a savage[1]—or as bad as ever?

Yr. aff.
VS

Mrs Michael MacCarthy

560: To Jacques Raverat   29 *Fitzroy Square, W.*

[late March 1911]

Dear Mr Raverat,[2]

On hearing of your important engagement, I was ready to let you off the other one. But Gwen says you will come, without cursing. The train is the 3.20 from Victoria on Saturday. We are going by that, so I hope you may be able to.

My congratulations are very warm. As I said, I have heard so much of you, that I can congratulate her too.

Yours,
Virginia Stephen

It will probably be ghastly uncomfortable at Firle. Take a week end ticket to Lewes.

Sussex

1. At the Post-Impressionist Ball.
2. The French painter, who was educated in England. He married Virginia's friend Gwen Darwin on 27 May 1911.

Little Talland House, Firle,
near Lewes, Sussex

[April 1911]

My dear Molly,

I'm so sorry I couldn't come to see you. Desmond asked me to come one day, but then we had a great presentation to manage—we gave the cook a clock.

I wonder whether possibly you and Desmond would come down and stay with me? I shall be at Firle till the 21st. There are two week-ends—8th and 15th. I wonder if you could manage either—only do come for more than a week-end.

I'm very ignorant about what one does after a child has been born.

I shall have a cook, but not great comfort to offer. Still the downs ought to be nice. The villa is inconceivably ugly, done up in patches of post-impressionist colour. I never thanked you for the furniture. The chair is the perfection of comfort. It was angelic of you.

It is delightful that you have another son. It's such a mercy to start fresh with no child in prospect. What about all our Clubs and performances.

We enjoyed Desmond's letter immensely.

Your affect.,

VS

Mrs Michael MacCarthy

562: To Vanessa Bell *Little Talland House, Firle,*
Lewes, Sussex

April 6th [1911]

Beloved,

I suppose you had a record bad crossing [en route to Turkey]. Really, luck is the very devil. However, its no use speculating now about it, as I shant hear; and you are crossing Europe.

I am alone; Ray [Rachel Costelloe] has just gone. We had meant to motor, but the snow kept us indoors. We went out once, and got bleached and drenched; she floundered like a calf. However, talk proved interesting. Here comes a piece of gossip which you *must* keep private. Talking of Oliver Strachey, she said "I can quite imagine falling in love with him". I said "I suppose you mean you *are* in love with him". She said "No: I only see that I might be—but dont want to be." I said "Is he in love with you?" She said "Oh no—not a bit. But he was very friendly." This morning however, she had a letter from him asking her to go over some railway works. This evidently pleased her very much. I'm pretty sure there will be an affair in that direction; she is either in love, or on the verge of it, so if it happens dont say "Poor Synge [Virginia]! snubbed again!"

At any rate, it seems clear that he is in a very susceptible state of mind, and you must therefore discount his attentions to me. The [Bertrand] Russells, Ray says, are trying to bring off a match between him and Isabel Fry [Roger's sister]. Poor wretch!—he has jumped into a kettle, as you would say. It promises to be a lively summer.

Ray told me that she is really very susceptible to men, though no man has been in love with her. She always stakes out the ground, as she calls it, with a new man; and considers the possibilities. "Could you marry Adrian?" I asked her. She said that would be impossible.

She is a good satisfactory creature, as downright as a poker, and very queer in the tremors of imagined love. But perhaps one would find her a little heavy? She told me that Mrs [Bernard] Berenson had treated old Costelloe[1] very badly, as he really had great merits. It now seems possible (this is further gossip, secret, and probably inaccurate) that she will leave B. as his temper has grown intolerable; and she is very unhappy. What a sheet of amorous gossip! But now that I'm alone you wont have anything but talk of trees and downs.

If only it would stop blowing and snowing, I should be very happy.

Having servants, turns this house into a comfortable respectable place. They are very goodhumoured, though Sophie seems to jam in the doors rather.

Ray is coming back next week. I've not heard from Saxon or the MacCarthy's; but I should rather like a week alone.

I feel a little worried about you. I see that the Ostend boat had to wait an hour at Dover. I feel pretty sure that I shall have to announce Olivers engagement to Ray in my next!

Yr. B.

Berg

563: To Vanessa Bell   *Little Talland House, Firle,*
                                        Lewes, Sussex

April 8th [1911]

Beloved,

Another card came this morning from Passau, which I told Sophie, is in Germany. Anyhow, you sound safe so far. I think Mother Sill [seasick remedy] is only bad if you take a quantity.

My news threatens to dry up—and there's always the doubt whether you'll get the letter.

I've had letters from Ray, Molly MacCarthy, and Saxon. I think Rays letter hints at possible mysteries: she says that fate is interfering with her plans—Can Oliver have proposed? She spent 4 days with him; and they met

1. Mrs Berenson's first husband, and Ray's father.

at Oxford—it might have happened. There can be no doubt, I think about her side of it. She said she'd felt much the same for 4 or 5 other men. But I thought there was something on his side too. What old gossips we are!

Molly and Desmond are in the Isle of Wight, so they cant come. Saxon sends a very exquisite letter in red ink; he talks of 'they' and 'he', and wishes me to propose another literary work for his evenings; he is feeling very cold, and cannot risk coming here. I shall probably be alone till the 19th. I am rather amused at being alone. I haven't been alone in the country since that summer at Wells, when I used to get letters from Hilton [Young].

I write all the morning, walk all the afternoon, and read and write and look out of the window the rest of the time.

The country is so amazingly beautiful, that I frequently have to stop and say "Good God!" I went to a mediaeval castle [Laughton Place] in the marsh this afternoon. Well—I wont describe; but promise me to come here the Sunday after you get back, and to say whether anything in Europe beats it.

The plovers were in a tremendous excitement. I met Lord Gage[1] in the village. He's not only crouch backed, but he is bitten by the same disease as Porchy [Lord Porchester]. He has a face like a dead hares, only white and scarlet. He was hobbling along on the Vicars arm, to inspect the tombs in the church. They looked at me; and I'd fallen into [a] dike, and got mud up to the knees! Happily, Maud had put a tuck into my petticoat.

The old gentleman, a clergyman, is being persuaded to bury the head of Cromwell.[2] They say its indecent to keep it in a box.

I have the greatest desire to see it; and even stroke it. Haven't you?

That is really the only news in England. If anyone praises me, say so. Its odd, retiring from the world like this. I feel as if I were 15 again—one begins to think of books and describing scenery just as one used. I am reading the Liaison Dangereuses[3] with great delight.

This is all very dull. Adrian has got to Marseilles, and suddenly discovers Hans' chain in his pocket. This causes a good deal of excitement in the kitchen. Sophie and Maud sit all day machining curtains in the dining room, and talking very comfortably and incessantly. What can they have to say, I wonder?

Yr. B.

You'll be at Constantinople today. How exciting! I suppose tomorrow I ought to write to Greece, but I'm not sure.

Berg

1. The 5th Viscount Gage, owner of Firle Place.
2. Canon Wilkinson was at this time the owner of Oliver Cromwell's skeletal head, and exhibited it in 1911 before the Royal Archaeological Institute. The head was buried in 1960 at Sidney Sussex College, Cambridge.
3. *Les Liaisons dangereuses*, by Pierre Choderlos de Laclos, 1782.

Little Talland House, Firle, Lewes, Sussex

9th April [1911]

Dear Jacques,

I've been long in writing, but I knew you would put that down to the infernal confusion of London—not to ingratitude. It was delightful of you to think of sending that book. In fact you have a delightful nature. Thank you so much. I've just been cutting the pages, and seeing several bold words which tempt me on, in spite of the Sabbath. I shall begin seriously after dinner.

We left London in a flurry, but now I'm here alone and shall be alone for a fortnight. I read furiously and write and walk. Its a very satisfactory life, and much more exciting, even than talking. As for the country, I never imagined anything so beautiful. I've discovered several new walks.

You and Gwen must come here again. By the way, would this house be any use to you both for a week or fortnight after 23rd? I shall probably be in France with Ka; away anyhow; and it seems a pity that all these sights shouldn't be seen.

One can put up six, as you know.

Thank you again.

> Yours ever,
> Virginia Stephen

I can't remember your address. I hope your walk was good.

Sussex

Little Talland House, Firle, Lewes, Sussex

April 13th [1911]

My dear Saxon,
　　The addresses are
> C/o Cook
> Place de la Constitution,
> Athens

from April 20th to 27th.
　　After that C/o Ionian Bank,
> Patras.

I dont know how late that may mean. Adrian is,
> C/o Cook,
> Galleria Vittoria,
> Via Chiatamone,
> Naples.

The weather being now divine I've spend a happy week alone. I think I shall be alone till Wednesday. I believe its the ideal life—one reads so much. I suppose you do that in London, certainly its very pleasant. George and Margaret [Duckworth] came yesterday, but thank God I was out, having fallen into the canal. Margaret was heard to say she'd never seen a prettier house. I am reading the Prelude [Wordsworth]. Dont you think it one of the greatest works ever written? Some of it, anyhow, is sublime; it may get worse. I am reading Liaisons Dangereuses. I wish you would bring out the classics facing an English translation; but that needing money, why not translate some Plato adequately? I suppose your taste though is for rare authors. I haven't seen H. O. Meredith's[1] poems. I should like to. I've heard from Nessa and Clive; they are very well; Clive at Dover determined to give up the tour, but Nessa got on to the ship and sat down, and would not move. Roger fell flat on his back, but did not injure his spine as they feared. This letter from Adrian may amuse you.

Yr. VS

Sussex

566: To Clive Bell   *Little Talland House, Firle,*
                                       Lewes, Sussex
18th April [1911]

Dearest Clive,

Before you get this you will, I hope, have been calling me a foolish creature for sending you a wire. My excuse is that I cant altogether quiet the alarm that Nessa has been taken ill in some way; and this made you stay on.[2] I agree that I ought to be easy with your tout va bien; but as I shant hear till Thursday or Friday, and the letter may miss me (you seem to think I'm in London—and I shall be at [Dr] Savages) well—I was extravagant. I am encouraged, by seeing that your plans seem to change a good deal. According to your list, you left Cple. on the 17th for good.

Having been kept awake till 4 this morning by dogs barking, and waked at 7 by pumps beginning and cocks, I am stupid and cross; though my head rides triumphant. Your letters have been falling in a shower—a great joy. I'm as uneventful as a parish magazine compared with you; but still, very happy. At any moment my Neo Pagan[3] Cox may descend. I had a shout

1. 'Hom' Meredith, a Fellow of King's College, Cambridge, and lecturer in Economics. His book was *Weekday Poems*, 1911.
2. At Broussa, Turkey. Virginia had read between the lines of Clive's letters that all was not well. Vanessa in fact had a miscarriage there.
3. This is Virginia's first use of the term invented by Bloomsbury to describe the intellectual group which included Rupert Brooke, Ka Cox, Gwen and Jacques Raverat, Frances Cornford and David Garnett.

from her yesterday. "O this Sun! I've been tramping all day, and singing. I want to talk to everyone I meet about the sun! They say its a fine Easter. Life's good."

I'm very reluctant to be broken in upon, by anyone; unless indeed it were someone I *couldn't* touch with a short stick! I've seldom enjoyed myself more than I have this fortnight. Perhaps theres vanity in it. Perhaps one's proud of being a self sufficient animal, like the camel of the desert, who eats his own hump. Nessa can tell you about him. I've found a new walk every day. You must come here and go there with me. There are plains, rivers, downs and the sea to choose from. You will wag your head, and say "Poor creature! Cornwall again!" I admit the Spring may have something to do with it. Its odd how completely one can withdraw from the world. I can hardly believe I was splashing about in Ott's drawing room only a fortnight ago. The succession of holidays, and the perfectly fine days, make one feel as though everything had gone to sleep. Jean [Thomas], indeed, comes knocking at the door. She had a river party yesterday with a very clever, but *not merely* clever, cousin who is fellow of Trinity Dublin; She asked me to go. What will be the end of Jean I cant think. My letters are scattered about Europe, so you mayn't have heard of her determination to study French history. Suppose this ends in Atheism, and she gives up lunatic keeping: well, her blood will be on my head.

I have had few letters of interest. Saxon writes, to draw my attention to the works of Theophrastus. I see that Saxon is now going to become a Grammarians Funeral.[1] He is going to edit some immense, corrupt, quite worthless work, in his leisure, just because other people wont do it. It will appear about 1950, he'll be made O.M. and the young will imitate his habits, as they do the habits of Fred Maitland.

Jacques writes to me, from Cornwall. He wants to settle about our Camp.[2] He is quite red, quite unshaven, hatless, with only one book—Rabelais; in two months, he says, . . . That I take to mean, bed with Gwen. It is portentous; I think the dots give the feeling rather well. How malicious we are about them! But I suppose they have their own brand of malice.

Yesterday I finished the 8th Chapter of Mel[ymbrosia]: which brings them within sight of the South American shore. That is a third of the book done, I think.[3] From sheer cowardice, I didn't bring the other chapters here. If I

1. She refers to Browning's poem of the same title.
2. Probably the plan realised in late August 1911, when Virginia and Ka Cox joined Rupert Brooke, Maynard Keynes and others on a camping expedition in Devon.
3. Virginia is referring to her latest draft of *The Voyage Out*. We know from Clive's letter to her of February 1909 that she had completed at least eleven chapters by that date, because he refers to the picnic, which occurs in Chapters 10 and 11 of the published novel. Therefore in speaking of 'a third of the book done', she means that she has rewritten a third of it.

thought "There! thats solid and done with" I'm sure I should have the palsy. Some of it, I'm certain, will have the pallor of headache upon it. But its no good attempting to rewrite. Eily [Darwin] comes tomorrow morning; I shall probably go up to London on Friday night; (21st) and to Savages on Saturday. I hope we shall start for France on the Monday—24th but when I have seen Ka, I shall know more. I mean to throw myself into youth, sunshine, nature, primitive art. Cakes with sugar on the top, love, lust, paganism, general bawdiness, for a fortnight at least; and not write a line.

What news is there to fill the page? I'm not engaged; the affairs of Ray and Oliver are, I suppose, at a standstill. She writes me from Corfe, where she is staying with Elly [Elinor Rendel]. Observing one day that Elly seemed low spirited, she looked and saw that Elly had gone blind; not only so, but was afraid of madness too. She had been walking with her eyes shut. Something suddenly went wrong; and she has to keep her eyes shut for a week, until she can get glasses. The madness was induced by brooding. As she has just failed to get some post, her gloom is profound.

This house has been turned into a very comfortable villa. "You wouldn't like to be public, Miss" said Maud; and put up thick curtains. I had been sitting naked before the Vicars gardener. The tailor having refused to make chair covers, I have persuaded the dressmaker.

Give the old creature an embrace—I wish I knew that she is quite well. But I shall hear this evening. "Firle, England" is address for wires.

Yr. VS

Quentin Bell

567: TO VANESSA BELL   *Little Talland House, Firle,*
                                             Lewes, Sussex
19th April [1911]

Beloved,

I've just come in from meeting Eily, and find your wire. As you say all is well, I suppose I am a fool to worry. At any rate all my doubts will be cleared up tomorrow or Friday, so I wont waste paper describing them. Only if you knew what anxieties you can send across the ocean, you would be excessively careful. You seem to do so much; aren't your males a little exacting?

I've had some intercourse with the world since I wrote. Ka came striding along the road in time for lunch yesterday; with a knapsack on her back, a row of red beads, and daisies stuck in her coat. Her innocent face was brown. We went for a walk; and lay on the grass, and surveyed the view. Then she began to tell me of her private affairs, which are very private; so dont share them. What advice would you have given I wonder? The state of the case is this.

Jacques, as you know, proposed to her, less than a year ago. She refused him several times. At last this autumn, thinking she would never care, she urged him to consider Gwen. Gwen quickly fell in love; and Jacques, seeing this, was overcome, proposed, and was accepted. He says now that he is in love with them both; and asks Ka to be his mistress, and Gwen to satisfy his mind. Gwen is made very jealous; Ka evidently cares a good deal for Jacques.

Obviously (in my view) J. is very much in love with K: and not much, if at all, with Gwen. Ought they to break off the engagement? J. has doubts, occasionally; Ka sometimes thinks she could marry him; Gwen alternately grows desperate, and then, accepting J's advanced views, suggests that Ka shall live with them, and bear children, while she paints.

There are endless possibilities of discomfort; but cynically considering the infantine natures of all concerned, I predict nothing serious. Ka will marry a Brooke next year, I expect. J. will always be a Volatile Frog. Gwen will bear children, and paint pictures; clearly though, J. and K. would be the proper match.

I've just seen Ka off, and fetched Eily here. Eily is very stout; but very nice. In the pauses between raptures over hills and clouds, she gave me her version of the affair.

She agrees with me that J. is much more in love with K. than with Gwen; she thinks the risks tremendous; but says that if it is broken off, Gwen will certainly go off her head.

I rather doubt that; but she would be very unhappy, and perhaps this is her only chance. The trouble is, to my mind, that they're none of them clever enough to carry the thing through successfully; and J. has muddied their minds with talk of the unchastity of chastity.

God! how I wish I knew about you! I am now going to take Eily for a walk. She has already told me that its a great bore marrying a man without taste. Having made a large sum by a story, Bernard [Darwin] bought her a picture, as a surprise; it was a work by a man called [George] Belcher, who draws for Punch. She says she found it very difficult to be grateful.

We shall go to France on Monday night, 24th. Address letters to Post Restante, Poitiers. until 31st. I shall come back on the 1st I think. All the places are close, so Poitiers will be our headquarters.

Yr. B.

The man at the post office has supplied me with this remarkable address.

Berg

463

Little Talland House, Firle,
Lewes, Sussex

April 20th [1911]

Beloved,

I'm writing in haste, before starting for an expedition to the sea with Eily. No letter has come from you, which is disappointing; but as Clive wires to London, you may think I'm there.

We have talked a good deal; she is a nice woman, in spite of her marriage. I have heard about Conder; and Bernards past. He was neglected as a small boy, by his stepmother; and this led him to take to golf, which Eily says has ruined his life. When he has enough to live on, he will do nothing but play.

One can only hope he will be struck dead on the golf course, for I suppose one can grow too old for golf. Her memories of [Augustus] John and [Charles] Conder are far more alive than anything else. But she is much agitated now about the Gwen and Jacques affair. Gwen comes to her and sobs, because she is so jealous, but wont say who she's jealous of. I'm sure J. will always be susceptible; and as Gwen will grow stout, he will roam widely.

The only other gossip was about Olive [Ilbert]. Hilton cut her at some party; she was desperate. She wrote to Fredegond[1], and said that if Fredegond did not bring about a meeting and a reconciliation before the end of the year, she would kill herself. F: doesn't even know Hilton; but was much agitated and went to Frances Cornford.[2] Frances, having seen Hilton, understood that Olives case was hopeless, and wrote to Olive a very strong letter; abusing her for preying upon Fredegond. All this has only just happened. Olive says there is something on her conscience, which she must put right by seeing him. Can this be anything to do with me? Eily of course, knew about my affair; she says Olive has told the story to all the young generation.[3]

I must stop, as we have to catch a train. Eily goes tomorrow. Oh dear, I wish I'd heard from you. I'm flourishing.

Yr. B.

I cant help wishing you'd be more explicit in your telegrams, but its no use wishing!

Eily sends this!

Berg

1. Younger daughter of Virginia's cousin Florence Fisher by her first marriage to F. W. Maitland.
2. Bernard Darwin's half-sister, married to Francis Cornford.
3. Virginia refers to Hilton's proposal to her.

Thursday [25 May 1911]

My Violet,

It is an age since I heard from you. Are you visible? Did you hear of our adventures in the East? Nessa managed to bring off a miscarriage in Broussa, a days journey from Constantinople. I went out, and found her surrounded by males, with a chemist for doctor. We had to get a litter made, and carry her stretched on it, through Constantinople and home by the Orient Express. It was the oddest parody of what we did five years ago [in Greece]. Since coming back she has recovered, and will get away for a bit I hope next week. But their holiday was more than ruined—all owing to the stupidity of a dreary little doctor who ought never to have let her start.

I daresay you've heard all this, and find it very dull. I wish you'd let me come and see you, if you are in London. I am now just settling to work again after these agitations. I know most of the parts of the female inside by now, but that is useless knowledge in my trade, the british public being what it is. We have been spending our days going to music lately. Today I ran into that elongated Miss Ponsonby, whose teeth continue long after her lip has stopped. I suppose that you have gone to Welwyn. My cottage is so beautiful that I can hardly stay in London. Would one be as foolish about one's baby? I suppose so.

I have now entered into a treaty with my widow who eats my scraps and cooks at a low rate, and also steals flowers off the great estate [Firle Place], and gives me a great bunch every Monday.

We had the oddest time abroad. I was there for a week. Roger put everything down to insanity, which was puzzling at first. There was also a crude Cambridge mathematician [H. T. J. Norton], who used to draw diagrams of the Ovaries on the table cloth, taking it for granted that a woman is the same shape as a kind of monkey.

Do write and say what has been happening. Aunt Minna hovers round, with new glasses, which enlarge one eye to the size of a cows. All my friends are getting married. We have to go to Cambridge on Saturday to see the last one of the Darwins.[1] I did my best by indiscretions to break it off—without success!

Your VS

D'you mind taking one of these prospectuses.

Berg

1. The marriage of Gwen Darwin and Jacques Raverat.

Thursday [8? June 1911]

Beloved,

A dreadful Whitsunday blankness has descended upon us. We hoped that the storm would lighten the air—far from it. The storm was terrific. As nearly as possible Synge [Virginia] was taken from you. A great flash almost came in at the window. A church was set on fire.

Did you feel horribly depressed? I did. I could not write, and all the devils came out—hairy black ones. To be 29 and unmarried—to be a failure—childless—insane too, no writer. I went off to the Museum to try and subdue them, and having an ice afterwards, met Rupert Brooke, with, presumably, a Miss Olivier.[1] Her beauty was marred by protruberant blemishes; as she wasn't beautiful, only a pretty chit, perhaps she wasn't Miss Olivier.

Today things are rather less sultry, in spite of the fact that we have just had Saxon to dinner.

Mauds brother has had four fingers cut off by a machine for making pear drops. The sweets stuck—he put his hand in to free them, and it was drawn into the mill. The misery of the lower classes impresses me very much. Think of losing a hand making pear drops!

Marjorie [Strachey] has just telephoned goodbye. Tomorrow she goes into a Rest Cure in Mecklenburgh Square. She has some strange symptoms which do not get better. At the same time Elly [Rendel] has broken down; she too goes into a nursing home.

I think a good deal about you. How are you feeling? What a mercy it would be if you came back completely cured! How the apes would rejoice.

The tea party is tomorrow. I will wire if Billy [Virginia] gets the first prize.

Please get Roger to settle what day he will come to Firle, and press him to. Then I will get Desmond. Everyone is away now I suppose.

I shall probably go down to Firle alone on Saturday, which will be rather a treat.

As it is very hot, and Adrian and Saxon are sweating at the opera, I am going up to Hampstead to see if I can drag old [Janet] Case out for a walk among the lovers on the heath.

This haste explains the dulness of this letter: nevertheless every word glows like a horseshoe on the anvil with passion. These June nights!—how amorous they make one. Tell me how you are and any adventures.

Yr. B.

Berg

1. One of the four daughters (Margery, Brynhild, Daphne and Noel) of Sir Sydney Olivier, Governor of Jamaica and Fabian Socialist.

Letters 571-592

Leonard Woolf returned on leave in June 1911, after nearly seven years' absence in Ceylon. He and Virginia had not corresponded during the whole of this period, but he soon slipped back into the company of his Cambridge (now Bloomsbury) friends, and on 3 July dined with Clive and Vanessa, and Virginia came in afterwards. He began to visit her at Firle, but the next offer of marriage came to her not from Leonard but from Walter Lamb, whom she turned down. She spent weekends with Lady Ottoline Morrell and Rupert Brooke, and with Brooke and other friends went camping in Devon in August. In September she was with the Bells, Lytton Strachey and Roger Fry at Studland. Then she changed both her houses in quick succession. Little Talland was given up for Asham, a pretty Regency house a few miles from Rodmell, of which Vanessa was her co-tenant. And in November she left Fitzroy Square for 38 Brunswick Square, which she shared with Adrian, Maynard Keynes and Duncan Grant. From 4 December they were joined there by Leonard Woolf, who rented the top floor.

571: To LEONARD WOOLF   *29 Fitzroy Square, W.*

8 July [1911]

Dear Mr Wolf,

Would you come down to Firle for a week end? It is a cottage in the Sussex downs. Either the 22nd or the 29th would suit.

I hope you will.[1]

Yours sincerely,
Virginia Stephen

Sussex

572: To LADY ROBERT CECIL   *29 Fitzroy Square, W.*

[July 1911]

Dear Nelly,

What a pleasure to be asked to tea with you! I will come on Wednesday with great pleasure. I've been explaining to your evanescent (which suggests phosphorescent) niece why it is that one cant ask to come and see you. Vanity we decided it was. If I hadn't been vain I should have shoved through the smoke and the feathered women that night and insisted upon asking you.

1. Leonard was not able to accept this first invitation to Firle.

Have you finished your novel? I hear you gave a dance, and a Suffrage Meeting, and I think it rather hard luck that I don't come under one heading or the other.

Yr. aff.
VS

This ink has had a slight admixture of strawberry jam so that it wont dry properly.

Hatfield

573: To Vanessa Bell

29 *Fitzroy Square, W.*

Wednesday [July 1911]

Beloved,

This is first of the new series of letters, which is written for you only; and Clive shall have letters for himself only, and so we shall all profit, by the gain in passion.

I suppose he described that vast melancholy party. What added to my depression was the fact that every watery matron of them all, as well as bald old gentlemen, invariably began 'Hows Vanessa? Where's Vanessa?''. All I could do was to invent a disease for you, which puzzled Mrs Booth herself. Half the child, I said, had miscarried in London—the other half, the legs presumably, miscarried at Broussa. This intrigued her considerably, as the case was not the same as Dodos [Antonia Macnaghten]: however, if you take the greatest care for six months she thinks there *may* be no danger in bearing a child next year—indeed sometimes one finds that that is the best cure of all. My Dodo etc. etc.

It was strangely like a Winkworth party,[1] only we were all 10 years older. I was glad to find that they are as vapid and commonplace as we used to find them, so that we [were] right to hate them.

The old passion to fly before them overcame me. Imagine Margy drifting —Bella trumpeting—Mrs Humphrey Ward shrilling—Imogen mincing— Meg flopping—Aunt Minna—she was almost impressive from her obvious nearness to death.

I have been to tea with Nelly [Cecil] this afternoon. There is no doubt that she is the best of those elderly aristocrats. I was very happy with her, sitting in the garden. What mind she has is quite honest. She told me that we had behaved very badly to Kitty [Maxse]. I said that Kitty was obsolete, and had to be dropped, but I denied that she had been dropped. She said that both Kitty and Leo were 20 years behind the times; and gave me to under-

---

1. Emma Winkworth. See page 33, note 3.

stand that Kitty is a foolish thimble-pated woman, living in a swarm of smart people she doesn't care about, but quite happy. You see Nelly is a good deal above that.

I feel a certain pathos in seeing these people again. Nothing seems to have happened, that one can talk about. However she reads a good deal. She has the illegitimate niece to stay with her. She also has several friendly char-women as crossing sweepers, but she doesn't patronise them as Kitty used to.

We went over Bedford Sq.[1] this afternoon. We mapped out rooms on paper. It would exactly do; the one drawback is that the 2 front rooms may be noisy. Duncan is going to have a great garden room, and I am to have a tremendous square room, at the back. There is a studio for you, adjoining a W.C.

Savage has asked me to dine, in 4 nights, to meet Jean [Thomas], [Harris?] Rackham and [Dr Seymour?] Sharkey!

Yr. B.

Are you feeling well?

Berg

574: To Vanessa Bell   29 *Fitzroy Square, W.*

Friday [21 July 1911]

Beloved,

It is a great devotion to write, as the heat is something awful.

We had our great expedition yesterday. It was all very odd. First of all it was rather strained; we lay under the trees and discussed the Bedford Sq. plan. Then we walked and he [Walter Lamb] began lamenting the lack of noble souls. We discussed love and women in the abstract. At last he sat down and said "Will you tell me if you've ever been in love?" I asked him whether he knew about the Lytton affair. He said "Clive told me a good deal", which made me angry, but cant be helped. Then I said I would tell him about it if he really wanted to know, and not out of curiosity. He said he wanted to find out what I felt, and would be glad to hear anything. I gave him an abstract. Then he said "Do you want to have children and love in the normal way?" I said "Yes". He said "I do care for you very much." I said "But you're quite happy?" He said, "There are such dreadful complications." I said "What." He said "You live in a hornets nest. Beside[s] marriage is so difficult. Will you let me wait? Dont hurry me."

I said "There is no reason why we shouldn't be friends—or why we

1 Virginia and Adrian proposed to take a large house in Bedford Square, which they could share with friends. The plan materialised, but at 38 Brunswick Square.

should change things and get agitated." He said "Of course its wonderful as it is."

Then we went rambling on; and I gathered that he felt he could not let himself fall in love because he doubted what I felt; and he also was puzzled by parts of my character. He said I made things into webs, and might turn fiercely upon him for his faults. I owned to great egoism and absorption and vanity and all my vices. He said Clive had told him dreadful stories to illustrate my faults (for God's sake, dont repeat this) I said that I liked him, and thought we could be friends. I tried to make this clear.

Then he talked a great deal about you—how noble and divine you were—how you frightened him—how he wished to talk to you, how he had an aesthetic love for you etc. etc.

We talked of general things after that—his gout a good deal—and then had tea and went home, and went to the opera. There was an enormous crowd of cultivated ones.—Sangers, Forster, Rupert, Ka, James, Wolf, etc. Walter walked home, and came in and drank here, as Adrian was out.

He began again about our relationship, and said he would like to live near me in the autumn, but didn't add much. It is uneasy, because he is always trying to find out what I feel, and I can only talk about the beauty of friendship.

Of course I liked him much better than I have ever done, as he was quite direct and really felt a good deal (unless I'm too vain to judge). But the thing is left in an uncomfortable state. He wants to come to Firle in September. I do like him, but the prospect of many long talks, rather appals me. There is something pathetic in him. He's so desperately afraid of making a fool of himself, and yet conscious that his caution is a little absurd.

I think I've told all I can remember—at least the gist of it. No doubt some further compliments to you will be washed up.

Oh how I'm damned by Roger! Refinement! and we in a Post Impressionist age. You dont deserve any compliments for sending me that one.

By the way, the last thing W. said before we were interrupted was that he could not see that I had a single fault! "Not even as a wife?" I said. "No: not even as a wife." In my opinion, he is in love with me; but that you must hush up.

I'm in great difficulties with my engagements. Eily won't answer; and I think she must have written to Firle. If she puts me off, I might come down next Thursday or Friday for the night (if you'll have me).[1] Case comes on Monday, and wont say for how long. Then Savage asks me for Thursday, and I accepted for Wednesday. Jean is in a fury—flings the telephone from her ear—because she thinks I'm trying to avoid dining with her. Saxon has become very pathetic about Bayreuth.

Altogether, its a hornets nest, as W. said. He meant that we lived in the

1. Vanessa was convalescing at Millmead Cottage, Guildford, conveniently near the home of Roger Fry.

centre of intrigues, which distressed him, and he asked about Harry [Norton] and Roger and Desmond. He asked whether I should flirt if I married. I said "not if I were in love with my husband." But that was bold.

Are you better? Does this heat hurt you? At lunch I compared you with a South American forest, with panthers sleeping beneath the trees. I also gave a passionate vision of our love—yours for me, I mean.

Yr. B.

Berg

575: To Violet Dickinson   *Little Talland House, Firle,*
                                             Lewes, Sussex

Sunday [23 July 1911]

My Violet,
Nessa is supposed to keep quiet, but she is practically all right. She is beginning to do things as usual. But the dr. says she ought to be very careful. The miscarriage went on for such an age, and it is very exhausting. I hope they'll take a house in the country next month. She has had no real holiday for an age. Happily the children both flourish.
I'm here for Sunday. A tremendous wind is blowing.
How are you? Should you call yourself fond of me, or merely indifferent?

Yr. VS

Berg

576: To Vanessa Bell   29 *Fitzroy Square, W.*

[25? July 1911]

Beloved,
I'm sorry if I wrote, as I gather is your opinion, with more maggots in my head than wits. Reports of talk, I agree, cant be taken as evidence; I was going by this. W[alter] told me he had talked to Adrian, who had given a sketch of my vices. "But, said W. "it was done kindly; and Clive blackened you with bitterness." Then he told me some of the things Clive had said. They were mixed with rhapsody, but they were unpleasant. I was angry at the impression it had made on W. for that is definite enough, and must have come there somehow and, after all, why should he be biassed? Clive quarreled with Lytton for that reason; but I don't mean to quarrel, only to cry out 'God! The gnats are biting!' as you do, almost perpetually throughout a summer evening.
Kiss my snout, beloved, you did tap it.
I have just come back from Firle, where I had an interesting time with

Case. She is a woman of great magnanimity, and even said some things in praise of you. (you can see me curling up to your side). She said how great your beauty was, and your dignity of character.

We talked incessantly.

I gathered that she has had several proposals, but, cherishing the image of a deceased father, who kept a school, she refused them all.

Doesn't it seem to you odd that she has never told either Emphie [Case] or Margaret [Llewelyn] Davies about any of them—"but we have sometimes discussed marriage in an abstract way." She had brought down a handsome reticule, into which she drops bits of torn lace from time to time; and this she takes away on visits. So she sat stitching with an expression such as Marny has when she goes watercolour sketching, and listened to a magnificent tirade which I delivered upon life in general.

She has a calm interest in copulation (having got over her dislike of naming it by the need of discussing Emphies symptoms with a male doctor) and this led us to the revelation of all Georges malefactions. To my surprise, she has always had an intense dislike of him; and used to say "Whew—you nasty creature", when he came in and began fondling me over my Greek. When I got to the bedroom scenes, she dropped her lace, and gasped like a benevolent gudgeon. By bedtime she said she was feeling quite sick, and did go to the W.C., which, needless to say, had no water in it.

I discussed the Bedford Sq. plan with her, the theory of which she thinks noble, but she thought we should get dirty.

If Adrian is with you, would you tell him that 2 or 3 sets of people have been to see the house, and one liked it so much that he was going straight back to Maples.

Of course, I half dread the moment when we let it; and the thing becomes serious. Sophie and Maud!

Do you think it would be a good plan to expose a letter, explaining it, and so break the shock?

I found a letter from Eily at Firle, who can have me some time later so I could come down to you on Thursday if that does.

I am also embroiled in one of my hottest broils with Jean [Thomas]. It is about a dinner at Savages: she says I offered 'to go on Wednesday, knowing that she' couldn't go that day; and thus showed callousness, brutality, immorality, lack of justice ("which one can see in your writings") and a "truly dreadful lack of consideration for the feelings and desires of your friends". To this I answered in sober fact; with one plain curse. I found a reply at Firle, which I read to Case. It was a masterpiece. It seems likely that one will have to give her a sharp rap—the sort you give me; only she would die, while I manage to survive.

I have also had 3 letters from W. [Walter Lamb]. What to say to him, I dont know. He wants to come here. I have written to say that I can only repeat what I said before, and that it seems not worth while to come up and hear that. However, as I said he could choose for himself, I must let him—this time.

With all my gross and inordinate vanity, my vampire like suction and (I know my faults by this time) I dont see that I can go on letting him praise me, unless I shall fall in love—and that seems as though one said unless I grow a beak. I've no doubt there is vanity in this too.

I would not write so much, except that I've got no one to talk to, and the night is so hot that I cant play, or read. Janet C. said suddenly in the train "What are you thinking of, Virginia?" Imprudently I answered "Supposing next time we meet a baby leaps within me?" She said that was not the way to talk.

I suppose Duncan has seduced A[drian]. I imagine a great orgy on the river tonight.

Yr. B.

Tell Adrian I had a long talk with Saxon about the Society [The Apostles] in the course of which he said "There is just a something about them—" and then giggled.

Berg

577: To Sir Sidney Lee   29 *Fitzroy Square, W.*

29th July 1911

Dear Sir Sidney,

I ought to have written before to thank you for your book.[1] I have read it with great pleasure. Of course I was very much pleased by what you wrote of my father. It was so sympathetic and fine. But I read it all with great interest. Thank you for sending it to me.

Yours very sincerely,
Virginia Stephen

Bodleian Library, Oxford

578: To Roger Fry   29 *Fitzroy Square, W.*

Monday [August 1911]

My dear Roger,

I'm afraid from what I hear that Nessa is still rather bad. Would you tell me if you think it better that I should not come? I had meant to come on

1. *Principles of Biography*, 1911.

Wednesday or Thursday; but I can see that it might be better not. Of course I want to, but I have a great fear of being too tiring.

We are callous—in the way we lay burdens upon you!

Yours ever,
Virginia Stephen

I must get my urinal. "A Venetian flower pot" I shall call it, to the chaste.

Sussex

579: TO ROGER FRY   29 *Fitzroy Square, W.*

[August 1911]

My dear Roger,

I expect I had better not come—at any rate now—if Clive is against it. I'm inclined to agree with you in thinking that it wouldn't do any harm, but his feeling is a reason in itself. I'm fearfully sorry that I allowed myself to talk and her to talk, only she doesn't make it easy to be discreet!

I'm going to Ottoline [at Peppard Cottage] on the 12th, and to Firle or Cambridge I think on Saturday, so I couldn't be at Guildford long anyhow.

I hope very much that you and Vanessa mean to come to Firle some time later. I think you'd forget all that outraged you, when looking at the cornfields.

Yours very sincerely,
Virginia Stephen

Sussex

580: TO LADY OTTOLINE MORRELL   *The Old Vicarage,*
                                         Grantchester

[16 August 1911]

My dear Ottoline,

It is the greatest difficulty to get pen and paper here, because Rupert [Brooke] apparently writes all his poems in pencil on the backs of envelopes. But I hope you'll be able to read this, because I enjoyed being with you so very much. It is such a relief that your feelings are not those of hatred mixed with contempt! I was very happy with you.

I am leading a queer life here, of perpetual conversation by day and by night. Yesterday we saw the Cornfords. I think you would like her, and him too, if only because he looks like something carved in green marble on a tomb. This has the effect of making him very silent; but she talks, and is better than her poems. Then there is a man—Sydney Waterlow—who has just separated from his wife, and is seeing life for the first time, being about 35. Otherwise Cambridge is empty.

I wonder if you are going abroad. It will be very nice to see you in the autumn.

Yr. aff.ate,
Virginia Stephen

Texas

581: To Vanessa Bell   *Little Talland House, Firle,*
                                            Lewes, Sussex

Tuesday [22? August 1911]

Beloved,

I am very sorry about Quentin. It does seem abominable that you should have all these bothers, and I'm afraid that you're not feeling very well—poor honey-buzzard. I wonder if your affairs have stopped.

It is very melancholy that you cant come, but we must fix our hopes on October, when this country will be even nicer, and we can carry our lunch to the top of the downs.

I've just heard from Frances Cornford, who is staying at Forest Row [the Freshfields' house] with Eily and wants me to go there, or to come here—its too annoying—I could have had you and Roger as well.

I am cursing domesticity too, but only in a very mild way. The servants have arrived, and made everything pompous and heavy-footed. Why we have them, I cant think. There is always a certain amount of grumbling to be lived down, because of the heat of the kitchen etc.

But of course this is a gnats bite to your miseries. I suppose though there is a kind of unity in marriage (barring children) which one doesn't get from liaisons. I'm thinking a good deal, at intervals, about marriage. My quarrel with it is that the pace is so slow, when you are two people.

As a painter, I believe you are much less conscious of the drone of daily life than I am, as a writer. You *are* a painter. I think a good deal about you, for purposes of my own, and this seems to me clear. This explains your simplicity. What have you to do with all this turmoil? What you want is a studio where you can see things.

If this is wrong, you might sent me a telegram. God! I shall enjoy talking to you again.

I saw as much of the strike[1] as anyone saw. They said there would be fewer trains at Victoria; as a matter of fact there was an extra one, and they were punctual. One or two stations were held by soldiers, who lay on their elbows smoking; and there was a soldier by a signal box. Otherwise there was no

1. A national railway strike, which began on 18 August and lasted two days.

difference, except for empty trains standing about. All this was what I foresaw. Rupert [Brooke] tried to work up some Socialist enthusiasm. He does not eat meat, except when he stays here, and lives very cheaply.

There was a great wedding here on Saturday, and I found a note from George in the dining room. "Beloved Old Goat—we have come over for Monk Bretton's wedding and hoped to have tea with you" etc.

They had mentioned Margaret's title to Mrs. Stephens [the cook] who was a good deal impressed. I have great luck in missing them.

Saxon writes that he wants to come over here from Haywards Heath where he has to spend what remains of his holiday with his parents poor wretch. I gather that the whole of Bayreuth was rather a failure, as far as the music went.

It is detestable, hearing servants moving about. Isn't it a good argument against Seend [Clive's parents] that it doesn't suit the children. I wish you'd gone straight to Studland. When would you like me to come there? I thought I could take a room. I do hope the brats are better, beloved creature.

Yr. B.

Berg

582: TO LEONARD WOOLF   *Little Talland House, Firle, Lewes, Sussex*

Aug. 31st [1911]

Dear Mr Woolf,
    (It would be much nicer to use Christian names).
    I am very glad you can come. Saturday week, the 9th, suits me very well, or any time, the week after. I shall be here, I expect, until the 18th. This is not a cottage, but a hideous suburban villa—I have to prepare people for the shock.

Yours sincerely,
Virginia Stephen

I will explain the trains, if you will say which time suits you.

Sussex

583: TO ROGER FRY   *Little Talland House, Firle, Lewes, Sussex*

[early September 1911]

My dear Roger,
    You can guess how grateful I am for the exquisite Pot which arrived without a flaw. It is now my chief ornament, and I think it will be the

instrument of much good, breaking down barriers, introducing the topics most worth discussing, etc. I couldn't thank you before, as I have been down in [Clifford Bridge, Drewsteignton] Devonshire living in a Camp with eleven other people. From my observations shaving is unknown among the younger generation. They were all densely wooded. Perhaps your pot will bring in that reform too. I wonder if you could possibly come here for next week end? Adrian and Duncan are coming. It would be a great pleasure—but dont bother to write if you cant. I had a very interesting time with Ottoline.

I think we have let Fitzroy Square, so that I shall probably be in London next week, and shall try to come down and see you. But I hope you may come here.

Yours very sincerely,
Virginia Stephen

Sussex

584: To Desmond MacCarthy   *Little Talland House, Firle,*
Lewes, Sussex

Sept. 4th [1911]

My dear Desmond,

Yes, I had been feeling a kind of instinct so that you ought to write to me.

Is there any chance that you would come here for the weekend on the 16th? L. Woolf is coming, and Marjorie Strachey, I think. The cook is here, so you would be more comfortable than last time.

I enjoyed my visit to Ottoline very much, and now, I hope we shall go on smoothly for the rest of our lives. Then I wandered about in various places, trying Camp life at one point—sleeping on the ground, waking at dawn, and swimming in a river. And all this time you have been earning your 16 pounds a week.[1] I do admire that, but aren't you worn and thin as a rake? I cant imagine anything more exhausting. Do keep it up: it makes Saturday much more amusing than it would otherwise be. It makes me feel a perfect amateur—sitting here before white sheets, every now and then chuckling at one of my own jokes—

Thank you for the name of the book—I have sent it on to Beatrice.

Yr. aff.
Virginia Stephen

Mrs Michael MacCarthy

1. Desmond MacCarthy was now writing regularly for *Eye-Witness*, which became *New Witness* in the following year.

Little Talland House, Firle,
Lewes, Sussex

4 September [1911]

Dear Leonard,

The 16th will suit me very well. If you can come on Friday, do.

Yours sincerely,

The station is Lewes. Virginia Stephen

Sussex

Firle [*Lewes,*
Sussex]

Postcard
Thursday [14 September 1911]

A fly will be at Lewes for the 11.6 on Saturday. Desmond MacCarthy and
Marjorie Strachey are coming by some train, I think.
Please bring no clothes.

VS

Sussex

2 Harmony Cottages, Studland
[*Dorset*]

[September 1911]

Dear Saxon,

Thank you very much for seeing about my ticket. I was putting my faith
in you.

I am coming up tomorrow and shall be delighted if you will dine with me
on Sunday. Where is Adrian, I wonder? How is he? He has completely
vanished. I spread a story that he is to be met with in the North of England,
leading a horse, attended by a flock of fowls, from which he chooses his
dinner now and then. Is this all a lie?

Lytton has been staying here, and left 2 days ago, to cross to Brest, in a
violent storm: nothing has been heard of him either. Roger has been here,
and we made a great expedition to Poole and got taken on a tug with two
barges up to Wareham, which is one of the most lovely towns I have ever
seen.

Everyone is well—and send (or sends) love.
Excuse pencil. My lodgings dont run to ink.

Yr. VS

Sussex

29 Fitzroy Square, W.

[21 October 1911]

Dear Leonard,

(I stupidly forgot to telephone) Thank you very much—I am going to this cycle [*The Ring*], but if I might come to your box for Siegfried on Monday I should like to. But perhaps you want to get the same person to go to all three. So write and stop me if you do.

I'm now engaged in a most spirited controversy about W.C.'s and E.Cs [earth closets] with Mr Hoper. Owing to you I've practically got that house.[1] The only question is whether Mrs Hoper—a very old woman—shall be made to clean out the E.C. or construct a private drain: which would be best? It seems to me that both must require cesspools: and W.C's are certainly pleasanter in wet weather. I had a splendid day down there investigating all this.

Yrs.

Sussex VS

589: To Lytton Strachey *29 Fitzroy Square, W.*

[6 November 1911]

Dearest Papa,

Will it suit you to come to the dancers[2] tomorrow night—dining here at 7.30 first? They're only amphitheatre this time; but when they do the other thing we will go to the stalls.

Life is very full—so full that my head is chock full down to the very nostrils, and strain as I may, nothing comes out. I've just come back from the [Francis] Cornfords—from the 7th Symphony, from a scene with —— ——[3], from an interview in a W.C. and, while I wash my teeth, a painter sings on a board outside my window.

Who was my mother by the way, Lady S. [Strachey]?

Yr. affectionate
daughter,
VS

If you can't come, telephone. Wrap up well—especially the left foot. Bring your muffler, blue spectacles, and lozenges.

Frances Hooper

1. Asheham (or Asham), near Beddingham, a few miles from Firle.
2. The Diaghilev ballet.
3. Dashes in original.

Thursday [9 November 1911]

My dear Ottoline,

I have wanted to come and see you—but we've been living in a desperate state of confusion—a great deal our own incompetence.

I'm afraid I shall be away this Saturday, and not back till Tuesday or Wednesday. We actually move in [to Brunswick Square] on Friday: and then we have to disappear to let the servants get straight. But if you're in London next week, may I come round some time? I should so much like to.

Our new address is 38 Brunswick Square. Its ever so much nicer than this—so quiet, and a graveyard behind. We are going to try all kinds of experiments. The one thing that seems certain is that a house is the cheapest way of living, and if you have a house you must have servants. We have spent a month discussing how to live.

How are you?

Yours affectionate,
Virginia Stephen

Texas

591: To Lady Ottoline Morrell

Little Talland House, Firle,
Lewes, Sussex

Monday [13 November 1911]

My dear Ottoline,

Next Tuesday would suit me very well. I will come to tea, unless you stop me.

I've fled here to escape the mess—but go back tomorrow. We are becoming boarding house keepers. It will mean keeping accounts, which begins to alarm me.

The country is amazingly beautiful, now that the leaves are off. Its a great question—where one ought to live. When do you move to the new house, I wonder?[1]

I must now go and make hare soup.

Your ever affectionate,
V.S.

Texas

1. The Morrells had sold the cottage at Peppard Common, and were to live temporarily at Broughton Grange, near Banbury. They did not find Garsington till 1913, and moved there in 1915.

9.30
The Vienna Café

Monday [20 November 1911]

Will you come to the dancers tomorrow? I hope to get stalls. You will sit between two seductive women.

If you can't come, would you telephone to Gordon Sq. If you can, will you meet us in the box office hall (I mean the ordinary big hall) at the opera, 25 minutes past 8—the opera beginning at 8.30, I presume, being out of the way of reading newspapers. My God!—whatever you do, put all your wits into few volumes. All day I've been lifting Swift, Dryden, Carlyle—such mountains they wrote, and only half an inch worth reading. I can't offer you dinner—but will you come to tea with me on Friday? There may be just room for your legs and a tea cup on the point of the knee by then. I've just been dining in this sordid place alone, and chose all the wrong things. The waiter has been cheeky to the young lady—she threatens to tell Mr Joseph.

Now I go back to break my first bed in Brunswick [Square], what is the right, yet delicate expression?

Yrs.
VS

Your ticket will be sent in the course of the day.[*This sentence is crossed out.*]
No: I will bring it with me.

Frances Hooper

Letters 593-638

The move to Brunswick Square was completed on 20 November 1911, and Leonard Woolf joined their establishment two weeks later. During the next month, Virginia received two further proposals of marriage. The first, from Sydney Waterlow, she turned down. The second, from Leonard on 11 January 1912, made her hesitate. Her indecision was partly due to her fear of marriage itself, with all that it involved, emotionally and sexually; and partly to a slight recurrence of her mental illness, which obliged her to return to the Twickenham nursing-home for the third time. Leonard was placed in a difficult position. His leave would soon expire, and he decided that if he could not win Virginia, he would return to Ceylon. Eventually, on 1 May, she wrote him a letter (615) which was sufficiently encouraging to make up his mind. He resigned from the Colonial Service, and on 29 May Virginia accepted him. She told her friends of her engagement with mingled pride and diffidence, as if fearing ridicule, and spent the next two months visiting his and her relations, and finally completing The Voyage Out. Virginia and Leonard were married at a Registry Office on 10 August 1912. She was 30 years old.

593: To VIOLET DICKINSON   *38 Brunswick Sq., W.C.*

Nov 20 1911

My Violet,

Would it bore you too intensely to have me to lunch one day this week—Tuesday, Wednesday or Thursday?

If it would, you need merely spit and say so.

I am now undertaking an entirely new branch of life, and if you can give me advice, so much the better.

What have you been doing? Why did you never answer my letters? At last I got to feel like a dog left out at night, barking at the moon.

We are still on the streets. Cant get rid of painters and plumbers.

Yr. VS

It would be very nice to see you again.

Berg

[November 1911]

My Violet,

Damn Ella [Crum]! Damn Margaret Lyttelton. Whats the use of my coming on the top of her? I cant dine with you on Wednesday or Thursday—I suppose Friday's no good? If not, I must wait till next week, which is mercifully free.

I'm now in the middle of putting my books up. You cant think what a job it is—but the Sq. is like Paradise, and there are the Foundlings [Hospital] for angels.

I didn't write about Hannah [More?]—didnt ever read her—but I suppose it must have been very very good.

Do settle a time. *What* a lying creature you are! Friendship!—

Yr. VS

That is the title of my novel by the way.

Berg

Dec 2nd [1911]

Dear Leonard,

Here is the scheme of the house. I think I told you about most of the things before. The servants are quite amenable. All they beg is that we shall be punctual. I'm expecting you to come in for tea on Monday. Your rooms are now papered white and look much nicer. There aren't any curtains; but there are blinds and I think we can rig something up. I hope it wont be very uncomfortable at first.

As to the rent of the room, Adrian and I think that probably 35/- a week would be about fair. This is to include light, coals, hot baths, and service.

We dont want to do anything but share the expenses of the house—Possibly this is too high a rent. I'm going to wait and examine the expenses after the first week, and then tell you, if you dont mind, what the cost of living and washing is.

I feel quite sanguine, because having gone into it all with the servants, they seem prepared and rather amused than otherwise. I want to ask you about other small things: whether you like fish—but that can wait.

Yrs.
VS

There is a book case in your room.

Meals are:

Breakfast	9 a.m.
Lunch	1.
Tea	4.30 p.m.
Dinner	8 p.m.

Trays will be placed in the hall punctually at these hours. Inmates are requested to carry up their own trays; and to put the dirty plates on them and carry them down again *as soon as the meal is finished.*

Inmates are requested to put their initials upon the kitchen instruction tablet hung in the hall against all meals required that day before 9.30 am.

If notice of absence is given before 6 p.m. the dinner can be cancelled; if given before 12 a.m. the lunch can be cancelled.

The meals will consist of tea, egg and bacon, toast or roll for breakfast: meat, vegetables, and sweet for lunch: tea, buns, for tea: fish, meat, sweet, for dinner. It is not possible as a general rule to cater for guests as well as inmates. If notice is given, exceptions can sometimes be made. Particular desires will be considered. A box will be placed in the hall in which it is requested that inmates shall place their requests or complaints.

It is hoped that inmates will make a special effort to be punctual, for thus the work of service will be much lightened.

The proprietors reserve the right of ceasing to supply service at any time: there will probably be holidays at Christmas, Easter, and in the summer. But at these times, a caretaker will be in the house, capable of supplying breakfast, and doing rooms.

Sussex

596: To Sydney Waterlow   38 *Brunswick Square, W.C.*

Dec. 9th [1911]

Dear Sydney,[1]

I meant to have answered your letter sooner. I'm very glad you dont reproach yourself, because I'm certain that there's nothing to reproach yourself for. All you say I think I understand, and it seems to me very reasonable.

But I feel that I must on my side make clear what I didn't make clear that night. I dont think I shall ever feel for you what I must feel for the man I

1. Sydney Waterlow had known Virginia and her friends for several years, and had joined them at Studland in September 1910. In November 1911 he proposed to Virginia, and was refused. At this moment in his career, he had temporarily resigned from The Foreign Office, and was working on a short book about Shelley. He was not then yet divorced from his first wife.

marry. I am very anxious that you should know this, so that you may take it into account. I feel that you have it in your power to stop thinking of me as the person you want to marry. It would be unpardonable of me if I did not do everything to save you from what must—as far as I can tell—be a great waste.

Please write and say whatever you wish to me at any time, and behave exactly as you wish. I hope we shall go on being good friends anyhow.

Yours ever,
Virginia Stephen

John Waterlow

597: To Lady Ottoline Morrell

38 *Brunswick Square, W.C.*

[December ? 1911]

My dear Ottoline,

I was so disgusted not to come last night. But I'd been foolish and got a headache, and am now a complete coward about headaches. Adrian and Duncan say it was most delightful—and I was hoping, of course, that something awful would happen—the teapot blow up, or the lights go out, or Lytton's beard catch in the candle—to spoil it all.

May I come and see you some time? I *am* cross about last night.

Yrs. V.S.

Texas

598: To Clive Bell

38 *Brunswick Square, W.C.*

Friday [December 1911]

My dear Clive,

This is going to be an infernally dull letter of business. Did I tell you about Mauds brother? He had 3 fingers cut off in a sweet making machine, 6 months ago. His firm is Kearly & Tonge, Whitechapel; the head of it is Lord Devonport.[1] He went to a solicitor who advised him not to take his half pay but to hold out for compensation. The firm said they would give him another job if he did not bring the case into Court. Now they have paid him £127 and tell him that they cant find him work. He has no written promise, and is completely up a tree.

Why I write to you is that I have written to George and Gerald; and George says that Lord Devonport is a strong Radical and that you must have had dealings with him. I dont for a moment think you have; but its just

---

1. Hudson Kearley, senior partner of Kearley and Tonge. He was chairman of the Port of London Authority, 1909-25, and was created Baron Devonport in 1910.

possible your father may know of the right thing to do. Anyhow, as they're in great straits, I thought I might ask. He can write and do accounts. Oh God how dull! This is the 4th time I have written about Mauds brother, and it becomes less and less credible every time. Once I had a clear vision of a knife sticky with raspberry drops sweeping off his finger, and the blood mixing with the cochineal. I've just come back from having tea with Richmond Ritchie,[1] who has lumbago. He became so lecherous that I had to leave. When old men are very lecherous, their beards and jowls are so unpleasant. He told a story of Queen Victoria congested with roast beef, which she eat all through the summer, surrounded by 4 great pillars of ice to keep the temperature down. Don't bother to write if there's nothing to say.

Yr.

VS

Quentin Bell

599: TO SAXON SYDNEY-TURNER [38 *Brunswick Square, W.C.*]

[23 December 1911]

My dear Saxon,

I could only get 5/6 tickets for Tuesday, but I got these. They are at the back—however they say one can see everywhere. I'm afraid I cant get dinner here early. So I'd better meet you there. Here is your ticket.

I saw Zimmern[2] on a bookstall today, and a pang of horror went through me remembering all the times I had forgotten it. If you've already had it, will you send it back, as it looks interesting, and I should like to read it.

Yr. aff.

VS

Adrian is going on very well and comes out [from a nursing home] on Tuesday. Happy Christmas! and Bright New Year.

I see that both tickets are in one. As you are less likely to lose it than I am, I send it. I will be in the booking hall at 5 minutes to 8. Or perhaps you will dine with me first at the Tower of Eiffel, bottom of Charlotte Street, 7 o'clock.

Sussex

1. Sir Richmond Ritchie (1854-1912), whose career had been in the Indian legal service. In 1877 he married Anne Thackeray ('Aunt Anny'), sister of Leslie Stephen's first wife.
2. Alfred Zimmern, *The Greek Commonwealth*, 1911.

Saturday [13 January 1912]

My dear Leonard,

I am rushing for a train so I can only send a line in answer.[1] There isn't anything really for me to say, except that I should like to go on as before; and that you should leave me free, and that I should be honest. As to faults, I expect mine are just as bad—less noble perhaps. But of course they are not really the question. I have decided to keep this completely secret, except for Vanessa; and I have made her promise not to tell Clive. I told Adrian that you had come up about a job which was promised you. So keep this up if he asks.

I am very sorry to be the cause of so much rush and worry. I am just off to Firle.

Yrs.

Sussex   VS

[January 1912]

My Violet,

Do come to tea on Friday. I am selfish and ask you to come here, because I now live like the Tortoise at the zoo—once a day I make an excursion for food—otherwise sleep.[2] But as you know, there was once a sleeping beauty, and some have been kind enough to hint—in short, I have no objection to being kissed.

Friday 4.30.

Yr. VS

Berg

7th February [1912]

My dear Ka,

I was just writing to you when your letter came. I've been ill, but I'm practically all right again now. It was a touch of my usual disease, in the head you know. I spent a week in bed, but now that's all over, except for miraculous

1. Leonard was staying with an old friend, the Vicar of Frome in Somerset. From there he had dashed to London on 11 January, and proposed to Virginia. She stalled. On his return to Frome, he renewed his proposal in two further letters.
2. In late January Virginia succumbed to a new attack of mental illness, and was obliged to rest for several days.

dreams at night. I live the life of an old old Tom cat. You would weep to see me. An old gentleman who by the formation of his hip has to trot or he would topple, trips round the Square with me every morning: but we never speak to each other. I can't give you much news. You would have been touched to know how often I've wished I heard your pad on the stairs, and your snuff snuffle at the door. At the very moment that I collapsed Nessa and Clive stayed with Hilton Young, who gave them influenza; so we could only send our love; but everyone is now established, though my novel—Oh God! it is a d——d bore not to be able to write at that.

Last Sunday we went down to housewarm Asheham. Adrian, Woolf, Marjorie and I went. It was the coldest day for 40 years; all the pipes were frozen; the birds were starving against the window panes; some had got in, and sat by the fire; the bottom fell out of the grates; suddenly Marjorie, who was reciting Racine, stopped dead and said "I have got chicken pox". We put her to bed, and I don't think its true, but Lytton, whom I saw today, forgot to ask what was the matter.

I'll write again and sketch the state of the world for you—only there's no point in that, as you say you know everything.

Do come back soon; you can't think how essential you are to the proper aspect of things; that is why animals were made; to balance human beings.[1] In spite of the frost, the accounts from the zoo are *thoroughly satisfactory*. They've come to the stage, I am told, when *they must be taught habits*; and you know how important this is, so come back on that account.

Ottoline floats about; but I'm not really in the swim now, and feel like an anemone at the bottom of an aquarium, seeing the fishes and the weeds—and not caring for anyone a damn—except B . . . [Bruin] and . . . [Leonard?]. A great excitement is now taking place in the dramatic world, engineered by Desmond so I have little hope—As you'll be back by the 21st, I'll say no more.

I'm very glad Rupert [Brooke] is better. Please give him my love.

Write again.

VS

Mark Arnold-Forster

603: To Violet Dickinson   [38 *Brunswick Square, W.C.*]

[7? February 1912]

My Violet,

I was just on the point of writing to you—only impeded by the loss of paper, ink and penny stamps—which miracle supplied all in a twinkling. I was going in that letter, which will never be written and was one of the

1. Ka Cox was in Munich with Rupert Brooke. Virginia had begun to call her 'the bear' or 'Bruin'.

wittiest and profoundest for its size of any in Europe—to have thanked you for the paper weight, which puzzles me as much as it charms. Is it Greek or Russian? Where from? What used for? Anyhow, it shall lie upon your letters: I've just fed it with that miserable Crumb.[1] No wonder Jesus starved.

We went to Asheham on Saturday—my God! What a day: all pipes frozen; grates with false bottoms; no E.Cs; one bedroom can supplied, for the purpose, which it needed a conjuring trick to hit; then the chicken pox broke out in the only guest. However, it was great fun.

Shall I come and see you? I'm now rampant, feeding on bullocks blood, and henbane; or the heads of red poppies which make me dream wild dreams —about you, and alabaster pillars, and dogs defiling them.

Yr. V.S.

Berg

604: To VIOLET DICKINSON   38 *Brunswick Square, W.C.*

[mid-February 1912]

My Violet,

I'm so sorry, but Savage is making me spend a fortnight in bed, as I cant sleep.[2] It is very ridiculous.

After that, I shall come and dine—if you'll have me.

I liked the pictures. Its quite obvious that Mrs C. [*unidentified*] was a solid provincial Lady, from the look of the house. One ought always to see peoples houses.

Yr. VS

Berg

605: To LYTTON STRACHEY   38 *Brunswick Square, W.C.*

[16 February 1912]

Address for Miss Berry
    is

        Burley
           Cambridge Park
             Twickenham.

Dear Lytton,

I've got to spend 2 weeks in bed. Could you be angelic and send me the

1. Possibly a letter from Ella Crum, who, like Violet, was intensely religious.
2. On 16 February Virginia returned to Jean Thomas's nursing home at Twickenham.

Memoirs of Miss Berry?[1] I expect they'd do splendidly: and I'll take immense care not to spot them.

I hope you are well.

Woolf has all your manuscripts and letters. Letters amazing! My God what an insight I have now in to that cosmogony![2]

Yr.

Frances Hooper

VS

606: To Leonard Woolf   *38 Brunswick Square, W.C.*

Tuesday [5 March 1912]

My dear Leonard,

You hit off my taste in reading very well. I should have thanked you before, but writing was forbidden. I shall tell you wonderful stories of the lunatics. By the bye, they've elected me King. There can be no doubt about it. I summoned a conclave, and made a proclamation about Christianity.

I had other adventures, and some disasters, the fruit of a too passionate and enquiring disposition. I avoided both love and hatred. I now feel very clear, calm, and move slowly, like one of the great big animals at the zoo. Knitting is the saving of life; Adrian has taken to it too. The wondrous thing is that it transmutes Stephenese into Saxonese, so much that the poor old creature thinks himself echoed, and suspects malice.

Today Lytton came to tea, and was very charming and amenable to all the strictures I made upon Cambridge life and the . . . ums [The Apostles]. He practically agreed with me that the Hearthrug was rotten, and the whales a-stink. I said you did too, and he groaned at the spread of light.

They have all gone to hear a concert at Gordon Square. I resisted, and now try to think that they'll all be a gabbling of fundamental realities and essential chords, which I should loathe.

I think the Chinese book is most interesting. There is such a delicacy in the commonest things, pork stuffed with hyacinths. Thank you very much for sending it and the others.

I must go out and post this. I have got 5/- which I am going to spend on chocolates and a sleeping draught, if the shops are open, and I escape molestation. I shan't want the sleeping draught—in any case.

Yr.

VS

Sussex

1. The journals and correspondence of Mary Berry, published in three volumes in 1866. She was the friend of Horace Walpole.
2. The nature of these manuscripts and letters is unclear. Virginia may be referring to the letters which Lytton had written to Leonard while he was in Ceylon, and 'the cosmogony' may be their group of friends at Cambridge.

607: To Lady Ottoline Morrell

38 *Brunswick Square, W.C.*

[March 1912]

My dear Ottoline,

I am so sorry that you have had this dreadful anxiety.[1] I hope it is going right, as the maid seemed to think this evening. I will call again to hear—but of course dont wake or take any notice. I know you must be exhausted. I am so very sorry for you and Mr Morrell.

Yr. aff.

V.S.

Texas

608: To Molly MacCarthy

38 *Brunswick Square, W.C.*

[March 1912]

My dear Molly,

I began a letter to you, and then went off to bed and never sent it. All I had to say was thank you for writing—advice and all!

I didn't mean to make you think that I was against marriage. Of course I'm not, though the extreme safeness and sobriety of young couples does apall me, but then so do the random melancholy old maids. I began life with a tremendous, absurd, ideal of marriage, then my bird's eye view of many marriages disgusted me, and I thought I must be asking what was not to be had. But that has passed too. Now I only ask for someone to make me vehement, and then I'll marry him! The fault of our society always seems to me to be timidity and self consciousness; and I feel oddly vehement, and very exacting, and so difficult to live with and so very intemperate and changeable, now thinking one thing and now another. But in my heart I always expect to be floated over all crises, when the moment comes, and landed heaven knows where! I don't really worry about W[oolf]: though I think I made out that I did. He is going to stay longer anyhow, and perhaps he will stay in England anyhow,[2] so the responsibility is lifted off me.

No, I shan't float into a bloodless alliance with Lytton—though he is in some ways perfect as a friend, only he's a female friend.

I saw Desmond the other day, who said you had gone off to Devon. I think that shows great determination. I wish you would write, if you dont hate writing, and say what you are doing.

1. Ottoline's daughter, Julian, aged six, was seriously ill and had undergone an operation.
2. Determined to resign from the Ceylon Colonial Service if Virginia would agree to marry him, Leonard had asked the Colonial Office on 14 February to extend his leave by four months, for personal reasons.

I spent a strange fortnight in bed, among faded old ladies, who might have been weeds at the bottom of a river, they were so placid and remote from everything, and yet alive. I am now leading a semi-invalid life, and it is very nice, when the days are fine, doesn't that sound old! I wish you would come for a day's outing with me to Richmond or somewhere, where after sitting by a flower bed for some hours, we could have an enormous meal.

Please go on being a friend, whatever I take it into my head to do.

Yrs. aff.

Mrs Michael MacCarthy   VS

609: To Sydney Waterlow   38 *Brunswick Square, W.C.*

March 21st [1912]

Dear Sydney,

I was very glad indeed to get your letter. I needn't say that your friendship will be a great delight, and the more I have of it the better. I've been a shameful time in writing, but one day after another has been knocked on the head by sleeping draughts. They are a good deal worse than sleeplessness, and the colour of the blood of bloated bugs.

My plans are rather vague; I do hate Easter, but if you're going to be in London, please suggest some time for coming. At this moment I'm kept from visitors, but in a week or two I shall be alright.

I read your article, guessing it must be you, and thought it excellent, because, imbecile as I am in such matters, I could understand and enjoy. I wish I'd known your facts about Gissing.[1] Desmond told me something, which was then contradicted and I felt I was writing about a ghost.

It's a great gain that you're going to live in London. I wonder where. My weekends in Cambridge [with the Quaker] make lurid pictures, like cheap lantern slides in my mind. Where are you going now?

Yours ever,

John Waterlow   Virginia Stephen

610: To Leonard Woolf   38 *Brunswick Square, W.C.*

[April 1912]

Nessa and Roger want to come to Asheham on Saturday—so, if you're not going to Cornwall will you come too.

I write this, as I vaguely think you may be starting at Dawn, and also Bob T: [R. C. Trevelyan] has arrived, and you may want an excuse.

Sussex

1. Virginia had also written about George Gissing's novels (*TLS*, 11 January 1912).

611: To Katherine Cox

[April 1912]

Dear Bruin Cox,

Are you coming to spend Sunday with me.

If the weather continues, we might see some wonderful things.

Anyhow, come to lunch at one, and we will invent something. What I should like best would be a great deal of eating in 18th Century houses by the river side, then a walk among daffodils and small blue flowers. Then more eating, this time in a great Inn on a hill with bow windows, where there is a nightingale outside. Then a return through market gardens by moonlight—the whole to include 8 hours of fresh air, 3 meals with a cost 1/9½.

Yrs.

Mark Arnold-Forster   VS

612: To Violet Dickinson

[April 1912]

My Violet,

I should like to come to tea on Friday, better than to lunch. I've not yet disappeared, except for Easter Monday. It was gorgeous down at Asheham. We spent two days laying tiles, and now every bone is stiff, and I can neither sit, stand, or write, owing to a great circle of bare flesh in my palm, where I flourished a hoe, and broke it. I see the management of the earth is a great art.

Yr. VS

Berg

613: To Katherine Cox

[April 1912]

Dear Ka,

What a singularly foolish letter! I mean about cleaning your head before you come here. Start on Friday, walk all night, and at dawn accept the first lift offered you by a South-going waggon. Anyhow, whichever way you go, you must arrive here on Saturday.

Marriages are happening so fast that you should look upon them merely as a natural act, and not write letters, make wills etc—But my God, your family seems to melt like the candle now perched on the arm of my chair.

Is the Stockbroker[1] practically the same as the Surgeon? Will Aunt Hester come up from Wimbledon? She's certain to have a stroke this time.

1. Ka's father was a stockbroker.

We came here yesterday, and since then we have scarcely moved out of the sun on the terrace except to eat and sleep. Mrs Funnell—but you don't know her—and how she brings puddings up with a rush, one end or t'other, that lie upon her like blankets—she has just been telling us how her Grandfather got a penny a tail for moles, and kept 100 tails in a tin box, which his wife hid in a cupboard in the corner.

I never saw the downs so splendid as they are now.

Why not wash your head here? Accident gave me this large sheet of paper; and now I can think of no gossip. Rupert and Bryn [Brynhild Olivier] came to tea the other day; she has a glass eye—one can imagine her wiping it bright in the morning with a duster. Rupert I thought slightly Byronic. Then I had a long walk with Walter [Lamb], which completely did for me, and I am only now un-freezing my wits. Why is it that he is like a deep well to draw words from? We went to Kew, and a leaden cloud at once overspread every bush, so bright a week ago. Vanessa's character remains very hard, and calculated to outlast the Sphinx. Marjorie is pursuing Yeats in Dublin, who is at No. 23 Southampton Row. Henry [Lamb] and Lytton rode in Dorset, and Henry was thrown again. But what's the use of telling you news—when every tremor reaches you by post or telegraph. What I should really like to do now, but must refrain, is to write a full account of the wreck of the Titanic. Do you know it's a fact that ships don't sink at that depth, but remain poised half way down, and become perfectly flat, so that Mrs Stead is now like a pancake, and her eyes like copper coins.[1] A curious fact, not to be circulated, out of respect for the relatives.

We are sitting over the fire, occasionally telling stories of our past.

Do come on Saturday, good, dear, Bruin Cox!

VS

Mark Arnold-Forster

614: To Leonard Woolf   *Asheham, Lewes*
                                              [*Sussex*]

Postcard
[30 April 1912]

A sad picture[2]—We dont appear in any of them, and Ka's photograph was mere smudge. Waiting for the train after a tremendous walk in record time.

VS

Sussex

1. The White Star liner *Titanic*, then on her maiden voyage, sank on 15 April, after striking an iceberg, with a loss of 1500 lives. Among the victims was W. T. Stead, editor of the *Pall Mall Gazette* and the *Review of Reviews*. Mrs Stead in fact survived him. Leonard took Virginia to the *Titanic* enquiry on 3 May.
2. On the reverse side of this postcard is a photograph of a funeral procession, probably of Lord Gage, who had died on 13 April.

May 1st [1912]

Dearest Leonard,

To deal with the facts first (my fingers are so cold I can hardly write) I shall be back about 7 tomorrow, so there will be time to discuss—but what does it mean? You can't take the leave, I suppose if you are going to resign certainly at the end of it. Anyhow, it shows what a career you're ruining!

Well then, as to all the rest. It seems to me that I am giving you a great deal of pain—some in the most casual way—and therefore I ought to be as plain with you as I can, because half the time I suspect, you're in a fog which I don't see at all. Of course I can't explain what I feel—these are some of the things that strike me. The obvious advantages of marriage stand in my way. I say to myself. Anyhow, you'll be quite happy with him; and he will give you companionship, children, and a busy life—then I say By God, I will not look upon marriage as a profession. The only people who know of it, all think it suitable; and that makes me scrutinise my own motives all the more. Then, of course, I feel angry sometimes at the strength of your desire. Possibly, your being a Jew comes in also at this point. You seem so foreign. And then I am fearfully unstable. I pass from hot to cold in an instant, without any reason; except that I believe sheer physical effort and exhaustion influence me. All I can say is that in spite of these feelings which go chasing each other all day long when I am with you, there is some feeling which is permanent, and growing. You want to know of course whether it will ever make me marry you. How can I say? I think it will, because there seems no reason why it shouldn't—But I don't know what the future will bring. I'm half afraid of myself. I sometimes feel that no one ever has or ever can share something— Its the thing that makes you call me like a hill, or a rock. Again, I want everything—love, children, adventure, intimacy, work. (Can you make any sense out of this ramble? I am putting down one thing after another). So I go from being half in love with you, and wanting you to be with me always, and know everything about me, to the extreme of wildness and aloofness. I sometimes think that if I married you, I could have everything—and then— is it the sexual side of it that comes between us? As I told you brutally the other day, I feel no physical attraction in you. There are moments—when you kissed me the other day was one—when I feel no more than a rock. And yet your caring for me as you do almost overwhelms me. It is so real, and so strange. Why should you? What am I really except a pleasant attractive creature? But its just because you care so much that I feel I've got to care before I marry you. I feel I must give you everything; and that if I can't, well, marriage would only be second-best for you as well as for me. If you can still go on, as before, letting me find my own way, as that is what would please me best; and then we must both take the risks. But you have made me very happy too. We both of us want a marriage that is a tremendous living thing, always alive, always hot, not dead and easy in parts as most marriages are. We ask a great deal of life, don't we? Perhaps we shall get it; then, how splendid!

One doesn't get much said in a letter does one? I haven't touched upon the enormous variety of things that have been happening here—but they can wait.

D'you like this photograph?—rather too noble, I think. Here's another.[1]

Yrs.
VS

Sussex

616: To Katherine Cox
Asheham [Rodmell,
Sussex]

May 2nd [1912]

Dear Ka,

Here is a cheque for the concert, though, considering I was in bed at Twickenham at the time, I didn't hear much ancient music for my money. I was up in London for a day, and retrieved your letter; 18 miles in 5 hours is good going; with a pack on the back I count it pretty fair, though that time I walked through the Marches of Wales taking one thing with another, bulls, morasses, declivities and precipices, I suppose I must have done about 20. But then I was 5 years younger than I am now. Janet never came, so I'm here alone, and go back rather melancholy this afternoon to settle in for the Summer, which will be absolutely dry, and all awhirl with Wagner, and Russian dancers. By the way, young Mr Funnell came running into his mother and said "I've just seen an old Trampwoman pass, with her bundle on her back". "That's not an old Trampwoman: that's Miss Cox" said Mrs F. looking out of the window. "She's walking to Woking." "That young woman's in need of a job" was all Mr Funnell could say.

I've heard about every household between this and Newhaven now, and I regret to say that the proportion of illegitimate children is quite amazing. Babies are born to old shepherds of 80, who never ask themselves what everyone's asking themselves all day long. So you see, gossip is not confined to the Ap . . . les [Apostles] and their satellites.

Come and see me soon.

Yr.
VS

1. This letter decided Leonard. He resigned from the Colonial Service, and his resignation was accepted on 7 May.

See what you missed! The young man with the pursed mouth is the new peer[1]. The elderly gentlemen, Uncles, military; and they didn't have tea, when they went back, but sherry and sandwiches.

Mark Arnold-Forster

617: TO LYTTON STRACHEY   38 *Brunswick Square, W.C.*

21st May [1912]

Dear Lytton,

How difficult it is to write to you! It's all Cambridge—that detestable place; and the ap-s-les are so unreal, and their loves are so unreal, and yet I suppose it's all going on still—swarming in the sun—and perhaps not as bad as I imagine. But when I think of it, I vomit—that's all—a green vomit, which gets into the ink and blisters the paper. How is your tragedy comedy? and are you aware that Walter's [Lamb] been satisfactorily delivered—are you aware of June 5th and the treat? We go up the river, swing, eat, make merry; that's plain sailing; but afterwards in the dusk, in the college garden, with Jane Harrison[2] to make proclamation, we have the tragedy from start to finish, and Choristers hidden in the Elms sing Walter's songs to Walter's music. There's no escaping. And after that, cold salmon and lemonade in the moonlight.

London is not rich in news—Dora's alive and so is Charlie [Sanger]; and they don't dress in black because their father's dead. Then Bobo Meinertz-hagen has broken off her engagement with Brother Mayor[3] because he lacks imagination, but still she exclaims, "He is the best man in the world!" Don't you think its time that ambling vague young ladies were taught their places? She is a sentimental Jewess—but you know her. Nessa has got over the measles, and they trail about Italy, rather uncomfortably I expect, and Clive takes the thermometer to bed with him.

As for Thomas Hardy, he's a great man; his style is not made to fit, but what of that? If we had but his ribs, his thighs, his stomach and his entrails! As a matter of fact this is more hearsay than anything else; and I dont know what vapours overcome me in Bedford Square [Ottoline]; I ramble like a drunken moth. Desmond, who is now dusty as a very old bottle of brandy, turns up for lunch—tea—dinner; and we go over the story of Donne's life. As the greater part of the history of England is somehow coming in, the book will be apoplectic. He is going to be as prolific as Miss [Rhoda] Broughton "One volume and a half every year" he says—What'll the half

1. The 6th Viscount Gage. Presumably Virginia enclosed the funeral postcard.
2. The classical scholar (1850-1928), who lectured in archaeology at Newnham.
3. But in this same year Beatrice ('Bobo') Meinertzhagen did marry Robert Mayor, a Fellow of King's, who became Secretary to the Board of Education.

volumes be d'you think?[1] Hom [Meredith] was here once, the attenuated [E. M.] Forster, and a very great writer called Bojer.[2] Ask Desmond about him when you meet. His theme is Conscience.

But the most interesting thing to observe, as I have often told you, is not these distinguished spirits, but the humble ones, the slightly touched, the eccentric. Alas! you're not interested in them, or I would tell you the story of Mary Coombes and the German student.

One more piece of gossip reaches me for your ear alone—that Pernel [Lytton's sister], after seeing several students wearing white spats, at once took to her bed, and sacrificed her ovaries.

Yrs.

VS

Frances Hooper

618: To Violet Dickinson   38 *Brunswick Square, W.C.*

22nd May [1912]

My Violet,

Next time you begin a letter: 'Are you pregnant, or married?' do for Goodness Sake, put the right number. Your envelope reached me open, and on it was written, "Opened by J. Stephen.'—who lives at 32, and when she saw what was in it, she promptly gave it back—but what of my character? The postman drew his own conclusions.

I will come down one day, if you will have me, and there is a train after lunch. But which day? Please tell me—not Whitsuntide—some day next week. We go on much as usual. Nessa started measles in Milan—isn't it amazing? Roger and Clive may still get it. Anyhow, the tour is ruined; though she is now all right. They are in Florence, I think. Every morning I write 500 words [of *The Voyage Out*]; and have already passed my natural limit; but must go on for another 5 chapters. The worst of it is, you wont like it; you'll tell me I'm a failure as a writer, as well as a failure as a woman. Then I shall take a dive into the Serpentine which, I see, is 6 feet deep in malodorous mud. By the way, *Are* you fond of me?

Yr. VS

Berg

1. In fact, Desmond MacCarthy wrote no major work, although seven volumes of his collected essays were published during his lifetime.
2. Johan Bojer (b. 1872), the Norwegian novelist.

[May 1912]

My Violet,

All next week is in a hopeless state of muddle, so might I come down the week after?

I should like to come down for the day, after lunch, and return when the nightingales are out. Please choose the day—all are now free.

I'm working very hard—in sight of the end.

Yr .VS

Berg

620: To Violet Dickinson   38 *Brunswick Square, W.C.*

[4 June 1912]

My Violet,

I've got a confession to make. I'm going to marry Leonard Wolf [*sic*]. He's a penniless Jew. I'm more happy than anyone ever said was possible—but I *insist* upon your liking him too. May we both come on Tuesday? Would you rather I come alone? He was a great friend of Thobys, went out to India—came back last summer when I saw him and he's been living here since the winter.

You have always been such a splendid and delightful creature, whom I've loved ever since I was a mere chit, that I couldn't bear it if you disapproved of my husband. We've been talking a great deal about you. I tell him you [are] 6 ft 8: and that you love me.

My novels just upon finished. L. thinks my writing the best part of me. We're going to work very hard. Is this too incoherent? The one thing that must be made plain is my intense feeling of affection for you. How I've bothered you—and what a lot you've always given me.

Yr. Sp.

Berg

621: To Madge Vaughan   38 *Brunswick Square, W.C.*

[June 1912]

Dearest Madge,

I want to tell you that I'm going to marry Leonard Wolf [*sic*]. He was one of Thoby's greatest friends. I'm very very happy—and I know you'll be glad.

May we come and see you some day? I want you to know him, and I dont mean there to be any lapse in our friendship, which has always been a joy, since—oh what years ago!

I've just finished my novel—all but one chapter—and I hope to publish it in the autumn. I will write to Mr Sully,[1] whom I well remember.

Leonard is far and away the most interesting and charming man I know, and I feel that I shall have to increase in virtue as his wife. We mean to do quantities of things. He wishes to know whether he may send his love—I've talked a great deal about you.

Yr. loving,

Sussex   VS

622: To Janet Case   38 *Brunswick Square, W.C.*

[June 1912]

My Dear Janet,

I want to tell you that I'm going to marry Leonard Wolf—he is a penniless Jew. He was a friend of Thoby's,—and I'm so happy—Its not at all what people say, but so much better. I dont think I'm nearly worth what he is. May we come and see you? You've always been angelic to me—no, much nicer than angelic, and I want you to like him. It has been worth waiting for.

Yours aff,

Sussex   VS

623: To Lytton Strachey   38 *Brunswick Square, W.C.*

6th June [1912]

Ha! Ha!

Virginia Stephen

Frances Hooper   Leonard Woolf

624: To Lady Ottoline Morrell

38 *Brunswick Square, W.C.*

[June 1912]

Dearest Ottoline,

This is to tell you that I'm going to marry Leonard Woolf. I'm very happy—and find him more necessary every day. Do you like him? I hope so, because I want to be a friend of yours all my life.

Forgive this scrawl written in bed, but I wanted to tell you.

Yr. aff.

Texas   V.S.

1. James Sully, the friend of Leslie Stephen.

625: To Violet Dickinson   38 *Brunswick Square, W.C.*

[June 1912]

My Violet,

Friday is no good—would Saturday do? If not, it must be one day next week. Please settle, (except Tuesday and Wednesday) It was idiotic to put you off—I've been rather headachy, and had a bad night, and Leonard made me into a comatose invalid.

We want very much to come. He is a most charming man, and I get steadily happier. By the way, my novel is getting on, in spite of interruptions, and L. wants me to say that if I cease to write when married, I shall be divorced.

Please have us.

Yr. VS

Berg

626: To Violet Dickinson   38 *Brunswick Square, W.C.*

[June 1912]

My Violet,

My head goes on aching stupidly, and we've decided to go off to the sea this week end and cure it. So will you let us come *Wednesday*—Please do— and nothing will induce me to put it off again. Work and love and Jews in Putney[1] take it out of one.

Yr. VS

Love to Nelly. I'm writing to her.

Berg

627: To Janet Case   38 *Brunswick Square, W.C.*

[June 1912]

My dear Janet,

Shall you be in tomorrow night about 9 or so?

We should like to come in if you are not too tired.

That seems the only time this week—relations have begun, and such a tea party at Putney.

"A sandwich, Miss Stephen—or may I call you Virginia?".

"What? Ham sandwiches for tea?".

1. Leonard had taken Virginia to meet his widowed mother, who lived in Colinette Road, Putney, with several of her children.

"Not *Ham*: potted meat. We don't eat Ham or bacon or Shellfish in this house."

"Not Shellfish? Why not shellfish?".

"Because it says in the Scriptures that they are unclean creatures, and our Mr Josephs at the Synagogue —— and ——

It was queer—

Yrs. aff.

VS

Sussex

628: To Madge Vaughan   38 *Brunswick Square, W.C.*

[June 1912]

Dearest Madge,

Thank you both for the telegram and for the letter.

We should like to come down some day after the 15th—Just now, everything's so unsettled—I mean work and engagements and so on—that we can't fix a day—but may I write later, and ask?

Meanwhile, how am I to begin about Leonard? First he is a Jew: second he is 31; third, he spent 7 years in Ceylon, governing natives, inventing ploughs, shooting tigers, and did so well that they offered him a very high place the other day, which he refused, wishing to marry me, and gave up his entire career there on the chance that I would agree. He has no money of his own. He has been living at Brunswick Sq. since December—we know each other as I imagine few people do before marriage. I've only known him 6 months, but from the first I have found him the one person to talk to. He interests me immensely, besides all the rest. We mean to marry in August, and he wants to find out about labour and factories and to keep outside Government and do things on his own account. He has also written a novel,[1] and means to write as well as be practical. We shall, I think, take a small house and try to live cheaply, so as not to have to make money.

O what an egoist I am! but you asked for details.

Do send me Janet's photograph. I've got all those of the children as babies which you gave me at Giggleswick.

At first I felt stunned, but now every day the happiness becomes more complete—even though it does seem a fearful chance—my having found any man who gives me what Leonard does.

You will come and see us, won't you, when we are married, and continue to be that eccentric but engaging animal, the Barbary Ape?

Yr. loving,

VS

Sussex

1. *The Village in the Jungle,* which was published in 1913.

Bell Hotel, Walberswick,
nr Southwold [*Suffolk*]

[June 1912]

My dear Nelly,

I wrote to you, but the difficulty of describing my husband overcame me, and I tore it up.

I quite agree that he ought to see something of the gardens at St Johns Wood, after 7 years in the East.

I think you will like him—though you will probably wonder why on earth he should marry me—considering that he has ruled India, hung black men, and shot tigers. He has written a novel; so have I: we both hope to publish them in the autumn.

I am very very happy, and I hope when I'm married that you will come and see me—or ask me to see you—oftener than in the past. Now please bear this in mind.

Yrs. Ever,
VS

I'm writing in an Inn, rain outside, 3 old spinsters discussing the beauties of river scenery.

Hatfield

630: To Lady Robert Cecil   38 *Brunswick Square, W.C.*

[June 1912]

My dear Nelly,

When I got home yesterday I found my first wedding present—yours. If they're all going to be as nice, I shall be in luck. I love your old glasses, which will adorn my table, directly I have one. You are extremely clever, as well as nice.

This is the prelude to asking whether we may come to tea with you—and would Tuesday next week suit? That seems the first afternoon. Heaven knows what happens to them—they melt away, and I shall soon find myself confronted by a wedding day. Is it an awful experience? Will you tell us truthfully all about it, when we come—that is if we may come?

Thank you again—I wish there was some new way of saying that which came out absolutely truthfully.

Your aff. VS

Hatfield

Monday [24 June 1912]

My Violet,

It was quite unnecessary to thank us for coming, considering that we both enjoyed it immensely. My husband says he never met anyone he liked so much as you. There is something very like Thoby about him, not only in his face. I feel I shall get fearfully spoilt—but at the same time he'll keep me in good condition as far as other things go. But wont it be awful if after all your care, my character, which promised so well, finally rots in marriage? We've been spending Sunday here—absolutely divine—but everything has over-grown during the week. We are now taking the garden in hand, and going to write for a longer lease. I'm inclined to start with only rooms in London, until we see how much we've got. It seems idiotic to put Leonard into an office, for the sake of a bigger income.

I hope you realise that I shall not talk less about myself and my own affairs now; I mean you must make up your mind to go on chastening me. Sophie [Farrell] was very proud of her flowers, which were put out in the middle of the bread she was baking. Shall we see you again? We go back this afternoon, and have to face Aunt Ritchie tomorrow. I'm having 2 dresses made by Nelly's woman.

Yr. VS

Berg

[July 1912]

My Violet,

Unluckily we've got some one coming down to Asheham this week, or we should have liked to come very much.

Shall you be in London at all? We're plucking up courage, now that we're more or less dressed to go and see George, but it does take a lot of virtue. Plans spin every day. I've just been riding in Richmond with L[eonard]. Great fun, though the horse was surprised.

Yr. VS

(working hard)

Berg

[July 1912]

My Violet,

I feel quite incapable of saying what I want for a wedding present, though I expect I want everything. At this moment we vaguely think of rooms in Grays Inn—they'd be very small, but cheap, and sufficient for a start. However, we haven't let these yet, and our plans depend on that. I think you must wait till the autumn.

Leonard hasn't yet got a profession—the Board of Trade would give him a job, but we should have to take it at once; and get no holiday till next June, and that doesn't seem worth while.

We're both writing hard; he has some journalism to do, and my novel is at last dying. O how sad when it's done! I think some of its very, or rather, amusing; and as it gets shoved out of my head, another begins; but next year I must have a child. I saw Nelly yesterday; it seemed to me the most ghastly fate imaginable, to sit and look on at other people talking all ones life.

Shall I see you again? We expect to marry about the 8th or 9th of August.

Yr. VS

My husband is much too good for me, but I'm very happy.

Berg

[July 1912]

Dear Ka,

Your growl, though slightly muffled, was very welcome. I'm in the midst of writing letters too intimate even for me; and feel inclined to write like Gwen, short sentences torn from the heart. Damn that woman! I've never answered her. Now the proposition I have to lay before you with all possible speed is this: will you come to Asheham this week, Saturday, and spend Bank Holiday? Leonard and I shall be alone. It would be a great joy... couldn't you leave the Aunts to the Americans who will welcome a touch of real life, real English ladies, real paralysis, real etc. Otherwise I shall not see you: wedding is 12th August, probably then Italy, Spain, and a steamer that crosses to Africa and Italy like an old lady making cats cradles. Iceland is in midwinter now, with yellow fog, and cataracts bursting out of rocks.

Do come.

Yr. V.

Shove[1] has just taken 2 rooms [at Brunswick Square]. 2 still going.

Mark Arnold-Forster

635: To Violet Dickinson   *Little Talland House, Firle,*
                                   Lewes, Sussex

[3 August 1912]

My Violet,

I suppose you are hunting or fishing somewhere or other. So I doubt whether you will ever get this, and it wont be much loss if you dont, because I am without ideas.

We are going to our registry office today week, attended by a singular old cousin[2], who trots if you whistle, and gallops if you sing, George in white waistcoat, Nessa in Turkish silk, and Aunt Mary with a crutch—she has again been blown over a milk cart—in her widows weeds. Then we go to the Quantock hills—where I dont know for 4 days—and then straight off to France, Spain and Italy.

We shall be back in October. At first we shall stay at Brunswick Sq: but we hope to take rooms somewhere this week. Everything has been left to the last—but the Novels are finished—and that is a great relief. In October we shall read them over, and decide whether they are to go straight into Hell. I shall write to you from some remote hill top—you might answer. L. sends his love.

                                              Yr. VS

Berg

636: To Emma Vaughan   *38 Brunswick Square, W.C.*

Aug 7th [1912]

Dearest Todger,

Its very exciting to have a present to look forward to. I shall remind you of it later. Iceland is, alas, knocked on the head—too late in the year. But we're doing Italy and Spain instead—We marry on Saturday, so this is the last letter you will ever have from your loving

                                       Virginia Stephen

Sussex

1. Gerald Shove, the economist, who had been at Cambridge. He married Fredegond Maitland in 1915.
2. Albert Venn Dicey, Professor of English Law at Oxford until 1909. He was distantly related to the Stephens through the Venns.

[8 August 1912]

My dear Duncan,

A rumour has reached me that you might come up for the wedding. I should like it very much if you did—but this is only to say that we are going to be done on Saturday—day after tomorrow—at 12.15 at St Pancras Town Hall, in case you had any thoughts. I believe that Dora Sanger, George, Richmond Ritchie, and old Albert Dicey[1] (for Gods sake dont whistle or he will run) are coming, so you might get a slight amusement. However, we've had such rows with poor old Mother Wolf, who says she never imagined such a slight as not being asked to the wedding, that its doubtful whether anyone will come.

I forgot to send on this letter; I hope its all right. I have an immense amount of gossip in my head, about all our relations, but I'm in such a rush that I cant tell you.

I hope you're enjoying yourself.

Yours,

V.S.

(God! this is the last of S!)

Duncan Grant

638: To John Maynard Keynes   38 *Brunswick Square, W.C.*

9th August 1912

Dear Maynard,

I enclose your bill—a curmudgeonly thing to do on the last night before ones marriage—but many bills have to be settled—board wages etc. As you see, April is doubtful—

Would you be so kind as to send the cheque to me at London Joint Stock Bank, 1 Woburn Place, Russell Sq. as I'm going away. Only a caretaker capable of bed and breakfast, but no more, will be here till 1st October.

Yours V. Stephen[2]

King's

1. In fact Albert Dicey did not come. The only guests at the wedding were Vanessa, George and Gerald Duckworth, Duncan Grant, Roger Fry, Saxon Sydney-Turner, Aunt Mary Fisher and Frederick Etchells.
2. Virginia Stephen and Leonard Woolf were married at St Pancras Registry Office on Saturday, 10 August 1912.

Appendix

NICKNAMES USED IN VOLUME I

Anny:	Anne Ritchie (Thackeray)
Apes, *Singes*:	Virginia
Aunt:	Violet Dickinson
Bar:	George Duckworth
Barbary Ape:	Madge Vaughan
Becca:	Stella Duckworth
Bee:	Beatrice Cameron
Billy Goat, Billy, B.:	Virginia (to Vanessa)
Bob:	R. C. Trevelyan
Bobo:	Beatrice Meinertzhagen
Boo:	Cordelia Fisher
Brotherboy:	Halford Vaughan
Bruin, 'the Bear':	Katherine Cox
Capra (Goat):	Virginia
Carrie:	Barbara Vaughan
Chief, The:	Madge Vaughan
Chipmonk:	Clive Bell
Cresty:	Thoby Stephen
Crumbos:	Walter and Ella Crum
Dodo:	Antonia Booth (Macnaghten)
Dolphin:	Vanessa Stephen (Bell)
Dotty, Dobbythinga:	Dorothea Stephen
Eily:	Elinor Monsell (Darwin)
Elly:	Elinor Rendel
Emmy:	Emmeline Fisher
Georgie:	George Duckworth
Ginia:	Virginia
Goat, Goatus, Il Giotto:	Virginia
Gribbs:	Thoby Stephen
Grim:	Thoby Stephen
Gumbo:	Marjorie Strachey
Herbert:	Thoby Stephen
Hom:	H. O. Meredith
Janet, Jan:	Virginia
Ka:	Katherine Cox (Arnold-Forster)
Kangaroo:	Virginia (to Violet Dickinson)

Katie:	Lady Cromer
Lellie:	Leslie Stephen
Lotta:	Charlotte Symonds (Leaf)
Madge:	Margaret Symonds (Vaughan)
Mango:	Adrian Stephen (?)
Maria:	Vanessa Stephen
Marny:	Margaret Vaughan
Mia:	Maria Macnamara
Minna:	Sarah Duckworth
Minny:	Harriet Thackeray (Stephen)
Nelly:	Lady Robert Cecil
Nessa:	Vanessa Stephen (Bell)
Nun:	Caroline Emelia Stephen
Old 'Un:	Vanessa (by Adrian Stephen)
Ott:	Lady Ottoline Morrell
Papa:	Lytton Strachey
Peter:	Clive Bell
Porchy:	Lord Porchester
Quaker:	Caroline Emelia Stephen
Ray:	Rachel Costelloe (Strachey)
Sheep:	Mary Sheepshanks
Sheepdog:	Vanessa Bell
Singes, the:	Virginia (the *Singerie*)
Snow:	Margery Snowden
Sparroy, Sp.:	Virginia (to Violet Dickinson)
Sym:	Mrs J. A. Symonds
Synge:	Virginia
Tawny:	Vanessa Bell
Thobs:	Thoby Stephen
Toad, Todkins, Toadlebinks:	Emma Vaughan
Tom:	Edwin Fisher
Totty:	Charlotte Pater
Uncles:	Thoby and Adrian Stephen
Wallaby, Wall:	Virginia (to Violet Dickinson)
Wattie:	Walter Lamb
Wombat:	Hans (dog)

INDEX

The numbers are page-numbers, except in the 'Letters to' section at the end of individual entries, where the letter-numbers are given in italics.

V. stands for Virginia Stephen (Woolf)

Bell, Clive—*contd.*
Letters to: Nos, *289, 292, 294, 297,*
299, 328, 345, 355, 378, 406-7,
410, 416, 421, 426, 429, 438,
442, 448, 451, 462, 471, 474,
481, 484, 498, 510, 513, 515,
523-4, 532, 534-5, 539, 541,
548, 551, 558, 566, 598
Bell, Florence (Lady Richmond),
34
Bell, Sir Hugh, 34
Bell, Julian: born, 323*n*; as baby,
328, 331, 342, 352, 367-8, 370,
372; as a boy, 428, 436
Bell, Mary (Lady Trevelyan), 34
Bell, Olivier (Mrs Quentin Bell), xi
Bell, Prof. Quentin: Biography of
V., xi, xvi; birth, 430*n*; as
baby, 435, 442, 475; name
changed from Claudian, 444,
448
Bell, Vanessa: *see* Stephen, Vanessa
Bell, William and Hannah (Clive's
parents), 265, 272, 274-5, 302,
447
Bemerton (Wilts), 91
Bentley, Richard, 386
Berenson, Bernard, 457
Berenson, Mary, 436*n*, 457
Beresford, Admiral Lord Charles,
298*n*
Beresford (photographer), 265
Berg Collection, New York, x-xi
Berryman, Mrs (Cornwall), 433
Bethlehem (lunatic asylum), 41
Bewick, Thomas, 165
Binyon, Laurence, 313
Birch, Una, 391
Birrell, Francis, 415
Bishopstone (Sussex), 454
Blatchfield (Surrey), 73-4
Blean (nr. Canterbury), 425-9
Blo' Norton Hall (Norfolk), 233-5
Bloomsbury: Stephens plan to live

in, 96; seek house in, 119-20;
135; buy lease of Gordon
Square house, 142*n*; V.'s
pleasure in district, 197-8;
respectability of Fitzroy
Square?, 284, 286-7
Bloomsbury Group: origins, 183;
V. finds them inanimate, 208;
bored by (1909), 415; *see*
Friday Club, Thursday Even-
ings
Boer War, 33*n*
Bojer, Johan, 499
Booth, Alfred, 184
Booth, Antonia: *see* Macnaghten,
Mrs Malcolm
Booth, Charles, 14*n*, 195, 208*n*, 276-7
Booth, Mrs Charles, 246, 276-7, 468
Booth, Imogen, 208-9, 348
Bordighera, 97
Boswell, James, 362*n*, 379
Bowen, Marjorie, 295*n*
Branfoot, Dr, 21-2, 25, 41
Brighton, 23, 443-4
British Museum, 253, 313
Brontë family, 159, 397
Brooke, Rupert: V. first sees, 328;
with Miss Olivier, 466; V.
stays with, 474-5; and camps
with in Devon, 467, 477; with
Ka Cox, 489*n*; tea at Asham,
495
Broomy Lodge (New Forest), 58*n*,
59
Broughton, Rhoda, 170, 498
Broussa (Turkey), 460*n*, 465, 468
Browne, Sir Thomas, 305
Brunswick Sq., No. 38: move into,
480, 481; house-rules, 484-5
Buchan, John, 248
Buffon, Comte de, 263
'Burley': *see* Twickenham mental
home
Burne-Jones, Edward, 107*n*, 169

76, 85, 245, 266; her ancestry, 89, 368n; their intimacy begins, 49; builds Welwyn cottage, 58, 73; smart social life, 63, 297, 368; relations with Crums, 70; hurts her back, 80-1; V. sends her essays, 82, 303; to Italy, 97; comforts V. during Leslie Stephen's illness, 114ff; seeks house for Stephens, 120; visits Leslie Stephen, 122; joins V. in Italy, 137n, 139; cares for her during her mental break-down, 141-3, 186; criticises her writing, 164; world-cruise with Lady R. Cecil, 198, 203-14; friend of Kate Greenaway, 210; goes to Greece with V., 239; cares for Vanessa in Athens, 239; ill with typhoid, 240ff; V. keeps from her news of Thoby's death, 248-66; she hears the news, 266; V.'s 'comic life' of, 304, 314, 336; in New York with B. Thynne, 331-2; 'estranged' from V., 367; car-accident, 379; V. tells of her engagement to Leonard, 500; she meets him, 505; gradual cooling of their friend-ship, xix

Letters to: *passim* from Letter *42* onwards (329 letters in this vol.)

Dictionary of National Biography, 1, 52

Dodd, Francis, 297, 313, 316, 324, 338, 348, 399

Dreadnought hoax, 422-3

Dresden, 39, 41, 149; V. in, 410-12

Drewsteignton (Devon), 477

Duckworth, Auberon, 283

Duckworth, George: attitude to V. in childhood, xvi, 3, 11, 472; V.'s later attitude to him, 101,

391, 438; gives family presents, 6; in Italy, 14; army camp, 17; takes Vanessa to Paris, 30-2; returns from Middle East, 46; takes Vanessa to Italy, 50-1; secretary to Austen Chamber-lain, 59, 100; manages V.'s finances, 67; friendship with Carnarvons, 74, 80, 98, 101; Leslie Stephen's illness, 95; to Manorbier with V., 130-2; marries, 142n; birth of sons, 194, 198, 283; secretary to Charles Booth, 208n; dis-courages Greek trip, 232, 235; sees little of V., 299; patronis-ing letter, 429; at V.'s marriage, 508n

Letters to: Nos. *12, 13, 21, 29, 30*

Duckworth, Gerald: character, 307; in V.'s childhood, 3; founds Duckworth & Co., 12n, 15; in Italy, 74; social life, 77; decides to live separately, 96; in Venice with V., 137-8; to Egypt, 262; in Rye with V., 307; at V.'s marriage, 508n; *mentioned*, 6, 13, 15, 21, 31, 54, 70, 101, 134, 161, 169, 208, 236

Duckworth, Henry, 194, 198, 201, 202

Duckworth, Lady Margaret (Her-bert): marries George, 142n; V. meets, 158, 180; makes better impression on V., 189-190; birth of sons, 194, 283; snubs V., 228; 'a good woman', 260; V. visits, 298-9

Duckworth, Sarah Emily ('Aunt Minna'), 13, 17, 18, 65, 68-9, 138-9, 167, 169, 215, 219, 359, 436, 448

Duckworth, Stella: 1, 3; marries, 4; takes V. to see Queen Victoria,

Maitland, Mrs F. W. (Florence Fisher), 26, 34, 145, 152, 154

Manchester: V.'s visit to, 223-4

Manners, Lady Marjorie, 214n

Manorbier (Pembrokeshire): Stephens' visit after Leslie's death, 130-6; V. gets idea for book there, 135n; Vanessa-Clive honeymoon at, 279n, 280; V. goes alone to (1908), 352, 355-68

Marlowe, Christopher, 45-6

Marsh, Edward, 387

Massingberd, Margaret, 15

Massingberd, Mildred, 40

Maugham, W. Somerset, 396

Maupassant, Guy de, 304

May, Admiral Sir William, 423n

Mayor, Robert, 498

Maxse, Leopold, 54, 156, 177n, 178, 209, 218

Maxse, Mrs Leopold ('Kitty'), 15, 37, 54n, 83, 94, 99, 100, 103, 112, 114, 126, 135, 145, 171, 208-9, 262, 468-9; original of Mrs Dalloway, 54n, 349n

Meinertzhagen, Daniel (and family), 409, 498

Melymbrosia: see *The Voyage Out*

Memoirs of a Novelist (by V.), 413n

Mendip Hills (Somerset), 340, 367

Meredith, George, 396

Meredith, H. O., 460, 499

Mérimée, Prosper, 304, 378

Methuen, Lord, 33

Michelet, Jules, 398

Milan, 393

Milman, Sylvia, 208

Milner, George, 100

Monsell, Elinor: see Darwin, Mrs Bernard

Montagu, Lady Mary Wortley, 337

Montaigne, Michel de, 66

Moore, G. E., 340, 347, 352, 357, 364

Moorsom, Kenneth, 281

Morants (owners of Ringwood house), 18

Morgan, Pierpont, 232

Morley College: xv; V. invited to teach at, 171-2; accepts, 173, 175; talks on Venice, 177; history, 191; composition, 210, 281; becomes librarian, 264; continues teaching, 292, 311, 312, 313; gives it up, 320

Morrell, Lady Ottoline: V. meets, 376; growing friendship with, 381, 394, 395, 398; V. visits, 451, 474; illness of her daughter, 492; told of V.'s engagement, 501

Letters to: Nos. *468, 475, 550, 553, 580, 590-1, 597, 607, 624*

Morrell, Philip, 381n, 448

Morris, William, 170

Murray, Gilbert, 351, 365

Murray, John, 215n, 231, 305, 332

Mürren (Switzerland), 44, 433

Mycenae (Greece), 239, 253

National Review, The, 177n, 266n

Nauplia (Greece), 239

Neo-Pagans, 460n

Netherhampton House (Salisbury, Wilts,), 89-94, 150

Newbolt, Henry John, 320-1

Letter to: No. *41*

Newcastle, Duke of, 438

New Forest (Hants.): V.'s visits to: 35, 43-4; 52-4; 168-72; 269-74; article by V. on, 173

Newnham College, Cambridge, 145, 328, 375

Newsome David, xviii

New York, 332

Noble, Miss (Warboys), 37, 43, 46

Noel, Fanny, 35

Noel, Frank, 228, 239

523

ness at Hove, 14-15, 21-2; at
Trinity, 34, 45, 72; advises V.
on Greek, 42; she asks him
about Shakespeare, 45-6; future
career, 76-7; decides to read
Law, 103; at his father's death,
127; to Manorbier with V.,
130*ff*; to Italy with V., 137-8;
writes pamphlet, 161; social life,
167, 180; Xmas in New Forest,
168-70; bird-watching, 192; in
Cornwall, 204-7; reads paper
to Friday Club, 225; sells
Thackeray MS., 232; in Italy
again, 235; and Greece, 239;
gets typhoid on return, 239;
serious illness, 240*ff*; worse,
246; dies, 248*n*; V.'s memory
of him, 303, 373-4, 434

Letters to: Nos. *2-10, 14-16, 36,
38-40, 47, 56, 66-7, 69, 81*

Stephen, Vanessa (Mrs Clive Bell):
V.'s love for, xvii, 147, 282,
345, 409; her character: courage,
16; volcanic, 31; competence,
213; health and vitality, 254,
276; no genius, 276; 'complete'
person, 408; early drawings,
5, 8; present from George
Duckworth, 6; runs Hyde Park
Gate, 9; learns painting, 10-11;
holidays at Hove, 14-15; dances,
16; wears trousers, 23; to Paris
with George, 30-2; weekend
parties, 39; at Royal Academy
Schools, 43, 54, 117; to Italy
with George, 50-1; in New
Forest with V., 53-4; works
with Sargent, 59, 60, 100; her
father's death, 127; at Manorbier with V., 130*ff*; in Italy
and Paris, 137-40; during and
after V.'s madness, 143; pre-
pares Gordon Sq., 147; with

V. in Cambridge, 147; social
life, 161, 166, 180; Xmas in
New Forest, 167-72; article on
Watts rejected, 178; portrait
of Lady R. Cecil, 188; and
of Lord Robert, 228; starts
Friday Club, 201; refuses Clive,
204*n*; exhibition of her paint-
ings, 210, 213; with V. in
Yorkshire, 224; in Norfolk,
234-5; ill in Greece and Turkey,
239; seriously ill, 239*ff*; recovers, 249; agrees to marry
Clive Bell, 250, 268; convalescence, 254-7; happiness
with Clive, 266, 268, 270;
meets her in-laws, 274-5

Marries Clive Bell, 278-9,
283; honeymoon, 279, 280;
in Paris with V., 290-1; at
Gordon Sq., 292; at Rye with
V., 308-11; birth of Julian,
323; joins V. at St Ives, 328;
in Bath, 347, 354; V.'s 'Life'
of, 353; in Highlands, 362,
365, 367; in Italy with V.,
393-4; at Studland, 411-12;
and at Canterbury, 426-7;
birth of Quentin, 430*n*; goes
to Turkey, 456; her mis-
carriage there, 460*n*, 468; V.
brings her home, 465; in love
with Roger Fry, 447, 470*n*;
measles in Milan, 499; at V.'s
marriage, 508*n*

Letters to: Nos. *390, 427-8, 432-4,
437, 439, 441, 444, 446, 488,
499-506, 512, 522, 529, 531,
546-7, 562-3, 567-8, 570, 573-4,
576, 581*

Stephen, Virginia (Woolf):
Life:
Childhood: mental breakdown,
aged 13, 1; sees Queen

Literary development: wants to write about Fens, 27; first unpublished essay, 28n, 29; plot for play, 60; early literary exercises, 82n, 103n, 150, 154-5, 163-4; idea for first novel, 135n; later literary exercises, 225n, 303; 'I must work', 140, 144; thinks of journalism, 148, 154-156; first published journalism, 158; 'comic lives', 163, 304, 314, 336, 353; memoir of her father, 165; reviewing, 167, 210, 211-12 and *passim*; searching for major subject, 168; contribution to Maitland's Life of Leslie Stephen, 172, 176, 180; lost early fiction?, 225n; *Voyage Out, The,* see separate heading

Literary method: sometimes writes standing up, 301, 343, 361; depressed by her writing, 223; sensitive to criticism, 167, 170, 295; and praise, 176, 383; 'I shall reform the novel', 356; her 'dreamlike world', 227, 320; writes in dreamlike state, 383; 'my boldness terrifies me', 383; 'no heart'?, 228, 379; rewriting, 383; her special attitude and use of language, xx-xxi

Her letters: handwriting, spelling, dating, etc., x, 195n; location of originals, x-xi; character of letters, xiii-xiv, xx, 198; her definition of a good letter, 264, 282; 'too formal or too feverish'?, 343; 'at a gallop', 362; 'burn them', 366; writing to Vanessa, 408

Opinion of other writers: Greek literature, 30, 35, 42, 46-7, 177, 378; Marlowe, 45; Shakespeare, 45-6, 77; the Bible, 96; Flaubert and George Sand, 229, 305; Renan, 271; Christina Rossetti, 272; Keats, 272, 273; Henry James, 304-5; Sir Thomas Browne, 305; Vernon Lee, 320, 400; Mary Coleridge, 324, 353; G. E. Moore, 357, 364; Bernard Shaw, 423; Trelawny, 445; Wordsworth, 460; Thomas Hardy, 498

Character and attitudes: analyses own faults (vanity, selfishness), 411, 441, 470, 473; sense of failure, 466; political, xv, 332, 441; trace of xenophobia, xv, 139, 403; Jews, 184, 394; admires few people, 271; hates grand houses, 10, 274; dislikes Society, 16, 43, 85, 217, 228; but admires aristocrats, 82, 84; despises humbug, 97, 108, 442; agnosticism, 63, 85, 148, 448; 'thank God I was born an Englishwoman', 139; attitude to working class, xv, 281, 350, 364; position of women, xv, 421; sex and marriage, xvi, 274, 276, 434, 469, 475, 492, 496-7; careful with money, 66-7, 68, 156, 252, 484-5; housekeeping, 261, 272; likes children, 157, 224, 325; dislikes babies, 328, 331; doctors, 148, 159, 306; academics, 385-6; clothes, 55, 100, 132; philanthropy, 441; travel, 235; loyalty to family, 272; mockery and malice, xiv, xx; gift for friendship, xv, xix; her beauty, xvii

Her insanity: attitude to, xv-xvi, 148; childhood attacks, 1, 7; 'the insane view of life', 42;

1904 attack, 141-3, 149; attempts suicide, 141; views on her doctors, 148, 159, 306; 'discharged cured', 175; 'manic' letter, 358-60; new threat (1910), 421, 424; sent to mental home, 428, 430-2; recovers, 434; further threat (1912), 488; returns to mental home, 490*n*, 493

Recreations and pleasures: skating, 4-5; moths, bugs, 7, 9, 10, 16, 42, 52; gardening, 7; bathing, boating, 15, 412, 477; bicycling, 15, 168; hunting (on foot), 54, 170; music, 17, 41, 88, 216, 263-264; opera, 293, 312, 331, 333, 384, 404-9; ballet, 479; dancing, 34, 43, 63, 181, 217; book-binding, 45*n*, 56, 64; pianola, 55, 57, 88, 395; drawing, 170, 172-3, 426; cards, 63; theatre, 396, 423; driving pony-trap, 36, 53, 94; motoring, 171, 219, 424; riding, 505; looking at pictures, 138, 410-11; silver-point press, 173; singing, 347; walking, 221, 234, 270, 360; knitting, 491; smokes pipe, 144; dogs, 59, 164, 224, 350; cat, 191, 201

Sterne, Laurence, 399
Strachey, Sir Edward, 46*n*
Strachey, James, 415, 433
  Letters to: Nos. *555, 556*
Strachey, Lytton: V.'s attitude to, xx, 344; first meeting with, 46*n*; his friendship with Thoby, 77; early meetings, 195*n*; visits V. after Thoby's death, 248; grow-ing friendship with V., 284, 311, 328, 333; V. criticises his poems, 344; in Scotland, 362; friend-ship 'platonic', 366; planning

a novel, 370, 381; in Cornwall with V., 373*n*, 374; V. 'not in love with', 377; proposes to V., 385*n*, 469; quarrels with Clive, 449*n*, 471; in Dorset with V., 478; 'a female friend', 492; told of V.'s engagement, 501
  Letters to: Nos. *302, 408-9, 414, 425, 445, 449, 456, 458, 461, 464, 469-70, 472-3, 492, 494, 508, 589, 592, 605, 617, 623*
Strachey, Marjorie, 401, 424, 449, 451, 466, 477-8, 489
Strachey, Oliver, 456-7, 462
Strachey, Pernel, 87, 156, 202*n*, 204, 406, 499
Strachey, Philippa (Pippa), 268-9
Strachey, Sir Richard, 44
Street Music, 177, 178, 180
Studland (Dorset): visit of 1909, 411, 412; (April 1910), 424*n*; (Sept. 1910), 435-6; (1911), 478
Sully, James, 356*n*, 501
Sussex University, xi
Swan, John Macallan, 54
Swendene, Mr, 25
Swift, Dean Jonathan, 255
Switzerland, 43, 44, 207*n*
Sydney-Turner, Saxon: character, 405-6, 410; his background, 443-4; early visits to V., 201*n*; with her in Cornwall, 208; visits her after Thoby's death, 252, 254, 257; in Rye with her, 307, 310, 311; writes letters in Latin, 328, 427; in Germany, 345, 353, 355; in Bayreuth and Dresden with V. and Adrian, 403-11; V. visits his parents, 443-4; at Firle, 454; academic plans, 461; at V'.s marriage, 508*n*
  Letters to: Nos. *431, 435, 443,*

scripts, 219, 220; V. at Giggleswick again, 220-5; V.'s criticism of her writing, 220-1, 318; her criticisms of V.'s writing, 226-7, 228; Henry James on, 318; *Story of Perugia*, 373, 393*n*; death of Barbara, 395-6, 397; at Wellington College, 433; V. visits her there, 436-7; V.'s engagement, 500-1; original of Sally in *Mrs Dalloway*, xviii

Vaughan, Margaret ('Marny'): learns Greek with V., 13, 19, 20, 25; with her at Warboys, 29; to Germany, 38; social work in Hoxton, 41, 93, 149, 179; V.'s feeling for, 88, 198-9; referred to in 'manic' letter, 359-60; *mentioned*, 23, 33, 56, 93

Vaughan, William Wyamar, 12*n*, 18*n*, 19, 33, 109; career, 157*n*; character, 156-9; headmaster at Giggleswick, 148, 156-60; 180; 223-4; at Wellington, 433

Vaughan Williams, Ralph and Adeline: married, 15; at Hove, 15, 30; reconciled to V., 149-50; concerts, 216, 312; *mentioned*, 17, 39, 57, 92, 102

Vaughan Williams, Roland, 14

Venice: V. in, 137-8; lectures about, 177; reviews book on, 373

Vermeer, 410-11

Verrall, Helen, 437

Victoria, Queen: V. sees, 6; Diamond Jubilee, 8; death, 42; story about, 487

Virgil, 2, 20, 215

Voyage Out, The (V.'s first novel): called *Melymbrosia* by V. throughout; relation of letters to, xxi; origin of title?, 186*n*; starts writing, 315-16; thinks it bad, 325, 330; 'struggling', 331; 'slashing at', 334; 'screwing it out', 340; seeks name for Rachel Vinrace, 341, 343, 345, 349, 356; writes and re-reads it at Wells, 343-4, 351, 354; 'so excited by', 355; invites Clive's criticism, 361; will 'carry it through', 366; done 100 pages, 367; sends them to Clive, 371; 'struggle with', 375; reply to Clive's criticisms, 382-3; resumes after illness, 438, 440; finishes 11 chapters, 461-2; interrupted by illness, 489; resumes, 499; 'in sight of end', 500, 506; finishes, 507

Walberswick (Suffolk), 504

Wales: *see* Manorbier

Warboys Journal, 28*n*, 29, 150

Warboys Rectory, Hunts., 26*n*, 26-29, 37, 43

Ward, Mrs Humphry, 60, 71, 137, 138, 219, 320

Wareham (Dorset), 478

Warr, Dr George: teaches V. Greek 13, 21; Latin, 20

Warre-Cornish, Francis, 231*n*, 407, 440

Waterfield, Caroline Lucie ('Lina'), 162-3, 373*n*, 393

Waterlow, Sydney, 424, 435; separates from wife, 475; proposes to V., 485-6

Watts, G. F., 71, 174, 178-9